Expository Reflections on the Gospel of John

Expository Reflections on the Gospel of John

Leon Morris

BAKER BOOK HOUSE
Grand Rapids, Michigan

One-volume edition
ISBN: 0-8010-6255-1

Originally published in four paperback volumes:

Vol. 1, *The Word Made Flesh* (John 1–5), 1986
Vol. 2, *The Bread of Life* (John 6–10), 1987
Vol. 3, *The True Vine* (John 11–16), 1988
Vol. 4, *Crucified and Risen* (John 17–21), 1988

Printed in the United States of America

Library of Congress Cataloging-in-Publication Data

Morris, Leon, 1914–

Expository reflections on the Gospel of John / Leon Morris.
p. cm.
ISBN 0-8010-6255-1
1. Bible. N.T. John—Commentaries. I. Title.
BS2615.2.M66 1990
226.5'077—dc20 90-964
CIP

Contents

Preface vii
1. The Word (John 1:1–2) 1
2. The Family of God (John 1:9–13) 10
3. We Saw His Glory (John 1:14) 17
4. Who Are You? (John 1:19–23) 27
5. The Lamb of God (John 1:29, 36) 35
6. The First Disciples: Andrew (John 1:35–42) 43
7. The First Disciples: Philip (John 1:43–46) 50
8. The First Disciples: Nathanael (John 1:45–51) 60
9. A Wedding in Cana (John 2:1–11) 69
10. The Temple (John 2:13–17) 78
11. Rebirth from Above (John 3:1–8) 87
12. The Death of Christ and the Life of Men (John 3:13–17) 95
13. Judgment: A Present Reality (John 3:18–19) 103
14. He Must Increase (John 3:25–30) 111
15. Samaritans and Jews (John 4:4–9) 120
16. Living Water (John 4:10–14) 129
17. Worship in Spirit and Truth (John 4:16–24) 137
18. The Great Harvest (John 4:32–38) 146
19. The Healing of the Officer's Son (John 4:46–54) 155
20. A Lame Man Healed (John 5:1–9) 164
21. The Sabbath (John 5:9–18) 171
22. The Son of the Father (John 5:19–24) 179
23. Life and Judgment (John 5:25–29) 187
24. Witness to the Son (John 5:30–47) 194
25. The Miracle of the Loaves and Fishes (John 6:1–15) 203
26. The Miracle on the Sea (John 6:16–21) 213
27. Manna from Heaven (John 6:25–33) 220
28. Living Bread (John 6:34–40) 227
29. The Flesh and the Blood (John 6:50–58) 234
30. The Spirit Gives Life (John 6:60–71) 243
31. The Feast of Tabernacles (John 7:1–13) 251

32. The Law of Moses (John 7:14–24) 259
33. "Where I Am You Cannot Come" (John 7:25–36) 267
34. "It Was Not Yet Spirit" (John 7:37–39) 275
35. Pride and Prejudice (John 7:40–52) 283
36. "Caught in the Act" (John 7:53—8:11) 290
37. The Light of the World (John 8:12–20) 299
38. Dying in Sin (John 8:21–24) 307
39. Pleasing the Father (John 8:25–30) 315
40. Freedom (John 8:31–36) 323
41. Children of the Devil (John 8:37–47) 329
42. Before Abraham Was (John 8:48–59) 337
43. Sight to the Blind (John 9:1–7) 345
44. Friends and Pharisees (John 9:8–34) 352
45. Faith in the Son of Man (John 9:35–41) 361
46. The Sheep and the Door (John 10:1–10) 368
47. The Good Shepherd (John 10:11–21) 376
48. "I and the Father are One" (John 10:22–30) 384
49. Unbelief—and Faith (John 10:31–42) 392
50. "Lazarus Is Dead" (John 11:1–16) 401
51. The Resurrection and the Life (John 11:17–44) 409
52. "One Man Should Die" (John 11:45–54) 418
53. The Anointing at Bethany (John 12:1–8) 425
54. The Triumphal Entry (John 12:9–19) 432
55. "But If It Dies . . ." (John 12:20–26) 441
56. "Lifted Up Was He to Die" (John 12:27–36) 449
57. Why Don't People Believe? (John 12:37–50) 457
58. Washing the Disciples' Feet (John 13:1–17) 465
59. Betrayal (John 13:18–30) 474
60. A New Commandment (John 13:31–38) 481
61. Christ, the Way (John 14:1–7) 489
62. Help from On High (John 14:8–17) 497
63. Going to the Father (John 14:18–31) 505
64. The Vine and Its Fruit (John 15:1–11) 514
65. Love and Hatred (John 15:12–25) 522
66. The Spirit—And the Persecuted (John 15:26—16:4) 531
67. The Work of the Spirit (John 16:5–15) 539
68. The Disciples' Joy (John 16:16–24) 548
69. The Disciples' Peace (John 16:25–33) 556
70. "Glorify Your Son" (John 17:1–5) 565
71. Prayer for the Disciples (John 17:6–11) 573
72. Disciples in the World (John 17:12–19) 582
73. Jesus' Prayer for All Believers (John 17:20–26) 591
74. The Arrest of Jesus (John 18:1–11) 601

75. Peter's Denials (John 18:12–27) 609
76. Jesus Before Pilate (John 18:28–32) 618
77. Jesus' Kingdom (John 18:33–40) 627
78. Power—And Sin (John 19:1–12) 636
79. No King But Caesar (John 19:13–15) 646
80. The Crucifixion (John 19:16–22) 654
81. The Death of Jesus (John 19:23–30) 662
82. Jesus' Pierced Side (John 19:31–37) 671
83. Jesus' Burial (John 19:38–42) 680
84. The Empty Tomb (John 20:1–10) 686
85. Mary Sees Her Lord (John 20:11–18) 695
86. Jesus' Appearance to the Disciples (John 20:19–23) 704
87. Thomas the Doubter (John 20:24–31) 713
88. A Wonderful Catch of Fish (John 21:1–14) 723
89. Peter Restored (John 21:15–19) 733
90. The Beloved Disciple (John 21:20–25) 743

Preface

For some years I have been very much occupied with John's Gospel. I have lectured on it, preached on it, written on it, thought about it, endeavored to live out its teachings. To audiences of various kinds, I have often tried to convey its message as I see it. This series of studies arises out of such ventures. It is an attempt to convey to today's reader the meaning of some of the great things John is saying to us. The tone is devotional, for I think that is the way John should be read. There is profound theology in this Gospel, and there are critical questions that have preoccupied the scholars through the centuries and still keep them busy. But we must always bear in mind that John wrote so that we might believe and in believing might have life (John 20:31). Some of the things he says are easier to grasp in the original Greek than in our translations, and I have tried to bring out some of these points, but I trust in such a way that the believer who has no Greek will not be at a disadvantage. Indeed one of my aims has been to make the meaning of such passages as clear as I can for the non-Greek reader. These, then, are some of the things John is saying to me as I read what he has written, and they are sent forth in the hope that they will also be of interest to others.

I have made my own translation from the New Testament. Though not a particularly good translation, it will help the reader to understand what the Greek text is saying to me. When quoting from the Old Testament, I have normally used the New International Version. My former secretary, Mrs. Dora Wellington, typed the manuscript, and I express my appreciation for her help.

Leon Morris

1

The Word

In the beginning was the Word, and the Word was with God, and the Word was God. He was in the beginning with God (John 1:1–2).

It was the end of a very hot day. I was leaning against a stockyard fence, talking to the overseer on a sheep station in the Australian outback. Suddenly and without anything that led up to it as far as I could see, he said, "You know, there's one thing in the Bible I don't understand."

"You're a lucky man," I said. "There are many things in the Bible I don't understand. But tell me, what is it?"

And while I was expecting a hoary old chestnut like "Where did Cain get his wife?" he replied, "'In the beginning was the Word'—what could that mean?"

If he was going to have just one biblical passage he could not understand, I think he chose well. These words from the opening of John's Gospel are certainly difficult. We often read them without giving them much thought. Exactly what do they mean? There is no obvious answer. The basic problem is that the expression comes from a way of thinking that we do not share. We must thus make a special effort and do a little digging if we are to overcome our problem and enter into the writer's meaning.

To us a "word" is a unit of language, the shortest thing we say or write. But people in antiquity sometimes used the term in ways different from ours. They could, of course, use it in much the same way we do, and they often did. But the Greeks in particular had other ways of using the term *logos* ("word"). To get technical for a moment, they spoke of the *logos prophorikos* and the *logos endiathetos*. (They also spoke of the *logos spermatikos,* but that expression we can afford to ignore in this inquiry.) The *logos prophorikos* was the word going out from someone, the uttered word, the word spoken or written with a view to communicating with others. Since this is substantially the way we use the term, it gives us no problems.

But we have nothing corresponding to the *logos endiathetos*. This was the word that was not spoken or written, not uttered in any way. It was the word that remained in the mind. It was something like our "reason," signifying what is rational, intelligible. Used in this way it stood for a most important part of any person.

This *logos* might also be used of what lay beyond man. As the Greeks looked out at the universe, they saw order. They did not live in a gigantic and frightening chaos. The sun rose and set predictably every day. The stars moved with regularity in their orbits and appeared when the mathematicians said they should. The seasons came and went in an orderly manner. What the farmer sowed, that (and not something else) was what he reaped. The Greeks found order everywhere.

Why? Why an orderly universe, not a chaos? When they thought about such questions, some of their philosophers said, "Because there is a *logos,* a 'word,' in the universe. Just as there is a *logos* ('reason') within a person, so there is a *logos* in this mighty universe." They conceived of a rationality, an ordering principle, effective throughout all that there is. It was only this, they thought, that makes sense of it all. Their "word" was something like a "soul" in the universe. It was infinitely wise, and now and then the thought appears that it was from this wise principle that wise men derive their wisdom.

Heraclitus, a philosopher of the sixth century B.C., could speak of the "Word" as God. He seems not to have put much difference between God, Fire, and Word. When he thought of God as the Word, he thought of him (in the words of James Adam) as "the omnipresent Wisdom by which all things are steered." But before we get to thinking that Heraclitus was thinking along lines similar to those we might use, we should notice that he had some curious things to say about God. For example, "God is day and night, winter and summer, war and peace, satiety and hunger. But he is changed, just as fire, when mingled with different kinds of incense, is named after the flavor of each." What are we to make of this?

Fortunately, our concern is not with the complexities of Heraclitus's thought. Since he is far from easy to understand, it is well that we are not called upon to make the attempt. We simply notice that Heraclitus thought highly of the *logos* and could even speak of the *logos* as God. For the most part, those who came after him did not use this terminology. Perhaps they were deterred by his abstruse way of putting things. For whatever reason, they spoke little of the *logos*. The term occurs now and then, but not often until we come to the Stoics, who made a good deal of use of the concept. They saw the universe as pervaded by reason and called this reason the *logos*. The terminology gave expression to their deep conviction that the universe is rational. The Stoics did not think of the *logos* as a person, but as a principle, a force. They thought of this principle as one that runs right through the universe. It originated everything and directs all things. Everything acts in accordance with it.

John, of course, was neither a disciple of Heraclitus nor a follower of the Stoics. Nor were those for whom he wrote his Gospel, though all of them knew that the philosophers who used the term thought highly of the *logos*. The prevailing attitude toward philosophers was not unlike the normal way of regarding scientists today. Ordinary people do not understand them, but they do realize that what they are saying is important. Most of us have learned a few scientific terms and use them now and then, terms like "evolution" or "bromide." Most of us could not give an accurate definition of such terms, certainly not in a form that would be acceptable to the scientists. But we know that these are scientific terms and that if a scientist speaks highly of anything, that thing is important.

It was something like this, I think, with the term *logos* in the first century. People did not understand exactly what the philosophers meant when they used the term. But they did understand that the philosophers used it of someone or something that was very important. So when non-Christian Greeks came across John's Gospel and read it for the first time, they would not have found his reference to "the Word" very strange. Certainly it would not have puzzled them as it did my overseer friend. They would not have understood all that John meant by it, but they would have recognized that he was referring to a being or a principle of the greatest importance.

The Jews

The Greeks were not the only people who read John's Gospel. Jews read it, too, and their background differed widely from that of the Greeks. Among other things, that meant that their understanding of "the Word" differed from that of the Greeks. For some Jews this came about as the result of speculation on certain Old Testament passages that speak of "the Word" or of "Wisdom" as being active. For example, they read: "By the word of the LORD were the heavens made" (Ps. 33:6).

Sometimes they read that the word of the Lord "came" to the prophets (Jer. 1:2; 34:1; Ezek. 34:1), or that the prophets "saw" the word (Isa. 2:1), or that the word was active in doing God's will: "So is my word that goes out from my mouth: It will not return to me empty, but will accomplish what I desire and achieve the purpose for which I sent it" (Isa. 55:11). We would not normally use the term *word* in this way, but the Jews found no difficulty in understanding "word" in a dynamic fashion. And they associated it with the activity of God.

The Jews had similar ideas about wisdom. There is a vivid personalization of wisdom in Proverbs 8:

> "The Lord possessed me at the beginning of his work, before his deeds of old; I was appointed from eternity, from the beginning, before the world began. . . . Before the hills, I was given birth, before he made the earth or its fields or any of the dust of the world. I was there when he set the heavens in place. . . . I was the craftsman at his side. I was filled with delight day after day, rejoicing always in his presence, rejoicing in his whole world and delighting in mankind" (Prov. 8:22–31).

This is a vivid picture of wisdom as in one sense separate from God and in another sense one with him. The Jews did not define this very closely. It is not unlikely that they had no precise idea in mind. But they were certainly fond of using this symbolism.

The Law was also highly esteemed and came in for this kind of semipersonalization. Sometimes it was thought of as very close to "the word," a development encouraged by some passages in Scripture. Thus we read, "The law will go out from Zion, the word of the Lord from Jerusalem" (Isa. 2:3; Mic. 4:2). In such a passage the parallelism shows that "the law" and "the word" mean much the same. As the Law was the most significant part of Scripture for the Jew, this put "the word" in a very significant place indeed.

Another interesting use of the term is found in the Targums, the name given to translations of the Bible as it was read in public. The Old Testament was written for the most part in Hebrew, and it was held that the Bible should always be read in the original language when used in worship, even when most Jews had ceased to speak the beautiful tongue. But, as a concession to the weakness of the flesh, the custom arose of giving a running translation into the language the worshipers spoke. Such a translation was called a Targum. At first the Targums were all oral, but in time some of them came to be written down. Those that survive give us some interesting insights into the way the Jews of the time understood the Bible.

Our concern is with the way they approached the divine name. They read in Scripture, "You shall not misuse the name of the Lord your

God, for the LORD will not hold anyone guiltless who misuses his name" (Exod. 20:7). At the time of which we are thinking, pious Jews had developed the custom of "putting a fence around the law." When God's law said, "You must not cross this line," they drew a line of their own well inside that specified limit. Then if in a bad moment they broke their own rule, they were still a long way from breaking God's rule.

The commandment about God's name was obviously one to be taken very seriously indeed. So the Jews put their fence about it with some care. In effect they said, "It would be a terrible thing to misuse God's name. Let us make sure that we never do this. Let us not speak God's name at all. If we never use the name, we will not misuse it!" So they never did.

But what were they to do when they came to God's name in the public reading of Scripture? They could scarcely pass it by. So they used some reverent alternative. They might say "the Lord" or "the Blessed One" or "the Holy One." And the Targums show that they sometimes said "the Word." For example, in Exodus 19:17 a Targum reads, "Moses brought forth the people out of the camp to meet the Word of God." This kind of thing is found frequently. William Barclay says that it occurs about 320 times in one Targum, the *Targum of Jonathan*. This, of course, is different from the Old Testament use of "the Word" to denote a separate entity working with God. But it is relevant to our study because it shows that where the Targums were in use, "the Word" was a well-known way of referring to deity.

The dynamic use of "wisdom" and "word" that we saw in the Old Testament continued in the period between the Old and New Testaments. For example, in the book entitled the *Wisdom of Solomon* there is a little prayer: "O God of the fathers, and Lord of mercy, who has made all things by your word and formed man by your wisdom . . ." (Wisdom 9:1–2). Clearly the writer used "wisdom" and "word" in much the same way, and equally clearly he conceived of both terms in dynamic fashion. Later he has a vivid passage that reads: "While gentle silence enwrapped all things, and night in its swift course was at mid point, your all-powerful Word leaped from heaven, from the royal throne." It goes on to speak of the Word as "a relentless warrior" and to say that the Word "touched heaven, while standing on earth" (Wisdom 18:14–16).

There were other usages of the term *word* among the Jews. The Alexandrian Jew, Philo, is said to have used the term thirteen hundred times and more. Sometimes he used it as a way of referring to God in action; sometimes he seems to be talking about a being separate from God. We need not go deeply into his usage. It is enough to notice that here once more we find "the word" used in close connection with God.

All this means that whether John's first readers were Greeks or Jews they would immediately perceive that the "Word" was very important. William Temple put it this way: The Word "alike for Jew and Gentile represents the ruling fact of the universe, and represents that fact as the self-expression of God. The Jew will remember that 'by the Word of the Lord were the heavens made'; the Greek will think of the rational principle of which all natural laws are particular expressions. Both will agree that this Logos is the starting-point of all things."

Christian Usage

But all this is background. We must bear in mind that John was writing as a Christian. His thought was essentially Christian. And while the other New Testament writers do not speak of Jesus as "the Word," they sometimes come very close to it. Thus Luke speaks of people who were "eyewitnesses and servants of the word" (Luke 1:2). Obviously it is difficult to be an "eyewitness" of a "word" in the way we use the term, and it is not easy to be its "servant." It seems that Luke has in mind the very close connection between Jesus and the Christian message. We see this also in the fact that he seems to view preaching the word (Acts 8:4) and preaching Jesus (Acts 11:20) as meaning much the same thing.

Paul is another to speak of preaching Christ: "We preach Christ crucified" (1 Cor. 1:23; 2 Cor. 4:5; cf. also Gal. 3:1). And he has a very interesting section in Colossians 1:25–27, where he writes of "the word of God," which is "the mystery," and proceeds to explain the mystery as "Christ in you" (i.e., the word of God = the mystery = Christ). Paul does not take the step of actually calling Christ "the Word," but he comes very close. He has the essential thought.

We should probably also notice the way Paul writes about Christ in passages like Philippians 2:5–11 and Colossians 1:15–20. These passages are not unlike those in which Jewish writers wrote about "the word" or about "wisdom." There was thus a preparation for John's use of the expression.

John's Climax

It is important to see that while John was using a term that would be widely recognized, he was not simply reproducing Greek or Jewish usage. Both Greek and Jew would be able to put meaning into what he was saying, but he was also going to surprise them. It is impossible for us to put completely out of our minds the thought that by "the Word" John means Jesus, but let us make the attempt. Let us try to read the opening to his Gospel as a non-Christian Greek or Hebrew might have read it in the first century. Bear in mind that Logos or Word meant some great rational principle running through the universe, or perhaps it was a poetical way of referring to God or one of God's attributes. We will not be precise, but just think of the Word in terms of undefined greatness and majesty.

"In the beginning was the Word," we read, "and the Word was with God, and the Word was God. He [or It, and so throughout] was in the beginning with God." So far, no problem. We recognize that the Word points to greatness and are not surprised to find this new writer linking the Word with deity. "All things were made through him," he proceeds, "and apart from him not one thing came into being that came into being. In him was life, and the life was the light of men. And the light shines in the darkness, and the darkness did not overcome it" (vv. 3–5). So far, so good. The Word, we see, is being pictured as active in creation. This is not greatly different from the cosmological speculations of which the reader had undoubtedly heard (whether or not he understood them is another matter).

Now comes a little interlude. "There was a man sent from God, whose name was John. This man came for witness, to bear witness to the light so that all should believe through him. He was not the light, but came to bear witness to the light" (vv. 6–8). Since this has to do with John the Baptist and not the Word, we pass it by.

Then we are back with the Word: "That was the true light that gives light to every man, and he was coming into the world" (v. 9). Our reader can understand this. Divine illumination is channeled through the Word. And there is no great problem with the great principle or spirit or whatever it was that was coming into the world. How else would illumination come to men?

"He was in the world, and the world was made through him, and the world did not know him" (v. 10). There was always a problem with people who did not recognize divine leading. "He came to his home and the home folk did not receive him" (v. 11). This brings out an all too common tragedy. Those who might have been expected to welcome the divine illumination have, regrettably, all too often turned away from it.

But this is not the whole story. There were some who responded: "But as many as received him, to them he gave the right to become children of God, even to those that believe on his name, who were born, not of blood nor of the will of the flesh nor of the will of man, but of God" (vv. 12–13). When people open their hearts to divine illumination, they are transformed.

Up to this point the intelligent first-century reader with no knowledge of Christianity has no real problem. He might not have chosen to express himself in this way and certainly does not understand John's full meaning. But what he reads makes sense to him.

The next words do not: "And the Word became flesh" (v. 14). This is staggering, unbelievable. It is a difficult line, something that the average intelligent first-century reader simply could not accept. "Flesh" is a strong term, almost a crude word in such a context. John does not say, "The Word became human," or "The Word took a body"; he says, "The Word became *flesh*"! This is a strongly emphatic way of saying that the Word entered this physical, human life. He came right where we are. He became one of us. How could the mighty principle of reason that runs through the universe ever become human? How could the God of Abraham, or any "Word" that stood close to him, ever become "flesh"? It made no sense.

When John starts his Gospel, then, by saying that this happened, he is not mouthing a commonplace. He is not repeating Greek or Jewish platitudes. His book is not to be about the kind of thing that was familiar to thinkers throughout the world of the day. He is writing about sheer miracle, about "incarnation." This familiar word derives from the Latin *carnis* ("flesh"). It means "enfleshment." "The Word became flesh." The One who was truly and fully God (v. 1) was so truly and fully man that the word *flesh* may be used of him.

It has been suggested that John may have been writing these words with people called Docetists in mind. ("Docetist" derives from a Greek word that means "to seem.") These were people who were so sure of the deity of Christ that they thought he only "seemed" to be man. They thought that he had no real physical body, but only "seemed" to have one. He did not eat and drink, but "seemed" to do these things. In the end he did not die on the cross to put away sin, but only "seemed" to die. In this way the Docetists preserved the deity of Christ but at a terrible cost. They lost the humanity altogether. So, some scholars think, John uses the strong word *flesh* to make sure that his readers have no doubt about the reality of the humanness of Jesus.

Whatever be the truth of this, we should be clear that right at the outset of his Gospel John makes two points and makes them emphatically: Jesus was God and Jesus was man. The Word of whom John writes was God. He leaves us in no doubt about that. He says plainly, "The Word was God." But at the same time he insists on the true humanity of the Word: "The Word became flesh." We will not make sense of John's Gospel unless we constantly keep in mind these two truths which he sets before us so emphatically at the beginning.

John is going to tell us what God has done for our salvation. He will devote a good deal of space to the events surrounding the crucifixion. Chapters 13–21, which represent a considerable proportion of his Gospel, are taken up entirely with Jesus' last night with his disciples, the crucifixion, and the resurrection. This is the heart of John's message. God took action in Christ to bring salvation to sinners.

Right at the beginning John makes it clear that Jesus can indeed do all this. He is nothing less than the Word, with everything that means for divinity. And the Word did nothing less than become flesh, with everything that means for humanity. Until we have grasped this we cannot begin to understand what John is saying in his Gospel. We must be clear about the person of Jesus Christ or we misunderstand his whole message. John is going to write about God, but his God is not some remote being living on the top of Mount Olympus (or, for that matter, hidden behind the curtain that screened the Holy of Holies). His God is love, and in love for sinful people he came to this earth. The true Godhead and the true manhood of Jesus Christ constitute the necessary preliminary to all that John has to say to us.

2

The Family of God

He was the true light that gives light to every man, and he was coming into the world. He was in the world, and the world was made through him, and the world did not know him. He came to his own, and his own people did not receive him. But as many as received him, to them he gave the right to become God's children, even to those who believe in his name, who were born, not of blood nor of the will of the flesh nor of the will of man, but of God (John 1:9–13).

John is writing about the incarnation. He is bringing to his readers' attention something of the significance of Jesus' coming into the world. He tells us that Jesus is the true light and that all who are enlightened get their enlightenment from him. John goes on to say that Jesus came into the world. "He was in the world," John writes, "and the world was made through him." This prepares us to hear something about a warm response to the coming of one who was God. But no. "The world did not know him."

John writes of the greatest of tragedies: "He came to his own, and his own people did not receive him." Here the tragedy of the rejection is put before us in stark simplicity.

"He came to his own" is a translation that we might perhaps put a little differently. The expression occurs again in John's Gospel, namely, when Jesus is hanging on the cross. Before him is his mother, Mary, and with her the beloved disciple. Jesus says to her, "Behold, your son," and to him, "Behold, your mother." The writer goes on, "And from that hour the disciple took her into his home" (19:26–27). "Into his home" is exactly the same expression as that used here. It means, literally, "into (the) one's own things." It was an ordinary expression people used to refer to home.

So we could translate John's words in this place, "He went home"; "He went home, and the home folk did not receive him." It might not have been so bad, we imagine John thinking, if Jesus had gone to the Romans or the Greeks or the barbarians and had had a bad reception. That might even have been expected. But he did not go to any such place. He went home. He went to God's own people, to those who had the Scriptures explaining how God had constantly dealt with his own people and worked out his plan for mankind through them. He went to those who had the message of the prophets. He went to those who had in the Psalms a priceless treasure of devotion and a continuing revelation of God's love for people and his dealings with them. He went to those who had been delivered by the Lord at the time of the exodus from Egypt and again in the return from the exile in Babylon. These were people who might be expected to know something of the ways of God. Would they not welcome God's Messiah? As it happens, no, they would not. When God's own Son came to them, his very own people did not receive him.

From my early days as a Christian I recall the way S. D. Gordon brought this out. When I was an undergraduate it was the fashion of the young Christians among whom I moved to read books by Gordon. This very popular writer had a series entitled *Quiet Talks: Quiet Talks on Prayer, Quiet Talks on Power, Quiet Talks on Service,* and so on. He seems to have spent quite a lot of time talking quietly. One of his books is called *Quiet Talks on John's Gospel,* and I have always found it very helpful.

When Gordon comes to this passage, he pictures someone coming home at the end of a hard day's toil. He is worn out by the exertions of the day, glad to be finished with his work, and looking forward to being at home with his family. His step quickens as he gets near his home. He feels in his pocket for his key, but it is not there; somehow he has misplaced it. But that does not matter; the family is at home. So he goes up to the front door and rings the bell. And nothing happens. No one opens to him. They are there and they know that he is there. The curtain at the window is drawn back a little, and eyes that he knows so well look out and see him. But they leave him standing there.

A silly illustration? Our immediate reaction is to say, "That's stupid. It isn't an illustration at all. It could not happen." No, it could not happen.

But it did happen to Jesus. He went home. He did not go to strangers. He went home. And it was the home folk—those who, above all people, might be expected to welcome him in—who did not receive him.

And the tragedy has been repeated again and again. Jesus continually comes to us who are his own, to us who have received so many blessings at his hand, to us who have the Scriptures so full of the revelation of his love and of what his loving purpose has done for us and expects from us. He comes to us whom he has created, whom he loves, and for whom he died. And all too often it is still true that his own people do not receive him. The tragedy of rejection is as much a part of our world as it was of the world of the New Testament.

The Children of God

Though the tragedy of rejection happened and thus must be mentioned, it is not John's theme. He knows that rejection is far from being inevitable. He goes on immediately to say, "But as many as received him, to them he gave the right to become God's children, even to those who believe in his name" (v. 12). There *are* people of faith, men and women who believe. There are people who receive Christ. That is what matters, and that is what John is writing about.

There are three important words here: "gave," "right," and "children." John is writing about God's gift. He is not writing about the tragedy of rejection but about the grace of acceptance. God accepts those who respond to Christ. To them he "gives." Entrance into the heavenly family is not achieved by human effort; it is always the gift of God. To those who receive Christ he gave (and he still gives) the gift of membership in the family of God.

The second great word is "right." Many translations have "power" or the like. We must be careful here, because there is power in the gospel message. Paul, for instance, frequently emphasizes this (for example, when he speaks of the gospel as "the power of God unto salvation" [Rom. 1:16]). All who have received Christ can testify to the power that has come into their lives. God does give power, but at this point that is not John's concern. He is talking about the "right" to membership in the family. He is saying that, of themselves, people have no right to a place in God's family. That is beyond any human achievement. John does not say that they achieve or attain or merit membership in God's family, as though they make their own way in. He says that they are given the right. The right is God's gift. Receiving this gift, they "become" members of the family. They were outside the family; they did not belong. Now they have been given the right to become members; they do belong.

The third word is "children." Those in the family can call God "Father." Here let us take notice of an interesting piece of Johannine terminology. John never calls men "sons" of God; his word is always "children." This is not the case with other New Testament writers; Paul, for example, cheerfully uses both words of believers. Thus he can say, "As many as are led by the Spirit of God, these are the sons of God" (Rom. 8:14), just as he can also say that the Spirit bears witness that we are "God's children" (Rom. 8:16). But for some reason John reserves the word *son* for Jesus Christ (unless, of course, he is referring to an ordinary human family; there he uses the term in the same way as anyone else; his distinctiveness is in the way he refers to people as members of the heavenly family). This seems to be part of the way in which he brings out the uniqueness of our Lord. He is the Son of God in a way that nobody else is, and John's language points to this truth.

The word *children* indicates those who share a common nature. That is what we expect in a family; it is what makes a family. A family is a group of people linked by ties of kinship; they share a common nature derived from their parents. John has the thought that believers are people whose essential nature comes from God. In chapter 3 of his Gospel he speaks of being reborn. The thought is that a divine miracle takes place whereby people are reborn into the heavenly family. Elsewhere we read of people becoming "partakers of the divine nature" (2 Peter 1:4), and it is something like that of which John is speaking here. Believers have the right to a place in the heavenly family because of what God has done in them.

John proceeds to bring this out by telling us how they get into that family (v. 13). He has three negatives and one positive. Three times he shows how people do not get in (no matter how strongly they feel that they do), and then he tells us of the one way in which they do get in. First, the negatives. Believers are born, John says, "not of blood nor of the will of the flesh nor of the will of man." "Not of blood" is actually a plural ("not of bloods"), which is puzzling. Some point out that there was an idea held by some people in antiquity that in the process of reproduction the father contributes seed and the mother blood. But though this would explain why blood is specifically mentioned (it points to the process of natural birth), it does not explain the plural. Some think that the reference is to the many drops that make up blood, or that it somehow refers to both parents, but neither suggestion carries conviction. Sir Edmund Hoskyns in his commentary holds that John could not have used the singular. He could not have said that Christians are not born "of blood," because in fact they *are* born of blood, the blood of Christ. That is true, but is it what John is saying here? It is not easy to think so. In the end I fear that we must content ourselves with remaining in some uncertainty about this point. That John means that we are not born into the heavenly family by any such process as natural birth is clear. Precisely why he uses the plural *bloods* to bring this out is not.

"Nor of the will of the flesh" continues the thought. Perhaps we should notice that John does not use the term *flesh* in quite the same way as does Paul. Paul often uses the word to bring out the inherent sinfulness of human nature. He says, for instance, "The mind of the flesh is death" (Rom. 8:6). When John uses this term he is usually thinking of the weakness of our nature rather than its sinfulness. That is the way it is here. The flesh is limited; its best efforts cannot secure entrance into the heavenly family. It is impossible for us to work ourselves up into such a state that we become fit for membership in the family of God. "Flesh" is not the way at all. As John tells us later in his Gospel, "What is born of the flesh is flesh" (3:6). It cannot be otherwise; "flesh" is not the way into the family of God.

Nor does one enter that family by "the will of man." The word John uses for "man" is often used in the sense of "husband" (John uses it this way, for example, in the story of the woman of Samaria [4:16–18]). If we insist on the meaning "husband" here, it will be taken as standing over against an implied reference to a wife in the use of the term *bloods*. But it may mean no more than simply a member of the human race. Our interpretation will depend on whether or not we think that John is making sharp distinctions. If he is, then at this point the meaning is that the husband in an earthly family cannot get the other members into God's family. His influence will help them in many areas but not in this one. We might also reflect that if a father wished to adopt a child into his earthly family, there was nothing to stop him. In that sphere what he said was law. But not so in the heavenly family; he has no jurisdiction there.

But it is perhaps more likely that John is not making such sharp distinctions. It seems to me that he is simply piling up one expression on top of another to bring out his point that entrance into the heavenly family is not the result of anything human. It is not what we do nor where we stand in the human scale of importance that effects our entrance. We can do a good deal for ourselves and for one another in the here and now, but membership in God's family is quite another thing.

S. D. Gordon, in the book to which I referred earlier (p. 11), makes the point that an earthly family has its limitations. He tells us that he knew people who had great pride in their families. Aristocrats the world over tend to boast of their ancient lineage and see themselves as important because of the families to which they belong. Gordon is not impressed. He says: "I come of a rather old family myself. It runs clear back without break or slip to Adam in Eden." This is a nice, humorous way of debunking pride in one's family. Our human family, after all, is something for which we can take no credit, however much we may appreciate it. We did not bring it about. John is saying that nothing of this sort counts. We do not get into the family of God because we happen to belong to some fine aristocratic earthly family. That is not the way.

We have a slightly ungrammatical saying, "It's not what you know, it's who you know," cynical words that point to the power of human influence. In this life it often matters to have the right connections, to know people who can pull strings for us. But however that may help in the furthering of human ambition, it does not help with the heavenly family.

John is saying that no human effort of any sort will get us into the family of God. Consider what people can do for themselves and for one another any way you will. That is not the way into God's family. Nothing human can bring it about.

Born of God

Now we come to John's positive. Believers, he says, "were born . . . of God." I guess "were born" is quite a reasonable translation, but the verb in Greek is one that is properly used of the action of the male parent rather than of the female parent. In old-fashioned language it means "were begotten." John is saying that membership in the heavenly family comes about because of the action of the Father, of God the heavenly Father. He does what must be done to make us "children of God."

John is saying with some emphasis that to get into the family of God there must be a miracle. It can be explained by no merely human mechanism. It is not in the control of men. It is what God does, sheer miracle.

As we shall see, John brings out a little more of his meaning when he comes to chapter 3. There he speaks of the necessity of being born all over again, of being reborn from above. To become a member of God's family does not mean to make the best of the ordinary human life. It is not a matter of dusting off a few of the worst habits of our present life to make it somewhat better. It is not a matter of a little moral improvement. It means a radical revolution. It means such a drastic change that it cannot be brought about by anything that we do, but only by what God does. It is not the way of human excellence, nor the result of some human philosophy; it is the way of God.

God's Action in Christ

A little later in the prologue, John speaks of the Word as becoming flesh and dwelling among men (v. 14). That is the way God began the process of bringing about the adoption of people into his family. In their natural state they are not fit to be members of the family, for they are sinners. None of their puny efforts can make them fit for membership in the family. For that a great divine action is needed, and that action began with the sending of the Son of God to become man.

It continued when the Son of God laid down his perfect life on Calvary's cross. John tells of this in the best-known words in the whole of Scripture: "God so loved the world that he gave his only Son, so that everyone who believes in him should not perish, but have life eternal" (3:16). That is the great divine action that puts away our sin and opens up the way into everlasting life, the life of the children of God.

John is not saying that everyone is saved. It is the person who believes who does not perish. Believing and eternal life go hand in hand. And not just believing as though it does not matter what one believes as long as one is sincere. This passage makes it clear that the saved are those who believe in Jesus' name.

When people trust God in this way, God acts within them. God takes them, transforms them, fills them with his Spirit, enables them to be the kind of people they could never be in their own strength or by their own wisdom or ability. John is saying that God's love for us is so great that he makes provision for us to leave the old self-centered way, the way that concentrates on our own success and our own happiness. He enables us to leave that way and to enter the new way, the way of membership in the family of God.

John is saying that God will take over our lives and put order into them. He will make them rich and full and significant. He will set us on the right way. John is putting before us early in his Gospel the possibility of living in the fullness of all that is involved in being able to call God "our Father."

3

We Saw His Glory

And the Word became flesh and lived among us, and we saw his glory, glory as that of the only Son from the Father, full of grace and truth (John 1:14).

One of the surprising things about the Fourth Gospel is that it does not mention the transfiguration of Jesus. All the other three Gospels do (Matt. 17:1–8; Mark 9:2–8; Luke 9:28–36). We might have expected John to emphasize this narrative because he is very interested in the idea of glory. He uses the noun *glory* eighteen times, which is nowhere near Paul's total of seventy-seven, but is more than that in any of the other Gospels (Luke is next with thirteen). John uses the verb *to glorify* twenty-three times, while no other New Testament writing has it more than nine times (Luke). These statistics show that John sees "glory" as one of the important elements in the life of Jesus. We might reason that it would be intelligible if John had included the transfiguration story with its revelation of Jesus' glory, and the other three had omitted it. But in fact it is the other way around. They tell us about it; and John, for all his emphasis on glory, omits it.

Some, it is true, see a reference to the transfiguration in the words "we saw his glory." They understand this to mean, "we saw his glory when it was revealed on the Mount of Transfiguration." But that is more than John actually says. In the light of the fact that he does not tell the story of what happened on that mountain, I do not see how we can find here a reference to that intriguing incident. If John meant us to see it in this verse, he would surely have said something specific about the mountaintop experience, either here or elsewhere. But he does not.

It seems to me that John has no intention of referring to the glorious transformation of Jesus before his disciples at any point in his Gospel. It simply would not fit into what he is saying. His idea of glory cannot be concentrated into any one incident. He has the distinctive idea of seeing glory everywhere in Jesus' life.

The Reality of the Incarnation

Let us begin with the fact that John tells us that "the Word became flesh." He is writing about One who is supremely great. He has already said that the Word was "in the beginning," that the Word was "with God," and that the Word "was God." He has used "the Word" as a name for One who is as great as can possibly be imagined. There is no way of thinking of anyone or anything as being greater than the Word. The Word is true God.

But John is saying also that Jesus is true man: "The Word became flesh." He came right where we are. He took our nature upon him. He underwent all that being human means. He did not play at being a man.

There is plenty of playing at being man in the legends of the Greeks. They would picture some god or goddess coming down from the lofty heights of Mount Olympus and looking just like an ordinary man or woman. The divine one would have all sorts of adventures. But in due course, when the situation became a trifle sticky, the deity would get tired of it all, throw off the disguise, perhaps perform a miracle or two to get out of whatever difficulty had arisen, and then return to the abode of the gods. That is all good clean fun. But it is not incarnation. Those gods are not really human, but only look that way. They do not undergo any real limitations, but simply disguise themselves. They do not put up with the trials and chances of a normal human lot, but are merely playing a game and doing so by their own rules.

John is writing about a genuine incarnation. The Word took upon himself our flesh, with all that that means. He accepted the limitations that are part and parcel of human existence. John does not spell out what those limitations are, but his choice of word leaves his readers in no doubt about the real humanity of the Word. He became *flesh*.

Not only so, but he "lived among us." John's verb *(skēnoō)* is connected with the Greek word for "tent" *(skēnē)* or, as some prefer to put it, "tabernacle." Some people think, accordingly, that John means "lived among us for a short time." Reasoning that people normally do not live in tents permanently, they understand John to mean "he pitched his tent among us for a while." They see the picturesque phrase as pointing to a temporary dwelling.

Of course, the incarnation was a temporary thing. Jesus did not live on earth as a man forever. But we cannot get that out of John's verb. While it referred initially to living in a tent, it came to be used of permanent dwelling. For example, it is used of those who dwell in heaven (Rev. 12:12), and there is nothing more permanent than that!

The Shekinah

If from the term John uses we cannot argue the temporary character of the incarnation, we can point to something else of great importance. To Jewish minds the reference to "tent" brings the thought, not of *a* tent, but of *the* tent, the tent or tabernacle of which they read in their Bible. In the wilderness wanderings of their ancestors, the place of worship was a tent called "the tent of meeting" or "the tabernacle of the congregation" (Exod. 33:7). It was a very holy place, and quite plainly the Israelites in the wilderness looked on it as a very significant place, a place where they could meet God.

Now when the tabernacle was first set up and was ready for worship, a wonderful thing happened: "Then the cloud covered the Tent of Meeting, and the glory of the LORD filled the tabernacle. Moses could not enter the Tent of Meeting because the cloud had settled upon it, and the glory of the LORD filled the tabernacle" (Exod. 40:34–35). That the Lord put his seal of approval (so to speak) on the place of worship meant a great deal to the Israelites, and subsequent generations loved to dwell on the way the "glory" came down. Nor was this only a kind of opening-day celebration, for at a later time "the glory of the LORD" appeared to all the people at this same tabernacle (Lev. 9:23).

The Hebrew word for "tent" is *mishkān,* which is related to *shᵉkīnāh*. For later generations of Israelites, this term *shᵉkīnāh* often referred to the glory of God as it is manifested to men. They saw it as bringing out the truth that God gloriously dwells among his people. At any time that he chose to make that truth manifest, he might do so by some public showing of his glory. This happened at other times than the setting up of the tabernacle. It happened, for example, on Mount Sinai, where "the glory of the LORD settled on Mount Sinai. For six days the cloud covered the mountain. . . . To the Israelites the glory of the LORD looked like a consuming fire on top of the mountain" (Exod. 24:16–17). It happened again during the wilderness wanderings. At a time when the people were ready to stone Joshua and Caleb, "the glory of the LORD appeared at the Tent of Meeting to all the Israelites" (Num. 14:10). This, of course, put a stop to the murderous enterprise. And it led on to the revelation that "the glory of the LORD fills the whole earth" (Num. 14:21).

John is saying to his readers, then, that the glory that had been manifested in one way or another in the wilderness wanderings and later, as at the dedication of Solomon's temple (1 Kings 8:10–11), was manifested in its fullness in the life of Jesus of Nazareth. All the previous manifestations had been partial. Now came that manifestation that was appropriate for the only Son from the Father.

A. M. Ramsey says of the use of the term here: "We are reminded both of the tabernacle in the wilderness, and of the prophetic imagery of Yahweh tabernacling in the midst of His people, and of the Shekinah which He causes to dwell among them. . . . The place of His dwelling is the *flesh* of Jesus." He goes on to say, "*All* the ways of tabernacling of God in Israel had been transitory or incomplete: *all* are fulfilled and superseded by the Word-made-flesh and dwelling among us."

The Place of Worship

The setup of the tabernacle and later of the temple tells us something about the glory of God as the Jews understood it. The architecture of the temple taught them something about the greatness and unapproachableness of God. There was first the outer court. There was no problem about that. Anyone could go there, even the Gentiles; indeed, it was called the Court of the Gentiles (each court was named for the people who could enter it, but go no farther). Then came the Court of the Women, which marked the farthest point the ladies might approach. The Court of Israel likewise stood for the limit beyond which the gentlemen of Israel might not go. It seems that in the wilderness tabernacle these distinctions were not made, but that the outer court was open to all Israelites in a ceremonially clean condition.

However, a common feature of the tabernacle and the temple was the Court of the Priests, into which no lay person might go. It was set apart for those who had been admitted to the sacred priesthood. It was "the Holy Place" (Heb. 9:2).

Finally, further on there was a place too sacred even for the priests to enter, "the Holy of Holies" (Heb. 9:3). This was entered on only one day in the year and by one man alone. On the great Day of Atonement, when suitable sacrifices had been offered, the high priest entered this very holy place and carried out prescribed rituals. Even so it was required that he take a censer and incense, and when he came inside the curtain that marked the Holy of Holies, he was "to put the incense on the fire before the LORD, and the smoke of the incense [would] conceal the atonement cover above the Testimony, so that he [would] not die" (Lev. 16:13).

The way the place of worship was constructed and the restrictions placed on access to the Holy Place and to the Holy of Holies emphasized the greatness and the majesty of God. The worshipers must not presume that they had the right to approach God when and how they pleased. Even the priests were limited and, of course, lay people even more so. That God's presence was among the people was not in doubt. That people could approach that presence as they chose was not a possibility.

Perhaps this is a lesson that we need to relearn. God is a great God. Man, as such, has no rights in God's presence. We often behave as though we can do as we like with God. I read about a church that had a sign outside: "The church is open. Come in. Sit, pray. It is never too late to talk to God." But underneath there was inscribed in smaller letters: "Hours: 9 A.M. to 12 noon." We do that with God. We say wonderful things about him. We say that he is great and wonderful and mighty. But then we act as though he were subject to our control. We even determine how he is to be approached and, of course, arrange things so that he is not going to be too hard to get along with.

But we cannot do that with God. The Old Testament teaching about God's glory should warn us away from our common approach. God is wonderful, majestic, a glorious being. He may choose to manifest himself to men, even to dwell among them. But that is for him to say, not for us to decide. There was a glory associated with the awe-inspiring spectacle of Mount Sinai that impressed on the people who saw it their own littleness (Deut. 5:24–25). There was a glory associated with the tabernacle that could even restrain a murderous impulse (Num. 14:10; 16:41–42). God is glorious. But men may not presume on that glory just because God is pleased to manifest it to them. They must retain a proper awe.

Humble Glory

John is well aware of what the Old Testament says about God's glory, but he is not simply repeating what the Old Testament says. He is saying something new. He says not only, "The Word became flesh and lived among us," but also, "we saw his glory."

What, then, did they see?

They saw the Carpenter of Nazareth. They saw a man who brought cheer to some lowly people at a wedding in an obscure Galilean village. They saw one whom Nicodemus thought he could patronize. They saw one with whom an unimportant Samaritan woman argued, as, for that matter, did many Jews in Jerusalem. They saw one who healed a lame man by the pool of Bethesda and was promptly denounced by the same man to his enemies. They saw him defend himself and his attitude toward the Sabbath.

They saw him feed a multitude of people with a few loaves of barley bread and some small fishes, and go on to be quizzed by an ignorant crowd of people who challenged him because he had not brought the manna from heaven as Moses did. They heard him speak at the Feast of Tabernacles and were interested spectators of the controversy that resulted. He healed a man blind from birth and stirred up more controversy. He raised Lazarus from the dead and stirred up yet more controversy.

And as John comes to the climax of his narrative, he tells of a long talk Jesus had with his disciples in the upper room, a talk that they clearly did not understand as they should have. Then he was betrayed into the hands of his enemies by one of his followers and disowned publicly three times by another. Finally he was tried before the Roman authorities, with his own people bringing the accusation. He was nailed to a cross and left to die.

John goes on to God's vindication in the resurrection and tells of how some of Jesus' followers saw him again. He relates a moving story of the way in which Peter was restored to his place of leadership and then of how that apostle immediately presumed on his place to poke his nose into the affairs of another follower of Jesus.

The Gospel of John is an interesting account with many ups and downs. It certainly is a long way from being a straightforward account of "glory" in anything like its Old Testament sense. Jesus does not appear as a lofty, unapproachable person, secure in his majesty from all assaults of his enemies. On the contrary. He is despised and opposed, and in the end his enemies get him. They crucify him.

This is not the way we understand glory. We can make sense of glory in the way we see it at the transfiguration. There we have Jesus overshadowed by the bright cloud and with his face shining like the sun. His clothing was white as the light, white as no one on earth could make it white. There were the heavenly visitants, Moses and Elijah, and the voice from heaven saying, "This is my beloved Son." That is glory that we can understand.

But a carpenter using a hammer and a chisel and a saw? What is glorious about that? That is no more than ordinary, everyday stuff. It happens all the time.

It is the same with Jesus' entire life. We can pick out a few glorious moments, but for the most part we would not call that life glorious. What, after all, did he do? He preached to a few people in an outlying province of an ancient, long since vanished empire. Even there he was not often in the capital, the center of affairs, but in a remote country area. He taught a few people, gathered a few disciples, did an uncertain number of miracles, aroused a great number of enemies, was betrayed by one close follower and disowned by another, and died on a cross. Where is the glory?

Centuries before, the prophet said of him: "He was despised and rejected by men, a man of sorrows, and familiar with suffering. Like one from whom men hide their faces he was despised, and we esteemed him not" (Isa. 53:3). That is the kind of life John is writing about. "Word become flesh" as he was, that is the kind of life he lived. And yet John says, "We saw his glory."

John is telling us that God does not need tinsel. There is no need for the outward trappings of majesty and pomp for God's purposes to be carried out. God does not see things as we see them.

The trouble with our vision is that we instinctively look for the glitter and the show. Public recognition and praise are important to us. We expect people to bolster their egos with claims to magnificence. We are a little like the opera singer Jan Klepura. It is said that on one occasion he complained to his publicity agent that another singer was getting much more publicity than he was. He did not want to be robbed of his share of glory. His agent said mildly, "The trouble is that the gentlemen of the press think that you are conceited and therefore they do not care to write about you." The singer was incredulous. He exclaimed, "Conceited? Me? The great Klepura?"

That's the way it is. We do not want people to miss our greatness. Even though our circle be a lowly one, we want all the kudos and the credit to which we are entitled, and a bit more if we can get it. We insist on being recognized and are upset when people do not accept us for what we think we are.

John is saying that God is not like that. Real greatness does not need to assert itself. Real glory is not to be found in pomp and circumstance and pageantry and show. That is just so much glitter. It does not matter. Real glory is different.

Real glory is to be seen in lowly service. When something must be done and someone so great and high that he need not do it nonetheless leaves his exalted place and does the lowly thing, that, John is saying, is glory indeed.

That is the kind of glory that the Fourth Gospel describes. It is that glory that we see on every page. Right at the beginning, John has left us in no doubt about the greatness of his Lord. The Word was in the beginning, he was with God, he was God. And it was that Word, that supremely great Word, who lived on earth in lowliness.

Where people needed help, he helped them. Where there were sick, he healed them. Where there were ignorant folk, he taught them. Where there were hungry people, he fed them. All the time he was seeking the needy. He did not haunt the palaces of kings and governors.

He was not found in the high places of the earth. Perhaps we may fairly say that people in such places felt that they had sufficient resource and could cope on their own. It was not to such that the Word came. All his life he was among God's little people, those who in one way or another felt their need. And wherever there was need, he was found doing lowly service. That is what Christ came to do. And that is glory.

Do you see why it would have been difficult for John to have included the story of the transfiguration? I do not say that it could not have been done, but in this Gospel it would have been difficult. It would have represented an attempt to concentrate in one incident the glory that John sees as spread out through a whole life. And it might have given a picture of glory in the sense of majesty and splendor. While John is not denying that there is a certain truth in the traditional understanding of the term as applied to Jesus, he is saying that real glory is not to be found in splendor but in humility. True glory is seen in lowly service, and John sees it in every moment of Jesus' lowly life.

Glory in the Cross

Particularly does John see glory in the cross. That was very hard for first-century people to take. For them the cross was an instrument of shame. There was nothing glorious about it. We Christians do not easily see the cross their way, because from early days we have been conditioned to see it as wonderful. We have made out of it an ornament. We work it into wonderful designs on the exterior and the interior of our places of worship. We wear it on our persons. We see it as a proper object of art, and innumerable artists have painted the crucifixion. The Red Cross is a symbol of humanitarianism. To make the sign of the cross is for many a pious religious act. Others of us reject this kind of symbolism, but we accept as our basic truth that it is the cross alone that gives us hope for time and for eternity. It was on the cross that our salvation was wrought. Piety, art, and humanitarianism combine to make the cross a valuable symbol.

But people in the first century did not see the cross that way. To die on a cross was painful, so painful that someone has called it "the acme of the torturer's art." The weight of the body on the arms, the pain of the wounds, the constriction of the lungs, the flies, the thirst—all these combined to make crucifixion one of the most uncomfortable ways of dying that man has ever devised. The pain of it all is obvious.

But many saw the humiliation involved as even worse. Crucifixion was considered by the Romans the most shameful way of dying. It was reserved for criminals and provincials and defeated enemies. A Roman citizen might not be crucified, no matter what he had done. That law was occasionally broken, but its force was clear. This was not a noble way to die. A Roman might be executed, but it would be in some honorable manner, say, by the sword. There was no honor in a cross. Crucifixion was for slaves and outcasts. It was not for good, honorable people like Roman citizens.

Yet John saw the cross of Jesus as glory. He tells us that Jesus introduced a teaching on his death with the words, "The hour has come for the Son of man to be glorified" (12:23), on which William Barclay comments, "Jesus did not mean by *glorified* what they meant. By *glorified* they meant that the subjected kingdoms of the earth would grovel before the conqueror's feet; by *glorified* He meant *crucified*." They defined glory as triumph; Jesus defined it as service. So for John the cross was not shame. It was glory. It was the glorious way in which God's Son brought life to people in darkness and death.

It was glory because it was the way in which the ultimate service was given to sinners. John reports the words of John the Baptist: "Look, the Lamb of God, who takes away the sin of the world" (1:29). By his lowly death Jesus dealt with the problem of the world's sin. John does not tell us why this should be the way that sin is dealt with, nor how the death of the Lamb of God takes away sin. It is enough for him that this *is* the way. Jesus must die to put away sin. John tells us that Jesus spoke of being "lifted up from the earth" and adds, "This he spoke signifying by what death he would die" (12:32–33). It may be that he has the same idea as Paul, that death by crucifixion meant bearing the curse spoken of in Deuteronomy 21:23 (see Gal. 3:13).

But whether or not this is the way John is thinking, it is not the central point. The central point is that he saw the death of Jesus on the cross as the supreme example of glory, not as the shameful thing his contemporaries thought it was. Jesus lived a life of humility, of lowliness, of rejection; then he accepted the most shameful of deaths. In that way he performed the ultimate service: he took away the sin of the world.

John is saying that this is what real glory means. Jesus had no need to come to earth. He might have retained all the joy and splendor of heaven. But he left it. And when he came to earth there was no necessity for him to live in poverty and rejection. But he did it. And when he came to the end of his life he was not compelled to die the painful and shameful death of the cross. But he did.

Could anything be more glorious? John speaks of this glory as "full of grace and truth." Perhaps a better understanding of his words is that the Word is full of grace and truth. But this is the Word in the capacity of which John has just spoken, and that means his taking the lowly way, the way of real glory. It is in that way that grace becomes a reality for mankind.

John is here putting before us a tremendous concept, one which is at the heart of the Christian faith. It is at the heart of the faith because it is by this glorious act of Christ that people are brought into salvation.

Perhaps we should also observe as a final note that this concept is at the center of Christian living. When we have entered into the meaning of the death of Jesus, we see that for us, as for him, real glory is in lowly service. The Christian way is not a way in which we look for people to praise us, to recognize us for what we think is the full extent of our merit. Real glory rather is finding some useful piece of service, no matter how lowly, and doing it as well as we can. Unless we see that, we do not understand what Christian service is. The call to Christian service is not a call to occupy some comfortable and eminent place. It is not the suggestion that if we go along in the right way, everyone will speak well of us. The call to Christian service is a call to take up our cross daily and to walk in the steps of him who for our sake took up his cross.

4

Who Are You?

And this is the testimony of John when the Jews of Jerusalem sent priests and Levites to ask him, "Who are you?" And he confessed and did not deny; he confessed, "I am not the Christ." They asked him, "What then? Are you Elijah?" And he says, "I am not." "Are you the prophet?" and he replied, "No." They said to him therefore, "Who are you? so that we may give an answer to them that sent us. What do you say about yourself?" He said, "I am a voice of one crying in the wilderness, 'Prepare the way of the Lord,' as the prophet Isaiah said" (John 1:19–23).

John the Baptist was preaching in the wilderness. The Fourth Gospel does not tell us, as the others do, that he was preaching a baptism of repentance, nor that the crowds were flocking to hear him. But it does tell us of the deep concern that John's preaching aroused among the official religious leaders in Jerusalem, for they sent a mission of inquiry. Here was a man claiming to speak in the name of God. This was doubly dangerous. In the first place, he should not have been speaking at all. They were the religious experts. If anyone was to speak in the name of God it was they. It would never do for people to get the impression that others could do the job as well! And in the second place, he might be the kind of man that would arouse enthusiasm. Then the multitudes would be stirred up, and who could tell what that would lead to? There might be riots or other behavior of the kind that would lead the Romans to intervene. And then where would the Jewish nation be? So the officials had to know all about it. They had to satisfy themselves that the Baptist was harmless.

The delegation was made up of "priests and Levites," suitably accredited religious men (incidentally, this is the only New Testament passage where the two groups are linked). They asked simply, "Who are you?"

The writer introduces John's reply with a solemn rigmarole: "And he confessed and did not deny; he confessed. . . ." He need have said no more than "He replied." This solemn, emphatic introduction to the Baptist's answer shows that it is important; the words should be listened to carefully. John's reply is, "I am not the Christ." The word *Christ* is our transliteration of a Greek word meaning "anointed." It is also the translation into Greek of a Hebrew word (which we transliterate as "Messiah") that has the same meaning. The words *Christ* and *Messiah,* then, both mean "the anointed one." John is denying that he is "the anointed one." Old Testament kings were anointed; hence the repeated expression "the Lord's anointed." Sometimes we read of "the anointed priest" (e.g., Lev. 4:3), and now and then a prophet was anointed (1 Kings 19:16). Anointing signified the setting apart of a person for the service of God; it was a solemn act of consecration. The Old Testament looks for the coming in God's good time of a special servant of God, one who would be not simply *an* anointed one, but *the* Anointed One, the Messiah. He would be God's agent in a very special way and accomplish some important service for the salvation of God's people.

John the Baptist's answer, then, is an emphatic denial that he was this special servant of God, the Messiah. We might ask, "Who said he was?" Well, no one had actually said this as far as we know (though some had wondered about the possibility [Luke 3:15]). John, being as perceptive as most, discerned what the mission of inquiry was all about. His questioners did not want people to be caught up in messianic speculations. They must have been wondering whether John would claim to be the Messiah. The inquiry cleared the ground for him to dispose of this possibility straightaway.

That led to a second question, "Are you Elijah?" This was not an easy question to answer. There was a sense in which the Baptist was Elijah; Jesus said that he was (Matt. 11:14). Jesus said that the Baptist fulfilled the prophecy that Elijah would come before the "great and dreadful day of the Lord" (Mal. 4:5). But the Jews were not looking for the Elijah of the prophecy ("He will turn the hearts of the fathers to their children, and the hearts of the children to their fathers"). They remembered only that Elijah had not died; he had been taken up to heaven in a chariot of fire (2 Kings 2:11). Maybe they did not expect the same chariot to bring him back, but they did expect that the same physical

Elijah would return. Since John was not Elijah in the sense in which the question was asked, he simply said, "I am not."

It is sometimes objected that if John was Elijah in one sense but not in another, he should have said so plainly instead of making this blank denial. There are two things to be said in answer to this objection. The first is that John may not have known that he was Elijah. Jesus' teaching that he was did not come until later. No man is what he thinks he is. He is what God knows him to be. John was a humble man and may well have refused to claim this exalted function for himself.

The other response is that to imagine the Baptist as going into a detailed explanation of the sense in which he was Elijah and the sense in which he was not is to miss the important thing that the Fourth Gospel is saying about him. In this Gospel the Baptist does one thing only: he bears his witness to Jesus.

We read in the other Gospels that John the Baptist called people to repentance. We read there that when they repented he baptized them. We read something of John's teaching to people like the tax collectors and the soldiers and the multitudes generally (Luke 3:10–14). For John's deeds and his teaching and his baptism and his imprisonment and his death we must look elsewhere. The writer of this Gospel is interested in only one thing about John—his witness. There can be little doubt that this Gospel does make reference to the occasion when Jesus came to the Baptist and was baptized by him (1:29–34). But it does not say so explicitly. It says only that the Baptist bore his witness to Jesus.

Witness

Quite apart from the activity of John the Baptist, our author is interested in witness. He stresses the idea in a way that none of the other Evangelists does. He uses the noun *witness* (or *testimony*) fourteen times, whereas Mark has it only three times, Luke once, and Matthew not at all. He uses the corresponding verb *to witness* thirty-three times, while Matthew and Luke each have it once, and it is absent from Mark. In both cases John uses the word more often than does anyone else in the New Testament.

I think he is saying two especially important things with his stress on this concept. The first is that what he tells us about Jesus is well grounded. He is aware that "witness" is a legal concept. The witness of at least two people is required to prove anything according to the law (8:17). He insists that there is not simply the testimony of two people to Jesus, though there is that (8:18); there is other testimony as well. There is the testimony of the works of Jesus (5:36; 10:25). There is the testimony of sacred Scripture (5:39). There is the testimony of each of the persons of the Trinity—of the Father (5:31–32, 37, etc.), of the Son (8:14, 18), and of the Spirit (15:26). There is the testimony of a variety of human witnesses, such as the disciples (15:27), the woman of Samaria (4:39), the multitude (12:17). And, of course, there is the testimony of John the Baptist. With all this weight of testimony, the writer seems to be saying that there should not be any doubt about Jesus; his attestation is formidable. Witness is a way of showing what the truth is, and in this case there is plenty of evidence as to what the truth about Jesus is.

The other thing John is saying arises from the nature of "witness." Witness commits. Suppose that you have seen an accident. Two cars have been involved in a collision. As long as you keep silent, you preserve all your options. You are free to come down on either side. As the protagonists argue and seek your support, both you and they know that you are uncommitted and may support either of them. But the moment you bear your witness the situation is different. You may say, "The Ford ran through a red light and crashed into the Chevy." Now everybody knows where you stand. You cannot afterwards say, "It was really the fault of the driver in the Chevrolet," without discrediting yourself. Witness commits.

So it is a striking thought that the Father has borne witness to Jesus. The Evangelist is saying that God has committed himself in Jesus. In the life and the teaching and the death and the resurrection of Jesus, he has said in effect, "This is what I am like." God has committed himself in Jesus. That is a staggering thought. It is important to this gospel writer, and, indeed, to the whole church of God.

But at the moment our concern is with the witness of John the Baptist. John told what he knew. That is the function of a witness. A witness is not there to give a beautiful oration adorned with magnificent periods and scintillating phrases. He is there to tell plainly and clearly what he knows. John was well aware of what was required of him: he was to bear witness to Jesus Christ.

But here were these wretched people from Jerusalem asking him about himself. He was not there to talk about himself. He was there to bear witness to Jesus. Notice how his answers get progressively more terse. To the first question he replies, "I am not the Christ." It may not be eloquent, but at least it is a decent sentence. It has a subject, a verb, and a predicate. The second time he is shorter: "I am not." The third time he is monosyllabic: "No." Since his interest is in Jesus, not in himself, he has no intention of being sidetracked into a discussion about himself. He does not matter. Jesus does.

The third question asks, "Are you the prophet?" Though not defined, this is plainly the prophet spoken of in Deuteronomy 18:15–19, the prophet like Moses that the Lord would raise up in due time. It is not clear why the Jews expected this prophet in connection with the Messiah. But the Messiah would be a wonderful person; he would come in splendor and be attended by many. They expected, for example, that Jeremiah would be there (Matt. 16:14), and "a prophet like one of the prophets" (Mark 6:15). So it is not really surprising that some of them thought of the prophet of Deuteronomy as well. But John was not this prophet either, so he simply answered "No."

A Voice Crying

So far the delegation had not done very well. They had been asked to get some information about John the Baptist, and all that they had was a string of negatives. Since they had to go back to Jerusalem saying who he was, not who he was not, they turned directly to the subject of their inquisition. They asked John, "Who are you?" and added, "so that we may give an answer to them that sent us." They had to take back some answer. Would John be helpful?

John told them how he saw himself. He quoted Isaiah 40:3, saying, "I am a voice of one crying in the wilderness, 'Prepare the way of the Lord.'"

It is interesting that the community responsible for the Dead Sea Scrolls took this same passage of Isaiah and found its fulfillment in what they were doing. But they understood the words differently, the difference depending on punctuation. In the very old manuscripts there is little or no punctuation and we must supply it. This is usually not too difficult. In this case we put a comma after "wilderness" (as in the way I have just quoted the passage).

But the men of Qumran put their equivalent of the comma earlier. They understood the words in the sense, "The voice of one crying, 'In the wilderness prepare the way of the Lord.'" Where were they? In the wilderness. What were they doing? Preparing the way of the Lord. How were they doing it? Sitting down and quietly reading their Bibles. Their whole emphasis was on looking after themselves and their own salvation. They had little thought for the multitudes outside.

John the Baptist was different. He was not primarily concerned with the salvation of his own soul. He was concerned for the needs of others. He was only a voice. But he kept on with his "crying in the wilderness." For him to prepare the way of the Lord meant getting out among the people and warning them so that they might be ready when the Lord came. He did not, it is true, go into the cities. His place was far from the big centers of population. But he did preach at a ford of the Jordan where many were coming and going. Crowds came to him. What he said would inevitably be widely known. So he called on people to be ready, because the Messiah was coming. It would not do for them to be found with all their sins about them. They must repent and accept his cleansing baptism, so that they would be ready.

Why Baptize?

John's questioners had elicited the fact that he made no claim to being the Messiah or a messianic personage. He was no more than a voice calling on people to repent. Why then, they asked, did he baptize? First-century Jews understood and practiced baptism. It was the proper thing for people who needed spiritual and ceremonial cleansing. It was used, for example, in the reception of proselytes (converts) to the Jewish faith from among the Gentiles. When a Gentile decided to become a Jew, he and all his family were baptized and all the males were circumcised. Baptism was necessary because during their life in the Gentile world they had picked up all manner of defilement. They had to be cleansed before they could begin their new lives as members of the people of God. So they were baptized. Their defilements were washed away in the waters of baptism.

The sting in John's practice lay in the fact that he was applying to Jews, members of the people of God, the very rite that they saw as appropriate for defiled people coming from the outside world into their number. Had John been the Messiah or someone closely associated with the Messiah, they might have seen some justification for the practice. Who could tell what the Messiah would do? But John had firmly denied being either the Christ or a prophet. It was all very puzzling. So they asked, "Why then do you baptize if you are neither the Christ, nor Elijah, nor the prophet?" (1:25).

Characteristically John answers in his own way. We have already seen that his interest was in Christ, not himself. So he says, "I baptize in water; in the middle of you there stands someone whom you do not know, he who comes after me and whose sandal-thong I am not worthy to unloose" (1:26–27). The question gave him the opportunity to speak about Christ.

His "I" is emphatic. It sets him in strong contrast with someone else. He does not name the other, but the comparison is plain. John acknowledges that he baptizes in water, but that is all that he can do.

What is important is that he is to be followed by someone far greater. The assertion that the someone greater will come after John is noteworthy. People in those days took it for granted that the ancients were the wise ones. Incredible as it sounds to the youth of today, young men then believed that their fathers were wiser than they. They really believed it. With us "Pop" is often a figure of fun. Our notions of progress tend to see the aged and those of previous generations as not attaining to our own achievements. "The good old days" are good for a laugh at any time. We simply do not believe that the old days could possibly compare with the present. But in the first century, most people the world over thought that there had been a golden age earlier in the history of the race, and that subsequent generations had not been able to reach that standard again. How could they? They were younger, and an ingrained respect for age forbade the thought.

So it would be expected that Jesus would be less than John. Coming later, he would look up to the older man, people would think. Not so, says the Baptist. Jesus came later into Judea, it is true, but that is not the whole story. In a more significant sense he was actually before John (vv. 15, 30). His essential being is such that he is far greater than John. In the sense that matters he existed long before John did.

The Sandal-Thong

John's humility comes to expression again when he says that he is not worthy to untie the thong of Christ's sandal. This takes us back into travel on the hot and dusty paths of Palestine. As one walked in the heat and the dust, one's feet inevitably became hot and dirty and smelly. When one came to a friend's house, the first courtesy provided was water to wash the guest's feet. But the host would not normally do this himself. To attend to the feet was a task fit for a slave, and it would be a slave who was expected to do the actual washing of the feet.

We may get a little help in appreciating the significance of John's words if we reflect on customs among students and rabbis. Rabbis were not paid for teaching their disciples. Their teaching was always in one way or another instruction in the Bible, and they held that it would be a dreadful thing to take money for teaching God's Word. So a rabbi's needs had to be met in some other way.

It was the custom for every Jewish boy to learn a trade. Sometimes we are told that this arose out of some grand notion of the dignity of labor. I greatly doubt this. In the case of people like rabbis it was sheer economic necessity. If the rabbi could not be paid for teaching, it was obviously important that he get a little money in some other way (cf. Paul and his tentmaking [Acts 18:3]).

But that was not the whole story. The rabbi could not work a full day and still have time to devote to his studies. Here the students could help. They were expected to perform all manner of little duties that freed their rabbi from preoccupation with the minor chores of life and gave him time to put into his books. There is a pertinent regulation which in its present form is dated about A.D. 250 but is probably much older. In view of John's words it is not unlikely that it went back to New Testament times. It reads: "Every service which a slave performs for his master shall a disciple do for his teacher, except the loosing of his sandal-thong."

The feet of even godly and learned rabbis got hot and dusty and smelly. It would be most unpleasant to perform the office of taking off the sandals and washing those feet. It was just too much to expect of a student. Anything else he would do. Cheerfully. But, please, not the sandal-thong!

It is fascinating that John selects precisely this duty which the student would not do for his rabbi and says of it, "I am not worthy."

I was reading of an airman in World War II who was a fine fighter pilot, but unfortunately a very obnoxious person. In his preoccupation with his own success, he got on well with nobody. It happened that he was transferred to another unit. His commanding officer passed on the message, "Splendid officer at 5,000 feet. Should never come lower."

John the Baptist was not like this. John knew how to take the lowly place. It was not for him to parade his own virtues. He came to bear witness to Jesus and never ceased to do so.

Later in chapter 1 we read of the time when Jesus appeared. John directed some of his own disciples to Jesus (vv. 35–37). Here we see the real greatness of this man. It is not easy in this life to gather followers around oneself in a good cause. But once they have been gathered, it is infinitely harder to say to them, "I have taken you as far as I can. Leave me and follow him." But this the Baptist did.

It is all summed up in words of his a little later in this Gospel: "He [i.e., Jesus] must increase, I must decrease" (3:30). That was John the Baptist. He was not the Savior and knew it. He was simply a voice, a witness. Consistently he called on his followers to follow Jesus instead. That was why he came. And those who were faithful to his teaching went after Jesus. Mission accomplished.

5

The Lamb of God

"Look, the Lamb of God that takes away the sin of the world. . . . Look, the Lamb of God" (John 1:29, 36).

"The Lamb of God" is an expression that has come to mean much to Christian people. It is embodied in some of the ancient liturgies of the church, and people still pray fervently, "O Lamb of God that takest away the sins of the world, have mercy upon us." Even where people do not use liturgical forms, they often find that "Lamb of God" comes easily to their lips. It is a meaningful way of speaking about (and to) Christ.

In view of its widespread use among Christians, it is all the more curious that no one knows exactly what it means. Of course, we are not lacking in suggestions. Many have pointed confidently to one meaning or another. The trouble is that there is no proof that any such suggestion is what the Baptist had in mind when he spoke the words, or what the writer of the Fourth Gospel meant when he recorded them.

For all the research that has gone into it, there is no agreement as to what the term originally meant. Some curious statements are made. One scholar thinks it "likely that the Evangelist is throwing back into John's words a title which, as applied to Christ, had in his own day become stereotyped." This conveys the impression that lots of people talked about "the Lamb of God." It suggests that at the time this Gospel was written this was a common title ("stereotyped"), and that the writer, with scant regard to what had actually happened, put it on the lips of John the Baptist. But if this is what happened, we have no way of knowing it. The difficulty with the expression is that far from its being stereotyped in the church before this Gospel was written, we have no knowledge of anyone at all, inside or outside the church, ever using it before John did. It is a standard method of procedure when we meet an expression like this to look back at those who used it previously. It generally happens that there is a clue to its meaning in the way people had employed the words. But with "Lamb of God" the trouble is that there is no previous example of its use. We cannot even take later examples and say, "Perhaps these are independent of the use in John and will help." The later examples, as so far known, all depend on this Gospel. Christians found the expression a meaningful one, so they took it from John and used it in their prayers and in other ways. To this day we know of no example of this expression that does not depend on John's Gospel.

It is true that Jesus is elsewhere referred to as a "Lamb." But he is said to be "like a lamb" or else a different Greek word is used, and in those examples the words "of God" are not added. We are left with a mystery. And while it is unlikely that with the evidence at our disposal we will be able to solve the puzzle, it may be profitable to consider some of the suggestions that have been offered. They may not clear up the problem, but they will teach us some important things about our Savior.

1. The Passover Lamb. Some of my friends are surprised that I find a problem here. To them it is plain that what John means is what they call "the Passover Lamb." They sometimes point out that, as John describes it, Jesus died at the time the Passover sacrifices were being offered. Further, this Gospel writer applies to Jesus as he died the words, "Not a bone of him will be broken" (19:36). This appears to be a reference to the regulation that the bones of the Passover victim should not be broken (Exod. 12:46; Num. 9:12), though we should notice that there are some who think the words refer to a passage in the Psalms that has nothing to do with the Passover (Ps. 34:20). On the whole the reference to the Passover seems probable. The argument then runs that John is using here at the beginning of his Gospel words which bring the Passover to mind, and then in his account of the crucifixion he quotes a Scripture passage which clinches the matter. It is John's way of saying what Paul put in these words: "Christ, our Passover, was sacrificed for us" (1 Cor. 5:7).

This suggestion can be made to sound convincing. But there are objections. One of them is that the animal offered in sacrifice at Passover was not necessarily a lamb at all; it might be a kid. Some retort, "But the use of a kid was exceptional; the victim was normally a lamb." As to that, I do not know. Nor do I know why those who put the suggestion forward are so confident. I have never seen it proved and do not know how anyone could possibly prove it. Scripture certainly allows for the use of either a kid or a lamb: "The animals you choose must be year-old males without defect, and you may take them from the sheep or the goats" (Exod. 12:5). It is perhaps worth noticing that a goat was offered at Passover time for a sin offering (Num. 28:16–22).

But in any case, whatever animal was offered, it was not called "the Passover Lamb." It was called simply "the Passover." Paul uses precisely this term when he writes, "Christ, our Passover, was sacrificed for us" (1 Cor. 5:7; his exact expression is "the Passover of us"). If that is what John means, there seems no reason why he does not use the term. Modern-day Christians often speak of "the Passover Lamb" or "the Paschal Lamb," but we should be clear that this is our contemporary way of speaking. It is not found anywhere in the Bible or in early literature.

A further objection is that John in fact says "Lamb of God." There seems no reason why we should take the words "of God" to mean "Passover." There are many things besides the Passover which connect with God (including all the sacrifices), and we need something more than a bare assertion that this is how we should interpret the expression.

Another objection sometimes made is that the Passover was not a sacrifice that took away sin; it was a memorial of a great deliverance. This may perhaps have been so when the Passover was instituted, but by the time the New Testament was written every sacrifice was held to put away sin, at least in some measure. Specifically this is said of the Passover, both in rabbinic writings and by the historian Josephus. So this objection has no real weight.

But the other objections remain and in my opinion are decisive. I cannot feel that it was the Passover that was in mind when the words were originally spoken or first recorded. Nevertheless it is profitable to reflect that the Passover commemorated a great deliverance. A slave rabble was taken out of Egypt and began the long road that would make them into a nation and that nation the people of God. And in Jesus there is also a great deliverance. People who were slaves to sin are set free. As John Bunyan put it in a memorable expression: "One day as I was passing in the field . . . suddenly this sentence fell upon my soul, Thy righteousness is in heaven. Now did my chains fall off my legs indeed." And by virtue of Christ's atoning work the chains have fallen off the legs of countless believers ever since.

While we cannot say that John's words are meant to point us to the Passover, we can say that there is at any rate one aspect in which Passover and "Lamb of God" come together. There is deliverance in both, and the deliverance from sin that Christ accomplished is a mighty deliverance indeed.

2. The Lamb Led to the Slaughter. In words that Christians have always seen as applying to Christ, Isaiah prophesies, "He was led like a lamb to the slaughter, and as a sheep before her shearers is silent, so he did not open his mouth" (Isa. 53:7). Clearly Isaiah is referring to a lamb's lack of resistance when it is brought to the place where it will be killed. This has some obvious links with the way Christ met death. Jesus made no resistance. When Peter struck out with the sword, Jesus told him to put it away, and Matthew adds that he asked, "Do you think that I am unable to petition my Father, and he will provide me with more than twelve legions of angels?" (Matt. 26:53). But Jesus did not make any such petition to his Father. He chose not to resist those who put him to death.

There is nothing to indicate that this is what John had in mind. The unresisting lamb of Isaiah 53 is not called the lamb "of God," and this seems to be a fatal objection to the proposal. This objection might possibly be overturned if it could be shown that there was a widespread belief that Isaiah 53 referred to the Messiah. In that case we could reason that the chapter would have been studied closely for every messianic application, and that accordingly the reference to the lamb would immediately have been seen as a reference to the Messiah. We could argue that, since the chapter refers to the Messiah, who is closely related to God, it would not be too difficult to understand the words "of God" in connection with "lamb." But there are too many assumptions along this line of reasoning. There is no real reason to hold that first-century Jews understood the passage in this way. H. H. Rowley seems to have shown conclusively that the Suffering Servant and the Davidic Messiah were not identified in pre-Christian times. Christians, it is true, have interpreted Isaiah 53 messianically, but it must have taken a little time for this interpretation to become widely accepted. It has not been shown that widespread acceptance was early enough to explain John's reference. There is no real evidence, then, that this is what he had in mind.

3. The Servant of the Lord. A very interesting suggestion put forward confidently by some scholars is that the expression is a mistranslation. John the Baptist spoke in Aramaic, they say, and he used an expression that means "the Servant of God." But he used a word for "Servant," namely *talyā*, that has two meanings. It means "lamb" and it also means "boy"; and "boy," of course, in many languages is used in the sense of "servant." So the thought is that John the Baptist called Jesus "God's Servant" but was misunderstood; *talyā* was meant as "servant" but was misunderstood as "lamb." If this is the explanation, John would have had in mind the Servant spoken of in a number of passages in Isaiah. When he added "that takes away the sin of the world," he had in mind more particularly Isaiah 53, with its statements like "Surely he took up our infirmities and carried our sorrows . . . he was pierced for our transgressions, he was crushed for our iniquities; the punishment that brought us peace was upon him, and by his wounds we are healed . . . the LORD has laid on him the iniquity of us all" (Isa. 53:4–6).

If this suggestion could be shown to be true, it would help us understand John 1. But unfortunately the linguistic basis is far from sound. In the Greek translation of the Old Testament, *taleh*, the Hebrew equivalent of *talyā*, is never translated by a word meaning "lamb." Nor is the Aramaic word used as the equivalent of the Hebrew word for "Servant" in Isaiah 53 (one Palestinian Syriac text is known to use the term in this way; but this is all the evidence there is in support and comes a long way short of proof).

The suggestion, then, lacks support. Though it remains just barely possible, the way people used the words in question in the first century makes it a highly unlikely explanation. Despite what is said in its favor, it seems that we should see the expression John used as referring in some way to a lamb, not to a servant.

4. *The Lamb of the Daily Offerings*. Every morning and every evening a lamb was offered in sacrifice in the temple (Exod. 29:38–42). It has been argued that everyone who was acquainted with the temple knew that this regular sacrifice was offered and would immediately think of this lamb upon hearing the words "the Lamb of God." And it has also been argued that there is nothing unlikely in the suggestion that this lamb of the daily sacrifices was called "the lamb of God."

It is true that the daily sacrifice would have been well known and that it was associated with God. But precisely because it was so well known we would expect that, if the sacrificed animal was indeed called "the lamb of God," there would be a record of this somewhere. But as far as our information goes, there is not one example of the use of the term "lamb of God" anywhere with respect to this sacrifice. Neither before nor after John's usage do we find the lamb in the temple called by this name. In any case, as it was a different lamb each time, it seems that it would have been called *a* lamb of God rather than *the* lamb of God if this expression was used of it.

We may fruitfully reflect that the temple sacrifices were a continual reminder of sin and of the necessity for doing something about it. We may go on to the thought that it is only the sacrifice of Christ that really puts away sin. But we cannot say that we have any real reason for holding that John had the daily sacrifices in the temple in mind when he used this expression.

5. *The Lamb That God Provides*. When Abraham took Isaac up the mountain to sacrifice him in accordance with the command of God

(Gen. 22:2), the lad asked a question: "'The fire and wood are here,' Isaac said, 'but where is the lamb for the burnt offering?'" To this Abraham replied, "God himself will provide the lamb for the burnt offering, my son" (vv. 7–8). Some suggest that John was drawing attention to this passage and to this lamb. He had in mind, it is said, the thought that the one sacrifice that really puts away sin would be that which God himself provided. It is the divine initiative in dealing with the problem of sin that is in mind.

This is supported by some considerations taken from Jewish thought about Genesis 22. That passage does not tell us how old Isaac was, but it speaks of him several times as a "lad." This word was used of Joseph when he was seventeen (Gen. 37:2), and while it may also be used of people somewhat younger and for that matter somewhat older, it does not suggest a small boy. Nor does the fact that on the trip up the mountain it was Isaac who carried the wood that was to be used for the fire in which the sacrifice would be offered (Gen. 22:6). The Jews in fact held that Isaac was a mature man at this time (one suggestion they made was that he was twenty-five years old, another that he was thirty-seven). Now Abraham was very old; he was a hundred years old when Isaac was born (Gen. 21:5). Add a few more years for Isaac to become a "lad" and it is plain that the old man could not have overcome the husky youth had he resisted being bound and placed on the altar (Gen. 22:9). The inference the Jews drew from this was that Isaac had consented to be offered, and they saw the submission of the young man as being just as important as the obedience of the old one. They dwelt so lovingly on this narrative that "the Binding" became a very familiar term. When they used this term, everyone knew what was meant; there was no need to add "of Isaac."

Since this was so well known and so well loved a story among the Jews, it is suggested that "the Lamb of God" is simply an allusion to it, pointing us to the fact that God would provide what is needed in sacrifice, just as he had provided so long ago in the case of Abraham and Isaac. In the end, of course, it was not Isaac who was offered on the altar, but a victim God provided, "a ram caught by its horns" in a thicket (Gen. 22:13).

One cannot but be respectful to this suggestion. It might just possibly be the answer to our quest. But difficulties remain. One is that, as far as we know, the term "Lamb of God" was never applied to "the Binding." Neither in Genesis 22, nor in the relevant Jewish literature about it, do we find the term used. Moreover, when the sacrifice was eventually offered in that incident, it proved to be not a God-provided lamb but a God-provided ram. It may also be relevant that in the many references to "the Binding" there is no indication that the attitude of Isaac (or, for that matter, of Abraham) or the offering of the ram was held to signify such a far-reaching atonement that it could be said to be the pattern for the taking away of the sins of the world. The suggestion is intriguing and opens up before us some profitable lines of thought. But we have no real reason for thinking that it was what John had in mind.

6. *The Triumphant Lamb of the Apocalypses*. In the last couple of centuries B.C. and the first couple A.D., there are several examples of a class of literature that the scholars call "apocalyptic." They make use of vivid symbolism of the kind we see in the canonical book Revelation. The exact meaning of this symbolism is not always clear, nor is the reason it was employed. But it is at least a reasonable suggestion that it was used so that enemies would not be able to get the meaning if by any chance the books fell into their hands. One surprising thing that emerges from a close study of this literature is the curious nature of the lamb symbolism. We would expect a lamb to stand for someone meek or gentle or lowly. Instead, a lamb, and especially a horned lamb, stood for a mighty conqueror. We see this in such passages as Revelation 5:8; 7:9–10, and indeed in the general picture of the Lamb throughout that book. Such symbolism is found in a number of other places. We can imagine that it would not have been easy for an uninitiated enemy to have made sense of it.

Some have thought that, since this use of "the Lamb" is so clear in Revelation, we should understand the same use in the Gospel of John. Why should there be a variation? This argument can be made to sound very convincing.

But there are a few difficulties. The first is the one we have been meeting all the way through: neither in Revelation nor in any other literature of the kind do we find the Lamb called "the Lamb of God." It is this linking of the Lamb with God that is so distinctive in John and so hard to find elsewhere. But without it we do not know whether we are dealing with the same imagery.

Another objection concerns the meaning. In apocalyptic literature the lamb, as we have seen, is a mighty conqueror. But there is no suggestion of conquest in John. There the thought is that of atonement for sin, not victory over enemies. It is true that in Revelation the Lamb that is so powerful is "the Lamb that was slain" (Rev. 5:12), but the problem remains. John's Gospel is not dealing with triumph but with sacrifice for sin. The two thoughts may be connected, but they are not the same.

7. *Other Suggestions*. Other suggestions are sometimes made. It scarcely seems necessary to try to canvass them all. But we should at least notice one or two of them. Some students see an allusion to the "gentle lamb" of Jeremiah 11:19. This lamb is a symbol of a righteous person being killed by the unrighteous. It stresses his harmlessness; he

does not resist. We are reminded of the attitude of Jesus toward those who arrested him. But the parallel stops there. John is concerned with putting away sin. There is no such suggestion in the passage in Jeremiah. Nor, of course, is there the use of the words "of God."

A suggestion difficult to take seriously is that it is the scapegoat of Leviticus 16 that is in mind. This would fit in quite well with the idea of taking away sin. But it suffers from the obvious and fatal objection that a goat is not a lamb, let alone "the Lamb of God."

Yet another idea is that there is a reference to the guilt offering. In support of this is the fact that on some occasions a lamb was offered as a guilt offering (e.g., Lev. 14:12, 21, 24; notice the expression "the lamb for the guilt offering"). But once again we have no reference to such an animal as being "of God." And further, while a lamb was sometimes offered in this way, more often the victim was not a lamb but some other animal. It is not likely that anyone hearing the expression "the Lamb of God" would think of the guilt offering.

It thus appears that there are objections to all of the suggestions that have been made. We cannot have full confidence in any one of them. But we can see points of truth in several.

Perhaps the best understanding is that the term is used with a general meaning. That is to say, it does not refer to any one specific lamb, but to the lamb as the sacrificial animal *par excellence*. A lamb was offered in many sacrifices; it was almost certainly the most common sacrificial animal. To the people of the first century, a lamb that takes away sin meant sacrifice. In what other way could a lamb take away sin? Our failure to tie down the expression to any one sacrificial offering may be due to the fact that it was intended to point in a general way to all that the sacrifices meant. If this is so, John is saying that in Jesus we find that divine victim who would perfectly fulfill all that the entire sacrificial system foreshadowed. That this Lamb is the "Lamb of God" means that he is closely related to God (John has just told us that he is with God and is God [1:1]). It also points to the divine initiative in bringing about the atonement for the world's sins.

Thus we may continue to use the expression meaningfully even if we cannot claim that we know exactly what John meant by it originally. At the very least it speaks to us of that divine sacrifice that put our sins away forever, a sacrifice that God provided and that we could never have found for ourselves.

When the two disciples of John the Baptist heard him say, "Look, the Lamb of God," they immediately followed Jesus (1:37). May our study of the expression do the same for us!

6

The First Disciples: Andrew

The next day again John was standing and two of his disciples. He looked at Jesus as he walked, and says, "Look, the Lamb of God." And the two disciples heard him speaking and they followed Jesus. . . . Andrew, the brother of Simon Peter, was one of the two who heard from John and followed him. This man first finds his own brother Simon and says to him, "We have found the Messiah" (which, being interpreted, is "the Christ"). He brought him to Jesus (John 1:35–42).

Of those who followed Jesus, Andrew is the first whose name we know. He came with a companion who is often thought to have been John, the beloved disciple. There seems little to be said against this, but on the other hand there is nothing to show conclusively that it was John. The name is not given and the man is not identified with the beloved disciple or with anyone else. But the beloved disciple was the author of this Gospel (21:24), and the story of the coming to Jesus has touches that many have thought indicate an eyewitness. It may be significant that no name is given to this man and that the same is true of the beloved disciple. Another question arises: Why should the author of the Gospel include this man if he is to play no further part? Be all that as it may, there is no doubt about Andrew. He is named, and there is no one known to have come to Jesus before him.

The name is a Greek one, with the meaning "manly." We do not read much about Andrew in the other Gospels, though we know from Mark that he and Peter had a house in Capernaum (Mark 1:29). Interestingly

Matthew and Luke speak of the house as Peter's and say nothing about Andrew's ownership (Matt. 8:14; Luke 4:38). Even in John, where we are told more about Andrew than anywhere else, Andrew is rather in the shadow of his brother Simon; the incidental notice about the house fits in with this fact. Andrew was not one for taking the center of the stage. We learn that he was a fisherman and that Jesus called him and Peter to become "fishers of men" (Matt. 4:18–20; Mark 1:16–18).

The only other information we get about Andrew in the synoptic Gospels is Mark's recording of the fact that he joined with his brother Simon and the sons of Zebedee in asking Jesus the question that touched off his apocalyptic discourse on the Mount of Olives (Mark 13:3). Neither of the other Evangelists specifies who asked the question: Matthew has "the disciples" and Luke simply "some" (Matt. 24:3; Luke 21:5).

Andrew Could Adapt

Most of our information about Andrew, then, comes from John's Gospel. There is a certain consistency about the references to this man that enables us to build up something of a picture of him. It is far from complete, and in the end there is much that we do not know about Andrew. But we know enough to see him as an individual, one who still teaches us important lessons.

The first thing we learn about him is that he was flexible; he could adapt. That he had been one of the disciples of John the Baptist indicates that he was not content with run-of-the-mill first-century Judaism. John the Baptist was preaching a baptism of repentance for the forgiveness of sins and announcing that the coming of the Messiah was near. For Andrew this was good news, so he attached himself wholeheartedly to John and accepted his preaching.

We do not know as much as we would like about the Baptist's preaching, but we do know that he was concerned to say a good deal about the one who would come after him, the Messiah. We know little about the terminology he employed, but it is plain that he told his disciples that it was the Great One to come who was important. When he came they should attach themselves to him.

He did his work so well that when the time came, Andrew and his friend knew what to do. When Jesus came along the Baptist did not say anything like "Follow this man." He said no more than "Look, the Lamb of God." We see Andrew's adaptability in that this was all he needed. He had learned from John so well that he simply left his teacher and followed Jesus.

Our interest in Andrew must not result in our overlooking the important thing that all of this tells us about John the Baptist. He had preached effectively and had gathered around him a group of people who wanted more than the conventional Judaism of the day. They were ready to repent and be baptized as a sign of their repentance, or at least many of them were. It must have been a source of great satisfaction to John to see so many attach themselves to him. But now he pointed them away from himself and directed them to Jesus. It is always a difficult thing for a preacher to direct people away from himself and to someone else, even when he knows that the other person can help them more. But this is what John did. The figure left by Andrew and his friend was a lonely one, but he was a figure of solitary splendor. It was a great thing that John did.

It is tempting to speculate on what meaning "the Lamb of God" had for Andrew. As we saw in our previous chapter, it is impossible for us at this distance in time to be sure of exactly what John had in mind. Presumably Andrew understood the expression far better than we do. But unfortunately he has not left a record of what he thought about it.

We have seen that at the very least a Lamb that takes away sin means sacrifice. It means rejection and suffering and death. Andrew could not have foreseen Calvary with all its horror, but he must have seen that John was pointing to a concept of messiahship far different from the one normally accepted in contemporary Judaism. The Jews were looking for a Messiah who would deal with the pressing problem of the Roman occupation. He would raise an army and drive the hated conquerors into the sea.

Now we cannot be sure how far Andrew had accepted such an understanding of the Messiah before he attached himself to John the Baptist. But it is not unreasonable to hold that his basic way of thinking was something like the contemporary understanding. It was not difficult to interpret the messianic prophecies of the Old Testament in terms of triumph, and in the first century over whom would the Messiah triumph if not the Romans?

It means a great deal that a man brought up with such an understanding of the Messiah came, as Andrew did, to such a fresh understanding that he was ready to attach himself immediately to one whose designation was "Lamb of God" and whose future was bound up with sacrifice. Obviously Andrew was not a mass of hardened prejudices. He could accept new thinking and act on it.

I do not mean that Andrew saw at once all the implications of "Lamb of God." No one could have done so at that time. Like the others who followed Jesus, he had a good deal of unlearning to do, and it must have taken time. But at least he was ready to make a beginning. He was not so set in his old ways that he could not change his thinking. Though "the Lamb of God" did not fit into the conventional understanding of the Messiah, that did not stop Andrew from accepting what it meant, as far as he could understand it.

Not only was he ready, then, to accept a sacrificial Messiah, but the words to which he responded spoke of the Lamb of God as taking away the sin of the world. This was something no political or military Messiah could do or would want to do. It was much more important, but it was not the kind of thing most people had in mind. Once more we see Andrew's readiness to adapt. He was not in a rut. He had learned many things from John the Baptist and responded to them. He learned from Jesus, too, and it is fitting that the last thing we hear about him in the Gospels is that he is asking Jesus a question (Mark 13:3).

Andrew the Evangelist

Andrew was not slow to bring his brother Simon to Jesus. There is a minor uncertainty about the Gospel writer's meaning at this point. We could understand his words to mean that Andrew "first found his own brother" (i.e., he found him before he did anything else). Or John could mean that Andrew "found his own brother first" (i.e., before he found anyone else; he found others, but Simon was the first). A slightly different reading in some manuscripts is, "He was the first to find his brother" (i.e., the unnamed disciple found *his* brother, too, but only after Andrew had found Simon). With a bigger difference, yet other manuscripts read, "In the morning he found. . . ." It seems to me that this last understanding of the passage is unlikely (though Moffatt and others accept it), but any of the other three is possible. They all indicate the promptness with which Andrew went about his task. In my opinion the first-mentioned meaning is likely the correct one, but whichever we adopt, we get a picture of Andrew as interested in bringing his brother to Jesus, so interested that he did so very quickly indeed.

This interest continued, for every time we come across Andrew in the Fourth Gospel he is bringing someone to Jesus. The next time we meet him is at the feeding of the five thousand. The other Evangelists tell us that the disciples wanted to send the people away so that they could get food for themselves in the neighboring towns and villages. It was Jesus who suggested that they should feed them. John tells us that he first asked Philip where they should buy bread for the crowd, only to be met with the information that two hundred denarii could not buy enough bread to give them all even a little. The situation was hopeless.

It is at this point in John's narrative that we again meet Andrew. "There is a young lad here," he said, "who has five barley loaves and two little fishes." He recognized the limitations of this meager supply: "but what are these among so many?" (6:8–9).

It cannot be said that Andrew foresaw what would happen, so we are left wondering why he brought the boy to Jesus. Perhaps he felt that at least Jesus ought to have something to eat after all his hard day's work. For whatever reason, he brought the lad to Jesus. He might not have been good at understanding all that Jesus could do, but he was good at bringing people.

The final occasion on which John mentions Andrew is toward the end of Jesus' public ministry, after the triumphal entry into Jerusalem. John tells us that there were some Greeks who had come up to worship at the Passover. It is not completely clear what the term *Greek* means in this context. Since they were going up to Jerusalem to worship, the first thing we think of is that they had become converts to Judaism (proselytes). But John does not say this. It seems likely that if this were the case he would have expressed himself somewhat differently. It seems more likely that these Greeks were what are sometimes called "God-fearers" or "half-proselytes" or "devout people." These were folk who were attracted to Judaism without being fully committed to it. They liked some things about it very much indeed. For example, the Jews taught emphatically that there is only one God, and this monotheism attracted some who had been brought up in an unsatisfying polytheism. The lofty morality of Judaism was also attractive in a world where moral values had slipped badly. Then there were the Scriptures, those tremendous words of the prophets, the riches of the Law, and the Psalms, and all the rest. They found much to attract them.

But they also found much to repel them. First-century Judaism was narrowly nationalistic with a firm belief in the superiority of all Jews to everyone else. Proselytes were accepted somewhat grudgingly and never seem to have had the same status as native-born Jews. Then again, Greeks found some of the ritual practices of Judaism repellent, for example, circumcision. Such considerations made it hard for them to become full Jews.

So they hovered on the fringe. They worshiped the one God and tried to live the life he demanded of his own people. But they refused circumcision and never became full members of Judaism. At the feasts they often came up to Jerusalem to worship, as in this case. They would, of course, not be allowed to go beyond the outer court, the Court of the Gentiles. But at least they would be in the house of the Lord at one of the feasts of the Lord.

It seems probable that John is talking about such people. They may have come from Greece, though not necessarily. Greeks lived in all sorts of places, and there were large numbers of them not too far away, in the region known as Decapolis on the other side of the Jordan. Wherever their homes were, they were not Jews by race.

They came to Philip and said, "Sir, we wish to see Jesus." Why did they come to Philip? Perhaps because he had a Greek name, but if so they were misled, because many Jews of the day had Greek names. For that matter, Andrew is a Greek name. However, whatever their reason, they came to Philip.

And they puzzled that good man. Could he bring Greeks to Jesus? *Greeks*? On the other hand, could he refuse? Did Jesus ever turn anyone away? Philip did not know what to do. So he went off and found Andrew.

Andrew had no problem. He was always bringing people to Jesus. And that was what he and Philip did now (12:20–22). There is a marvelous consistency about Andrew. Every time we meet him in the Fourth Gospel he is bringing someone to the Lord. It is a noteworthy characteristic.

William Temple is reported to have said that the church is the one organization among men that exists purely for the benefit of nonmembers. In this striking way he brought out the truth that mission is of the essence of the church's existence. The function of the church is not to be a cozy club for like-minded people who prefer not to go along with everything in contemporary society. It is a group of people committed to proclaiming the gospel and bringing others to Christ. Andrew understood this function of the church very well. He seems not to have tried to fasten attention on himself, but was concerned simply with getting people to come to Jesus. That, for him, was the thing that mattered.

A Lowly Man

Andrew is not usually held to have been one of the really outstanding early Christians. It is noteworthy to see him called "Simon Peter's brother" (John 1:40; 6:8), and not named for his own achievement. The first of these references is especially striking, for at that point Peter had not yet been brought into the narrative. He came in only after Andrew brought him to Jesus, but even then Andrew was in the shadow of his greater brother.

But people without great gifts are sometimes strikingly effective. I like the story of the man who for a long time had been a very poor fisherman, but who then started to bring home some fairly good catches. Thereafter he rarely failed to fill his basket. It happened that one day his wife decided to go with him when he went off to try a new spot.

When they arrived, the husband kept looking around. His wife was puzzled. "What are you looking for?" she inquired.

"An old man."

"What old man? You don't know anybody here, do you?"

"No, of course not. But I have discovered that old men know where the fish are. So I generally find one and watch where he goes. Then when he is finished, I take over his spot. It usually works."

The husband was not brilliant; he seemed to have learned practically nothing about how to go about the task for himself. But his method worked. It made him a respectable fisherman, instead of one who had to content himself with stories of the ones that got away.

Andrew was perhaps a bit like that. There is nothing to indicate that he was a great man, and much to indicate that he was rather a humble person. But he had one thing going for him—he could and did bring people to Jesus. That is what counts.

Lowly service is important. Let us never forget that it was Andrew who brought Peter to Jesus, an act which William Temple says was perhaps "as great a service to the Church as ever any man did." Andrew may not have been able to do great things, but he brought Peter to Jesus, and Peter did great things. From a human point of view, it is impossible to see how those great things would ever have been accomplished had not Andrew played his part so well.

Has not this been consistently true in the history of the Christian church? Ananias of Damascus, for one, is scarcely a celebrated name in Christian annals, but he introduced Saul of Tarsus to the Christians.

And the story has gone on. Who can tell even the name of that monk at Erfurt who taught Martin Luther the doctrine of justification by faith? He himself did little, but Luther made the teaching ring through Europe.

Or think of that Sunday-school teacher who felt led to speak to a young man about his soul. He was hesitant and not at all sure how to go about it. He spent time outside the shop where the young man worked, not quite knowing what to say. But in the end he plucked up his courage, went in, and stammered out words that told of the love of Christ for people and the love people should have for Christ. The result was the conversion of Dwight L. Moody, one of the greatest evangelists of modern times.

We could go on. Again and again we see in the shadows of great Christian leaders humble people who themselves could never do great deeds, but who knew the importance of bringing men to Christ. Without them the history of the church would have been very different and far less successful.

It is still the case that there is need for people like Andrew. Lots of them. The Lord raises up very few great leaders, but he calls many followers, people who will work humbly in lowly places and in this way set his great purpose forward. Few things are more important for the Christian than lowly service well done.

7

The First Disciples: Philip

The next day he wished to go out into Galilee and he finds Philip. And Jesus says to him, "Follow me." Now Philip was from Bethsaida, from the city of Andrew and Peter. Philip finds Nathanael, and says to him, "We have found him of whom Moses (in the law) and the prophets wrote, Jesus the son of Joseph, who is from Nazareth." Nathanael said to him, "Out of Nazareth can any good thing come?" Philip says to him, "Come and see" (John 1:43–46).

I once heard a bishop of the church say, "Apparently Philip was a rather stupid man." This rather took the congregation aback, for it is not the way we expect bishops to talk about apostles. The apostles were the great leaders of the church in its early days. The bishops are leaders in the church in these latter days. We expect that one lot of leaders will be respectful to another lot. So the congregation was surprised, to say the least.

Now I am not a bishop, so I will not say such a dreadful thing. But when you look at the record, it does seem that Philip was not very bright. I think I understand why the bishop spoke as he did.

We depend on John for most of our information about Philip. This apostle is mentioned in the lists of apostles in the first three Gospels, but that is all they tell us about him. They say nothing about what Philip said and did. For that we must go to John.

The first thing John tells us is that Jesus "finds" Philip (v. 43). This is unusual. All the others who are said in John 1 to have come to Jesus either came of their own accord or were brought by their friends. Only in the case of Philip is it said that Jesus took the initiative. This has been developed by some scholars into an argument about sources. In this chapter, they say, disciples "come" to Jesus or "are brought" to him. There is something wrong, they suggest, when we read that Jesus "finds" this man. So there is a different source behind this part of the chapter. Or perhaps there has been some editorial work. Perhaps originally Peter (who is mentioned in the previous verse), having been brought to Jesus by his brother Andrew, carried on the process by finding his fellow townsman Philip and bringing him.

But I wonder. Elsewhere John does not proceed in such a mechanical way that we can safely say, "All who come to Jesus must come in much the same way." He is not at all averse to variety. Nor does he depict Jesus as a passive personality who simply waits for things to happen. There is nothing out of character in Jesus' finding Philip, even though this is a different process from that recorded of the others.

It is also interesting that it is Philip, of all those spoken of in this chapter, whom Jesus found. Simon Peter was really a great man, the outstanding leader in the early church. Andrew was not of the same caliber, but he was a man of initiative, always bringing people to Jesus. Nathanael, of whom we read at the end of the chapter, is not a man about whom we know much, but the little we do know reveals him to have been a guileless person. As we shall see, he had at least one memorable experience under a fig tree. Since the shade of a fig tree was often used as a place for prayer and meditation, we may conclude that he was a deeply spiritual man, perhaps something of a visionary.

But it was not Andrew or Peter or Nathanael whom Jesus went out and found. It was Philip, this perfectly ordinary man, one who, as far as we know, had no outstanding quality. Jesus is not interested only in the great. He went out to enlist this humble, ordinary man personally, to number him among his apostles.

Philip of Bethsaida

The name *Philip* is a Greek name meaning "lover of horses." But we should not think that it shows that Philip was a Greek. Many Jews bore the name. For example, the tetrarch who governed the region was called Philip (some have even guessed that the apostle was named after him). Our man may well have had a Hebrew name as well as this Greek name, but if he did we have no information about it.

There seems to have been nothing wonderful about Philip. Every time we meet him he seems to be out of his depth. We do not understand what John is telling us about him if we see him as some spiritual supergiant. He is a humble, ordinary man, one with whom most of us might well feel quite at home.

On the first occasion that we meet him, he was found by Jesus. It fits in with all the rest we know about Philip that he took no initiative in this matter. It apparently did not occur to him that he should seek Jesus out. It is not quite certain when Jesus found him. John tells us that Jesus wanted to go into Galilee and he found Philip. Does this mean that he in fact went into Galilee and found Philip there? William Barclay thinks so, for he translates, "And there He found Philip." This is certainly a possible understanding of the Greek text, and it may be supported by John's reporting that Philip went on to find his friend Nathanael, who was a Galilean (21:2). It is, of course, possible that Nathanael had come into the region where John the Baptist was active, but this Gospel does not say so. So Philip may have been at home when Jesus found him. If so, it is all the more remarkable that Jesus sought him out.

But it seems to me that this is a somewhat unlikely reading of the evidence. It looks as though John 1, after the prologue, is concerned with what happened in the area where the Baptist was busy. We have his witness to Jesus, then his pointing of two of his disiciples to the Lord. This is followed by one of them bringing his brother. The most natural reading of the chapter is that Jesus went on to find Philip in that area and that Philip completed the process by finding Nathanael. This would make Philip one of the group that had gathered around John the Baptist. He may have gone along with his fellow townsmen, Simon and Andrew; that would be in character. And it would also be in line with what we read of Philip elsewhere that he followed Jesus only after having received the kind of preliminary teaching that came from the Baptist. Given Philip's nature, it is unlikely that Jesus simply found him at home and, with little advance preparation, immediately persuaded him to follow.

Philip's home was Bethsaida, a Galilean town. The exact site of the place is not known, and indeed there are some who think that there were two towns of that name, "Bethsaida of Galilee" (12:21) and "Bethsaida Julias." This latter name was given to a town rebuilt by the tetrarch Philip, who added "Julias" to "Bethsaida" in honor of the daughter of the emperor. However, our best understanding of the evidence is that there was but one Bethsaida, situated somewhere near the place where the Jordan runs into the lake of Galilee. Perhaps it had a suburb on the other side of the river, and this may have given rise to the confusion about the names. The name means "house of fishing," appropriate enough for a place on the shores of the lake where so many fishermen plied their trade.

Philip and Nathanael

Jesus said to Philip, "Follow me." John does not say that Philip did follow him, but this is the clear implication of the passage. There would be no point in recording Jesus' command if nothing had happened. It is also the case that Philip immediately went looking for his friend Nathanael. When he found him he said, "We have found him of whom Moses . . . wrote," which indicates that he was already classing himself with the disciples of Jesus. There is no real doubt that Philip followed Jesus, nor that for Philip this meant attachment to the Messiah (however he understood that term).

His first reaction was to go to his friend with the news. He said to Nathanael, "We have found him of whom Moses (in the law) and the prophets wrote, Jesus the son of Joseph, who is from Nazareth." His "We have found" may in the circumstances be a slight exaggeration, but it is understandable. The others had indeed "found" Jesus, and when Philip followed him he aligned himself with them.

He does not speak of Jesus as "the Messiah" or use a similar title. He refers to him as the one of whom Moses and the prophets wrote. The fact that these words come first in the Greek gives them emphasis. This may mean that they were important words for Nathanael and Philip, and this in turn that the two friends were of the number of the Israelites who searched the Scriptures for information about the Messiah. It seems as though they were interested in the topic and had had many discussions. They would not have lacked material; Alfred Edersheim informs us that the rabbis found as many as 456 passages in Scripture that spoke of the Messiah. We need not think that all of these would have been known to Philip and Nathanael, or even that all were thought of as messianic as early as this time. It is enough that, in the opinion of many first-century students, there were many messianic passages. These two gentlemen would not have lacked passages for study.

Philip specifies the Law as one of the places in which the prophecies were to be found. In strict usage this refers to the first five books of our Old Testament, Genesis to Deuteronomy, the books of Moses. Sometimes the expression is used loosely, with a meaning like "Scripture." But the addition about the prophets here shows that Philip has in mind the books of Moses. "The prophets" probably means more than it does with us. The Jews spoke of "the former prophets" (by which they meant what we call the historical books; e.g., Joshua, Judges, 1 and 2 Samuel) and "the latter prophets" (what we call the prophetical books; e.g., Isaiah and Jeremiah). There were some differences from our classification, for they did not include Chronicles among the former prophets, nor Daniel among the latter prophets. But the division I have given answers fairly well. What Philip is saying is that a considerable part of the Bible points forward to the Messiah. And "Moses . . . and the prophets" may be a shorthand way of referring to the whole Old Testament (cf. "the law and the prophets" [Matt. 7:12]).

Philip may be saying more by his use of but one singular verb to cover the two subjects. He may be emphasizing that it was one person of whom Moses and the prophets wrote. Their messianic passages agree. They point to the same person, and that person is Jesus.

Philip calls Jesus "the son of Joseph," but we should not read too much into this. Certainly we should not argue, as some have done, that John in reporting this is denying the virgin birth. In the first place, we cannot expect a man who has been a disciple for no more than a matter of hours to know the intimate details of the birth of Jesus. Philip could not have known more at that time than that Joseph was the legal father of Jesus.

And in the second place, it is quite in John's manner to put down a statement which his informed readers will know to be in error, and leave them to work it out for themselves. G. Salmon points out that "no one understands better the rhetorical effect of leaving an absurdity without formal refutation, when his readers can be trusted to perceive it for themselves." This kind of irony is common in John's Gospel. A good example occurs in the discourse about the Bread of Life. At one point Jesus refers to being the bread that comes down from heaven, and his opponents say, "Is not this Jesus the son of Joseph, whose father and mother we know? How does he now say, 'I have come down from heaven'?" (6:42). Had they known the truth of the matter, they would have known that this very point of Jesus' parentage, far from being a difficulty, was itself proof that Jesus had come from heaven. But John does not stop to point this out. He is content to make his point more effectively with the use of irony. So here as well.

But Nathanael is not impressed. He retorts, "Out of *Nazareth* can any good thing come?" One of the little problems that preoccupy the scholars is why Nathanael should have been so contemptuous of Nazareth. True, it was a small and insignificant place, but we have no evidence at all for thinking that there was anything evil about it, such that it would be disqualified from being the hometown of the Messiah. Nathanael's poor opinion of the place is not reflected in any other source known to us. But for some reason Nathanael was very critical. As Hoskyns puts it, "Nathanael uses intelligent human observation to set a firm limit to the power of God," a process intelligent humans have been repeating all too often ever since.

The best suggestion that has been made, it seems to me, is that there was probably a rivalry between Nazareth and Cana. They were small places not far apart, and such centers often know a local rivalry (for that matter, such rivalry is not unknown between large cities). There is not much reason behind it, and many are quite amused at it, not taking it seriously. But there always seem to be some who do, and sometimes they are not the people we would expect to indulge such whims. Some scholars hold that such a rivalry is an improbable explanation; they feel that John is not likely to have chronicled a petty local jealousy. The trouble is that the reasons they suggest for Nathanael's words are even less convincing. Until a better explanation comes along, we may as well go along with this one.

Whatever the reasoning behind it, how do you meet a question like that? Philip did not know. He made no attempt to answer the question but simply said, "Come and see." Philip thought that if Nathanael could be persuaded to see for himself, it would work out all right. He knew his friend and had come to know Jesus. Seeing no way of overcoming the difficulty Nathanael had raised, he hoped that Jesus would do it for him. We may well reflect that under the circumstances this was probably as good an answer as could be given. But nothing in what we read of Philip leads me to think that he worked through all sorts of possibilities and came up with this one as the best. I think he felt hopeless. He could not argue the point convincingly, so he could only suggest that Nathanael come and see for himself.

So Nathanael came and Jesus convinced him. The story ends well. We may profitably reflect that it is not necessary to know all the answers before we can render acceptable and fruitful service to God.

Philip and the Loaves

The next time we meet Philip in John's Gospel is at the feeding of the five thousand with the five loaves and the two fishes (6:5–7). John tells us that Jesus lifted up his eyes and saw the crowds. Then he said to Philip, "Where will we buy bread so that these people may eat?" Philip was the natural person to be asked, because he came from nearby Bethsaida (1:44). It was not that Jesus meant the purchase of bread as a serious option. Clearly the quantity needed would be enormous, and it would not be easy to get it to this deserted place even if it were purchased. John explains that the question was simply to test Philip; it was not to be taken as an indication of the way Jesus would in due course provide for the people's needs.

So Philip faced the question. It was a large crowd, and Jesus' disciples were a small band. John tells us that Philip's answer was in effect, "If we had two hundred denarii (which, of course, we have not), and if we were to spend them on bread (which, of course, we cannot do as there are no bakers' shops in this area), there would not be enough to give all of them a little taste."

That was Philip's contribution to the solution of the problem. Once again we have a man out of his depth. He could see the difficulty; that was not hard for him. But he had no idea how the problem could be solved.

Philip and the Greeks

The third time we meet Philip in this Gospel is on the occasion when some Greeks came to him at Passover time in Jerusalem (12:20–22). Jesus had entered Jerusalem in triumph, and there had been a good deal of enthusiasm among those who followed him. Knowing what Jesus had done in their territory, doubtless many of the Galileans who had now come up to the feast were full of hope that he would proclaim himself Messiah. (Did not the fulfillment of prophecy through his triumphal entry into the city point to this?) They saw him as one who could get rid of the hated Romans and begin a new era for the Jews and for Palestine. Jerusalem was always excited during the great feasts, with crowds from all over the world thronging the streets. The triumphal entry must have heightened the normal state of excitement. What would happen next?

The Greeks who came to Philip may have been proselytes or converts to the Jewish religion, but, as we saw earlier (p. 47), this is improbable. They were more likely to have been "God-fearers," people who were interested in the Jewish way and specifically in serving the God the Jews worshiped, but who were deterred from becoming full members in the Jewish community of faith because of ritual practices like circumcision. They were religious people, for John tells us specifically that they had come to Jerusalem to worship (v. 20). The fact that they were Greeks meant that they could worship only in the Court of the Gentiles. Yet the prospect of worshiping there had brought them to Jerusalem.

These Greeks heard about Jesus. We have no information, however, about precisely what it was that they heard. John brings them into his narrative without introduction or explanation. He says only that they were among those who had come up to Jerusalem to worship at the feast and that they came to Philip. It is not clear why they selected Philip, but it may have been because he had a Greek name. If so, this is only a partial explanation, for his was not the only Greek name among the apostles (Andrew, for example, is also Greek). In any case there were many Jews who had Greek names. Greek was spoken throughout the world of the time; it was the common language of communication. Many people from a variety of nationalities accordingly provided themselves with a means of identification in this common language.

We cannot, then, determine the reason for their choice. But we are told that when they came, they "asked" Philip, "Sir, we wish to see Jesus" (v. 21). The words are not strictly a question, but a question is implied. Clearly they wanted to know whether Philip would help them in their quest. They spoke of "seeing" Jesus, but they had in mind more than physical sight. It was not difficult for anyone to see Jesus as he went about Jerusalem. The Greeks wanted more than this. They wanted an interview with Jesus and looked to Philip to arrange it.

From where we sit this was no big deal. We know that Jesus was full of love for all and, indeed, that he was about to provide in his death an atonement for the sins of the world. We have so fully accepted the idea that the gospel is a message for all men that we do not often stop to think how strange that must have seemed to some early disciples. It certainly was a problem for Philip.

Could he possibly bring Greeks to Jesus? Greeks? All of Jesus' ministry had been among the Jews. Jesus was a Jew himself. All the apostles were Jews. All the disciples Philip knew were Jews. Jesus and his friends had come to Jerusalem to keep the Passover, a feast of the Jews. The feeling that Jesus' people were Jews was so strong that for many years after this quite a few Christians held that if a Gentile wished to join them, he had to be circumcised and keep the law of Moses, that is, become a Jew in the full sense (cf. Acts 15:1). In the face of all this Jewishness, how could Philip possibly bring Greeks to his Master?

But, on the other hand, how could he turn them away? After all, Jesus had occasionally taken trips outside Jewish territory, such as that to Caesarea Philippi (Mark 8:27). He had healed the daughter of the Syrophoenician woman (Mark 7:24–30). Quite apart from such specific instances, Jesus habitually welcomed those whom the Jewish establishment regarded as outcasts. How would he view it if Philip turned the Greeks away?

It was all so very perplexing. Philip did not know what he should do. There were convincing objections to either course of action. So he went to Andrew and told him all about it. But, as we have noted, Andrew had no doubts. He was always bringing people to Jesus, and now he and Philip brought the Greeks. As in the case of Nathanael, it all ended well. But Philip was certainly puzzled in the situation in which he found himself.

Philip in the Upper Room

We get just one more glimpse of Philip in John's Gospel. It is in the upper room on the night before the crucifixion. Jesus is talking to the apostles and says in a reply to Thomas, "I am the way and the truth and the life; no one comes to the Father except through me. If you had known me you would have known the Father; and from now on you know him and have seen him" (14:6–7). This may have been clear to Thomas, but it was a puzzle to Philip. What does Jesus mean? We know the Father? We have *seen* the Father? That is just too much.

So Philip blurts out, "Lord, show us the Father. That's all we want" (14:8). Thus he draws down on him Jesus' gentle rebuke, "Have I been with you for such a time and you still do not know me, Philip?" He goes on to explain, "He who has seen me has seen the Father."

Thus in all the events involving Philip, we find him out of his depth. There is a consistency about Philip, just as there is a consistency of a different sort about Andrew.

A Humble Disciple

Obviously Philip had his limitations. And I, for one, find that comforting. We generally think of our Lord's twelve apostles as something special. They represent the inner circle, the aristocracy of the Christian church. There is nobody we can set alongside the apostles. And very naturally we make giants out of them. We see them as some kind of super-Christians, people infinitely higher than the likes of us.

But were they? Philip wasn't. And maybe some others weren't either. How many of us can recall offhand the names of the Twelve? We get off to a good start because we know Peter, James, and John. After our last two studies we think readily of Philip and Andrew. Most of us remember Thomas the doubter, and Judas who betrayed his Lord. The first part of the list is not difficult, but when we get down to "Lebbaeus, whose surname was Thaddaeus," we are hesitant, and with numbers ten, eleven, and twelve most of us are struggling.

Why do we find it so hard to remember them? Perhaps because some of them were simply not memorable men. Quite unreasonably we think that Jesus must have chosen spiritual giants for his Twelve. But he seems not to have done so. Some of them certainly were great men. I think that Peter would have been a great man in any company; probably John also in a different way, and perhaps some of the others would have been, too. But it seems that some of the Twelve were perfectly ordinary men, people about whom there was nothing special. People like Philip.

God does not need great men or women and great names to get his work done. He can, and often does, use very ordinary people. It may not seem to be anything wonderful when God picks out some really outstanding people like Peter and Paul and does great things through them. But when he takes humble, unimportant people like Philip, and makes of them the very saints of God, that is really wonderful.

I find Philip very encouraging. I can find no outstanding quality about him, nothing that makes him great. But there he is among Jesus' chosen Twelve. And ordinary people like me can learn that God has a place in his service for the lowliest. He still wants and uses the service of his Philips. Let us then not be discouraged by our limitations, but let us be encouraged and go forward to do whatever small piece of service God has for us to do.

8

The First Disciples: Nathanael

Philip finds Nathanael, and says to him, "We have found him of whom Moses (in the law) and the prophets wrote, Jesus the son of Joseph, who is from Nazareth." Nathanael said to him, "Out of Nazareth can any good thing come?" Philip says to him, "Come and see." Jesus saw Nathanael coming to him and he says of him, "Look, truly an Israelite in whom there is no guile." Nathanael says to him, "Where did you get to know me?" Jesus answered him, "Before Philip called you, while you were under the fig tree, I saw you." Nathanael answered him, "Rabbi, you are the Son of God, you are the King of Israel." Jesus answered him, "Because I told you that I saw you under the fig tree do you believe? You will see greater things than these." And he says to him, "Truly, truly, I tell you, you will see heaven opened and the angels of God going up and going down on the Son of man" (John 1:45–51).

The last of those recorded in John 1 as having come to Jesus at this time was Nathanael. Very little is known of this man. In fact, we read of him only in the incident in which Philip brought him to Jesus and on the occasion of the fishing expedition in John 21. But in the fishing story we have no more than his name and the information that he came from Cana of Galilee (21:2). If Nathanael did anything on that fishing trip, it is not recorded. Accordingly, all that we really know of him is what happened when he first met Jesus.

Some hold that we do not even know this. They point out that the name *Nathanael* (like its Greek equivalent, "Theodore") means "God has given." They argue from this that we are meant to see here not an individual, but an ideal disciple, or perhaps a typical incident. This would mean that the story is a pictorial way of telling us about what "God has given," a good gift that is repeated again and again in Christian experience. But there seems little reason for taking up this position. No concrete evidence is cited. The fact that the name has a meaning is surely not enough. Many first-century names had edifying meanings, but that does not mean that they were not real names of real people. On this occasion the story of Nathanael is the last in a sequence of stories of people who came to Jesus; there is no reason for thinking that it is less factual than any of the others.

Other people attempt to enlarge our knowledge of Nathanael by identifying him with someone else. They point out that we read of this man only in John, and they argue that he may well be identical with someone known in the synoptic Gospels by another name, all the more so as the name *Nathanael* does not occur in the Synoptics. The usual candidate is Bartholomew, who is not mentioned in John. "Philip and Bartholomew" are linked in that order in the lists of the names of the Twelve in all three Synoptics (Matt. 10:3; Mark 3:18; Luke 6:14); this fits in with the fact that in John it is Philip who brings Nathanael to Jesus. In the list in Acts 1 the order is "Philip and Thomas, Bartholomew . . ." (Acts 1:13); those who advocate the identification point out that Nathanael follows Thomas in the list of fishermen in John 21:2.

Their position is supported by the fact that the name *Bartholomew* is not really a personal name at all. "Bar" is a prefix meaning "son of," so that Bartholomew means "son of Tolmai." Anyone with a title like this almost certainly had a personal name of his own as well. We find such a title in the name of the great apostle Simon Peter, who is called "Simon Barjonah" (Matt. 16:17; i.e., he was Simon, son of Jonah). So Bartholomew almost certainly had another name. It is further pointed out that all the others mentioned in John 1 became apostles; from this it is inferred that Nathanael did too. If so, he is likely to have been Bartholomew.

All this is interesting but highly speculative. We can perhaps say that if we assume that Nathanael was in fact one of the Twelve, he was probably the same man the Synoptists call Bartholomew. But why should we make that assumption? There is nothing in John 1 to indicate that he would become one of the Twelve, though that proves little, since there is not much to show that the others would become apostles either. We have that information from other sources. But I see no reason for holding that in this chapter John is writing about the Twelve as such. He seems rather to be writing about men who became followers of Jesus; whether or not they became apostles is irrelevant. Jesus had many disciples outside the Twelve, and I cannot imagine a reason why John should not write about one from this wider circle in the opening section of his book.

"Come and See"

When we were thinking of Philip, we saw that he was the one responsible for bringing Nathanael to Jesus. The narrative reads as though the two were friends. They seem also to have been interested in studying the Bible, specifically the passages in Scripture that told of the coming of the Messiah. So Philip's opening words to Nathanael were, "We have found him of whom Moses (in the law) and the prophets wrote, Jesus the son of Joseph, who is from Nazareth" (1:45). Though Philip does not say so, the impression we get is that the two friends had often discussed scriptural passages about the Messiah, which they had found in the writings of both Moses and the prophets. They had been looking for the coming of God's Great One, and Philip was now enthusiastic: "We have found him!" What a wonderful thing that the prophecies they had studied and sought out for so long should now be fulfilled. And not only fulfilled in their own day, but right where they were, and in a person whom Philip himself had met! Philip was a very happy man and he told Nathanael all about it so that he could come to share in the joy.

But Nathanael was not impressed. Presumably he had been just as interested as Philip in searching out the relevant passages in the Bible. But it was quite another matter when it came to seeing them fulfilled in someone from Nazareth. Nathanael wanted more than Nazareth. "Out of *Nazareth* can any good thing come?" he asked (v. 46). We have already seen (pp. 54–55) that there is nothing discreditable about Nazareth as far as we know, and that Nathanael's objection probably came from nothing more than the fact that it was a little village not far from Cana, Nathanael's hometown. For Nathanael, the Messiah would be an impressive figure. He would come with the aura of being the fulfillment of countless prophecies of Scripture. How, then, could he come from a little place like Nazareth? Why, it was no bigger than Nathanael's own Cana! Great people simply do not come from the Nazareths of this world.

Nathanael's scepticism must have been a surprise to Philip, who clearly had been so mightily impressed by Jesus that he went right off to tell his friend. But the friend was less than enthusiastic; he was downright cool. What was to be done, then? Philip could not argue him out of his scepticism, but he could, and did, invite him to come and see for himself. "Come and see" was a stock phrase among the rabbis. They seem to have used it when they found a somewhat difficult problem to which the solution was not at all obvious. But it was possible, and the words are an invitation to join in a search for it together. It seems also to have been an invitation to look for something new or important or both. Philip, of course, was not a rabbi. But it is not without interest that he used this expression which meant so much to the rabbis.

An Israelite Without Guile

Nathanael was sceptical, but not too sceptical to avail himself of Philip's invitation. It would do no harm to go along with his friend and meet this Nazarene.

There was a surprise for him straightaway. Jesus saw him coming and greeted him with the words, "Look, truly an Israelite in whom there is no guile" (v. 47). The word for "guile" is an interesting one. Originally it seems to have meant the bait used in catching fish. Now the art of the angler is to deceive the fish. He presents the fish with a bait that seems quite acceptable (indeed, desirable), but in fact serves the interests not of the fish but of the fisherman. It deceives the fish. The word came in time to mean any cunning device, especially one for catching something or someone. For example, it was used of the Trojan horse and of Penelope's robe. It tended then to signify not so much "bait" or the like, as "deceit" or "craftiness." It pointed to an object that would effect someone's purpose by seeming to be other than it was, and this in such a way that the simple were beguiled.

There is an interesting example of its use in the Greek translation of the Old Testament. Jacob, it will be recalled, put hairy skins on his hands and wore Esau's robe to deceive Isaac into thinking that it was his elder son and not Jacob who came to him with savory meat. This resulted in the aged patriarch's giving Jacob his blessing. In due course Esau came in from his hunting and sought Isaac's blessing for himself. When Isaac realized what had happened, he said to Esau, "Your brother came deceitfully and took your blessing" (Gen. 27:35). The word translated "deceitfully" ("with subtilty" in KJV) is translated into Greek by the same word we have here *(dolos)*. This is what Jesus says Nathanael lacks. Nathanael was not like Jacob. Not for him the cunning contrivance that deceives. He was a plain, straightforward person. William Temple brings out the resemblance to the passage in Genesis by translating at this point, "An Israelite in whom there is no Jacob!" Nathanael was an Israelite indeed. But he was not like Jacob.

It may be worth noticing that this is the only place in John's Gospel where the word *Israelite* occurs. John speaks often of "the Jews" but only here of any Israelite. He may mean us to discern that Nathanael was really all that an Israelite ought to be. Paul reminds us that a man is a true Jew if he is one inwardly (Rom. 2:29). That is what Jesus is saying about Nathanael.

This greeting astonished the man. Nathanael had never seen Jesus before and was quite sure that Jesus had never seen him. How then could he possibly know anything about him? So Nathanael explodes in an incredulous question, "Where did you get to know me?" (v. 48). Incidentally this reaction neatly proves the truth of Jesus' point about his guilelessness. A guileful person would have affected a modesty leading him to say that he really was not worthy of such a description. Not Nathanael. Since he really had no guile, he accepted the accuracy of what Jesus had said and simply asked how Jesus knew.

Under the Fig Tree

Jesus replied, "Before Philip called you, while you were under the fig tree, I saw you." This clearly meant a lot to Nathanael, but it is not at all obvious to us. We notice first that the words "before Philip called you" are put first in Jesus' reply and are thus given a certain emphasis. Jesus is not speaking of something that took place as a result of Philip's call. What he is speaking about had taken place at an earlier time.

And that is about the end of our certainty. We can engage in speculation, based on what we know of fig trees and of people and their habits. Fig trees were very much a symbol of home, especially of home in a time of peace and prosperity. Micah has an apt description of peace: "Every man will sit under his own vine and under his own fig tree, and no one will make them afraid" (Mic. 4:4). Zechariah similarly looks forward to a time of peace and prosperity: "'In that day each of you will invite his neighbor to sit under his vine and fig tree,' declares the LORD Almighty" (Zech. 3:10). Fig trees and grape vines were very common throughout Israel, and every man wanted to have them about his home. Jesus' reference, then, almost certainly points to something that took place at Nathanael's home.

We can perhaps say more. Palestine could be hot in the summer, and there were no such amenities as air conditioning. So people looked to shady trees to help them through the hot weather. The rabbinic writings give evidence that scholars often used the shade of a fig tree as a good place to study and meditate and pray. A large fig tree gives a very acceptable shade, and as the tree was common, it was a widespread practice to use its shade for pious purposes.

It seems fair to say that Nathanael had had some outstanding experience as he studied his Bible or prayed in the shade of a fig tree at his home. What it was we do not know. But Jesus knew; his words showed that.

John Calvin comments: "We should also gather from this passage a useful lesson, that when we are not even thinking of Christ we are observed by Him; and this must needs be so, that He may bring us back when we have withdrawn from Him."

The King of Israel

What is not clear to us was abundantly plain to Nathanael. He knew immediately what Jesus meant and was deeply impressed by his knowledge. He exclaimed, "Rabbi, you are the Son of God, you are the King of Israel" (v. 49). Clearly he found Jesus' words totally unexpected and totally devastating to his scepticism.

I was reading of a father who was quite out of sympathy with his long-haired modern son's interest in conservation, protest marches, and the like. But one day the father scored a neat point by remarking: "Do you realize that when you wash your hair you use four times as much shampoo as I do? And all that excess is foaming away into the ecosystem and polluting the environment!" It was a completely unexpected statement.

So with Nathanael. He had not anticipated anything like Jesus' answer, and so it had a profound effect on him. The first thing we notice is the respectful "Rabbi" which begins his response. He had not been this polite when he asked whether anything good could possibly come out of Nazareth. His opening word indicates a change of heart.

He proceeds to affirm that Jesus is the Son of God. He uses the emphatic pronoun *you*. It singles Jesus out from all others. What follows in the statement is distinctive to him.

"Son of God" has different meanings. It may be used of man, as when Paul writes, "As many as are led by the Spirit of God, these are the sons of God" (Rom. 8:14). A similar thought is implied also in the family prayer of all Christians, when we say, "Our Father." As we have been adopted into the heavenly family, we may rightly be called "sons" (and, of course, "daughters") of God.

But the expression may also be used in a more limited sense. Instead of referring to a son of God in general, we may use the term in a restricted sense to denote the unique Son of God. This marks one person as God's Son in a special way. He is Son of God in a way different from that in which all of God's people may be called sons. Nathanael is using the term in this second way. He is not saying that Jesus shares with all pious men a good relationship with God, but that Jesus' sonship is different. He is not a son of God, but the Son of God.

We noticed earlier (p. 13) that John does not use the word *son* (of God) to refer to pious people who are members of God's family; he reserves this term for Jesus. He does, of course, use "son" in the ordinary way—for human sons of human fathers; it is when speaking of the heavenly family that his terminology is distinctive. When he wants to refer to human membership in the heavenly family, he uses the word *child* (as he did in 1:12). By keeping the word *Son* for Jesus he brings out his deep conviction that Jesus is God's Son in a special way, a way different from that in which anybody else may be called a son. A good example is John's reporting of Martha's confession: "I have believed that you are the Christ, the Son of God, who comes into the world" (11:27). Obviously this was not meant as a commonplace; Martha was saying that Jesus stood in a very special relationship to God. It is the same with Nathanael. He is saying that Jesus is different, the Son of God as no one else is.

Nathanael goes on to speak of Jesus as "the King of Israel." This expression is found only three times in the whole of the rest of the New Testament. One such occurrence is in Matthew's account of the mockery as Jesus hung on the cross. The chief priests and scribes and elders called on "the King of Israel" to come down from the cross (Matt. 27:42). It is not without interest that Nathanael here uses in sincerity at the beginning of Jesus' ministry a title that others would use in mockery at the end!

Mark also records the incident reported in Matthew. But in Mark the words "the Christ" and "the King of Israel" seem to mean nearly the same thing (Mark 15:32). Jesus is no ordinary king, but the messianic King, the Christ of God, the Deliverer whom God sent.

The only other passage containing the expression is the record of the triumphal entry. John tells us that as the people came to meet Jesus, they took branches from palm trees and cried out, "Hosanna, blessed is he who comes in the Lord's name, even the King of Israel" (12:13).

It is obvious from these passages that "the King of Israel" was a title of grandeur. We might be inclined to think that to go from "Son of God" to "King of Israel" is anticlimactic. But this is not the way it would have seemed to Nathanael. For him, "King of Israel" was as high a title as could be given. It denoted the sovereign ruler over the people of God, and thus someone who had an especially close relationship to God and a special task from God. We should also bear in mind that Jesus had just greeted Nathanael as "an Israelite." Accordingly, when Nathanael calls him "King of Israel," he is expressing his own allegiance and submission. As William Barclay puts it, "Nathanael capitulated for ever to the man who read and understood and satisfied his heart."

Heaven Opened

Jesus proceeds to assure Nathanael that this is but a beginning. Nathanael had been impressed by Jesus, as we see from the fact that

Jesus' use of just one expression had caused such a reversal in the attitude of the man from Cana. But, Jesus says, he will see greater things than these: "You will see heaven opened" (1:51).

This is not a commonplace, for it is consistent biblical teaching that heaven is beyond man's grasp. The story of the Tower of Babel, back in Genesis 11, illustrates the foolishness of man in his proud assurance that a tower could be built that would bring him to heaven. It firmly makes the point that God forbids this. He puts obstacles in the way. To attain heaven by our own effort must remain forever an impossible dream. Man may want to bring it about but he never can. A little later in John's Gospel we read that "no one has gained the heights of heaven except him who came down from heaven, the Son of man" (3:13). That remains true. Man is limited; heaven may be in his aspiration, but it is beyond his grasp.

But God can open heaven if he so chooses. Three times we read in the New Testament that he has done so. It happened at the baptism of Jesus (Luke 3:21). On that occasion heaven was opened for the visible coming of the Holy Spirit in a form like a dove. This was accompanied by the voice from heaven that affirmed that Jesus is God's beloved Son. Clearly that opening of heaven was very special.

So, in different ways, were the other two. When Stephen's speech met a hostile reception, he had a vision of "the glory of God and Jesus standing at the right hand of God." He said, "I see the heavens opened and the Son of man standing at the right hand of God" (Acts 7:55–56). This was a significant occasion in the life of the church. Stephen was about to become the first man martyred for the new faith. Heaven's opening assured him that, despite what men might say, God would receive him. He might be condemned by his opponents, but he had divine approval.

The third occasion was in Peter's vision. He saw "the heaven opened" and a great sheet let down full of all sorts of creatures that Peter could not class as "clean" (Acts 10:11–16). This was God's way of bringing home to the apostle the great truth that Gentiles are as important in his sight as are Jews, a most important lesson for the early church. For that matter, it is still important. Not all Christians have come to learn that race does not matter. If God opened heaven to make this clear, why are we so slow to learn it?

Jesus is saying, then, to Nathanael that his ministry would make the realities of heaven known to men. People can never attain heaven of themselves, but God can open heaven. He has sometimes done so, and preeminently was this the case in the ministry of Jesus. He has met us where we are. He has disclosed to us what we could never know of ourselves.

Jesus also says that Nathanael will see "the angels of God going up and going down on the Son of man." Notice a small point: Jesus speaks of the angels as first "going up." We would expect him to say that they would first come down from heaven and then return. But that is not the order. And it is not the order in Jacob's vision when that patriarch saw a ladder set up from earth to heaven and angels going up and down on it (Gen. 28:12). What can this mean but that the angels are here already? God has never forsaken the people he made. His love is so strong that it is always exercised toward us. We must not think that our sin or our stupidity can ever stop God from being active among us. His angelic messengers are constantly with us.

The other significant thing is that the angels ascend and descend not on a ladder (as in Jacob's vision), but on the Son of man. Jesus is the one Mediator between heaven and earth. He brings the realities of God to us, and he lifts us up to God. It is to be his work both to teach people the way to God and to be the way to God (cf. John 14:6). He will in due course lay down his life that we may be given that life that is life indeed. This is foreshadowed in the conversation with Nathanael. Nathanael could not have understood all that was involved in the mission of Jesus. But he could understand that he was no more than at the beginning of his knowledge of Jesus. Jesus had already shown him that he knew much about him and knew something of his intercourse with God. Now Nathanael learns that Jesus has much more to show him. Jesus would be the Mediator between heaven and earth.

9

A Wedding in Cana

On the third day there was a wedding in Cana of Galilee, and the mother of Jesus was there. Jesus and his disciples had been invited to the wedding. And when the wine ran out the mother of Jesus says to him, "They have no wine." Jesus says to her, "Lady, what have I to do with you? My hour has not yet come." His mother says to the waiters, "Do whatever he tells you." Now there were set there six stone water jars for the Jewish purification rites; each held two or three measures. Jesus says to them, "Fill the water jars with water." They filled them right up to the brim. And he says to them, "Draw out now and take it to the master of ceremonies." So they took it. When the master of ceremonies had tasted the water made into wine, and did not know where it had come from (though the waiters who had drawn the water knew), the master of ceremonies calls the bridegroom and says to him, "Everyone puts out the good wine first, and when people get drunk the worse. But you have kept the good wine until now." This Jesus did as the beginning of signs in Cana of Galilee, and manifested his glory. And his disciples believed in him (John 2:1–11).

We do not know a great deal about the way a wedding was conducted in first-century Palestine. A good number of regulations survive, so that we know about things like preliminary arrangements, contracts, and so on. We know who might marry whom and who might not marry whom. In sum, we know quite a bit about weddings in general.

But what happened on the great day? Here our knowledge is limited. We have no information about who performed the marriage ceremony, for example. We do not even know whether it was a religious or a civil ceremony (if indeed there was a distinction in those days). We may reason that among a people as religious as the Jews it is unthinkable that anything as significant as a wedding would take place without a solemn religious ceremony. But the fact is that we do not know. We can reason about it. We can say, "Such and such must have happened," but we cannot point to evidence. Would there have been a rabbi there? Or a priest? A Levite perhaps? Who would conduct the ceremony? What part would the heads of families play? We do not know.

Yet there are some things we do know. The wedding was preceded by a betrothal, which was a very solemn affair and much more binding than is an engagement with us. To break an engagement in modern times is not, as a general rule, much more difficult than simply returning the ring. But in first-century Palestine it required the same procedure as divorce.

The day of the wedding was a Wednesday if the bride was a virgin and a Thursday if she was a widow. The wedding was often held in the evening, because there were processions and these were more spectacular if they were held by torchlight. First the bridegroom and his friends went in procession to the home of the bride. The bridegroom and a few of those close to him went into the bride's home, while the others waited outside (like the ten young ladies in Matt. 25:1–13). The actual ceremony, whatever its form, took place inside the bride's home. Then there was another procession, this time with all those interested going to the home of the bridegroom.

Here the marriage feast was held. This was a very important part of the proceedings. It was often a lengthy affair and might go on for a week. It was important that everything be done properly. One thing that seems strange to us is that there was a strong element of reciprocity. If one gave a feast of such and such a quality (and quantity!) when his son was married, he was entitled to an equivalent when his neighbor's son was married. If the neighbor did not provide it, he could be taken to court and sued; a wedding feast was not simply a social occasion, but involved a legal obligation. This is important for our present study. It is quite possible that the bridegroom of John 2 and his family were financially unable to provide all that was necessary for the wedding feast. It is often said that it is unlikely that Jesus would have performed a miracle like this simply to rescue people from a minor social embarrassment. Quite so. But it may well have been much more than that. It may be that Jesus rescued a young couple from a financial liability that would have crippled them economically for years.

The Wine Failed

We are told that this marriage was at Cana of Galilee. This place is rarely mentioned in early literature; in the New Testament it is referred to only here and in John 4:46 and 21:2. Each time "of Galilee" is added; apparently people needed some indication of its location. We may fairly reason that it was not an important place.

And the participants were not important people. Important people did not live in places like Cana. We are not even told the name of anyone in either of the families being linked by this wedding. Plainly the people were poor; otherwise they would have made ample provision for the wedding. They were certainly a long way from being like the customers of a New York bank of whom I read recently. For people who like to use only clean, fresh bank-notes, quite untouched by human hands, the bank provides new notes in books with tissues between the notes. This service is provided free for customers who keep a minimum balance of $25,000. Our wedding party would not have qualified. But it was for this humble, obscure, unnamed group of poor people that Jesus did his first miracle. God's priorities are not ours.

John tells us that the mother of Jesus "was there" (v. 1). Incidentally it is one of the minor mysteries about this Gospel that the author never uses Mary's name. He uses some other names freely, but he always refers to Mary as "the mother of Jesus." No satisfactory explanation of this has been given; we must simply take it that John omits the names of some people. John the son of Zebedee is himself nowhere mentioned by name (cf. John 21:2), and these two facts may be linked. John tells us that on the cross Jesus commended Mary to the keeping of the beloved disciple (19:26–27). If this man was the author of the Gospel and his practice was not to mention the name either of himself or of his brother, he may well have extended this habit to include Mary, who at the time of writing was, or had been, a member of his household.

John does not say so, but he leaves the impression that Mary was a friend of the family, and that she had been in residence with them to help with the preparations for the wedding. By contrast, Jesus and his disciples "had been invited" to the wedding (v. 2). Some, it is true, hold that they simply came by and, being there, were "invited" on the spot. They further conjecture that it was this unexpected addition to the guest list that caused the wine to run out, so that Jesus' miracle was a means of rescuing people from a difficult situation that he himself had helped to bring about. But this is to read a great deal into the passage. The plain meaning of the words before us is that Jesus and his friends had been invited in the customary way.

Evidently the family was a poor one. They had had to make the minimum preparation for the wedding, hoping that everything would work out all right. But it didn't. They miscalculated the amount of wine needed (or perhaps they could not afford more), and there was not enough.

That was a serious matter. There is a rabbinic saying, "Without wine there is no joy." We should not misinterpret this as evidence that the rabbis were given to much drinking. They were not. They were highly critical of drunkenness, and they required that when wine was drunk it should be diluted with water in the proportion of three parts of water to one of wine. The saying reflects the fact that in the first century there was not much choice of beverages. Quite unreasonably we tend to read back our rich variety; we think that if they did not have our tea, coffee, Coca-Cola, and the like, they had their equivalent. But in the first century one drank water or one drank wine. For ordinary people there was nothing else. A wedding or other feast was a special occasion. So while some people evidently had the habit of drinking water as their normal practice (cf. 1 Tim. 5:23), this was felt to be inappropriate at a feast. On such an occasion there must be wine. No one, then, could dismiss the absence of wine at a wedding feast as a matter of no importance. In that time and in that place it mattered very much.

As we saw earlier, it is likely that the family responsible was in a difficult financial position. That the wine ran out is itself evidence of the fact that they were poor. Had they not been in straitened circumstances, they would never have allowed such an occurrence. It is almost certain that some of the guests were people who had previously entertained the present hosts and were thus entitled to demand an equivalent hospitality. There may even have been the prospect of a lawsuit. We must not think of the situation as a very minor affair, with nothing much hinging on the outcome.

In this crisis Mary approached Jesus. She did not ask explicitly for a miracle, but her words seem to look for nothing less. At the least she knew Jesus to be resourceful, and she put the problem before him. But we should perhaps see more than that in her words. Mary knew the circumstances of the birth of Jesus, and she had had visits from the shepherds and the wise men. Whatever the case with other people, she knew Jesus to be God's Messiah. It may be that we should see here some natural motherly pride and perhaps a small trace of exasperation. From Luke's Gospel we know that Jesus was about thirty years old when he started on his public ministry (Luke 3:23). Mary may well have been asking herself, "When will he begin his work as Messiah?" Surely it was time. Moreover, there was the excitement arising from the events described in John 1. Disciples were gathering round Jesus. He was being hailed as the Messiah. Why then does he not do something? Mary, proud of her son, gives a gentle push. Here is a fine opportunity for him to make a beginning.

This is probably behind Jesus' words, "Lady, what have I to do with you?" (v. 4). These words are not as distant in Greek as they sound in English. For example, Jesus used the same form of address, "Lady" or "Woman," in speaking to women for whom he was doing miracles (Matt. 15:28; Luke 13:12), the woman at the well (John 4:21), the woman taken in adultery whom he rescued from being stoned (John 8:10), and Mary Magdalene at the tomb (John 20:15). And, of course, it was this form of address that he used when he spoke to Mary from the cross (John 19:26). There is no harshness in the term on any of these occasions.

Yet we should bear in mind that it was a very unusual form of address for a son to use in speaking to his mother. Apart from the examples in this Gospel, no one seems to have noticed any. Neither among the Jews nor among the Greeks is this form of address attested.

We should probably infer that Jesus, though speaking politely, is putting a distance between them. As long as he lived in the home at Nazareth he was subject to his parents as a dutiful son. But when he began his public ministry he was God's Messiah. He must now act as God leads him. His relationship to his mother is changed, and she must not presume on her position. This is also the thrust of "what have I to do with you?" It points to a changed relationship. There is no longer the tie to which Mary appealed. Jesus is now not simply her son, but God's Messiah, who must be active in doing the will and the work of God.

Jesus adds, "My hour has not yet come." This must surely mean, "It is not yet time for me to act." We would leave it at that, were it not that this is the first of a series of references to Jesus' "time" or his "hour." His time has not yet come in John 7:6, 8, 30; and 8:20. But when the cross is in immediate prospect Jesus says, "The hour has come that the Son of man should be glorified" (John 12:23; there are similar statements in 12:27; 13:1; 16:32; 17:1). In other words, this series of statements running through the Gospel up till the time of the crucifixion is a way John has of bringing out the fact that the purpose of God is worked out in the life of Jesus, a purpose that is to culminate in the cross. Until the crucifixion Jesus' hour had not arrived. At the crucifixion his hour came. This is an unobtrusive but impressive way of indicating the centrality of the cross. We are not to see the cross as a sad accident coming at the end of a life full of the promise of better things. We are to see it as the culmination, and as the intended culmination, of all that Jesus did. That for which he came into the world would be accomplished on the cross and nowhere else.

Water into Wine

Clearly Mary did not take Jesus' words to her as a sharp rebuke. She went on to instruct the servants to do whatever Jesus told them (v. 5).

Incidentally, the fact that she could give such an instruction shows that she had some standing in the household and underlines our impression from verse 1 that she was in the house at the time to help with the wedding preparations.

John now inserts a little explanation of the scene. He specifically refers to some water jars. They were made of stone and were of considerable size. He tells us that they had a capacity of "two or three measures" each. This is the only passage in the New Testament where this word for "measure" is found, but in other literature it was in frequent use (often in connection with a quantity of wine). It denoted eight to nine gallons, so that two or three measures would amount to something like twenty gallons. Six such jars would hold about 120 gallons of water. If this seems a lot, we must bear in mind the continuing need for ceremonial purification. Before eating, each guest would have a servant pour water over his hands. If the feast went on for a number of days, the process would be repeated every time the guest ate, for in the meantime he might well have contracted defilement in some way. So, with any sizable number of guests, there would be the need for a fair quantity of water.

Jesus' first instruction to the servants was to fill up these water jars. This is presumably a way of ensuring that there would be no doubt about what happened. With the jars filled right up to the brim with water, there was no chance of inserting anything else into them.

Some have seen some symbolic significance in the number six. They point out that seven was regarded as the perfect number and suggest that six should be seen as a symbol of coming short. This leads us to think of the Jewish approach as coming short, and of Christ's way as the perfect way that replaces it. I suppose that a symbolic significance of this sort is not impossible, but it is not the kind of thing we meet elsewhere in this Gospel. Against it also is the fact that there is nothing to indicate the number seven. Jesus does not produce a seventh jar, for example. Moreover, we cannot be certain that six would be recognized as an indication of falling short. The Alexandrian Jew Philo, who wrote shortly after this, thinks of six as the perfect number. He gives as his reason that it is equal to the sum of its factors ($3 \times 2 \times 1 = 6$ and $3 + 2 + 1 = 6$). We are not impressed by his logic; nonetheless, we are not in a position to say, without some indication in the context, that John is pointing to something imperfect when he uses the number six. That is not given in the number itself.

Next Jesus instructs the waiters to draw water and bring it to the master of ceremonies (v. 8). He does not say from what the water should be drawn, and some people have thought that he meant that they should draw water from the well. It is true that the verb here is often used of drawing water out of wells (though not exclusively; there are other uses). But there is nothing to show that this is the meaning here. If it is this that is in mind, why does John tell us about the water jars? And why does Jesus command that they be filled? It seems curious that they should be mentioned if they are to play no part in the story. Everything points to the water as being taken from the water jars.

John puts no particular emphasis on the miracle. In fact, he does not even say when it happened. For that matter, he does not say how much water was turned into wine, but simply assumes the miracle and says, "When the master of ceremonies had tasted the water made into wine. . . ." Some have thought that his meaning is that the whole 120 gallons became wine, others that only what was brought to the guests was so changed. If the former was the case, the change probably took place before the waiters started bringing it in; if the latter, then the transformation would have been at the time of bringing the beverage to the guests.

Some have objected to the idea that all 120 gallons were changed, on the grounds that this would be far too much for a wedding feast and would be an encouragement to drunkenness. But that is probably the wrong way to understand it. We have already seen that wine was heavily diluted on such occasions, and if we are to think of the entire amount as being changed (which I think we should), the point is that it was more than was needed for the wedding. The young couple would be able to sell the excess and start their married life with an asset instead of facing a crippling liability. While we cannot be sure which of the views is to be preferred, it seems to me that the mention of the capacity of the water jars turns the scale. If all the water was changed into wine, this tells us how much there was; it is an important piece of information. But if only what was drawn out was changed, what is the point of mentioning the size of the jars? In this view it would not matter what size they were.

One point of the miracle is that Christ makes abundant provision. There was an immediate need at the wedding, but when he supplied that need he did more: he helped the young couple get off to a good start in their married life. He gives with no niggardly hand. Paul speaks of God as supplying his people's need "according to his riches in glory" (Phil. 4:19), not simply according to their need at one particular moment.

The Result

The first result of the miracle was the comment of the master of ceremonies. He called the bridegroom and pointed out that he was not behaving as a host usually did. Evidently this man had had a wide experience of festivities (as we would expect of someone appointed to preside). He remarked that the usual practice was for people to put out their best wine at the beginning. At that time the guests' palates are still sensitive, and they can remark on the quality of what they are drinking. When they have drunk a quantity (actually he says, "when people get drunk," which is a comment not on the state of the guests at this particular feast but on what happens at feasts in general), then the worse wine is brought out. When palates are no longer sensitive, people are less aware of what they are drinking.

But on this occasion the best wine had been kept back until later. It would seem that neither the master of ceremonies nor the bridegroom knew where the wine in question came from. We are told only that the waiters who brought it in knew. The master of ceremonies was not consciously commenting on a miracle; he was simply impressed by the taste. But John's readers will pick up the point that Jesus does not do things by halves. Not only is the wine that Jesus provides abundant in quantity, but it is also of excellent quality. There is nothing to equal it.

John adds a comment of his own. He tells us that Jesus did this "as the beginning of signs" (v. 11). He has his own terminology for Jesus' miracles. He never calls them "mighty works" as do the other Evangelists. He calls them "signs" or "works." The latter term points to the fact that what to us is a miracle is to Jesus no more than a work. And, as John uses the term for both miracles and the nonmiraculous, it points to the further truth that for Jesus there was no great difference between the one and the other. His life was a unity. Being who and what he was, he did some things we can class only as miracles, as well as more ordinary things. But we ought not to think of Jesus as though he on occasion transformed himself into a magician, into another person so to speak. All that he did he did as one person.

But here John uses the term *sign*. This is a way of saying that Jesus' miracles were not simply works of wonder. The essential characteristic is not that we cannot explain them, but that they are meaningful. They convey spiritual truth.

A New Creation

Accordingly, we should look for the spiritual significance of this first sign. Right at the beginning of his account of Jesus' ministry, John tells a story of transformation. He is not writing about Jesus as though he were simply a wonder-worker. He is telling us about the way Jesus transforms lives. He will go on in chapter 3 to the necessity for being reborn; there he will set forth the same truth in a different way. The divine power will transform the life of whoever comes to Christ.

We should not overlook the fact that John says specifically that the water jars in this story were set there "for the Jewish purification rites" (v. 6). It was precisely this water of Jewish purification that Jesus changed into wine. John surely means us to see that the water of Jewish ceremonial observance, water used in accordance with Jewish concentration on the law as the way of salvation, is changed by Christ into the wine of the gospel. Jesus had not come to tidy up an old system. He came to change people, to change them radically, to put a new power in them.

This may be indicated also by some unobtrusive notes with which John starts his Gospel. After his prologue, he begins his account by telling us what happened on one particular day (1:19). In verse 29, the words "the next day" move us on to Day Two. A similar expression in verse 35 advances us to Day Three. Then in verse 39 two young men come and stay with Jesus, beginning at around 4 P.M. This seems to mean that they stay the night, bringing us to Day Four. In verse 43 the words "the next day" take us to Day Five. There is no reference to Day Six, but in John 2:1 we read "on the third day," which, by the inclusive method of counting in use at the time, brings us to Day Seven. John puts no emphasis on it, but he thus begins his Gospel with an account of the happenings of one momentous week, the week that inaugurated Jesus' ministry.

We recall that the opening words of this Gospel are "In the beginning," exactly the words with which Genesis commences its description of the seven days of creation. Surely John is doing much the same thing. By his choice of opening words and by arranging his first narratives in a way that recalls the creation story, he is making the point that he is writing about a new creation. This is not a creation in the physical world, but one in the hearts of men. Jesus does not take sinners as they are and leave them like that. He transforms them. He brings a new power into life and makes them new.

John goes on to say that Jesus "manifested his glory." The sign showed something of who and what he is. He is fully man, but he is more. This "more" might be hidden from the casual observer. But John goes on to say, "His disciples believed in him." He says nothing about the effect of it all on the guests or the wedded couple or the master of ceremonies or the waiters, though these last at least knew that water had been changed into wine (v. 9). None of these saw the significance of what had happened.

But the disciples did. They were interested and committed people, and they looked into the meaning of what Jesus did. And because they looked for spiritual meaning, their faith was deepened. God always responds to the genuine seeker.

10

The Temple

And the Passover of the Jews was near, and Jesus went up to Jerusalem. And he found in the temple men selling oxen and sheep and doves, and all the moneychangers sitting. He made a whip of rushes and drove them all out of the temple, both the sheep and the oxen, and he poured out the money of the moneychangers and overturned their tables. He said to those who sold doves, "Take these things away from here; do not make my Father's house into a shop." His disciples remembered that it is written, "Zeal for your house will devour me" (John 2:13–17).

The Passover was one of the three great festivals of the Jewish year. It commemorated the great deliverance of the people from Egypt and was accordingly a time of special solemnity. It was one of the three occasions each year when all adult Jewish males were required to go up to Jerusalem (Deut. 16:16). So it is not surprising to find Jesus keeping it in the usual way and going up to the capital city.

John speaks of it as "the Passover of the Jews," from which some have drawn the conclusion that there was another Passover, the Passover of the Christians (which would in time develop into the Easter festival). But this seems highly unlikely. In the first place, it is reading too much into the words "of the Jews." John refers to Jewish customs often. In our last study we saw how naturally he referred to the water jars for the Jewish purification rites, where his expression is like that here: "the purification of the Jews" (2:6). He also uses this kind of language with respect to the Feast of Tabernacles; it is "the feast of the Jews" (7:2). Are we to think that the Christians had their own purification ceremonies and their own Feast of Tabernacles?

In the second place, this would attribute to the early Christians a greater interest in liturgical observances than the New Testament warrants. There is evidence that those among them who were Jews observed some of the Jewish liturgical requirements, such as the feasts. Some even kept the Jewish Sabbath. But there is little evidence of any specifically Christian liturgical observance. It seems reasonably clear that Sunday was kept as a day for worship (1 Cor. 16:2; Rev. 1:10), though there is not as much evidence even for this as we might have expected. And it is not easy to find any other day that the Christians kept as holy. Sometimes their language is hard to reconcile with any real concern for special days (e.g., Gal. 4:10–11).

In the third place, for the Christians the Passover could be said to have been sacrificed already (1 Cor. 5:7). This would be a very strange statement if the Christians were in the habit of keeping an annual Passover of their own.

It seems clear, then, that John simply means that the Jews held a Passover each year, and that on the occasion of which he is writing Jesus went up to Jerusalem to keep it. Not all Jews went up each year, of course, but many did. It was a great festival, and people liked to be in Jerusalem for it.

Traders in the Temple

On this occasion, when he came up to Jerusalem Jesus found a busy bazaar in the temple courts. There were people selling oxen, sheep, and doves, which would have been necessary for those who wanted to offer a sacrifice. Obviously, for people who came from a distance, perhaps from over the sea, it would be difficult and in some cases impossible to bring with them the animals needed for sacrifice. So it was important that there be those who would provide the necessary victims somewhere handy to the temple. Then the worshipers could come up to Jerusalem with their money, purchase the animals or birds on the spot, and offer their sacrifices in the normal manner.

If the sacrificial system was to be continued and if it was to be available for people who came from distant parts, it was necessary that there be provision for them to purchase what they needed for their offerings. But the point is that there was no necessity for the animals and the birds to be in the temple precincts. They needed only be somewhere handy. But the traders were evidently eager for business and set up their stalls in the temple itself. This means in the outermost court, the Court of the Gentiles. For the traders it meant good business; they were on the spot and in a position to make many sales. But for any Gentile who came up to the temple to worship it meant that prayer had to be offered in the middle of a cattle yard and money market. It is true that the service these businessmen provided was useful, but they should have provided it somewhere other than in the temple itself.

The moneychangers were needed because offerings in the temple were to be made only in approved currency. A surprising number of commentators say that this was because some coins had stamped on them the image of the emperor or some other great person or some heathen emblem. Pointing out that the Jews refused to make any representation of the human form, they hold that heathen coinage with such images was unacceptable for the temple offerings. But this overlooks the fact that it was not only permitted, but required, that offerings be made in Tyrian currency, and the heathen Tyrian coins bore representations of the human form.

The reason for stipulating Tyrian coinage is never given, but it probably concerns problems that arose when people were not strict enough with their currencies. In many states coins were of uncertain alloy. When times were hard, rulers were able to stretch their available gold and silver by making the coins a little less valuable, either by simply reducing the amount of precious metal in them or by substituting some cheaper metal for part of the gold or silver. But the Tyrians were traders and knew the value of a stable currency. So they insisted that their coins be of exactly the right weight and contain exactly the right amount of precious metal. People knew that they could trust Tyrian currency. If a Tyrian coin was supposed to contain a certain amount of silver or gold, then it would certainly contain that amount of precious metal.

The temple authorities probably insisted on this coinage for temple dues and the like because they knew what they were getting. In any case they seem to have melted down the coins and cast them into ingots, so the heathen symbols did not matter; they did not last long. Whether or not that is the reason, there is no doubt as to the practice. Anyone making an offering in the temple had to do so in Tyrian coins. So moneychangers were needed. Worshipers came from all over the world bringing their local coins, and the moneychangers exchanged their coins for Tyrian.

Driving the Traders Out

When Jesus came up to the temple, then, he found himself confronted with commercialism run riot. Instead of a quiet courtyard where people from all over the world could pray, there was this noisy trading center.

So he made a whip, probably out of rushes, though some hold that it was of cords. They find support in the fact that in the only other place where the word is used in the New Testament, it certainly means the ropes on a ship (Acts 27:32). Either way, it was not a particularly formidable weapon. But armed with this alone, Jesus proceeded to drive the traders from the temple.

Obviously one man with such a small armament could not prevail physically over a crowd of traders. There can be little doubt that he had an ally in the consciences of the traders. They knew deep down that whatever the legalities, they should not have been there. Had they combined to resist Jesus, it is not easy to see on the human level how he could have overcome them. But his selfless anger and their uneasy fears combined. They fled before his onslaught. He drove out the traders with their sheep and oxen; he poured out the money of the moneychangers and overturned their tables.

He said to the sellers of doves, "Take these things away from here; do not make my Father's house into a shop" (v. 16). The word *shop* is more literally "house of trade," and the double reference to "house" is noteworthy. They had forgotten in whose house they were and were making a house meant for the worship of God into a house for their own profit.

There is an account of a cleansing of the temple in all three synoptic Gospels. But they tell us that on that occasion (which seems to be different from the one John describes; it is at the end of Jesus' ministry, whereas John is describing what happened near the beginning of it), Jesus quoted Isaiah 56:7 and went on to complain that the traders had made the house of God into "a den of robbers" (Mark 11:17). He was complaining about the dishonesty of the traders, and there was indeed room for that. Enough examples are attested of their exorbitant charges to make it clear that they took advantage of their privileged position. But in John it is not the dishonesty of which notice is taken, but the practice itself. Whether honest or not, they should not have been there. The temple was meant as a place of worship and should not have been used as a means of amassing profits.

Notice further that Jesus speaks of "my Father's house." He does not class himself with men and speak of "our Father's house." Throughout this Gospel he never links himself with people in such a way that we can say that his relationship to the Father is the same as that of men. God is our Father, but he is Jesus' Father in a special way. We may become "sons of God"; he is "the Son of God"!

The disciples remembered the words of Psalm 69:9: "Zeal for your house will devour me." We should probably understand these words to mean that Jesus has that all-consuming zeal for God and for God's house that is characteristic of the Messiah. All that Jesus does arises from his special relationship to God and his vocation to be God's Messiah. John writes his whole Gospel to bring this out (20:31), and narrating this incident is part of the way he fulfills his plan.

Raising the Temple

The Jews answered him, "What sign do you show us, that you do these things?" Jesus replied, "Destroy this temple and in three days I will raise it up." The Jews said to him therefore, "This temple was built in forty-six years, and you will raise it up in three days?" But he was speaking about the temple of his body. When accordingly he was raised from the dead, his disciples remembered that he had said this and they believed the Scripture and the saying that Jesus had spoken (John 2:18–22).

The Jews recognized the messianic significance of what Jesus had done. Interestingly, they did not question the deed itself, but Jesus' right to do it. They expected that when the Messiah came, God would do miraculous things through him; presumably they thought that the Messiah could do more or less what he wanted to in the temple. So they asked Jesus for a sign that would accredit him. If he was going to act like the Messiah, let him produce a sign that would show him to be the Messiah. John says that they "answered" him, which means that they answered his action. What he had done spoke louder than any words. They made reply to that devastating action.

Jesus responded, "Destroy this temple and in three days I will raise it up" (v. 19). This puzzled them, but in some form or other it was remembered and distorted. When his enemies arrested him years later, they produced witnesses who said, "We heard him say, 'I will destroy this temple made with hands and in three days I will build another not made with hands'" (Mark 14:58). This is not exactly what Jesus said, and indeed in this form it is something very different. But it resembles his actual statement sufficiently for us to see that it is based on what Jesus had said. Unfortunately for their purpose, the witnesses could not agree on the exact words; this is natural if they were trying to recall a cryptic statement made some years before. Mockers also recalled the saying as Jesus hung on the cross (Mark 15:29), and Stephen's opponents seem to have had the same words in mind (Acts 6:14). In the synoptic Gospels there is no narrative relating the actual event at which Jesus spoke these words. It would seem that behind all these passages there are fragmentary and imperfect recollections of what Jesus said on this occasion.

The Jews had asked Jesus for a sign, but throughout his ministry he consistently refused to give a sign when he was asked for it in this way (cf. Mark 8.11–12). Jesus said that the only sign that would be given to the people who looked for one was the sign of Jonah, who was three days and nights in the belly of the whale, just as the Son of man would be in the heart of the earth (Matt. 12:38–40). That is to say, the resurrection would be the sign.

It is along this line of thinking that Jesus here says, "Destroy this temple and in three days I will raise it up." The language is different, but the meaning is the same. The Jews would bring about his death, and on the third day he would rise. Ironically they would themselves be the means of bringing about the sign they were demanding. Another irony is that when the sign in fact came, they did not recognize it, because they refused to recognize the resurrection.

We should notice a change of vocabulary that seems significant. In the earlier part of this account, John uses for "temple" the word *hieron* (v. 14), which is an inclusive word. It refers to the whole of the temple precincts, with the courtyards, vestries, and whatever else belonged to the temple complex. But in verse 19 Jesus uses the word *naos,* which means "the sanctuary." It was used of the central place in any temple, the shrine, the place where deity dwells. This word is sometimes used metaphorically of the believer, who is the "temple of the Holy Spirit" (1 Cor. 6:19). But its use here of Jesus probably points to the fact that God was in him in a special way.

The Jews were astonished. They thought about their temple, a magnificent structure that had been in process of construction for a long time. They spoke of forty-six years, which may mean that at the end of that period of time a certain stage in the work had been completed, so that they could speak of the temple as "built." Actually the temple was begun by Herod but not completed until A.D. 64, well after the time these words were spoken. But even forty-six years is a long time and stands for a considerable amount of work. They found it incredible that Jesus would accomplish in three days what had taken the workmen so many years.

But they had not understood Jesus. He was not talking about the stones and mortar that preoccupied them. He was talking about "the temple of his body" (v. 21). This pattern—a statement by Jesus, a misunderstanding, then a further explanation that brings out more truth—is repeated a number of times in this Gospel (and is not unknown in the others). It is an effective way of driving a point home.

John does not say that the disciples understood all this straightaway. It was only after the resurrection that they remembered the saying and saw what it meant. The result was that they believed (v. 22). John's linkage of believing "the Scripture" with believing "the saying that Jesus had spoken" shows that he put the words of Jesus on the same level as those of the Bible, the Word of God. This is instructive for understanding his view of Jesus.

John sees the words as pointing to Jesus' resurrection. We should perhaps notice that there have been other interpretations. Some students think that the "body" refers to the church. They remind us that the church is explicitly said to be the body of Christ in passages like Ephesians 1:23 and 4:16. They suggest that Jesus meant that his death would result in the appearance of the church. There is, of course, truth in this, since apart from the death of Jesus, there would have been no Christian church. The atonement is the great act on which the very existence of the church depends. But it is not easy to think that it is this that John has in mind when he reports these words of Jesus. John does not call the church the body of Christ in any other passage, and we have no reason for thinking that in this Gospel a reference to the "body" without further explanation would lead his readers to think of the church. There must be a further meaning.

Others hold that Jesus was referring to the literal temple and speaking of its ultimate destruction. But he would not refer to the rebuilding of this material, physical structure, for in fact it was not rebuilt after it was destroyed in A.D. 70. So they maintain that Jesus said something about the destruction of the temple that was not fully understood. They think that the exact words have been lost in the process of transmission, so that it is now impossible to be certain of what Jesus said or what he meant. Probably, they suggest, he said something about the new way that he would bring to pass, a new way that would replace the temple and all it stood for.

The Resurrection

Such explanations are put forward sincerely, but it seems they are no improvement on what John tells us, namely, that the words refer to the physical body of Jesus, which would be destroyed, but which would be raised up in the resurrection. Let us bear in mind a number of relevant facts.

In the first place, all the other Gospels tell us that Jesus predicted his resurrection (e.g., Matt. 16:21; Mark 9:31; Luke 18:33). It is clear in all the Gospels that Jesus knew that he would be rejected by the Jews and that in the end they would succeed in having him put to death. But it is equally clear that he did not regard their triumph as permanent. He foresaw that he would rise from the dead and said so. John's explanation of his words here fits in with what we know from elsewhere.

It is also clear that Jesus said something about the temple that his enemies thought involved its destruction and used against him at his trial (as we saw earlier). They could not remember the exact words (Mark 14:58–59). This would be very natural, for the statement was made at least a couple of years before Jesus' arrest and trial; and in addition it is the kind of enigmatic saying that they would not have understood and thus might have difficulty in recalling exactly.

It is also the case that when in any Gospel Jesus speaks of "three days," he usually means the period leading up to the resurrection. He does this often and in fact does not refer to "three days" in any other way (except for one saying about people who had been with him for three days [Matt. 15:32; Mark 8:2]). It is not easy to see why anyone should attach "three days" to a saying about the literal destruction of the temple. It is much the best explanation that Jesus himself linked "three days" to a reference to the temple in a statement that foretold his rising from the dead.

A New Way

We should take the words, then, as an unusual way of referring to the resurrection after the Jews had helped bring about the death of Jesus (the "destruction" of his body). But John often has sayings that may be understood in more ways than one, and not uncommonly it seems as though he intends us to see a double meaning. This may well be the case here.

For the fact is that the death and resurrection of Jesus did mean the destruction of the temple as a viable religious system. After Jesus had offered the sacrifice that would put away the sins of the world, what place would there be for a temple in which the central act was the offering of the bodies of animals on the altar? When Jesus died, the temple died as the center of a religious system.

John is surely tying all this together. He tells us how Jesus cleansed the temple, an act that vividly rejected the Jewish system as it was practiced, with its externality and its exaltation of the profit motive. When he goes on to Jesus' words about the destruction of the temple, he seems to be saying that in due course the death and resurrection of Jesus would spell the end of the way of approach to God that his contemporaries accepted so uncritically.

R. H. Lightfoot has this to say:

> There is in this story, thus set before us here, a triple depth of meaning. First, the Lord performs an act by which He condemns the methods and

> the manner of the existing Jewish worship. Secondly, this act, as set forth by St. John, is a sign of the destruction of the old order of worship, that of the Jewish Church, and its replacement by a new order of worship, that of the Christian Church, the sanctuary or shrine of the living God. And thirdly, intermediate between the old order and the new order is the "work"—the ministry, death, and resurrection—of the Lord, which alone makes possible the inauguration and the life of the new temple.

To see the words in this way is to see John as setting forth a grand conception. He sees the work of Jesus as the critical event in the working out of the plan of God for man's redemption. He sees what God has done as a call to us to bow in adoring worship before him who has wrought out our salvation in what his dear Son taught and did. The death and resurrection of Jesus have transformed our whole conception of the way to God. In the light of what Jesus has done, there is no place for the kind of thing that the temple symbolized. As the writer to the Hebrews put it, "no longer is there an offering for sin" (Heb. 10:18).

11

Rebirth from Above

There was a man of the Pharisees, Nicodemus by name, a ruler of the Jews. This man came to him by night and said to him, "Rabbi, we know that it is from God that you have come as a teacher, for nobody can do the signs that you do unless God is with him." Jesus replied, "Truly, truly, I tell you, unless anyone is reborn from above he cannot see the kingdom of God." Nicodemus says to him, "How can a man be born when he is old? He cannot enter a second time into his mother's womb and be born, can he?" Jesus answered, "Truly, truly, I tell you, unless anyone is born of water and Spirit he cannot enter the kingdom of God. That which is born of the flesh is flesh, and that which is born of the Spirit is spirit. Don't be astonished that I told you, 'You must be reborn from above.' The wind blows where it wants to, and you hear the sound of it, but you do not know where it is coming from or where it is going. So is everyone who has been born of the Spirit" (John 3:1–8).

Jesus' conversation with Nicodemus is fascinating. In the first place it is quite unexpected that a man of this kind would want to talk to Jesus. John tells us that he was a Pharisee, a ruler, and "the teacher of Israel" (vv. 1, 10). This is not the kind of person that the Gospels tell us was usually found where Jesus was. But Nicodemus came.

When he came he spoke with some condescension. "Rabbi," he began. Jesus was not really a rabbi, but it doesn't hurt to be polite (especially if one's friends know nothing about it!). "Rabbi, we know that it is from God that you have come as a teacher. . . ." Is there here a note of conscious superiority? Is he implying, "Some of us are disposed to think quite well of you"? Though Nicodemus was condescending to talk to the Galilean teacher, he was still very mindful of his own position and who he thought Jesus was.

I am reminded of an incident in an American law court. A flamboyant figure strode to the witness box and was sworn in. He was instructed, "State your name," and replied, "Frank Lloyd Wright." "Occupation?" "I am the world's greatest living architect." Afterwards one of his friends said to him, "Frank, how could you say such a thing in court?" To which he replied simply, "I had to. I was on oath."

Do I detect something of this in the attitude of Nicodemus? He was not coming to Jesus (he thought) as to a superior or even an equal. He was very conscious of the relative positions of a Pharisaic ruler and a preacher from Galilee. Nicodemus might be polite, but he knew where they both stood.

But Jesus was not concerned with the kind of thing that mattered to Nicodemus. He wanted none of the polite exchanges that rested on such a foundation, but came straight to the real need of the Pharisee. His opening words are the solemn "Truly, truly," which in this Gospel introduce and emphasize important statements. "Truly, truly, I tell you, unless anyone is reborn from above he cannot see the kingdom of God" (v. 3). I am adopting here the common translation "born," but it might be noticed that the Greek verb is more naturally understood of the male parent than of the female. It is the "begotten" of old-fashioned speech. The point is that what Jesus says more naturally refers to the male parent than the female, and in this context refers to the action of God the Father. The way to the kingdom is not the way of human striving or of human excellence of any sort. We enter the kingdom because of what God does.

"The kingdom of God" is the most frequent topic of Jesus' teaching in the Synoptics, but it is rare in the Fourth Gospel. It is generally accepted that the term is to be understood dynamically; that is to say, it means "reign" rather than "realm." It points to something that happens rather than something that exists. It is the rule of God actively at work. Obviously it is important for religiously minded people that they see this kingdom, so the words were important for Nicodemus.

There is a problem for us as to the precise meaning of the expression I have translated "reborn from above." The adverb *anōthen* is held by some to mean "again." The word can mean either "again" or "from above," and the difficulty is that either translation gives a good sense in this passage. But John has the habit of using words that have more than one meaning in a way that shows he wants his readers to see multiple meanings. So it is, I think, here. The begetting of which John is writing is something new, so we should understand the adverb as "again." But it is not an earthly renewal that is in mind, a fact which is brought out with "from above." If we understand the adverb in the sense "reborn from above," we get both meanings and save ourselves the problem of trying to differentiate between them.

Clearly Nicodemus did not like the way the conversation was going. He asked, "How can a man be born when he is old? He cannot enter a second time into his mother's womb and be born, can he?" (v. 4). This is surprising. Jesus quite obviously did not mean this, and an intelligent man like Nicodemus can scarcely have thought that he did.

It is possible that it was the form of expression that bothered Nicodemus. The words are not unlike those often used of a convert to the Jewish religion. When a Gentile decided to become an adherent of the Jewish way and was admitted by way of baptism and circumcision, it was often said that he was like "a child newborn." To use terminology that fitted the latest convert to Judaism would have seemed to Nicodemus the last thing that should have been said about such a distinguished person as he, a Pharisee and a member of the governing body, the Sanhedrin. J. Alexander Findlay says it was "as though in modern times an Anglican dignitary or eminent Nonconformist divine were told to go and get converted in an evangelical mission hall!" It may be just what he needs, but he is unlikely to welcome the proposal. It may be this sort of thing that bothered Nicodemus.

But I wonder whether perhaps he was being wistful rather than just plain difficult. He may have been thinking that the past grips us with an all too firm grasp. I am what I am today because of the nature with which I was born and then what all my yesterdays have done to me. Some of them have strengthened me and made me a better man, but all too many have weakened me and dragged me down. I have learned all sorts of bad habits and made mistakes innumerable. When I try to do good, I am hindered by the fact that I am so used to doing evil.

Perhaps Nicodemus was reasoning: "How wonderful it would be to shake off the dead hand of the past! I would like to have such a 'new birth' and thereafter not be limited by all my sins and errors and mistakes. It would be tremendous to make a completely new beginning, quite unhindered by the handicaps the past has built into me. But, of course, it is impossible. The lesser miracle, the physical one of going back into one's mother's womb for birth, is impossible. How much more the greater miracle, that of breaking with the past and starting all over again! It would be wonderful. But—."

Water and the Spirit

Jesus repeats what he said before, but with slight differences. Once again he uses the emphatic "Truly, truly." What follows is important and must be listened to carefully and heeded: "Unless anyone is born of water and Spirit he cannot enter the kingdom of God" (v. 5). We should probably not read much difference between "seeing" the kingdom (v. 3) and "entering" it (here). It is John's habit to introduce slight variations of expression with no great difference of meaning. In both places the meaning is that the way into God's kingdom is not a way worked out by man. The natural man always likes to think that he can merit acceptance by God by the kind of life he lives, the great deeds he does, or some other aspect of human striving. But twice over Jesus says that nothing of the sort is the way. The way is by regeneration, by being reborn by the power of God.

A further difference is that whereas before Jesus had spoken of being "reborn from above," here the process is described as being a birth "of water and Spirit." This is not an easy expression, and commentators have tried to explain it with a fascinating diversity of results. But the many explanations tend to fall into one or another of three groups.

One interpretation sees "water" as referring to cleansing of some sort. It may be the kind of cleansing that John the Baptist preached. He called on people to repent and accept his baptism as a sign of their repentance, with a view to the forgiveness of their sins. Some scholars place no stress on the connection with John the Baptist, but simply see "water" as a natural symbol for being made clean. According to this view Jesus is saying that to enter the kingdom one must first be cleansed from one's sins and then be given the positive endowment of the Holy Spirit of God, who enables people to live uprightly. There is a negative aspect to salvation (cleansing by water) and a positive aspect (the work of the Spirit). This view is attractive and must remain a possibility.

A second view sees "water" as connected with natural birth. This view may take more than one form. Thus "water" may refer to the fluid that surrounds the unborn child and from which it emerges during the process of birth. If this is the way to understand it, the expression is simply a reference to the natural process of being born.

Another way of understanding "water" is quite foreign to us, but seems to have been quite congenial to first-century Jews and, for that matter, to quite a number of other people at that time. Words referring to something wet were often used as euphemisms for the male semen: "water," "dew," "drop," "rain," and other words were all used in this way. We could take this meaning here and understand the expression in much the same way as that which we have already noted. It would then simply mean natural birth. In both cases the meaning would be that the way into the kingdom means (1) natural birth ("water") and (2) birth from the Spirit.

But there is another way of understanding "water" as a reference to the male semen. In the Greek text, "water" and "Spirit" go closely together in this passage (there is one "of" that covers them both). Some have thought accordingly that the birth in question is one of water-and Spirit, that is, a birth of "spiritual seed"; one must be born with the birth the Holy Spirit provides. It is a support to this view that a little later Jesus speaks of being born "of the Spirit" (v. 8); and as we noted earlier, it is John's habit to use expressions that differ from one another slightly but have essentially the same meaning.

A third way of understanding the expression is to see a reference to Christian baptism. Then the meaning would be that the Holy Spirit is at work when one is duly baptized, and it is this that brings entrance to the kingdom. The strongest reason that can be urged in favor of this view is that at the time when this Gospel was written this meaning might well have occurred to many readers. The weakness is in seeing how Nicodemus could possibly have understood Jesus if that was what he meant. Christian baptism had not yet begun, and it is not easy to see why Jesus should puzzle an inquirer with a reference to a nonexistent sacrament. So, while this view is popular in many circles today, it seems best not to accept it. The words must have made sense to Nicodemus.

It seems to me that the second way of taking the expression is the best way, and that in the sense of being "born of spiritual seed." This way of understanding the words would be natural for a learned Pharisee like Nicodemus, and it makes excellent sense. Jesus would then be saying that the way into the kingdom is the way of divine action. We enter a completely new existence by virtue of what the Holy Spirit does in us. So thoroughly are we remade that the process can be described as a being born all over again, a spiritual rebirth. It is quite distinct from the natural process of birth or, for that matter, from any natural process. Jesus is referring to the power of God to remake people.

Flesh and Spirit

Jesus proceeds to develop the thought. "That which is born of the flesh is flesh," he says, "and that which is born of the Spirit is spirit" (v. 6). Sir Edmund Hoskyns brings out the meaning of these words neatly when he says, "There is no evolution from flesh to Spirit."

The word *flesh* is used in more ways than one in the New Testament. In Christian teaching it is often associated with "the world" and "the devil" (as in "the temptations of the world, the flesh, and the devil"). We find this meaning sometimes in Paul, for example, when he tells us that "the mind of the flesh is death" (Rom. 8:6; in the next verse it is "enmity against God"). But we do not find it in John. He prefers to use the term to point us to the physical weakness that is an inevitable part of this mortal life. It may refer to limitations on the way people carry out actions like judgment (8:15). But it may also refer to Jesus' becoming human for us (1:14), or to "the flesh" that he would give "for the life of the world" (6:51).

If John does not use the term for what is sinful, he certainly does use it for what is limited. That is his meaning here. We like to dwell on those things that we can accomplish. Human achievement means much to us. But Jesus is saying that it is limited to this earth. When it comes to entrance to the kingdom of God, the best human efforts are of no use. For that we need divine energy.

Jesus goes on to say, "Don't be astonished that I told you, 'You must be reborn from above'" (v. 7). In view of the principle just set forth, there is nothing really surprising in the statement that it is necessary for a rebirth to take place if anyone is to enter God's kingdom. Jesus makes it clear that what he is saying applies not only to Nicodemus. In Greek there is a distinction between the singular and the plural of "you," just as in old-fashioned English we had "thou" as well as "you." Here Jesus uses the singular when he says, "I told you" (i.e., "I told thee"), but the plural in the words, "You must be reborn from above." This is not a private principle that applies only to Nicodemus, a kind of solution to his own personal problems. It did have its personal application to Nicodemus, but it applies universally as well. It is true of us all that rebirth from above is the one way into the kingdom.

Notice also the strong word *must*. Jesus is not saying that rebirth is on the whole a good idea. He is not just recommending it for people in some special situation, perhaps with difficult problems of their own. He is making it of universal application. This is true of everybody. There is no exception.

It is said that George Whitefield, who was associated with the Wesleys in the Methodist Revival, preached on this text again and again. When one of his friends asked him, "Why do you preach so often on the text, 'You must be born again'?" he replied, "Because you *must* be born again." It was a good answer, and one that brought out this great evangelist's firm grasp on this central spiritual truth.

The Spirit and the Natural Man

There is a little uncertainty about the way to understand Jesus' next words. The difficulty is that the word we have translated "spirit" up till now, has also in Greek the meaning "wind" or "breath." It would seem that from the earliest days people noticed that when anyone ceased to breathe he died. Now breath seemed nonmaterial; it was not like, say, a piece of wood or metal, which could be seen and handled. Equally the spirit of man could not be seen or handled. So the same word came to be used in a number of languages for "spirit" and "breath." Since wind is no more than a lot of breath going somewhere in a hurry, the word was used to mean "wind" as well. It is only the context that enables us to say which meaning should be understood in a given passage.

Jesus' words in verse 8 may accordingly be understood as "the wind blows where it wants to" or as "the Spirit breathes where he wills." A point in favor of the second translation is the fact that the same word has been understood earlier in this chapter in the sense "spirit." We would thus expect it to have this meaning here also. The meaning of the verse would then be that the Spirit moves as he wills. People cannot predict what he will do. Nor do they know what motivates anyone who has been reborn by the agency of the Spirit. Just as the Spirit of God is unpredictable to the natural man, so the person remade by the Spirit is quite incomprehensible to him. He does not know the Spirit, so he does not know the Spirit-led man.

This understanding of the words is consistent and gives a good sense. It would unhesitatingly be accepted were it not for the fact that Jesus goes on after the difficult words to say, "and you hear the sound of it." Now the unbeliever can scarcely be said to hear the "sound" or the "voice" of the Spirit. How can he possibly do that? Because of this difficulty it seems necessary to look at the other way of taking the words. They will then mean, "The wind blows where it wants to, and you hear the sound of it, but you do not know where it is coming from or where it is going." This gives an excellent sense also, and is free from the disadvantage attending the first interpretation. We should surely take Jesus' words in this way.

He is saying to Nicodemus, then, that the familiar wind is mysterious. Was there a gust of wind at this point in the conversation? It would underline the point that it is possible to hear the wind without knowing either its origin or its destination. It is like that for the unspiritual person. He may indeed come into contact with one who is indwelt by the Spirit of God, but he cannot understand him. It makes no sense to him when the Spirit-filled man or woman forsakes a life of ease and comfort for difficult and demanding and lowly service. For the true Christian it is a commonplace that the site of one's service may be in slums, among the down and outs (or, for that matter, in the penthouses, among the up and outs!). Or it may be among some primitive tribe in a distant land. It may mean forsaking comforts and prospects and friends. For the worldly-minded the question always arises, "What do you get out of it?" Such people cannot understand those who prefer to ask, "What can I put into it? How can I best serve?"

The Radical Novelty of Christianity

The mystery of rebirth points us to the great distinctive that separates the Christian way from other ways. In antiquity, as in modern times, there were many religions that emphasized the importance of good works. But Jesus says that no one can so live that eternal life is owed to him. It is neither a reward for good conduct nor the result of diligent search. It comes from being reborn.

We noticed earlier that the figure of rebirth was sometimes used of the proselyte, the convert to Judaism from among the Gentiles. But though the figure of rebirth might be used of him, he did not enter into eternal life in the way Jesus was teaching. The proselyte thought that when he became a Jew it was necessary that he merit his salvation by the life he lived. He was still bound by the idea of good works. He thought that he earned his salvation by his own efforts.

So it was with other religious systems. There were, for example, a group of religions that today we call "the mystery religions." Not as much as we would like is known about them, but it is known that the novice went through some horrifying experience by way of initiation and then was brought into a condition of peace. In a way this was a gift. But in a way it was also his reward. He had of his own free will submitted to the rites of initiation. He had done the right thing; he had performed all that was prescribed for him and thus earned his salvation.

This continues in the modern world. There are "religions" like communism and humanism that hold out before people a very limited idea of salvation. But common to them, and to every purely human system, is the thought that in the end salvation depends on what we do. We must, for example, cease to rely on superstition. Instead we must educate people; we must work to establish communism or humanism. This is the supposed way of "salvation." In both cases the end result is proportional to the effort we make.

The fact is that it comes naturally to the human animal to rest his ultimate salvation, however he may understand it, in his own strong right arm. In the end, he thinks, everything depends on what he does. But in the end, Jesus says, that will never do. At best, what we finish up with is "flesh," some human system with all the typical faults of a human system. He is saying that reform is not enough. It is a noble ideal, but it operates only on fallible human flesh. Over against that he insists that "you must be reborn from above." It is in being remade by the Spirit of God, not in dusting off a few of our worst habits, that the way of salvation lies.

It is as true of our generation as it is of all others: "You must be reborn from above"!

12

The Death of Christ and the Life of Men

"No one has ascended into heaven except him who came down from heaven, the Son of man. And just as Moses lifted up the snake in the wilderness, even so must the Son of man be lifted up, so that everyone who believes may have eternal life in him. For God so loved the world that he gave his only Son, in order that everyone who believes in him should not perish, but have life eternal. For God did not send his Son into the world to condemn the world, but so that the world should be saved through him" (John 3:13–17).

Jesus is still talking to Nicodemus. He has made it clear that the way to life is the way of being reborn from above. Nicodemus's puzzlement upon hearing this (v. 9) leads Jesus to refer to the Pharisee's position as "the teacher of Israel" and to the contrast between heavenly and earthly things (vv. 10–12). If Nicodemus could not understand earthly things, how could he comprehend the heavenly?

Then Jesus proceeds to the truth that rising to heaven is not a human achievement (v. 13). In a way this is the thrust of the previous section. The point about being reborn is that man in his natural state cannot attain the highest. Jesus now puts the same basic truth in another way. He says that no man has ever gained the heights of heaven. That belongs only to "the Son of man." This is the way Jesus normally refers to himself. It is a puzzling expression, but we need not go into all the problems it presents and for which the scholars have no agreed solutions.

What is clear is that Jesus uses it of himself in his official capacity, so to speak. Where people today often speak of Jesus as the Messiah, he preferred to refer to himself as the Son of man. This term has an obvious reference to his humanity, but it is also a way of bringing out his heavenly origin, for the expression seems to have been taken from Daniel 7:13–14, where we read that "one like a son of man [came] with the clouds of heaven," and "approached the Ancient of Days." To this Son of man were given "authority, glory and sovereign power; all peoples, nations and men of every language worshiped him. His dominion is an everlasting dominion that will not pass away, and his kingdom is one that will never be destroyed." Clearly the Son of man is a divine person with great dignity.

But since this term seems not to have been in common use in Jesus' day, most people would not have seen him as claiming any particular place for himself when he used it. It was a way of both concealing and revealing his messiahship at the same time. It concealed it from those who did not look too hard, yet revealed it to those who saw a link with the passage in Daniel. Nobody else seems to have referred to Jesus in this way, with the exception of the dying Stephen (Acts 7:56). It was Jesus' own way of referring to himself, and he used the term frequently.

In this passage, then, he is saying that it is his work to come from heaven to save people. People cannot attain heaven, but he can come down from heaven and raise them up. In Isaiah 14:12–13 we read that the "morning star, son of the dawn," said in his heart, "I will ascend to heaven; I will raise my throne above the stars of God." But he could not bring this desire to pass. No created being can rise to heaven by his own efforts. But the Son of man is on a different level. He could and did come down to raise men to heaven.

The Snake in the Wilderness

Jesus goes on to explain something of what this means (v. 14). He reminds Nicodemus of the story in Numbers 21, where some fiery snakes were biting the Israelites with fatal results. Moses prayed for the people, and God told him to make a fiery snake in bronze and put it up on a pole. Whoever looked at it would live (Num. 21:6–9). The lifting up of the bronze snake in this way was clearly connected with life and salvation.

So now Jesus likens this to what would happen on the cross. He speaks of the Son of man as being "lifted up." Though he does not explicitly mention the cross at this point, it is clearly in mind in the following verses, and we need not doubt that this is so here as well. In a later part of his Gospel, John appears to give an explanation of what he understands by this term. Telling us that Jesus said, "I, if I be lifted up from the earth, will draw all men to me," John proceeds to add his own explanation of what this meant, "This he spoke, signifying by what death he would die" (12:32–33). This is an intelligible way of referring to the cross, though an unusual one.

It is unexpected for another reason. The verb John uses is rarely employed in this way. It is much more usual to find it employed in a sense that we would translate by "exalt" or the like. We find it, for example, in Peter's sermon on the day of Pentecost, when that apostle said of Jesus, "Having therefore been exalted at the right hand of God . . ." (Acts 2:33). And it occurs in a compound form when Paul writes, "Therefore also God has highly exalted him" (Phil. 2:9).

In an earlier study (pp. 21–26) we saw that John has a highly individual use of the term *glory,* applying it freely not to majesty and splendor, but to lowly service. It is like that here. The supreme exaltation is that on the cross, for there the Son of God laid down his perfect life for others.

Notice further the little word *must*. Jesus is not saying that there are various possibilities before him and that from them all he chooses this one (though he might have chosen one of the others). That is not the way of it at all. He says that he "must" be lifted up in this way. We do not know in what the necessity lay, but we find the word *must* used a number of times in connection with what Jesus would do in carrying out his mission. So here. It points to a compelling divine necessity. It was the way people would be saved, and so, though it meant pain and grief and difficulty, Jesus chose to endure it. Being who and what he was, there was no alternative. He would save people, even though it meant dying for them on a cross.

Faith and Life

Jesus goes on to speak of the purpose of his death. It was "so that everyone who believes may have eternal life in him" (v. 15). Faith—or more exactly, believing—is a very important concept in John. The verb *to believe* is found ninety-eight times in this Gospel (though interestingly, the corresponding noun *faith* does not occur at all). It is clear that the idea of trusting Christ or God (John puts little difference between these two activities) is supremely important. Its importance arises from what we have seen in our earlier studies, that men cannot attain salvation by their own efforts. This is something that must be brought about by God if it is to happen. To receive salvation, people need simply trust God. If we do not trust him, we place ourselves outside the salvation he offers. If we trust him, we enter into all that this salvation means.

Sometimes John speaks of "believing in" Christ (v. 16), sometimes of believing that what Christ or God says is true (e.g., 5:24). Sometimes he sees faith as having content, and refers to "believing that . . ." (e.g., 8:24), and sometimes he uses the term absolutely, speaking of people as simply believing (9:38). So fundamental is faith that it is not necessary to say in whom we believe. When we take God's way we become believers.

It seems likely that this is the meaning here. I know that some translators and commentators take the words in the sense "everyone who believes in him. . . ." But the construction found here is unusual; it is certainly not John's normal way of saying "believes in him." It is probable that "in him" should be connected with "eternal life" rather than with "believes." John then means us to understand the words in the sense "everyone who believes may have eternal life in him." In any case this is a small point, because elsewhere it is said that people are to believe, that they are to believe in Jesus, and that life is in him. All these points are taught in this Gospel; it is only a question of which of them is found here.

John often refers to "eternal life." To see what he means we must refer to the Jewish concept of time. For the Jews all time could be divided into three ages: the age before the creation, the present age, and the age to come. The age to come is the age that would be ushered in by the coming of the Messiah. There is an adjective that literally means "pertaining to an age" and that might theoretically be used of any of these ages. But in practice it is always used of the age to come. It is this adjective that John uses here. It gives the meaning "life appropriate to the age to come."

The traditional translation "eternal" draws attention to one aspect of that age: it never ends. But that is only one aspect. Much more important is the quality of life that people will then have. As B. F. Westcott put it, "It is not an endless duration of being in time, but being of which time is not a measure." It is this life of quality of which Jesus is speaking. Elsewhere in this Gospel he brings out the point by saying, "I came that they may have life and have it abundantly" (10:10). The point, then, is that to believe in Christ "lifted up" for us is to enter a wonderful life, a life whose quality nothing earthly can produce or match.

The Love of God

This leads on to John 3:16, the best-known text in the whole of Scripture: "God so loved the world. . . ." The love of God is the great basic reality on which the whole Christian edifice is built. Without that great love there would be no Christianity. That love is not aroused by some great merit in the beloved. It is emphasized throughout the Bible, in the Old Testament as well as the New, that God loves sinful people. We are not required to overcome evil before God will begin to love us. Twice we read, "God is love" (1 John 4:8, 16), which assures us that love is God's essential nature. God loves, if we may put it that way, because he can do no other. It is his nature to love. Fundamentally he loves because he is love.

This truth is of priceless value to all of us, full of shortcomings as we are. We can know with certainty that God's love does not depend on our being good. If that were the way of it, we might well despair. But because his love depends not on what we are but on what he is, we may have confidence. God loves because he is a loving God. That being so, he will never cease to love us.

John assures us here that God loves "the world." This was a new thought. Though it is often said in earlier writings that God loves his own people, there appears to be no Jewish writing from those early days that says that God's love reaches out to all mankind. It is a new idea, and a wonderful one, that God loves everybody in this sorry old world. Elsewhere we read that God sends his sunshine and his rain upon the wicked and the good, upon the just and the unjust (Matt. 5:45). It is like that here. God's good gifts are bestowed because it is his nature to love: they are not bestowed on account of human merit.

The Gift of God

Not only did God love the world, but he gave the world a gift. He gave his Son. There is an interesting construction in the Greek which means not simply that God loved the world enough to give his Son, but rather that he loved the world so much that he actually gave his Son. The fact of the gift receives emphasis.

We may say that God gave this gift in part when he sent the Son into the world. This is a truth that John insists on over and over again. More than any of the other Gospel writers he brings out the truth that God sent the Son. Quite often he reports Jesus as referring to "the Father who sent me"; in fact Jesus characterizes the Father as "the having-sent-me-Father" (an expression he repeats several times). The mission of the Son is of great importance in this Gospel. The coming of the Son into the world means, of course, that illumination has come to men. John often uses the figure of light to bring out what Jesus has done: he has revealed to us what God is like (1:18).

But there is more than revelation. The gift of God was brought to its climax and consummation on the cross. It was there that our redemption was wrought out, the central act that made salvation possible.

It is noteworthy that the cross is here said to show the love of the Father. It is possible to see it also in terms of the love of the Son (as in Gal. 2:20). This is a very true and very meaningful part of our understanding of the cross, but we should not overlook the fact that the love of the Father is there as well as that of the Son. Christians have not always given due attention to this. They have sometimes pictured the Father as somewhat stern, laying it down that sin must be punished and holding out before unrepentant sinners nothing but doom. When Christians think of the Father in this way, they tend to stress the fact that it was the Son who came to die for them.

But it is important to see that the love of the Father is involved as well as that of the Son. God is love. It was he who sent the Son to be the Savior of the world. The great act of atonement was not in defiance of the will of the Father but rather the outworking of that will. Paul gives expression to this tremendous truth: "God was in Christ, reconciling the world unto himself" (2 Cor. 5:19). It is because the Father loves us that we are saved.

William Temple points out that the passage we are discussing "is the heart of the Gospel. Not 'God is Love'—a precious truth, but affirming no divine act for our redemption. *God so loved that He gave.*" This is the essential point. Love is not to be thought of as some beautiful but helpless thing wringing its hands, so to speak, in the face of evil, but unable to do anything about it. The love of God is active, and we see it in the cross (Rom. 5:8; 1 John 4:10). God so loved that he gave.

Sir Harry Lauder told a story that brings this out well. He spoke of a man who, during the difficult days of World War I, was taking his small boy for a walk. The lad noticed that there were stars in the windows of some of the houses they passed.

"Daddy, why are there stars in some of the windows?" he asked.

His father replied, "That comes from this terrible war, laddie. It shows that these people have given a son."

The little fellow went on silently digesting this information. Then he looked up and there was the evening star, shining brightly in the sky. He said, "Daddy, God must have given a Son, too."

That is it. In the terrible war against evil, God gave his Son. That is the way evil was defeated. God paid the price.

Life Eternal

This, John tells us, was "in order that everyone who believes in him should not perish, but have life eternal." Again we have a reference to believing, this time with the addition "in him." This is a frequent construction in John, one that brings out the importance of a personal faith in a personal Savior. To believe in someone in John's terminology means to give one's full trust. It means to rely wholeheartedly on the object of the trust.

The means whereby sin was dealt with is the gift of God, the death of his Son. The means whereby this becomes effective in the life of any one person is believing in him. The "him" may refer to God himself or to the Son, but in John there is no great difference. Throughout his Gospel he depicts the Father and the Son as so close that to honor one is to honor the other, to despise the one is to despise the other, to believe on one is to believe on the other. The point being stressed is that salvation comes through the gift of God, not through the effort of man. All that is required from the human end is that we trust. This is not a meritorious action so that we are rewarded, so to speak, for being trusting people. Rather our trust is the means whereby we receive God's good gift.

John goes on to speak of not perishing but having life eternal. We saw earlier that "life eternal" is life appropriate to the age to come, life of a different order from anything we see here on earth. Here it is set over against "perishing." John does not explain what he means by this, but obviously it is a most unwelcome fate. It is a reminder that it is a very serious thing to refuse the gift of God.

Throughout the New Testament there is emphasis on this truth, though not always with the same terminology. Jesus spoke of hell (Luke 12:5), and of "the hell of fire" (Matt. 5:22). He spoke of cutting off hand or foot or casting out an eye rather than going to hell (Mark 9:43–47). On the last occasion he added, "where their worm does not die and the fire is not quenched." He spoke of evildoers being "cast into the outer darkness; there there will be wailing and gnashing of teeth" (Matt. 8:12). Elsewhere we read of sinners for whom "the blackness of darkness" is reserved (Jude 13). Or they may be "lost" (2 Cor. 4:3), or lose their souls (Mark 8:36). Again, the fate of the wicked is death (Rom. 6:23).

It is not easy to see what that state can be that is capable of being described in so many ways. Fortunately we are not called upon to understand it, but to escape it. John is saying that when we trust God in Christ, we are delivered from the ultimate horror. We pass from death to life (5:24).

God's Purpose

John has set before us the alternatives of "perishing" and "eternal life." He has shown us that God gave his Son to deliver those who trust him. He goes on to the thought that while the condemnation of the finally impenitent is a reality, that is not the purpose of God. "For God did not send his Son into the world to condemn the world, but so that the world should be saved through him." There is a little problem in that elsewhere John tells us that Jesus said, "For judgment I came into this world" (9:39). On the surface these two statements do not agree, but only on the surface.

John's basic idea is that God sent his Son and gave him on the cross in order that people might be saved. That purpose of salvation runs through John's Gospel, as through the rest of the New Testament. But it is also the case that the offer of salvation divides people. Some gladly trust God and accept his offer. Some turn away from it. The latter enter into judgment (or condemnation), just as surely as the former escape it.

Someone has said that it is not the purpose of the shining of the sun to cast shadows. But if the sun shines on opaque objects, shadows are inevitable. The shadows are, so to speak, the other side of the sunshine. So it is with condemnation and the coming of the Son of God. He did not come in order that people be condemned. But there are great moral issues involved, and those who refuse salvation thus condemn themselves. The condemnation is as real as the salvation.

The last words of this verse are "through him." We may well close this study by reflecting that God's purpose is salvation. This stems from the love of God and is brought to us "through" the Son. Both are involved, for both love sinners.

13

Judgment: A Present Reality

"He who believes in him is not condemned; but he who does not believe has been condemned already, because he has not believed in the name of the only Son of God. Now this is the condemnation, that the light has come into the world, and men loved the darkness rather than the light, because their deeds were evil" (John 3:18–19).

He who believes in him is not condemned." John has just been speaking about the love of God for the world. God's love gave Jesus so that people might be delivered from perishing and brought into eternal life. John has said that the reason that God sent his Son into the world was not condemnation, "but so that the world should be saved through him" (v. 17).

Now he goes on from that point. First, he makes it clear that, from the human side, salvation is a matter of faith only. Nothing more is required. John brings this out by a couple of his favorite stylistic devices. One is repetition. Every now and then he emphasizes a point by the simplest of all devices: he simply repeats it. So here. "He who *believes* in him is not condemned; but he who does not *believe* has been condemned already, because he has not *believed*. . . ." The verb occurs three times. The thought is hammered in. Believe, believe, believe. That is the important thing. It is *believing* and not some other thing that matters.

The other device John uses here is the placing together of a positive statement and a negative one. This brings out the truth by putting it two ways. First, "He who believes in him is not condemned." Then the other side of that particular coin, "he who does not believe has been condemned already."

John's verb is in the present tense; he is speaking of a reality here and now. But this carries with it, of course, the thought that the present reality continues. The believer need not fear, not now and not in eternity. There is for him no condemnation. His deep need has been met.

In a story among the legends of India of a time long ago, two kings were about to go to war. They appeared before the god Krishna prior to the battle. He said, "To one of you I will give ten armies of soldiers, to the other myself unarmed." One king was very happy to have chosen the ten armies of soldiers and went off congratulating himself. The other seemed just as happy to have the god alongside him. Krishna asked him, "Why did you choose me?" To which the king replied, "Because I need a Great Companion."

A profound truth is enshrined in this legend, a truth that comes home to all of us from time to time. Life is not easy. There are problems, perplexities, difficulties. It is not unusual to feel alone, unsupported, vulnerable. If I am without anyone to stand by me in a hostile and difficult world, I am in an impossible situation. I need a Great Companion. It is not simply that it is advisable, that it would be a help. For to live life in the conviction that I am on my own, that there is no one to stand with me, is disaster.

John is saying that this disaster never happens to the believer. To put one's trust in Christ means to have that constant companionship that suffices for all of life, life now and life in the hereafter.

"He who believes in him is not condemned." The believer has quietness and calm and peace. He knows that no condemnation lies before him. He is not condemned now, and he will not be condemned in the life to come. Anyone who has Christ as his companion can walk through life serenely. Nothing in life can disturb him deep down.

This does not mean that the believer will not have troubles. Of course he will. Christians have all the troubles that other people have. Becoming a believer does not mean taking out a kind of insurance policy so that God now shields from every unpleasantness. That is not the way the Christian life works out. The Christian is in the same world as the non-Christian. Probably every saint at one time or another has wanted to be taken out of the world, but it is right here in the world that he belongs. The believer is sent to live a life of service, service to God and to his fellow creatures, and he is sent to live it amid the same kind of difficulties everyone else has. Indeed, he has a few more, because it is characteristic of the world to mock believers and sometimes to persecute them.

But all this is external. It belongs to the outward circumstances. It does not get to that place where trouble really counts, deep down inside one. When there is inner turmoil, a feeling that we cannot cope, then we are in real trouble. I am not saying that the believer never knows this sort of thing. Believers are fallible and sometimes they take their eyes away from their Lord (as Peter did [Matt. 14:30]). But this is out of character. It is not the Christian way. Believers characteristically trust Christ and in trusting find serenity. There is no condemnation and no sense of condemnation.

Unbelief

John goes on to the point that the condemnation that the believer never knows is not a phantom. It is a grim reality for the unbeliever: "He who does not believe has been condemned already." John is not saying that the unbeliever will be condemned on judgment day. That is a truth he expresses elsewhere (5:28–29), but it is not what he is saying here. Rather he is saying that the unbeliever is condemned here and now. Because of his unbelief he has entered the state of condemnation, of life without Christ. He does not have the Great Companion. He lives a life of an altogether different quality from that of the person who has come to believe. John places a great emphasis on the here and now. Without ever overlooking the fact that eternal realities are more significant than anything that happens to us in this present life, he yet brings out the truth that spiritual attitudes are important for life here on earth. He does not postpone either bliss or loss to a distant world beyond the grave. Life right now is what it is because of our spiritual attitudes.

Why is the person condemned? "Because he has not believed in the name of the only Son of God." Perhaps we should notice a little point about the Greek construction John employs. The two verbs translated "has been condemned" and "has not believed" are both in the perfect tense. In Greek that points to something permanent, a lasting state. John is not talking about a passing moment of doubt or unbelief. He is talking about the person who has entered a continuing state of unbelief. That person no longer keeps open the possibility that Jesus might be the Son of God and the Savior of the world. Unbelief is the atmosphere in which he lives. He knows of Christianity as a way of life some people choose, but for him it is irrelevant. He knows that Christians talk about faith, but for him it is just a word. He is not really interested, and he certainly does not know what it is to trust in the sense in which Christians trust Christ. That for him is totally unknown territory. He lives in unbelief, continuing unbelief. He wants nothing else and accordingly he gets nothing else.

John says the unbeliever has not believed "in the name" of the Son of God. Among the people of antiquity, names meant far more than they do with us. With us a name is simply a label, a distinguishing mark whereby we separate one person from another (we have a problem when we meet two people with the same name). A number would serve as well, and in fact many institutions today identify us by number rather than by our name.

But not all people use names merely as distinguishing labels. In my younger days I read stories about American Indians who had wonderful names like Hawkeye or Deerfoot or Sitting Bull. I did not know then, though I have since been informed, that the Indians thought that the name and the quality somehow went together. When an Indian brave gave his little boy the name Hawkeye, he thought that the little fellow would see just a bit better because of the name, while the little chap called Deerfoot would run a bit faster. The name and the quality somehow went together. (To this day I have never been quite sure exactly what the father had in mind when he called his son Sitting Bull, but I have no doubt that it was something great and meaningful.)

I am not saying that the men of antiquity regarded names in the same way as the American Indians did. They did not. Their concept of names was quite different. I am simply drawing attention to the fact that our way of regarding names is not the only possible one. There have been others.

In antiquity there was a widespread view that the name and the person were somehow bound up together. There was an interesting application in the realm of magic. Among the papyri that have come down to us from the ancient world are some that record the spells used by magicians. Sometimes these scrolls contain a long string of names, which may be followed by a string of nonsense syllables, apparently on the theory that a spirit might well have a name very different from any that the magician might know. The reasoning behind all this was that the name and the spirit went together. If, somewhere in his list, the magician had managed to hit on the name of a powerful spirit, then that spirit would do his will. To have the name meant to have power over the spirit. The name and the spirit went together.

If the name and the person are bound up together, then to believe "in the name" means to believe in all that the name stands for, to trust the whole person. "The name of the only Son of God" points us to him who for our salvation came down from heaven. It points him out as the one whose love was so great that he left all that heaven means and lived a life of service and rejection, a life that would end in a death that atoned for sinners. For us. John has written of the cross, which is a vivid illustration of God's love and the means of bringing salvation to us. To believe in the name means to put one's trust in a God who loves like that.

The Condemnation

To choose not to believe in the name is to condemn oneself. "Now this is the condemnation," writes John, "that the light has come into the world, and men loved the darkness rather than the light, because their deeds were evil" (v. 19). An interesting point arises from his choice of word for "condemnation"; he uses the Greek word *krisis* and passes over *krima*. The two words are often used without much difference of meaning and, as John shows a marked preference for *krisis*, there may not be much significance in his choice here. But nouns ending in *-ma*, like *krima*, strictly denote the concrete embodiment of the verbal action; *krima* thus denotes the sentence of judgment. Nouns ending in *-sis*, like *krisis*, point to the activity in process—in this case the process of judging.

John is not saying, "God has passed judgment, and this is his sentence." Rather he is saying, "This is what judging means. This is the way judgment works out." The condemnation goes like this: light has come into the world, and men loved darkness. He could have said, "One day men will be judged for what they have done. One day God will come down on sinners like a ton of bricks, and he will punish them because they loved darkness and rejected light." But he does not say this. Rather he says that to love darkness is itself condemnation.

John is writing about the sentence of judgment that people impose upon themselves. Elsewhere he speaks of judgment day and, for example, refers to the resurrection to life and the resurrection to judgment (5:28–29). But here his concern is with the present, with what people do to themselves. They choose darkness and not light, and in doing so they sentence themselves.

I do not know how to bring this out better than by drawing attention to a little rhyme I came across in C. J. Wright's book on John's Gospel. It has to do with Judas Iscariot and his betrayal of Jesus:

> Still, as of old,
> Man by himself is priced.
> For thirty pieces Judas sold
> Himself, not Christ.

Consider Judas at the moment when his betrayal of Jesus was completed. As he stood there with the thirty pieces of silver in his hands and Jesus in the grip of the enemy, he had succeeded perfectly in what he set out to do. He had received his price; he had the money. He had sold his Master; Jesus was in the hands of the enemy. All had gone as Judas planned it.

But that is a superficial view. There is a very real sense in which Judas did not do anything to Jesus. Centuries before Jesus was born, the prophet wrote of him: "He was despised and rejected by men, a man of sorrows, and familiar with suffering. Like one from whom men hide their faces he was despised, and we esteemed him not" (Isa. 53:3). Then he went on with a surprising revelation:

> Surely he took up our infirmities and carried our sorrows, yet we considered him stricken by God, smitten by him, and afflicted. But he was pierced for our transgressions, he was crushed for our iniquities; the punishment that brought us peace was upon him, and by his wounds we are healed. We all, like sheep, have gone astray, each of us has turned to his own way; and the Lord has laid on him the iniquity of us all (Isa. 53:4–6).

Right from the beginning of his life, the cross lay before Jesus. God had always intended that his Son should come and die to put away men's sin. That is the way sin would be dealt with and overcome. Had Judas remained faithful and loyal and true, that would not have meant that Jesus would not have been crucified. Some other way would have been found to get him to the cross. That is what he came for. Salvation at the cost of his life was the purpose of God for his Son.

In a very important sense, then, Judas did not do anything to Jesus. But if he did not sell Jesus, how irrevocably he sold himself! And the price Judas put on his immortal soul? Thirty pieces of silver.

"Still, as of old,/Man by himself is priced." To this day it is all too often the case that our attainment of our aim is itself our ultimate condemnation. We set out to do something, as Judas did. And we succeed in what we aim at, not realizing that it is simply our form of loving darkness rather than light. We write our own sentence of condemnation.

Years ago I was a curate working in a parish that had a new housing area. I recall that one day, when I was walking through the area, I came to a house just as the new people were moving in. The moving van was at the curb and the furniture was being carried in. It was not the right time for a lengthy speech, but I greeted the man and his wife, welcomed them to our area, assured them that the church was a going concern and that we would be glad to see them any Sunday.

The new arrival smiled a funny little smile as he said, "We might send the kids to Sunday school, but I don't think you'll see us."

"Oh," I said. "Why on earth not?"

He looked at me astonished. "Look," he said, "we're just moving in! The house is new; I've got to paint it. There's no garden; I've got to plant one. There's no shed; I've got to build one. And the only day I have to do things like this is Sunday."

I pointed out to him that the only day he didn't have to do those things was Sunday: "Six days shalt thou labor and do all that thou hast to do. . . ." But I rather felt that I was on the losing end of that one.

And so it proved. I passed by the house from time to time, and it was very obvious that the householder was at work. He planted his garden, and a very attractive garden it was. He built his shed, and from the outside it looked a neat and competent piece of work. I never did get inside the house, so I don't know from personal observation what the painting was like, but I have no doubt that it was well done. And from what I could see, most of this work was done on Sundays. It took the man years, and by the time he was through, any lingering affection he may once have had for the house of God and the things of God had long since vanished.

Now it would be quite wrong to think of God as a grim tyrant looking down from heaven at this man and saying, "You make your house nice and I won't have you in my heaven!" That's not it at all. God is love. God sent his Son to die for us. He is not bent on shutting people out of heaven.

No. "Still, as of old,/Man by himself is priced." The man of whom I am writing chose to pursue his own aims and not the service of God. He put his house before his God. And the price he put on his immortal soul? A garden, a shed, and some buckets of paint.

"Still, as of old,/Man by himself is priced." We see this sometimes in the business world. Here is a man who decides that he will get to the top of his particular tree. He applies himself with great diligence and builds up his business. He finds it easier (and financially more profitable) if he cuts a few corners; his determination to be rich is greater than his concern for uprightness. His commercial success and his moral failures are alike great. He succeeds in what he set out to do, but his very success is his failure. He has priced himself out of the kingdom of heaven. He has set his love on darkness rather than light. He has condemned himself.

John's imagery is that of a man in a dark room. All the walls are black. The ceiling is black. The floor is black. There are no windows, and the door is shut. It is absolutely dark, and the man is shut in there with no light at all. He has an impoverished, limited, narrow existence with only what the darkness can give him.

But he need not stay there. The door is not locked. All he has to do is give it a push and walk out into God's good sunshine. But he does not do it. He "loves the darkness rather than the light." To love darkness rather than light is itself the condemnation. It is to shut oneself up in a cramped, mean, narrow existence in place of the liberty and the love and the light that God freely offers us.

That says something to every one of us. "Still, as of old,/Man by himself is priced." We are all quite capable of writing our own sentence of condemnation, and far too many of us do just that. The thing in which we succeed is so often the thing that condemns us. We have our goals. We may want to make a million dollars or be popular or powerful. We may aim at sporting or social success, at community achievement, at any one of a hundred goals each of which we may dress up to look acceptable. And in the process we may sell our souls. We set a price on ourselves by that for which we sell our lives. When we put anything before our Lord, that is our equivalent of the thirty pieces of silver.

At a time when our Lord is calling us to be his servants and to stand up for him in the middle of a generation that is all too often materialistic, secular, racist, insensitive, unloving, sensual, and just plain selfish, all too often we simply go our own way. We choose our particular piece of darkness and love it so much that we refuse to come out into the light of the gospel of Christ. By that refusal we write our own binding sentence of condemnation, for "Still, as of old,/Man by himself is priced."

14

He Must Increase

A dispute about ceremonial cleansing arose between John's disciples and a Jew. They came to John and said to him, "Rabbi, he who was with you on the other side of the Jordan, to whom you bore your witness, look, this man is baptizing, and everyone is coming to him." John replied, "A man can receive nothing except what is given him from heaven. You yourselves bear me witness that I said, 'I am not the Messiah,' but rather, 'I have been sent before him.' It is the bridegroom who has the bride. The bridegroom's friend, who stands and listens for him, is full of joy at the bridegroom's voice. This is my joy and it is full. He must increase, but I must decrease" (John 3:25–30).

The Dead Sea Scrolls have shown us that there was a very great deal of interest in ceremonial purification at the time the Christian movement began. The Qumran covenanters evidently went in for ceremonial washings in a big way, and there were others who showed an interest in this sort of thing. The movement associated with John the Baptist came under this heading because John called on people to repent and to be baptized. His very title, "the Baptist," shows the emphasis he put on the rite. Since different people had different ideas about what was effective in the way of ceremonial purity, it is not surprising that disputes should arise from time to time about what was the right thing to do. So we read that one day some of John's followers had a dispute with a Jew on this subject. It may be significant that it was John's disciples and not John himself who were caught up in the discussion. Followers are often inclined to be more pernickety about minor matters than are their leaders.

I am reminded of the tourist who, having spent some time in a rather sleepy little village with very few inhabitants, remarked to one of the local people, "I see you don't have much of a population problem here." To which the local replied, "That's where you're wrong. Almost all of the problems round here are caused by the population!" It would seem that on this occasion John's problem was caused by the population.

There is no indication of the precise question at issue. We know no more than that there was a difference of opinion. Perhaps the man argued that all the talk about baptism was most confusing. Here was John making disciples and calling on people to be baptized, while Jesus, whom John had baptized, was now busy making disciples of his own and perhaps even having them baptized (4:1–2). Maybe the man was asking why he should get baptized by John when Jesus was doing so much better. Perhaps he was saying that with different leaders operating at the same time it was not easy to see who was right. All that we can be sure of is that in some way Jesus' success was drawn into the discussion.

So some of John's people came to John and complained. Evidently they had not been able to refute the Jew with whom they had been arguing, so they came to John to try to get things set right. Clearly they were very loyal to their leader. They were glad to be his followers and wanted to see his cause advanced. They knew that he had borne witness to Jesus, but apparently they had taken little notice of what he had said. John had told them plainly that he was not the Messiah and that they should follow Jesus. Many, including Andrew and his friend, had done just that—they had left John and followed Jesus (1:35–37).

Not these people, however. They had attached themselves to John so firmly that they refused to be detached. This appears to have been a problem among the followers of the Baptist, for at a much later time some men who had been baptized with John's baptism apparently still counted themselves as his followers. They had not gone on to link themselves with the followers of Jesus (Acts 19:1–7).

It is easy to be so happy with whatever good we have that we cut ourselves off from anything further. We have a proverb: "The good is the enemy of the best." It would seem that these followers of John are an apt illustration of what is meant. They had heard John's preaching, they had realized their sinfulness, they had repented and been baptized. They had also heard John's teaching (see Luke 3:7–17). All this must have been a wonderful spiritual experience for them.

The Baptist had spoken of the near approach of the kingdom of God and had said that he himself was no more than the herald of the kingdom. It was the Mighty One who would follow who would bring in the kingdom, not John. As plainly as a man can do it, the Baptist had pointed people to the Messiah who would come. But these people were well content with where they were. It was wonderful that they had come to grips with the need for repentance and had experienced all that John's baptism meant. They were thrilled to hear their leader continue with his exhortations to people to turn from their sin. But there they stayed.

They might have gone on to all that fellowship with Jesus meant. They might have entered into the kingdom of God. They might have known continued spiritual growth under Jesus. Instead they chose to remain at the early stage of repentance. Let nothing be said to diminish the importance of repentance. It is the necessary preliminary to all that forgiveness means; as long as people commit sin, there is the necessity for them to turn from it in repentance. But repentance is no more than the preliminary. It opens up the way to many blessings, and if we do not go on, we cut ourselves off from them all.

That is what these disciples of John were doing, and that, alas, is what many of us still do in different ways. It is well to reflect that we are called to spiritual growth. If we are still at the stage at which we entered the Christian life when we were converted, if we have not gone on to maturity, we are repeating the mistake of those well-intentioned followers of John.

They come to John with their complaint. They do not speak Jesus' name, but complain about him "who was with you on the other side of the Jordan" (v. 26). They are clear that their John had done his part; for they say, ". . . to whom *you* bore your witness" (their "you" is emphatic). It is as though they are saying, "It's not fair! You did your part. You bore your witness and did it well. Why can't he help you instead of building up a large following of his own?" They are indignant. The tense of their verb *bear witness* is perfect, which conveys the meaning that there was something permanent about the witness John bore. He had left it on record, so to speak. Even these people who are so upset about the success of Jesus are clear that John had spoken well of him. And indeed John did speak well of Jesus. Much later, when Jesus came into the area where John had baptized, people were able to remember that while John had done no miracles, "all things that John said about this man were true" (10:41). And John's testimony at that late time brought people to believe in Jesus.

What Is Given from Heaven

John's followers might be upset and angrily determined to uphold the place of their master, but John himself was not of that opinion. He had come to bear his witness to Jesus, and single-mindedly this is what he did. It would not have been surprising if he had delivered a sharp rebuke to those who had so misunderstood the central point in his teaching. But, after all, they are his followers, and he speaks to them kindly. He simply points out to them that God is in control of everything. "A man can receive nothing except what is given him from heaven" (v. 27). This last expression means "from God." The Jews out of reverence often avoided using the name of God, and "heaven" was a regular substitute. John is saying that one has only what God gives to him.

This might be understood in either of two ways. It might refer to the Baptist himself. There is no point in his followers' getting upset because he does not have the supreme place. God did not give him that supreme place. He has what God gave him, the place of the forerunner. That is a very significant place. Indeed Jesus said that there is nobody among those born of women who is greater than John (Matt. 11:11). His following statement that the least in the kingdom of heaven is greater than John is to be taken as a mark of the wonderful thing that membership in the kingdom is, not as a criticism of John in the slightest degree. But John's point here is that, great or small, the place he has is the place that God has assigned him. It is true of all of us that God has given us such and such gifts, those and no more.

It is important that we make the best use of our gifts. We will certainly do more in the service of God and find life more rewarding if we do use them to the full than if we spend our time complaining that we do not have such and such a gift. The Baptist's calm acceptance of the place God has assigned him is an object lesson to all of us.

It is possible, however, that John was speaking more of Jesus than he was of himself. It was true of Jesus, as it was true of John, that in his incarnate life he had what God had given him. There was no point in anyone's complaining about Jesus' success, for that is what God had given him. John had always taught that God would send the Great One who would bring in the kingdom. And when he saw the Holy Spirit descend on Jesus at his baptism, he had hailed him as that Great One. Let his followers recognize that, and then they would not be so upset about what was happening. What was happening was what God was doing in the world. It was not some man's interfering with God's plan and striving after kudos that he did not deserve. There is never a reason for being unhappy about the success God gives, especially about the success that he gives to his beloved Son.

John goes on to remind his followers of what they already knew. He had borne his witness to Jesus as they had said (v. 26). In their turn they could bear witness to John. They had heard him say that he was not the Messiah. They could testify to it. Why then should they be upset when the Messiah made his appearance and was acclaimed by some of the people? John's "you yourselves" points out that they had the answer in the facts of which they had knowledge if only they would give attention to them. John had made it very clear that he was not the Christ, the Messiah (1:20). When he was asked to tell the delegation from Jerusalem who he was, he had replied that he was "a voice," that and nothing more. And that voice moreover was a voice bearing witness to the coming of the Christ. John never claimed more, and it was sheer misunderstanding on the part of his followers if they thought anything else. They just weren't listening.

Listening

Failure to listen is a fault to which we all are prone. It is much easier to hear what we want to hear than what someone is really saying, especially if what is being said is something we do not greatly like. John's followers had attached themselves to him because they thought he was a very great person and was giving very important teaching. Having done the right thing (so they thought) and attached themselves to this superb teacher, it was unsettling to be told that they should leave him. Why should they leave him? He was a great man, and they had left whatever it was they had been doing before simply in order that they might be near him. They listened with eagerness to John's preaching. Wasn't it wonderful to hear him call the religious leaders "sons of snakes"? And how he thundered out his warnings about an angry God who would soon be showing people what he did when he was angry! And those calls for repentance! The priests and the Pharisees certainly did not want to hear any of that. There was never a dull moment when John was telling people off.

So these followers of John were very happy with his preaching and did not want to go anywhere else. It was so wonderful to stay where they were. If he spoke of some coming Great One, this was probably no more than politeness. For them it was John who was the Great One. If he said something about leaving him and following someone else, they were probably hearing it the wrong way. It would be better to stick around with John till they got it clearer. Being John's loyal men, they were not going after someone else.

So when the man from Nazareth started preaching and teaching and people began to follow him, John's disciples thought this could not be anything other than a rival movement. This Jesus had even been baptized by John. They had seen it happen. Did it not follow that he was a disciple of John? Now a disciple has no business branching out on his own. His job is to follow his leader. In their opinion, Jesus should certainly have remained loyal to John. That was surely what they were going to do.

John had said that he was "sent before" the Great One, meaning that he was no more than the forerunner, the man who was to prepare the way for the Greater One who would follow. But in antiquity there was often the thought that the greatest person was the one who came first. People held to the idea of "the good old days." They thought that in the infancy of the race there had been a golden age when things were wonderful and men were incredibly wise. History was all downhill from then on. Each generation was apparently a bit worse than its predecessor. So it was with teachers. The great teachers were those of earlier ages who had established the body of teaching that was handed on from generation to generation.

Probably reasoning in this way, John's disciples made out a case for his being a greater and wiser teacher than Jesus. Did he not come first? Had he not baptized Jesus? Did this not mean that Jesus had publicly declared himself to be a follower of John? Since John must be the greater of the two, it would be folly to leave John for Jesus. So they misunderstood John's teaching about being the forerunner.

Now the Baptist repeats it. And he repeats it in a way that must make them think again. Over against the Christ he is no more than the one who has "been sent" before him (v. 28). The idea of being sent certainly contains the idea of subordination. John is in no doubt that he is a lowly person, not the great man that his followers have made him out to be.

The Bridegroom

John proceeds to an illustration that should make the point clear. "It is the bridegroom who has the bride," he says, and goes on to speak of the best man, with his important, but subordinate, place (v. 29). The New Testament writers do not often speak of Jesus as the Bridegroom, but we read a number of times of the church as the bride of Christ, which, of course, means the same thing. There are several picture words used to bring out the relationship between Christ and his people: the church is the body of Christ, the church is a building, and so on. Each tells us something important about the way we should see the church and the way the church relates to its Lord.

The imagery of the bride and bridegroom emphasizes the place of love and commitment. A tender love binds bride and groom in any rightful marriage, and this is of the essence of the relationship of the church to Christ. The thought of the church as a body or a building does not bring out this aspect as well. But we are all familiar with the importance of love in a true marriage. Indeed, without love we have no real marriage at all but a travesty. Love is of the essence of marriage. The church is the object of the love of Christ, a love so great that Christ died for the church. It is important that church members respond to this love with love. There is nothing more important in the living of the Christian life than love.

Commitment is likewise important. In marriage the bride gives herself wholeheartedly to the bridegroom. She pledges herself to him and to him alone. So with the church. Christians do not think of Christ as merely one of a number of interesting religious teachers. They are not religionists but *Christ*-ians. They have attached themselves to Christ, not to religion. They see Christ as their Savior. It is central to the Christian way that Christ died on the cross to put away our sins. He is our teacher certainly, but he is more. He is our Savior. We may have many teachers, but there is only one Savior. To see the church as the bride of Christ is to see her as pledged entirely to the Bridegroom, the Bridegroom who saved her at the cost of his own blood.

This imagery springs from the closest tie between human beings. No two people are bound so closely together as are husband and wife. We are thus reminded that the church is closely bound to Christ. Sometimes the thought is that the bride should prepare herself (Rev. 19:7). A young lady will certainly put everything into her preparation for her wedding. On that day everything must be done in the best possible way. So Christians are called on to prepare themselves for Christ and the glorious consummation that awaits us at the end of the age. One great scholar reminds us: "A Marriage is the union of two which grows into perfect unity through love." That tells us something very important about the church and its relationship to Christ. And John's use of the term *bridegroom* tells us something very important about the place he gave Christ. At a wedding no man is as important as the bridegroom. For John, Jesus is the central figure, the one round whom everything else revolves.

The Friend of the Bridegroom

And that helps John bring out his own place. He is the "bridegroom's friend," the equivalent of the best man at our weddings. But the best man in antiquity did some things that today's best man does not. He was often responsible for arranging the wedding in the first place and subsequently had other duties, the most important being that of bringing the bride to the bridegroom. He was a well-known and highly respected figure.

John's point here is that he was not the bridegroom. For all his importance, he was necessarily number two. No one can compete with the bridegroom for center stage. A wedding is about a bridegroom and a bride. It is not about a best man. The best man is no more than someone who helps to bring the marriage about. John is emphatically making the point that he is a subordinate. He is not minimizing his own place, for, after all, at a wedding the best man is a very important person. But it is the bridegroom who matters. John does not want his followers to be in any doubt about that.

He adds a very important point. The friend of the bridegroom is a very happy man at a wedding. He is neither torn by jealousy because he does not have the bride, nor concerned because people are more interested in the bridegroom than they are in him. He sees the wedding as a very happy occasion, one on which he rejoices with his friend. It is precisely because he is the friend of the bridegroom that he is happy. His friend has the bride, and the best man is delighted. His rejoicing is brought out with an emphatic expression that means literally "he rejoices with joy." It is not that the best man merely puts up with what is going on with as good a grace as he can muster. No. He is genuinely happy, filled with joy because of his friend's joy. He is there for that reason—to promote the joy of the bridegroom—and when that is realized, his own joy is complete.

And that is what the Baptist says about himself. He is not jealous of the success that his followers tell him Jesus has had. That is what John has come for. He is there to set forward the coming of the Messiah. Now that he has come, John can say, "This is my joy and it is full." He is not simply mildly pleased that Jesus has come and is having success. He is deliriously happy. He is full of joy. That is what the mission of John is all about. His followers may be distressed and displeased, but not John. What they tell him about Jesus is just what he wants to hear.

"He Must Increase"

John goes on to some of the greatest words ever to fall from the lips of mortal man: "He must increase, but I must decrease" (v. 30). John had not come in order to be a leading figure. His message had always been that one greater than he was coming. He never wavered in his conviction that he was no more than the forerunner of the Christ.

We should not view this as though it were the most natural thing in the world. It is not natural. What is natural to all of us is to want the best place for ourselves. We may have very different ideas as to what that place is, but there is no wavering in our desire to have it.

Somewhere I read a story of a new nation that in its endeavor to keep up with the developed world set up a national television service. There was but one channel, and through it the government told the people the things it thought they should know. In time it became apparent that the people were not completely happy with this arrangement, and their discontent became so strong that the powers-that-be in their wisdom decided to arrange for a second channel on which more popular programs might be viewed. But one night the president had a specially important message for the nation, and everyone was commanded to watch Channel One. One citizen loyally watched his president for an hour, but then felt that he had had all he could stand. So he switched to Channel Two, only to find that on that channel he was confronted with a soldier pointing a gun at him and saying, "Switch back to Channel One!" The story is apocryphal, but it certainly illustrates our natural penchant for wanting to have things our own way. Be we presidents or ordinary citizens, we want to be number one in our own circle, and we tend to take what action we can to see that this is brought about.

But John was wiser. And humbler. He was not consumed by a passion for popularity and success as the world counts success. He saw clearly that he was to be the Messiah's forerunner, that and nothing more. And he rejoiced in that role, which meant that as time went on people would increasingly put Jesus at the center ("He must increase") and John at the periphery ("I must decrease"). So be it. John would then be doing what God had for him to do, and God's purpose would be set forward.

It is good when God's servants today are content to serve well in whatever place he has assigned to them and do not set their hearts on some higher place that is not theirs. Humility and the conviction that what matters is that God's purpose be set forward, not that I should be seen to be wonderful, are still essential in the work of God.

15

Samaritans and Jews

He had to pass through Samaria. He comes then to a city of Samaria called Sychar, near the piece of land which Jacob gave to Joseph his son. Now Jacob's well was there. Jesus then, being wearied from the journey, was sitting thus at the well. It was about noon. A woman from Samaria comes to draw water. Jesus says to her, "Give me a drink." (For his disciples had gone off into the city to buy food.) The Samaritan woman says to him, "How is it that you, being a Jew, ask a drink from me, being a Samaritan woman?" (For Jews do not use [*drinking vessels*] *with Samaritans)* (John 4:4–9).

He had to pass through Samaria." This reads strangely in a writing about Jews, for the Jews of the time normally had as little as possible to do with the Samaritans. Most Jews seem to have hated Samaritans on principle and avoided all contact with them. Strict Jews, for example, when traveling from Galilee to Jerusalem, would cross the river Jordan, travel south on the eastern side of that river, and then cross it again for the ascent to Jerusalem. Though this meant going extra miles, it also meant that they avoided the territory of the Samaritans. If the need was pressing, they might go through Samaria, but not otherwise. The Jewish historian Josephus uses language much like that of John here when he says, "For rapid travel it was necessary to take that route [i.e., through Samaria]." But only dire necessity would cause strict Jews to do this.

The quarrel between the two nations went back a long way. It is not unlikely that at the time when the Hebrews were divided into two kingdoms, those in Judah had a feeling of superiority towards those in Israel because the one temple for the worship of God was in their territory, in Jerusalem. There were shrines in northern Israel and the golden calves that King Jeroboam had made, but the one place where the true God was to be worshiped was in their great city. Those in the north had to come there or else go astray in their worship.

Then came the dreadful time when the mighty Assyrians came down with all their awesome military power and destroyed forever the northern kingdom, Israel. The Assyrians (and some other conquerors in antiquity) had a habit of moving large numbers of conquered peoples. The theory appears to have been that if they broke up the subject nations into small groups, there would not be the cohesion for them to launch revolts. So they took large numbers of the people in the ten tribes in the northern kingdom and set them down in other parts of the vast Assyrian Empire. They could not leave the land of Israel depopulated, of course, so they moved other peoples in there, people from Babylon, Cuthah, Avva, Hamath, and Sepharvaim (see 2 Kings 17:24).

These new settlers ran into trouble. Lions killed some of them, and this made the survivors feel that they needed instruction about how to worship the God of the land. Evidently they felt that each god had a territory of his own. They had been quite happy with their own gods back in the lands from which they had come. And indeed they thought that those gods still had some power where they were, for they continued to worship them. They made idols in their usual fashion and followed their old customs, like the dreadful one of burning their children in the fire as sacrifices to their gods (2 Kings 17:30–31). But since worship of their own gods did not prevent them from being killed by lions, they sought information about the God the Israelites had worshiped.

The Assyrians sent back an exiled Israelite priest, and this induced the new population to add the worship of the true God to their other religious practices. "They worshiped the Lord, but they also served their own gods" (2 Kings 17:33). But as the years passed the worship of these other gods seems gradually to have dropped out, and the people in Samaria and the surrounding regions worshiped only the God of the Jews. It might have been expected that this would create some form of bond between them. After all, it was only the Jews and the Samaritans in all the world who worshiped this one God. But it did not work out that way. While the Jews were glad that the Samaritans worshiped the true God, they were not happy with the way they went about it. Take, for example, the Bible. The Samaritans had as their Scripture the five books of Moses—the books from Genesis to Deuteronomy—these five and no more. They knew nothing of the teachings of such wonderful books as the Psalms and all the books of the prophets. The Jews saw the Samaritans' worship as impoverished.

Bitterness grew. There came a time when the people of Judah, like the northerners earlier, were defeated in war and taken to the land of the conqueror as captives. This time the conquerors were not the Assyrians but the Babylonians. But in due course Persians defeated the Babylonians and allowed the Jews to return to their own land. They found it a shambles. Their cities had been overthrown and apparently not rebuilt. There was destruction everywhere.

One thing that particularly worried them was that their beautiful temple had been destroyed. So they set about rebuilding it. When the Samaritans heard of this, they offered to help. Did they not worship the same God? Was it not proper that they should assist in the construction of the new temple? But the Jews wanted no help from Samaritans. Were they not astray in many of their ideas? Would God be pleased with a temple built with the help of heretics? So the Jews refused to let the Samaritans help them, and the Samaritans in turn refused to worship in Jerusalem. The Samaritans in due course built a temple of their own on Mount Gerizim. But when the Jews became strong again, they were able to control Samaria and burned down the Samaritan temple. For them it was basic that there could be only one temple to God, and that temple was at Jerusalem.

Not surprisingly all this created an atmosphere of bitterness. There were some notable exceptions, but for the most part the two nations detested each other. In one of the apocryphal books, written between the Old and the New Testaments, we read: "With two nations my soul is vexed, and the third is no nation: those who live on Mount Seir, and the Philistines, and the foolish people that dwell in Shechem" (Sirach 50:25–26). Shechem was an important Samaritan city, and "the foolish people" are the Samaritans.

All this means that at the time of Jesus there was a strong mutual antagonism between the two peoples. It was not an antagonism that Christians shared. There is not much about the Samaritans in the first two Gospels. Luke, however, has the parable of the good Samaritan and also the information that one of the ten lepers Jesus healed was a Samaritan (the one who came back to thank him). Luke also tells of a time when the people in a Samaritan village refused to receive Jesus and his disciples because they were clearly going up to Jerusalem, an attitude that distinctly annoyed James and John. Not sharing their annoyance, Jesus rebuked them (Luke 9:52–56). John's Gospel adds to our information. In addition to this story of the Samaritan woman at the well, he tells us of an occasion when the Jews called Jesus a Samaritan (8:48). Clearly they discerned a friendliness in Jesus' attitude toward these people, a friendliness of which they did not approve.

It should not surprise us that there is little about the Samaritans in the Gospels, since Jesus' whole life was spent among the Jews. But enough is said for us to see that he strongly opposed the Jewish attitude. And when the early Christians began their work of preaching the gospel, it was not long before they were evangelizing the Samaritans (Acts 8:5–25).

But the antagonism so common in Jesus' day makes it noteworthy that John says that Jesus "had to" go through Samaria. We are surely to understand this as pertaining to his mission, not to the necessities of his journey. Jesus could scarcely have been in such a hurry that he had to take a shortcut. If he was, John tells us nothing about it. No, the necessity lay in who Jesus was and what he was doing. For the Son of God the bitterness that divided the two nations was not something to be complied with but something to be overcome. God loves Samaritans as well as Jews, and it was necessary accordingly that the Son of God should go through Samaria and meet the needs of Samaritans.

Jacob's Well

So Jesus came near a village called Sychar, the exact location of which is not known for sure. But near it was a well that people thought was dug by Jacob centuries before. Jesus rested by this well while his disciples went into the village to get some food. Whether Jacob really was responsible for the well is, of course, not known. He did buy some land in the general area (Gen. 33:19) and later he did give some land to Joseph (Gen. 48:22), though we have no way of knowing whether it was the same land. There is no record of his having dug a well there, but there is nothing improbable in the suggestion. And the fact that this well is a very deep one (over a hundred feet) has been drawn into an argument that it was in fact Jacob who dug it. Since there is normally plenty of water in the area, it is suggested that only a stranger in the land would have gone to all the trouble to dig so deep a well! Be that as it may, there was a well there, and Jesus rested by it.

That he was weary is an interesting detail. It shows that he had been working hard and traveling much or both. It also brings out the true humanity of our Lord. John consistently shows us that Jesus is the divine Son of God; it is impossible to read his Gospel without seeing this. But John is equally sure of Jesus' genuine manhood. The Son of God came right where we are. If we are wearied with what this world does to us, let us reflect that Jesus knows all about that. He was weary too.

Water at Noon

John quite often tells us the time of day when things happened, and he does so here. It was about "the sixth hour," that is, noon. A woman from the village came to draw water. It was not unusual that a woman should do this; after all, the drawing of water was a common chore for the women, as it still is. What was unusual was the time. Mostly the women came at around sunset, when the heat of the day was over. It could be very hot in the middle of the day, and few women would venture forth for the heavy work of carrying water at such a time. Yet we should bear in mind that there is at least one other record of water being drawn at this hour. In Exodus 2:15–17 we read of Moses helping some young women with watering their flock from a well; the Jewish historian Josephus says this happened at noon. We have no way of knowing whether this is accurate, but the fact that he says so shows that in his day drawing water at noon was not thought of as impossible. But it was certainly unusual.

Indeed this may be the reason why the woman chose to come at noon. She could be sure that there would not be many others drawing water at that time, and it may be that that suited her fine. As we see from later stages in the narrative, she was not a woman of good reputation and may have been more comfortable in getting her supply of water when there were few other women around—or better, none at all. At least she would not hear what they were saying about her!

And that may be the very reason she chose to use this particular well. There would have been other wells closer to her home than this one (people do not usually carry water farther than they have to). It has been suggested that the quality of the water in this well may have been better than that in other wells closer to her home. This may have been the case, but if so we have no way of knowing it. John says nothing about it. Some believe that the woman may have been attracted by the association of the well with the name of the great patriarch and thought that a well bearing his name would be better than other wells. Again this is a possibility, but since the woman did not say why she came, in the end we are left to guess.

What we do know is that Jesus asked her for a drink (v. 7). It was usually women who drew water, so from one point of view it is not surprising that Jesus should ask her. From another it is, as the woman's reply in verse 9 shows. She recognized that Jesus was a Jew, though John does not tell us how. Was it the way he dressed? Or the way he spoke? At any rate she knew. And she knew that Jewish men did not normally ask her, or for that matter any other Samaritan, for something to drink. The reason is usually translated, "For Jews have no dealings with the Samaritans," or words to that effect.

But we have been told that the disciples had gone off to the village to buy food (v. 8). If that is not having dealings with the Samaritans, I do not know what is. The expression will bear closer examination. The verb is an unusual one and is found only here in all the Greek New Testament. It is a compound that means literally "use with," so that the expression means "Jews do not use with Samaritans." People have reasoned that "use with" must mean something like "associate with," "meet up with," and thus in general "have dealings with."

But it might have been better had they asked, "What is it that Jews do not use with Samaritans?" In this situation the answer must be drinking vessels. Jesus did not have anything with which to get water from the well (v. 11), and presumably this means that he had nothing like a cup either. If the woman were to give him a drink, he would have to use a drinking vessel that she supplied. And she knew that Jews did not do this.

Ceremonial Defilement

In our culture we do not have the concept of ceremonial uncleanness, so the point of this is not as obvious as it would have been to a Jew or a Samaritan of the first century. For them it was accepted as obvious that contact with anything ceremonially unclean brought defilement to the person who made contact. A well-known example is contact with a dead body. Anyone who had contact with a corpse was unclean for seven days according to a Jewish law (Num. 19:11). It was not even necessary to make physical contact. If anyone even entered a tent where there was a dead body, he became unclean (Num. 19:14). The same passage tells us that everything in the tent became unclean and, of course, contact with an unclean object conveyed defilement. Moreover, when a person became unclean he would make unclean any clean person he touched. And the unclean could not engage in religious activities like worship. All in all, ceremonial uncleanness was to be avoided. It made life intolerably complicated and cut one off from all sorts of useful and interesting activities.

Unfortunately nobody in antiquity seems to have set down exactly how relationships between Jews and Samaritans were organized. At that time everybody knew, so why write about it? The result is that we do not know today. We are left to gather our information from statements about other things. Sometimes there was a comparatively friendly attitude between the two groups. There was a Jewish regulation that if three people ate a meal together, they must say grace together. That is to say, none of them must say grace for himself, but a common grace would be said by one of them to cover them all. And one rule says that a Samaritan might be included in the number. That would mean that sometimes Jews and Samaritans shared a common meal and prayed together. Indeed a Samaritan might be the one who said grace for them all, for it is laid down that in that case Jews must not say "Amen" until they have heard the whole prayer (who can tell what heresy a Samaritan might introduce before he finished?).

But some Jews were more strict. Rabbi Eliezer used to say, "He that eats the bread of the Samaritans is like to one that eats the flesh of swine." Clearly this godly man was taking no risks! And from the general tone of references in the writings of the rabbis it seems that the hard line was not uncommon. We must not build too much on the "friendly" references. It seems that many had as little to do with Samaritans as they could. Certainly the woman at the well had no high expectations of a Jew. She expected that a Jewish man would not want to use her drinking vessels and was surprised that Jesus evidently did not take this attitude.

Don't Talk with Women

Actually Jesus' request was the beginning of a lengthy conversation, and this too must have surprised her. We today scarcely realize the extent to which women were excluded from important aspects of religion. To start with, there was a strong feeling among the Jews that women should not be allowed to study the Law, which meant that they were cut off from education, for it was the Law that was studied in the rabbinic schools. Rabbi Eliezer said, "If any man gives his daughter a knowledge of the Law it is as though he taught her lechery." It was not only that women were in fact not educated; many rabbis thought it was a sin to educate a woman.

This extended beyond formal education to ordinary conversation. Rabbi Jose ben Johanan of Jerusalem pointed out that "the Sages have said: He that talks much with womankind brings evil on himself and neglects the study of the Law and at the last will inherit Gehenna." I like the little story about a pious woman who had learned this lesson well. Rabbi Jose the Galilean was once uncertain of his route and happened to meet this woman. He asked her, "By what road do we go to Lydda?" She rebuked him by retorting, "Foolish Galilean, did not the Sages say this: Engage not in much talk with women? You should have asked: By which to Lydda?" If he had put his question this way, he would have saved a few words and thus have talked less with a woman!

The rabbis had a firm view that women were inferior to men in every way. There is an ancient prayer, "Blessed art thou, O Lord . . . who hast not made me a woman," which takes this view into worship and gives expression to a lordly sense of male superiority. There is a corresponding prayer for a woman, "Blessed art thou, O Lord, who hast fashioned me according to thy will." Presumably this prayer was composed by some male and was meant to convey the thought that it is good for a woman to reflect that, though she does not have the great privilege of being a man, she still has some place in God's scheme of things. If we look closely at the two prayers, we may well feel that the woman had the better of it. It is certainly much more a matter for thanksgiving that one is made according to the will of God than that one is not a member of the opposite sex. But that is a modern and Christian attitude, not an ancient Jewish one.

All One in Christ

Jesus was not bound by the prejudices of his time. From a number of incidents in the Gospels, it is plain that he did not share the common view regarding the Samaritans. Did he not have a Samaritan as the central figure in one of the greatest of the parables? And when he healed ten men who were lepers and one came back to thank him, did he not speak appreciatively of this man, Samaritan though he was? Racial prejudice might have been common in Jesus' day (as, alas, it has been common in most periods of human history), but he had none.

This is a lesson that the early church learned. Paul writes, "There is neither Jew nor Greek, there is neither slave nor free, there is neither male nor female, for you are all one in Christ Jesus" (Gal. 3:28). He does not, of course, mean that there is no difference between Jew and Greek, between slave and free, between male and female. Of course there are differences. What he is saying is that these differences give us no ground for taking up an attitude of lofty superiority. He is saying that there is a unity in Christ that transcends all kinds of human barriers.

To be a Christian is to know that you are a sinner, but that your sin has been put away at terrible cost, the cost of the death of the sinless Son of God. Really to take that in and to put your trust in Christ means to enter into a new way of living. Among other things, it means that you see racial prejudice as sinful. Racial prejudice erects barriers that are meaningless in a context where the whole human race needs salvation, where the really significant problem is sin, not race. If we understand what the death of Christ means, we understand that racial prejudice has no place in our lives.

And we understand that sexual prejudice likewise has no place. As that ancient Jewish prayer reminds us, women are fashioned according to the will of God. The most ardent male chauvinist cannot claim more. The sexes are not in some form of competition but are created in fulfillment of the divine purpose. In this world they belong together, and each is impoverished without the other.

Paul could write, "Receive one another, as Christ received you, to the glory of God" (Rom. 15:7). In this he showed that he had learned an important lesson from his Master. Because of what Christ has done for us, we are to act toward other people in the way he acted. That means an end to stupid practices like racial prejudice and sexual harassment. Unity in Christ is an important Christian concept.

16

Living Water

Jesus answered her: "If you knew the free gift of God and who it is that says to you, 'Give me a drink,' you would have asked him, and he would have given you living water." The woman says to him, "Sir, you have no bucket and the well is deep; from where then do you have the living water? Are you greater than our father Jacob, who gave us the well and drank from it, he and his sons and his cattle?" Jesus replied, "Everyone who drinks of this water will thirst again; but whoever drinks of the water that I will give him will never thirst again, but the water that I will give him will be in him a fountain of water leaping up into life eternal" (John 4:10–14).

Jesus asked the woman of Samaria for a drink. This led to her expression of astonishment that a Jew would make such a request of a Samaritan woman. We have looked into the mutual antagonism of the two races and seen something of the tolerant attitude that Jesus brought into a tense and difficult situation. But the woman's statement was there, and we now resume our study of the incident by going on to the further conversation.

Jesus points to some things that the woman did not know. The first is "the free gift of God" (v. 10). Jesus here uses a word *(dōrea)* that is somewhat unusual among the Evangelists (this is the only place in any of the four Gospels where it is used to denote a gift, though it is used adverbially with the meaning "freely, in the manner of a gift"). He does not explain what the free gift is, but in view of the context it seems likely that he means the living water of which he goes on to speak. The woman in her remote Samaritan village and with her inadequate knowledge of the ways of God knew nothing of the living water that God could give her. She was in danger of rejecting a good gift that she was not yet in a position to evaluate.

The second thing of which she was ignorant was the identity of him with whom she was speaking. The whole conversation gives the impression that she did not take Jesus seriously. She was evidently not in a hurry and found it pleasant to spend some time gossiping by the well. The stranger was unusual for a Jew, but until later in the conversation she thought no more of him than that. She had at this time not the slightest idea of the great privilege that was hers.

This is a mistake that many of us make. Of course, if we were to see our Lord in all his splendor, we would bow down to him. If he appeared in his heavenly majesty, we would do anything he asked and do it gladly. But do we not often fail to recognize him when he comes to us in a way that we do not expect? And are we not at times guilty of failing to do for him the things we should? Jesus said that on judgment day there will be some very surprised people. On that day some will be rewarded for feeding the Lord when he was hungry, for giving him something to drink when he was thirsty, for welcoming him when he was a stranger, for clothing him when he was naked, for visiting him when he was sick, and coming to him when he was in prison. This will puzzle them, for they will have no recollection of doing any of those things. Then they will be told, "Inasmuch as you did it to one of the least of these my brothers, to me it was you did it." And others will be equally surprised at being condemned for failing to do these things for the Lord, only to be told that when they did not do these things for the least of his brothers, they did not do them for him (Matt. 25:31–46).

It is not given to most of us to walk in high places, to be constantly in the presence of the great. Mostly we live and move and have our being among very ordinary people. Indeed they are sometimes far too ordinary for our tastes! We perhaps create fantasies of the wonderful service we would render if our lot were cast in different places. What the Samaritan woman did not realize was that she stood in the presence of the Lord of all. It is important that we realize that when we have the opportunity of meeting human need, even the need of very lowly people, we too are in the presence of the Lord of all.

Flowing Water

Had the woman known the realities of the situation, she would have asked for the gift of "living water." This is not an expression that we use very often (unless we are talking about this part of the Bible or a similar passage). But the expression was not uncommon among people who lived in first-century Palestine.

It was used of water that flowed, water in a river, or water poured out, that is, water in motion as opposed to stagnant water, water in a pool or a cistern or a basin. "Living water" was vital in the many ceremonies of purification that mattered so much to the people of that day. When a person contracted ceremonial defilement and had to be cleansed, it was "living water" that was needed. For example, scrupulous people commonly washed their hands before a meal. For they might have accidentally picked up some defilement as their hands touched many things, and if they conveyed that pollution to the food they ate, they would be entirely defiled.

But washing did not mean, as with us, washing in a basin of water. The water had to be poured over the hands. Elisha could be described as the one who "used to pour water on the hands of Elijah" (2 Kings 3:11); that is to say, he helped him in the process of washing. It had to be "living water," water that moved, if it was to remove defilement.

The rabbis do not seem to have used the expression "living water" in metaphorical senses. For them it was always water that flowed. They often used the word *water* metaphorically, mostly to refer to the Law, the first five books of our Old Testament. They found this revelation of God so necessary and so refreshing that "water" was a natural way of referring to it. But "living water" was different. That was always flowing water, water that moved.

We rarely find this expression in the Old Testament, but there are some passages that come close. Thus we read, "The words of a man's mouth are deep waters, but the fountain of wisdom is a bubbling brook" (Prov. 18:4). Again, "The teaching of the wise is a fountain of life" (Prov. 13:14). Water is a natural symbol of what is invigorating and refreshing.

There are some other Old Testament passages that associate "living water" closely with God. Twice Jeremiah speaks of him as "the spring of living water" (Jer. 2:13; 17:13), and the psalmist prays, "With you is the fountain of life" (Ps. 36:9). In Ezekiel's vision there was the mighty stream that flowed from the temple, and though we do not have a specific statement that this was living water coming from the Lord, we are not far from such a statement. We should also notice that the bride is "a garden fountain" and "a well of flowing [literally, living] water" (Song of Sol. 4:15). Such passages link "living water" with God, and we should not overlook this scriptural teaching when we find Jesus claiming to give the living water. The claim he makes here is one that puts him very close to God the Father. It is a striking claim indeed.

But Jesus seems to be putting more meaning into the words "living water" than do the Old Testament passages. He does not explain here what "living water" stands for, but he uses the concept again later in this Gospel, when he says of the believer, "Rivers of living water will flow from his innermost being." John goes on to explain, "He said this about the Spirit which those who believed on him would receive" (7:38–39). This later passage is very important and will repay close study. But here we simply notice that it explains for us the meaning of "living water." Jesus is talking about the gift of the Holy Spirit.

"Our Father Jacob"

But the woman is not thinking in terms of deep spiritual realities. She is polite as she addresses him, "Sir." (This word could be used in the sense "Lord." Indeed it is often used in that way in the New Testament, but there is no reason for thinking that the woman as yet saw Jesus in that light. She is simply being polite.) The word has perhaps a note of formality about it when used in this manner. She is putting a distance between them.

Her sternly practical mind goes to the fact that Jesus has no bucket. (Her word in verse 11 means anything that could be used for drawing water; most travelers would probably have a skin bucket to meet such needs as they journeyed.) "The well is deep," she adds. The water did not lie near the surface, and a person without equipment would not be able to get at it. She is taking Jesus' reference to water quite literally; she sees it as the kind of water that she would draw from the well. As Jesus had no way of getting at the water in the well, she dismisses his words. No bucket, no water. That's all there is to it!

But Jesus had spoken of "living" water, and now she asks where he will get this "living" water. She has made it clear that she is thinking of ordinary water and has pointed out to her own satisfaction that the water Jesus is talking about is not going to come from the well. Where, then, could it come from? She sees no other source of water in that place.

She raises a further objection that seems to her to make Jesus' position quite impossible: "Are *you* greater than our father Jacob?" (v. 12). Her "you" is emphatic. It is ridiculous to think that such a person as Jesus appeared to be could possibly be greater than Jacob. But he would have to be much greater if he was going to get water in this place without so much as a bucket. She reminds him that Jacob had not come up with a tiny quantity of water. He had produced enough to provide not only for his own drinking needs, but also for those of his sons and his cattle. That was a lot of water. It would require someone much greater than she thought Jesus to be to do that.

This is a good example of the irony that John introduces from time to time. To the woman it was impossible that Jesus was greater than

Jacob, but the truth was that he was indeed greater by far than that patriarch. John often leaves statements like this one unrefuted if his informed readers would immediately recognize the truth. The woman did not realize it, but her words pointed to an important truth.

It is perhaps curious that the woman speaks of Jacob as "our father." As we saw in an earlier study, the Samaritans were a mixed race and had no real claim to descent from Jacob. But the claim was certainly made, and the historian Josephus, for example, tells us that the Samaritans considered that they were descended from Joseph through his sons Ephraim and Manasseh. Evidently the woman was repeating a claim that Samaritans were fond of making, though, as far as we can see, without historical justification.

J. C. Ryle has a sharp comment that brings out another aspect of the situation: "Dead teachers have always more authority than living ones." It is a common failing of the human race to think that those of an earlier time were greater and wiser than those more recent. The woman clung to the thought that the well from which she drew was sanctified in some way because Jacob dug it. Jacob was the ultimate source of her supply, and she was not going to let anything interfere with that comforting thought. She would not look past Jacob, even though this meant cutting herself off from the most wonderful thing there is, the gift of life from the Son of God himself.

I like the story of the comedian who gave one of his children a birthday gift of a bulldog. A friend asked why he had chosen such an unusual and downright ugly gift. "He will see that ugly face," replied the father, "and in time he will discover all the love behind it. He'll never take anything at face value again." Whether it worked with that child I do not know. But I do know that it is important not to put our trust in surface impressions, as the woman was doing at this point. She was in danger of missing out on the best there is because of her casual impressions of Jesus and her firm commitment to a great one of the past.

Never to Thirst Again

The woman is determined to keep to the kind of water that is in Jacob's well. So Jesus continues to talk about it. He makes the single devastating point that whoever drinks of that water will certainly thirst again (v. 13). That is the nature of that water. There is nothing about it that even raises the possibility of a permanent quenching of thirst. That the woman was there to draw water was a witness to the fact. The water she had drawn previously was exhausted. She had drunk it and now was thirsty again. There is no permanent satisfaction that way.

Perhaps it is not inappropriate to point out that this is characteristic of the world. It is not only the water supply that must be renewed every day and the food supplies that must be obtained again. The way of worldliness is the way of permanent dissatisfaction.

There was a commanding officer in a certain army unit who had been a heavyweight boxer in his pre-army days and was held in a good deal of respect accordingly. On one occasion he was dealing with a group of soldiers who were guilty of various military offenses. Having received his sentence, one of them told a friend who was waiting to be dealt with, "He offered me the choice between seven days of confinement to barracks and three rounds in the boxing ring with him. I chose the seven days of confinement, and he roared at me, 'Coward, take fourteen days of confinement to barracks.'"

When his turn came, the friend was glad of a little inside information. "Will you take seven days of confinement to barracks or will you go three rounds in the ring with me?" the officer asked.

Thankful that he had some idea of what was involved, the soldier promptly replied, "I'd prefer the three rounds with you, sir." But to his consternation the officer shouted, "You'd take advantage of an old man, would you? Fourteen days in barracks for you!"

The way of worldliness is a bit like that. There is no means of ultimately pleasing it and meeting its demands. No matter which way we try, we cannot attain final and lasting satisfaction. The modern world is a study in dissatisfaction; with all its sophisticated pleasures it is a classic example of boredom and discontent. Surely never in the history of the race have there been so many ways of attaining pleasure, so much in the way of technical devices to make life easy and enjoyable (think of all the gadgets with which our homes are adorned). And never have so many been bored and unhappy, seeing life as a frustrating business, an exercise in futility. I do not want to give the impression that I can state the world's problems in one sentence and give the solution in another. Life is too complex for that. But there can surely be no doubt that part of the difficulty arises from the fact that "everyone who drinks of this water will thirst again." There is nothing lasting about this world's satisfactions.

Jesus contrasts with this the drinking of the water that he will give. We might notice an interesting change of tense in the Greek. When he says, "Everyone who drinks of this water . . ." (v. 13), the verb *drinks* is in the present tense, a tense that can depict continuous action. This kind of drinking goes on and on. It has to, because of the kind of water that is involved.

But when Jesus says, "Whoever drinks of the water that I will give him . . ." (v. 14), the verb *drinks* is in the aorist subjunctive, with a meaning like "whoever has drunk once for all." He is talking about a decisive happening. When anyone comes face to face with Christ and, abandoning an old way of life, turns to him for salvation, for the "living water" that he alone can give, then something permanent has happened. That person has entered into an experience from which he will never want to go back. He has drunk of the water that is permanently satisfying.

This does not mean that the Christian life is a kind of flat, bovine contentment, such that the believer has nothing to reach out for, no attainment in the service of Christ that is yet before him. Jesus pronounced a blessing on "those who hunger and thirst for righteousness" (Matt. 5:6). The believer is always aware that he has not yet attained the standard which he ought to attain. He is never ignorant of the fact that there are greater experiences yet before him. With Paul he cries out, "Forgetting the things that are behind and stretching out towards what is before, I press on toward the mark for the prize of the high calling of God in Christ Jesus" (Phil. 3:13–14).

The Water That Leaps

The water that Jesus gives "will be in him [who drinks of it] a fountain of water leaping up into life eternal." The Spirit-filled life is dynamic. Jesus brings out something of what this means by the use of an unusual word for the action of water. His verb for "leap" is not normally used for the action of inanimate things, but rather for living beings, people or animals, that jump in the air. There does not appear to be another example of its use for the action of water. It is true that a fountain is water in motion in a way that might aptly be described as "leaping," and we do sometimes speak of a fountain in this way. But that was not the way the ancients described it. They used other verbs. Jesus is not referring to an ordinary process, a natural force, but to something that is very unusual. When the Holy Spirit enters the life, there is vital force that finds vigorous expression.

This may perhaps be indicated by another piece of John's language in this chapter. He has used the word *pēgē*, "spring," of the source of the woman's water supply (v. 6). It is uncertain why this word would be used of a well. Theoretically there might have been a spring at the bottom of the well, and if so the well would have had a magnificent source to replenish its supplies. There is no spring there now, so if the word is being used strictly, the spring has since dried up. But it seems more likely that the word simply means "well." It is apparently used without regard to the way the water got into the well. But the more usual word for a hole in the ground is *phrear*, and this is used in verses 11 and 12. There is something static about this word. It simply refers to a ditch, a hole in the ground.

But when Jesus refers to the living water he uses *pēgē* again, and there is a point in his choice of word. This is a real fountain; it contains vital force as it leaps up. And that corresponds to the life of the believer. When the Holy Spirit comes into anyone's life, there is a new power as well as a new sense of direction. Jesus is not calling people to a worldly life with one or two of its worst habits eradicated. He is calling them to something radically new.

He speaks of this radically new existence in terms of eternal life. As we saw in an earlier study (p. 98), this refers to life that is proper to the age to come, but it is life that Jesus has made available here and now. The wonderful thing about the gift of the Holy Spirit is that those who have it do not live out their lives solely in the possibilities of this present world and its resources. Something of the power and the vision of the age to come is theirs now.

It is this wonderful prospect that is held out to the woman of Samaria. There is nothing extraordinary about her. As we read the chapter we do not see her as a woman with outstanding achievement or potential. We have already seen that Jesus does not always choose outstanding people. Many of his miracles of grace are worked in what the world would count as very unpromising people. That is one of the things this chapter is saying to us. The gift of the living water is not a reward for meritorious service. It is a gift that brings to anyone who receives it, no matter how insignificant and limited he or she may be, a totally new experience, a new power, a new life—the life that is life eternal.

17

Worship in Spirit and Truth

He says to her, "Go call your husband and come here." The woman answered him, "I have no husband." Jesus says to her, "Well did you say, 'I have no husband,' because you have had five husbands and he whom you now have is not your husband; this you said truly." The woman says to him, "Sir, I see that you are a prophet. Our fathers worshiped in this mountain, and you say that in Jerusalem is the place where we must worship." Jesus says to her, "Believe me, woman, an hour is coming when neither in this mountain nor in Jerusalem will you worship the Father. You worship you know not what; we worship what we know, for salvation is from the Jews. But an hour is coming and is now present when the true worshipers will worship the Father in spirit and truth, for the Father seeks such as his worshipers. God is spirit, and those who worship him must worship in spirit and truth" (John 4:16–24).

When Jesus spoke of living water that would give permanent satisfaction, the woman asked for it so that she would not have to come to the well to draw water (v. 15). Clearly she was not serious. The water Jesus was offering was not the kind of water that would relieve those who drank it from having to make visits to wells. She did not think that Jesus had anything in particular to give; rather, she was simply humoring an unusual acquaintance.

But Jesus saw that the time had come to bring things home to the woman and he asked her to bring her husband (v. 16). It has well been pointed out that the gift Jesus would give is not a gift to be enjoyed alone, but it is to be shared with other people. And with whom could the woman share better than with her husband? This may have been part of the reason for Jesus' request. But it seems more likely that he wanted to bring home to the woman the fact of her sin and the importance of doing something about it.

She said, "I have no husband," to which Jesus replied, "Well did you say, 'I have no husband,' because you have had five husbands and he whom you now have is not your husband; this you said truly" (vv. 17–18). Clearly the woman was an expert at divorce! We, by contrast, know little about divorce among the Samaritans of the time, though it seems a fair assumption that their customs did not differ greatly from those of the Jews.

According to the law of Moses, a man could divorce his wife, but a woman's rights were more limited: she could not divorce her husband. That, however, was not the whole story. She was sometimes allowed to petition the court, and if the judges thought it right, they could direct the husband to divorce her. Some wealthy women were known to have paid their husbands to divorce them. So there were ways that women could get around their nominal inability to get rid of unwanted husbands.

Theoretically there was no limit to the number of valid marriages anyone could contract, but the rabbis thought that a nice girl would not have more than two husbands, or three at the most. Jesus may mean that the woman had had more than the allowable number of marriages, so that her present union was not legal. Or, in accordance with the way he looked at marriage (Matt. 19:3–9), he may be saying that she was not really married at all. Or again, it may be that the woman had become so used to getting in and out of marriage that in the last case she had dispensed with the formality of marriage altogether.

Wonderful Mount Gerizim

Whatever the precise circumstances, the woman's home life clearly did not bear close examination. She wanted to get off the topic, so she tried to pick an argument on a religious theme. A good argument is often a useful way of avoiding an unpleasant subject. She paid Jesus a compliment, "Sir, I see that you are a prophet," and went on, "Our fathers worshiped in this mountain, and you say that in Jerusalem is the place where we must worship" (vv. 19–20). That should end the unpleasant topic of husband or no husband!

There was continual dispute between the Jews and the Samaritans over the right place for worship. The Jews held that the only place in the whole world where a temple could rightfully be built for the worship of God was Jerusalem. They did not mind synagogues in all sorts of places, but the temple must be in Jerusalem. The Samaritans, by contrast, held that Mount Gerizim was the right place. They found in their Scripture that Abraham and Jacob had made altars in the general vicinity (Gen. 12:7; 33:20). They found also that Mount Gerizim was the place where the people were to be blessed (Deut. 11:29; 27:12), and that God had commanded that an altar be made on this mountain (Deut. 27:4–5). In our Bibles the mountain where the altar was to be made is Mount Ebal, but in the Samaritan Scripture the mountain is Gerizim. They thus felt that they had good grounds for seeing Gerizim as important. They added to their argument by understanding Gerizim to be in view whenever an expression like "the goodly mountain" occurred.

With this way of reading the Bible, Mount Gerizim became a most significant and historical spot. The Samaritans thought that almost every important happening in the days of the great patriarchs took place on or near Mount Gerizim. They accordingly had strong feelings about their beloved holy mountain. This is illustrated in a story that was told about a Samaritan who got into conversation with a traveler, evidently a Jew. The traveler said that he was going up to Jerusalem to pray. The Samaritan replied, "Would it not be better for you to pray in this blessed mountain rather than in that dunghill?" With emotions like this so easily aroused, we can see that the woman might well feel that if she could get a good argument going over the rival merits of Jerusalem and Gerizim, her family circumstances would be forgotten.

"You Worship You Know Not What"

But Jesus was not going to be drawn into the kind of discussion the woman wanted. He had something more important to do than engage in futile argument. He pointed out that the place of worship is not important and further that times were changing. They lived in a troubled era, and soon people would worship neither in Gerizim nor Jerusalem. So they should not put too much emphasis on the place.

Then he drew attention to a defect in the whole Samaritan approach. "You worship you know not what," he said (v. 22), drawing attention to the poverty in spiritual things that necessarily followed from the Samaritan refusal to use any part of Scripture other than the first five books of our Old Testament. That meant that they did not have the historical books, Joshua and Judges, the books of Samuel, Kings, and Chronicles, and those of Ezra and Nehemiah. They did not know of the way God had watched over his people through the centuries, working out his purposes in both blessing and judgment. They did not know of the people whom God had raised up to do his will, nor did they know of the way God's demand for righteousness had worked out in history.

And they did not have the Psalms. To cite but one, the Shepherd Psalm (Ps. 23) is surely one of the great devotional treasures of Scripture, and to be without it is to be impoverished. So with other psalms that give an insight into the heart and mind of the true worshiper of God. To lack the psalms is to be robbed of truths of inestimable value. And think of Proverbs, that storehouse of practical wisdom, with its insights into the way God would have his people live.

The books of the prophets are part of the treasures of the whole human race. All sorts of people, whether or not they are worshipers of the God of the Bible, find these writings unique in their insight into the ways of God and man and the relationship between the two. The prophets have much to tell of the way God regards our sins and spiritual ineffectiveness, and of what is necessary in the path of service to God.

The Samaritans did worship the true God. But they had turned their backs on much of the revelation that God had given, and thus they incurred the condemnation, "You worship you know not what." Since Jesus says "what" and not "whom," it may be that he is pointing to the whole system of worship as well as to the God being worshiped. It was good that they were worshiping the true God, yet tragic that they did not know what they were doing. They had rejected too much of the revelation to know what they were about.

Perhaps we should ask ourselves how all this applies to us. It may well be that of many modern worshipers it can also be said, "You worship you know not what." Certainly God has made a rich and full revelation for us in Scripture, but when we go to church on Sunday, all too often it seems that our approach to God ignores much of it. It is easy to have our minds firmly made up as to what God is like and then not listen to what God says about himself in Scripture. How many of us, for example, take seriously such words as "our God is a consuming fire" (Heb. 12:29)? But they are part of the Bible, and when we worship we should bear in mind God's vigorous hostility to everything that is evil. So with the rest of the revelation. When we come before God, it is not good enough to be hazy and uncertain about what has been revealed. Worship is too serious a matter for that.

But we seem often to be in a state of ignorance. If we were truthful about our knowledge of God, many of us would have to confess that we are somewhat like a certain weatherman who was called as a witness in a trial. He was to give expert testimony as to the amount of the snowfall at the time of the crime. He gave his evidence competently and answered crisply all the questions asked of him. Then as he was about to leave the witness box the judge inquired, "What's the weather going to be like for the rest of the day?" "I'd rather not say," replied the weatherman. "I'm under oath."

An uncertainty like that tends to creep into much of our worship. It is all too easy to drift into a customary pattern without giving it any real thought. But God has revealed a great deal in the Bible, and it is plain that he expects us to take that revelation seriously. If we are to worship acceptably, it will be because we have come to know God as fully as we can and because our worship flows from that knowledge. It is a terrible thing if it can be said of us that we do not know what we are doing when we engage in worship.

"We Know"

Over against the uncertainty of the Samaritans, Jesus sets the certainty the Jews had. He is not saying that every Jew worshiped more acceptably than every Samaritan, but rather that the Jewish system took account of all of Scripture and thus, in principle at least, the Jews had a better knowledge of him whom they worshiped than did the Samaritans. Of course an individual Samaritan might be more sincere and might worship more acceptably than an individual Jew. But that is not what Jesus is talking about. He is talking about the approaches of the two groups taken as a whole.

There is a calm confidence in Jesus' words, "We worship what *we know*." The Jews' worship of God was not based on their desires, their hopes, the opinions of their liturgical experts, or anything like that. Jesus is saying that their worship was based not on speculation but on knowledge. This is an indispensable part of true worship. Thus David could say, "The Lord is my Shepherd" (Ps. 23:1), and Paul could say, "I know whom I have believed" (2 Tim. 1:12). There is a quiet certainty about the approach of the worshiper who takes seriously what God has revealed in his Word. It is there for our information. Since God means what he says, we may have confidence when we approach him in accordance with his revelation.

Assurance is an important part of the Christian faith. God has made certain promises and he will keep them. We may rely on that. We are not meant to be left uncertain, wondering whether in the end we will or will not be saved. There is a whole book of our New Testament written to bring us this assurance. As John comes toward the end of his First Epistle he says, "These things I have written to you who believe on the name of the Son of God in order that you may know that you have life eternal" (1 John 5:13). He is not writing to the general public, nor is he penning an evangelistic tract. He is writing to believers. And he wants believers to be in no doubt. They are to *know* that they have eternal life. God has promised it to those who believe (John 3:16; Acts 16:31). Well, then. Let them act on the certainty that God will do what he says he will do. The assurance of salvation is one of God's good gifts.

Salvation Is from the Jews

When Jesus goes on to say, "Salvation is from the Jews," he is not engaging in some narrow nationalism. His word *salvation* is actually preceded by the definite article: he says "*the* salvation." He is not speaking of any kind of salvation that people might think of, but THE salvation, the salvation prophesied in the Old Testament, the messianic salvation. When the Samaritans refused to accept most of the Old Testament writings as sacred Scripture, they cut themselves off from an understanding of the salvation that God would provide in due course.

Jesus' words are not to be understood as ascribing some great superiority to the Jewish nation as such. He is pointing to the prophecies of Scripture about the Messiah and saying that those prophecies meant that when the Messiah came he would come from among the Jews. There is no way of reading the Old Testament and concluding that the Messiah would be a Samaritan. In his great purpose God chose the Jewish nation as the one to which he would make his supreme revelation and among whom in due course he would send his Messiah. The other nations have their gifts and their callings in the life of the world. But it is only to this nation that God would send the Messiah. People may argue as they will about the merits of Gerizim and other holy places. Nothing can alter the fact that God has determined that his Messiah and the salvation that the Messiah would bring would come to this one nation, the Jews.

And that salvation is desperately needed. There is in every modern nation, just as there was in the Jews and Samaritans, that which shrieks aloud of our inability to make this world the kind of place in which we would like to live. I have a certain sympathy with the ninety-four-year-old man who was told that he needed a hearing aid. He declined with decision, saying, "No, I've heard enough!" Unfortunately we cannot keep out the world's evil by simply refusing to listen. The evil is real. And our need of salvation is real.

True Worshipers

Jesus moves on to what real worship means. Disputes between Jews and Samaritans might stir people like the woman to whom he was talking, but they had no real substance. Things were changing, he said.

"But an hour is coming and is now present" (v. 23) points to the entrance of something new into human life. And that new thing is, of course, the coming of Jesus. Before his time people could dispute about Gerizim and Jerusalem as rival places of worship, but his coming means the end of the old ways. He would in due course die on a cross to put away people's sins and thus make obsolete the ways in which people worshiped in the rival shrines. The coming of Jesus means the end of ways of worship like those in Jerusalem and on Mount Gerizim.

The woman could not have been expected to work out all that the presence of Jesus in this world means. She had just met him and had no way of understanding the nature of his messianic vocation. She could not know that in due course he would lay down his life on a cross, but she could understand more than she had so far evidenced. Her talk of worship had centered on place. She was interested in whether Gerizim or Jerusalem was the better *place* to approach God. Jesus now turns her thoughts to the better *way* to approach him.

He speaks of "the true worshipers." It is possible, of course, to approach God mechanically and formally, but such worship is not true worship. If the woman wants no more than formality, let her keep on with discussions about the better place for a temple. But if she is really concerned with approach to God, if she wants to be a true worshiper, then she will have to take a different tack. It is easy enough to be a false worshiper, to be concerned simply with being in the right place at the right time. Which of us has not felt the temptation to be preoccupied with the outward? It is so easy to concentrate on being in our customary place of worship, on taking up our habitual position, on standing and sitting and singing and speaking (and, of course, taking part in the offertory) at the usual times.

But all of that is not worship. True worship is done "in spirit and truth." Some have thought that "spirit" here refers to the Holy Spirit, but this seems unlikely. It is true that the Holy Spirit is involved in our worship. Paul writes of the way the Spirit helps us in our weakness in prayer; we do not know what to pray but the Spirit himself makes intercession (Rom. 8:26). So, too, we are to pray "in the Spirit" (Eph. 6:18). But it is not this sort of thing of which Jesus is speaking. He is surely referring to the human spirit and saying that true worship can never be accomplished in what is merely outward. True worship means right inward dispositions; it means being involved at the deepest level of our natures.

When we come to worship, other people may see whether we are in our usual place, whether we have a reverent demeanor, whether we are joining in the hymns and responses. But only God knows whether our spirit is involved and thus whether we are really worshiping or merely going through the motions. In our worship we must always keep in mind the truth that we cannot deceive God. We can deceive our neighbors and we can deceive ourselves. But God always knows whether our worship is "in spirit and truth" or whether it is a sham.

Jesus says that right worship is done "in spirit and truth" (not only "in spirit"). In John's Gospel truth has a large place. It is linked in some way with Jesus himself, for he said, "I am . . . the truth" (14:6). We should bear this in mind when we think of worship, for it is only because of what Jesus has done that we Christians can approach God in the way we do. We close many of our prayers with "through Jesus Christ our Lord," and rightly. It is because of what Jesus has done that we can come to God. And it is in the measure that we see the truth in Jesus that we will worship as we should.

We generally think of truth as a quality attaching to words; people speak the truth or they tell lies. This, of course, is quite biblical, but there is also the idea that truth can be a quality of action; people may "do the truth" (3:21). It is perhaps something like this that is meant here. If we are to worship rightly, we must "do the truth" as we worship. We must be completely sincere.

We should notice another small point. Some translations, as, for example, the King James Version, read "in spirit and in truth." This reads well in English, but in Greek there is only one "in." The preposition is not repeated before "truth." In other words Jesus is not saying two things: we must worship in spirit *and* we must worship in truth. He is expressing one complex idea: we must worship in spirit and truth. The two go together. They make up one acceptable attitude.

God Is Spirit

We should understand Jesus' words about God in verse 24 in the sense "God is spirit" rather than "God is a spirit." In Greek there is no indefinite article like our "a." When we translate we put the article in or leave it out according to the general sense of the passage. Here Jesus is not saying that God is one spirit among many, which would be the meaning of "God is a spirit." Rather he is saying that God's essential nature is spirit. Jesus' statement is like "God is light" (not "a" light) or "God is love." The word order puts emphasis on "spirit." It is important that we understand this truth about God.

It is important because our worship must be the kind of worship that accords with the nature of God as he is. Since God is spirit, our worship must be in spirit; it must be of a spiritual kind. Of course, the outward does have its place. Jesus is not saying that it does not matter. But he is saying quite firmly that its place is a minor one. What matters in the most important sense is that we realize something of God's nature as spirit and that our worship accordingly must proceed from our inmost being. It must be worship in spirit.

Notice the word *must* in this verse. Jesus is not saying merely that it would be a good idea for people to worship this way. He is saying that it is absolutely necessary. In our free and easy democratic ways we often feel that worship is an individual matter. Each of us may worship when and how he or she chooses. It is all up to the individual.

But Jesus is denying this. He is saying that our worship must accord with the kind of being God is. He has just rebuked the Samaritans with the words, "You worship you know not what." It is something like that which is in mind here. It is important to know what God has revealed of himself if we are to worship acceptably. I am not saying that we must have a full and perfect understanding of God before we can worship acceptably. If that were the case, nobody could ever worship, for our knowledge is always partial (1 Cor. 13:9, 12). But we are not in control of worship. It is not the worshiper who determines what shall be done and how it shall be done. Worship must always be such as to agree with the kind of God being worshiped. Since God has revealed to us something of his essential being, our worship must be such as accords with that revelation.

Worship is a great privilege that God has given us. Let us then use it rightly.

18

The Great Harvest

Jesus said, "I have food to eat which you do not know about." The disciples therefore said to one another, "Surely no one has brought him anything to eat?" Jesus says to them, "My food is to do the will of him who sent me and to accomplish his work. Don't you say, 'Four months yet and the harvest comes'? Look, I tell you, lift up your eyes and look at the fields, because they are white, ready to harvest. Already the reaper is receiving his wage and gathering fruit to life eternal, so that he who sows may rejoice with him who reaps. For in this is the saying true: 'One man sows and another man reaps.' I sent you to reap that for which you did not labor. Others have labored and you have entered into their labor" (John 4:32–38).

The disciples had come back from the village with the food they had bought. They were surprised that Jesus was talking with a woman (v. 27). As we have seen, men in general did not talk much with women, and this was especially true of religious teachers. But the disciples had been with Jesus long enough to know that he did not always do what people expected. In any case he was their leader. They could scarcely say to him, "Why are you talking with her? Don't you know that a teacher like you does not talk to women?" Nor could they very well rebuke the woman for talking to a great religious figure (though they probably felt like doing so). Since Jesus accepted her, they could scarcely drive her away. So they said nothing. But the problem was solved for them when the woman decided to go back to the village and tell people of her great discovery. So she left her water pot (the reason for her journey in the first place!) and went off (v. 28).

The disciples reasoned that Jesus must be hungry (they had probably been clean out of food when they went off to do their shopping), so they tried to get him to eat something. They were met with the surprising statement: "I have food to eat which you do not know about" (v. 32). Not unnaturally, they interpreted this to mean that somehow Jesus had obtained some food while they were absent. But how? Who could have given him anything? There were no people about. No one could have done it! Perhaps we should notice in passing that in John's Gospel we often read of people who took literally words that Jesus used of spiritual realities. The Jews did this when Jesus spoke of destroying and raising the temple (2:20), Nicodemus did it with the new birth (3:4), and the woman did it with the living water (4:15). Now the disciples do it with the food that Jesus eats. This kind of misunderstanding persisted to the end (14:8; 16:17–18). The revelation that Jesus brought is not obvious and open to everybody. There is mystery about it, and we do not recognize its meaning unless Jesus explains it.

This episode shows us an important truth about the way that Jesus used his miraculous powers. Since he had already done a number of miracles (2:23), the disciples would not have been unaware of his abilities. But it never occurred to them that he might work a miracle to meet his own needs, even legitimate ones. The miracles were always worked for other people; they were never used for selfish purposes, whatever the personal needs of Jesus might have been. And the disciples knew this. They knew that Jesus would not have worked a miracle for himself. If he had had food, someone must have brought it to him.

Doing the Will of God

But how could it have happened? Jesus explained: "My food is to do the will of him who sent me and to accomplish his work" (v. 34). We should notice that Jesus is speaking specifically about himself. His "I" is emphatic when he says, "I have food to eat," and the word *my* is emphatic when he says "my food." However it might be with other people, this is the way it is with him.

His food was to do the will of God. It was meat and drink to him to set forward the divine purpose. That was why he had come to this earth, and fulfilling the divine purpose was more important to Jesus than the food the disciples had gone off to buy. He does not say "God," but "him who sent me." This is characteristic of the Fourth Gospel. Again and again in this Gospel we read of the Father as having sent the Son. John has two Greek verbs for "to send," one of which he uses twenty-eight times and the other thirty-two times. In many of these instances he refers to the Father as sending the Son. Clearly the thought of mission is important to this Evangelist ("mission" is derived from a Latin verb which means "to send"). It is possible to speak of the Son as "coming" into the world, and John does this. It matters to him that for our salvation Jesus came. But it matters also that in this Jesus was at one with the Father. The Father is involved in this work of salvation. He *sent* the Son.

Jesus speaks of "accomplishing" the Father's work. The verb shows something of his persistence. He is not speaking of an occasional good impulse, but of carrying through right to the end the good work that he does. It is easy to grow weary in well-doing and to decide that we have done enough. Not so is the work of the Father accomplished. That demands persistence. It may also be implied that this is work that the Father began and that Jesus now carries on. If that is in mind, it would fit in very well with the saying "one man sows, another man reaps," which comes a little later. And it would also see the whole life of Jesus as one great "work." Sometimes in this Gospel we read of the "works" that Jesus did. That takes his deeds one by one and looks at them as individual acts. But this way of speaking sees his whole life as a unity, as one great act of God. Both ways of looking at what Jesus did are important.

Four Months to Harvest

It looks as though Jesus proceeds to quote a proverb in verse 35. His "you" is emphatic: "Don't *you* say . . . ?" This is not his saying, but theirs. Some reject the view that this is a proverbial saying on two grounds: such a saying is not found anywhere in the extant literature, and in any case it takes longer than four months to get a crop to the stage of harvest in Palestine (six months is more likely). The first objection is not a strong one. When I worked in a remote parish in the Australian bush, I found that the farmers had a lot of sayings that I have never read in any book. This is surely true of people everywhere. Not only farmers but city-dwellers tend to evolve short, pithy sayings that arise out of their way of life.

The second objection is a bit stronger, but not much. It does take longer than four months to grow a crop in Palestine. But it seems that the men on the land in ancient Israel tended to divide the year into six two-month periods: sowing time, winter, spring, harvest, summer, and extreme heat. And in what is probably the oldest Hebrew inscription in existence, commonly called the Gezer Calendar, we read that there were two months of sowing, two months of late sowing, one of pulling flax, another of barley harvest, then the general harvest. From both the general practice and the Gezer Calendar, we see that from the end of sowing to the beginning of harvest there are four months. While the saying does not mean that crops grow in four months, it does mean that a period of at least four months intervenes between the end of sowing and the commencement of harvest. "Rome was not built in a day," we say—some things just can't be hurried. A proverb like this makes good sense.

The alternatives do not look attractive. Some suggest that we have here a remark made by the disciples as they looked at the crops. But a chance remark like that is not the kind of thing that is recorded in the Gospels. A further objection is that if in fact it was four months before the harvest, the crops would be in the early stages of growth, and that is not a time of scarcity of water. A weary traveler would find water on the surface; he would not depend on a woman coming to the well to draw water if he wanted a drink.

On all counts it seems better to think of the words as a proverbial saying which conveyed the thought that some things cannot be hurried. There is plenty of time. The farmer must just wait for the months to pass. He cannot get his harvest until the right amount of time has elapsed. Now this has a certain force in the processes of agriculture. There is a limit to what can be done to get the crop in early. We may use fertilizers and irrigation and chemicals, but in the end we must still wait for the plants to grow. Patience is a necessary virtue for the farmer, as James points out (James 5:7).

The Harvest of Souls

But the spiritual harvest does not run on the same lines as a crop of wheat. It is all too easy to think it does and to use that as an excuse for doing nothing. I like the comment of Campbell Morgan on this verse: "If those disciples had been appointed a commission of enquiry as to the possibilities of Christian enterprise in Samaria I know exactly the resolution they would have passed. The resolution would have been: Samaria unquestionably needs our Master's message, but it is not ready for it. There must first be ploughing, then sowing, and then waiting. It is needy, but it is not ready." Can't you hear many of our ecclesiastical assemblies passing such a motion? We are always ready to recognize needy areas, but just as ready to find perfectly good reasons why we should do nothing for the present.

And it is that kind of attitude that Jesus is opposing. "Look," Jesus says, "lift up your eyes and look at the fields, because they are white, ready to harvest." The imagery is plain enough, but there is a problem as to the detail, namely the use of "white" as indicating readiness for harvest. What crop is white at harvest time? Certainly not wheat, and even the city-dweller knows of "the golden grain." Some of my farmer friends point out that if wheat is not reaped when it is ripe, it turns a whitish color (they call it "rotten ripe"!). If this is in mind, Jesus is saying that the harvest is overdue. But I am not aware of any writer in antiquity who sees wheat as white, nor is the color associated with any other crop.

I think that H. V. Morton may give us the clue. He speaks of being in this very vicinity: "As I sat by Jacob's Well a crowd of Arabs came along the road from the direction in which Jesus was looking, and I saw their white garments shining in the sun. Surely Jesus was speaking not of the earthly but of the heavenly harvest, and as He spoke I think it likely that He pointed along the road where the Samaritans in their white robes were assembling to hear His words."

The harvest of which Jesus is speaking is surely to be understood in terms of people. He is not directing the apostles to agriculture, but to the harvest of souls in which they should be interested. In that harvest there is no reason for waiting. The harvest is there to be reaped, and there is an urgency about it. They must give themselves to the work of harvest and not comfort themselves with the reflection that there is no hurry because a harvest takes time to ripen. This harvest must be reaped now.

Urgency

There is an "already" at the end of verse 35, which many translations take with the preceding words: "the fields are already white. . . ." But this does not accord with the way John normally uses the word (he puts it early in the sentence, not at the end). And the sense of urgency in the passage seems better conveyed by taking it with what follows. It seems much more likely then that "already" goes with verse 36: "Already the reaper is receiving his wage." Since the normal procedure was for the laborer to be paid for his work at the end of each day, this indicates that the disciples are far behind. The day has gone, the energetic reaper is already being paid, and what have they done? We should probably not try to identify those who are already being paid. They form part of the imagery Jesus is using, and the point is simply that time is going on—there must be no delay.

There is a fine sense of urgency in a saying of Rabbi Tarfon (*c.* A.D. 130): "The day is short and the task is great and the laborers are idle and the wage is abundant and the master of the house is urgent." That is the way it always is in the service of our Master. In Christian work there never seems to be enough time, and there is always more to be done than we can easily accomplish. And is it not true that all too often the laborers are idle? We can so easily find good reasons for not doing the work that God sets before us. But the wage is abundant; our Lord never begrudges his people anything (cf. Luke 10:7). And the Master is urgent. We may be slack in our obedience, but the command to preach the gospel is plain enough, and the obligation to live the Christian life is abundantly clear.

Jesus brings out the overwhelming importance of the task by saying that the reaper gathers fruit "to life eternal." The task is not some insignificant one, where it does not matter much whether or not it is done. Jesus is talking about work in a field where the eternal welfare of people is at stake. Christians are called to work for the eternal well-being of those to whom they bring the gospel.

We are never to take the attitude that it does not matter much whether people respond. There are many invitations given in any normal society where it does not matter whether people accept them. When I am invited to a party, I may choose to go or not go. That is up to me. If I do not go, I miss the party. But that is all. I may have something better to do with my time. There may be other parties I can attend later. And if worse comes to worst and I simply stay at home and am miserable when I could have been rejoicing with my friends, that is soon over. In the long run it does not matter greatly whether or not I attend a particular party.

So it is with a multitude of organizations. There are innumerable clubs and societies which we receive invitations to join. If we accept, there are certain consequences, many of them beneficial. But we are not permanently handicapped if we do not. We may be impoverished by our refusal and may cut ourselves off from the possibility of doing useful service for our community. But whether we accept or decline, the results do not last forever.

It is otherwise with our work as Christians. The issues at stake here are eternal. If we are able to bring someone to trust Jesus, then we have accomplished something lasting. As James puts it, "He who converts a sinner from the error of his way will save his soul from death" (James 5:20). *From death!* That is a tremendous result. And of course, if a sinner refuses to turn from his evil way, that too is of lasting significance. When we evangelize we should be clear that we are doing something of great and permanent significance. Our concern is with eternal issues.

The Sower and the Reaper

The sower and the reaper rejoice together. They must never forget that they are working together for the same end result. The work of one would not be worth much without that of the other. If someone sows and no one comes along to reap in due course, the sower has wasted his labor. And if someone comes to reap where no one has sown, there is nothing he can do. The sower and the reaper are partners. Each depends on the other.

Sometimes Christians forget that. They did at Corinth. There they had developed cliques in the church, grouping themselves around the names of their favorite preachers. There were those who said they went along with Peter, those who aligned themselves with Paul, those who said that Apollos was the man, and even those who, apparently disgusted with the other factions, said they belonged to Christ (but don't all Christians?).

Paul would have nothing to do with such nonsense. He did not even congratulate those who put him in first place. He asked, "Has Christ been divided up? Was Paul crucified for you? Were you baptized in the name of Paul?" (1 Cor. 1:13). It is ridiculous to think of any but Christ as having brought salvation and accordingly as having first place. People like Peter and Apollos and Paul are nothing more than "servants through whom you believed." Paul goes on to explain a little more fully: "I planted, Apollos watered, but it was God who gave the increase" (1 Cor. 3:5–6).

That is the way it must always be in Christian service. There is no place for rivalry or jealousy. We are engaged together in a great work, the work of God. One may plant and another water, one may sow and another reap. But it is God and only God who can give the increase. We are all partners in doing God's work, channels through whom he accomplishes his purpose. If we understand what we are doing—and, more importantly, what God is doing in his world—we understand that the harvest is the important thing, not the part that this worker or that plays in bringing it about. As long as the harvest comes, sower and reaper can rejoice together.

So Jesus goes on to quote another proverb: "One man sows and another man reaps" (v. 37). It often happens on a small farm that the one who sows is also the one who does the reaping. But sometimes this is not the case; it matters little as long as the crop is got in. In the metaphorical application of the proverb it often happens that the one who sows is not the one who reaps. And again we may say that it matters little as long as the crop is got in. The task is the important thing, not the part of it that any particular worker accomplishes.

Entering the Labor of Others

It is often the case in life that people enjoy the fruits of the labor of others. Perhaps someone does a lot of hard work and then dies, and it is his heirs who enjoy the fruit of his labor. Or it may happen in other ways. When I retired I was able to buy a house with a very lovely garden. It had obviously been prepared with loving care by someone who knew much more than I do about the wonders and beauty of plant life. Every day I rejoice in the beautiful surroundings in which I live. And the beauty is not of my creating. It has been brought about by someone who is no longer here. He labored, and my wife and I have entered into his labors.

In the Christian task, one person often does a good deal of "spade work" and is then transferred, leaving it to others to reap the benefits of the hard work that they themselves did not do. Though the principle is clear, it is not easy to see in detail what Jesus meant here.

Some suggest that we must apply the words rigorously to the scene John is describing. It was Jesus and the woman who labored. Jesus taught the woman about the living water, and the woman passed on the good news to the people of the village and brought them to Jesus. All that the disciples did was go into the village and buy food. But now a crowd of believers was being formed and would enter into fellowship with them. The disciples had done nothing but would enjoy much. We must accept this as part of Jesus' meaning.

But others think that we must look back beyond the current happenings. Since John the Baptist had worked in this area, it is suggested that Jesus and his disciples were building on the work of John. This too is true. The Baptist had called on his hearers to repent because the kingdom of God was drawing near. He had told them of the coming of the Great One who would follow him and baptize with the Spirit. Where people accepted this teaching they were ready to respond to what Jesus and his followers said. Here it is true that John the Baptist labored and those who came later reaped.

For some this is not going back far enough. They see a reference to the prophets of the Old Testament, who had spoken in the name of God and prophesied of the Messiah whom God would send in due course and of the salvation he would bring. Those who read the ancient Scriptures with spiritual perception were prepared for the coming of God's own Son and responded to him when they met him.

Still others suggest that we must look to the future rather than to the past. Jesus would send the apostles ("apostles" means "sent ones") in due course, and they would reap what he had sown. This view reminds us of a truth we should never forget, that Christianity depends on the cross. There is but one way of salvation, and that way depends on the fact that Jesus died to put away our sins. Later Jesus said that a grain of wheat that does not fall into the ground and die produces nothing, "but if it dies, it bears much fruit" (12:24). It is the death of Jesus that results in Christian "fruit." Without that death there is nothing.

Many notice that in later happenings in that very area we have an excellent illustration of the principle involved. Philip went to Samaria and preached, with the result that many Samaritans believed. Only after that did the apostles Peter and John come down and enter into Philip's labors (Acts 8).

It is not difficult, then, to see many applications of this principle in the work of the servants of God. But for us the primary thing must always be the work that Jesus has done. Paul speaks of him as the one foundation (1 Cor. 3:11). His atoning death is the necessary basis of the Christian life. Without his taking away of our sins we would still be in the ways of death. In a very real sense Jesus is the basis of our every Christian activity. In everything we do we enter into the work Jesus did. We could go further. When we try to win people for Christ or to build up those who know him, we always find that Christ has been there before us. "I sent you to reap that for which you did not labor," he said to the apostles (v. 38). The same is true for us today. We go, not because it seems a good idea to us necessarily, but because he sends us. And when we go we find that all our reaping is done in a field that he himself has prepared.

19

The Healing of the Officer's Son

So he came again to Cana of Galilee, where he made the water wine. And there was a royal officer whose son was sick in Capernaum. When this man heard that Jesus had come out of Judea into Galilee, he went to him and asked him to come down and heal his son, for he was at the point of death. Jesus then said to him, "Unless you people see signs and wonders you will not believe." The royal officer says to him, "Sir, come down before my little lad dies." Jesus says to him, "Go, your son lives." The man believed what Jesus said to him and went off. As he was now going down his slaves met him and said that his child was alive (and well). He inquired of them therefore the hour at which he recovered. So they said to him, "Yesterday at the seventh hour the fever left him." So the father knew that it was at that very hour at which Jesus said to him, "Your son lives." And he believed, he and all his household. This is now the second sign that Jesus did when he had come out of Judea into Galilee (John 4:46–54).

His work in Samaria finished, Jesus completed his journey to Galilee and went to the village of Cana once more. Up till this point John has recounted only one miracle, which he now recalls by reminding his readers that Cana was the place where Jesus had turned the water into wine. That had been an outstanding event, and John expects it to linger in the memory of his readers.

He now introduces a gentleman whom he calls a *basilikos*. This word is connected with the idea of royalty (*basileus* means "king"), and some feel that here it means someone of royal blood, a member of the royal family. As far as the language is concerned this is possible, but there is nothing in the narrative that points to anyone so exalted. It seems much more likely that it means someone in the royal service, so I have translated it "royal officer."

Exactly what position the man held is not clear. Elsewhere we read of people in Herod's service, such as Chuzas (Luke 8:3), but the word used of that man is not the same as that here. We also read of Manaen, "the foster-brother of Herod the tetrarch" (Acts 13:1). Of this title F. F. Bruce says, "The title 'foster-brother' was given to boys of the same age as royal princes, who were brought up with them at court." It does not seem as though that is meant in the present passage. Some suggest that the officer was the manager of Herod's estates, others that he held some political office the exact nature of which has not come down to us. We do not know. All that we can say for certain is that he was a trusted official.

Some have felt that Chuzas or Manaen was the person meant here. This is, of course, possible, and it is pointed out that if Chuzas was the father of the boy who was healed, that might explain why his wife was later found among the group of women who followed Jesus and supported him out of their means. But since John says nothing that will enable us to link this man with anybody else in the New Testament, all such identifications must remain pure speculation. For John what mattered was what Jesus did and how the man and his household came to believe, not the satisfying of our curiosity about just who the man was.

A little bit of human nature comes out in the use of the word *basilikos* ("royal"). In this context it must refer to someone in the service of Herod, even though Herod was not really a king at all. He was a "tetrarch," which means "ruler of a fourth part." This title seems to have been used originally in Macedonia, where it denoted the rulers of the four regions of Thessaly, but the Romans used it more generally for the ruler of almost any part of a province. When King Herod ("Herod the Great") died, his territory was divided among his sons. Archelaus received Judea, Samaria, and Idumea; Herod Antipas got Galilee and Peraea; while Philip's lot was Trachonitis, Ituraea, Batanaea, and Auranitis. It could be said that Archelaus got about half, and the other two about a quarter each, which would make the title *tetrarch* very appropriate. But, as I have said, the Romans did not use this title with exactness. Whatever he ruled, the Herod of this story was not a king at all but a tetrarch. Human nature being what it is, Herod remembered that his father had been a king, and he fancied the title for himself. And so he was sometimes called King Herod (see Mark 6:14 for an example).

The father in our story, then, was in all probability one of the officers of Herod the tetrarch. He lived in Capernaum, about twenty miles away from Cana. His son had a fever (v. 52), though this is not a very precise description of his illness, as the term was used for a variety of ailments. Still we can see the general character of his illness. Clearly the boy was in a bad way. His father feared that he would die. Hearing that Jesus was in Cana and evidently knowing that at an earlier time Jesus had worked a miracle there, the father now sought Jesus out with a view to having him cure his son.

He asked Jesus to "come down," which is a little mark of accuracy, for Cana is in the hills, while Capernaum is by the lake. He asked Jesus to heal his son and brought out the urgency of this request by saying that the boy was at the point of death. It was this that had caused the father to undertake the twenty-mile ride on horseback in an endeavor to get the boy cured.

Signs and Wonders

Jesus' response is unexpected: "Unless you people see signs and wonders you will not believe" (v. 48). His plural (which I have tried to bring out by the translation "you people") shows that he is not speaking particularly about the man who made the request. It is not even clear whether Jesus is including him. He may be making a general remark about the reaction of the people to his ministry. In every age, not least our own, people have loved the spectacular, and it would seem that this was true of first-century Galilee. Jesus looked for people to trust him and follow him in faith. But many were more interested in spectacular miracles than in their spiritual need and the importance of following Jesus, whether or not that was popular.

We have already come across John's use of the word *sign* (p. 76). It is one of his important words for Jesus' miracles, a word which points to the fact that there is spiritual truth demonstrated in the miracles. In the literal sense of the word, miracles are "*sign*ificant." They have meaning. The careless and superficial rejoice in the wonderful happening and do not get down to the spiritual truth to which it points; it is this to which Jesus is objecting. "Wonders" is a term that directs attention to the marvel in the miracle. It is something that people see but cannot explain. They can only stand before it in awe and amazement. The word occurs sixteen times in the New Testament. It is noteworthy that it is never used alone, but is always joined with "signs," as it is here. The point is that although the miracles are surely wonderful and we certainly cannot explain them, that is not the most important thing.

That is subordinate. The important thing is what God is doing through them.

When people came to Jesus simply on the basis of the wonderful miracles they saw him do, they lacked the genuine trustfulness that is the mark of the true disciple. It is still the case that people who look for the spectacular and the sensational have not understood what the Christian way means. Perhaps that is the reason why so many in these days do not walk in the way of Christ. Loving the spectacular, they find uncongenial the humble, quiet, steady service that is the lot of the servant of God. I do not want to dismiss the spectacular altogether. Certainly the hand of God is in the extraordinary. But that is not the usual way in which God does his work in the world. And for most of his servants it is in what the hymnwriter calls "the trivial round, the common task," that the path of true service lies.

Faith

Jesus looked for faith, a truth that John makes clear over and over and is seen here in his "you will not believe." It was faith that was important, not an attitude that looked for signs and wonders. In the Gospels as a whole we see that Jesus normally did his miracles in response to the faith of those who came to him. "Do you believe that I am able to do this?" he asked the two blind men who sought sight (Matt. 9:28). "All things are possible to him who believes," he said to the father of the boy who had fits (Mark 9:23), which drew from the man the classic reply, "I believe; help my unbelief" (v. 24). "Don't be afraid, only believe and she will be saved," he said to Jairus when that man had been informed that his daughter was dead (Luke 8:50). It was trust in him that mattered, and Jesus demanded it constantly.

But Jesus' power could also operate when there was no faith. We shall see an example of this when we come to the next chapter, where Jesus heals a man who has been lame for thirty-eight years. The interesting thing about this miracle is that the man did not even know the name of the One who healed him, let alone trust in him. Sometimes faith followed the miracles, and we can trust that this happened in the case of that lame man. Certainly Jesus speaks of people who sought him out after the miraculous feeding because they had eaten the food and not because of the signs (6:26). Clearly Jesus thinks it would have been better if it had been the signs that had moved them. And in the upper room Jesus said, "Believe me that I am in the Father and the Father in me, but if not, believe on account of the works themselves" (14:11). While Jesus looked for the faith that simply trusted him without any support other than a knowledge of him, it is better to believe on the basis of the miracles than not to believe at all.

We should not despise such lowly faith. I am reminded of a wise college president who was addressing a gathering of fellow presidents. "Always be kind to your *A* students and your *B* students," he said. "One day one of them will come back and make a good professor for you." He went on, "And always be kind to your *C* students. One day one of them will come back and build you a two-million-dollar science block!"

We need not have quite this outlook to see that there is value in the lowly. All faith, even that which brings people to Christ for imperfect reasons, is precious before God. But this Gospel makes it clear that, though he welcomes all who come, it is better to come in simple trust in Christ for what he is than for the wonders he can perform.

Yet Jesus was prepared to welcome all who came to him, no matter if their coming was with inadequate motives. And who of us ever does come with the completely right motive? We are simply too imperfect. Yet he always welcomes us. He takes us with what little faith we have and makes us into the very saints of God.

The Gift of Healing

But the father in the story was desperate. He had come because his boy was dangerously ill. He needed help urgently. So he did not proceed with a discussion of how much or how little faith he had, nor did he try to defend himself against a possible accusation that he had come with a view to seeing Jesus do "signs and wonders." "Sir," he said, "come down before my little lad dies" (v. 49). Earlier John had used the term *son* of the sufferer, as did the father when he first spoke to Jesus (vv. 46–47). But his affection comes through when this time he speaks of "my little lad." The diminutive may be used to express smallness of size but is also used affectionately, and we need not doubt that this is the case here.

Jesus' reply must have been totally unexpected: "Go, your son lives" (v. 50). It is plain that the father was anxious that Jesus should return with him to Capernaum and was hoping that he would be able to get him there in time. It apparently had not occurred to him that Jesus could heal without being there. The centurion of whom we read in Matthew 8:5–13 was different. He was used to giving commands and knew that when he told a soldier to do something, that something would be done. He did not have to be there supervising. So he did not ask Jesus to come to his home. He wanted no more than that he speak the word. But this kind of faith was unusual. "I have found such faith in no one in Israel," Jesus said (Matt. 8:10). The royal officer here in John's Gospel certainly did not have it. He wanted Jesus to "come down."

So Jesus' words represented a hard test for the father. He had nothing to go on except Jesus' assurance. Jesus did not give him a sign of any sort. He simply said that the boy lived and told the man to go. The man passed the test. Without anything other than Jesus' word he went on his way: "The man believed what Jesus said to him and went off." He had his values right and acted on his faith in Jesus.

I have read that the singer Marian Anderson was once told by Toscanini that she had the voice of the century. On one occasion she gave a concert at the While House for the king and queen of England and the Roosevelts. On one Easter Day she sang beneath the Lincoln statue in Washington to a crowd of more than seventy-five thousand, including many of this world's great ones. So, when a reporter asked her what was the greatest moment of her life, she had plenty to choose from. But her answer was, "The day I went home and told my mother that she needn't take in washing any more." For all her greatness, Marian Anderson had her sense of values right.

So with our royal officer. He knew enough about Jesus to trust him. And he was prepared to act in accordance with that trust.

We should not misunderstand Jesus' words. Modern translations often have something like "your son will live" (Revised Standard, New English Bible, Good News Bible) or "your son is going to live" (Goodspeed). Such translations can be defended, but they miss the point that Jesus is not just giving an optimistic forecast of how the fever will turn out. He is speaking a word of power. The fever did not gradually clear up but left the boy at the moment Jesus spoke. John is not giving an account of an interesting prognosis Jesus made, which was vindicated by later events. He is telling us of a "sign" that Jesus accomplished.

The Hour of Recovery

As the man was going home, some of his slaves met him with the news that the boy was better. The boy is described in three ways. At the beginning he is the man's "son" (vv. 46–47). Later the man uses the affectionate "little lad" (v. 49). In verse 51 the slaves call him the "child." Godet comments that the slaves "in their report, use neither the term of affection *(paidion),* which would be too familiar, nor that of dignity *(huios),* which would not be familiar enough, but that of family life: *pais, the child.*" John has preserved these lifelike touches.

The father immediately asked when the boy got better and received the answer, "Yesterday at the seventh hour the fever left him" (v. 52). This raises the question of the way time is measured in this Gospel. First-century Jews measured time from sunrise or sunset and spoke of "the first hour of the day" or "the first hour of the night" and so on. On this reckoning the seventh hour would be about 1 P.M. If that was the hour at which Jesus told the man to go, he would have had plenty of time to get back to Capernaum that day. And he would no doubt have been anxious to see for himself that what Jesus said had indeed happened. Why would he stay in Cana overnight?

So some have suggested that John is using a different method of computing time. They suggest that he is using the Roman method, which counted hours from midnight and from noon. On this reckoning the seventh hour would be our 7 P.M. At such an hour the man might well decide to stay the night rather than return home immediately. This would make good sense, except for the fact that the so-called Roman method does not seem to have been used in ordinary life. It was a legal method of computing time, used, for example, in determining when a lease expired. But though fairly common in such circumstances, it does not seem to have been used in daily life. Roman sundials, for example, have VI and not XII for the middle of the day.

So it would seem that we must see the miracle as taking place at around 1 P.M. We can only guess at the reasons why the man did not immediately return home. His anxiety had been relieved, for he believed what Jesus had said to him. There may also have been the practical problem of his horse. No doubt he had ridden the animal hard in order to get to Jesus before the boy died, and the animal might not have been in a fit state to begin the long journey home. For whatever reason, the man stayed there overnight and went home the next day.

It was on the way home that his slaves met him with the great news that the boy was well again. Evidently the household had been so thrilled at the sudden recovery that they could not wait for the master to return but sent slaves to let him know. And when they told him the time of the sudden recovery, he recognized that it had occurred at the very hour when Jesus had spoken his word of healing. Jesus spoke in Cana, and the healing took place in Capernaum. Distance is no barrier to the power of God. Jesus could do works of healing without being physically present.

Notice that the words "your son lives" in verse 53 are exactly repeated from verse 50, and almost exactly the same expression is found in verse 51. John has a habit of repeating words and phrases for emphasis (usually with some small variation). So it is plain that he regards these words as important; they are the key to our understanding of the miracle. They are words of power, not simply a prophecy that the boy would get well in due time.

A Household of Faith

The result was that the man "believed, he and all his household." The fact that the man went on such a journey to get Jesus to come and heal his boy shows that he had some kind of faith. Then, when Jesus spoke his words of power, we are told that "the man believed what

Jesus said to him" (v. 50). That involves some kind of trust, but the expression itself means no more than that he took the words Jesus spoke at face value. He accepted Jesus' saying and believed that what he said had happened.

But when John now says, "He believed," this means that he had a genuine trust in Jesus. He had come to faith in the full sense. He no longer simply looked for a miraculous cure; he had faith in the person. John's whole Gospel is written in order that people may come to put their trust in Jesus (20:31), and here we see an example of what is meant. The man believed. And not only the man; his whole household believed as well. We have no way of knowing how much they knew of Jesus and how much they trusted him before the miracle. But the healing made a tremendous difference to them. They recognized that what had happened showed the power of God, and that made full believers out of them too. The whole household came to a place of faith.

The Second Sign

John rounds off this story by telling us that this is "the second sign that Jesus did when he had come out of Judea into Galilee" (v. 54). But he has already told us that Jesus had done "signs" in Jerusalem, so that many believed (2:23). How, then, is this the second sign? Some scholars think that John is making use of a book someone had written about Jesus' miracles, a "Book of Signs." This is not impossible, for the miracles are always attractive to Christian people; to this day we love to hear of how Jesus made people well. Some early Christians may have decided to write a book telling of the miracles. But this does not seem likely. The fact is that all the books we have from the early Christians include teaching as well as miracles, and it is not easy to think that anyone would want to write about Jesus as simply a miracle worker. He was that, but he was much more.

It seems more likely that we should understand John as Rieu does when he translates, "Thus once again Jesus wrought a miracle after leaving Judaea for Galilee." It was not Jesus' second miracle, but it was the second time he had worked a "sign" after he had gone from Judea into Galilee. It may indeed have been the second one he did in Galilee. We must bear in mind that there is a great deal that Jesus did that we know nothing about. The Gospels record only a few of the many things he did. But as far as our information goes, this was Jesus' second Galilean miracle, and both were done after he had been to Judea and returned.

The earlier miracle was the changing of water into wine (chapter 2). Perhaps John wants us to notice something of an advance. That was a miracle done on the spot; this one was done at a distance. That was a change in an inanimate substance (water was changed into wine), but this one concerned a living being. That one marked a continuance of social life. This one took a boy as good as dead and gave him life.

20

A Lame Man Healed

After these things there was a feast of the Jews and Jesus went up to Jerusalem. Now there is in Jerusalem by the Sheep Pool a pool that has five colonnades, called in Hebrew "Bethesda." In them there lay a crowd of sick people, blind, lame, paralyzed. Now there was a man there who had been thirty-eight years in his illness. When Jesus saw this man lying there and came to know that he had been like this for a long time he says to him, "Do you want to be made well?" The sick man answered him, "Sir, when the water is stirred up I have no one to help me into the pool; while I am coming someone else gets down before me." Jesus says to him, "Get up, pick up your pallet and walk." Immediately the man became well and he picked up his pallet and walked (John 5:1–9).

The miracle of healing we have been considering in the previous study took place in Galilee. John now moves to Jerusalem. His "after these things" is a time note he uses now and then to convey the thought of an indefinite interval. He is not telling us everything that happened nor does he let us know how long an interval elapsed before the next incident took place. He is interested in the things Jesus said and did, not in the precise sequence.

It happened at "a feast." This time John does not tell us which feast it was, as he often does. He is very interested in the Jewish feasts; in fact, there is more information about them in this Gospel than in any of the others. John uses the word *feast* a total of seventeen times. Matthew and Mark each have it twice and Luke three times, so John's use is distinctly exceptional. Not only does he use the general term *feast* often, he names particular feasts. We read of three Passovers in this Gospel (2:13; 6:4; 11:55; the third Passover is mentioned several times). We read also of the Feast of the Dedication (10:22) and the Feast of Tabernacles (7:2). Each of the feasts, of course, had deep religious significance and pointed to important spiritual truths. Apparently one of John's minor aims is to show his readers that Jesus perfectly fulfilled all that the feasts typified. What they symbolized he brought into existence.

All Jewish adult males were required to go up to Jerusalem for the three most important feasts of the year, the Passover (or Feast of Unleavened Bread), the Feast of Weeks, and the Feast of Tabernacles (Deut. 16:16). They often tried to go up also on other occasions, for there was clearly something special about observing a feast in the capital city, the one place where there could be a temple. As John does not tell us which feast this one was, we do not know whether or not it was one of the great feasts. We have nothing to go on, so the suggestions that are made are mere guesses. Since John does not mention the disciples in this incident, it is possible that Jesus went up without them. Though they often accompanied Jesus, we should not suppose that he never went anywhere without taking them with him.

The Pool

"Now there is in Jerusalem . . . ," says John, and his use of the present tense ("is") may be significant. It has been drawn into discussions of the date of the writing of this Gospel. The city of Jerusalem was destroyed by the Romans in A.D. 70, and if the present tense is used in its normal sense, this would mean that this Gospel was written before that date. In my opinion it was written before A.D. 70, but we cannot put much emphasis on this line of reasoning. People sometimes use the present tense when they are talking about things in the past, and John may be doing just that.

He goes on to talk about a pool, but the way he locates it leaves us uncertain about his precise meaning. He says, "Now there is in Jerusalem by the Sheep—," but he does not say what goes with "Sheep." The people who read his Gospel in the first century would have understood this perfectly, and John did not need to spell it out. But we do not, so we have to guess. The most common conjecture is "gate." Hence "Now there is in Jerusalem by the Sheep Gate" is adopted by translations like the Revised Standard, the New International Version, and the Good News Bible. One objection is that no ancient writer takes it that way. (C. K. Barrett says that no one takes it that way before A.D. 1283.) If it were correct, we would expect writers in antiquity to show that they understood it this way. Another suggestion is "market" (King James). There is nothing improbable about this, and it may be correct.

But on the whole the best suggestion seems to be that we should understand the word *pool* (as do most ancient writers). John is saying, then, "Now there is in Jerusalem by the Sheep Pool a pool. . . ." Somewhere near the Sheep Pool there was another pool, and it is at this other pool where the action takes place. The word used for "pool" means it was quite large; we should not think of it as a little pond. The word is connected with the verb "to swim" and means a pool big enough to swim in.

There is another problem with the name of the pool, this time due not to what John wrote, but to what the scribes did with his Gospel. The name varies in the ancient manuscripts. It seems that some of the scribes either did not understand the name or thought it was wrong, so they tried to correct it. For whatever reason, the pool is given a variety of names in the manuscripts. The name with the best support is Bethsaida (which means "house of fish" or "house of the fisher"). Another name found is Bethzatha, which appears to be a variant of Bezetha, and this, according to the Jewish historian Josephus, was the name of the part of the city where the pool was located. Belzetha, which appears in other manuscripts, is probably another variant of the same name. The name in the King James Version is Bethesda, which means "house of mercy," a beautiful and appropriate name when we think of the sick people who came there for help.

The problem is a difficult one, but it seems to have been solved for us by the Dead Sea Scrolls. One of them has references to a number of places in and around Jerusalem, one of which is "Beth Eshdatain." Now in Hebrew and Aramaic, in addition to the singular and the plural of nouns with which we are familiar, there is a form for the dual, that is to say, there is a special form of nouns that denotes two. And "Eshdatain" is dual. The ancient monastery near which the scrolls were found was destroyed in the war of A.D. 66–70, so we have here evidence contemporary with the New Testament, and its reference to the two pools seems to make it clear that we are to think of Bethesda as the correct name.

Archaeologists have found a double pool which in modern times is known as St. Anne's. There is little doubt that this is the place where the healing took place. There were five colonnades, one between the two pools and the other four around the perimeter.

People Waiting to Be Healed

John tells us that in these colonnades there was "a crowd of sick people, blind, lame, paralyzed." The true text of the Gospel does not tell us why they were there, but in some manuscripts it is made plain that they were there to try to find healing. These manuscripts go on to say that sometimes an angel went down into the pool. The waters of the pool were agitated, and whoever went into the pool first was healed. So the people were there, each hoping to be the first into the pool when the angel came, and thus be cured.

There can be no doubt that this is not part of what John wrote; it is quite out of character in the New Testament. Nowhere in Scripture do we have anything like an angel's coming and doing works of healing on a haphazard basis, with the first of a group of sick people to get into a pool being chosen and all the rest ignored, no matter how needy. It simply does not fit into the Christian way of understanding things. But there is little doubt that many people in Jerusalem believed this, and that was why the sick were there at the pool. They really thought that there was a chance of a cure if they could be first into the pool when the water was stirred.

Nobody knows what caused the disturbance of the water. Some think there was a spring that bubbled up intermittently, and this may well have been the case. There is no spring there now, but it is not impossible that there was such a spring in Jesus' day and that it dried up over the centuries. Others think that water was piped into the pool from some external source (from the temple area perhaps) and that when this happened the waters were agitated. We do not know. But there is no reason to doubt that there was something that caused the waters to move at unpredictable times, and that this was interpreted by the people of Jerusalem as meaning that an angel came and gave the sick the chance of being healed.

A Lame Man

Among them there was a man who had had some complaint for thirty-eight years. John does not tell us what the trouble was, though from verse 8 there can be little doubt that it was some form of lameness. Some exegetes draw spiritual lessons from the duration of the man's illness; they point out that it was the length of time that the Israelites wandered in the wilderness after their disobedience of God (Deut. 2:14). They see in this account a picture of the Jews paralyzed because of their lack of faith, and of Jesus giving healing to those who believed. Others think of the passage as applying generally to all those without spiritual power and not to the Jews in particular. They reason that the wilderness symbolism shows that such people have no spiritual home unless they turn to Christ. But while it may be possible to discover some edifying symbolism along such lines, it is not easy to think that this was what John had in mind. He seems rather to be bringing out the fact that this lameness, being of such long-standing nature, was not going to be easy to cure. For thirty-eight years neither the healing waters not anything else had been able to make the man well.

Jesus saw the man lying there by the pool. John does not tell us how Jesus knew that the man had been there for so long; he simply says that Jesus "came to know" this. Jesus may have asked the man, or somebody may have told him. The main point is that he knew. In contrast to what happened in the case of many other healings, the man does not approach Jesus; Jesus approaches him (v. 6).

He begins by asking, "Do you want to be made well?" It may seem to us that the answer is obvious. Of course the man would want to be cured. But it is not quite so simple. A man who had been disabled for so many years had settled into a pattern. He knew what his disability allowed him to do and what it stopped him from doing. Almost certainly he was a beggar, since there was no other way he could get a living. People would know him and where to find him if they wanted to help him.

If he was to be made well, he would lose all this. He would be adventuring into an unknown life. He could no longer depend on other people, but would have to take the responsibility for his own life. He would lose all his present securities and, being no longer a beggar, would have to earn his own living. How? He had not been trained to do anything; he had no special skills. People might help a lame person, but who would help an able-bodied man? To be healed meant to enter a completely new life, a life with wonderful possibilities but also with unknown perils. What did the man really want?

What we really want is not always what we say. There is a story about a man who lost out to a rival for promotion in the organization in which they both worked. The loser felt that he ought to do the right thing, so he dictated a telegram to his secretary: "Congratulations on your success. Permit me to extend heartiest congratulations and pledge my sincere, wholehearted support." The secretary took the message down in shorthand, then said, "Shall I read it back?"

"No, no," said the man. "I couldn't stand it!"

We are left wondering whether the congratulatory message was really meant. To say a thing and to mean it deep down are not the same. We are likewise left wondering whether the lame man really wanted healing. Jesus' question concerns the man's will, deep down. Did he really want health, with all its responsibilities as well as its privileges?

William Barclay reminds us that there is a contemporary application. "The first essential towards receiving the power of Jesus," he says, "is the intense desire for it. Jesus comes to us and says: 'Do you really want to be changed?' If in our inmost hearts we are well content to stay as we are there can be no change for us. The desire for the better things must be surging in our hearts." One reason why some people have nothing to do with Christ is that they do not wish to be disturbed out of their comfortable, selfish ways. To be a Christian introduces us to a life that none who have experienced it ever want to lose. But there is a price. To enter this life means leaving the old one.

Healing

The man's thoughts are concentrated on the pool. He makes no real answer to Jesus' question, though perhaps he implies that his endeavors to get into the pool over all those long years show that he did want healing. But quite clearly he does not think of Jesus as someone who might heal him. He has his mind made up about the way healing would come and does not allow anything to disturb him from that course. John Calvin comments, "This sick man does what we nearly all do. He limits God's help to his own ideas and does not dare promise himself more than he conceives in his mind."

The sick man explained to Jesus why he had not had healing, though he had looked for it for so long. Clearly he believed firmly that the one way in which he would be healed would be by getting into the pool right after the waters moved, so that the angel's healing work would be done on him. But his infirmity made it difficult for him to move fast, and someone always beat him to it. If he had had someone to help him, he would have had more chance. But he had no one. Actually, unless he could swim, he really did need help, because the pool was quite deep and there was no shallow end.

Jesus did not discuss the pool or its alleged curative properties. He simply told the man to get up, take up his pallet, and walk (v. 8). The word I have translated "pallet" means a camp bed. Some see it as a mat, and Moulton and Milligan, who produced a Greek lexicon giving the meaning of the words of the New Testament when they occur in the papyri and inscriptions, speak of it as "the poor man's bed or mattress." It was evidently quite light and portable, as we would expect from its being by the pool. There was no absolute need for him to pick it up. The man would have been just as truly cured if he had sprung to his feet and gone around the pool, "walking and leaping and praising God" like the lame man healed in Acts 3:8. But the taking up of the poor bed on which he had lain for so long was no doubt symbolical. No longer did it carry him through the day; he carried it.

The cure was immediate. Straightaway the man was healed, and he did what Jesus told him: he took up his pallet and walked. The power of the Lord was greater than that of the lameness. With one word of command, Jesus dispelled the paralysis that had lasted for thirty-eight years.

An interesting feature of this healing is that there is nothing comparable to "your faith has saved you," which we find so often in the accounts of healing miracles in the other Gospels. Not only is there no mention of faith on the part of this man, but there is no room for it. When he was asked who had healed him, this man did not know. Far from trusting Jesus, he did not even know his name. And later, though obviously the religious authorities were hostile to the man who had healed him, he did not hesitate to go and tell them who it was. He does not stand out as an attractive personality at all.

We may well reflect that while Jesus commonly acted in response to faith, this was not a necessary precondition of the power of God being at work in him. He could and sometimes did do a mighty work when, as far as we can see, there was no faith.

21

The Sabbath

Now that day was the Sabbath. The Jews therefore said to the man who had been healed, "Sabbath it is and it isn't lawful for you to carry your pallet." But he answered them, "The man who made me well, that man said to me, 'Take up your pallet and walk." They asked him, "Who is the man who said to you, 'Take (it) up and walk'?" But the man who had been healed did not know who it was because Jesus had gone off, there being a crowd in the place. After this Jesus finds him in the temple and said to him, "Look, you have been made well; sin no longer, lest something worse happen to you." The man went off and told the Jews that it was Jesus who had made him well. For this reason the Jews persecuted Jesus, because he was doing these things on the Sabbath. But Jesus answered them, "My Father works right up till now and I work too." On account of this, then, the Jews tried all the more to kill him, because he was not only breaking the Sabbath, but was calling God his own Father, making himself equal to God (John 5:9–18).

The lame man had been healed on a Sabbath day, and that led to trouble. There were pernickety Jews who were more interested in the letter of the law than in deeds of mercy, and they took offense at what had happened. In verse 10 John speaks simply of "the Jews," which is a way he has of referring to the religious leaders of the nation, especially those who were hostile to Jesus. Sometimes, it is true, he uses the term in a neutral sense or even a good sense, as when he reports the words of Jesus, "Salvation is of the Jews" (4:22). But generally, as here, he does not mean the whole nation, but that section of it that was in authority and opposed what Jesus was doing.

These Jews addressed the healed man. Incidentally, John has the word *healed* in the perfect tense, which indicates that the cure was permanent. In all probability many of the "cures" that took place at the pool did not last very long. John is not talking about a sham healing, but about something that had made a permanent change in the man. He was healed and would stay healed.

But that did not matter to these Jewish leaders. They drew attention to the day and indeed put emphasis on it: "Sabbath it is," they said, "and it isn't lawful for you to carry your pallet." By putting the word *Sabbath* first, they gave it emphasis. For them what mattered was that the day was holy. They ignored the healing altogether and did not even mention it. Their precious regulations mattered to them much more than the plight of a man who had been lame for thirty-eight years!

Sabbath Regulations

The Jewish teachers made a very thoroughgoing attempt to stop all work on the Sabbath, and some of their regulations were really extraordinary. Thus in the Mishnah tractate *Shabbath* we read of thirty-nine classes of work forbidden on the Sabbath (*Shabbath* 7:2). This was not, however, a complete list: both at the beginning and the end it is insisted that these are "the main classes of work," which leaves open the possibility that other activities were prohibited as well.

And they certainly were. A man might not go out on the Sabbath wearing one sandal, unless he had a wound in his foot (*Shabbath* 6:2). The reasoning was that this would give rise to suspicion that he was carrying the other sandal under his cloak (a forbidden "work"). If he was wounded, however, nobody would think he had another sandal with him. Again, while it was quite in order to borrow wine or oil from a neighbor on the Sabbath, one must not say, "Lend me them" (*Shabbath* 23:1). To say this would imply that a transaction was being made, and a transaction might involve writing, which was one of the thirty-nine forbidden classes of work.

A man should not search his clothing on the Sabbath looking for fleas, nor should he read by lamplight (*Shabbath* 1:3). The point of this latter is that he might be engrossed in his reading and, forgetful that it was the Sabbath, might perform the work of tipping the lamp to make the oil flow into the wick so that he would have a better light. A woman was forbidden to dress her hair or paint her eyelids (*Shabbath* 10:6), for she would then be engaged in the forbidden work of building or dyeing.

One regulation that I rather like was concerned with toothache: One must not put vinegar on one's teeth in an attempt to soothe the ache (that would be a forbidden act of healing). But it was permitted to take vinegar in the ordinary course of a meal, and the rabbis added philosophically, "If he is healed he is healed" (*Shabbath* 14:4).

It is obvious from such regulations that there were many ways in which the unwary might fall into a breach of the Sabbath. But it was also the case that the knowledgeable were able to get around many of the regulations. It was stipulated that one must not carry things in either hand, in one's bosom, or on one's shoulder. These were ordinary methods of carrying things and were clearly "work." But a regulation says: "If [he took it out] on the back of his hand, or with his foot or with his mouth or with his elbow, or in his ear or in his hair or in his wallet [carried] mouth downwards, or between his wallet and his shirt, or in the hem of his shirt, or in his shoe or in his sandal, he is not culpable since he has not taken it out after the fashion of them that take out [a burden]" (*Shabbath* 10:3). None of these was a normal way of carrying things, so none was classed as work. We are reminded of Jesus' castigation of those who put heavy burdens on other people but did not lift them themselves (Matt. 23:4). Clearly anyone with a very good knowledge of the regulations would not only be able to forbid other people from doing many harmless things, but would find ways of doing most things he wanted to do himself.

"He Told Me to Do It"

It was in such an atmosphere that the healed man was interrogated. He was examined by the experts and, while he himself would not have known all the regulations, he knew that all sorts of work were forbidden on the Sabbath. He knew also that his judges were in a position to do him harm if they judged him guilty of a transgression. So he was in a difficult position.

He defended himself by saying that it wasn't his fault. The man who healed him had told him to take up his pallet and walk (v. 11). What else could he do? One of the regulations provided that if a man was carried on a couch, "he is not culpable by reason of the couch, since the couch is secondary" (*Shabbath* 10:5). But apparently a couch by itself was quite another matter. It was not secondary, and the man was therefore culpable. Our lame man presumably did not know the regulation, but his judges did. So he was in danger.

The Jews naturally asked him who it was who had told him to take up his pallet and walk (v. 12), but the man could not help them. He had not known who it was. It was enough for him that he was healed. He simply did what he was told. Nor could he point Jesus out. There was "a crowd in thc placc" and, human nature being what it is, the people had doubtless flocked around the healed man to see for themselves what had happened to him. Jesus would have been lost in the crowd, and the man himself would have been so taken up with his newfound health that he would not have been looking for Jesus or for anyone else. So there was no way he could answer their question.

"Sin No Longer"

It was otherwise a little time later. John tells us that Jesus found the man in the temple. He may well have gone there to offer thanks to God for the wonderful healing he had received. Jesus sometimes told people to give thanks in this way (Mark 1:44; Luke 17:14), and it is not unlikely that the man was doing something of this sort. He certainly had cause for thanksgiving.

It is plain that he was not in any sense a follower of Jesus. He had not been healed on account of his faith or anything of the sort. He was a man in need, and Jesus in his compassion simply met that need. But it was also important that the man be brought to face spiritual realities. So Jesus sought him out.

"Look, you have been made well," he said; "sin no longer, lest something worse happen to you" (v. 14). "You have been made well" is in the perfect tense, which means that the cure was permanent. He would not relapse into his former lameness. But Jesus points to his sin and urges him to abandon it. What the sin was we have no way of knowing, but it must have been real enough, and Jesus knew what it was. He does not say, "Don't begin to sin, now that you have a new life," but rather, "Stop sinning—sin no longer." The expression implies that the man had been sinning and that his sin continued. He had a new physical life. Jesus bids him start a new spiritual life.

In this Gospel it is made clear that suffering is not necessarily the result of sin. Jesus told the disciples that the man born blind had not suffered his disability because of sin (9:3). But this does not mean that suffering is never the result of sin. Thus it is possible that in the present case there was some sin that lay behind the lameness. Some have felt that the "something worse" of which Jesus spoke was a further physical disability that the man would undergo if he kept on in an evil way. This cannot be dismissed as altogether impossible, but it seems more likely that Jesus is pointing out that the eternal consequences of sin are worse than the lameness from which the man had been delivered. He had escaped from a crippling physical handicap. Let him not now live in such a way that he would incur a far worse consequence and an eternal one.

We do not always take the "something worse" seriously enough. There is a story told of Bishop Warren A. Candler that illustrates this point. He was preaching on the way Ananias and Sapphira lied to God and pointing to the seriousness of sin. "God does not strike people dead these days for lying," he said. "If he did where would I be?" A ripple of laughter went through his amused congregation. The bishop paused for a moment and then roared right back at them, "I'll tell you where I'd be. I'd be right here, preaching to an empty house!" We do not give enough contemplation to the consequence of sin. If we think about it at all, we think it will happen to someone else. We should take Jesus' words more seriously. His warning is as relevant to us as to anyone.

Persecution

The healed man was not a very nice person. When he found out that it was Jesus who had healed him, he went off to the authorities and told them. He knew that they were incensed at the healing and wanted to know who had performed it in order to take action against him. One would think that simple gratitude would have impelled the man to keep quiet. The authorities had done nothing to him; they had questioned him and let him go. Why then should he go out of his way to let them know the identity of his benefactor?

Perhaps he thought he was still in danger. We do not know what penalties were inflicted at that time on those who broke the Sabbath, but whatever they were the man was liable. The death penalty was theoretically possible, so he may have thought that he was in considerable danger. His defense at his examination had been that the man who healed him told him to carry his pallet. Now that he could name him, he could make his case. Though it meant trouble for the Healer, the man may have reasoned that it secured his own safety. It was not an admirable action.

There is an interesting difference in the way what happened is described by the authorities and by the man. They asked him who it was who told him to take up his pallet and walk (v. 12). Now he answered their question by saying that it was Jesus who had healed him (v. 15). For them it was the offense that mattered. For him the important thing was the healing. Augustine acutely commented: "They sought darkness from the Sabbath more than light from the miracle."

"For this reason the Jews persecuted Jesus, because he was doing these things on the Sabbath" (v. 16). John does not tell us exactly what they did in this persecution, but it must have been unpleasant. Note that John says that Jesus "was doing these things on the Sabbath." The verb denotes continuous action; Jesus kept on doing things like this. It seems that John is not going to tell us of a great number of activities of

Jesus on the Sabbath. He has apparently chosen this one as a representative action, one that enables us to see Jesus' attitude toward the Sabbath.

We should notice that according to the Jewish leaders Jesus had a totally wrong attitude toward the Sabbath. In the usual translation of their accusation, Jesus "broke" the Sabbath, but this may not be strong enough. The verb is the ordinary word for "loose"; this can be in the sense "loosen the cohesion," and thus "loosen into its component parts," that is, "destroy." It is used of destroying the temple in 2:19, and of the ship breaking up in Acts 27:41. Where physical objects are not in mind, it may be used in this way for destruction, for example, Christ's destruction of the works of the devil (1 John 3:8). It seems that it is some such meaning as this that the Jews had in mind. They thought that Jesus was not simply making a single breach of the Sabbath regulations; he was destroying the whole institution. They were concerned about what had happened on this one day, but they were more concerned because they thought that what Jesus was doing meant the end of the Sabbath. In their view, if people acted as he did, then the Sabbath was gone.

It is plain from the synoptic Gospels that Jesus' attitude toward God's day was very different from that characteristic of the Pharisees. It is interesting that people from Jerusalem went up to Galilee to oppose Jesus (Mark 3:22, etc.). That was a long way to go, and we wonder why they did it. This story may give us part of the reason. Jesus came into conflict with the authorities in Jerusalem on what they saw as a major issue. Accordingly they opposed him strongly wherever they could.

The Sabbath

Jesus' defense is interesting. He does not refer directly to the Sabbath, but to the Father: "My Father works right up till now and I work too" (v. 17). He calls God simply "My Father," which is a more intimate form of address than the Jews would use. They might call God "Father," but they would usually add something like "in heaven" to make it clear that they were not being too familiar. But Jesus does no such thing. Here and in other places he uses the ordinary language of the family when he is speaking of the heavenly Father. This is a claim to a special intimacy, and the Jews recognized it as such.

The creation story in Genesis ends with the statement: "By the seventh day God had finished the work he had been doing; so on the seventh day he rested from all his work. And God blessed the seventh day and made it holy, because on it he rested from all the work of creating that he had done" (Gen. 2:2–3). The Sabbath rest thus derives from God's resting from his creating activity. But that does not mean that God rested from everything. There might be no more creating, but unless there was a sustaining activity from God, creation could not last. He continually upholds everything.

Jesus' attitude to the Sabbath derives from that of God. As we have seen, he claims a special closeness to God. In the synoptic Gospels he justifies what he does on the Sabbath with the words: "So the Son of man is Lord even of the Sabbath" (Mark 2:28). While the wording is different, the two defenses are basically very similar. Jesus has a special relationship to the Father, a relationship that issues in his being "the Son of man" and having a special position that enables him to do what he does. And that relationship justifies him in doing on the Sabbath what God does. This close personal relationship is significant throughout the Fourth Gospel.

As we shall see in the next study, it leads to Jesus doing what God does (v. 19). We should be clear on this. When he rejected the attitude of the Jews to the Sabbath, he was not saying that they were too restrictive and that their regulations should be eased. He was saying that they had the wrong attitude altogether. They objected to his healing on the Sabbath. Why? God did not cease from works of mercy, nor should his people. If they really understood what God was doing in the world and doing all the time, they would see that deeds of compassion, like the healing of the lame man, were not simply permitted but required. That was the kind of thing God did, and therefore it was the kind of thing that God's people should be doing.

Equal with God

But the Jews were not impressed. To them it seemed that Jesus was adding another offense: not only did he continually break the Sabbath, but now he was claiming that God was his Father in a special way. They saw that as "making himself equal to God" (v. 18). On both counts he was a blasphemer.

They never seem to have asked themselves whether what he said was true. It contradicted their cherished ideas, and that was enough for them. It had to be wrong. So does prejudice blind people. The coming of the Son of God into their midst was the most wonderful thing that had ever happened to them. But they did not see what had happened. They did not recognize what God was doing. Prejudice always blinds people and robs them of their opportunity to receive the richness of God's blessings.

Right through his Gospel, John is insisting that God was in Jesus in a special way. He would have agreed with the Jews that in his claims with regard to the Sabbath and his relationship to the Father, Jesus was making himself equal with God. But he would have gone on to say that those claims were justified. The error of the Jews lay not in a failure to understand Jesus' meaning, but in a failure to see that what he said was the truth.

22

The Son of the Father

Jesus replied, "Truly, truly, I say to you, the Son can do nothing of himself, only what he sees the Father doing; for whatever he does, these things the Son does likewise. For the Father loves the Son and shows him all the things that he himself does. And greater works than these he will show him so that you will marvel. For as the Father raises the dead and gives them life, so also the Son gives life to whom he will. For the Father judges no one, but he has committed all judgment to the Son so that all may honor the Son even as they honor the Father. He who does not honor the Son does not honor the Father who sent him. Truly, truly, I say to you that he who hears my word and believes him who sent me has life eternal. He does not come into judgment, but has passed out of death into life" (John 5:19–24).

The discourse that follows the healing of the lame man is rather strangely neglected. It does not have striking expressions like "the Logos," nor sustained dialogue full of human interest like the conversation with the woman at the well. But it is critically important. As Bishop Ryle says, "Nowhere else in the Gospels do we find our Lord making such a formal, systematic, orderly, regular statement of His own unity with the Father, His divine commission and authority, and the proofs of His Messiahship, as we find in this discourse." Here we have Jesus setting forth in orderly fashion the truth of his relationship to the Father and something of what that means in his daily life. He makes it clear also that this has consequences for his listeners. It is because of his relationship to the Father that they ought to give heed to what he says. And much of what we read elsewhere in this Gospel depends on the truths here set out. Certainly it was because of the kind of claim that he made here that his enemies finally killed him.

The discourse is a unity, but we may divide it into three sections. In the first (vv. 19–24) Jesus is concerned with his relationship to the Father, in the second (vv. 25–29) with his work of judgment, and in the third (vv. 30–47) with the witness borne to him in a variety of ways, which shows that what he claims about himself is well supported. We will consider them in order.

Doing the Same Things

John introduces this discourse in a way that shows it is important. The expression I have translated "Jesus replied" is somewhat longer and more formal in the Greek: "Therefore Jesus answered and said to them." It is followed by "Truly, truly" (which occurs again in vv. 24–25). All this is a way of emphasizing the importance of what follows. It is not a casual utterance but a considered statement of great significance.

Jesus begins by saying that he "can do nothing" other than what he sees the Father doing (v. 19). Notice the word *can*. He is not saying that he does not do things other than those the Father does, but that he cannot do them. This is reinforced with an emphatic negative. In the Greek there is a double negative, literally "cannot do nothing"; in English two negatives cancel each other out, but in Greek they strengthen each other. Jesus is saying that he can do absolutely nothing apart from the Father; he is quite helpless without the help the Father gives.

Today we more or less take it for granted that God is to be spoken of as "Father," but this was not the way it was in the first century. As we saw in an earlier study (p. 176), the Jews did sometimes call God "Father," but they kept their distance all the same. They usually added something to remove any suspicion of undue familiarity, for example, "our Father in heaven." They were sure that God had a special relationship to the Jewish nation, but they were also sure that they must take care not to presume on this relationship. One wit has complained that in modern times people tend to think of God as a celestial Grandfather rather than as the heavenly Father. First-century Jews did not make that mistake.

But Jesus often called God "Father," using the language of ordinary family life in his approach to God. Nowhere is this more apparent than in the Fourth Gospel. John has the word *Father* 137 times, of which no fewer than 122 refer to God. This is far and away the most frequent use of the term anywhere in the New Testament (Matthew comes closest with sixty-four examples of "Father"; in all the Pauline letters it is found only sixty-three times). It is to John more than anyone that we owe our use of "Father" when we think of God. He has the word fourteen times in this discourse alone. Here Jesus is concerned with his relationship to God in a very special way.

It is what the Son sees the Father doing that he himself does. Notice that he does not say that he does similar things or that he copies the Father's deeds. He does the *same* things. The Father and the Son are at work together. What the Son is doing the Father is doing, and what the Father is doing the Son is doing likewise. R. H. Lightfoot brings out this point: "The union, therefore, is absolute. It is not, for instance, as though the Son reveals the Father in certain particular ways or in certain remarkable actions; no moment of His life, and no action of His, but is the expression of the life and action of the Father." The point is important. It is easy to think of the Father as at work in the Son, say, at the moment of the healing of the lame man. But Jesus is claiming something far more than that. He is saying that in his whole life he and the Father are at one and are doing the same things. He never acts independently of the Father. The relationship between them is very close and intimate.

The Father Loves the Son

And the relationship is one of love (v. 20). The Father loves the Son, a statement that is repeated elsewhere in this Gospel (10:17; 15:9; 17:23, 24, 26; the verb is different in these passages, but they all point to a deep and constant love). Love is important throughout this Gospel, and the love that links the Father and the Son is at the basis of it all. The use of the present tense indicates a continuing love. The Father never ceases to love the Son.

Now it is of the essence of love that it gives. The gift here is one of knowledge: the Father keeps showing the Son all that he does. This "showing" on the part of the Father corresponds to the "seeing" on the part of the Son (v. 19). "All the things" indicates that there is no withholding. The love of the Father for the Son means that he opens up to him all that he himself is doing. There is full and complete mutual disclosure.

And there are greater things ahead: "greater works than these he will show him." Jesus does not explain what these greater works are; as a result, the passage has been variously understood. Some draw attention to the greater miracles that Jesus would do, miracles described by John in later chapters: the giving of sight to a man born blind (ch. 9), and the raising of Lazarus from the dead (ch. 11). Others think of the spiritual resurrection involved in Jesus' gift of life to the spiritually dead, or point to what he would do through his followers in later times, the "greater works" of 14:12.

But we should surely understand "greater works" as referring to the works of which Jesus goes on to speak: his giving of life and his work in judgment. Notice that he speaks of them simply as "works." What to us is a stupendous miracle is to him no more than a work. John often uses this term for the miracles Jesus does; indeed, in this Gospel Jesus more often calls them works than anything else. John speaks of them as "signs," for they have meaning, and Jesus uses this term sometimes. But his usual word is "works."

He will do these greater works "so that you will marvel." The doing of a miracle shows that there is a power at work that we do not usually see. The point of the greater works of which Jesus is speaking is that they bring people to see something of the power of God in action. Jesus can call on people to believe "for the works' sake" (14:11). Of course, faith that rests on the works is not the highest kind of faith, but it is better than none.

Life for the Dead

Jesus points out that the Father raises people from the dead and gives them life (v. 21), a truth that his hearers would have readily accepted. There was a saying of the rabbis: "Three keys are in the hand of God and they are not given into the hand of any agent, namely that of the rain [Deut. 28:12], that of the womb [Gen. 30:22], and that of the raising of the dead [Ezek. 37:13]."

But Jesus says that the Son gives life to whomever he wills, and this was something that his hearers would have found highly offensive. Life is the gift of the Father; it is not given by any of God's agents. So this saying is something that Jesus' audience would have rejected decisively. They could not accept the fact that God was in Christ in a very special way, that what Jesus was doing was what God was doing. But it was true whether they accepted it or not, and Jesus confronts them with it.

The question arises as to whether Jesus is here speaking of the life that will be given when the dead are raised on the day of judgment, or whether he means his present gift of eternal life. There can be no doubt that a little later he is speaking of the last great day, for he refers to calling people out of their graves (vv. 28–29). But since his verbs here are in the present tense, it seems that he is referring to his present gift of life, after which he goes on to the further thought of life at the last day.

Jesus takes those who are spiritually dead, people whose whole horizon is bounded by the affairs of this life in which they are immersed, and to them he gives life. This is the great miracle of which John writes so often. It is one of the great themes of his Gospel that Jesus gives eternal life and gives it here and now. Here, in this life, we may know what it is to experience the life of the world to come.

Judgment

The thought next moves to judgment. This is apparently only a preliminary to the fuller treatment that will be given the subject a little later (vv. 25–29). But here we have what for the Jews would have been an astonishing new thought: Jesus said that the Father has "committed all judgment" to him (v. 22). It was accepted Jewish teaching that at the last day we all face judgment. There was nothing new about that.

But Jesus went on to say that the Father has committed all judgment to the Son, and this the Jews would have found very difficult to accept. They held firmly that the Judge on the last day would be God himself, that no one else would have this authority. We might think that perhaps the Messiah would be the Judge and that the Jews had simply gone astray in failing to see that Jesus was the Messiah. They did fail to see that, but there was another difficulty for them: they did not expect the Messiah, whoever he was, to be the Judge. Strack-Billerbeck, the standard authority for the writings of the rabbis, maintains that in the whole range of rabbinic literature there is no passage that says the Messiah will judge the world. This was not an accepted idea at all. Jesus was claiming that he would exercise a function that the Jews universally held belongs to God alone.

The Christians did not see Christ as in any way opposed to the Father in this matter of judging. They did not deny that the Father would be the Judge, but they held that the Father would judge the world through the One he had appointed for this task (cf. Acts 17:31). The Father gave assurance of this in that he raised him from the dead (Acts 17:31). This view sees the Father and the Son as very closely related; and that, of course, is the point of the present passage.

Judgment will be done in this way, says Jesus, "so that all may honor the Son even as they honor the Father" (v. 23). For a king is dishonored if his messengers are dishonored. There is a well-known example of this in the Old Testament (2 Sam. 10). When Nahash the king of the Ammonites died, David reflected that this man had showed him kindness, so he sent messengers to express his sympathy to the new king, Hanun the son of Nahash. But Hanun's advisers told him they were sure that there was no friendship in David; he had simply sent people to spy out the land, they said, preparatory to an invasion. Convinced by this reasoning, Hanun had half of each man's beard shaved off and half of his clothing cut off. Then he sent them back. David took this insult to his messengers as an insult to himself and responded with the war that Hanun's advisers thought they were warding off.

Likewise, people who dishonored the Son dishonored the Father who sent him. To ill-treat the messenger of God is to fail to honor the God who sent him. But John is saying more than this. The passage we are considering keeps emphasizing the unity of the Father and the Son. These two do not act separately. It is what he sees the Father doing—that and nothing else—that the Son does. They do not exist separately: the Father is in the Son, and the Son is in the Father (14:10). When people do dishonor to Jesus they are not simply dishonoring a peasant from Nazareth; they are dishonoring God. What is done to the Son is done to the Father. The close unity of the two means that it is an exceedingly serious offense to do dishonor to Jesus. People are to honor the Son just as they honor the Father.

Salvation

That the Father and the Son are one is seen in the way people are saved. Jesus introduces the next saying with "Truly, truly," which is a way of drawing attention to the importance of the words. They are solemn and very significant.

Then he says, "He who hears my word and believes him who sent me has life eternal" (v. 24). He does not say, "He who hears my word and believes it." Nor does he say, "He who hears the word of God and believes it." The Father and the Son are so much a unity that Jesus speaks of hearing what he says and believing the Father. What he says is what the Father says.

We have seen in our earlier studies that John often speaks of "believing in" (e.g., 3:16). This is a way of bringing out the importance of trusting a person. It means believing in Jesus so wholeheartedly that, so to speak, we are taken out of ourselves and come to be one with him. We come to be "in" him, as Paul would put it. Here John does not use that construction, but one that means "accepting as true." He is talking about believing what God says to us, really believing it. Now if we really believe that what God says is true (not simply say we believe), then we trust him. While the two constructions draw attention to different ways of looking at faith, in the end they come to much the same. We are to believe what God says and are also to trust him. The two are inseparable.

The person who so believes, Jesus says, "has life eternal." Notice the present tense. He does not say the person "will one day have life eternal," but his words mean that the believer has it now. Of course it would be legitimate to use the future tense, because there is much more to eternal life than we can know here and now. We will enter into its fullness in the life to come. That is true. But it is not what Jesus is saying here. He is saying that the believer has eternal life and has it now. Eternal life is endless life. That is important. But what is more important is that it is life of the highest quality.

A person who is stranded on a desert island or lost in a tropical jungle might well manage to stay alive. He might manage to find food and water and even to be healthy. But such a life would be limited and impoverished when compared with the rich and full life that is possible in a civilized community. So it is with the person who is badly injured and comatose and kept alive on life-support systems. He is alive in the sense that his heart is beating, and he cannot be said to have died. But life in the sense of a rich and meaningful existence is not his.

There are different kinds of "life." Jesus is saying that the wonderfully satisfying life that is proper to the world to come, the kind of life that is lived in eternity, is made available to those who believe. That there is more to be experienced in the afterlife goes without saying. But that we enter into something of that life here and now is the wonderful gift that Christ gives his own.

No Death

For those who believe, there is no condemnation. John's word is "judgment," but here the meaning is negative judgment or condemnation. The believer need never fear that, for Jesus has delivered him. He has already passed out of death into life.

We have just seen that the person stranded on a desert island or lost in a jungle or in a coma is not experiencing a very full life. What Jesus is saying here is that people who lack faith are not really living at all. They may go through the motions, but their existence is so impoverished that compared to the life he came to bring, they are dead. They lack the peace of God. They do not know divine forgiveness. They have no experience of the dynamic of the Holy Spirit and are strangers to fellowship with God. They do not enjoy the rich and warm fellowship of the redeemed. "Life" means ever so many things of which they have no knowledge.

It is that kind of living that Jesus calls "death." It is a shallow and empty form of existence. To be limited by one's sins and unable to get free of them is a form of death. To know that in the next world one faces their consequences is a form of death. To be ignorant of the life of the world to come is another form of death. "A man wrapped up in himself makes a very small parcel," some wit has said, and it is so true. Any way of living that cuts us off from God and confines us to what we are in ourselves and can achieve of ourselves is not life in the full sense, but a form of death.

The salvation Jesus comes to bring delivers us from death. We will die (unless the Lord comes back soon) in the sense that we will pass from this life. But this is a transition from one form of living to another. In the full sense of the word, the believer will never die (11:26). Already he has passed out of death and into life.

23

Life and Judgment

"Truly, truly, I tell you that an hour is coming and now is, when the dead will hear the voice of the Son of God and those who hear will live. For as the Father has life in himself, so also he has given it to the Son to have life in himself. And he has given him authority to do judgment, because he is the Son of man. Do not be astonished at this, for an hour is coming in which all who are in the tombs will hear his voice and will come out, those who have done good things to the resurrection of life and those who have done bad things to the resurrection of judgment" (John 5:25–29).

Truly, truly," shows that we are coming to another very significant saying. Jesus uses the expression to emphasize the importance of the words that follow, so there is no doubt that these words are meant to be taken with full seriousness.

But they can be taken in more ways than one, and different students of the Gospel do in fact interpret them differently. The major dispute is over whether we are to understand the judgment of which Jesus speaks as a judgment that takes place here and now, or whether he is referring to a judgment at the last day. A present judgment is certainly found in this Gospel, for example, in 3:19, where we read that to love darkness rather than the light is itself judgment. And the judgment at the end of this world is certainly in view in some passages, for example, when Jesus refers to the word he speaks as judging people "at the last day" (12:48). Both are Johannine thoughts. The question is, Which is in mind in this passage? Advocates of both present and future judgment are certainly to be found.

Life

Jesus begins this section by speaking about the life he gives to the dead (v. 25). This could be understood as his calling of people from the tombs at the last day were it not for the fact that he says not only "an hour is coming," but also "and now is." The addition makes it very difficult for us to see this as a reference to the end of the world. Jesus is talking about something that happens now. We find exactly the same expression in 4:23, when Jesus is talking to the woman of Samaria about true worship. So there can be little doubt that here at any rate we should understand Jesus to be speaking about the present.

"The dead," then, are the spiritually dead, those about whom we were thinking in our last study, people who walk and talk and go through all the motions of being alive here and now, but whose spiritual lives are such that they can be spoken of only as dead. If we take this Gospel seriously, we must see that spiritual death is a grim reality. Unless people receive the life-giving touch of the Savior, they are dead where it counts.

John's use of the Greek verb *to hear* should be noticed. For the technically minded let me say that sometimes he uses the accusative case after the verb and sometimes the genitive. For those not so minded, it is enough to know that he has two ways of expressing himself. When he uses one of them (the accusative), he means that the sound is heard and that is all, like hearing the wind in 3:8 and not understanding. But when he uses the other (the genitive), at least with sounds like voices, he means that the sound is heard with understanding and appreciation, like the sheep hearing the voice of their own shepherd (10:3).

It is this second construction that John has here. When spiritually dead people hear Jesus, some of them at any rate hear with understanding and appreciation. There are, of course, others who do not give him this sort of hearing, but John is not talking about them here. Of those who hear rightly we may say that God is at work in their hearts and they do not reject the message. They take it in and are glad of it. Those who hear in this way "will live." Life is the gift of the Son of God, as we see so often in this Gospel.

Notice that Jesus refers to himself here as "the Son of God." We often use this expression when we speak about him, but he does not often use it himself. In fact, in John's Gospel he does so three times only, here and in 10:36 and 11:4. The Jews apparently took good notice, for they told Pilate that he said he was the Son of God (19:7). Towards the end of the Gospel, John tells us that he wrote it so that people may believe "that

Jesus is the Christ, the Son of God . . ." (20:31). It is interesting accordingly that he so rarely refers to Jesus as making this claim. John prefers to make his point by letting what happened speak for itself. When his readers see what Jesus did and what he taught, they will see for themselves that he was indeed the Son of God.

But here Jesus is speaking about the giving of life to the dead. In speaking of this kind of activity, it is appropriate for him to refer to his relationship to the Father. Anyone less could not do this. It is because he is the divine Son that he is able to give life. So it is that those who hear will live. This does not mean that everyone who heard him was saved. This Gospel makes it very clear that there were people who heard Jesus and yet rejected him wholeheartedly. Their response to the word of life was a preference for death. So they continued in their self-centered ways and in the end hounded Jesus to his death.

But John's interest at this point is not in those who preferred death to life, but in those who responded to Jesus. For them it was life, eternal life, the life of the coming age. They were done with the ways of death.

Life in Himself

Jesus goes on to point out that God's relation to life is not the same as that of anyone else. The Father "has life in himself" (v. 26). We have life because our parents came together and God gave them the gift of life. No one gave God the gift. Our life is a fact, but not a necessary fact. The world would have gone on without us if we had not been born. But the life of God is not like that. His life is a necessary life. It is impossible for him not to exist. If he did not exist, nothing would exist. God's life is of a different quality from ours.

Augustine, a great theologian of the ancient church, reflected on this passage. God did not "borrow" life, he thought, nor partake of a life other than his own: "The very life is to Him His very self." Augustine used a candle as an illustration. When it is night and we have a lit candle, we are not in the darkness. But if the candle is put out, we are in darkness; we have no light in ourselves. So with life. We do not have it in ourselves, but it is a gift given to us. Not so with God. His life is his own. He needs no one to give him life. With him is "the fountain of life" (Ps. 36:9); "the Lord is your life" (Deut. 30:20). We are reminded that "God gave us life eternal and this life is in his Son" (1 John 5:11).

And God has given the Son, Jesus continues, the same gift. He too has life in himself. His is a necessary life. Peter called him "the Prince of life" (Acts 3:15), which brings out the same thought from another angle. Jesus is sovereign over life, not subject, as we are, to all sorts of limitations if it is to continue. Augustine saw no difference between the kind of life the Father has and that which the Son has, except that the Father has life in himself that nobody gave him, and the Son has life in himself that the Father gave him. That the Father is the ultimate source of all life, including that of the Son, is perhaps a way of assuring us that ultimately there is but one life. We are not to think of two eternal sources of life.

It is this assurance about the nature of the Son's life that gives believers assurance about the eternal life Christ gives to them. He shares with the Father in having this life that does not depend on some external source. Since his relationship to life is sovereign, he is thus able to bestow it where he wills. The eternal life we have is the gift of the One who is in a position to make the gift because he has life "in himself."

Authority for Judgment

The thought moves on to judgment. The Father has given to the Son authority to exercise judgment "because he is the Son of man" (v. 27). Some have taken the last expression to mean "man," and understand Jesus to be saying that it is the fact that he is genuinely human that is his qualification for judging. But this is scarcely adequate, for as Chrysostom pointed out centuries ago, if that was the meaning, we would all be qualified to judge. There is a small difference between the expression used here and "the Son of man" as used elsewhere, but the difference should not be regarded as significant. Jesus is saying that it is because he is all that "the Son of man" means that he is qualified to be the Judge of us all (cf. Dan. 7:13–14).

Judgment, like life, belongs with the Father. Abraham could refer to God as "the Judge of all the earth" (Gen. 18:25), and Jephthah could speak of "the Lord, the Judge" (Judg. 11:27). As we saw in an earlier study (p. 183), the Jews grasped this truth firmly and held that in the end it is God and God only who will be our Judge. They did not even allow the possibility that the Messiah would engage in judgment. The thought that the Son of God would in the end be the Judge was a distinctively Christian thought. It did not spring from first-century Judaism, but was in fact strenuously resisted by the Jewish leaders when they heard Jesus make his claim. So we should not accept Jesus' words here as commonplace, as though he were saying something that everybody knew. He was making a great and unusual claim.

That the Father has given him the authority to judge is a way of making it clear that nothing Jesus says about himself takes away from the supreme place of the Father. We are not to think of the two as in any sort of conflict or rivalry, nor are we to think of them as acting independently of one another. Just a few verses back we saw that the Son does what the Father does and that this means not that he copies the Father, but that they are together doing the same thing. Now we have something of the same thought with regard to judgment. It is not that Jesus displaces the Father; it is rather that the Father does the judgment but does it through the Son. So it is with all the authority of the Father that the Son does his work of judging.

Resurrection

Jesus goes on to the thought of the resurrection at the last day (vv. 28–29). There are, it is true, some who hold that in this section of the discourse, as in the preceding one, we are to think of the present time rather than the end of the age. The whole is to be understood, we are told, as referring to the giving of life to the spiritually dead. That seems clearly to be the meaning in the earlier verses, but the language is against it in this part of the discourse. Jesus speaks of those in the tombs and of resurrection to judgment as well as of resurrection to life. A resurrection to judgment is certainly not the giving of spiritual life to the spiritually dead.

Jesus calls on his hearers not to be astonished at what he has just said, because there is something perhaps even more wonderful to take place in the future: he will be God's agent in bringing about the resurrection of the dead and final judgment. He speaks of those in the tombs as hearing his voice. His will be the voice that wakes the dead and ushers in the final judgment.

He goes on to speak of "those who have done good things" as called "to the resurrection of life," while "those who have done bad things" are summoned to that of "judgment." It puzzles some Christians that final judgment is linked with our deeds, when the New Testament is so insistent that our salvation is all of God's grace. But while the New Testament always regards salvation as springing from grace, it just as consistently sees judgment as proceeding on the basis of works.

We should be clear that none of us ever merits salvation. As Christians in the New Testament sense, we have come to see ourselves as sinners and yet as the objects of God's love. We are those who have been died for, and we receive God's good gift by faith. But saving faith does not leave us as we were. The saved do not go on in their sins as though nothing has happened. They repent and turn away from all evil. They live in the strength that God supplies, and their new lives are the evidence that they have been saved by grace. The lives we live are the proof of the faith we profess.

It is true that we do not always live as we should, even though we are convinced Christians. Paul deals with this problem when he tells the Corinthians that there is but one foundation, namely Jesus Christ, but that those on this foundation (and thus saved) may build with what is valuable, like gold or silver or costly stone, or on the other hand with worthless things like wood or hay or straw (1 Cor. 3:10–12). Judgment day will test our work, Paul says, "for it will be revealed in fire, and the fire will test each person's work, of what sort it is" (v. 13). He goes on to point out that the person who has built well will receive accordingly, while the person who has put in only shoddy work will suffer the loss of it, "though he himself will be saved, but so as through fire" (vv. 14–15).

This helps us to see that judgment is a reality, even though it is grace that saves us. We who are Christians are responsible people; one day we must give account of ourselves to God. The way we serve God is important, and we must never take lightly the importance of doing good works.

Condemnation

But there are others, those who have done bad things. The word I have translated "bad things" occurs in 3:20 and nowhere else in John. It is not the usual word for "evil." It means "worthless," "of no account," though we should probably not insist on the literal meaning. John often uses words with more or less the same meaning without making sharp distinctions, and this is the way we should understand this term. The Evangelist is referring to those who have rejected Christ and to the kind of lives they have lived in consequence. They have not set themselves to the service of God and of their fellows, which is the lot of every faithful believer. In one way or another they have lived lives with self at the center. The result is that in the end, when they stand before the Judge in the last great day, what they have done will be accounted worthless.

They will be raised, Jesus says, "to the resurrection of judgment." Strictly this means a resurrection at which they will undergo judgment, which theoretically might result in either condemnation or acquittal. But "judgment" may sometimes mean "adverse judgment," and that is surely the case here. Evildoers can look for no great success when they are given just judgment.

The two resurrections remind us that we are responsible people. God has set us in the world with many opportunities for helping others and generally cooperating with his purposes. We should not think it a matter of indifference whether we make use of our opportunities or not. To whom much has been given, of them will much be required. Life is a wonderfully joyous affair, but it is also wonderfully solemn. It is a one-way street; we cannot go back and do anything over again. We get just one shot at it. Let us then make the most of it.

One more thing before we leave this section of the discourse. For Jesus to speak as he did that day was a very courageous thing. He was saying things which he knew the religious people of his day would regard as blasphemy and for which they would oppose him relentlessly. But they were true and they were important, so he said them. William Barclay well says that "the man who listened to words like this had only two alternatives—the listener must either accept Jesus as the Son of God, or he must hate Him as a blasphemer and seek to destroy Him. There is hardly any passage where Jesus appeals for men's love and defies men's hatred as He does here." The sad thing is that the religious leaders simply rejected what Jesus said. There is no indication that they weighed the evidence or gave serious consideration to what Jesus was saying. They simply opposed him more strongly than ever. G. Campbell Morgan says, "On the human level, what Jesus did that day, and what He said that day cost Him His life. They never forgave Him."

24

Witness to the Son

"I can do nothing of myself. I judge as I hear and my judgment is just, because I don't seek my own will but the will of him who sent me. If I bear witness about myself, my witness is not true, but there is another who bears witness about me and I know that the witness that he witnesses about me is true. You sent to John and he bore witness to the truth; now I do not receive witness from man but I say these things so that you may be saved. That man was the light that burns and shines and you were willing to rejoice for a time in his light. But I have the witness greater than that of John; for the works which the Father has given me to do, the very works themselves that I am doing, bear witness about me that the Father has sent me. And the Father who sent me has borne witness about me. You have never heard his voice, you have never seen his form, nor do you have his word abiding in you because you do not believe him whom he sent. You search the Scriptures because you think you have eternal life in them. And it is they that bear witness about me, and yet you are not willing to come to me so that you may have life.

"I do not receive glory from men. But I know you, I know that you do not have the love of God within you. I have come in my Father's name and you don't receive me. If another should come in his own name you would receive him. How can you believe, receiving as you do glory from one another, and yet you do not seek the glory that is from the only God? Do not think that I will accuse you to the Father. It is Moses, on whom you have set your hope, who is your accuser. For if you believed Moses you would believe me, because he wrote about

me. But if you do not believe his writings how will you believe my sayings?" (John 5:30–47).

Throughout his Gospel, John emphasizes the importance of witness. As we have seen in our earlier studies, this is noticeably more frequent in this Gospel than in any other book in the New Testament. John uses the concept in several ways, but the passage to which we now turn is noteworthy for the way in which he brings out the variety of the testimony borne to Jesus. Witness is borne to Jesus by the Father (vv. 32, 37; this is the testimony that carries conviction to Jesus), by John the Baptist (v. 33), by Jesus' works (v. 36), by Scripture (v. 39), and by Moses (v. 46). This is a very strong combination, and while it is not all the witness to Jesus that this Gospel records, it makes a powerful argument that people ought to believe in Jesus. The evidence is there.

The Witness of the Father

Jesus begins this part of his address by disclaiming that his actions are ever done independently of the Father. He uses the strong expression "can do nothing"; it is not simply that he does not act independently of God, he cannot do so (cf. 5:19). This does not, of course, mean that he is an automaton, unable to do anything unless someone from outside pulls the strings. It means that being who and what he is it is unthinkable that he should do anything that does not have the approval of the Father. We do not understand what Jesus' ministry was all about unless we see that it was the Father's work that he was doing. He came to do the Father's will and the Father's work. Precisely because of this, it was impossible for him to act independently. He always acted in the closest connection with the Father.

Jesus has just been talking about judging. He has said that it is his voice that will wake the dead and bring people from the tombs to face judgment. We saw that this is an extraordinary claim, because the Jews firmly believed that final judgment would be given by God alone. Now we see something of how and why Jesus would do this work of judgment. He is not speaking of an independent judgment which he would give and of which God might or might not approve. He cannot act independently of God. His judgment is as he hears, that is, "hears from God." He is in constant and intimate communion with the Father; this means that the judgment he gives is the judgment of God and as such is perfectly just.

He reinforces this with the firm disclaimer that his will is set to do anything other than what God wills. The present tense shows that he is referring to what happens in his life day by day. He is not referring here to final judgment. His aim throughout his life is to do the will of God. His own will is not set up in opposition to God's.

Jesus now comes to the thought of witness and points out that if he bore witness to himself, that witness would not be accepted (v. 31). There is a sense in which this is true of anyone. The law of Moses provided that there must always be two or three witnesses (Deut. 19:15). The rabbis said emphatically, "None may be believed when he testifies of himself"; and again, "None may testify of himself." Law everywhere agrees that a man's testimony to himself is not sufficient. There must be others to establish the truth.

But Jesus is saying something more than this. Several translators and commentators miss something of his point by taking the text to mean, "If I testify about myself, that testimony is not valid." But Jesus does not say "valid"; he says "true." He is not talking about the conditions under which testimony is adjudged valid. He is talking about what is true. He is making the claim that if there were nothing but his own word, it would not be true. Unless the Father supported what he said, not only would it be invalid testimony, but it would be erroneous.

William Temple has a valuable comment: "If His word stood alone, it would not be true at all. For divine revelation did not begin and end in Him, though it reached its crown and finds its criterion in Him. There must be other evidence, not only to support His own, but because the nature of His claim is such that it can only be true if all the work of God—the entire universe so far as it is not vitiated by sin—attests it."

We should be clear on this. If Jesus was what he said he was, then his claim had to be supported by other testimony. It could not stand by itself. This does not mean that there was anything lacking in it, but simply that it was a claim of such magnitude that it involved something more than himself.

And Jesus says that such testimony does exist: "there is another who bears witness about me" (v. 32). He does not say who this other is, but there is not the slightest doubt that he is referring to the Father. Notice that he uses the present tense. He says that this other "bears witness," and he speaks of "the witness that he witnesses." He is appealing to present fact. If his opponents only had eyes to see, they would discern that the Father was bearing witness in the whole life of Jesus. The things Jesus did and the things he said were done and said only because the Father was with him. This testimony is the only testimony that mattered to Jesus. It, and only it, was sufficient for him.

A little later he comes back to the thought of the Father's testimony (v. 37). He points out that his opponents do not hear the voice of God, even though they claim to be followers of Moses and Moses heard that voice (Exod. 33:11). The disciples differ from the Jews in the way they hear the words of Jesus. They not only listen to them, but they receive them and recognize Jesus' divine origin (17:8). But despite their great claims, the Jews do not recognize the voice of God when they hear it.

They have never "seen his form." Jacob saw God and his name was changed to Israel (Gen. 32:30; cf. v. 28). But though they claimed to be descendants of Israel, the Jews were not true Israelites. If they had been, they would have recognized that he who has seen Jesus has seen the Father (14:9).

Jesus also says that they did not have his word "abiding in" them (5:38). The psalmist hid God's word in his heart (Ps. 119:11). But though the Jews gave high honor to the psalmist, they did not follow his example. They professed reverence for the word of God and had a great knowledge of facts about Scripture. But it was not in their hearts. Had it been, they would have been open to receive the word of God from Jesus as the disciples did (17:14).

They did not receive him whom the Father sent (v. 38); this was both their basic error and the evidence that their high-sounding claims were false. The Father bears witness to Jesus. The Jews of the day for the most part did not recognize what God was doing. The reason they did not was their lack of will (v. 40). They willed not to come to Jesus and accordingly found all sorts of reasons for rejecting the divine witness. Let us be warned.

The Witness of John the Baptist

Immediately after introducing the thought that Jesus had another to bear witness to him (namely the Father), the Lord goes on to the witness of John the Baptist. "*You* sent to John," he says; his pronoun is emphatic (v. 33). This is not something he is bringing up of his own accord; it was the Jewish leaders' own idea that they should send to John. There is also the thought that the notion of someone's bearing witness to Jesus is not so strange. They themselves had a witness.

The Baptist bore his witness to the truth. The verb *bore witness* is in the perfect tense, which carries the suggestion of a witness that continues. Jesus is not speaking about ancient history, something of value only as a reminder of long-since-vanished events. John bore his testimony, and it continues to be of force. People remembered what he said. He bore his witness to "the truth." We would have expected that Jesus would have spoken of this witness as being borne to himself. But we must keep two things in mind. The first is that Jesus himself is identified with the truth; he said, "I am . . . the truth" (14:6). It would therefore not be possible to bear witness to what this Gospel means by "the truth" without bearing witness to Jesus. In the Christian system there is no such thing as an abstract truth totally unrelated to Jesus. In the most meaningful sense of "truth" it is one with Jesus.

The other thing we must remember about "witness to the truth" is that Jesus would in due course tell Pilate that this was why he himself came into the world (18:37). The Baptist and Jesus were in a sense bearing witness to the same thing. Jesus went on to say to Pilate, "Everyone who is of the truth hears my voice." It is necessary to have a commitment to truth before one can take in what Jesus is saying. Because many of his contemporaries did not have that commitment, they rejected him and finally had him put on a cross.

Jesus gave the bearing of witness to the truth as the reason for his being born and coming into the world, and it is not without interest that the Baptist was a man "sent from God" and that he came to bear witness, in this case "to bear witness of the light" (1:6–8). Again we reflect that Jesus was "the light of the world" (8:12), so again John's witness points to Jesus. In this Gospel John the Baptist does but one thing: he bears witness to Jesus. We may see this in what is termed his bearing witness to the light or to the truth, or we may see it in John's referring to the Lamb of God or to a greater than he who would follow him or to one who would baptize in the Holy Spirit. But look at him how you will; for this Evangelist, John the Baptist was simply a witness.

Jesus goes on to say that it was not John's witness that brought conviction to himself (his "I" is emphatic). He received testimony from no man (v. 34). Since he had the testimony of the Father, why should he rely on John the Baptist? His reason for reminding them of John the Baptist was to benefit them: "so that *you* might be saved" (the emphatic pronoun again). If they had taken notice of what John was saying, they would have been started on the way that leads to salvation. That had in fact happened to some of the disciples. They had been among the followers of the Baptist and had obeyed him when he told them to go after Jesus. Why had these Jews not done the same?

When Jesus goes on to say that John was the burning lamp, he uses the past tense (v. 35). It may be that John was dead at this time or at least in prison. His ministry was in the past. Of course the lamp burns; it is consumed by shining. There may be a hint here that John's ministry was costly. He burned himself out, but he gave light to those about him.

Yet another emphatic pronoun *you* is used to draw a contrast between the Jews and the Baptist. John had such a sense of serious purpose that he gave himself wholeheartedly to his burning and shining, but they were happy to rejoice in him only "for a time" (literally, "for an hour"). They were casual merrymakers, not earnest seekers for truth. Though they had in their midst that man of whom Jesus said a greater than he had never arisen among those born of women (Matt. 11:11), they refused to take him seriously.

People often do not take the trouble to appreciate the truth when it is before them. I was reading of a woman who had trouble with her gas bill. She always paid what she saw on the bill, but some months she was told that she had underpaid, some that she had overpaid. She put this down to the inscrutable ways of the gas-company personnel, perhaps assisted by a computer or the red tape in which they were entangled. Then one day her latest check was returned along with a standardized card on which were printed various possible reasons: name of payee incorrectly entered, signature missing, and so forth. All of the usual explanations were crossed out and at the bottom was written: "You have been paying the date. *Please* pay the amount."

It was a little bit like that with the Baptist's contemporaries. They had firm ideas about the way to God and were not going to be sidetracked by a preacher like John. They were so sure that what they were doing was the right thing that they never asked whether what John was saying was true. So they missed the greatest blessing that God was offering them.

The Witness of the Works

The third form of witness is the witness of "the works" (v. 36), a witness that Jesus says is "greater than that of John." The majestic "But I" with which the verse begins sets Jesus apart from men. His "I" is emphatic again. Though John's witness was important and Jesus was happy to commend it, it was not what carried conviction to him. The works he did were evidence that God was at work in his ministry. These were works that "the Father has given me to do." God was in them.

We have seen that John in his Gospel often calls Jesus' miracles "signs," an important word, for it tells us that these are not simply works of power, but that they are meaningful. They point beyond themselves and convey spiritual truths. But John also often calls them "works," which is a more general term not confined to the miracles but covering all sorts of deeds. It indicates that the whole of Jesus' life (all his "works") mattered, for God was in it all, the nonmiraculous as well as the miraculous. It also indicates that what to us is a miracle was to Jesus no more than a work. There is no distinction between the miraculous and the more ordinary when this term is used; God is seen in it all. God is in the life Jesus lived, in his sinlessness, in his compassion, in his words of kindness, in all that he did. And because his whole life in all its variety showed forth God, it was all part of the witness borne to Jesus.

The Witness of Scripture

Jesus then referred to the attitude toward Scripture of those to whom he was speaking (v. 39). The verb I have translated "you search" might possibly be an imperative (as it is in the King James); the form of the Greek verb could be either an indicative or an imperative. We should probably take it as indicative, for Jesus was speaking about what they were doing. But is it fanciful to think of the imperative as in the background? Jesus was certainly encouraging the right attitude to the Bible.

During the early years of our era, the scribes had amassed a vast amount of curious learning about the Bible. We do not know exactly how much of this goes back to the time of Jesus, but certainly some of it does. These scribes knew how many verses and even how many letters there were in each of the books of the Bible, which verses had all the letters of the alphabet, what was the middle verse of a given book, and so on. They had compiled an incredible mass of useless information, while at the same time they failed to come to grips with what the Bible was saying.

Jesus says plainly that the Scriptures "bear witness about" him. Rightly read, the Old Testament leads to Christ. But the scribes of his day, with their wooden reverence for the letter of Scripture, failed to understand the wonderful thing it was saying and thus were quite unable to recognize him to whom the Scriptures pointed.

The fundamental trouble was that they did not want to see. Their will was set in a different direction. Jesus was in their midst, the messenger sent by God, the one who would accomplish salvation. Their tragedy was that despite the deference they paid to the Scriptures, they did not want to come to someone like Jesus. "You are not willing to come to me so that you may have life," he says (v. 40). And because they did not come, they cut themselves off from life.

The Witness of Moses

The end of the chapter includes a most unexpected line of reasoning. Jesus tells his hearers not to think that when they stand before God they will find that he is their accuser. No. Their accuser will be Moses

(v. 45). For the Jews, Moses was the great lawgiver, and because they so highly valued the law he gave and saw it as the law of God, they were sure that Moses would be on their side. Their attitude to the law of Moses secured his support. No matter who would be against them before God, they could surely rely on Moses, who gave the law that they made central in their thinking and living.

They had set their hope on Moses. The verb is in the perfect tense, which points to a continuing state of affairs: they had put their hope in Moses at some time in the past and there it rested. Hope in Moses was a permanent feature of religion for them.

Jesus does not say that Moses "will be" their accuser, but that he "is" their accuser. Most take this to look forward to the last day, the great day of judgment, and we should probably see this as included in the meaning. But the present tense also points to the state of affairs at the time of speaking. Moses is a standing witness against them.

The reason, says Jesus, is that Moses wrote about him (v. 46). This is in agreement with what Jesus has been saying about the witness of Scripture as a whole. What is true of the Bible generally is true of the books of Moses in particular. The Jews, however, were not holding to what Moses wrote but to what they thought he meant. Their prejudice prevented them from seeing the fulfillment of the writings of Moses when it took place before their eyes. Hoskyns wrote, "The law of Moses is not a religion of salvation, it is the categorical imperative of God by which men are accused and exposed as sinners." They are shown to need a Savior, and Jesus comes as that Savior. To read the law in the way the Jews of that day did is to miss what Moses was really saying.

So they did not really believe their great lawgiver. Jesus asks how, in view of that, they could be expected to believe what he himself says. They had put a good deal of time and energy into the study of Moses' words, words in written form which they could look at again and again and pore over in an effort to extract their meaning. And if they still did not believe what Moses had written, they would not (and they did not) believe the words that Jesus was speaking.

This section of John's Gospel makes the important point that there is adequate testimony borne to Jesus. If anyone does not believe, it is not because there is a lack of evidence. It is because of a lack of will. This sobering truth is still worth pondering.

25

The Miracle of the Loaves and Fishes

After these things Jesus went off to the other side of the sea of Galilee, that is of Tiberias. A great crowd followed him because they saw the signs he was doing on the sick people. Jesus went up into the mountain and sat there with his disciples. Now the Passover, the feast of the Jews, was near.

Jesus then looked up and saw that a great crowd was coming to him. He said to Philip, "Where will we buy bread in order that these people may eat?" He said this by way of testing him; for he himself knew what he was going to do. Philip answered him, "Two hundred denarii worth of bread would not be enough for each of them to have a little." One of his disciples, Andrew the brother of Simon Peter, said to him, "There's a little boy here who has five barley loaves and two small fishes. But what are these among so many?"

Jesus said, "Make the men sit down." Now there was a lot of grass in that place so the men sat down in number about five thousand. Jesus then took the bread and when he had given thanks he distributed it to those who were seated, also as much as they wanted of the fishes. When they had had enough he said to his disciples, "Gather up what is left over so that nothing be wasted." They gathered it up therefore and filled twelve baskets from the fragments of the five barley loaves which were left over by those who had eaten.

Therefore the men who had seen the sign Jesus did said, "Truly this is the prophet who is to come into the world." Jesus then perceived that they would come and seize him in order to make him a king and he withdrew back into the mountain, by himself, alone (John 6:1–15).

Apart from the resurrection, this is the only miracle found in all four Gospels. Clearly it made a great appeal to the early church. We may wonder why, and it is perhaps worth reflecting that bread occupied a greater part in the life of people in first-century Palestine than it commonly does with us. We may speak of bread as "the staff of life," but in practice it occupies a small place in our diet. It was otherwise for most people in Bible times. The wealthy might have a variety of foods, but for ordinary people bread was the most significant daily food. And getting enough to eat was not a matter of course; the poor man often went hungry. Eating and drinking could be used metaphorically of the good life: ". . . nothing is better for a man under the sun than to eat and drink and be glad" (Eccles. 8:15a). God's blessing on the poor can be described in terms of his giving them bread (Ps. 132:15). It is interesting that the New International Version here (and in many other places) translates the Hebrew word for "bread" as "food." We think naturally of a variety of foodstuffs; the ancients thought equally naturally of bread.

Eating and drinking may symbolize blessing, for example the blessing that would follow when the people entered the Promised Land: it would be "a land where bread will not be scarce" (Deut. 8:9). On a day that was "sacred to the LORD" Nehemiah called on the people to "go and enjoy choice food and sweet drinks" (Neh. 8:10). Ezekiel looked forward to a great time in the future when among other things the prince will "sit inside the gateway to eat in the presence of the LORD" (Ezek. 44:3). In such a moment as the vision of God we would be inclined to concentrate on some "spiritual" aspect, but when the elders of Israel were given their great privilege "they saw God, and they ate and drank" (Exod. 24:11). More could be cited, but this is enough for us to see that in first-century Palestine a meal could have much greater significance than it normally does with us. Food could be a symbol pointing to many blessings, and when Jesus met the need of the great crowd this pointed to him as the One who could supply their deepest need.

The Gathering of the Crowd

John tells us that, following the events of chapter 5, Jesus went off to the other side of the lake. His "after these things" (v. 1) is not precise. It does not mean that what now follows took place immediately. John uses the expression with a meaning like "some time later." He gives the lake two names, "the sea of Galilee," which he follows with "of Tiberias." The former would be the name by which it was known in the Christian church and also in all probability locally. The other name would derive from the fact that on its shore there was a town named Tiberias, after the Roman emperor. This town was founded about A.D. 20, so it does not seem likely that people called the sea by this name during the lifetime of Jesus. It may have been the official name and the name by which it was known when John wrote his Gospel. For whatever reason, he gives two names for the body of water and thus ensures that his readers know what he is talking about.

John does not say much about it, but he refers to a sustained ministry of Jesus. His verbs in verse 2 are all continuous, and we would get the force of the statement if we understood it in the sense that the crowd "kept following him because they kept seeing the signs he continually did. . . ." John knows of a large number of miracles Jesus did, though he tells his readers of only a few. These he has selected for his own good reason (20:30–31), but incidental references like this show that Jesus did many wonderful things of which we know nothing. Jesus' compassion for the sick is specially to be noted.

As often in this Gospel, the miracles are called "signs." For John the important thing about the miracles was not the element of wonder, the fact that Jesus was doing things that people could not explain, but that these things were sign-ificant. They had meaning. They pointed beyond themselves. This does not mean that all the people who saw them saw them as signs. The people seem often to have been impressed by the element of the miraculous and to have followed Jesus simply because some of the things he did were so wonderful. John consistently takes the line that it is better to follow Jesus for some inadequate reason than not to follow him at all. But it is better to follow him for what he is, rather than because the signs were so wonderful.

On the occasion on which he is about to concentrate John says that Jesus went up "into the mountain" (v. 3). This expression may mean simply mountainous country in general, in which case the thought will be that Jesus went up from the land around the lakeshore into some more hilly place. But I am intrigued by his use of the definite article, "*the* mountain," especially as it occurs elsewhere (e.g., Matt. 5:1; Mark 3:13). I wonder whether there was some place that Jesus and his followers frequented, so that they spoke of it in this way. If so, we have no way of knowing where it was. But in any case the expression need mean no more than that they went into hilly country.

John adds a little time note. It was near the Passover, and for his Gentile readers he adds that this was a Jewish feast (v. 4). John has a great interest in the Jewish feasts; he has more references to them than has anyone else in the New Testament (he uses the word for "feast," *heorte,* seventeen times, whereas no other writer has more than three). He mentions three distinct Passovers and it is this that gives us the clue that Jesus' ministry lasted for about three years. John does not tell us why he mentions the feasts so often, but the probability is that he saw Jesus as fulfilling all that the feasts pointed to. The Passover was a memorial of a great deliverance in Israel's past, but Jesus would bring a greater deliverance and one available to people everywhere, not just those in one nation. At this point we might also reflect that the original Passover led to the wilderness wanderings and God's gift of manna to sustain his people. The manna will be before us later in this chapter, and the mention of the Passover may be in part to prepare us for this. In passing we may notice that in this verse we have three characteristic marks of John's style, a time note, a reference to a feast, and his mention of "the Jews."

The Problem

John concentrates his attention on the miracle. He does not tell us that Jesus had withdrawn with his disciples in order to be alone, nor that the multitude saw where he was going and followed, so that he spent the day in teaching them and healing those who were sick. He does not tell us that what he narrates took place at the end of the day. These things we find out from the accounts in the other Gospels. John starts at the point when Jesus looked up at the crowds and thought about feeding them.

He lets us see something of the difficulty in the situation by telling us of Philip's suggestion and of Andrew's finding of a small boy who had a little food. Philip was a native of Bethsaida (1:44), and we learn from Luke 9:10 that these things happened near that city. Thus Philip would be the logical person to know what food resources there were in the area and how they could be employed to meet the needs of the hungry people. John wants us to know, however, that this was not a serious attempt on the part of Jesus to obtain the necessary food supplies through Philip. Jesus knew what he was going to do. His question was apparently meant to show that there was a real problem. What he was about to do was to meet a genuine human need, which normal human resources were unable to satisfy. He was "testing" Philip, and the result of the test would be to show that from the apostle's point of view the problem was insoluble.

Jesus asked where they could get the bread, but Philip does not even try to answer that question. Instead he points to the sheer impossibility of feeding the people. They were, of course, in wilderness country. There were no bakers' shops and thus they could not buy bread. But Philip concentrates on the matter of purchase. If they had a lot of money (which presumably they did not) and if they were able to spend it all in buying bread (which in the circumstances they could not do), they would not have enough to give everyone a little taste (v. 7). That was Philip's contribution to solving the problem!

Plainly he had in mind a great deal of money, but just how much is not clear. Early translations often specified a number of dollars or pounds as the equivalent, but these days most do not. Presumably the fluctuations of currencies in modern times are such that any amount that sounds reasonably possible at the date of publication may be wildly erroneous a few years later. Philip specified two hundred denarii, and we can best understand his meaning if we reflect that one denarius was the normal wage for a workman for one day. It was the wage agreed upon, for example, by the owner of the vineyard and his workmen in Jesus' parable (Matt. 20:2). When we allow for Sabbaths on which men did not work, two hundred denarii would be the wages for something over thirty-three weeks, about eight months. When we put it this way we see that Philip was talking about a considerable sum of money.

Clearly he was not giving a possible solution but saying in effect, "It can't be done!" From another point of view so was Andrew, but his approach was not mathematical. Andrew is called Simon Peter's brother, just as he was when we first met him, back in chapter 1 verse 40. Again we see him in the shadow of his great brother. He may not have been an outstanding person and thus may be known more because of this relationship than from his deeds, but we should not overlook the fact that Andrew has a consistency of his own and that consistency is his bringing of people to Jesus. He did it at the beginning with his brother Simon and he does it now with a little boy.

John does not tell us who the boy was, nor how Andrew found him. He does not say whether the lad offered his lunch or whether Andrew persuaded him. Throughout this narrative John concentrates firmly on what he sees as the essential points and passes over a number of things that we in our curiosity would like to know. But his procedure means that the essence of the story stands out in massive simplicity.

The boy, Andrew told Jesus, had five barley loaves and two little fish (v. 9). We should not misunderstand the word *loaves*. Andrew is not referring to the kind of loaf that we might buy in a modern bakeshop. He is talking about something much smaller, like a roll or a biscuit or a scone (the different terminologies in different parts of the English-speaking world make it hard to find one expression that we can all understand; but it should be clear that it was a small piece of bread). John tells us (as the others do not) that these little loaves were made of barley flour. This was cheaper than wheaten bread, and it means that the little boy came from a poor family.

The word we translate "fish" is not the usual word for fish swimming in the water *(ichthus),* but a word that really means prepared food, usually cooked food. It was used of anything eaten with bread and often of a "tidbit." But what was mostly eaten with bread was fish, and that is the meaning the word has in this place. The five little loaves and the two little fish were, it would seem, the provisions the boy had made (or had had made for him) for his own meal. Now he was offering it to Jesus. But, while Andrew is quite prepared to bring the boy and his offering to Jesus, he does not see this as anything of a solution to the problem before them. "What are these among so many?"

The Miracle

Jesus is not recorded as having said anything to either Philip or Andrew. They appear in the narrative simply to show the impossibility of meeting the situation from human resources and with human wisdom. Jesus began by getting the crowd seated (v. 10). We speak of being "seated," but of course the verb means "recline." At that time people reclined when they went to their tables for meals, and it was this posture that they naturally adopted when they used the grass as their resting place. John tells us that there was a good deal of grass in the place, so it would have been a comfortable enough posture.

John uses two different words for "men." The first time he has *anthropos,* which may mean "human being," and the second time it is *aner,* which may mean "husband." Some see a difference in the meanings here, with John first of all speaking of the totality of the crowd and then speaking of only the men as seated. But this seems highly unlikely (why would Jesus have the women and children stand?). If the change is significant, the meaning rather will be that, while Jesus told them all to recline, the number of men involved was five thousand. This would agree with Matthew's account, for that Evangelist expressly says that there were five thousand men apart from women and children (Matt. 14:21). But John often uses synonyms with no great difference in meaning and this may be another example. While he is certainly not contradicting Matthew's version, he may not be writing about the number of men apart from women and children, but simply varying his terminology.

John describes the miracle very simply. Jesus took the bread and gave thanks over it in the manner of any host beginning a meal (v. 11). Then he distributed it to the people and did likewise with the fishes. From the other Gospels we learn that it was the disciples who actually gave the food to the people. John, of course, does not mean that they did not do this and that Jesus did it all himself. But his way of expressing himself puts the emphasis on Jesus' action. It was what he did in multiplying the loaves and the fishes that mattered, not the actions of the disciples as he permitted them to share in the wonderful event.

John's verb for Jesus' giving of thanks is *eucharisteo,* and to some students it seems significant that he uses this verb rather than *eulogeo,* which is used in the other Gospels. John's verb was used in the early church with respect to the Holy Communion and indeed gave it one of the names whereby it came to be known, "eucharist." It is suggested that John wants us to see a reference to the Holy Communion here. But against that we should notice that Matthew and Mark have John's verb when they refer to the feeding of the four thousand (Matt. 15:36; Mark 8:6), so it has no particular application to this miracle. Further we must bear in mind that John never refers explicitly to the communion. While he has far and away the longest account of what went on in the upper room on Jesus' last night, he does not tell us that Jesus then began this service. Again, he uses the verb *eucharisteo* of Jesus' prayer of thanksgiving at the time he raised Lazarus (11:41). There is no reason at all for thinking of a sacramental reference here.

John goes on to say that Jesus gave the people as much fish as they wanted. A meal of bread and fish would have been very satisfying to those Galileans, and John goes on to speak of them as being "filled" (v. 12); this was no token meal but a substantial repast.

What Happened?

In modern times there has been a good deal of discussion of this miracle, and many scholars have asked the question "What really happened?" While a variety of answers have been given, three in particular stand out.

A favorite with those who are sceptical about Jesus' miracles in general runs like this. There was really plenty of food there, for many people had brought lunch packets with them. But they were selfish. They did not want to share with those who had nothing. So they all kept their food to themselves and refrained from eating. But when the little boy brought his lunch to Jesus they were all put to shame and began to produce their food and to share it. When this was done it proved to be enough and more than enough. Everybody had enough to eat and there was a good deal left over. This makes a big appeal to some, but it has the fatal objection that it is not what John says (or for that matter any of the other Evangelists). It originates in the fertile imaginations of modern people, not in the story told in the Gospels.

A second view is that what took place was something like a service of Holy Communion. It was not really that service, because Jesus had not yet begun it. But the suggestion is made that we have a kind of forerunner. Fellowship was important for Jesus and his followers, and eating together was a significant mark of fellowship. So it is suggested that from time to time Jesus may have had a token meal with his followers. They took a little piece of bread (and here of fish) and ate together as a sign of the fellowship they enjoyed before God. It is pointed out that the verb *eucharisteo* used here is that used of taking a token piece of bread in the communion and thus quite appropriate in a token meal. Again, Moses gave the manna and Elisha fed a hundred men with twenty barley loaves (2 Kings 4:42–44); it is suggested that it was proper that Jesus likewise be seen to be the provider of what was needed and that this was done in a symbolical way. But again it is important to see that this is not what the Gospels are telling us. This view originates in the mind of modern people, not in the Gospel story. There we read of people being "filled"; the meal was not a token, but a genuine reception of a satisfying quantity of food. And the verb *eucharisteo* simply means "to give thanks"; it has no necessary reference to food, nor to a small quantity. Its use proves nothing.

So we come to the third view. What happened was a real miracle. Jesus, being the incarnate Son of God, was able to do things that others cannot, and on this occasion he provided the food that was needed to satisfy the hunger of a large number in a way that we can only call miraculous. If we see Jesus as really God Incarnate, this will provide no difficulty. And if we do not so see him, then we will not see a creative act, whatever the evidence.

What Was Left Over

Jesus was able to use his powers to supply the needs of a great number of people. But that did not mean that he was indifferent to waste. He told the disciples to gather up what the people had left so that nothing be wasted (v. 12). Good food was important. It must not be lost.

When the disciples did this they filled twelve baskets with the pieces of food that remained over (v. 13). This shows plainly enough that John is talking about a miracle; it is astounding that there should be so much at the end when there was so little at the beginning. There is more than one Greek word for "basket," and some maintain that the word used here *(kophinos)* means a small basket, such as a traveler might use to carry his food. They contrast it with the word used in the accounts of the feeding of the four thousand *(sphuris),* which they hold means a large basket; it could be large enough to hold a man, for it was in such a basket that Paul was lowered from the wall at Damascus (Acts 9:25).

But in fact the difference between the two words appears to refer to the material of which the baskets were made, not to size. The *kophinos* was made of stiff material, like wicker, whereas the *sphuris* was rather made out of some flexible material, like hemp. The *kophinos* may indeed have been small; but, if so, we gather this from the probability that the reference is to baskets that the disciples might have had with them to carry their food, not to the use of this word rather than another. John, incidentally, speaks only of fragments of the bread, but Mark makes it clear that there was fish to spare as well.

Prophet and King

The people were impressed. They may not have understood all that is involved in what John calls a "sign," but they did see that what Jesus had done was wonderful. So they gave their verdict, "Truly this is the prophet who is to come into the world" (v. 14). They do not speak of "a" prophet, but "the" prophet, which points us to that great prophet that Moses said would come in due course, a prophet like himself (Deut. 18:15–18). It is perhaps curious that they thought of Jesus as this prophet rather than as the Messiah, for the Jews in general seem to have distinguished the two (the Jews asked John the Baptist whether he was the Messiah, and when they found that he was not they asked whether he was the prophet, 1:20–21). But perhaps this group of Galileans was somewhat confused about the finer points of theology and put the two together.

Jesus saw that they wanted to make a king out of him, so he withdrew (v. 15). The Jews in general hated being under Roman rule and longed for the day when they would be free and would have their own king to rule over them. There is no doubt that many people of this time looked and longed for a militant Messiah who would lead an army and defeat the Romans. It would seem that the people who had just seen the miracle felt that Jesus would be just the man for this. If he could make five barley loaves and two small fish into a meal for thousands, what could he not do in the way of military supplies and army tactics?

But Jesus was not a king of that kind. He regarded the setting up of an earthly kingdom as a temptation of the devil (Luke 4:5–8) and he would have no part in it. He is king in the hearts of his followers, but that is a very different thing. The tragedy of these Galileans was that they tried to make Jesus into their kind of king. They did not get what they wanted and in the process they lost the kind of king Jesus really is. People still make that mistake. They insist that Jesus be the kind of king (or savior or whatever) that they want. They try to force him into a mold of their own choosing. They can never succeed, but while they are trying they lose the wonderful gift that Jesus is offering. Let us learn to see him as he is and to submit to his kind of kingship.

26

The Miracle on the Sea

When evening came his disciples went down to the sea. They embarked in a boat and were going across the sea to Capernaum. It had become dark already, and Jesus had not yet come to them. A strong wind was blowing and the sea was rising. When they had rowed about twenty-five or thirty stadia they see Jesus walking on the sea and getting near the boat. They were afraid, but Jesus says to them, "I am. Don't be frightened." They wanted to take him into the boat, and immediately the boat came to be at the land to which they were going (John 6:16–21).

Both Matthew and Mark have the story of the storm and of Jesus walking on the sea right after the feeding of the multitude. Their accounts are somewhat fuller than that of John and, for example, Matthew includes the incident of Peter's walking on the water. Many have found in John's account an edifying story meant to teach that Jesus comes to us in our trials when we least expect him. It is edifying and we may profitably engage in such reflections. But we should not think of the story as a pious invention. A comparison with the other Gospels leads us to see that John included the story at this point because it happened straight after the feeding of the five thousand. His narrative is brief and lacks anything superfluous. He is apparently not trying to point a moral but giving in the simplest terms a brief account of what happened. Many have pointed out that this story is a very suitable introduction to the teaching in John 6, but that is another matter.

The Disciples' Departure

The previous incident concluded with an attempt by some in the crowd to make a king out of Jesus, so that the Master withdrew into the mountain to get away from them. John says nothing about the disciples in that connection, but we learn from Matthew and Mark that Jesus "compelled" them to get into the boat and go across the lake. Their verb is a strong one; its meaning is given in Abbott-Smith's lexicon as "*to necessitate, compel* by force or persuasion, *constrain*." Clearly Jesus was determined to get the disciples away from the scene as quickly as possible, and once in the boat they would have been effectively removed from the scene.

None of the Evangelists tells us why Jesus did this, but it is not hard to see. We know that the disciples were not immune from the temptation to see Jesus as a king like earthly kings. There was that occasion when James and John and their mother came to Jesus to ask that the young men might sit one on Jesus' right and the other on his left in his kingdom (Matt. 20:20–23). Even in the upper room at the very end of Jesus' earthly ministry, there was a quarrel among them as to which of them would be the greatest (Luke 22:24). It took the death and resurrection to teach them what sort of kingdom Jesus had in mind, but right up till then they were looking for some form of earthly empire. And they had the natural, healthy ambition of young men. Each wanted a big place in the kingdom when it came.

Many who profess to follow Jesus have surprising ignorance about what is involved. I am reminded of the new minister who in the Sunday school decided to ask a few questions to test the knowledge of the students. He asked one boy, "Who made the walls of Jericho fall down?" and received the answer "It wasn't me, and that's for sure."

The minister turned to the somewhat embarrassed teacher. "What do you think of that?" he asked.

"Tommy's a good boy," she said. "He doesn't tell lies. If he said he didn't do it, I believe him."

The minister thought his church council ought to know of the appalling incapacity of the Sunday school so that he could rely on their support in a program to improve matters. So he reported what had happened. They considered the matter and in due course sent the result of their deliberations to the minister: "We see no point in making an issue of this incident. It will be best simply to repair the walls. We are prepared to pay the cost and charge it up to vandalism."

The story is no doubt apocryphal, but it reminds us that people who call themselves Christians often show surprising ignorance of what they might be expected to know of the Christian way. The disciples in due course gave the church magnificent leadership, but at this point they were certainly lacking in a full understanding of what Jesus was doing for our salvation. At least some of them would have been glad to see him as an earthly king.

It is obvious that the kingmakers among the crowd who had been so impressed by the miracle would have had some active supporters among the apostolic band. The hotheads in the crowd and the hotheads among the disciples would have formed a strong alliance. Jesus wanted none of that sort of trouble and he sent the disciples off early. Without their involvement he dealt with the crowd and went back into the hill country. Accordingly there was no nonsense about starting a rebellion against Rome.

So as the day was ending the disciples came down to the sea. They got into their boat and started off across the water to go to Capernaum. John tells us that it was already dark and that Jesus had not come to them. But, if they were in the boat going across the water, how could he come to them? They were certainly not expecting him to join the boat in the middle of the lake, so these words are unexpected. It would seem that Jesus probably told the disciples to start off immediately and to put in at a certain place along the shore where he hoped to join them. But evidently the instruction included the provision that they were not to wait beyond a certain time. Getting rid of the kingmakers and going into the mountain country took time, so that Jesus did not in fact join them. So they set off across the lake without him.

A Storm

The sea of Galilee is not a large body of water, and there are some considerable mountains close by, which can cause strong wind squalls. It is possible for storms to arise suddenly and evidently that was what happened on this occasion. With a strong wind blowing and a rising sea, the voyage came to be a difficult one. Mark tells us that the wind was contrary and that would have made their rowing a hard task. Rowing is not the easiest of pastimes and rowing against a strong wind can be wearying. Clearly the disciples were in an unenviable situation.

John tells us that they saw Jesus when they had rowed about twenty-five or thirty stadia (v. 19; Mark simply locates the boat "in the middle of the sea," which is not precise but shows that they were still a long way from land). A stadion was about six hundred feet. The lake was about sixty-one stadia wide at the greatest breadth, but they were not crossing at this point, so their voyage would have been somewhat shorter. How much shorter we do not know, because of our ignorance of their precise route. But they were certainly well on their way and may have been about three-quarters of the way across.

They saw Jesus. John's language becomes vivid and he uses the present tense: "They see Jesus, walking. . . ." It was near Passover, so that the moon must have been near to the full and thus there would be light. The wind may have blown up clouds and therefore we do not know how much light, but plainly there was no difficulty in seeing Jesus.

Walking on the Sea

According to most translations Jesus was walking on the sea, though perhaps we should notice that there are some scholars who think we should understand the Greek as "by the sea." They point out that the identical expression is found in 21:1 where it must mean "by the sea." They maintain that with twenty-five or thirty stadia covered the journey must have been nearly over. Further, at the end of the story, when the disciples wanted to take Jesus into the boat, "immediately" the boat came to be at the land. They suggest accordingly that there was no miracle and they see what happened in this way: The sailors were in a difficult position in a storm at sea and in fact were terrified. They thought they might well be wrecked; their lives were in danger. In the dim light they saw Jesus walking on the shore and in their overwrought state thought he was walking on the waves. But, in fact, the reasoning goes on, he was not, and in a few minutes there they were on the shore, safe and sound.

But the matter is not as simple as that. The Greek preposition *epi* is rather like the English "on." The basic meaning refers to one thing being on top of another, though it is not impossible to use it of "being close by." Thus if you say, "I live on Fourth Avenue," you really mean that your house is beside Fourth Avenue; you do not mean that it is in the middle of the avenue. But the fact that "on" may have more than one meaning does not bother us. The context shows us which one is meant, and we cheerfully use the word in whichever way the need of the moment dictates.

So the fact that in 21:1 the expression means "by the sea" does not give its meaning here. We must take the context into account. It is relevant also to see what the other accounts say, and we find that Matthew has exactly the same expression as John. In his case the subsequent request of Peter that he be bidden to come to Jesus "on the waters" (Matt. 14:28) employs the same preposition *epi*, "on," which makes it very plain that in this story the meaning is "on the sea" and not "by the sea."

There is also the fact that the disciples were afraid. Some of them were skilled fishermen; their trade was to catch fish on that very lake. They knew it intimately and must have been familiar with its storms. There is no indication that their fear was due to the wind and the waves. It was the sight of Jesus getting near the boat when they were well out from land that scared them. Men do not approach ships in the middle of the sea, so it did not occur to them that this was their well-known and well-loved Master; they thought they were seeing a ghost (Mark 6:49). There is no reason at all for associating their fear with the storm; it was the sight of Jesus on the water that made them afraid. They could not explain it, and the unknown filled them with fear.

Reassurance

Jesus reassured them immediately (v. 20), though it is not quite certain how we should translate his words. The traditional way of doing this is "It is I" (KJV); the words simply identify the speaker. However we understand the passage, it certainly includes this. Jesus calmed his followers by assuring them that what they were seeing was no wild phantom, but their well-loved Master. And it is not easy to see how else he would say the equivalent of our idiomatic "It's me!"

But the words may have a further meaning; they are emphatic words, spoken in the style of deity. In the first volume of these *Reflections* we had occasion to notice that in Greek it is usually not necessary to use the personal pronoun to indicate the subject of a verb. We are familiar with this in our use of the English word *am;* the only possible subject of "am" is "I." The Greeks took this a lot further. Their verbs normally showed (by the forms they took) what the subject was. So they did not use the pronoun as a general rule. But if they wanted to emphasize the subject, if they wanted to say "*I* am" rather than "I am," they used the pronoun.

But there was a difference when they came to set down divine speech, the words of God. The Old Testament is, of course, written in Hebrew, but in time it was translated into Greek, and it was this Greek translation that was normally used at any rate by Jews outside Palestine and often by those inside it. When the translators came to words of God they apparently thought that these should be translated differently from the words of men. They tended to use the emphatic form with the pronoun "*I*."

It is this emphatic form that John uses here. It is not improbable that he wants us to see Jesus as using the kind of speech that is appropriate to God. It would all fit in. The storm that could not conquer or even impede him, the fear of the disciples, the help he was about to bring them, his coming to them walking on the water as men cannot do, all these things made the language of deity appropriate. John may well have felt that in the circumstances it was only right that he should convey to his readers the fact that Jesus was more than a man, and accordingly he used the language of deity. He does this a number of times (8:24, 58; 13:19; 18:5, 6; cf. Exod. 3:14; Deut. 32:39; Isa. 41:4; 43:10, 25). It is beyond doubt that sometimes John uses the words to hint at the truth that Jesus was more than a man, and it may well be that he is doing this here.

It is this expression that calms the fears of the disciples and forms a suitable introduction to the "bread of life" passage that follows. There again Jesus uses this form of words and there it is made plain that he fully meets the needs of his own.

The End of the Story

John goes on to say that the disciples wanted to take Jesus into the boat. That is very natural, but did they do so? John does not say so, though some translators are so sure that they did that they translate that way. Mark tells us that Jesus went up into the boat and that the storm ceased (Mark 6:51). John may well mean this, but it is curious that he does not say so in set terms. However, the difficulties if we suppose that Jesus did not enter the boat are so many that few adopt that understanding of the passage. We should understand that Jesus did get in with the disciples, even though we cannot explain why John does not say so explicitly.

Then he adds "immediately the boat came to be at the land to which they were going" (v. 21). Does this mean that there was another miracle? It is possible to take the words as meaning there was not. Those who see no miracle, of course, welcome this statement. For them it indicates that the disciples were closer to the shore than they thought, and as soon as they recognized Jesus they found themselves safely arrived at land. But we have seen that this is not a good explanation of what John says. He may mean, however, that the coming of Jesus put new heart into the rowers. Before he came they had been disheartened with their hard rowing against a fierce headwind. Now that they had him on board they bent their backs and it was not long before they found themselves at their destination. This would be all the more likely if we bear in mind what Mark tells us about the cessation of the storm. That would have made their work so much lighter.

But many commentators think John means that there was a second miracle. Godet puts this well: "One can scarcely imagine, indeed, that, after an act of power so magnificent and so kingly as Jesus' walking on the waters, He should have seated Himself in the boat, and the voyage should have been laboriously continued by the stroke of the oar? At the moment when Jesus set His foot on the boat, He communicated to it, as He had just done for Peter, the force victorious over gravity and space, which had just been so strikingly displayed in His own person."

This does appear to be what John is saying (cf. Moffatt, "so they agreed to take him on board, and the boat instantly reached the land they were making for"). We are reminded of Psalm 107, which speaks of God's care for sailors, who see God's "wonderful deeds in the deep" (v. 24). God stills storms and delivers them from their distress, but specially important are the words "he guided them to their desired haven" (v. 30). It is something like this overruling care of God of which John is writing.

Through the centuries this passage has been a source of comfort and strength to God's troubled people. We all go through the storms of life, and these can be discouraging affairs when we are tried to the limit of our strength. It is good to know that at all times we are the objects of God's love and care and that in his own way and in his own time he brings us through our trials.

We should also reflect that Jesus comes to us in ways we do not expect. When the sailors were tossed about on that boat there is little doubt that some of them at any rate thought, "If only Jesus were with us!" That would be just what was needed. He would find some way of seeing them through. But when he came he came in a way that they did not expect, and instead of welcoming his appearance they were frightened. And is that not sometimes our experience, too? Jesus often comes to us in the guise of "one of the least of these, his brothers," and we do not expect to see him like that. Sometimes he comes to us in trials and difficulties, and we do not expect that either. It is well that we look for the spiritual perception that will enable us to recognize him and to welcome him in whatever guise he comes. One thing is certain. The Christian way is full of surprises, and Christ constantly comes to us in ways that we do not anticipate. Unless we welcome him, however he comes, our spiritual experience will always be the poorer.

27

Manna from Heaven

And when they had found him on the other side of the sea (the people) said to him, "Rabbi, when did you get here?" Jesus replied, "Truly, truly, I tell you, you seek me out not because you saw signs, but because you ate of the loaves and were filled. Do not work for the food that perishes, but for the food that remains into eternal life which the Son of man will give you; for him did God the Father seal." They said to him therefore, "What shall we do in order to work the works of God?" Jesus replied, "This is the work of God that you believe on him whom he sent." So they said to him, "What sign do you do then so that we may see it and believe you? What do you work? Our fathers ate the manna in the wilderness as it is written, 'He gave them bread from heaven to eat.'" Jesus said to them then, "Truly, truly, I tell you, it was not Moses that gave you the bread from heaven, but my Father gives you the true bread from heaven. For the bread of God is he who comes down from heaven and gives life to the world" (John 6:25–33).

Curiously the crowd asks Jesus, "When did you get here?" (v. 25). John has told us that they were puzzled about what boat he could have come in, and we might have expected them to ask, "How did you get here?" Indeed, so strong is that expectation that some commentators say that this was what they did ask. We know that it was the significant question. If they had asked that and understood the answer, they would have been in a better position to understand who Jesus was. But like so many of us they asked the wrong question (like the little girl who saw some ballet dancers cavorting on their toes and asked, "Mummie, why don't they just get taller girls?"). They had the opportunity of finding out something wonderful and instead asked only about the time.

Jesus' reply is a solemn one, preceded as it is with the "Truly, truly." This expression indicates that what follows is important, sometimes that it is not what the hearers would expect. Jesus points out that his hearers were not really interested in "signs," sign-ificant happenings, events that showed that God was at work. These people had had a splendid free meal and it was this that made them interested in Jesus. But they had not asked themselves, "What does it mean? What does it tell us about Jesus and about what God is doing in Jesus that he is able to do such a wonderful thing?" If they had given consideration to the sign, they might well have learned an important spiritual lesson and have come to believe in Jesus. Throughout this Gospel faith that is based on the miracles is never seen as the highest kind of faith, but it is better than no faith at all.

But these people did not even have that kind of faith. They were interested in having their hunger satisfied, and it was that that kept them talking to Jesus. It was their need as they themselves saw it and not as Jesus saw it that occupied their whole attention. It is easy to make the same mistake. Most of us are so sure that we know what we need in this life that we pursue it single-mindedly and never stop to ask whether it is this that is important, this that matters in the sight of God.

The food in which these people were interested was a perishable commodity. There was nothing lasting about it. They had had a good meal of bread and fishes but now they needed another meal. Their very hunger was evidence that the food of which they were thinking has no lasting results. They should not keep working for what is at best temporary (v. 27). The verb *work* has a continuous force. Jesus is saying that they are constantly working for what is not lasting.

Guy de Maupassant has a story about a young woman in modest circumstances who was invited to go with her husband to an important function. Not having suitable jewelry, she borrowed a necklace from a rich friend. Unfortunately somehow the necklace was lost and the young couple were in despair. The wife, however, found a duplicate in a shop and, though it was very expensive, bought it with borrowed money so that she could return it to her friend. Then she and her husband had to work for years to raise the money to repay the loans. When they had at last succeeded it happened that one day quite by chance she met her friend and on an impulse told her what had happened. The friend replied, "But my necklace was paste; it was worth only a few francs!"

That is a parable about life for many people. They labor for the food that perishes, for that which has no permanent value. Like the couple in the story they give the best years of their lives in working for what is worthless.

Eternal Life

Jesus counsels his hearers to look instead for "the food that remains into eternal life." There are things that last, and they are more important than the transient things on which we spend so much time and energy. Jesus' words form an unusual Greek expression that appears to combine two meanings: the food of which he is speaking is forever in contrast to the perishable food that so preoccupied his hearers, and further it gives eternal life to those who receive it. While Jesus invites the people to concentrate on this food, he does not say that by doing so they will merit eternal life. Eternal life is his gift. It comes in no other way.

The Father has "sealed" Jesus. In antiquity a seal was much more important than it is with us (even when we allow for the importance of the seal in some commercial transactions). It was an age when many people could not read. It was thus useless to write one's name on one's property. Since the rascals who would be tempted to take what was not theirs could not read, they did not know whose it was. Thus an important man used a seal. He had a device, a representation of a bull or another animal or perhaps some geometric design, something that was distinctive. With a signet ring or the like this mark could be impressed into a soft material like wax, which retained the design when it hardened. The potential wrongdoer could see the design and know what it meant. He might be very wary about tampering with the property of a powerful man.

The seal, then, was a mark of ownership. But it was used more widely. It might be affixed to a document, for example, and then it gave attestation. The man who affixed his seal by that fact declared his agreement to what was in the document. It was a mark of approval.

Jesus is saying, then, that God the Father has given his approval to him. The word order in the original is of interest: "him the Father sealed, the God." While we frequently read of "God the Father," this is the only place in the New Testament that has the order "the Father, God" (8:41 is slightly different). It is not clear why the unusual order is adopted, but we should see at least that Jesus is saying that his Father is none less than God. That God has given his seal means that we are not to think of Jesus as simply a peasant from Nazareth giving an interesting personal point of view on certain religious matters. He was one with God and God was at work in him. The seal means that God has given his mark of agreement, of approval. It is an error to dismiss Jesus as no more than just another man.

That brought from his hearers the question "What shall we do in order to work the works of God?" (v. 28). The fact that they asked the question indicates that they had some real interest in serving God. The fact that they put their whole emphasis on what they themselves would do indicates that they had not understood what Jesus was telling them. Like many people through the centuries they were firmly convinced that their salvation depended on what they themselves did. They put their trust in their own strong right arm. They ask "what shall we do?"; they say "to work the works." They entirely overlook the fact that Jesus has just said that the Son of man "will give" eternal life. Eternal life is a wonderful thing, so wonderful that none of us can ever merit it, no matter how hard we try or how great our human achievement. It is always a gift.

Jesus answers their question in terms of faith. They had asked about working "the works" of God; Jesus replied by speaking of "the work" of God (v. 29). The singular is important, for as Jesus told Martha one day, only one thing is needed (Luke 10:42), and that one thing we find here is "that you believe on him whom he sent." God has chosen to work out our salvation in the life and death and resurrection of his Son, and there is no other way. If we are to have eternal life, we must put our trust in the Son. Characteristically the Son is here described as "him whom he sent." It is important that Jesus was not engaged in some self-chosen activity, but that he was on a mission; he had been sent by God. Both the Father and Son are interested in bringing eternal life to sinners, and it is not possible to separate them. So Jesus speaks of believing in such a way as to involve the Father as well as the Son.

The Manna

That evokes a question about a "sign" (v. 30). It is curious that these people, of all people, should ask, "What sign do you show us?" for they had just seen a marvelous sign in the feeding of the multitude with a few loaves and fishes. They could also have known of the walking on the water if they had made inquiry among Jesus' disciples. And Jesus indicates that they had seen a number of miracles as his plural "signs" (v. 26) shows. It scarcely seems that they would need a further sign.

But that is what they ask for. "What sign do you do," they ask, "so that we may see it and believe you? What do you work?" (v. 30). They imply that if only Jesus produced a satisfactory "sign" they would believe him. Of course, had he done so, they would doubtless have found some other reason for not believing. As Ryle put it, "It is want of heart, not want of evidence, that keeps people back from Christ." But they persuaded themselves, and tried to persuade Jesus, that all that was needed was the proper "sign" and they would become believers. Such a demand was made more than once (Matt. 16:1; Mark 8:11–12; Luke 11:29), but Jesus always refused it.

On this occasion Jesus' interrogators pointed to the manna in the wilderness as the kind of thing they had in mind (v. 31). When the Israelites passed through the wilderness they had problems getting enough food, and Scripture tells us that God met their need, sending them each day (except the Sabbath) "thin flakes like frost on the ground" (Exod. 16:14). The name *manna* was given to it (from the Hebrew for the question they asked, "What is it?"), and we are told that it "was white like coriander seed and tasted like wafers made with honey" (Exod. 16:31). This daily gift lasted through the forty years of the wilderness wanderings (Exod. 16:34–35). The manna was called "bread from heaven" (Exod. 16:4; cf. Ps. 78:23–25).

There was an idea among the Jews that God would send the manna again in the latter days. "It will happen . . . that the treasury of manna will come down again from on high, and they will eat of it in those years" (2 Baruch 29:8). Very importantly, there was an idea that the Messiah would be associated with the renewal of this gift. "As the former redeemer [i.e., Moses] caused manna to descend, as it is stated, *Behold, I will cause to rain bread from heaven for you* (Ex. XVI,4), so will the latter Redeemer cause manna to descend, as it is stated, *May he be as a rich cornfield in the land* (Ps. LXXII,16)" (Ecclesiastes Rabbah I.9).

Plainly the Jews who talked with Jesus had something like this in mind. They read of the manna in their Bible and they looked for the Messiah to be in some respects a second Moses. So they thought that he would accredit himself by bringing down the manna from heaven. The Jews were not content with the sign that Jesus had given. They demanded that the sign be the one that they wanted.

This is a natural human tendency. We seem always to want things our own way. I was reading of a man who went into a restaurant in Sydney and ordered from the seafood list a big mud crab. When the dish arrived the diner found that it had only one claw so he asked why that should be. The waiter explained that these crabs are very pugnacious and often engage in fights in some of which claws get torn off. This crab had clearly had a misfortune in fighting another crab. The diner immediately pushed the plate aside and demanded, "Bring me the winner!"

The Jews were a bit like that. They were not content with what they had seen Jesus do, but demanded what they thought would be something better. In their judgment the Messiah must produce the manna. It did not matter whether the Messiah thought that or not. They were sure that they knew what the Messiah would do. It is easy to put a human limitation on what God must do. We must all learn that God does things his own way, not the way we lay down. We would have thought that Jesus' feeding of the great crowd of people from such limited resources would surely be the kind of miracle that must accredit him. But quite plainly the Jews found it insufficient. After all, Moses fed a whole nation; Jesus merely five thousand people. Moses fed them for forty years, whereas Jesus had given them only one meal. Jesus supplied ordinary bread and fish, while Moses gave them "bread from heaven" and, since there is none of that available for sampling, there is no limit to what people can imagine about its delicacies.

True Bread from Heaven

Jesus refutes the position they were taking up. Again he begins with the emphatic "Truly, truly" (v. 32); what follows is important. He points to three errors they had made and he gives the correct position:

1. Moses did not give the gift; God did.
2. God's gift is not only in the remote past; he gives now.
3. The bread from heaven that matters is a spiritual gift; it is not something physical like the manna. They were in error in looking for such a gift.

It is always a mistake to confuse the divine Giver with the earthly instrument through whom he makes his gift. Moses was a faithful servant of God, but it was not in him to supply the manna and in fact he never did. He simply told the Israelites what God would do and passed on God's commands concerning its use.

And it is important to see that God's gifts continue. It was said of one great man that he believed in a God who lived until the days of Oliver Cromwell. Many of us have an attitude something like that. We do not doubt that God once worked in this world. We are sure that he acted among men in Bible days and we are ready to take that a little further. God attested the preaching of the early missionaries with miraculous signs. Some of us take that down perhaps to the Reformation and think of the way God used spiritual giants to set forward his purpose. Others of us come closer to modern times, depending on whom we see as people through whom God delighted to act in days gone by. But when we look at our own problems and the problems of our church in the modern turmoil and the needs of our modern world, it seems so much easier to concentrate on what people can do and are doing. But that is not a Christian position. Jesus is teaching us that God is a present reality. Continually he gives his good gifts. Continually he acts in the fulfillment of his purpose.

But the most important part of Jesus' answer is that in which he says "the bread of God is he who comes down from heaven and gives life to the world" (v. 33). He speaks of "the bread of God" rather than "bread from heaven," thus putting emphasis on the Giver. But the really significant thing is that the gift is Christ himself, "he who comes down from heaven." The Greek could be understood either as "he who" or as "that which." It is likely that the Jews took it in the second sense, for they were thinking of a material kind of food. But Jesus was speaking of himself, and he points them to the deeper truth that the real heavenly bread concerns a person. God has supplied the need of his people by sending them, not something to eat like the manna, but a Savior.

The Savior "gives life to the world." The manna could satisfy bodily hunger, but it could not give life to the dead. Jesus can and does. Throughout this Gospel there is an emphasis on the gift of life. Sometimes it is spoken of as "eternal life," sometimes, as here, it is "life." There is no great difference. Jesus brings to us the life of the world to come and makes it a present reality.

28

Living Bread

They said to him, then, "Sir, give us this bread always." Jesus said to them, "I am the bread of life. He who comes to me will never hunger and he who believes in me will never thirst, never. But I told you that you have both seen me and not believed. All that the Father gives me will come to me and him who comes to me I will certainly not cast out, because I came down from heaven not to do my own will but the will of him who sent me. And this is the will of him who sent me that I should not lose any that he gives me, but raise it up at the last day. For this is the will of my Father, that everyone who sees the Son and believes in him may have life eternal and I will raise him up at the last day" (John 6:34–40).

The woman at the well did not understand what the living water was, but she asked Jesus to give it to her all the same (4:15). The crowd was a little bit like that. They certainly did not understand that Jesus was himself the living bread, but he had been speaking of bread from heaven and they apparently liked the sound of it, even if they did not really believe in its reality. They may even have been a bit sarcastic when they asked that they might be given the heavenly bread always (v. 34). They had spoken to Jesus of the manna, and it may be that they had in mind something of the kind. When the Messiah came the gift of the manna would be renewed, and Jesus claimed to be the Messiah. "Let us ask him, then, for the food from heaven" seems to be the way they were thinking. "Let us see whether he can give us the bread he is talking about!" The manna had been a constant source of supply, and, while Jesus had done something wonderful in giving a meal to five thousand people out of five loaves and a few fishes, if he were the Messiah he would be able to keep it up. So they ask not only to be given the food, but to be given it always.

"I AM the Bread"

Jesus' reply shows that the gift is not to be separated from the Giver. He is himself the bread of which he has been speaking. When we were considering the walking on the water we saw that in Greek the expression "I am" with the emphatic personal pronoun is the style of deity (p. 217). It is this that we have here. Jesus is claiming that he can give a great gift, and his form of words indicates that he is big enough to give such a great gift. He does not say, "I am divine," but this form of words is such that the perceptive listener will understand what he is saying about himself.

Dr. G. Campbell Morgan links this passage with that which tells of Moses at the burning bush. There that patriarch asked the name of him who spoke to him out of the fire and was told, "I am who I am. This is what you are to say to the Israelites: 'I AM has sent me to you'" (Exod. 3:14). Dr. Morgan thinks that on this occasion Jesus "took the name of the burning bush, and linked it with the symbol of perfect sustenance for human life. 'I am the Bread of life.' Thus He employed the simplest of terms, with sublimest significance." Whether or not there is this definite link with the burning bush, the words certainly convey a high claim.

This is the first of seven great "I AM" sayings in John's Gospel, some of them repeated with slight variations. Jesus says emphatically that he is "the light of the world" (8:12), "the door" (10:7, 9), "the good shepherd" (10:11, 14), "the resurrection and the life (11:25), "the way, and the truth, and the life" (14:6), and "the (true) vine" (15:1, 5). This is a tremendous series of claims, and together they point to someone who is far greater than any mere man. Clearly John has gathered a collection of sayings that show very plainly that the Savior of whom he writes is one with God.

Jesus, then, is "the bread of life." This "I AM" saying is repeated with several variations. Thus we read, "I am the bread that came down from heaven" (v. 41); "I am the bread of life" (v. 48); "I am the living bread" (or "the bread which lives," v. 51). We also have some variations on the theme of bread without the "I AM," as "the bread of God is he who comes down from heaven" (v. 33), and "this is the bread which [or who] comes down from heaven" (v. 50). There are many facets to this teaching. Common to them all is the thought that, just as bread is basic to sustaining this bodily, physical life, so is Jesus basic to the eternal life of which this Gospel says so much.

We should notice that "bread of life" could be understood in more ways than one. The genitive "of life" is not precise, but means something like "a 'life' kind of bread." This might mean bread that gives life or bread that is itself alive. Both are true, and in the Johannine manner it may be that we are meant to understand both.

Jesus adds a statement that brings out what receiving the bread of life means. Interestingly he does not say "He who eats it" but "He who comes to me" (v. 35). He is talking about a spiritual experience, and our earthly metaphors do not describe it with precision. There are more ways than one of putting it. If we use the metaphor of food, then bread is to be eaten, and Jesus speaks a little later of people eating the living bread (v. 51). That is the way they get life. But the life of which Jesus is speaking is a spiritual life and is to be understood in terms of knowing God and Jesus himself (17:3). To know him we must come to him, and this is the way Jesus puts it here. We should not try to put fine distinctions between these various ways of expressing it. They are all ways of saying that eternal life is a gift of God and that it comes through Jesus Christ.

Here Jesus explains it in negative terms: the person who has this life will never be hungry or thirsty. Both expressions are emphatic, with the use of the double negative. The one who comes to Jesus will certainly never hunger; the bread he imparts is completely satisfying. Bread normally has nothing to do with thirst, but eating and drinking go naturally together, and thus Jesus adds the information that this person will never thirst either. In any case he has earlier said that he gives the living water (4:10, 14). This expression is even more emphatic than the one that tells of the bread; in addition to the double negative there is added an adverb, which with a negative means "never, not at any time." Jesus is affirming in the strongest terms the satisfying nature of the life he brings.

Elsewhere Jesus speaks of those who "hunger and thirst after righteousness" (Matt. 5:6), but the emphatic denial that believers will ever hunger and thirst is not in contradiction. In Matthew Jesus is speaking of the yearning that is an inevitable part of entering into the salvation of God. When we know something of his righteousness we long for more. It is so wonderful that we cannot do otherwise.

But this is not inconsistent with a deep satisfaction. It is this of which Jesus is speaking in the present passage. When our soul's deep need has been satisfied we are delivered forever from the emptiness and dissatisfaction that are an inevitable part of the life of the worldly, who may rebel from time to time. They attempt to find alternative lifestyles in the face of the frustration and the futility of so much in modern communities. But in the end such rebellion is rarely successful. As Augustine put it in his prayer: "Thou hast made us for Thyself and our hearts are restless till they rest in Thee." It is in this sense that our need is met in Christ. We still long for more and more knowledge of him. But the world's restlessness has gone forever.

The Will of God

Jesus has been speaking of the wonderful gift of life that those who come to him receive. Now his "but" introduces a strong contrast (v. 36). Those to whom he was speaking had not believed in him, had not come to him, and accordingly they had not received the life he was offering. He says that he had "told" them, though it is not clear when. Some think he is referring to verse 26, but it is perhaps more likely that he is speaking of some quite different (and unrecorded) occasion. What he emphasizes is that they saw him, as indeed they were still seeing him, but they did not understand who it was they were seeing. For them he was just another man, and they put no trust in him. Their failure to believe was the critical factor that cut them off from the blessing he was offering.

Perhaps the reason was that they were not included in "all that the Father gives me" (v. 37). There is mystery here. The New Testament consistently teaches that our salvation is the gift of God. It is not that we do something and then God is able to do something. It is not that God stands on the sidelines, a helpless spectator until we decide that we would like to believe, and only then does he come into the process. No one can come to Jesus unless the Father draws him (v. 44). From first to last our salvation is something that God brings about. That is what is in mind when Scripture refers to predestination. It is the divine activity that is the first and most significant thing.

But, along with this, Scripture affirms our responsibility. We are called on to repent and believe. We are warned that those who do not put their trust in Christ will inevitably perish. Nowhere do the Bible writers give the impression that the saved are just automatons, moving like puppets when the strings are pulled. We are responsible people and must one day give account of ourselves.

Both these truths receive emphasis, but nowhere, I think, do the Bible writers attempt to bring them together. That is not one of the things that has been revealed. And Christian theologians have not been conspicuously successful when they try to harmonize them. They usually emphasize one group of passages at the expense of the other. I suspect that the problem is too big for our little minds.

Here Jesus is not giving a reason for the Jews' lack of faith but assuring those who come to him of the warmest of welcomes. When he speaks of what the Father gives, his word *all* is neuter (= "everything") where we might expect the masculine "everyone." The construction (which occurs elsewhere in John) puts emphasis on the universal application of the words. There is no exception. "All," then, that the Father gives to Jesus come to him, but it is the Father's gift that is important. Without that they would not come.

When they come Jesus always receives them. Again we have an emphatic double negative: "him who comes to me I will certainly not cast out." We may come in confidence, knowing that the Giver and the Receiver of the gift are at one.

In this world this is not so. There was the small boy who just after Christmas went to Macy's in New York to exchange a doll that had been given him as a Christmas present for some water pistols. There was no problem with the exchange, but the assistant asked, "Who would give you a doll?" To which the boy replied, "My uncle. He always does. He thinks I'm a niece!" We constantly make misjudgments of one sort or another, and our gifts do not always work out as we would like. John is telling us that this is not so with the Father and the Son. When God's gift is made to the Son it is always received. "I will certainly not cast him out."

Such casting out is unthinkable because the whole reason for the incarnation was that the Father's will be done. We should not think of Jesus as somehow setting up his will as something distinct from that of the Father and then going ahead to do what his own will suggested. No. He came to do the will of the Father. There is no disunity there.

The divine will is further explained. Not only does Jesus not reject anyone who comes to him, but he sees to it that no such person is lost. This is the will of God, and because it is the will of God Jesus sees to it that it is done. We should be clear that there is no disunity in the Godhead and that our salvation is a matter in which both Father and Son are involved. Sometimes in the history of the church believers have overstressed the activity of one or the other. Some have been so impressed with the love of the Father that they have given the impression that all that is necessary for our salvation is that we repent and believe. God will not let us down. And Jesus is not brought into the picture at all.

Others have gone to the opposite extreme. They have seen God as a mighty God, a righteous Judge who will certainly punish all sinners. Since we are certainly sinners, that means that we are in trouble. Into that picture comes the compassionate Son who interposes himself between the wrathful Judge and the doomed people. We are saved from the Judge because the Son loved us enough to die for us and take on himself the consequences of our sin.

Both these pictures are caricatures of what Scripture says. It is God who so loved the world that he sent his Son. And it is Christ who died on the cross for our salvation. When we believe, it is the Father who has chosen us and drawn us and the Son who never casts us out. We should be clear that both the Persons are involved in the work of salvation. It is the will of God, who sent his Son into the world, that none of those he gives to the Son be lost.

This is all sheer grace. It is not like the lawyer who was rather fond of lecturing his son. The young man, in pursuit of his aim to be a lawyer, in due course worked for his dad during vacation periods. One day the father happened to overhear the lad talking to one of his friends. "I hear you'll be working for your father these holidays," said the friend. "How much is he paying you?" "Three thousand dollars" was the reply. "Seventy bucks a week and the rest in legal advice."

God's good gift is not like that. In his grace he freely gives to sinners what they could never merit, never obtain from their own resources. He gives freely, generously, without finding fault.

The Last Day

Jesus says that he will raise up the saved person on "the last day" (v. 40). He speaks about the last day several times in this chapter (vv. 39, 40, 44, 54); it is an expression found only in John in the New Testament. John puts a good deal of emphasis on present salvation and present judgment. He sees both as operative in the world here and now, and from this some have drawn the conclusion that he is interested only in the here and now. It may well be that he sees more importance in what happens in this life than do some other writers, but it is a mistake to think that this is all he is concerned with. We saw when we were looking at chapter 5 that he looks for a day when Christ will call the dead from the tombs. And here he is sure of a day that will end this world and usher in the life to come. He is equally sure that the believer has nothing to fear when that day comes. Jesus will raise him up, and he will go in to the fullness of the life of the world to come. Far from salvation in this world being all that there is, John looks forward to the end of the world and to Jesus as the one who will raise the redeemed and bring them into life eternal.

This part of his Gospel is greatly taken up with the will of God, and it comes out again here. Life eternal is the will of God. Jesus spoke previously of God as having sent him, now as "my Father." The two, of course, go together. It is because he is the Father (with all that this means) that he sent the Son. It is because he sent the Son that we see what it means that he is the Father.

The saved person here is the one "who sees the Son and believes in him." It is not common to have "seeing" connected with salvation. The Jews were earlier blamed for having "seen" Jesus and not having believed (v. 36). They saw Jesus but they did not appreciate the significance of Jesus. It may be something like this that is meant here. Jesus wants people to see him for who he is, to have the heavenly vision that is inseparably linked to faith. With the grace of God at work, and with this vision and this faith, the result is life eternal. And as in the previous verse this is linked with being raised on the last day. The resurrection of believers is important, and Jesus repeats it. Eternal life is wonderful here and now. But we should not think that its meaning is exhausted in this life. Its full unfolding awaits the life of the world to come.

29

The Flesh and the Blood

"This is the bread that comes down from heaven in order that anyone may eat of it and not die. I am the living bread that came down from heaven. If anyone eats of this bread he will live forever and the bread that I will give is my flesh, for the life of the world." The Jews therefore began to argue among themselves, "How can this fellow give us his flesh to eat?" So Jesus said to them, "Truly, truly, I tell you, unless you eat the flesh of the Son of man and drink his blood you have no life in you. He who eats my flesh and drinks my blood has life eternal and I will raise him up at the last day. For my flesh is true food and my blood is true drink. He who eats my flesh and drinks my blood abides in me and I in him. As the living Father sent me and I live because of the Father, so he who eats me, that one will live because of me. This is the bread that came down from heaven, not such as the fathers ate and they died. He who eats this bread will live forever" (John 6:50–58).

Throughout this discourse Jesus has continually referred to himself as "bread," and here the thought is that, in contrast to the manna by which the Jews set such store, he came from heaven. Despite the fact that the Jews spoke of the manna as "bread from heaven," it was not genuinely from heaven. It did not exist in heaven before they received it. It could be spoken of in terms of heaven only in the sense that it was God, the supreme heavenly Being, who sent it to them. But its entire existence was here on earth. Its total function was to sustain earthly life, and it did even that only partly, for the whole wilderness generation (with the exceptions of Joshua and Caleb) died before they reached the Promised Land.

Jesus is bringing out the fact that his hearers had some serious misconceptions about the manna. They did not understand its limitations: those who ate it necessarily died in due course. It only delayed death. And they did not understand that the gift he was offering them was incomparably greater: those who received it would never die. It overcame death. Jesus says that the bread of which he is speaking came down from heaven "in order that" *(hina)* those who eat it may not die (v. 50). That bread is given in order that it may be eaten.

We must not think that it does not matter to God whether people are saved or not. It is the very purpose of his sending of the Son that people enter life. So now Jesus says that his coming to earth is for the purpose of bringing people into salvation. The meaning of "die" here is different from that of the same verb in verse 49. There the point is that in the wilderness the manna was not able to sustain life indefinitely. Those who ate it died in due course. But the bread of life of which Jesus speaks is different. Those who eat this bread have eternal life. They never die. They do, of course, die in the sense that they complete this earthly, physical life. But their reception of the bread of life means that they have been given the life that is eternal, the life that goes on in the age to come and never has an ending, the life that is of a different quality from ordinary, worldly life, for it is the life proper to the age to come. In the sense of spiritual death they will not die.

Once again Jesus speaks of himself as "the living bread" (v. 51) though this time with a slight difference, for he speaks of the bread as "living," and not of "the bread of life." In this Gospel there are many occasions when a word or a phrase is repeated with some slight change but with no apparent difference in meaning. It is a mark of John's style; that is the way he writes. So we should not look for any great significance in the fact that he now speaks of "living" bread, whereas he previously referred to "the bread of life." It perhaps ties in the thought that life is specially associated with Jesus (cf. 1:4; 5:26) a little more clearly, but we can scarcely say more. To eat of this bread is to live forever. We have here a typical example of Johannine emphasis. In verse 50 he says will "not die"; here it is will "live forever." He puts the negative and the positive side by side to reinforce one another in such a way as to leave no doubt about the point he is making. The living bread means to its recipient life and not death. Let there be no misunderstanding about this. The kind of life of which the Jews were thinking is not life in the full sense. The kind of life Jesus was offering is.

"Flesh"

Now comes one of Jesus' "hard" sayings: "the bread that I will give is my flesh" (v. 51). It would have been easier for the Jews (and for us) if the bread of which Jesus is speaking were to be understood in a purely "spiritual" way. Then we could think that Jesus is claiming to be a prophet, one who comes with a heavenly message, such that those who receive it will have a profound spiritual experience and find themselves alive with a vibrant new form of existence. There is, of course, a measure of truth in this, but it is not what Jesus is saying. He uses the harsh, strongly physical word *flesh*. He could have said "my body," as he did when he began the service of Holy Communion. He could have said "myself." But he chose to use the word *flesh*, which puts a strong emphasis on this physical corporeality. It was this body of flesh that Jesus would give for the life of the world.

Some see a reference to the Holy Communion here, but it is not easy to see this in the words Jesus used. As we will see a little later, this is not the way the early church referred to that sacrament. Jesus is referring to Calvary, not to any liturgical service, no matter how solemn.

He will give his flesh, he says, "for the life of the world." The preposition "for," *huper*, is one over which there has been a good deal of dispute. Some scholars hold that it means no more than "on behalf of," and they contrast it with *anti*, "in place of." But this is too simple. There is no doubt that *huper* can be used in the general sense of "on behalf of." It is used in this way, for example, when Jesus says, "Pray for those who persecute you" (Matt. 5:44), or that he who is not against us is "for us" (Mark 9:40).

But the word can convey a substitutionary meaning, as when one person does something "in the place of" someone else. This is common in the papyri, when one person says he is writing *huper* another. The second person is illiterate; he cannot write the letter himself, so someone else writes it in his place and in his name. However we choose to translate it, in such a context it means substitution. This usage is undoubtedly found in the New Testament, for example when Paul writes to Philemon and speaks of Onesimus serving *huper sou*, "in your place" (Philem. 13).

There seems not the slightest doubt that John has this usage. He tells us that the Good Shepherd gives his life "for the sheep" (10:11, 15). He reports the words of Caiaphas that it is expedient that one man die "in the place of the people" (11:50) and goes on to explain that in this way the high priest prophesied that Jesus would die "for the people . . . and not for the people only" (11:51–52) but in order to gather together God's people into one. John reminds his readers of this when he characterizes Caiaphas as he who said it was expedient that one should die in the place of the people (18:14). He has Peter's statement that he would lay down his life "for" Jesus if need be (13:37) and Jesus' question with the same expression (13:38). He tells us that Jesus said there is no greater love than to lay down one's life for one's friends (15:13) and that the Lord in his prayer spoke of sanctifying himself "for" his own (17:19).

From all this there seems to be no doubt at all that John sometimes uses the preposition in a substitutionary sense. That is the way we should take it in the present passage. When Jesus gives his flesh "for" the life of the world he is speaking of his death in the place of sinners, that death that would give life to the world.

Not surprisingly, the Jews found this a difficult saying. However, there was not unanimous opposition, for they "argued" or "disputed" among themselves (v. 52). It was not easy to see how Jesus could die "for the life of the world," and some of them spoke of him contemptuously as "this fellow." If anyone could do something "for the world," they apparently thought, it would not be this man. So they argued.

Eating the Flesh and Drinking the Blood

This led Jesus to repeat what he had just said, but in a stronger form. He prefixes what he has to say with "truly, truly," which we have seen before is a way of putting emphasis on what follows and marking it out as important and significant. He goes on to speak not simply of his giving of his flesh or of their eating the bread of life, but of eating his flesh and drinking his blood (v. 53). This is the sort of thing that would arouse horror in a pious Jew, who would not even eat meat in his daily food unless the blood had been drained from the carcass. But Jesus says that apart from this eating and drinking there is no life. It is a strong and emphatic statement.

This passage is held by many to refer to the Holy Communion. John has no account of the institution of this service, but his language in this part of the Gospel, with its references to eating the flesh and drinking the blood, seems to many people to be so much like the language of the communion service that this must be the equivalent. They think that for reasons of his own John has omitted the institution but has given his teaching about the sacrament in this chapter. Usually no evidence is cited for this. It is taken as axiomatic; the language is held to apply obviously to the communion service, and that is all there is to it.

But there are difficulties with this position. One is that, despite the confident assertions, the language is not that of the Holy Communion. There one reads of eating the body, here of eating the flesh. The difference may not be great but it is real. The early church did not speak of "flesh" in the communion service, but of the "body." It is sometimes said that Ignatius used "flesh" in this connection, but not much can be made of this because of the way this gentleman used language. Thus he says, "I desire the bread of God, which is the flesh of Christ," which many take to refer to the communion. But Ignatius goes on immediately, "and for a draught I desire his blood, which is love incorruptible." The language looks like the communion at first, but the context is concerned with martyrdom, not liturgy, and in any case the ending shows that Ignatius is simply using metaphors to bring out spiritual truth.

There is a similar problem with his statement that "the eucharist is the flesh of our Savior Jesus Christ," which looks explicit enough. But then Ignatius says, ". . . which flesh suffered for our sins, and which the Father of his goodness raised up." He also speaks of the gospel as "the flesh of Jesus" and of faith as "the flesh of the Lord." It is clear that Ignatius does not use "flesh" as a way of referring to the communion. He uses it in a wide variety of ways, most of which are metaphorical.

The Christian writers of antiquity tend to use "flesh" as a way of referring to the incarnation, as when Justin Martyr spoke of Christ as "having been made flesh by the Word of God." When they refer to the Holy Communion they speak of the "body" of Christ. I do not mean that no example at all can be found of the use of "flesh" in this connection. I mean that such usages are very hard to find and must be thought of as distinctly exceptional. We cannot take the use of "flesh" in John 6 as obviously a reference to the communion. It would be a most unusual way of referring to the sacrament, one completely without parallel in the New Testament and extremely hard to document in the early church.

Even more significant is the strength of Jesus' language. He says that without the eating and drinking of which he speaks "you have no life." It is very difficult indeed to think that Jesus is saying that the one thing necessary for eternal life is to receive the Holy Communion. That would be out of harmony with his teaching in all four Gospels. But here his language is unqualified in any way. He allows of no exception. This is the one way into life. To take the sacramental view of this passage is to say something very serious, for it would disqualify from eternal life whole communities like the Salvation Army and the Quakers and a significant proportion of Christian families, and children who have not yet been admitted to Holy Communion. Those who accept the view I am criticizing should examine the calamitous consequences of their interpretation.

They should also bear in mind that the Jews of that day often used the language of eating and drinking when they wanted to refer to taking teaching into their innermost being. It is easy to listen to a teacher's words in a superficial way. We may say, "What a fine teacher!" but take no notice of what he says. We may perhaps say of someone who profits from the teaching that he takes to heart what he has heard: the Jews of the day spoke of eating or drinking the teaching (do we not sometimes also speak of "drinking in every word"?). For example, there is a rabbinic treatment of Proverbs 25:21: "If your enemy is hungry, give him food to eat; if he is thirsty, give him water to drink." This is said to mean: Resist your enemy "with the bread of the Torah [i.e., the Law of God], as you read 'Come, eat of my bread' (Prov. 9:5); and 'if he be thirsty, give him water to drink'—the water of the Torah, as in the verse, 'Ho, everyone that thirsteth, come ye for water' (Isa. 55:1)." Such statements could be multiplied. The word of God is often likened to food or drink, which must be taken within oneself.

Jesus is then using language that people would appreciate and understand as something quite different from Holy Communion. He has already spoken in this discourse of people coming to him as the bread of life (v. 35) and of believing in him (vv. 40, 47), and he is saying much the same when he invites his hearers to take him into their innermost being. There is the addition in this part of his address that the separation of flesh and blood points to his death, as do different words in 3:16. He is saying that he will die for the people and inviting people to feed on him in a heavenly and spiritual manner.

Those who here see a reference to Holy Communion do not explain why Jesus should have given teaching about that sacrament to a group of Jews who were largely antagonistic to him, and moreover why he should have given it long before he instituted the service. They could not possibly have understood him, and Jesus surely intended his audience to understand what he was saying.

Life

For such reasons, then, we must reject the view that Jesus was talking about the Lord's Supper in this passage. We could say that he was speaking of how people should receive him and that when we understand this we can say that this, too, is how we should receive him when we receive the communion, i.e., by faith. But we can scarcely say more.

Jesus is saying, then, that his death is the one means of salvation and that we appropriate his dying for us when we come to him in faith. That is the one way of salvation, for unless we receive him in this way we "have no life" in us (v. 53). This is a strong and emphatic statement. The cross is at the heart of the Christian way, and it is only by the death of Jesus that we are able to enter into the life he died to bring.

In a way characteristic of this Gospel we have the negative, "unless you eat . . . and drink . . . you have no life," followed by the positive, "He who eats my flesh and drinks my blood has life eternal" (v. 54). The twofold form of expression puts emphasis on the truth being stated. We are left in no doubt that the life of which Jesus is speaking comes only in this one way. Without the eating and drinking, we have no life. If we eat and drink, we have life. That is the great, central truth that Jesus is bringing out throughout this entire discourse.

There is a different verb for "eat" in this verse, and we see it again in verses 56, 57, 58. Strictly it applies to a noisy eating, like "munch," and some have held that it must mean a literal feeding and thus refer to Holy Communion. But this makes no sense. It is nonsense to say that the word means literal eating and that therefore we must understand eating the flesh of Jesus to mean eating the communion bread. The communion bread is not literally the flesh of Jesus. To hold that it is his flesh is to abandon the literal meaning. John often uses words of similar meaning without significant difference of meaning, and we must see the same thing here. The change of verb is a point of style, not a change of meaning.

"I will raise him up at the last day," Jesus says (v. 54). In much of this Gospel there is the precious truth that eternal life is something that we enjoy right now. It is a very wonderful part of the Christian way that the moment we believe we enter into life and that in this eternal life we have the constant presence of God with us, whatever our circumstances. It has been the strength of many a Christian in troubled circumstances that he knows that God is with him and will never leave him. That is true and it is important. But it is not the whole story. John also has the thought that at the last day Christ will raise all his people, and he has that thought here.

True Food

Jesus goes on to say that his flesh is "true food" and his blood "true drink" (v. 55). There have always been people who have offered as spiritual sustenance that which does not sustain. In this very chapter we read of people who suggested that the manna that came down in Moses' time was bread from heaven and that if Jesus really was the

Messiah, he would provide bread like this. But the manna was not food for the soul; it did not give eternal life. In the fullest sense it was not "true" food. It sustained the body but did nothing for the soul. The bread that Jesus is offering is different. It is the true food that we all need and that will sustain us eternally if we receive it.

Yet once more Jesus refers to eating his flesh and drinking his blood, this time connecting it with the thought of abiding (v. 56). John delights in the language of "abiding" and has the verb forty times in all. We see something of how important it is to him when we notice that Matthew has this verb three times, Mark twice, and Luke seven times. Clearly it is an aspect of Christianity that appealed to John and to which he kept coming back. It is important that Christians do not simply have a fleeting contact with Jesus but that we "abide" in him, just as he "abides" in us. We do not know what life has in store for us. There may be wonderfully happy experiences or terribly depressing ones before us. We have no way of knowing. But we do know that as our trust is in Christ we will always be in him and he will always be in us. That will increase our joy in the happy experiences, and it will give us strength in our times of difficulty. John's thought of abiding is a part of Christianity that we cannot do without.

This leads on to another characteristic Johannine thought, that of mission. The living Father sent Christ (v. 57). This runs through this whole Gospel, though not usually with that exact language. But Jesus is speaking about life, and it helps us to see that God is "the living Father." We are not to think of some dead idol, but of the living God, who is himself alive and is the source of all the life that others live. We are alive physically only because the living God gives us physical life, and we are alive spiritually only because the living God gives us spiritual life. That living Father is so interested in giving us spiritual life that he sent his Son into the world to live and to die for us.

Jesus says that he lives "because of the Father." This may be understood in more ways than one. There is the sense that it is the Father who has life in himself and he has given to his Son also to have life in himself (5:26). The life of the Father and the life of the Son are inseparable. There would be no life in the Son if there were no life in the Father. We cannot put a difference between them, for example, by appealing to the one against the other. They belong together.

There is also the sense that on earth the incarnate Son lived to do the will of the Father. That is his necessary food (4:34). It is unthinkable that he should be busy about anything but his Father's business.

Which leads to the thought that this should be our business, too. Notice that Jesus speaks now not of eating his flesh and drinking his blood but of eating him, but the difference in meaning is not great.

There is still the thought of taking him into our innermost being. When we do that we will enter into the experience of living for Christ in the same kind of way that he lives for the Father. Both aspects will be true for us. We owe our spiritual life to him; it is not something we achieve by our own efforts. And when we have that gift of life we will live to do service to Christ. We will live "because of" him.

Jesus ends his discourse by repeating the main thought in a slightly different way (v. 58). His hearers had been obsessed with the manna and wanted the Messiah to bring it down from heaven again. Jesus has told them that they have the wrong idea, and he does so again. The bread from heaven is not the manna. Israel of old had that food and Israel of old died in the wilderness. The true bread from heaven of which Jesus has been speaking throughout this discourse is different. Anyone who eats this bread "will live forever." Real bread from heaven has nothing to do with the sustaining of physical life, as his hearers wrongly thought. It is concerned with something infinitely more important: eternal life, life that is a wonderful gift of God now and that will gleam and glow through all eternity.

30

The Spirit Gives Life

Many of his disciples, therefore, having heard this said, "This saying is a hard one; who can hear it?" But Jesus, knowing in himself that his disciples were muttering about this, said to them: "Does this trouble you? If then you see the Son of man going up where he was before—? It is the Spirit who gives life; the flesh profits nothing at all. The words that I have spoken to you are spirit and they are life. But there are some among you who do not believe." For Jesus knew from the beginning who they were who would not believe and who it was who would betray him. And he said, "For this reason I told you that no one can come to me unless it be given him from my Father."

From this many of his disciples went away backward and no longer walked with him. Jesus therefore said to the Twelve, "You don't want to go away, do you?" Simon Peter answered him, "Lord, to whom should we go? You have words of life eternal and we have believed and have known that you are the Holy One of God." Jesus answered them, "Did not I choose you, the Twelve? And one of you is a devil." He was speaking about Judas, son of Simon Iscariot, for this man was going to betray him, being one of the Twelve (John 6:60–71).

Let us begin this study by noticing that John often speaks of "Jesus' disciples" or "his disciples" or the like, and that this is a mark of earliness. When Jesus was alive there were all sorts of rabbis who had disciples, so those who followed him were marked off from all others by some expression that showed that they were following him and not someone else. When the church had settled down and Christians spoke of "disciples," there was no need to say whose disciples they were, "*the* disciples" being, as Bernard puts it, "a Christian phrase which no one would mistake." The earlier expression is found at times in all the Gospels, and John almost invariably has it.

Many disciples found what Jesus had been saying in the discourse about the bread of life a "hard" saying. This probably means "hard to accept" rather than "hard to understand." Some of the sermon is not easy to comprehend, but the real difficulty does not lie there. As Calvin put it, "The hardness was in their hearts and not in the saying." They had their own ideas about the way to God and they were not going to be shaken out of it.

I am reminded of the very modern boy who went off to Sunday school. When he came home his mother asked what he had learned. "Well," he said, "we had a story about Moses. God sent him behind the enemy lines to rescue the Israelites from the Egyptians. When they got to the Red Sea Moses called for the engineers to build a pontoon bridge to get them across. When they were all over Moses saw the Egyptian tanks coming. Quick as a flash he sent headquarters a message on his walkie-talkie radio, asking them to send dive bombers to blow up the bridge. They did and the Israelites were saved."

His rather dazed mother inquired, "Is that really the way your teacher told the story?"

"Well, not exactly," admitted her offspring, "but if I told it the way she did, you'd never believe it!"

We're all inclined to be a little bit like that. We have a firm idea of how God should act, and we persist in seeing his actions the way we imagine them instead of listening to what in fact he has chosen to do. That was the way it was with Jesus' hearers that day in Capernaum. They were sure of the way God acted. Were not they and all the Jews the people of God? Had he not sent his prophets to their nation? Did they not have fine official interpreters of his word? Jesus, they thought, could not possibly be believed when what he said contradicted their understanding of the way God acts. They did not say all this openly, but "muttered" to themselves (as is still often the way with the discontented). But Jesus knew.

The Son of Man Going Up

"Does this trouble you?" he asked (v. 61), where his verb is a picturesque one taken from the practice of trapping birds or animals. The trap would be set with a stick (called a *skandalon*) propping it open.

When the bird sat on the stick and moved it the trap was triggered off and the capture made. The verb *skandalizo* means "to trigger off the trap," and it is this verb that is used here (as in a number of places in the New Testament; it is difficult to find a satisfactory English equivalent, and there are many suggestions: "to cause to stumble," "to offend," and others). Matthew and Mark have this verb often, but John has it only twice (again in 16:1). Jesus perceived that what he had said meant trouble, not enlightenment, to his hearers. They would not accept it; they could not imagine that Jesus was in fact the one way of salvation. So they did not accept what he was saying. They found his words too difficult.

Jesus poses a question for them (v. 62), and there is a problem for us in that he does not complete it. Evidently they were able to fill in the missing bit whereas we, from a different background, find it hard to do so. Our translations put in something to make the sentence grammatical in English. Thus the King James Version inserts "What": "What and if ye shall see . . . ?" (similar are NIV, JB, NEB, RSV; GNB has "Suppose, then, that you should see . . . ?). But Jesus says no more than "If then you see . . . ." but leaves his hearers to work out for themselves what would be the result of their seeing. He speaks of the Son of man "going up where he was before." This must refer to his going back to heaven, for Jesus has made it clear in the discourse just ended that he came down from heaven (vv. 33, 38, 41, 42, 50, 51, 58). There seem to be two possibilities. He may be saying in effect, "If you see me returning to heaven, will you not be troubled even further?" Or he may be saying, "If you see me returning to heaven, will not that solve your difficulty?" But there are problems with each interpretation.

Both seem to refer to the ascension, but John does not record this. And if we turn to Luke's accounts of the ascension, it is plain that it was not seen by very many and evidently was not intended to be seen by the public at large. It was apparently meant to give encouragement to the disciples, not to bring conviction to unbelievers. So it is hard to think that Jesus means that the ascension, as such, will be the means of persuading these unbelievers of the truth of his words. But it is not much easier to think that he is saying that the ascension would bring them more trouble. Why should it?

Perhaps we should see the "going up where he was before" as a kind of shorthand summary of the climax of Jesus' way of saving us. It would then include the cross, the resurrection, and the ascension in one great saving act that culminated when Jesus went back to where he was before. This would make it easier to see their being troubled, for to unbelievers it was only the cross that registered. They could not conceive of anyone who was crucified as having the approval of God.

Rather, they thought of crucified people as being accursed (in accordance with Deut. 21:23).

Neither view is completely satisfactory. But we should bear in mind that it is only when Jesus has died for sinners and risen and been exalted to heaven again that we can see him for what he really is. Until then, people could have no more than a partial view of who he was and what he stood for. Unbelievers would see the cross and stop there. It was necessary to believe, if people were to see that the cross leads on to the resurrection and the ascension. And it was necessary to believe, if people were to understand what "the living bread that came down from heaven" means. Whatever else Jesus' words mean, they are a reminder that faith is necessary if we are to understand what he is saying and doing. And they are an appeal for that faith.

The Spirit and the Life

Jesus' next words pose a difficulty of a different sort. He speaks of "Spirit" and "flesh" (v. 63), and this would lead us to think of the contrast between our spirits and our bodies. But he speaks of the Spirit as giving life, and that must mean the Holy Spirit, for our human spirits do not give life. But Jesus also speaks of his "words," and this may point to the "spirit" of what he is saying, as against the literal meaning of the words. Plainly several contrasts are possible, and it seems likely that John expects his readers to see more than one of them.

It is clear in the first place that Jesus is saying that life is the gift of the Holy Spirit. This is in accordance with, say chapter 3, with its insistence on the necessity for being born of water and the Spirit, or simply born of the Spirit. It forms a marked contrast with that aspect of rabbinic teaching that insists that it is the Law that gives life. Thus we read, "Great is the Law, for it gives life to them that practice it both in this world and the world to come" (Mishnah, *Aboth* 6:7). Jesus is saying that life is a gift from God. We have life in the most meaningful sense only when the Spirit of God works within us to produce that life. This is a thought to which John gives expression a number of times (see 3:5f., 8; 4:23f.; 7:38f.), and it is of central importance. People always like to think that they can bring about their own salvation by their own efforts. But it cannot be done. The whole purpose of Jesus' coming to earth was to undo the effect of our sins, and the eternal life he made available to us is effected by the work of the Spirit. The "flesh," which is the best of which we are naturally capable, "profits nothing at all." There is no life in it.

Jesus goes on to speak of his words as "spirit" and as "life" (there is a somewhat similar connection in 3:34). We are not to think that a wooden literalism is the way to profit from Jesus' words. We should not take the attitude to them that the Jews so often took toward the Law. But his words, rightly received, bring about the wonderful transformation. As we take in Jesus' words, see them as they are, the words of God (8:26, 28; 12:49f.; etc.), and respond to them, we find new life from the working of the Spirit within us. It is only as we accept the words of Jesus that we know the life that the Spirit gives.

There is an unusual repetition of the verb *are* in this verse. We would have expected "are spirit and life," but we have "are spirit and are life." This means that "spirit" and "life" are not to be regarded as the same thing. They are distinct. It also means that there is some emphasis on "are." Jesus is talking about facts. We should not take the expression to justify a scheme of allegorical interpretation. This has been beloved by many pious people through the centuries, and it is astonishing what meanings some still find in the Bible by allegorizing difficult passages. Jesus is not justifying such approaches. He is saying that his words are creative. Take them as they are meant and they bring about new life in the believer. The Spirit and the words of Jesus are to be seen as in the closest connection.

Unbelievers

But while Jesus thus offers eternal life to those who hear him, he knows that there are unbelievers listening to him (v. 64). They will not respond. The life of which he has been speaking is not for such people. But these words show that the fact that some did not believe did not take Jesus by surprise. He knew that this would be so, and he knew who they were who would not believe.

It is a little surprising that John says at this point that Jesus knew who would betray him. The thrust of the discourse has been on life, on Jesus as the bread of life, and on the importance of receiving him, of believing in him, of eating his flesh and drinking his blood. All this makes it clear that the life of which Jesus speaks is not a gift made to all. Believing is of fundamental importance. And it is important that Jesus was not deceived by an outward profession. He accepted Judas into the apostolic band, but that does not mean that he did not know what sort of person Judas was.

The problem of Jesus' knowledge in this Gospel is not an easy one. Sometimes it is clear that he did not have knowledge of a particular point and asked a question to find out (e.g., 1:38; 18:34). But on other occasions he had unusual knowledge (e.g., his knowledge of the woman of Samaria's five husbands, 4:18). It seems that his perfect humanity meant that there were areas in which, like all mankind, he was ignorant and had to find out in the same way as others. But there were areas of life in which his unique mission demanded unique knowledge, and such knowledge was given to him. So now we find that he knew who would not believe and specifically knew of Judas's future treachery. Judas would surprise the apostolic band in due course, but he would not surprise Jesus.

This brings us to a repetition of the thought we met earlier in this discourse, that it is not a human achievement to come to God (v. 65; see v. 44). Left to ourselves we continue in our sin. It is only as God does a work of grace in us that we have the desire and the strength to turn away from evil and respond to the message of salvation. People come to Jesus, not because they are gifted with unusual spiritual perception, but because it is "given" them from the Father. The whole of our salvation, from start to finish, is a gift of God.

Backsliders

"From this" (v. 66) is ambiguous. It may mean "from this time" or it may mean "arising from this," "because of this." Either makes good sense and perhaps, in the Johannine manner, both are in mind. Up till this time there had been many who had followed Jesus. Here was a new teacher with some fascinating things to say. And he did some amazing miracles. He was certainly worth following. So the crowds were there. But this last discourse has made it abundantly clear that Jesus was not just another rabbi. He did not teach in the way people expected, and in particular his claim to have a special relationship to God and to be the only one who could bring life to sinners proved a stumbling block to many of his hearers. So they ceased to applaud and simply left him. They were not the genuine article and did not appreciate teaching from God when they heard it.

Knowing the genuine article is not always easy. There was an art student who was a bit lost in an exhibition of abstract and cubist works. But he felt that he should get something out of such a fine exhibition to improve his collection and further his acquaintance with this form of art. Some pieces did not appeal to him and some were out of his price range. But then his eye lighted on a work of striking simplicity. There was a black dot on a field of white, framed in brass. He hailed an attendant and asked, "How much is that?" "That, sir, is not for sale," the attendant replied. "It's the light switch."

It is easy to be pretentious without having a genuine appreciation. It was that way with some of the people who followed Jesus. But when in the end they found out something of what he was driving at they left him. John says they "no longer walked with him," which gives us a little glimpse of Jesus' peripatetic ministry. He walked with his disciples. But these people ceased to walk with him.

The Twelve

That raised the question of how far this movement of backsliding was going to go. So Jesus asked the Twelve whether they wanted to join it (v. 67). In Greek it is possible to put a question in such a way as to show whether a negative or a positive answer is expected, and Jesus' question looks for the answer "No." He was confident of his close followers. He looked to them to remain, and though the question had to be asked in view of the defections, he expressed in it his expectation that they would remain. His "you" is emphatic: "Whatever be the case with others, *you* will not go away, will you?" is the thrust of it.

The question is addressed to them all, but as often happened it is Peter who is the spokesman. He has a question of his own, "Lord, to whom should we go?" (v. 68). He and the other apostles had had enough experience of Jesus by this time to be sure that they did not want anyone else. It was unthinkable that they should abandon their fellowship with him for anything else on earth. Jesus had spoken of his words as life-giving, and Peter shows that he and his friends had understood this: "You have words of life eternal." The words that repelled the halfhearted followers were full of meaning to committed believers, and they pointed to a life with Jesus that believers could not think of abandoning.

Peter goes further. "And we have believed and have known," he says, "that you are the Holy One of God" (v. 69). He uses the emphatic pronoun *we:* whatever be the case with others, *we* have believed. The Twelve have made their decision. In both the following verbs Peter uses the perfect tense. The thrust of this is that they have come to a place of faith and they remain in it; they have come to a state of knowledge and remain in it. Peter is emphasizing the certainty he and his friends had, a certainty of both faith and knowledge. They had put their trust in Jesus, and that meant that they would not abandon him as these halfhearted people had done. Their loyalty was beyond question. They also had knowledge. When people come to know Christ they have a piece of knowledge beyond price. To know him is to lose the uncertainties that are so much a part of worldliness.

"The Holy One of God" is a most unusual expression. In fact, it is used of Jesus on only one other occasion, when a demon-possessed man used it in the synagogue at Capernaum (Mark 1:24; Luke 4:34). It occurs occasionally in the Old Testament, as when Aaron is spoken of in a similar way (Ps. 106:16), but it reminds us of the frequent expression "the Holy One of Israel," which is a way of referring to God. There cannot be the slightest doubt that as Peter used it he gave it the fullest possible meaning. It was a way of showing that he and his friends put Jesus in the highest place they knew. This is one of the high points of John's whole Gospel.

Judas

Jesus knew that what Peter said was true, but that it was not true of the whole Twelve. These were the men that Jesus had chosen, and the implication is that they, of all people, might be expected to be faithful. But even here all was not sweetness and light. "One of you is a devil" (v. 70). John speaks of Judas as having his place in Satan's schemes (13:2) and of Satan as entering him as he went about the betrayal (13:27). He was clear that Judas acted in such a way as to set forward the purposes of evil; he was not wholeheartedly committed to Jesus even though he was numbered among the Twelve.

John adds his own words of explanation. He tells us that Jesus was speaking about Judas, and he speaks of him as "son of Simon Iscariot" (v. 71). The word *Iscariot* is apparently a place name meaning "Man of Kerioth," and it thus applies equally to Judas and to his father. We know of two Kerioths, one in Judah (Josh. 15:25) and another in Moab (Jer. 48:24). Either way it would mean that Judas was not a Galilean, apparently the only one of the Twelve of whom this could be said.

John adds his reference to the betrayal, not implying that Judas had this in mind so early, but as saying that the thing that marked Judas out was the fact that in the end he betrayed Jesus. In the Greek there is a touch of certainty about it. That is what Judas would do in due course. The enormity of this is brought out with the words "being one of the Twelve." It was bad enough that anyone should betray Jesus, but that one from this intimate group should do it is horrible beyond words. It is worth noticing that this is the worst thing any of the Evangelists says about Judas. Nowhere do they speak of him as a wicked villain or anything of the sort. They simply record what he did and let the facts speak for themselves. They are interested in letting their readers know what happened, not in passing their own verdict.

31

The Feast of Tabernacles

After this Jesus was walking in Galilee, for he would not walk in Judea because the Jews were trying to kill him. Now the feast of the Jews, the Feast of Tabernacles, was near. His brothers therefore said to him, "Leave here and go into Judea so that your disciples may see the works that you do, for no one does anything in secret and seeks to be known publicly. If you are doing these things, show yourself to the world." For even his brothers did not believe in him. So Jesus says to them, "My time has not yet come, but your time is always present. The world can't hate you, but it does hate me because I testify about it that its deeds are evil. You go up to the feast; I am not going up to this feast because my time is not yet fulfilled." When he had said these things he remained in Galilee (John 7:1–9).

After this" (really "after these things") gives no indication of how long a time had elapsed; it is an indefinite interval. But the previous chapter has been taken up with what happened at Passover time, and this goes on to the Feast of Tabernacles, which we know took place six months later. John is not trying to give a full account of Jesus' ministry. He selects the incidents that will further his purpose and is quite capable of passing over considerable intervals of time without saying anything about them. He tells us those things that will help us see that Jesus is the Christ, the Son of God, the things that will help us believe (as he tells us in 20:31). And he passes over without comment quite long stretches of Jesus' ministry that do not fit his purpose.

The repeated use of "walking" gives us a little glimpse of the way Jesus lived. His ministry was not confined to any one place and he kept moving among the people. But he traveled in the humblest way: he walked. He did not ride in a chariot or even on a donkey. He walked from place to place and those who traveled with him must walk, too.

Notice further that his walking at this time was done in Galilee, not Judea, on account of the hostility of "the Jews." This avoidance of Judea was not due to lack of courage. When the time came Jesus would go up to Jerusalem and die for us all. But he would do this in his own good time. Till the proper moment he would not rush headlong into danger. That was not the way in which the purpose of the heavenly Father would be set forward. John is not saying that Jesus would not go to Jerusalem at all before it was time for him to die. John will go on in this very chapter to tell us that Jesus did go up to the capital to observe the Feast of Tabernacles. He is saying that Jesus was aware of the dangers that beset him and that he acted accordingly. If he chose to go to Jerusalem at this time, he must do so with proper caution.

John Calvin has an interesting comment. He says that it was not right for Jesus to rush into danger but also that "He did not turn aside a hair's-breadth from the course of His duty." This Calvin sees as having a moral for us as we seek to serve God. We too may have to face danger, and we will be tempted to put a high value on our lives. In such a situation he warns us that "we must always beware that we do not for the sake of life lose the purpose for living." That is good advice still.

John uses the expression "the Jews" in more ways than one. Sometimes it is used in a good sense, as when he says, "Salvation is from the Jews" (4:22), and sometimes it is neutral, as it is here when he speaks of "the feast of the Jews." But mostly he uses it to denote the Jews who were hostile to Jesus, especially the leaders of the Jews in Jerusalem. They were "the Jews" *par excellence*. So it is here, when he speaks of "the Jews" as trying to kill Jesus. This does not mean all the Jews, for Jesus himself was a Jew and so were his disciples and those who followed him. But the Jewish leaders, those who were outstanding Jews, were hostile to Jesus and were the ones who were seeking his death. So Jesus stayed in Galilee.

But the danger was very real. John repeatedly speaks of the attempts being made to kill or arrest Jesus (7:1, 13, 19, 25, 30, 32, 44; 8:37, 40, 59). He has concentrated in these two chapters a good deal of what he has to say about the hostility of the leading Jews to our Lord. It seems that in the early days of his ministry the crowds flocked around Jesus. They loved to listen to the new teacher from Galilee and to see the miracles he did. But then, as we saw in chapter 6, they came to understand something of the demands he made on his followers, and they did not like them. So their ardor cooled. The Jewish leaders saw in Jesus a man who might well claim to be the Messiah and in the process start a rebellion that would bring trouble on the province. So they opposed him vigorously.

We saw at the beginning of this study that it was John's aim to show that Jesus was the Messiah. He seems to have used the Jewish hostility to bring out the objections that were urged to Jesus' messiahship and to show that there were answers to every objection urged. Chapters 7 and 8 are thus an important part of the way John accomplished his aim.

The Feast

John proceeds to tell us that the Feast of Tabernacles was near and speaks of it, not as "a" feast of the Jews, but as "the" feast (v. 2). It was the great occasion in the Jewish festal year. Modern Christians are apt to miss this. The feast about which we hear most in the Gospels is the Passover, and when we read about the feasts in the Old Testament it is Passover that grips our attention. It leads us into the fascinating story of the way God delivered his people from their captivity in Egypt, with the suspense built up through the call of Moses, the series of plagues, and the departure of the people in haste when they had observed the first Passover. There is nothing of the kind in connection with the other feasts in the Jewish ecclesiastical year. The result is that we think of Passover as the outstanding occasion of the year.

But that was not the way it seemed to first-century Jews. They did, of course, delight to observe the Passover. That was a perpetual memorial of God's wonderful deliverance of their fathers and of their emergence as a nation. Nothing should be said that would for one moment diminish the splendor of the occasion. But the high point of their year was not there. It was the Feast of Tabernacles. We see what it meant when we reflect that the Hebrews of the Old Testament were an agricultural people. Their lives were closely bound up in the sequence of the seasons. Passover, it is true, was one of the three great festivals for which males were required to appear before the Lord (Exod. 23:17), but the other two were the Feast of Harvest, when the firstfruits were brought in, and the Feast of Ingathering or Tabernacles, when the harvest was completed (Exod. 23:16). It was the great feast at the culmination of the year's activities. At any earlier time there might be a calamity that would prevent the harvesting of the crops, but Tabernacles marked the successful completion of their labors. The harvest was in the barns; the people could relax and rejoice. It was *the* feast for an agriculture people.

The name "Tabernacles" was due to the custom of celebrating the feast in leafy shelters built for the occasion. These might be in courtyards or on the flat roofs that were so common. Goodspeed translates "the Jewish camping festival," which may help us see something of the attitude people would take to this feast, though we should also bear in mind that it had deep religious significance. It was a thanksgiving for all God's mercies in the harvest and the provision that this meant for all the coming year. Living in temporary shelters put rich and poor on a level while the feast lasted and reminded worshipers that all are of equal status before God.

The feast was primarily a harvest thanksgiving. But other associations developed. There was thanksgiving also for all that God had done for the nation of old throughout the wilderness wanderings. And, with one harvest successfully completed, farmers looked forward to the coming year and used the time of thanksgiving as a time of prayer that God would continue his mercies and send the rain that was needed in the year that lay ahead.

There is a little confusion as to the duration of the feast. It was said to last for seven days (Lev. 23:34; Deut. 16:13, 15), but there is also mention of an eighth day (Lev. 23:36). We should probably understand that originally it went for seven days, but that in time an eighth day was added. But, for whatever length of time it was celebrated, it is clear that it was the high point of the year.

Jesus' Brothers

In time Jesus' brothers came to believe in him, and we find them gathered with the apostles and some believing women soon after the ascension (Acts 1:13–14). But during the time of his ministry they appear to have been very sceptical. Certainly that is the way they were at this time. As the Feast of Tabernacles approached they urged him to go on up to Judea (v. 3). It does not appear that they were sincerely interested in setting forward what he was doing. Apparently they were being sarcastic. They said he should go to Judea so that his disciples might see his "works." That word is often used for Jesus' miracles and is its probable meaning here. The brothers seem to be implying that they know what the "works" are, but that the "disciples" do not. This presents a problem, for there do not appear to be any "works" that the brothers had seen but the disciples had not. Perhaps they are implying that they know Jesus far better than the disciples do. And they know how a public figure should act. He should conform to *their* way of doing things.

I am reminded of the bright young lady who, at a time when it was fashionable for everyone to have a "shrink" of their own, said to a friend, "You've never been to a psychiatrist? You must be crazy!" In this spirit the brothers affirm that they know what Jesus ought to be doing.

Or it may be that they are saying that it is important that Jesus become known in Jerusalem. "If you are going to be a Messiah," their thoughts may run, "then go up to the capital and make your claim. You can't be the Messiah of Israel if you stay in the remote countryside, far from all the centers of population and of power." Their unbelief may be impelling them to urge Jesus to go to the big city where (they thought) his claims would be shown as shams.

They point to the impossibility of acting in secret and expecting to be known publicly (v. 4). They knew enough about what Jesus was doing and about the people who were following him to know that he was making a claim to some public status, be it Messiah or something else. "Let him go to where it counts," they are saying. "No public figure is established in Galilee. Show yourself to the world."

The words could possibly be understood as genuine encouragement. The reader might think that the brothers were urging Jesus to do something that would genuinely set forward his cause. But that would be a misunderstanding, so John adds his little explanation that they did not believe (v. 5). Whatever their motive in saying these things, it was not faith.

Jesus' Time

Jesus declines to do as they say. The brothers do not understand what he is doing; they do not believe in him; their advice does not spring from a sincere desire to forward his mission. Jesus begins by saying that there is a difference between him and them, and he expresses it in terms of "time" (v. 6). His word for "time" is *kairos,* a word that often has about it the idea of "the right time," "the appropriate time." In the first volume of these *Reflections* we saw that there is an impressive series of statements throughout this Gospel that inform the reader that Jesus' "time" or his "hour" had not yet come. These references persist until the eve of the crucifixion, when we find that his hour had come (12:23; 13:1). This saying fits into the series and means in part that Jesus was still pressing on towards that for which he had come into the world. But in the context there will also be the meaning that it was not time for Jesus to go up to the feast in the way the brothers suggested.

Some suggest that we should not see here a reference to the coming of the consummation of Jesus' mission, because John normally uses the word for "hour" for that, not *kairos*. This is so, and the possibility must be kept in mind that he means no more than that Jesus was selecting the most appropriate time to go to Jerusalem. But the contrast with the brothers favors the linking of this passage with those that refer to Jesus' "hour."

It was different for the brothers. Their "time" was always present. They were not sent by God on a mission like Jesus. So they did things when and as it seemed good to them. They neither submitted everything to the plan of God nor accomplished any worthwhile and lasting result.

The World's Hatred

In this matter the brothers line up with the world. They lived their lives in much the same way as the world in general, that world that sets itself in opposition to Jesus and all that he stands for. The world in that sense "can't" hate the brothers (v. 7); they belong to it and share its inability to hear the call of God to mission. The world loves its own (15:19), so the brothers are secure from its hatred. They belong to it.

But Jesus does not. John insists on this over and over again. He is "from above" (3:31); the Father sent him (6:38f.) He came on a mission of salvation (3:17). This is not the way of the world. Indeed, when the world sees what Jesus is doing it hates him. It does not share his love for sinners, his deep concern at the plight into which sin has led them. The world is not prepared for the kind of self-sacrifice that we see on the cross. It knows nothing of winning salvation for others at the cost of one's own life. So it is opposed to Jesus because of what he is and does.

It is opposed to him also because he testifies about it. As we read the Gospels we see this again and again. Jesus did not tolerate the world's evil. He denounced it unsparingly. He called down "woe" on the scribes and Pharisees and did not leave this a general denunciation but singled out specific misdeeds (cf. Matt. 23). There is no harmony between Jesus and "the world" as there is between the brothers and "the world." They cannot appeal to a community of interest because they do not understand what Jesus is doing.

So Jesus declines their invitation and urges them to go up to the feast (v. 8). That was the natural thing for them to do, and they should set about it before it was too late. "I am not going up to this feast," he says, and this presents a problem, because a little later he did go up. It also was a problem for the early Christian scribes, because some of them apparently altered "not" to "not yet" (*ouk* to *oupo*) as they copied out this Gospel. Indeed there are some scholars who accept "not yet" as the right reading, reasoning that as Jesus did in fact go up that must have been what John wrote.

But John's point seems to be that when Jesus went up to Jerusalem he did not go up as one of those who kept the feast. He was not a member of a company of pilgrims who went up together in good time so that they would miss none of the wonderful festivities. He went up privately and of set purpose missed the opening part of the celebrations. He went up, not as a pilgrim, but as the messenger of God. He went up, not to keep the feast, but to deliver the message that God had for him to deliver. The feast was the occasion for the message, not the reason for his journey. It was the means of gathering together those that God intended should hear what Jesus had to say. So, in the sense in which the brothers meant it, Jesus never did go up to this feast. And that is what he means when he says, "I am not going up to this feast."

He adds a reason: "My time is not yet fulfilled." The right moment would come and he would then be there. But his "time" was not the time the brothers suggested. So he stayed in Galilee (v. 9).

The People at the Feast

When his brothers had gone up to the feast then Jesus himself also went up, not publicly but as it were in secret. The Jews then were looking for him at the feast and were saying, "Where is he?" And there was a muttering about him among the crowds. Some people were saying, "He is a good man"; others were saying, "No. But he deceives the people." No one, however, was speaking openly about him for fear of the Jews (John 7:10–13).

At an unspecified time after the brothers went up to the feast, Jesus went up to Jerusalem, too (v. 10). But there was a difference. They went up as pilgrims to keep the feast; he went up incognito. People did not know that he was coming. This does not mean that Jesus traveled stealthily, but that he went by himself without being a member of a party of pilgrims. Such a caravan could be quite large. We are told that when the boy Jesus was separated from Joseph and Mary they spent a whole day looking for him among the company (Luke

2:44). Clearly the pilgrims from Galilee traveled in large groups, and it would be impossible to be inconspicuous in such a group. Jesus went up in such a way that he did not attract attention.

At a feast like Tabernacles crowds of religious Jews went up to the capital to keep the feast, and clearly many in Jerusalem expected that Jesus would be among those who attended. "The Jews" were looking for him (v. 11). This probably refers to the enemies of Jesus; it is a favorite Johannine way of speaking of them. They anticipated that Jesus would come up for such an important feast and they kept their eyes open so as not to miss him.

Evidently the hostility was becoming known and people realized that it might be dangerous to speak too openly about Jesus, for John goes on to say that there was a "muttering" about him (v. 12). Not only the leaders but other people as well wondered about him. When John says "the crowds" he seems to mean neither the disciples nor the enemies of Jesus, but the multitudes who were not committed to his cause, yet were not hostile either. Some of them thought Jesus a good man, while others thought of him as a deceiver. These would largely be pilgrims from a variety of places, and probably a good number of them had never seen nor heard Jesus. They would be relying on what they had heard from others, and their verdicts would depend on their source of information. They knew enough to know that it could be dangerous to speak too openly, so they kept their voices low. Clearly "the Jews" were the dominant people, and it was wise not to antagonize them, the pilgrims thought. So, though there was considerable interest in Jesus, there was little open discussion.

32

The Law of Moses

When it was now the middle of the feast Jesus went up into the temple and began to teach. The Jews were astonished and said, "How is this man learned when he has never been educated?" Jesus answered them, "My teaching is not my own but that of him who sent me. If anyone wills to do his will, he will know about the teaching whether it is of God or whether I speak of myself. He who speaks of himself seeks his own glory; but he who seeks the glory of him who sent him, this man is true and there is no unrighteousness in him.

"Did not Moses give you the Law? And yet none of you keeps the Law. Why are you trying to kill me?" The crowd replied, "You have a demon; who is trying to kill you?" Jesus answered them, "I did one work and you are all astonished. For this reason Moses gave you circumcision—not that it originates with Moses, but with the fathers—and on the Sabbath you circumcise a man. If a man receives circumcision on the Sabbath in order that the Law of Moses be not broken, are you angry with me because I made an entire man healthy on the Sabbath? Do not judge superficially, but judge righteous judgment" (John 7:14–24).

We have seen that Jesus declined his brothers' suggestion that he go up to the Feast of Tabernacles (vv. 3–8). He never did go up as they suggested, as one of the throng of pilgrims, going up to Jerusalem to keep the feast. But he did make his appearance at "the middle of the feast" (v. 14). This may be meant to be taken literally and signify the fourth day. But it is more likely to be a general statement and indicate that Jesus came on the scene somewhere about the middle of the festivities.

There was a prophecy that God would send his messenger to his people: ". . . 'suddenly the Lord you are seeking will come to his temple; the messenger of the covenant, whom you desire, will come,' says the LORD Almighty" (Mal. 3:1). The prophet Zechariah puts a great deal of emphasis on the importance of the Feast of Tabernacles (Zech. 14:16–19). Jesus, it would seem, goes to the temple at the Feast of Tabernacles in fulfillment of such Old Testament prophecies. He is not there simply as one of the pilgrims: he is there as the messenger of the Lord. He will speak the message God has for his people at that significant time.

He "began to teach," which appears to mean that he sat with a group of people and instructed them. Later in the feast he will stand and shout a message to the assembled throng (v. 37), but here the meaning appears to be that he engaged in a quieter session of instruction of a smaller group. As they listened they were astonished. It seems as though these people had not heard Jesus before, and this would not be surprising. John has not spoken of Jesus as teaching in Jerusalem before this time. He has done some miracles there (2:23), and we need not doubt that he did some teaching, too. Nevertheless, all the teaching that John has recorded up till now seems to have taken place in Galilee. In any case we should bear in mind that Tabernacles was the greatest of the feasts and that Jews came up to Jerusalem from many places. The people Jesus was teaching would doubtless have been pilgrims, and most of them may never have been in a position to hear him before this.

Education

Their astonishment was apparently at the way Jesus handled his subject. The expression I have translated "How is this man learned?" (v. 15) is more literally "How does this man know letters?" where "letters" will be understood in the sense "sacred letters," i.e., the Bible. There would have been no problem in Jesus' knowing something of the Bible. It was read in worship in the synagogue, Sabbath by Sabbath, and any attentive person would pick up a good deal simply by taking in what was read. And some parts of the Bible were learned by heart. Thus every little Jewish boy was taught to say "Hear, O Israel . . ." (Deut. 6:4f.). Certainly Jesus knew enough to read the Scripture in the synagogue service (Luke 4:16ff.). Some knowledge of "letters" was widespread and would not be surprising.

But more advanced education would take place in the rabbinical schools. The student would attach himself to a rabbi and the rabbi would teach him the accepted lore. This put a good deal of emphasis on memory work. In a day when all books had to be laboriously written by hand, books were always in comparatively short supply and much was necessarily committed to memory. Indeed, for some people it seems that this was held to be all that was necessary. A term of abuse sometimes used was to call such a scholar "a bag of books." He had committed whole books to memory and could at need recite them. But he had no real grasp of what they meant and no wisdom in handling his knowledge. There were others whose learning led them to concentrate on points that other people might well not know, but which were of no great importance. Some of the Jews showed great ingenuity in their handling of the regulations of the Law, seeing the bare minimum that had to be performed in order to comply with the regulations and the ways in which loopholes might be found for those who did not want to be "overrighteous" (Eccles. 7:16).

Jesus had not been through the rabbinic training, and it would not be expected that he could sustain a continuing argument from Scripture. It was this that seems to have astonished his hearers. They would not have expected a man who came from a carpenter's home in Nazareth to have been able to teach like Jesus taught.

This is a fine piece of Johannine irony. He made it clear at the beginning of the Gospel that Jesus is the divine Logos, the Word of God. Now he sees the Jews confronted by the Logos incarnate and calling him "this uneducated fellow" (Moffatt). They could not recognize the divine wisdom when they heard it.

Teaching from God

Jesus' response is to say that his teaching is not his own (v. 16). We should notice here that in the first century there was a different attitude toward teaching from our customary view. We prize highly an original teacher, but the ancients did not. There was a widespread idea that there had been a Golden Age in the remote past and that at that time men had been greater and wiser and stronger than their successors. Indeed, since that time it seems that history had been all downhill. So, if anyone produced highly original teaching, teaching that could not be traced back in some way to the great days of the race, then obviously that teacher must be in error. When an original teacher appeared he had to perform some intricate mental gymnastics to pin his teaching on some illustrious predecessor. If he could do this, he was accepted. If not, no one took much notice of him.

Thus, if Jesus had claimed that his teaching originated with himself, he would have been immediately discredited. Not, of course, that he took the position he did simply because of the effect it would have on his hearers. He took his position because it was true. It is a consistent piece of Johannine teaching that there was a oneness between Jesus and his heavenly Father such that what he said came from God. And that is what he tells his hearers now.

He does not speak of God but of "him who sent me." Again and again we have this truth repeated in this Gospel. God sent his Son. This is something very different from what was normally accepted in the ancient world. The Greeks thought of their gods as remote from ordinary people, living a serene existence on the top of Mount Olympus, and far too great to be affected by what insignificant mortals might do. They were not moved by our sin unless it in some way managed to outrage one of them personally. And their attitude to the human race was not one of love. How could such great and lofty deities love puny, unimportant, mortal humans?

It was better with the Jews, because they had learned well from the Old Testament that God concerns himself with his people, and that through the centuries he had sent his servants the prophets, the psalmists, the lawgivers, and others, and had worked out his purpose for his own. But for the Jews of the first century it seems that all this was in the past. That God had acted in days gone by they accepted. That God would act in the end of time they fully agreed. But now? That was another matter altogether.

But Jesus kept saying that God had sent him. That means not only that God had acted in love in the past and that he would act in love in the future, but that he was acting in love now. The mission of Jesus meant that God was taking action to bring about salvation, and that colored everything he said and did. Specifically, his teaching was the teaching of the God who sent him on his mission of salvation.

Knowing God's Teaching

Jesus, then, is saying that his teaching should be accepted because it was God's teaching. He knows that, but how are his hearers to know it? He says it is a matter of the will. The set of the life is important. If anyone really "wills to do his will," that person will know the truth of Jesus' teaching (v. 17). It is a matter of being completely sincere. It is easy to delude ourselves into believing something that we very much want to believe. And it is not hard to persuade ourselves that something is erroneous if it is going to be uncomfortable to accept it. Self-delusion is widespread and is a source of many errors. Specifically, if someone does not wish to accept the teaching of Jesus, there will always be some reason he can dredge up that will make his rejection of it plausible.

But the genuine person, the one who simply wants to do what is right and who wills to do the will of God, that person will have an inner certainty. The Spirit of God will be at work with his spirit and will lead him into the ways of truth (16:13). He will have a divinely given certainty, and that is above all price. Jesus is emphasizing that the right attitude towards God is all-important. God will never let the genuine seeker be led astray permanently. He may have his difficulties along the way, but he will be in no doubt that Jesus is the One sent by God and that the teaching he gives is from God.

Long ago the great Augustine uttered some wise words. He pointed out that it is faith that is supremely important in the attitude of the Christian. This great African theologian said, "Do not seek to understand in order to believe"; Christianity is not a religion primarily for the intelligentsia. We do not need to fight our way through an intellectual maze before we can become acceptable to God. That is a matter of trust, not of massive intellect. "What is 'If any man be willing to do his will'?" he asks and then answers, "It is the same thing as to believe." But Augustine is clear that faith does not mean the abandonment of intellectual activity. "Believe that thou mayest understand," he wrote. Understanding follows faith, and Augustine's impressive literary output bears ample witness to this truth. But, massive as his intellect certainly was, Augustine was sure that it is faith that is of central importance.

Jesus goes on to the attitude of the teacher (v. 18). He is speaking primarily of himself, for it is his teaching that is being questioned, but what he says applies in lesser measure to all who teach in the name of God. The person who has his eye fixed on "his own glory" will necessarily speak "of himself"; such an attitude is incompatible with speaking the message of God. As we see from Jesus' lowly life and from his lowly service in going to the cross for sinners, he had no self-seeking. His teaching was genuinely from God. And as we seek to speak in God's name the same attitude is sought from us. One wise man has well said that "it is impossible at one and the same time to give the impression that Jesus is a great Savior and that I am a great preacher." If the Christian teacher is anxious to draw attention to himself, he cannot point people to Christ. On the other hand, if he is concentrating on pointing people to Christ, he cannot keep his interest on himself.

The person with this right attitude, Jesus says, "is true." He does not say that he speaks the truth (though that, of course, is also the case), but that he *is* true. Truth can be a quality of people as well as of words. In a special sense this was true of Jesus, for he could say, "I am the truth" (14:6). But there is a sense in which every believer must be a "true" person, one whose faith is translated into a thoroughly reliable way of life. That person will avoid unrighteousness of every kind.

Moses and the Law

When Jesus goes on to speak of the Law (v. 19) he is not turning to a new and unrelated subject. For the Jews of his day it was the Law that Moses gave (the first five books of our Old Testament) that was the special subject of study. They revered Moses as possibly the greatest of men; certainly the giver of the Law was a highly significant figure. The Jews exhausted their superlatives in seeking to bring out the importance of the Law.

Jesus' opponents have been criticizing him and rejecting his teaching. They maintained that they were doing this because they held to what Moses taught, and everyone knew that God had spoken through Moses. Now Jesus points out that their loyalty to Moses was suspect. "None of you keeps the Law," he says. That would have been a shocking accusation to them. The Law was more than a subject that they thought of only occasionally. It was the center of their study and their model for living. Constantly they tried to live as the Law directed.

But now Jesus asks, "Why are you trying to kill me?" This was certainly not in accordance with the Law. He does not mean, of course, that they are all caught up in the plot, but there are enough for his question to have a point. And it certainly shows that there were those who were far from keeping the Law.

The crowd did not understand. As we have seen earlier, the multitude in Jerusalem at that time would have been largely made up of pilgrims for a wide area. It was not they, but "the Jews," those who lived in Jersualem and particularly their leaders, who were trying to get rid of Jesus. The crowds from so many places did not know what the leaders were trying to do. But killing Jesus sounded crazy to them, and accordingly they accused him of having "a demon" (v. 20), an accusation made on other occasions (8:48–52; 10:20f.; cf. also Mark 3:22, etc.).

The Sabbath

Jesus proceeds to develop his point that none of them keeps the Law. The pilgrims did not know of the plot to kill him (which was one way of breaking the Law). But the way the Sabbath was observed was common knowledge, and he goes on to show them that they were not really keeping the Sabbath in the way they should.

He starts with "one work" that he had done (v. 21). He does not explain which work this is, but the context makes it clear that he is referring to the healing of the lame man who had waited for thirty-eight years for healing, healing that he had sought in vain from the healing waters (5:1ff.). That miracle had been performed on a Sabbath, a fact that had caused the powers-that-be a good deal of concern and had led to a spirited discussion with Jesus (5:16ff.). As he often does, Jesus speaks of his miracle as a "work"; what to us is an inexplicable miracle is to him no more than a "work." Being who and what he is, this sort of thing is what he does so naturally. But it was a miracle that made them all "astonished." There was no explanation for it that they could see, and this led to amazement.

Jesus goes on to one of the central requirements of the Law as the Jews practised it, the requirement of circumcision (v. 22). Moses laid it down that this ceremonial act should be carried out, but he did not originate the practice. God had commanded Abraham to circumcise every male child as a sign of the covenant that he was making with that patriarch (Gen. 17:9ff.). This had been done by the patriarchs, so that the command in the Law was to perpetuate what God had commanded long since, not a new provision initiated by Moses. The exact date of its institution is not important; Jesus simply points out that it was not their highly revered Moses who began it, but "the fathers."

Now the Law required circumcision to be carried out on the eighth day of the baby's existence. It also required that people do no work on the Sabbath. Circumcision was regarded as work, so this posed a little problem: What happened when the eighth day fell on the Sabbath? Should the Sabbath be regarded as of overriding importance, so that circumcision be postponed till the next day? Or was circumcision so important that it took precedence over the Sabbath regulations? Should they go ahead and circumcise the baby even though it was the Sabbath? Moses did not say what should be done under such circumstances, but the Jews were clear: "Great is circumcision which overrides even the rigour of the Sabbath," said Rabbi Jose (Mishnah, *Nedarim* 3:11), and this was the accepted understanding. Circumcision was extremely important. The Law was understood to mean that nothing must stand in the way of its performance, not even the Sabbath.

Jesus reminds his hearers of this well-known fact in order to make clear his attitude to the Sabbath. When he healed on that day it was not in an anti-Sabbatarian attitude. He was not saying that the Sabbath should not be kept. Nor was he saying that the rules for the Sabbath were too strict and that there should be some relaxation.

He was saying that his critics did not understand what the Sabbath meant and why it had been instituted. He was saying that if they reflected on the meaning of their regular practice with regard to circumcision, they would see this for themselves. The Law of Moses provided for circumcision on the eighth day, and the need of the little baby to be included among God's covenant people by the use of this rite overrode the requirements of Sabbath observance. Think what this means. Think. The person is more important than the rules. The Law itself bears witness to this.

So with Jesus' healing. It was concerned not with one member of the body (as circumcision was), but with the "entire man" (v. 23). It was unthinkable to Jesus that the man should be allowed to remain any longer in his helplessness and his hopelessness. If his critics understood what the Law meant, they would see that the kind of thing he had done in healing the lame man was not only permitted but required by the Law. The Law was meant for the good of the people who were under the Law. Good deeds, deeds of mercy, *ought* to be done on the Sabbath. His enemies were in the wrong. They were not really keeping the Law at all when they objected to his healing.

There is an interesting change of tenses in Jesus' two uses of the word *judge* (v. 24). The first is a present, which with the negative conveys the force of "stop judging superficially." There is the implication that they have been doing this, and Jesus commands them to stop it. "Judge righteous judgment" employs the aorist (at least in many good manuscripts), which concentrates on the specific case and tells them to make a right judgment about it. They should, of course, do this all the time, but the way Jesus puts it places emphasis on the specific example before them. They should make a right judgment about this, and that would help them to a better understanding of the ways of God.

33

"Where I Am You Cannot Come"

Some of the Jerusalemites therefore said, "Is not this he whom they are trying to kill? And look, he is speaking openly and they are saying nothing to him. Do the rulers by any chance know that this man is truly the Christ? But we know where this man comes from. But as for the Christ, when he comes, no one knows where he comes from." Jesus therefore cried out in the temple as he taught saying, "So you know me and you know where I am from! And I did not come of my own accord, but he who sent me is true, One whom you do not know. I know him, for I am from him and he sent me."

Therefore they tried to arrest him, and yet no one laid a hand on him because his hour had not yet come. But many of the crowd believed in him and said, "When the Christ comes will he do more signs than this man has done?" The Pharisees heard the crowd muttering these things about him and the high priests and the Pharisees sent officials to arrest him. Jesus then said, "Yet a little while am I with you and I go to him that sent me. You will look for me and you will not find me, and where I am you cannot come." The Jews therefore said to themselves, "Where will this man go that we will not find him? He won't go to the dispersion among the Greeks and teach the Greeks, will he? What is this saying that he spoke, 'You will look for me and you will not find me, and where I am you cannot come'?" (John 7:25–36).

There are different groups of people in Jerusalem referred to in this chapter. As often, there are references to "the Jews," which normally mean those Jews who were hostile to Jesus and more especially the Jewish leaders in Jerusalem. Then there is "the crowd," which seems to mean mostly the pilgrims who had come up to the capital and specifically to the temple in order to keep the feast. They were uninformed about Jesus, but many of them were ready to listen to his teaching and some of them were so impressed that they believed in him (v. 31). Now another group is mentioned: "the Jerusalemites." This is a very unusual expression, being found elsewhere in the New Testament only in Mark 1:5. Obviously it means people who lived in Jerusalem, but it seems to be used not of the whole population but of the city mob. They had more information than the pilgrims, for they knew of the plot to kill Jesus (v. 25), though it was not their plot; an undefined "they" were responsible.

The mob was impressed by the fact that Jesus was teaching publicly and openly and that nobody was doing anything about it. The word that I have translated "openly" (v. 26) is an interesting one. It is made up of two words, which literally mean "all speech," so that it points to an attitude of being completely at home, a comfortable feeling wherein the words come freely and easily. From this basic meaning the word comes to be used in two common ways. It may mean "boldly," "courageously" (when we feel quite at home we are not afraid); or it may mean "openly" (when we feel at home we feel no urge to cover up and keep things secret). It is the second meaning that is used here, though, the hostility of the enemies of Jesus being what it was, the first meaning might also apply.

Why, then, were the rulers doing nothing about Jesus' public teaching? The Jerusalemites raise the possibility that these rulers knew that Jesus was in fact the Christ. They do not rate this possibility very highly. The way they express it in the Greek implies that a negative answer should be given to their question. There has to be some explanation. So they suggest this one. But they dismiss it; there is no probability in it.

They toy with the idea of "the Christ." Many Jews seem to have held that when the Christ came he would burst on the scene suddenly and people would not know where he had come from. There was certainly the idea that the Messiah would be "revealed," and this seems to have been understood at any rate by some to mean that nobody would know anything about him until the revelation took place. Another view was that he would arise out of the sea, which meant, of course, that prior to his sudden appearance nobody could have any idea of him or of where he would come from. Again there was a rabbinic saying that held that three things come quite unexpectedly: Messiah, a windfall, and a scorpion. It is an interesting trio, but it leaves no doubt that whoever originated it did not see how Messiah's arrival could be forecast. That was completely unknown. Justin, a Christian writer from the middle of the second century, quotes a Jew as saying that even if the Messiah had come, that Messiah would not know he was the Messiah until Elijah came to anoint him.

There was thus no shortage of ideas, and, while we cannot be sure which one these men of Jerusalem held, clearly they were not going to allow the possibility of Jesus being the Messiah. Despite what the rulers might hold, despite the miracles Jesus did, there was always something that could be alleged as an obstacle. There was no satisfying them.

I am reminded of a little family that went to a restaurant for a meal. When the waitress came for their orders the wife said she would like a salmon sandwich with white bread. The waitress said, "You'll like our chicken better. And brown bread is better for you than white." Then when the daughter decided on a green salad with no dressing, and coffee to drink, the waitress responded, "There's not much nourishment in that. Why not have a cottage-cheese salad. And milk is better than coffee." The man in the party, thoroughly cowed by this time, said timidly, "What would you suggest?" To which the waitress snapped, "Suggestions! Who's got time for suggestions?"

You can't win with some people. Whatever line you take, they disagree. It seems that the Jerusalemites were something like this. They did not know as much about Jesus as they perhaps might. But they certainly weren't going to be found out saying that he was the Messiah. If one objection wouldn't do, another could surely be found. As it happened, the one they settled on was that they knew Jesus' origin. This is another piece of John's irony. If they had really known where Jesus came from, they would have known that he was indeed the Messiah. But all that they knew was that he came from Nazareth, an unimportant village in Galilee. They were quite ignorant of the virgin birth, of the truth that Jesus was "from above," and that he was where he was because the heavenly Father had sent him.

Sent by God

Jesus used this as a starting point for some important teaching. He "therefore cried out" (v. 28), and the verb shows that he wanted to give the greatest publicity to an important statement. This verb is used a number of times in this Gospel to introduce important teaching; look at the way it comes in in 1:15; 7:37; 12:44, for example. Jesus begins with an ironical agreement with what the Jerusalemites had just said. They knew where he came from. This was certainly true in the sense that they knew that he came from Nazareth. But it was not true in the deeper sense that he came from God.

So Jesus goes on: "I did not come of my own accord." This does not mean, of course, that he did not want to come, that his own desires lay elsewhere. It is an important part of the teaching of this Gospel that the Father and the Son are one, that in the salvation that Jesus was in process of working out they were in perfect harmony. But his point here is that he is not, as his hearers think, an upstart. There were many who claimed positions of eminence and even some who claimed to be Messiah. But these were all motivated by their own impulse. They came on their own initiative. They had the support of their own adherents, but that was all. The critical thing was that they had no divine mission. They might claim it, but God had not sent them.

It mattered everything to Jesus that God had sent him. It was this that gave him assurance in the face of the hostility of so many people who might have been expected to be genuine servants of God, the leaders, especially the religious leaders of the nation that rejoiced to be "the people of God." But while they might reject him, he rejoiced in the nearness of "him who sent me," of whom he now says that he "is true." Goodspeed translates this "someone who is very real." The "reality," the "truth" of God was very important, but these people did not know God. Because they did not know God they did not know Christ. It is impossible to know the one without the other, and consequently to be ignorant of one is evidence that one is ignorant of the other.

It is another truth insisted on throughout this Gospel that Jesus knows the Father. In fact the three expressions that come together here, "I know him," "I am from him," and "he sent me," sum up a great deal of Johannine theology: knowledge, origin, and mission.

Attempted Arrest

These words of Jesus led to different reactions. Some decided that Jesus had gone too far and that he should be arrested (v. 30). John says "therefore," which shows that this was the consequence of what Jesus had just said. He does not tell us in what the attempt to arrest him consisted, nor who did this. He simply says "they" sought to arrest him, but in Jerusalem the only people with the power to bring about an arrest were the Romans and the temple authorities. There is no question of Roman might at this point, so it must be the priests and their allies. John makes it plain that there was strong hostility and that Jesus' enemies were prepared to take action.

The attempt, however it was made, was completely unsuccessful. Not a hand was laid on Jesus. As we do not know exactly who was trying to make the arrest or how they went about it, we cannot know what went wrong with the attempt. But we do know the basic reason for the failure—Jesus' "hour had not yet come." As we have seen more than once in these studies, John is clear that Jesus had come to discharge a divinely given mission. He must do what was necessary to bring about the salvation of sinners, and in due course that would mean dying for them. But that death would be at the time and in the way that God planned it all. Puny tyrants would not be able to interfere. Till the time came for Jesus to die, nobody could prevent him from going about his business in the service of God. Of course, when his "hour" came, nothing would be able to prevent him from going forward to death either. But that is another matter and it will be developed in another place. Here John is content to leave us with the thought that in the will of God it was not yet time for Jesus' enemies to succeed. So, whatever the attempt they might make to arrest him, it must be unsuccessful.

So much for the reaction of Jesus' opponents. But there were also many of the pilgrims there, "the crowd" (v. 31). These people were more open-minded. They had probably for the most part not known Jesus and perhaps even not known of him before they went up to Jerusalem for this feast. But they were ready to listen to him and to watch what he did. John tells us that many of them came to believe in Jesus, the attitude for which John is looking throughout. He wrote his Gospel, he tells us, so that people would believe. These pilgrims then were doing what people, in John's judgment, ought to do.

But if their faith was praiseworthy, perhaps the reason for it was not quite so admirable. They ask, "When the Christ comes will he do more signs than this man has done?" In this Gospel "signs" is a characteristic word for the miracles; it marks them out as significant happenings. For John faith that is based on the miracles is not the highest kind of faith, but it is better than no faith at all. It was this "miracle faith" that the pilgrims had. To record this in such a context is, of course, to confer high praise, for there was hostility to Jesus and his enemies were taking strong action against him. It must have taken some courage to profess faith in him accordingly, but this these pilgrims did. It is interesting that they think of the Messiah primarily in terms of the doing of miracles. For us it is his love for sinners, his work of salvation, his atoning death, that matters most. But we view what happened in Palestine with the benefit of centuries of hindsight. For those pilgrims it must have been difficult to know how to recognize the Messiah. The miracles were a useful guide.

Though they professed belief, the pilgrims evidently did not speak very openly about it. But the Pharisees heard them "muttering" and took notice of it (v. 32). There is an interesting little mark of John's accuracy here. He speaks of the Pharisees as hearing what the crowd was saying, but of the high priests and the Pharisees as trying to make an arrest. The point is that the high priests were aristocrats. They did not know what the common people were saying. But the Pharisees, the religious leaders, were much more in touch with what was going on. They tried to teach people what they saw as the right way. They were sufficiently in touch to hear these quietly spoken words. But they had little power. They did not control the police; they had no power of arrest. That belonged rather to the high priests. Quite clearly the Pharisees went off to the high priests and told them what was going on. Then, when those who had the power decided on an arrest, the Pharisees are linked with them in sending the officials. They gave their religious sanction to what was being done.

Going Away

Evidently it took a little time for the officials to get busy. It may be that there were no officers immediately available and some had to be sought. Perhaps the crowd around Jesus was thick and it took time for them to make their way through to the place where he was. It may be that their instructions included a warning that the situation was tense and that they should be careful how they went about their work. For whatever reason, Jesus continued for a time with his teaching and we do not hear of the arresting posse again until verse 45, when they report that they had not done what they had been ordered to do. But John says little about them. His interest is in Jesus, not in a posse of policemen.

Jesus' teaching takes a surprising turn. He speaks of being with them for a short time and then of returning to the One who had sent him (v. 33). Perhaps this is a logical follow-up from the last words John has recorded of Jesus, back in verse 29. He said then that he was from God and that God had sent him. Now he speaks of returning to him who had sent him, his mission complete. It is also possible that we should see the words as a reaction to the attempted arrest. It would not be long before Jesus was removed to a place out of the reach of any arresting party. It may even be that the words are a response to the faith John has just spoken of. That faith was based on the miracles, and some hold that Jesus is referring to his death, which was much more significant for faith than the miracles were.

His enemies will look for him, Jesus says, and will not find him; he will be in a place where they cannot come (v. 34). We do not find it overly difficult to understand this, for we are on this side of the cross and the resurrection. But it puzzled those who heard it. How could Jesus possibly go to some place where they could not follow? If he could go, surely so could they?

The speakers now are "the Jews," the enemies of Jesus (v. 35). They express their wonderment at such a destination and proceed to a suggestion, "the dispersion among the Greeks." At that time there were many Jews who lived outside Palestine. Most of the big cities of the Roman Empire had sizable groups of Jews, and there were also many in some countries outside the empire. All these Jews outside their own country were called "the dispersion"; they were the dispersed members of the people of God. They do not suggest that Jesus will teach the dispersion, the Jews scattered abroad, but the Greeks. This may be another example of John's irony. Jesus himself never did go to the dispersion and teach Greeks, but his followers did. In due course the early Christian preachers traveled all over the empire, making the synagogues their jumping-off points in the cities to which they went as they preached the gospel message to the Greeks (and others). What the Jews here dismiss as fantastic became in fact the method by which the Christian way was spread throughout the empire.

It is easy to make blunders based on misunderstanding. I was reading of a shopkeeper who lived next door to his shop. He was often troubled by people using the parking lot alongside his shop, though he saw it as meant for his customers and certainly not as a free public parking lot outside shop hours. Coming home late one night, he saw the lot just full of cars. He felt this was too much, that he must do something about it. So he hunted up a police officer and did not rest until there was a ticket on every car. Satisfied and rejoicing at a job well done, he went inside, only to find that his wife was hostessing an evening for the ladies of the church, who had been very happy to find parking available so close to the home where they were meeting!

So with these people. They did not realize what they were doing when they rejected Jesus of Nazareth and in doing so rejected the incarnate Son of God. Like the man in the little story, they would have been well advised to have made more inquiries before they settled on their course of action. They thought of the Greeks and they thought of the dispersion. But they did not think of the possibility that in Jesus of Nazareth they were being confronted with a messenger sent by God, nor that the going away might be a going away not simply from Palestine but from this whole earth, a going back to God.

So John leaves this part of his story with these people repeating the words of Jesus in puzzlement (v. 36). In this Gospel words are very rarely repeated exactly, and this is one of the few places where this happens. We should see the words as important. Probably John also means us to see that the words haunted these hearers. They knew that they did not understand and they knew that the words did have a meaning. Jesus understood quite well what he was saying. What could he mean? John leaves us with the picture of people who were not willing to submit to the voice of God and who accordingly did not understand. Which is not exactly unknown in our own day.

34

"It Was Not Yet Spirit"

On the last day, the great day of the feast, Jesus stood and cried out saying, "If anyone is thirsty, let him come to me and drink. He who believes in me, as the Scripture said, rivers of living water will flow out of his innermost being." He said this about the Spirit whom those who believed in him would receive. For it was not yet Spirit, because Jesus was not yet glorified (John 7:37–39).

You would think it would be easy to know when "the last day" of the feast was, especially since it is also called "the great day." But this is not the case. In Deuteronomy 16:13 we read, "Celebrate the Feast of Tabernacles for seven days . . ." and this is repeated in verse 15, "For seven days celebrate the Feast to the LORD your God. . . ." But in Leviticus 23:36 we read with respect to this feast, "For seven days present offerings made to the LORD by fire, and on the eighth day hold a sacred assembly and present an offering made to the LORD by fire. It is the closing assembly. . . ." It is not unlikely that an original seven-day festival was at some time lengthened by a day. Or perhaps there was a closing assembly on the eighth day from the very first. We do not know. But the uncertainty leaves us wondering whether John regards the seventh or the eighth as the last day.

At this feast there were ceremonies with the pouring out of water and the lighting of great candelabra, which were said to have illuminated every house in Jerusalem. But these seem to have finished by the seventh day; they were not used on the eighth. So also the leafy shelters in which people lived during this feast were taken down on the seventh day. It can thus be argued that the eighth day was not really a part of the feast, being rather an addendum.

But perhaps we should say that if the eighth day was observed at all, the seventh day can scarcely be called the last day. Moreover, the absence of the water and light ceremonies on the eighth day may have given greater point to Jesus' words about living water and about the light of the world. It seems best to understand John as speaking about the eighth day.

Ceremonies at the Feast

Tabernacles was a very happy feast. It marked the end of the year's work, with the harvest safely in, so everyone was merry. Living in leafy shelters for the duration must have been a lot of fun. People carried bunches of leaves, which they called *lulabs,* in accordance with the way the Pharisees interpreted Leviticus 23:40: "On the first day you are to take choice fruit from the trees, and palm fronds, leafy branches and poplars, and rejoice before the LORD your God for seven days." The Sadducees took this to be an instruction about the material out of which the leafy shelters were to be constructed. The Pharisees, however, took the words as an instruction to the worshipers to carry fronds from the trees named. The Pharisees were closer to the people and had a better reputation as religious leaders, so it is not surprising that their interpretation of the passage prevailed.

A. Edersheim says that the worshiper carried in his right hand the "*lulab* or palm, with myrtle and willow branch on either side of it, tied together on the outside with its own kind, though in the inside it might be fastened even with gold thread." Rabbi Ishmael maintained that the requirements for a *lulab* were three branches of myrtle, two of willow, one palm, and one citron. Whichever was right, the people made their *lulabs* and carried them in their right hands, while each had a citron in the left hand. At certain points in the reciting of psalms they all shook their *lulabs,* which thus featured in the observance. The observances included dancing and the music of flutes. Young branches of willow were brought in and arranged round the altar in such a way that the tops formed a canopy over it.

Each day for seven days a priest would convey water from the pool of Siloam in a golden vessel and bring it in a happy procession marked by the blowing of trumpets till they came to the temple. This was a very joyous occasion about which there is a rabbinic saying: "He that never has seen the joy of the water-drawing has never in his life seen joy." At the temple the water was poured out into a bowl beside the altar, from which a pipe conveyed it to the bottom of the altar, while at the same time wine was poured in a similar fashion on the other side of the altar. This water ceremony was an acted prayer for rain. A saying reputed to go back to Rabbi Akiba (who died in A.D. 134), and which may be much older, asks "Why has the Torah commanded: Pour out water on the Feast of Tabernacles?" and answers "The Holy One, blessed be He, has commanded: Pour out water before me on the Feast of Tabernacles, in order that the rain (of the coming year) may bless you." Whether the saying had been formulated in New Testament times we do not know, but there is no doubt that this is the way the people understood the water ceremonies. Indeed, the idea goes back at least as far as the time of the prophet Zechariah, who associated rain with the observance of the Feast of Tabernacles (Zech. 14:16–19). The reciting of Psalm 118:25 as a prayer for prosperity is also thought to be a petition for rain. Some words from Isaiah were also used, probably during processions: "With joy you will draw water from the wells of salvation" (Isa. 12:3).

Let the Thirsty Drink

It is against this background that we should understand Jesus' words. The people were in a happy mood as they joined in the celebration of this most joyful feast. But the acted and spoken prayers for rain reminded them of their dependence on the goodness of God. They were not able of themselves to provide for the coming year. Unless God sent the rain, the Feast of Tabernacles next year would be a grim occasion.

The water ceremonies had been dutifully carried out for seven days. On this day there were none. But now Jesus speaks (v. 37). It is a solemn occasion and he stands up to issue his invitation. Teachers usually sat with their disciples, so that his posture was unusual. This may be to mark an unusual occasion, and it is also the case, of course, that by standing he put himself in a position to be heard more widely. John says that Jesus "cried out"; the loud shout would mean that the maximum number of people would hear him.

Jesus speaks of the thirsty and invites them to come to him and drink. Clearly he is not speaking of thirst after the water that sustains our physical life, but of thirst after spiritual things. It is that thirst that is of first importance, and it is that thirst that Jesus satisfies. Up till this point Jesus seems not to have given specific teaching of his own at the feast. John has recorded Jesus' replies to questions put to him, but not any teaching he gave spontaneously. That has been reserved until now, the climax of the whole observance, and Jesus brings out the deep significance of the feast. It points to him as the giver of the water that really satisfies. The people have been thinking of their need of rain; Jesus reminds them that they have another and a deeper need, the need of their souls. It is likely that he has in mind God's giving of water from the rock to the people in the wilderness (Exod. 17:6; Num. 20:7–11). After all, at Tabernacles water was poured out by the altar, but the people did not drink it. In the wilderness they did drink the water that came from the rock. Jesus is the Rock from which his people's need is abundantly satisfied.

There is a problem of punctuation here and this affects the sense. There is very little punctuation in the most ancient manuscripts; the reader was expected to supply it himself. Usually this presents no problem, but now and then there is uncertainty. In this place we usually put a comma after "thirsty" and a full stop after "drink." But some suggest that we should put our full stop (or semicolon) after "me" so as to read (with NEB), "If anyone is thirsty let him come to me; whoever believes in me, let him drink." But, though many accept this understanding of the text, there are some strong objections. Thus the words about being thirsty look for something about drinking. It is the thirsty person, not the believing person, whom we expect to drink. The words about faith go better with coming to Jesus than with drinking.

There is also a grammatical point. When we come to the expression "rivers of living water will flow out of his innermost being" (v. 38), the word "his" must refer to the preceding "he," the believer. It cannot refer to "me" (i.e., Christ), as most who adopt this punctuation prefer. Indeed, one of the main reasons for accepting the variant punctuation is that those who adopt it understand the passage to mean that it is Christ who is the source of the living water.

Rivers of Living Water

The question that arises then is "Do the rivers of living water flow from the believer or from Christ?" It is because it seems so obvious that they come from Christ that many scholars take "he who believes" with the preceding verb "drink." And, of course, it must be accepted that it is Christ who supplies the living water, not the believer. But there is a sense in which the believer can be the source of blessing to others, a truth given expression in the prayer of the humble man who prayed, "Lord, I can't hold much, but help me to overflow lots." It has often been the case in the history of the church that people of small capacity have been the source of blessing to many.

We should notice, moreover, that Jesus speaks of the giving of living water as taking place "as the Scripture said." Now it is very difficult to find a passage that meets this situation. People sometimes appeal to the story of the water coming from the rock (Exod. 17:6), but it is not easy to understand this passage as a prophecy that the Messiah would give living water. It is no better with "He opened the rock, and water gushed out" (Ps. 105:41), or with the water coming out from under the threshold of the temple in Ezekiel's vision (Ezek. 47:1), or with Joel's prophecy that "all the ravines of Judah will run with water. A fountain will flow out of the LORD's house and will water the valley of acacias" (Joel 3:18). Each of these passages has been appealed to, but none ascribes living water to the Messiah. The same is true of other passages. If we adopt this understanding of the text, we are left with Jesus' appealing to "the Scripture" in a way that we cannot follow.

It is true that the Old Testament does not say in precise words that rivers of living water will flow from the believer. But it does speak of God's people as the source of blessing to others and uses the imagery of water to make the point. For example, "You will be like a well-watered garden, like a spring whose waters never fail" (Isa. 58:11b). A spring, of course, is outgoing; it is not like a well that simply accumulates water. The spring sends it forth. This may be involved also in calling the heart "the wellspring of life" (Prov. 4:23). Other passages could be cited; the Old Testament often uses water to bring out the thought of God's good gift to his people, and sometimes, as in the passages quoted, there is the thought that the believer is outgoing.

Of course this comes short of producing a proof text that does away with all argument. I am simply saying that there does not appear to be any Old Testament passage that says that the Messiah will be the source of living water, but there are some that are naturally interpreted along the line that the believer can pass on the blessing he has received from God.

It goes without saying that the believer is never thought of as originating the living water, neither in the Old Testament nor in Jesus' words. That is always a divine gift. But Jesus does appear to be saying that when the believer has this gift he will not be a self-centered person. He will be outgoing, and the blessing he has received from God he will pass on to other people.

John Bunyan has the old gentleman, Mr Honest, say,

> A man there was, though some did count him mad,
> The more he cast away, the more he had.

Over against which we may set the "rule" of the pool that takes in but does not give out. Of this rule it can be said, in the words of the poet Wordsworth,

The good old rule
Sufficeth them, the simple plan,
That they should take, who have the power,
And they should keep who can.

But this rule is self-defeating, as the Dead Sea shows. Where water keeps flowing in and none flows out, there is stagnation and death. It is the pool out of which water flows as well as into which water flows that sparkles with life.

The Spirit

John adds the explanation that Jesus was speaking about the Spirit (v. 39). He was not saying that the believer is naturally a source of blessing to others. That is not so. The Christian does not somehow become a great and wonderful person, full of life and vitality in his own right. But the Holy Spirit within him enables him to be outgoing in such a way that he will be of help to others.

Now the Holy Spirit is not given only to great and outstanding people. We are not to think of great saints as empowered by the Spirit while ordinary Christians are left to struggle on as best they can. The Spirit is given to "those who believed in him." Every believer receives this great gift. That is the wonderful thing about the Christian way.

Many of the religions of antiquity had the thought that from time to time a divine spirit would come upon people. But they held that this was a gift given only to the outstanding. The recipients of this great gift would be priests or others standing in a specially close relationship to the god. They would not be ordinary worshipers. It was something new when the Christians said that the Spirit would be given to every believer. Paul can go so far as to say, ". . . if anyone has not the Spirit of Christ, he does not belong to him" (Rom. 8:9; he also puts it the other way round, "As many as are led by the Spirit of God these are sons of God," Rom. 8:14). To be a Christian is to have the Holy Spirit. That is a precious and wonderful truth.

Another difference from the religions of antiquity was the way the Christians understood what the Spirit would do. The worshipers in other religions held that the presence of the divine spirit would be known by ecstatic behavior of some kind. People on whom this spirit was bestowed would engage in "holy roller" kinds of activity; they would speak strange gibberish, and there would be other curious physical manifestations.

But the Christians held that the presence of the Holy Spirit would be known by the way people lived. "The fruit of the Spirit," Paul wrote, "is love, joy, peace, longsuffering, kindness, goodness, faith, meekness, self-control" (Gal. 5:22–23). The Spirit makes people better people. He does not simply make them unpredictable people, as the heathen thought.

So it was that in the first century humble, ordinary people came to believe in Jesus and became different people. The Holy Spirit within them guided and strengthened them so that their lives were transformed. Instead of going in the ways of selfishness and sin they became loving people, doing all they could to help others. The transformation was obvious and left even the heathen saying, "Behold, how these Christians love one another!" The Spirit enabled quite ordinary people to live up to what is meant by being members of "the people of God."

"Not Yet Spirit"

Next John has a very unusual expression, which I have translated "it was not yet Spirit." Most translations have something like "the Spirit was not yet given," which makes a better English sentence and seems to translators to be what John must have meant. But there are references to the Spirit's activities among people in earlier days. Thus Luke speaks of John the Baptist as filled with the Holy Spirit from his mother's womb (Luke 1:15). Elizabeth was filled with the Spirit (Luke 1:41), and the Holy Spirit was upon Simeon (Luke 2:25). As we saw in our study of John 3, Jesus taught that it is necessary to be "born of the Spirit" if we are to enter the kingdom of God (John 3:5). So it is clear that the Spirit was active in people before this time. When John has said things like "So is everyone who has been born of the Spirit" (John 3:8), he surely cannot mean that the Spirit has not yet been given.

He goes on to say that the reason for his statement about the Spirit is that "Jesus was not yet glorified." We have seen in our earlier studies that John uses the concept of glory in an unusual way. He does not see glory in terms of majesty and splendor and the like, but in terms of humble service. When we see someone who could rightfully claim a position of ease and honor leaving all that this means in order to engage in lowly service of the needy, there we see true glory as John understands it. And especially do we see glory in the cross of Jesus, for Jesus' death is the supreme example of taking the lowly place to meet the needs of others. So John speaks of Jesus as being "glorified," where other people would say he was "crucified." Thus, with the cross immediately before him, Jesus says, "The hour has come that the Son of man may be glorified," and again, "Now the Son of man is glorified" (12:23; 13:31).

The New Testament makes it clear that things were very different after Jesus died and rose again. In the second chapter of Acts we read of the coming of the Holy Spirit in mighty power on the early church, and from then on references to the Spirit are frequent, much more frequent than in the Old Testament or the Gospels. It has been said that Acts is wrongly named; it is not so much "the Acts of the Apostles" that the book is about as "the Acts of the Holy Spirit." Throughout that book it is the Spirit who is constantly active. And in the Epistles that follow in our New Testament we see that the Spirit was a vital presence for the early Christians.

Putting all this together, we can see that what John is saying is something like this. It is true that the Spirit was active in some measure in Old Testament days and in the days when Jesus was on earth. But he did not come in all his fullness until the work of Jesus had been done. In the providence of God the work of the Son preceded that of the Spirit. The era of the Spirit, the time when the full scope of the Spirit's work would appear, was "not yet."

Jesus invited people to come to him in faith. That was the way they would enter into salvation. Their sins would be forgiven because in due course Jesus would die on the cross as their Savior. And the Spirit of God would take them and transform them. He would make them into loving, outgoing people, people from whose innermost being blessing would flow to others.

This is still the order. Justification precedes sanctification. We do not find our lives transformed by the power of God's Holy Spirit and after that come to believe in Jesus Christ. First we believe, we appropriate what is meant by "Christ crucified." Only then do we come to know what it means to experience the presence of the indwelling Spirit. John is pointing us to an order that is important in the working out of the Christian life.

35

Pride and Prejudice

Some of the crowd, when they had heard these words, said, "This is truly the prophet." Others said, "This is the Christ." But some said, "The Christ does not come from Galilee, does he? Has not the Scripture said, 'The Christ comes of the seed of David and from Bethlehem the village where David was'?" There was a division in the crowd because of him . Now some of them wanted to arrest him, but nobody laid hands on him (John 7:45–52).

The teaching Jesus gave at the feast made a big impression on some of his hearers. "The crowd" is evidently still the pilgrims who had come up to Jerusalem for the feast, not the Jerusalem mob. They were more open-minded than the people of Jerusalem, but not necessarily well informed. They were not unanimous, and John records two different verdicts that they gave after the teaching.

Some of them were sure that Jesus was "the prophet," i.e., the prophet to whose coming Moses looked forward (Deut. 18:15). In earlier passages in this Gospel we have seen references to this prophet, and it is clear that there were quite a few Jews who expected that prophet to appear. Why they should think of Jesus as fulfilling the role is not clear, but then we have no information about what the Jews of the first century thought that prophet would do. Clearly he would be an important person, for otherwise the great Moses would not have prophesied of him centuries before.

There were others who went further and spoke of Jesus as the Christ (v. 41). This we know to be a true perception, though of course we have no way of knowing what they meant by "the Christ." Some people used the term but had strange ideas about who the Christ would be and the kind of work he would do. Some thought he would be a warrior who would push the Romans out of their country. This was probably a fairly widely held idea, because patriotic Jews hated having the Romans rule them and thought that when the Messiah came he would be a very powerful person. Surely then he would get rid of the hated conqueror? Whether or not these people had such a concept of the Messiah we do not know. But at least they saw Jesus as the Christ and we must appreciate that.

But there was prejudice in the air. There were others there who could not possibly think of Jesus as the Messiah, the Christ, because they were so convinced that he came from the wrong place. They held that the Messiah would come from Bethlehem (v. 42), and as Jesus was a Galilean he could not be the Christ. It did not matter how impressive his credentials, how outstanding his teaching, how wonderful his miracles; he came from Galilee and that was that! So does prejudice blind people.

They ask a question about the Christ and Galilee, but the way they put it looks for a negative answer. They rejected the possibility of a Galilean Christ altogether. They speak of "the" Scripture, which normally means a specific passage from the Bible. But it is difficult to find a passage that says exactly what they claim. We can say that the general thrust of many Old Testament passages is such as to suggest that the Christ would be a descendant of David. There are passages like God's message to David: ". . . I will raise up your offspring to succeed you, who will come from your own body, and I will establish his kingdom. . . . I will establish the throne of his kingdom forever" (2 Sam. 7:12–13). Such words point to a great king descended from David, but later words in this passage are hard to apply to the Christ: "When he does wrong, I will punish him . . ." (v. 14b).

There are passages in the Prophets, such as Isaiah 9:2–7, which speaks of the wonderful child who would be born (though without calling him the Christ) and says, "He will reign on David's throne" (v. 7). Again, "A shoot will come up from the stump of Jesse; from his roots a Branch will bear fruit" (Isa. 11:1). Again we read in Jeremiah: "'The days are coming,' declares the Lord, 'when I will raise up to David a righteous Branch . . .'" (Jer. 23:5).

Another possibility is Psalm 89:3–4, where God says, "I have made a covenant with my chosen one, I have sworn to David my servant, I will establish your line forever and make your throne firm through all generations." But this is not a very promising passage for our purpose. While we may well say that it is only Christ who will rule "through all generations," the passage does not specifically mention him. We can certainly say that the name of David is firmly linked with what God would do when he came in blessing (see, for example, Jer. 30:9; 33:15, 17, 22; Ezek. 34:23f.; 37:24; Hos. 3:5; Amos 9:11). We do not doubt that such passages refer to the Christ, but the difficulty is that they do not mention him in set terms and thus we cannot be sure that any of them is "the Scripture" of which the people speak.

There are also passages that point us to Bethlehem, but there is none that says in set terms that the Christ will come from that village. Most Christians think of Micah 5:2, which speaks of "one who will be ruler" as coming from Bethlehem and which goes on to say that his "origins are from of old, from ancient times." This is enough to convince most of us, and I certainly agree. But the point is that the passage does not mention the word *Christ,* and thus we cannot be certain that the people had these words in mind.

In the end we are left wondering. Clearly these people were certain that their Bible connected the Christ with David and with Bethlehem. And we think they were right. We are sure that our Bible does the same. But we cannot find any one passage that does this, so we cannot be sure of exactly what Scripture they had in mind.

So there was a division among the crowd. Some were sure that Jesus was the Christ and some were sure he was not. The second group was so sure and so much in opposition that they wanted to arrest him. They almost certainly did not have the power to do this: John is telling us of people in "the crowd." But they wanted to do so; they were firmly opposed to Jesus.

Failure to Arrest Jesus

The officials therefore came to the chief priests and Pharisees and these said to them, "Why didn't you bring him?" The officials replied, "Never did man so speak." The Pharisees answered them, "Are you deceived too? Have any of the rulers or of the Pharisees believed in him? But this crowd, which does not know the Law, is accursed." Nicodemus, who came to him formerly, said (being one of them), "Does our Law condemn a man if it does not first hear from him and come to know what he is doing?" They answered him saying, "Are you from Galilee too? Search and see that a prophet does not arise from Galilee" (John 7:45–52).

The mention of failure to arrest brings us back to the fact that earlier the chief priests and Pharisees had sent a posse to arrest Jesus (v. 32). Now John tells us what happened when they reported back. They evidently did not say anything at first, but it was obvious that they had no prisoner, so those who had sent them off asked why.

The manuscripts differ a little in reporting their reply (v. 46). Many read: "Never did man speak like this man," and this is accepted by many scholars. But there is good reason for accepting the shorter reading: "Never did man so speak." The officials would have meant that Jesus' teaching impressed them; there had never been a teacher like him. But John probably means us to see a deeper meaning in the words: Never did *man* so speak. The words of Jesus were such that they are not to be thought of as the teaching of a mere man. They are more than that. They are words that come from God.

This is an interesting defense of their failure. It is curious in the first place that they did fail to arrest Jesus. We know that in the providence of God it was not yet time for him to confront the Sanhedrin. But people who are sent to make an arrest are subordinate people and they normally simply carry out instructions. It is not for them to make the big decisions, so they do what they are told. Of course, sometimes they are confronted with circumstances beyond their control, such as the hostility of the crowd. But there were apparently no such circumstances in this case. As far as we can see, there was nothing that physically prevented them from making the arrest.

And people who fail to carry out instructions usually present some excuse. On this occasion we know that there was a division in the crowd, with some people holding that Jesus was the Christ and some rejecting the idea. The officials could have defended themselves by saying that with the crowd divided there was the danger of stirring up trouble if they made the arrest. But they said nothing of the sort. They simply said that no man ever spoke like this.

It was the Pharisees who answered (v. 47). Evidently the chief priests were not as much involved as the Pharisees were. The Pharisees could not go along with the officials for one moment. The only explanation of such outrageous conduct is that they had been "deceived." But that is incredible. So they put their question in a form that means "You aren't deceived, too, are you?" Earlier we noticed that some of the crowd were governed by prejudice in that their idea of the origin of the Messiah prevented them from seeing Jesus as he really was. They rejected his messiahship, not because anything was lacking, but because their own prejudice ruled out the possibility. Now we see the prejudice of the Pharisees. They were the religious experts. They knew.

In their view the common people or the arresting officers could not possibly be right. Prejudice blinded the Pharisees, too.

They go on to point out the stupidity of believing in Jesus by asking whether any of the rulers or Pharisees had believed (v. 48). For them to ask the question was to answer it; no important person could possibly believe! "Rulers" is a general term, but here it seems to mean people like the Sadducees or the leading priests. It is the politically-minded over against the Pharisees, who were religious leaders. What they are saying is that nobody of any consequence has believed in Jesus. It is true that he has a following of a sort. But for the Pharisees this following comes only from the rabble, from people who have no real knowledge. They are certainly not the kind of people who should influence the officials. Actually the officials had not mentioned the crowd, but the Pharisees are not influenced by that. It is enough for them that their own party and the people they respected, such as the "rulers," had not believed in Jesus. Therefore the officials were in the wrong when they took notice of the nobodies who followed Jesus.

The Pharisees go on to speak of the crowd as "accursed" (v. 49). They perhaps have in mind such words as those of Deuteronomy 27:26: "Cursed is the man who does not uphold the words of this law by carrying them out." Whether or not it was this passage that was meant, there cannot be the slightest doubt about the contempt felt by people like the Pharisees for the common people. Those who gave time to the study of the Law regarded this as the highest good open to man (they did not allow women to study it!). They studied it in minute detail, often, alas, missing its important teaching while they concentrated on things like the number of words in a book. But there is no doubt about the way the Pharisees looked down on people who did not accept their view, people like those in the crowd of pilgrims. So they tell the officials that they are quite wrong to be impressed with Jesus. Only accursed people are influenced by him.

A Hesitant Defense

They must have been greatly surprised to find Nicodemus, one of their own number, speaking up in mild opposition to the rest (v. 50). John tells us that this man had come to Jesus earlier, and he repeats now what he told us then, that Nicodemus was 'one of them,' i.e., a ruler. It was the last thing the other Pharisees would have expected.

Actually Nicodemus's defense is very tentative (v. 51). He simply takes up the reference to the Law, which the Pharisaic spokesmen have made, and points out its relevance to their view of Jesus. He does not even make a categorical statement but asks a question, though the way he puts it looks for a negative answer. It is as though he were saying, "Our Law does not condemn a man, does it, if it does not first hear from him . . . ?" The Jewish laws did not provide for automatic condemnation of the kind of Pharisees were engaging in. A man had to be examined and given a chance to defend himself. The judges had to know what he was doing, not what his opponents thought about him.

There is irony here. The Pharisees' question implied that no important person believed in Jesus, and straightaway Nicodemus, "a ruler of the Jews" (3:1) spoke up. They spoke of the people who did not know the Law as "accursed," and immediately they are reminded that they were not acting in accordance with the Law. They were prejudging the case. In the literal sense they were prejudiced.

Prophets and Galilee

And that prejudice prevented them from paying serious attention to what Nicodemus was saying. They were angry men, and people who have lost their temper do not usually weigh arguments carefully. They use another question expecting a negative answer and an emphatic pronoun to give the sense, "Surely *you* aren't from Galilee, are you?" (v. 52). They recognize that Nicodemus is a resident of Jerusalem in good standing. They do not suggest that he is a provincial from the country districts. But they make it clear that they see it as incredible that anyone who is anyone could think for one moment that Jesus, the Galilean, was worthy of credence.

They go on to invite Nicodemus to search for a prophet from Galilee. He will see that there have never been any. Actually they use the present tense, and it is just possible that they mean that no prophet comes from Galilee in their own day. That would mean little, because there was no prophet from anywhere else at that time either. But they may possibly mean that the Galileans of their day were specially unspiritual. "Look for yourself," they may be saying. "You will see that a prophet never comes from people like these Galileans."

If that is not their meaning, if they are saying that there has never been a prophet from Galilee, they are mistaken, for Jonah came from Gath Hepher (2 Kings 14:25), a town in that district. Other prophets may also have come from Galilee; our knowledge of the origins of the prophets is not as full as we would like. But it is certain that Galileans were looked down on by many of the dwellers in Jerusalem (it is not exactly unknown for other city people in other times and other cultures to have a poor opinion of people they regard as country bumpkins).

This attitude was not universal, however, and some of the Rabbis could do better than the Pharisees in our incident. There is a saying of Rabbi Eliezer: "There was not a tribe in Israel from which there did not come prophets." God, of course, raises up his messengers where he will. Prejudiced and self-opinionated people like these Pharisees are not good guides to what God has done and is doing in his world.

It is interesting to notice another possibility. Years ago Rudolph Bultmann, a great German scholar, suggested that we should understand the text to mean not "a prophet" but "the prophet," i.e., the Messiah. Jonah was so obviously from Galilee that the Pharisees should not have made such a glaring mistake as to say that *no* prophet came from that province. But the context is one in which people are talking about the Messiah, and the suggestion is that they are saying that, whatever be the case with other prophets, *the* prophet, the Messiah, does not come from Galilee.

At the time Bultmann and others made this suggestion there was no support for it in the manuscripts. All without exception read "a prophet." But since then a very old papyrus has come to light (which the scholars call P66) and it does have the definite article: "the prophet." This seemed to some a confirmation of Bultmann's conjecture and they have been inclined to accept it.

That is an interesting incident in scholarly activity. But it still remains that every Greek manuscript except this one reads "a prophet," and no good reason has been suggested why this one manuscript should be right and every other Greek manuscript in existence should be wrong. It still seems that we should accept the reading "a prophet." The Pharisees were making Galilee out to be the kind of place from which spiritual leadership can never come. So does prejudice blind even people as religious as these Pharisees.

36

"Caught in the Act"

And they went each to his own home, but Jesus went to the Mount of Olives. Now early in the morning he made his way to the temple. All the people were coming to him and he sat down and taught them. The scribes and the Pharisees bring to him a woman taken in adultery. They stood her in the middle and they say to him, "Teacher, this woman was taken committing adultery, caught in the very act. Now in the law Moses commanded us to stone such women. What, therefore, do you say?" They said this to test him so that they might have something wherewith to accuse him. But Jesus stooped down and wrote on the ground with his finger. Then as they continued to ask him he straightened up and said to them, "Let him that is without sin among you be first to throw a stone at her." And again he stooped and wrote on the ground. Now when they heard this they went out one by one, beginning with the elders, and he was left alone, and the woman in the midst. And Jesus straightened up and said to her, "Woman, where are they? Did no one condemn you?" "No one, sir" she replied. And Jesus said, "Neither do I condemn you. Go, and from now on sin no more" (John 7:53—8:11).

There seems no doubt that this story forms no part of John's Gospel. It is found in only one of the oldest manuscripts, and scholars agree that this one manuscript cannot be held to be right, against the overwhelming weight of the others. When the story does begin to appear it is found in various places: it is found after verse 36 or after verse 44, sometimes at the end of this Gospel, or again after Luke 21:38. More manuscripts put it after verse 52 than anywhere else, but the divergence makes it plain that there were scribes who thought the story ought to be retained but did not know where it ought to go. So they put it where they thought best, and their ideas varied.

The language convinces many that the passage does not belong in this Gospel. For example, it speaks of "the scribes" (v. 3), an expression familiar to us from the first three Gospels, but which John does not use at all. There are several Greek words which occur in this little story, but which are found rarely or not at all or which are used in different ways in the Fourth Gospel.

Such considerations seem decisive. There is no real reason for thinking that John included this story in his Gospel. But that does not mean that it did not happen. The story has an authentic ring to it. As we read it we feel, "This is what Jesus would have said!"

If it is not the account of something that actually happened, the question arises, "Where did the story come from?" It is not the kind of tale that the early church would have made up, for it might be taken to mean that adultery did not matter very much, and the early church took up no such position. Indeed, the story seems not to have been very popular in the early church and it would seem to be for this reason. Christian leaders apparently felt that it might encourage people to engage in sexual adventures, which they themselves resolutely opposed. So it seems that this is a true story, a story of something that really happened, which for some reason the writers of our Gospels chose not to include. But it persisted in the early church and in time tended to become attached to John's Gospel. We may profitably study it as an incident in which we see Jesus' compassion and the way he handled ingenious and hardhearted opponents.

The Accusation

Clearly the story once belonged to a longer narrative. As we have it, it starts with a statement that everyone went home, but it does not tell us who these people were, nor from where they went home. It goes on to say that Jesus went to the Mount of Olives, so evidently the preceding narrative was set in Jerusalem. And if we do not know much about the place, neither do we know the time. But Luke tells us that when Jesus was in Jerusalem in the days just before he was arrested, he used to teach in the city during the day and go out to lodge in the Mount of Olives at night (Luke 21:37; Mark speaks of Bethany, Mark 11:11, but this would be seen as part of the Mount of Olives). It would all fit in if we thought of the incident as taking place at Jerusalem during Jesus' last days.

The story goes on to say that early in the morning Jesus went to the temple, and we are reminded that Luke says that the people went to the temple early to hear Jesus teach (Luke 21:38). "All the people" came to hear (v. 2), so evidently there was quite a large crowd. "Were coming" is continuous: it gives a picture of people continuing to come over quite a period. Jesus sat down to teach, for sitting, of course, was the normal posture for a teacher in those times. Standing before a class seems not to have been usual.

Now "the scribes and the Pharisees" come on the scene. Scribes were people who could read and write, quite an accomplishment in a day when the majority were illiterate. We should not exaggerate this, for there were many who could read in the first-century Roman Empire, but we should not read back into the situation anything like the degree of literacy in a modern Western community. Being members of a profession concerned with reading and writing, the scribes themselves did a good deal of reading, and many of them were learned. And as the Law, the first five books of our Old Testament, was the principal subject of study, they tended to be religious men as well. This, of course, formed a natural link with the Pharisees who were wholeheartedly concerned with the way God should be served. While the scribes were not all Pharisees (some were linked with the high priests and their associates, e.g., Acts 4:5), it is never surprising to find them mentioned together.

On this occasion they come to Jesus, bringing with them a woman they said had been caught in the very act of adultery, and they go on to ask whether she should be stoned. This raises some very difficult questions.

Proving Adultery

One of the questions concerns the proving of adultery. Let us notice first of all that in Judaism at that time adultery meant sexual relations outside marriage on the part of a married woman. Her husband was not regarded as committing adultery unless his sexual partner was married. In the male-dominated society of that era there was a wider permissiveness for the husband than for the wife.

But adultery was an offense very hard to prove. This is so in the nature of the case, for lovers the world over and the centuries through tend to seek solitude. In all its forms lovemaking is a private activity of two persons. It is easier to suspect a breach of marriage relations than to prove it. This difficulty was intensified by the way first-century Jews conducted their legal system. They insisted on much more rigorous standards of proof than those accepted elsewhere. For example, it was required that there be two witnesses, and it was not enough for the witnesses to have seen the offenders in a compromising position, such as coming out of a room in which they had been alone. Even lying on a bed together was not sufficient proof. The witnesses must be able to testify that the movements of the people in question allowed no other interpretation. And, of course, the evidence of the two witnesses must agree.

There was moreover a legal rule, "No penalty without a warning." This meant that in the case of any crime it was necessary that a potential offender be warned not to do such and such a thing. He must be aware that a certain action was wrong. He was not regarded as in breach of a law if he did not know what the law provided. An interesting provision is that a scholar need not be warned orally. It is presumed that his study of the Law made him aware of what he should and should not do. But lesser mortals had to be told.

In the case of adultery this meant normally that the husband expressly told his wife, in front of witnesses, of her duty. Of course, it could be argued that even a young bride knows what she should do in marriage and this knowledge made legal arguments possible. But the maxim was there and must be borne in mind in such a situation as the one with which we are dealing. It added to the difficulty of proving adultery, however it be understood. However, on this occasion the scribes and the Pharisees appear to imply that the conditions had been fulfilled. They had the necessary witnesses and the woman had been taken in the very act.

A Trap?

All this leads us to ask some questions. First, it is impossible for a woman to commit adultery all by herself, so the question arises, "Where was the man?" If the woman had been taken in the very act, as her accusers said, then there should have been a male offender who was taken, too. Of course, if there had been a trap set for the woman, arrangements might well have been made to enable the man in the case to make good his escape. It is not easy to see how he could have avoided capture otherwise.

We do not know why a trap should have been set for the woman, but clearly the accusers were bent on having her executed. It may well be that the husband wanted her out of the way and had engaged helpers to secure that end. In Jewish law he could, of course, have divorced her without any difficulty. All that was necessary was for him to write "a bill of divorcement" and send her away. But if she had property she would take it with her when she was divorced, whereas if she died it would revert to her husband. We know nothing of her circumstances, and the situation may have been very different. All that I am saying is that the story reads as though a trap had been set for the woman, and it is not difficult to envisage circumstances in which an unscrupulous husband might seek to entrap his erring wife with a view to having her executed.

Another feature of the story is the lack of proper legal officials. There is no mention of any officer of the court, and the accusers may well have been trying to bring about a lynching. They faced a problem because, while the Law of Moses provided for an execution as they claimed, it was not possible for the Jews to execute anyone without the permission of the Romans (see 18:31), and the Romans would never give their permission for an execution for such an offense as adultery. But if a lynching took place, and if this was discovered and the perpetrators brought to book, they could always claim that they were following the provisions of their religion and hope that they would not be treated too harshly (this was evidently what happened when Stephen was stoned). In any case the Romans would not be able to bring the woman back to life.

But if this is the way the events should be understood, it was well for the lynching party that they should make out as good a case as they could for the woman's guilt and for her punishment according to their law. So they had their witnesses. And they went through the form of consulting Jesus, who was a religious teacher, even if not one recognized by the rabbinical schools.

"What Do You Say?"

But if the participants in the plot had ends of their own to secure, at least some of them were Pharisees and strongly opposed to Jesus. They decided to use the woman to try to score against him. So they submit the case to him and ask for his opinion. It seems that rabbis were often asked to settle knotty points in the interpretation of Scripture. Rabbis were the great expositors of the Law of Moses, and when a difficult point arose it was standard procedure (and very convenient!) to look to the experts for their opinion. There are many such interpretations scattered through the Mishnah and the Talmud. They are not put in the form of decisions in legal cases, but in that of interpretations of passages of Scripture as in the present case.

They begin politely by addressing Jesus as "Teacher" (v. 4). They go on to explain the circumstances. There is apparently no doubt about guilt. The woman was "caught in the very act." The problem was what their course of action should be. They say that Moses prescribed stoning in such cases (v. 5), though it should be noted that they do not quote Moses exactly. In both Leviticus 20:10 and Deuteronomy 22:22 it is provided that both guilty parties be executed, whereas these zealots use the feminine form and confine their attention to the execution of the woman in the case. They also specify stoning as the method of execution, whereas the Law of Moses says no more than that the guilty couple should be put to death. Stoning was prescribed for the couple when a man had sex with an engaged girl (Deut. 22:23–24), in circumstances where her consent could be assumed, but for only the man if circumstances were otherwise (Deut. 22:25–27). It is true that the Jews had come to the view that stoning was to be used where Scripture spoke of the death penalty without prescribing the method. But the point is that here the accusers in their zeal ascribe to Moses words that he did not utter.

For them the position in Scripture was plain. But would Jesus agree? They use the emphatic pronoun, "What do *you* say?" On the surface of it, this is a perfectly normal question. They were about to do something that the Romans might not approve of, and they were consulting a religious teacher to make sure that they were doing the right thing.

But the narrator goes on to tell us that they were not sincere (v. 6). They asked their question as a test for Jesus, with a view to getting him to say something of which they could accuse him. It is not quite certain what the nature of the trap was. Perhaps they thought that if Jesus said, "Stone her," he would be in trouble with the Romans, for only they had the right to execute and they did not execute for adultery. If on the other hand he said, "Do not stone her," he might well lose influence with many of the Jews, for he could then be pictured as urging people not to obey the Law. It is objected that the Romans would not have taken action, but we do not know enough about their views on such situations to be definite.

Another suggestion is that the zealots were simply concerned with Jewish opinion, not that of the Romans. Those who hold this view maintain that, while death was the penalty for adultery in the Law, there was a strong body of opinion that opposed this. There is evidence that adultery was fairly prevalent during the first century, but executions were uncommon. Thus, were Jesus to favor stoning, he would alienate a considerable number of people who thought the penalty too severe. But if he rejected it, he would be held to be soft on sin and a breaker of the Law.

His enemies clearly felt that whichever way he answered they had him. Of course, he could have avoided giving a decision. He was not in an official position. He was not required to make pronouncements and he was not a recognized teacher. He could simply have refused to answer. But if he had taken this option, the woman would certainly have been killed. In any case it was not Jesus' way to avoid hard questions.

Writing on the Ground

But at first he said nothing. He stooped and wrote on the ground with his finger. The narrator does not tell us what he wrote, but Christian expositors have not let this deter them. In the early church it was suggested that he wrote the sins of the accusers, but this does not attract much support in modern times. Some have felt that Jesus was following the practice of Roman judges, who wrote their sentence first and then read it out. On this view what he wrote was "Let him that is without sin among you be first to throw a stone at her." Another view is that Jesus simply did not wish to look at these professedly godly men who were so intent on killing a woman; the writing was incidental.

An interesting modern view is that Jesus wrote some words from the Old Testament. The Hebrew alphabet consists of consonants only, the reader supplying the necessary vowels. A system was devised of using dots and dashes above and below the consonants to indicate vowels, but the text of sacred Scripture is consonantal. Sometimes more than one set of vowels can be supplied to the same consonants, and in the first century it was held that a given set of consonants may be understood to include all the meanings given by the different sets of vowels that might be supplied. If Jesus spoke the words, the reasoning runs, he was limited to the meaning of the vowels he actually spoke, whereas if he wrote them, he could include all the possible meanings of those consonants.

It has accordingly been suggested that Jesus wrote some words from Exodus 23:1: "Do not help a wicked man by being a malicious witness." With different vowels "a wicked man" becomes "wickedness." If this is in fact what Jesus wrote and if this is why he wrote it, he is warning the accusers (a) to be careful lest they be guilty of being malicious witnesses, and (b) to make sure that they are not associating themselves with wickedness, with an unsavory business. People who themselves were not giving false witness might find themselves in legal trouble if they associated themselves with what false witnesses were doing.

Witnesses

The apocryphal Book of Susanna emphasizes the importance of truthfulness in witnesses and the danger attending the bearing of false witness. In the story two wicked elders tried to persuade Susanna to have sexual intercourse with them, and when she refused they accused her of this misconduct with a young man. She was sentenced to death, but as she was being led away to execution a young man called Daniel prevailed on them to go back to the place of judgment. There he examined the witnesses separately and showed that they were lying. The result was that the punishment the elders had tried to have administered to Susanna was inflicted on them and they were executed. This insistence on true witness and the danger of false witness must be kept in mind as we proceed to the next stage of the story.

When Jesus said nothing, but wrote in the dust, apparently his enemies felt that they had him in trouble. They pressed him to give them an answer. His answer has become a classic: "Let him that is without sin among you be first to throw a stone at her" (v. 7). It could not be said that Jesus was soft on law and order. He definitely told them to throw a stone. But, by confining his invitation to the man among them who was without sin, he effectively stopped the execution.

His words invited them to think again. And among the thoughts that went through their minds there must have been the importance of being sure the witnesses were trustworthy. If no proper warning had been given to the woman, for example, the witnesses might well be in danger. And anyone who associated with a false witness could be penalized.

Jesus resumed his writing on the ground while they thought about it. One scholar thinks that this time he wrote, "Have nothing to do with a false charge" (Exod. 23:7). Those who read these words would be able to finish the verse: ". . . and do not put an innocent or honest person to death, for I will not acquit the guilty." These very words had been used by Daniel in the story of Susanna to convict the lying elders and bring about their deaths. Whether Jesus wrote these words or not we cannot know, but the truth they expressed must have occurred to his hearers. At first they had been eager for a stoning, seeing nothing but the opportunity for killing off someone who could not strike back. Now they realized that it was not so simple. If they joined with false witnesses to bring about an execution, their own execution might well follow.

Exit the Accusers

As the realities of the situation dawned on them they went out (v. 9). None of them were guiltless, and they came to see that they were in no position to throw stones. How many of them were deterred by the simple realization that they were sinners themselves, and how many were thinking of the penalty of associating with false witnesses, we have no way of knowing. All that we know is that they went. The elders went first. They would have the greater responsibility. In the culture of the day they would be expected to take the lead, which meant that they had to be very careful. If there was anything amiss, they would be expected to take a stand against it, so their place was more precarious than that of the younger men. But when the elders went off, the younger saw that their position was impossible and they went away, too.

Jesus stood up and saw that the woman alone remained. "In the midst" may mean that Jesus' original hearers were still there and that those who had gone were the people who had accused the woman. But the important point was that there was nobody there who wanted to stone the woman.

Jesus asked her, "Where are they? Did no one condemn you?" (v. 10). "No one, sir" was her answer (v. 11). We could take the last word in the sense "Lord," but there is no evidence that she was a follower of Jesus, so it is probably better to take it in its more usual sense. She is polite and doubtless deeply grateful.

Jesus declined to condemn her, but this does not mean that he countenanced her sin. "From now on sin no more" implies that she had been sinning and is a call to her to amend her ways. Jesus does not say that she is forgiven. She has given no evidence of penitence or faith. She was still an unregenerate sinner. But he had been merciful to her, and his call to her to cease from sin is a way of indicating that the way is open wide if she would but come.

37

The Light of the World

So Jesus spoke to them again saying, "I am the light of the world. He who follows me will certainly not walk in the darkness, but will have the light of life." The Pharisees therefore said to him, "You are bearing witness about yourself; your testimony is not true." Jesus answered them saying, "Even if I do bear witness about myself my testimony is true, because I know where I came from and where I am going. But you do not know where I come from or where I am going. You make your judgment according to the flesh, I judge no one. And if I do judge, my judgment is true, because I am not alone, but I and the Father who sent me. And in your law it stands written that the testimony of two men is true. I am he who bears witness about myself and the Father who sent me bears witness about me." Therefore they said to him, "Where is your Father?" Jesus answered, "You know neither me nor my Father. If you had known me, you would know my Father too." He spoke these words in the Treasury, as he was teaching in the temple, and no one arrested him, because his hour had not yet come (John 8:12–20).

Most scholars hold that this chapter continues to refer to what happened at the Feast of Tabernacles. That was a great festival and its observance was not hurried. The ceremonies with light and with water were picturesque and were clearly the center of attention. As this chapter is taken up at least in part with the importance of light and the way light helps us see something of the significance of Jesus' person and mission, it is thought that it would naturally refer to what happened and what was said at the feast. It would certainly fit in.

But we should notice that nothing is said about the feast in this part of the Gospel. Nothing is said about the crowds either, and the crowds at the feast were large and were a significant part of the celebration. Tabernacles was not a private occasion, but one when the gathering of large numbers of people made it clear that this was a national celebration. Now the crowds are mentioned constantly in chapter 7 (eight times in this one chapter), but John does not mention them again until 11:42. It is, of course, possible that they were there but it just happens that he says nothing about them. But it is more probable that he does not mention them because they were not there. It seems that the feast was over and the crowds had gone off home. This is all the more likely in that throughout this part of the Gospel Jesus is confronted by his enemies. They hassle him and try to trip him up in some way. They are there throughout. We would probably not be far wrong if we thought of the events of this chapter as taking place after the Feast of Tabernacles, though not long after it. The crowds have gone, but people's thoughts are still taken up with the wonderful ceremonies. And without the crowds to inhibit them, the enemies of Jesus use the occasion to try to overthrow him.

Jesus' Great Claim

The "so" and the "again" (v. 12) mean that this followed on some previous incident. As we saw in our last study, there is no real reason for holding that the story of the woman caught in adultery formed part of the original Gospel, let alone that it stood just before these words. And if we go back to what immediately precedes it, we find a meeting of Jewish leaders. There is no obvious connection.

But the last words in that incident were the retort of the leaders to Nicodemus in which they ask whether he is a Galilean and invite him to search and see that no prophet ever arises from Galilee. It may be that we are to take John as meaning that Jesus' great claim is to be understood over against that contemptuous rejection. They saw him as an insignificant provincial, not even a prophet. John immediately records that Jesus is the light, not just of Galilee, not just of all the land of the Jews, but of the whole world. It is the kind of ironical situation that John delights to record.

Jesus' "I am" is in the style of deity (v. 12). In an earlier study I pointed out that in Greek it is not necessary to give the personal pronoun on most occasions (p. 217). The verbal forms differ with different personal subjects. And, as the form of the verb thus showed what the subject must be, people did not bother to state it. They let the verb tell what the subject was.

But if they wanted to put some emphasis on the subject, if they wanted to say "*I* am" rather than "I am," they included the personal pronoun. The use of the pronoun points to emphatic speech.

Now when pious Jews were translating their Scriptures from Hebrew into Greek they evidently thought that they ought to use some emphatic form of speech when they were giving us the words of God himself. We can still feel the force of this when we reflect on the form in which we have traditionally received the Ten Commandments. There is a series of commands beginning "Thou shalt not—" a form we would not normally use at all. But it sounds right in the Commandments. In line with this the translators quite often used the emphatic pronoun when recording words that God himself had spoken. "I am," with God as the speaker, would be the emphatic "*I* am."

This is what we find with the saying "I am the light of the world." The "I" is emphatic. This is the way God speaks. The form of the expression is making a claim, quite apart from the meaning of the words.

Light

And the words do make a staggering claim. We are probably to understand them against the background of the Feast of Tabernacles. The words were evidently spoken not long after that feast, and John has recorded them right after his account of the feast. Now a very spectacular part of the feast was the use of the great candelabra. There were four of them and they were filled with oil by young men who to do this climbed ladders that, according to the Talmud, were fifty cubits high. The light from the lamps was brilliant and the Mishnah says that "there was not a courtyard in Jerusalem that did not reflect the light." Such brilliant illumination was a great occasion and seen but rarely in the ancient city. When the feast was over, of course, the great candelabra were not lit. This formed a marked contrast, and it was in the darkness of the post-festival period that Jesus spoke.

He spoke not only of being a light to Jerusalem, which, spectacular as it was, was all that the light of the feast could mean. He spoke of being a light of the world. The imagery implies that the world is in darkness, in the darkness of sin. Men left to themselves cannot overcome that darkness. But Jesus claims that he can bring them the illumination that will banish the darkness in which they habitually live, and this wherever they are in the whole wide world.

There is some foreshadowing of this in the Old Testament, for example, when the Servant of the Lord is called to be "a light for the Gentiles" (Isa. 42:6; 49:6; cf. 51:4). It seems that the idea did not die out completely in Israel, but on the whole the nation did not make much of it. In the first century the evidence is that most Jews were inward-looking. They were very happy that their nation was the chosen nation and that they were the chosen people. But they saw that as a privilege rather than a responsibility. Such a group as the community in which the Dead Sea Scrolls were written was very particularist. They saw themselves as the people God chose and all outside their sect as lost. Other Jews were not so extreme, but most of them tended to confine the love of God to his chosen people.

So Jesus' teaching that he was the light, not simply of his followers, nor even of Israel, but of the whole world, was breathtaking. It implied that God had a love for all mankind and not only for Israel. No one is beyond the love and the care of God. The coming of the Son of God is to bring light to all people, whoever they may be and wherever they may live. He is the light of nothing less than this whole world.

The Light of Life

People are expected to react to the light. They are not simply to be happy because it has reached them, as the people of Jerusalem were happy in the illumination of the great candelabra. Jesus immediately speaks of people following him. The light is to bring them out of the darkness, and that means that they must now follow the right road; they must follow Jesus.

In first-century Palestine a teacher like Jesus moved about from place to place and his disciples went with him. So to "follow" Jesus for people like the Twelve (and others, see Luke 8:1–3) meant literally following him as he went from place to place. But the word, of course, could also be used in the sense "follow as a disciple." While there was often in Jesus' lifetime a literal, physical following, the term was used from the first in the sense of becoming an adherent of Jesus and seeking to live according to his teaching.

When anyone does this, Jesus says, he will certainly not walk in the darkness. There is an emphatic double negative here, which emphasizes that it is impossible for anyone who follows the light of the world to find himself walking in the dark. Darkness is often used in antiquity, in Judaism and elsewhere, for negative things, things like obscurity, concealment, deception, error, and the like. Sometimes it is used of the darkness of death. Jesus is saying that anyone who follows him is delivered from all such things.

On the contrary, the follower "will have the light of life." This means more than that he will walk in the light. That way of putting it, of course, expresses an important truth, but it views light as something external, an illumination coming from some external source that enables the traveler to see where he is going. To "have" the light means something extra, for now the light is not something external that may or may not be present when it is needed. The follower of Jesus *has* the light.

And this light is "the light of life." That is to say, it is light that excludes death, light that is intimately involved with life. We have seen repeatedly in this Gospel that these two concepts are closely connected. Now we see this repeated and at the same time see that Jesus is the source of the light that means life.

Testimony

But Jesus' opponents are not listening, or if they are hearing the words they are not taking notice of what they mean. They do not concern themselves with light and darkness; indeed, these two great concepts are not mentioned again in the rest of the chapter. Instead the Pharisees turn immediately to the question of the rules of evidence. They say that Jesus is not to be believed because he is talking about himself (v. 13). Of course, when a man talks about himself, his detractors will always think that he has a bias and that what he says must be weighed carefully. But these Pharisees go further than that. They simply reject Jesus' whole testimony because it comes from him personally. "Your testimony is not true," they say. By "true" they seem to mean "valid"; it is testimony that does not conform to the rules and therefore is not to be accepted. They would have agreed in any case that it was not true, but their point is that self-testimony is not valid testimony and cannot be accepted when anyone is trying to establish a point in a court of law.

So they want to talk about testimony. Jesus proceeds to show that they do not really know what they are talking about. He points out that he is qualified to talk about himself whereas they are not. Jesus is aware of his heavenly origin and destiny, but these Pharisees know neither (v. 14). The great point that is insisted on throughout this Gospel is that Jesus is sent by God. The two Greek verbs for "to send" occur with great frequency. In fact John uses both of them more often than does anyone else in the New Testament. And his most frequent use is for the Father's sending of the Son. It is a basic teaching of this Gospel that in Jesus we see none less than the One whom God has sent into the world to do his will and bring salvation to sinners.

But God has not sent him with a blare of trumpets and an army of angels so that it would be impossible to deny his heavenly credentials. The self-satisfied, the proud, the smug, are in no position to appreciate the great spiritual realities, and they do not recognize the Son of God. The lowly in heart are in a different position. They do believe in Jesus and they recognize that God has sent him. They may not know all about him and their capacity to carry on a theological discussion may be minimal. But it is not great intellectual capacity or years of theological education that matter. Such things neither bring people close to Jesus nor compel them to stay at a distance. It is spiritual perception that counts and it is this that the Pharisees lacked. They did not have the humility or the self-knowledge or the close walk with God that would enable them to appreciate what God was doing in Jesus.

Their judgment was "according to the flesh" (v. 15). "Flesh" is, of course, the soft part of the body and in itself is neither good nor bad. In some parts of the New Testament it is used of what is sinful (cf. our expression: the temptations of "the world, the flesh and the devil"), but John does not often have such a usage. The term can refer simply to what is weak about human life, and this human life of ours is inevitably weak in its knowledge of ultimate spiritual things and in its ability to understand and act on them. The trouble with these Pharisees was that they were making a judgment on profound spiritual realities (the Father's sending of his Son into the world) on the basis of human weakness and human limitation. They did not understand Jesus' heavenly origin and destination and were thus unable to judge him.

His attitude was so different from theirs that he says, "I judge no one." In the sense in which they were judging (with their minds closed to fundamental spiritual realities) he was not judging. It would be wrong to use the same verb for two such different activities. So Jesus says simply that he judges no one.

This presents us with a problem, for Jesus later says that he has many things "to speak and to judge" (v. 26), that he came into the world for judgment (9:39). Indeed, the Father has committed all judgment to him (5:22). We should probably understand this in the sense that judgment was not his aim. He came not to judge but to save (12:47), and this is constantly in view throughout this Gospel. But the salvation he died to bring is not something automatic. There were many who refused to have anything to do with Jesus or his salvation. Did he then judge them? In one sense, not at all. They judged themselves. They turned away from the salvation that God was offering them, and that meant that they called down judgment on themselves. We get it all wrong if we think of Jesus as a grim tyrant looking around for people he could send to hell. He came to rescue people, not to sentence them, and John never lets us forget this. This is what is in mind at this point. Jesus, the Savior, judges no one. Those who reject him judge themselves.

The Testimony of Two

So Jesus claims that when he judges his judgment is true (v. 16). This is because he does not stand alone but is to be seen always in conjunction with the Father who sent him. Notice how the Father's sending of the Son is stressed. For John this is one of the great truths and again and again he reports sayings of Jesus that bring this out. So Jesus' judgment is never to be thought of as a merely personal judgment. All he does he does together with the Father.

This enables him to go on to the validity of his testimony, even as judged by the criteria of the Pharisees. They disregarded the testimony of Jesus because it stood alone. Very well. Jesus reminds them that "in your law" testimony is valid when there are two witnesses who agree (v. 17). His "your law" sets him apart from them (cf. the way Nicodemus can say "our law," 7:51). At the same time it reminds them of what was valid even from their point of view. The law required two witnesses (Deut. 19:15), and even when a man's life was at stake two witnesses were sufficient to send him to execution (Deut. 17:6). It was specifically laid down that the testimony of one person is not sufficient (Num. 35:30), and the Jews were so impressed by this that even when the number of witnesses was not mentioned they took it that at least two were required.

Two witnesses would establish a position. Jesus goes on to say that in his case there were two witnesses, the Father and himself (v. 18), and once more the Father is characterized by the fact that he sent Jesus. Mission is very important throughout this Gospel. It was this testimony that carried conviction to Jesus. For him what men said mattered little; it was the Father's testimony that mattered.

But for the Pharisees that was another matter. They asked where Jesus' Father was (v. 19). They were doubtless looking for a human figure, someone they could see and question. Such a figure was not available. But then what difference did it make? They could see and question Jesus and they still refused to believe him. The point was that they lacked spiritual perception. They could not recognize that the wonderful teaching Jesus was giving was true, nor could they recognize that it was endorsed by the Father they professed to serve. As Jesus had just spoken of himself as "the light of the world" (v. 12), it may not be inappropriate to say that the Pharisees' preoccupation with darkness disqualified them from a worthwhile verdict on the light with which they were confronted. They never did come to see that there was a unity between Jesus and the Father. If they had come to see the truth of what Jesus was saying, if they had really come to know him (as his disciples had done), they would have known the Father as well. The two are inseparable. It is impossible to know the one without the other. The Pharisees never did learn this.

Jesus' Hour

John rounds off this section of his narrative by telling us that Jesus was teaching "in the Treasury" (v. 20). This can scarcely mean the place where the temple treasures were actually stored. It must refer to that part of the precincts where people came when they wished to make their offerings. There was a part of the Court of the Women where there were thirteen trumpet-shaped collection boxes into which the devout would cast their offerings. Each one had an inscription to show to what use the offerings cast into that particular box would be put. That the court was called "the Court of the Women" does not mean that men would not be there, for each of the courts was named for the people who could go no farther. Thus Israelites as well as Gentiles were in the Court of the Gentiles, but the Gentiles could not go into the Court of the Women. Israelite males and females could both be found in that court, but women could not go into the next court.

John goes on to say that nobody arrested Jesus. He implies that some would have liked to do this, and in view of the hostility of the Pharisees throughout the section we have been looking at we can see that this was certainly justified. But "his hour had not yet come" and until it had come he was safe from all his enemies. As we have seen in earlier studies, this is a note that begins as early as 2:4 and recurs from time to time throughout the Gospel until we come to the eve of the crucifixion. John is clear throughout that Jesus moves towards his "hour."

38

Dying in Sin

Therefore he said to them again, "I am going away and you will look for me and you will die in your sin. Where I am going you cannot come." The Jews said therefore, "He won't kill himself, will he? Because he says, 'Where I am going you cannot come.'" And he said to them, "You are from below, I am from above; you are of this world, I am not of this world. Therefore I told you that you will die in your sins. For if you do not believe that I AM, you will die in your sins" (John 8:21–24).

We have seen that John has a great interest in life and specifically in eternal life. It is one of his great interests to bring out the wonderful difference Jesus made by bringing to people the news of what God has done to give them life. He emphasizes that the whole purpose of the death of Jesus was to bring life to all who believe. In studying John we must bear this well in mind and indeed put strong emphasis on it.

But the other side of that coin is that there is such a thing as death. People may refuse the offer of eternal life. Some did in John's day and some do in our day. John does not overlook the fact that the offer of life is made against a background of death. If people are not brought into life, then they die. John is a realist. He does not gloss over unpleasant facts. And one such unpleasant fact is that if people do not enter eternal life, they die.

John pays a good deal of attention to this. For example, he uses the verb *to die* twenty-eight times in all, which is more than in any other book in the New Testament. Nearest is Romans, which has it twenty-three times, a book that, like this Gospel, gives serious attention to the issues of eternal life and death. The other Gospels have the verb much less frequently: Matthew five times, Mark nine, and Luke ten times. Clearly John's use of the word is exceptional. He also has the noun *death* more than the other Gospel writers, but as all four come within the narrow range of six to eight this is not specially significant.

John speaks of sin seventeen times, while Matthew has it seven times, Mark six times, and Luke eleven times. This emphasis is not always noticed. For example, one scholar has written, "The fact of sin ceases to be the dominant fact in his theology, but here and there he recognises it and makes some partial attempt to connect it with his own doctrine of the work of Christ"; and again, "the doctrine of sin, in the sense that it meets us elsewhere in the New Testament, is almost wholly absent from the Fourth Gospel."

But this is just not true: it does not square with the facts. John has so many great thoughts that apparently this scholar did not notice that he is not oblivious to the problem of sin. John has his own way of dealing with it, and it would be a mistake to hold that, because he does not treat sin in the same way as does Paul, for example, he does not see it as serious. He does. And in the passage we are studying today we see this clearly. Here he links death and sin in such a way as to make it clear that both are serious and that the one leads inevitably to the other. The only way of escape is to respond to the fact that God sent his Son to be the Savior of the world.

Going Away

"Therefore he said" links the words that follow to those that precede, but the link is not such that we can say exactly how they are related or whether they were spoken on the same occasion. We do not know exactly when Jesus said them, but John knows that they are important and he includes them. The words about going away are similar to what Jesus said earlier (7:33–34), though there he spoke about a short time while here that is not expressed. It may be held to be implied, but here Jesus concentrates on the facts of his departure, their inability to find him, and their death in sin. The verb *to go away* can be used of the ordinary goings and comings of life (e.g., 4:16; 21:3), but John uses it quite often in a special sense. Perhaps that is not the best way of putting it, for this use is never in John's own words, but always when he is reporting what Jesus said.

Several times Jesus said he was "going away," mostly without saying anything about his destination. Sometimes he says he is going to the Father (16:10, 17), sometimes to him who sent him (7:33; 16:5), and once he says he is going to God (13:3). He tells the disciples that he is going away and that where he goes they cannot come (13:33, 36). He assures them also that, though he is going away, he will come back to them (14:28). And, while this going is clearly mysterious, Jesus knows very well what his destination is (8:14).

Thus the idea that is put before the people in the passage before us is not an unusual one in this Gospel, but one that we meet a number of times. And it is clear that it puzzled the hearers. We are not always told of their reaction, but whenever we hear of it they do not understand.

Here Jesus simply says that he is going away. Now the words "I am going away" need mean no more than that Jesus was about to remove to another part of the country. But it would not be true of such a destination that his hearers could not come there, so the words must have a different meaning. In the light of the other passages that refer to Jesus as going to God or the Father or him that sent him, there can be little doubt that here he is referring to his going away from this world in death. Of course, his enemies would die in due course, but their death would not be like his. There was something voluntary about Jesus' death, and it was a death that would restore him to the life with the Father he had enjoyed before coming to this earth. They could not come to God in such a passing from this world.

"You will look for me," Jesus says. This probably is meant to bring out the importance of the passage of time. By then it will be too late. During the time that he moved among them they had ample opportunity for accepting his message, for becoming his disciples, for entering into salvation. But in due course their opportunity would be over. Jesus would return to the Father and, search as they would, they would no longer be able to hear and see him. No matter how hard they looked, they would not find him. There is no substitute for using the opportunity while we have it.

"You Will Die in Your Sin"

Jesus tells them that they will die in their sin. This does not mean simply that they will be sinners all their days until they die. It means that they will face that death that is the due reward of sin (Paul can speak of "the wages of sin" as death, Rom. 6:23). Jesus does not go into detail and there remains something mysterious about the saying. But it is clear enough to be devastating. To die in sin is the ultimate disaster. Jesus speaks of dying "in sin," whereas in verse 24 he has the plural "sins." This may be nothing more than the variation without significant difference in meaning that we have seen a number of times in John. But the words about dying in sin are placed before the verb here, which gives them special emphasis, and it may be that we are to understand that rejecting Jesus is the sin of all sins.

There is an application to physical death. In due course these people would come to the end of their earthly lives and go through the portal we call death. That would mark the end of the time open to them to repent and believe in the Savior. It is the consistent teaching of the New Testament writers that there is something decisive about life here on earth. Here we face the critical choice and we carry the result with us into the afterlife. As the writer to the Hebrews puts it, "It is appointed to men to die once and for all, and after this—judgment!" (Heb. 9:27). It is now that is the day of salvation, and we do well to pay good heed to this aspect of scriptural teaching.

Jesus' words also apply to death in the sense that death is the wages of sin. The link with sin in this saying is plain. Sin cuts us off from that life that is life indeed and shuts us up to the full horror of death. It may be worth reflecting that John has just recorded Jesus' words about being the Light of the World and his assurance that the person who follows him will not walk in darkness, but rather "will have the light of life" (v. 12). The death of which he is now speaking is the reverse of all this. It means a rejection of the Light of the World. It means a refusal of discipleship of the Son of God. It means doing without "the light of life" and doing without that light by one's own deliberate choice. It means shutting oneself up to all that darkness means.

Suicide

It is curious that Jesus' opponents do not give a moment's thought to all this. I suppose that this is the way of the world all through the centuries. It certainly is the case today. The world's tragedy is that with the way of salvation before them people choose to concentrate on the world's fading attractions. It is not so much that they deliberately weigh the claims of Christ and reject them, as that, like the people in this passage, they do not take him seriously. They fix on something quite irrelevant and give no thought to where that leaves them, nor to the magnitude of the opportunity they are slighting.

Instead of facing what it means to die in their sin, the people talking to Jesus wonder whether he will kill himself (v. 22). The form in which they put their question shows that they do not take this very seriously (it expects the answer "No"). But it is the one thing they face out of what Jesus has said.

Suicide was regarded as a very serious matter by first-century Jews. They were impressed by the words of Genesis 9:5: "And for your life-blood I will surely demand an accounting. . . . ." They remembered, too, the dreadful fate of Ahithophel (2 Sam. 17:23). An occasional exception was made, for example in the case of Samson, who slew so many Philistines in a way that brought about his own death. Nearer to New Testament times there was praise and admiration for the defenders of the fortress of Masada who killed themselves and their families rather than fall into the hands of the Romans. But such exceptions were rare. Generally speaking, suicide was thought of as desperately wicked and as inevitably bringing the punishment of hell on its perpetrator.

Josephus, the first-century Jewish historian, speaks strongly about taking one's own life: "But as for those who have laid mad hands on themselves, the darker regions of the nether world receive their souls, and God, their father, visits upon their posterity the outrageous acts of the parents." He goes on to point out that, though even the bodies of enemies are given decent burial, the bodies of suicides remain unburied until sunset (as a form of punishment). He also says that in other nations a suicide's right hand must be cut off, "holding that, as the body was unnaturally severed from the soul, so the hand should be severed from the body." It is interesting that the Jews should take such a strong line when the philosophers of Greece could regard suicide as a permissible, even a praiseworthy, way of bringing to an end a long and honorable life that had now become burdensome.

Even though they strongly opposed him, Jesus' enemies could not think that he was talking about suicide. Hatred of such a crime was too deeply entrenched in the nation for anyone to contemplate it. They mention the possibility only to dismiss it.

But there may be something more. Granted that they did not really think Jesus would commit suicide, why do they raise the possibility? Perhaps as a deliberate misinterpretation with a sting in its tail. They may be reasoning, "He is talking about suicide. That means going to hell. Well, we certainly can't come where he is going, if that is what he's planning."

"From Below" and "From Above"

We should probably understand Jesus' reply in the light of such an understanding. His enemies were talking about hell, about the nether regions. Jesus invites them to reflect on where their real affinities lie. On another occasion he spoke of the scribes and Pharisees as going to great lengths to make a convert, and when they have done so, he said to them, ". . . you make him twofold more a child of hell than yourselves" (Matt. 23:15). His "from below" has a somewhat similar meaning here (v. 23). He is saying that these people who were so ready to sneer at him and to suggest that he would go to hell were in fact speaking of their own domain. They were "from below"; they belonged to hell. Jesus' "you" is emphatic. They were linking him with hell and in so doing they inadvertently showed what their own proper place was.

By contrast, Jesus is "from above." His proper place is heaven. Right through this Gospel John insists that Jesus had come from heaven, from God. He keeps telling us that it was the Father who sent Jesus. His appearance on earth was not because he was of the earth, for he was not. It was because the heavenly One came to this place to save the sinful denizens of earth. They should not misinterpret the reason for his presence.

Almost the same contrast is made in terms of "this world" and "not of this world." There is a great deal about "world" in this Gospel (the Greek word for "world" is used seventy-eight times; the most in any other book is twenty-three, in 1 John). It is used in a number of different ways, but one important way is the one we see here. This world can be a very attractive place for those who live in it, and there is a constant temptation to make it the center of everything in life. To be "of this world" in this way is to miss the greatest good. There is, of course, no reason why we should not enjoy this world. It is a good world, made by a good God, and the people of God legitimately find much of value in it. But when it becomes the focus of the whole of life it is a snare and a source of error. It is this concentration on the things of this life that Jesus is blaming in those to whom he is talking.

We so readily accept the world's values, even when we are seeking to do good. I like the story about the thirteen-year-old boy who, in a time of heavy snow, decided to make a few dollars by clearing driveways. Before he began his father pointed out that there was a good deal of snow in their own driveway and it would be nice if he started there.

"How much is it worth?" asked the boy.

"Son, this is your home" said his father. "I leave it to your sense of honor how much you ought to charge. Or even whether you ought to charge at all. Let your conscience be your guide."

So the youth got to work. With the driveway nicely cleared he confronted his father and said, "Dad, I've made a decision. I will charge you nothing at all. I leave it to your sense of honor how much you ought to pay. Or even whether you ought to pay at all. Let your conscience be your guide."

Despite their high-sounding words we get the feeling that both father and son were moved by a worldly consideration—how to get the best deal for himself. And is this not rather widespread in our modern communities? It comes natural to us all to look for the best for ourselves and to avoid, if we can, the kind of confrontation with the challenge of the service of God that will make life a little less easy. That was what Jesus' opponents were doing.

In both his contrasts, "below"–"above" and "this world"–"not of this world," Jesus uses emphatic pronouns for both *you* and *I*. He sets himself in strong contrast with the enemies to whom he is speaking. They should not blur the difference between them. Jesus is not talking about a minor difference of opinion. He is taking about the ultimate cleavage between the people of God and the people of Satan, between those whose place is heaven and those who belong to hell.

"I AM"

"Therefore," Jesus says, "I told you that you will die in your sins" (v. 24). The reason for this fearful death is the fearful lives they are living. They belong to this world, to "below," and thus they disqualify themselves from being with God in the world to come.

Jesus explains this further with a reference to faith. "For if you do not believe that I AM," he says, you will undergo this death. The thought that people must believe is a common one in this Gospel, and indeed John tells us that he wrote it in order that people might believe and in believing might have life (20:31). We have noticed in our studies that he uses a variety of constructions with his verb *'to believe'* and may give expression to the thought that people must trust Jesus, accept what he says as true, and so on. Here he speaks of believing "that." Faith has content, and unless we see this we shall never believe as John understands the term. It is not a matter of producing just any kind of faith, as though faith were itself a merit. It is faith in Jesus as he is that matters, faith that recognizes the wonderful truth behind his "I AM."

In earlier studies we have seen that the personal pronoun is not used in Greek in the way we use it. The form of the verb tells us sufficiently what the subject is. But where God is the speaker the pronoun is used. This emphatic way of speaking was seen as suitable when a divine person is doing the speaking.

In the Old Testament the emphatic "I AM" is used a number of times. There was an important occasion when God revealed himself to Moses and sent him to say to the Israelites, "I AM has sent me to you" (Exod. 3:14). "I AM" is the very name of God in this passage. There are other relevant passages, such as the one in which God says to Isaiah, "I am he" (Isa. 43:10). We could assemble quite a group of such passages. They make it clear that "I AM" was closely connected with God's revelation of himself.

And that is surely the significance of what Jesus is saying here. He is taking the expression so firmly linked with God's self-revelation in the Old Testament Scripture and using it of himself. He is saying that God is revealed in him in a special way. Unless we recognize this revelation and respond to it in faith, we place ourselves outside the sphere of salvation. As Jesus put it, if you do not believe this, "you will die in your sins."

39

Pleasing the Father

So they said to him, "Who are you?" Jesus said to them, "Why do I talk to you at all? I have many things to say and to judge about you, but he who sent me is true and as for me, the things I heard from him, these are the things I speak to the world." They did not know that he was speaking to them about the Father. Jesus therefore said to them, "When you have lifted up the Son of man, then you will know that I AM. And I do nothing of myself, but as the Father taught me, I speak these things. And he who sent me is with me. He has not left me alone, because I always do the things that are pleasing to him." As Jesus said these things many believed in him (John 8:25–30).

The people to whom Jesus had been talking probably did not understand all that he was saying, but they understood enough to see that what he said implied a big claim about his own position. He was "from above," whereas they were "from below"; they were "of this world," whereas he was "not of this world" (v. 23). Unless they believed "that I AM" they would die in their sins (v. 24). This certainly meant that Jesus was claiming to be on a very different level from the one where they stood. So they asked him, "Who are you?" They put some emphasis on "you" by placing the pronoun first; "You, who are you to talk like this?" is the force of it. One commentator sees the expression as meaning "Why do you give yourself such airs?" They rejected utterly any idea that Jesus was different from or better than they were. They saw him as just another Jew, and one from the provinces at that. He could not possibly know more about God and the way God should be served than they did.

Jesus' reply is one of the most difficult pieces of Greek in the New Testament and it is translated in a variety of different ways. The King James Version reads "Even the same that I said unto you from the beginning," and essentially the same translation is given by the Revised Standard Version with "Even what I have told you from the beginning." But this version has an alternative in the margin, "Why do I talk to you at all?" This is not the reading of other manuscripts; it is a different attempt at translating the same piece of Greek. The New English Bible faces the same problem but puts its solution the other way round. In the text it reads "Why should I speak to you at all?" and in the margin it has "What I have told you all along." The Good News Bible has essentially the same translation as the Revised Standard, with "What I have told you from the very beginning" in the text and "Why should I speak to you at all?" in the margin.

The problem is that we have the Greek word that means "beginning," but it is used in a very unusual way. Used in the way John employs it here, it really means "at first," "at the beginning." But "What I am saying at the beginning" is not an easy expression. We see something of the problem translators have if we consult the commentary of C. K. Barrett. This writer notes that the expression means "at first," "at the beginning," but goes on to say that we must choose between "I am from the beginning what I tell you" and "I am what I tell you from the beginning." But the trouble with this is that Barrett substitutes "from the beginning" for "at the beginning," and these two do not mean the same thing at all. And the expression we are thinking of means "at" not "from." John sometimes says "from the beginning" (6:64; 8:44; 15:27; 16:4), but in none of these places does he use the expression we have here.

Now it happens that this expression is sometimes used by the Greeks with a meaning like "altogether." But they use it with a negative. We would get the force of this if we were to see it as "at all" in the phrase "not at all." A great preacher of the early church, John Chrysostom (which means "John of the golden mouth"), explains the passage this way: "What He saith, is of this kind; 'Ye are not worthy to hear My words at all, much less to learn who I am.'" We must always take what Chrysostom says seriously, for Greek was his native language and he read the Greek New Testament in his native tongue. Despite this, not many have gone all the way with him, though the "at all" that he saw is taken up in several translations. Mostly those who take this view see the words as a question, "Why do I talk to you at all?" or the like. The Berkeley version, however, sees it as a statement, "I am exactly what I tell you."

The trouble with this way of taking the expression is that in Greek writings generally it seems to be used with this meaning only with a negative. It is the "at all" in "not at all," but it does not seem to have been used with this significance without the negative. So, while this remains as a possibility, it cannot be said to be without difficulties.

The earliest manuscript of this Gospel that survives, the Bodmer papyrus which the scholars cite as P66, reads "I told you at the beginning what I am also telling you." There is always a great respect for the earliest manuscript of any part of Scripture, and most of us would like to feel that this manuscript is right. The reading is without difficulty and gives a clear and acceptable meaning. The problem here is the question "If this is what John wrote originally, how does it come about that every other manuscript in existence is wrong?" It seems easier to think that the scribe who wrote this manuscript found the reading so difficult that he said to himself something like this: "This does not make sense; someone must have made a mistake. Now what would make better sense? I know. . . ."

Other suggestions have been made. Barclay translates, "Anything I am saying to you is only the beginning" and Rieu, "So we go back to our starting-point!" There are other renderings. But none of them impresses us as an adequate way of putting the Greek into English.

So in the end we must confess that we simply do not know the precise meaning of what John has written. Until some further evidence comes to light we must be content to remain uncertain. There are two main possibilities: it may be the question "Why do I talk to you at all?" or it may be the statement "What I say to you at [or "from"] the beginning." But there is nothing that enables us to say definitely which is right or whether there is a better solution.

Jesus evidently means that there is no point in explaining further what he has said; his hearers have such closed minds that they will not understand. Either way of taking the words fits in with this. So he says, "Why do I talk to you at all?" Or perhaps he is saying that he has said it all before; there is nothing to add. If they did not believe him before, no further words will enable them to do so now.

What the Father Said

Jesus goes on to refer to other things he has to say to them. If he is going to say no more about himself, he has a lot more to say about *them*. And those other things concern judgment. This is one of the great themes of this Gospel, as we have seen in our previous studies. He does not develop the thought at this point, but it recurs (cf. 8:50; 12:48; 16:8, 11, etc.). Jesus did not come primarily for judgment (8:15; 12:47), but judgment is one of the important truths. Jesus' hearers were responsible people. One day they would give account of themselves to God, and they should not complacently shelter themselves under the security blanket of the conviction that they belonged to the people of God. Nor should we.

Jesus goes on with "he who sent me is true" (v. 26). He does not say "the Father" but "he who sent me." Once again we see that the mission of Jesus is important. Again and again we find him referring to the great truth that the Father "sent" him. John will not let us miss the truth that in Jesus we see not merely human wisdom, but one sent from none less than God the Father. Truth is a very important concept in this Gospel, and it is connected with Jesus (14:6) and the Spirit (14:17) as well as with the Father. Here the thought is that the Father is utterly real and completely reliable. Jesus' hearers might quibble about the things he said and might fancy that they knew more about spiritual realities than he did. But he is pointing them to God as real truth. The trouble with the hearers was that they were substituting their ideas about God for the reality. No matter what they might say and no matter what we may say, no matter what their or our contemporaries may say, the truth of God still stands.

And it is that truth that Jesus proclaims because what he says are the things he heard from the Father. Again we have a consistent thought in this Gospel. Again and again John reports words of Jesus that bring out the truth that his message is not of human origin. He brings a revelation from none less than the Father.

And this revelation he speaks "to the world" (v. 26). This means that the message is worldwide in its scope. As it is the message of God's way of salvation obviously it has no restricted application. Jesus spent his earthly life in Palestine and his preaching was very largely restricted to the Jews. It was only after his ascension that the Holy Spirit came at Pentecost and led the church to proclaim the gospel among the Gentiles. But words such as these make it clear that the worldwide application of the gospel was in view from the first. It moved out in God's good time to the lands outside Israel, but the nature of the message is such that it is meant for all and in due time must go to all.

We should also bear in mind that "world" has another meaning. It can mean the worldly-minded, those whose horizon is bounded by the things of here and now. It is not unlikely that, as is the case with so many expressions in this Gospel, we should see "world" here as having a double meaning. It points to people in the lands beyond the sea but also points to those who would normally take no notice of a religious message. The gospel is to be preached not to the converted but to the unconverted, and Jesus is setting the example with his preaching.

There is yet another possibility. The word I have translated "to" also means "into" and in New Testament times was sometimes used in the sense of "in." It is possible that we should see Jesus as saying that this is what his message is as he speaks "in the world."

But the Jews did not understand. They did not know God nor did they know that he is in a special sense Jesus' Father (v. 19). So it is not surprising that they did not catch the allusion to "the Father" (v. 27). With their views about Jesus they did not care who his father was; they had no idea that he had been sent by the heavenly Father. Their spiritual blindness meant that they did not recognize the mission of Jesus. Indeed, it is the basic fault of the enemies of Jesus right through this Gospel that they lacked spiritual perception and failed to recognize the wonderful thing that had happened in their midst, when the Son of God himself came to live among them. When Jesus spoke about his "Father" they did not recognize that the message came from the One they called God. So can prejudice blind people.

Lifting Up the Son of Man

So Jesus took the discussion further. He spoke of the time when they would have "lifted up the Son of man" (v. 28). John uses this verb *to lift up* in an unusual way (as we saw in our study on 3:14). The word means "to raise on high" and is used of elevating physical objects, as when Moses lifted up the bronze snake in the wilderness (3:14). It could also be used figuratively, as it is when it is used of Capernaum's thinking it was "lifted up to heaven" (Matt. 11:23). Similarly Jesus said that "everyone who exalts himself will be abased," while it is "he who humbles himself" who "will be exalted" (Luke 18:14).

This idea of exaltation in the heavenly realm is often the meaning of the word in the New Testament. It is used of Jesus' being exalted to God's right hand in heaven (Acts 2:33) and of God's exalting him to be a Prince and Savior (Acts 5:31).

John, as we have seen, uses the word of Moses' lifting up of the bronze snake in the wilderness. He has it four times more, and on each of these four occasions it refers to Jesus' crucifixion. In a sense that was a physical lifting up, so we can understand it being used of death in this way. Yet at the same time we should bear in mind that what was so obvious to John was far from obvious to his contemporaries, and the word was not normally used of crucifixion at all. John probably chooses the term because of its other associations. It could refer to the physical elevation of Jesus on the cross. But John also surely has in mind the truth that it was this being "lifted up" on the cross that was Jesus' supreme glory. We have seen that John has the great idea that to serve in a lowly place when one could readily take a higher place is real glory. That is surely his idea here. Presumably Jesus spoke in Aramaic, but when John put his words into Greek he chose to use a verb that spoke of physical exaltation but also of exaltation in the heavenly region.

Jesus used his favorite self-designation, "the Son of man." This is a title that is used by no one in the Gospels except Jesus, but he uses it again and again. It is generally agreed that it points us back to "one like a son of man" in Daniel 7:13. It was not a recognized title of the Messiah, and Jesus seems to have used it as a way of both concealing and revealing his messiahship. Those who did not heed his message would see nothing in the expression, but to Jesus himself it expressed something of his mission and his relationship to the Father.

When this "lifting up" takes place, Jesus says, "you will know that I AM" (v. 28). This means that the cross is not only the means of our redemption, but that it has a revelatory function. We have seen a number of times that "I AM" is a title of divinity and points to the highest place. The cross, where the Son of man died to bring salvation, shows who he is.

There is a problem in that many of those at the crucifixion did not come to know anything of the sort. There were mockers there who did not take Jesus seriously and there were his enemies who rejoiced in his death. It seems that what Jesus means is that the cross forces people into a final decision. Face to face with the cross his hearers would come into either a place of salvation or of final condemnation. They would accept him as God's own Son and the Messiah who was bringing salvation. Or they would turn away from him with finality.

The cross always does that. When we come face to face with it, when we see the One who died on it for us, then either we respond with penitence and faith and so enter salvation, or we harden our hearts, reject the revelation, and shut ourselves up to the eternal consequences of our action.

The Father and the Son

From the cross Jesus moves on to another thought we meet many times in this Gospel: that he does not act independently of the Father. "I do nothing of myself," he says (v. 28). Most translations take "and I do nothing of myself" as part of the previous sentence, and this must remain a possibility. In that case Jesus is saying that part of the revelation that the cross would bring is that Jesus does nothing alone. Always the Father is with him.

But it seems more likely that the revelation is simply "that I AM." Then Jesus goes on to say that now, long before the cross, it is true that he does nothing in isolation from the Father (cf. 5:19, etc.). We misunderstand his whole life if we see him merely as someone who set out to follow high ideals and to do things of which the heavenly Father would approve. For Jesus (and for John who records it) it is important that he had never been at work in separation from the Father. He could do nothing apart from God. There was a close unity between them right through his earthly life.

This is brought out first with respect to his teaching. His message was not an earthly message on which God was pleased to set his seal of approval. It was a message right from God. It was only what the Father taught him that he spoke (v. 28).

Then he moves on to his fellowship with the Father. Jesus lived an earthly life with all that this means in terms of trials and tribulations, of joys and sorrows, of achievement and opposition. But he was never left to do all this by himself. The Father, who is again characterized as "he who sent me" (v. 29; the thought of mission keeps coming up), is with him. The thought that God will be with his people is one that is found often in the Old Testament and is carried on in the New. People of faith can rely on that presence. But especially is that presence given to Jesus, and he says here that God has not left him. The Father never leaves the Son. Even in the shadow of the cross, with the malignancy of his enemies at its worst and with his closest followers about to desert him, Jesus could say that he was not alone (16:32). The Father never deserts the Son.

The third thing is that the Son always does the things that please the Father. His life is spent entirely in doing those things of which the Father approves. Christians often speak of the sinlessness of Jesus, which is a fact and an important fact. But it is negative; it tells what Jesus did not do. Here we have the positive. Not only did he avoid evil, but he actively did the good. Always he did the things that please the Father.

Faith

As Jesus spoke, "many believed in him" (v. 30). John does not tell us whether these were people from among Jesus' opponents who had been changed as a result of what he said to them or whether they came from among the uncommitted who were listening to what was going on. Either way the point is that not all who heard him were hostile or indifferent. Even in a chapter like this, where there is so much opposition to Jesus and all he stood for, many came to trust him. And, in a world that is as hostile and indifferent as ours is, it is heartening to reflect that there are still many who come to believe. It encourages all God's servants to persist in their mission as Jesus did in his and to trust the same heavenly Father who did such things in and for and through him.

40

Freedom

Jesus therefore said to the Jews who had believed him, "If you remain in my word you are truly my disciples and you will know the truth and the truth will set you free." They answered him, "We are Abraham's seed and have never been slaves to anyone; how do you say 'You will become free'?" Jesus answered them, "Truly, truly, I tell you that everyone who commits sin is the slave of sin. Now the slave does not remain in the house forever; the son remains forever. If then the Son makes you free, you will be really free" (John 8:31–36).

This passage is a dialogue between Jesus and some Jews who "had believed him" (v. 31). It is plain from the exchange that their faith did not go very deep. In fact it can scarcely be called faith at all. We are reminded that there are degrees of conviction. Evidently these people had been impressed by some of Jesus' sayings. They believed them, and they counted themselves as followers of Jesus. This may mean only that they agreed that some of Jesus' teachings were true. The Greek construction John uses could mean no more than that they accepted as true what Jesus had said. Some scholars press this literal meaning. But John uses a variety of constructions when he refers to believing, and he does not seem to put much difference between them. It is better to see these people as folk who claimed to be disciples of Jesus, but whose commitment did not go very deep. Jesus now speaks to them about the meaning of true discipleship.

The first point is that it is necessary that they "remain." Discipleship is not a sudden enthusiasm, not something that flares up quickly but is soon over. Discipleship means remaining with Jesus. It means remaining in his "word," too. The "word" of Jesus means his whole teaching, not this aspect, nor that, but the teaching as a unity. The teaching of Jesus is to be taken seriously. Many of us delight to call ourselves Christians but then go on to manufacture a religion of our own, perhaps taking up some aspects of what the Master said and which we find attractive. But we like to keep firmly in control. What we approve we see as right, and what we find uncomfortable we reject as no part of authentic Christianity. We decide what we think is suitable and do not dream of comparing that with the teachings of the Lord we profess to obey. So we evolve a religion of respectability or, if we are younger, of non-respectability, and label that Christian.

Jesus is insisting that this is not the way to go if we really want to be disciples. That involves the discipline (do not miss the connection of "discipline" with "disciple") in the first place of learning what the teaching is, and in the second of putting it into practice. Discipleship means taking with full seriousness the fact that Jesus is the Master.

Free

It is easy to grasp this part of Jesus' teaching and to go on from there to the thought that being a Christian is a grim business in which we are shut up on a kind of treadmill. It means, we so easily think, that we are always trying to learn a little more and then to put that into practice. And as soon as we have done this some further demand is made of us. We are never able to escape the grind of learning and then trying to put what we learn into living. We make our Christianity into a very trying, very unpleasant, and very grim way of being right with our Maker.

Wherever we got that idea, it was not from the teaching of our Lord. It is, of course, true that there is always something more to learn and something more to do in Christian service. But this is no dull grind. Rather it is an ever-new adventure. To remain in Jesus' word is to know the truth, and to know the truth is to be free. Truth is an important concept in John's writings and is used especially about the truth of God, the truth that is expressed in the gospel and finds its embodiment in Jesus who said, "I am the truth" (14:6). It is the truth that God sent his Son to live for us and to die for us. It is the truth that we reach our full potential and enjoyment of life only when we live in harmony with God who made us. It is the truth that it is the Son's death on Calvary's cross that puts away our sins. It is the truth that it is only as we trust him that we know the calm of sins forgiven and the entrance into a life of satisfying service of God and man. This final truth we never know apart from Jesus. His "word" brings us the knowledge of things eternal that was forever beyond our unaided grasp.

"And the truth will set you free" (v. 32). Jesus was well aware of the fact that sin blinds people, shuts them up to a cramped, narrow experience and prevents them from enjoying real freedom. Jesus' words are often misunderstood in modern times by people who see them as a charter for liberty in research and in intellectual pursuits generally. Truth is then seen as the one compulsory quest; to follow the way of truth is a liberating experience.

It is not to be denied that there is a sense in which this is true. Dedication to the quest for knowledge, for a better understanding of truth, is a liberating thing. But that is not what Jesus is saying. His concern when he uttered these words was not for science or philosophy or the like, but for the deep needs of the soul. He was not even speaking of freedom from sin in the sense of a way of liberation from what we see as shackling us, so that we could use his teaching to get free from something that we could not defeat in any other way. Jesus is not a tool to enable us to get personal success, even in respectable, religious ways.

Jesus is talking about liberation from the whole way of the world, with its concentration on the things of here and now. He is talking about the liberation that brings us near to God, so that our concern is with him, with the doing of his will. We no longer are caught up in our own selfish concerns, in the darkness of sin and evil, of alienation from God, of concentration on "the world." The liberation of which Jesus speaks brings us into fellowship with the Father.

Abraham's Seed

Jesus' hearers did not like this at all. It seems pretty clear that they did not really understand what he was saying. Perhaps their gorge rose at the suggestion that they were not free. Sometimes the use of a word riles us so that we find it difficult to pay attention to the flow of an argument because of our resentment at the word we do not like. It seems that it was something like this that happened to the Jews, because they did not reply to what Jesus was saying but to something that they thought up themselves.

"We are Abraham's seed," they said, "and have never been slaves to anyone" (v. 33). "Seed," of course, means "descendants," and the Jews took great pride in being descendants of the great patriarch Abraham, the man whom God called "my friend" (Isa. 41:8). There is a saying of Rabbi Akiba (who was a little later than this; he died about A.D. 135):

"Even the poorest in Israel are looked upon as freemen who have lost their possessions, for they are the sons of Abraham, Isaac, and Jacob." The whole nation, Akiba felt, had a dignity that rested on relationship to the great patriarchs and not to any worldly wealth. This attitude was undoubtedly to be found in the days of Jesus as well as in the next century.

There is something admirable about this patriotic view, for those who held it were not going to be too depressed about life's little troubles. But it all too easily led to a depraved kind of patriotism whereby one's own nation is regarded as the only one that counts and all others are despised. And it could lead to a failure to reckon with reality. Thus on this occasion the Jews showed a superb disregard for the facts of life as typified by the presence of the Roman soldiers in their very midst. They were not slaves in the sense of being the personal possession of any one Roman or group of Romans. But they were slaves in that their destiny was not in their own hands. It was what the Romans said that dictated Jewish conduct. It is unrealistic to call a nation occupied by enemy troops free. But that is what these Jewish leaders did.

They also disregarded their history. We have "never" been slaves, they said. Not when they were in Egypt before Moses led them out? Not when the Philistines invaded their land and, in their determination not to allow weapons, regulated even the way axes and sickles were sharpened (1 Sam. 13:19–22)? Not when the Assyrians carried off as captives the people of the northern kingdom (2 Kings 17:6–7)? Or when the Babylonians did the same to those in the kingdom of Judah (2 Kings 25:11)? So can prejudice blind people to the truth.

It is one of the melancholy facts of life that the spiritually blind think that there is nothing to see and the spiritually bound deny that there is any freedom beyond their condition.

Slavery

Jesus' answer begins with the solemn "truly, truly" (v. 34). This is a formula that Jesus uses often to prefix statements of special importance and solemnity. It is a warning to take very seriously the words that follow. There is a division among the manuscripts as to exactly what follows, but the best reading is probably "everyone who commits sin is a slave." Other manuscripts have "is the slave of sin," but the longer reading appears to be the result of an attempt by some scribes to make unmistakably clear what they saw as Jesus' meaning. Now there cannot be any doubt that Jesus is referring to slavery to sin. But the way he puts it gives emphasis to "slave." The sinner is not free.

The more we think about it, the more we see that it is true. The first time anyone commits a particular sin there may have been a terrible struggle with temptation. But if the person gives way, then the next time there is not such a hard struggle. And if he continues in that path, there comes a time when there is scarcely a ripple of temptation. The person has become the slave of the sin that once was so strongly resisted.

We see the same thing if we reflect on what happens when we try to break a bad habit. It is not easy. We are well aware that we are in the power of the evil thing. It may be that by God's grace in the end we succeed, but that does not alter the fact that until God helps us we are in the grip of the habit. In our own experience we know what it is to be enslaved to evil.

Our very attempts to assert our freedom all too often lead to a worse bondage. One of the saddest features of modern life is the growth of violence over almost the whole of the world. People decide that they will not be bound by the petty restrictions that they find so frustrating and so limiting. So they assert themselves to the maximum of their strength to get what they want by the exercise of their power. But that does not lead them into a glorious life where they can get all they want. It provokes other people to be violent in return, and the end result is the loss of peace for all. Evil never brings freedom. It brings bondage.

The drug habit is another illustration. For an increasing number of people, life seems impossible without the use of heroin or some other drug. The habit was begun in all probability as an attempt to assert freedom, to show that one is not bound by the petty conservatisms that govern the lives of the "straight." But the freedom is illusory. It leads straight into slavery.

The list could go on and on. There is an almost endless number of evils to which we in modern times have made ourselves slaves as we assert our freedom. But we are no more free than the previous generations against whom we rebel. We have simply exchanged one form of conformity for another; we have found a new kind of slavery to take the place of an old one.

The Son

Jesus goes on to point out that there are differences between a son in a household and a slave. He begins with tenure. "The slave," he says, "does not remain in the house forever" (v. 35). A given slave, of course, might remain in the one household all his life. But that is an unusual occurrence. It depends on the nature of the services he can render, on the character of his owner and his own character, and on a host of other things. The point is that he has no security. He can be removed at any time. He can be transferred temporarily or permanently. He can be retained by the present owner or given away or sold.

But the son is always a son. Normally he will remain in the house as an honored member all his life. Should he journey abroad or should he be expelled from the household, he is still a son. His status as a son is permanent. He has his responsibilities and his privileges and in both is distinctively different from a slave.

There is a story of an old man and a twelve-year-old boy who passed through customs in New York after a trip to France. A friendly customs man asked if they had enjoyed the trip, whether they had seen the Louvre, Versailles, and the like. The man replied that he was blind and had seen nothing. He went on, "I want my son to see as much as he can, so that his life will be rich and full. But first he has to tell me all about what he sees. That ensures that he sees much. And in a way I see them, too, as he tells me about them." The boy carried his notebook in which he had written all the things he wanted his father to "see." For both of them the relationship (and the trip) was meaningful. There is a permanent link between father and son.

A Son and *The* Son

In Jesus' saying the son in question is the human son, the son in any household. But John's interest is in *the* Son, the Son of God, and, while he uses an expression that has its application to any human family, in the fullest sense it applies to Jesus. He is the Son who "remains forever." His sonship is a heavenly sonship and it is never-ending.

And just as his sonship is distinctive, so the freedom he brings is distinctive. The person who is made free by Christ will be "really free" (v. 36). John uses a word for "really" that he uses nowhere else. It carries the idea of "in essence"; there is that about Christ that means he can give a freedom that is qualitatively different from the lesser freedoms people enjoy.

This will be connected with the slavery to sin that Jesus has been speaking about. That is a slavery that no man can break. No man can give another freedom from sin, because he himself is caught up in the same bondage. But Jesus is not, and the great thought that John hammers at over and over again is that Jesus came to bring salvation, a salvation that may be understood in terms of freedom from the sin that besets us all.

41

Children of the Devil

"I know that you are Abraham's seed; but you are seeking to kill me because my word has no place in you. I speak the things I have seen with my Father, and you therefore do the things you have heard from your father." They answered him saying, "Abraham is our father." Jesus says to them, "If you were children of Abraham you would do the deeds of Abraham. But now you are seeking to kill me, a man who has told you the truth which I heard from God. Abraham did not do this. You are doing the works of your father." They said to him therefore, "We were not born of fornication; we have one Father, God." Jesus said to them, "If God were your Father you would love me, for I came out from God and have come; and I did not come of my own accord, but he sent me. Why do you not understand my speech? Because you cannot hear my word. You are of your father, the devil, and the lusts of your father you will to do. He was a murderer from the beginning and did not stand in the truth because the truth is not in him. When he speaks the lie he speaks of his own, because he is a liar and the father of it. But because I speak the truth you do not believe me. Which of you convicts me of sin? If I speak the truth why do you not believe me? He who is from God hears my sayings; for this reason you do not hear them, that you are not from God" (John 8:37–47).

The Jews had claimed that they were "Abraham's seed" (i.e., descendants of Abraham, v. 33). This was a matter of great importance to many of their race. They looked back with pride to their great ancestor, but this was more than a matter of being thrilled at the wonder of their connection with so great a man. They held that it brought them many blessings.

Sometimes they connected this with the inspiration it gave them to be worthy of so great an ancestor. Thus in the tractate "Aboth" ("The Fathers") we read: "He in whom are these three things is of the disciples of Abraham our father; but [he in whom are] three other things is of the disciples of Balaam the wicked. A good eye and a humble spirit and a lowly soul—[they in whom are these] are of the disciples of Abraham our father. An evil eye, a haughty spirit, and a proud soul—[they in whom are these] are of the disciples of Balaam the wicked" (Danby's translation). There are other such sayings drawing attention to other qualities, such as compassion.

Now to see oneself as a descendant of Abraham in matters like these is a very good thing. It is to take delight in the outstanding merits of Abraham and to model oneself on the great patriarch. It is to see Abraham as one whom it is important to imitate. When the Jews took pride in Abraham in this way it meant that they were striving to be better people, to be more like Abraham in the things they did day by day.

But it was possible to fasten attention on the advantages people thought they would get from belonging to Abraham. Thus the saying we were looking at a moment ago goes on to ask how the disciples of Abraham differ from those of Balaam and, instead of answering in terms of upright conduct or of careful attention to the service of God or the like, says simply: "The disciples of Abraham our father enjoy this world and inherit the world to come. . . . The disciples of Balaam the wicked inherit Gehenna and go down to the pit of destruction." To belong to Abraham means the blessings of heaven, whereas to belong to anyone else (like Balaam) means hell.

This attitude is the end of any genuine attempt to serve God, and it was this attitude that was characteristic of the Jews to whom Jesus was talking. They took pride in their connection with the great patriarch and were confident that because they were descended from him they were sure of God's blessing in the here and now and also of a place in heaven in the hereafter. Since Abraham would take care of them, they saw no need to be very much in earnest about their service of God. They could thus ignore the challenge in Jesus' teaching and refuse to take him seriously. They simply refused to think about what Jesus was saying and to ask whether it was true.

Murder

Jesus agrees that they are "Abraham's seed." They were the patriarch's physical descendants and in this sense were certainly his seed. But conduct is another matter. We have just seen that among the Rabbis there were those who saw descent from Abraham as a reason for cultivating qualities of character: because they were Abraham's seed they must be humble, compassionate, and the like. But this meant nothing to the people to whom Jesus was speaking.

He brings this out by saying "you are seeking to kill me" (v. 37). This has come before us several times in this part of the Gospel. John mentioned it in his narrative section (7:1), Jesus referred to it himself (7:19), the people spoke about it (7:20, 25), and attempts were made to arrest him (7:30, 32, 44). Plainly his life was in danger and equally plainly it was people like those to whom he was speaking who were responsible. A little later they would take up stones to stone him (v. 59). They may have been descendants of Abraham in the sense that they were his physical progeny, but in spirit they were as far from Abraham as was conceivable. At heart they were murderers.

The reason for their rejection of Jesus, he says, was that "my word has no place in you." Jesus' "word," as we have seen, was his teaching; it is a short way of referring to the essential message that he brought from God. And the tragedy of his hearers was that they had no room for this message. Their hearts were too full of pride and self-sufficiency, too taken up with their own importance to give consideration for a moment to the possibility that a teacher from the provinces, and from an obscure village in the provinces at that, could possibly have anything to say that would be worth hearing for these grand folk who lived in the capital city, in God's own Jerusalem.

Yet what Jesus said came directly from God. Interestingly he does not speak of the things he "heard" from the Father, but says, "I speak the things I have seen with my Father" (v. 38). His vision of God is unobscured and constant. He speaks because his message reflects this vision. He brings a message direct from God.

Another Father

Notice Jesus' "therefore." It is precisely *because* his message came directly from God that they did not receive it. His message was one of love and humility and compassion, and it was because it was the kind of message it was that they would not receive it. The way Jesus puts it is "you do the things you have heard from your father" (v. 38). Their conduct reflects their parentage. Jesus does not say who their father is; he leaves it that they are acting as they are because their father is who he is. Now what father would lead his sons to plan murder?

This is a question his hearers do not attempt to answer. It was fundamental to these Jews that they were descendants of Abraham. For them everything depended on that. Their hope for this life and the next did not depend on God's grace or their piety or their moral achievement or anything of the sort. It depended on their relationship to Abraham. No descendant of that great patriarch, they thought, could ever be lost. Because of their father, they were safe.

So they gratefully go for the opening they think Jesus has left them. "Abraham is our father," they say simply (v. 39). For them that was all that mattered. If they were doing the things they had heard from their father, then all was well because Abraham was their father.

Consistently Jesus is taking the position that what we do shows who our real father is. So he immediately retorts that their deeds show that it is not Abraham who is really their father. If they were Abraham's children, they would do Abraham's deeds. This, of course, was recognized by the better minds in Israel, people who said things like those we noticed earlier about the disciples of Abraham being humble and compassionate. But these people were too self-opinionated for that, too certain that they had to be right and Jesus had to be wrong.

So Jesus goes on to say, "But now you are seeking to kill me" (v. 40). He is aware of the intention to murder him and brings the plot out into the open. And who are they trying to murder? "A man who has told you the truth which I heard from God." This is as far as could possibly be conceived from doing what Abraham did. It shows that it was not Abraham who was their father but someone else. And for the second time Jesus says that they are doing the works of their father. If they thought about what they were doing, they might possibly come to see who their real father was.

God's Children

That leads the Jews to change their position in a hurry. Somewhat curiously they say, "We were not born of fornication" (v. 41; Moffatt translates "We are no bastards"). Their "we" is emphatic: "we, in contrast to others." It is not easy to see why they say such a thing. Possibly they had heard something about the virgin birth of Jesus. They would not have accepted this for a moment, but, recognizing that there was something unusual about the way Jesus came into the world, they may be putting the worst possible construction on it. So they took the opportunity of being scornful of him, while at the same time they asserted their own superior position.

Another possibility is that they were thinking of the way the Old Testament prophets so often denounced idolatry by likening it to adultery or fornication. False religion is faithlessness and may be illustrated by thinking of faithlessness in marriage. These Jews were perhaps beginning to see something of the way Jesus' argument was running and they tried to counter it. That may be why they ceased to call Abraham their father and said instead, ". . . we have one Father, God" (v. 41). Malachi had asked, "Have we not all one Father? Did not one God create us?" (Mal. 2:10). It was a nice thought to fall back on.

But it drew the response "If God were your Father you would love me" (v. 42). The way in which this is expressed in the Greek implies that both propositions are wrong: "If God were your Father (as he is not) you would love me (as you do not)." There runs right through Jesus' teaching in this exchange the thought that our conduct reflects our paternity. It was nice that these people claimed now that God was their Father. But would the claim stand up to the test of facts? Did their deeds show that this was true or false? Jesus begins with love. John tells us in his first Epistle that "God is love" (1 John 4:8, 16), and it follows that those who are God's children will be distinguished by the love they show to others. These Jews were not characterized by love; it followed that it was not God who was their Father.

It is critical that they did not love Jesus, for he "came out from God" (v. 42). His divine origin is emphasized throughout this Gospel, and those who belong to God, those who are God's children, will recognize this. He adds "and have come," which is somewhat curious. But there is some evidence that this second verb was used by people claiming to have come from a deity or even when the heathen said that one of their gods had "come." It may be that Jesus is asserting by his use of the word that his origin was divine.

It goes with this that he was not self-impelled. That he came from God meant that he was on a mission from God (as John says so often). Jesus did not come completely of himself. God sent him. It was this that was so basic for Jesus and this that his opponents so consistently refused to see.

There is a problem in the difference between Jesus' "speech" and his "word" (v. 43). Both terms can denote what anyone says. Rieu seems to give us the meaning with his translation, "Why do you not understand my language? Because you cannot comprehend my thought." They are not in tune with Jesus' basic position. They do not comprehend what he means by coming from God, by being sent from God and the like. And, because they never get to grips with what is basic in his teaching, they find the words of a particular discourse impossible to understand. They can "hear" in the sense that the words fall on their ears and are registered. But this is not the same thing as appreciating the meaning of what is said. It is in this latter respect that they fall short.

The Devil and His Sons

Now Jesus says bluntly, "You are of your father, the devil" (v. 44). When he has previously spoken of their father he has clearly meant the evil one, but this is the first time he has said this explicitly. Consistently there has been the thought that parentage dictates actions. Those who are of God do the things that please God. Those who are sons of Abraham do the deeds of Abraham. And those who are of the devil do the devil's deeds. So, Jesus says, "the lusts of your father you will to do" (v. 44). The word *lusts* means any strong desire. It can occasionally be used of good desires, but mostly it speaks of a yearning for evil. Clearly that is the meaning in this verse. The evil desires that are characteristic of the devil are characteristic also of his sons. Jesus says not only that they do such evils, but that they "will" to do them. They have set their wills on the evil course they have chosen, a course that is identical with that of the devil. In this way they show that he is indeed their father. As John says in his first Epistle, "He who does what is sinful is of the devil, because the devil has been sinning from the beginning . . ." (1 John 3:8).

The devil "was a murderer from the beginning." This takes us back to the story of Eden. There the devil tempted our first parents and caused them to do what God told them not to do. God said plainly to Adam and Eve, "You must not eat from the tree of the knowledge of good and evil, for when you eat of it you will surely die" (Gen. 2:17). Eve had this in mind when the devil approached her (Gen. 3:3), but the evil one threw doubt on this and led her and Adam into the sin that brought death to them both and thus to the whole human race. The evil one was thus a murderer on quite a scale. And in a different sense he was the murderer of Adam's son Abel. When Cain was angry at Abel's acceptance with God, God said to him, ". . . sin is crouching at your door; it desires to have you, but you must master it" (Gen. 4:7). But Cain did not master it. He yielded to it and murdered Abel. Right from the beginning the devil has brought about murder.

Jesus moves to the thought of truth. We have seen before that truth is an important idea throughout this Gospel and that it is to be seen as a quality of action as well as of speech (3:21). It is closely linked with Jesus, who would in due course say, "I am the truth" (14:6). But the devil had nothing to do with the truth. He "did not stand" in it. He took up his stance elsewhere, for he had nothing to do with truth. He found truth utterly alien.

It is an easy step from there to the thought that the devil has a natural affinity for lying. "When he speaks the lie he speaks of his own" (v. 44). He is a natural liar "and the father of it." The Greek here could be translated "and so is his father," from which some have engaged in curious speculations about the devil's father. But we have no information about such a being and there is no real reason for thinking that this is the meaning of Jesus' words. Rather he is saying that falsehood takes its origin in the devil. He is utterly false and he deals in falsehood. He moves people to be as false as he is.

Truth

That puts Jesus apart from his hearers. He speaks the truth, he says, and because he speaks the truth they do not believe him (v. 45). Notice that he does not say "although I speak the truth . . ." but "because I speak the truth. . . ." The presumption all God's people make is that when the truth is spoken people will believe. And so they will if they are from God.

But Jesus is speaking of evil people. Because they are who and what they are, because they are the children of the devil, because the devil and all his helpers are false and love falsehood, therefore they do not believe the truth when they hear it. They have nothing to do with truth. We should be clear that good and evil are separated by a great chasm. We must not expect that the evil will believe the good. They will not believe unless there is a miracle of grace wrought in them.

Jesus goes on to challenge his hearers. They are opposing him and maintaining that he is not from God. So he asks them, "Which of you convicts me of sin?" (v. 46). It is interesting that none of them replies. This is striking, and we may well say that if even Jesus' enemies could not find sin in him, then his life must have been really outstanding.

But perhaps it is the issue of the challenge rather than the silence of the hearers that is the really wonderful thing. It indicates that Jesus had a perfectly clear conscience. He knew that there was no sin in him. Even a good man, a man far better than the average among God's servants, could not ask such a question if he knew that there was sin in him, even if his enemies did not know about it. A good man would not rely on the ignorance of his opponents. For Jesus, then, to ask such a question means that he knew that there could be no answer. Only one who lived very close to the Father could utter such words.

In the light, then, of the fact that they could not bring evidence of even one sin, in the light of the fact that he spoke the truth, Jesus can ask, "Why do you not believe me?" They ought to have believed one who came in the way Jesus did.

Jesus rounds off this section of the discussion by pointing to the two groups of people we so often find in this Gospel. The one who is "from God" hears Jesus' sayings. This group of people do not hear them because they are not "from God" (v. 47). They have argued that Abraham was their father. Then they shifted their ground a little and said that God was their "Father." These are both ways of saying that they were faithful Israelites, loyal members of the people of God, and Jesus emphatically denies their claim. They do not recognize God's messenger. They are therefore shown to be not God's people.

42

Before Abraham Was

The Jews answered him saying, "Do we not say well that you are a Samaritan and that you have a devil?" Jesus replied, "I have no devil, but I honor my Father and you dishonor me. But I do not seek my own glory; there is One who seeks and judges. Truly, truly, I say to you: if anyone keeps my word he will certainly not see death, not for ever." The Jews therefore said to him, "Now we know that you have a devil. Abraham died, and the prophets, and you say, 'If anyone keeps my word he will certainly not taste death, not for ever.' Are you greater than our father Abraham, who died? And the prophets died; whom are you making yourself?" Jesus answered, "If I glorify myself my glory is nothing. It is my Father who glorifies me of whom you say that he is our God. And yet you do not know him, but I know him. And if I should say that I do not know him I would be a liar like you. But I do know him and I keep his word. Abraham, your father, rejoiced to see my day, and he saw it and was glad." The Jews therefore said to him, "You are not yet fifty years old, and you have seen Abraham?" Jesus said to them, "Truly, truly, I say to you, Before Abraham was, I AM." Therefore they took up stones to throw them at him. But Jesus was hidden, and went away out of the temple (John 8:48–59).

Why did the Jews say that Jesus was a devil-possessed Samaritan? We can see why they said he had "a devil." They did not like his teaching and it suited them to ascribe it to the evil one. But

"Samaritan"? There is no serious suggestion that Jesus was anything other than a Jew, born in Bethlehem of a Jewish mother and brought up in Nazareth in a Jewish home. But we have seen that the Jews did not like the Samaritans. Though the two groups worshiped the same God, the Jews felt that the Samaritans were too ill-informed about him and too lax in the way they approached him. So they had as little to do with them as they could.

There is a saying reported in the Talmud in which three scholars criticize someone who has picked up some learning but has not been to one of the rabbinical schools. One Rabbi says that this man is just one of "the people of the land" (i.e., the common people who did not observe the religious regulations properly), a second that he is "a boor" and a third that he is "a Samaritan." Clearly the scholars had no high view of the Samaritans.

It is probably something like this here. Jesus' opponents may well have in mind the fact that he did not go along with them in observing their detailed regulations. They are saying in effect, "You are no better than a Samaritan! And a demon-possessed Samaritan at that." It is a way of repudiating his teaching and, by classing him with a despised nation, saying that what he taught would not be accepted by any right-thinking person.

Honoring God

Jesus completely ignored the charge that he was a Samaritan. It was not important. The Jews of his day might be narrow nationalists, but he was not. He was quite ready to pass through Samaria and talk with a Samaritan woman (chapter 4). He told a parable about a good man from Samaria. So it probably did not worry him in the slightest that he should be accused of being a Samaritan.

But he did deny that he was demon-possessed. So far from following the dictates of a demon he said, "I honor my Father" (v. 49). It was important that he had come to do the will of God, and he did not allow the accusation that he was demon-possessed to stand for a moment. He uses emphatic pronouns for "I" ("*I* have no devil, but honor my Father") and "you" ("*you* dishonor me"). This sets the Jews apart from him. He consistently gave honor to the Father, but they gave no honor to the one the Father sent. They are in opposite camps.

Jesus further differentiates himself from his opponents when he says, "But I do not seek my own glory" (v. 50). There is the implication that they do seek their own glory: he is not like them. "Glory" is a complex concept in this Gospel and Jesus will return to it later in this conversation. Here the point is that there are people who continually try to get others to think well of them. His Jewish opponents are like that. But Jesus is saying that this is not true of him. His aim is to do the will of God and it is God who "seeks and judges." The language is that of the law court. A just judge would seek out the truth of a matter and give a true and just verdict on the basis of the evidence. The implication is plain. It is his opponents and not Jesus who will be condemned by God. His enemies have not understood the situation in which they find themselves. They think that they are able to hound Jesus with their accusations of being a Samaritan and having a devil. But in fact they are people who stand under judgment, and it is God who will pass judgment on them in due course.

Death

Consistently in this Gospel Jesus' teaching is derived from God, and it is the revelation God gives whereby people enter life. So Jesus moves to the point that his teaching brings life. It is life that his opponents are refusing by taking up their attitude of hostility to him. He prefaces his words with "Truly, truly," which we have seen is his common way of introducing something that is both solemn and important. And with an especially emphatic form of expression he says that anyone who keeps his "word" will never die: "not for ever" (v. 51). His "word" stands for the whole body of his teaching (as in vv. 31, 37, 43). To give heed to that teaching, to accept it and act on it, is to enter God's salvation and that means no eternal death.

Far from impressing them, these words confirm the worst suspicions of these Jews. "Now we know that you have a devil," they say (v. 52). They take Jesus' words to apply to this physical life and see it as quite impossible that his "word" can prolong this life indefinitely. Since this is so, what he says must be wrong, they reason, and to make such a farfetched claim without any real basis proves that he has a devil.

They appeal to the example of Abraham, their great ancestor. Abraham had been a wonderful servant of God (was he not even called God's "friend" [Isa. 41:8]?). If anyone could avoid death, they seem to say, it would be this man. But did he?

No, he did not. Abraham died, as everyone else dies. For good measure they add the prophets. The prophets were the nation's great heroes. The Jews, almost alone among the nations of antiquity, saw the prophets (rather than warriors of some kind) as their great ones. And these, the Jews now say, are all dead. If the great ancestor of the nation died and if the great teachers of the nation died, then what is this heresy that anyone who keeps Jesus' word will never die? To them it was nonsense.

They ask, "Are you greater than our father Abraham?" and "Whom are you making yourself?" (v. 53). The recording of these words is another example of John's irony. He knows, and his readers know, that Jesus is greater by far than Abraham and the prophets. But he leaves the objection in the form in which it was made. It is ironical that the Jews are drawing attention to the really significant point, though without realizing its significance.

"My Father Glorifies Me"

Jesus has already said that he does not seek his own glory (v. 50). He repeats more or less the same point in slightly different language by saying that if he were to "glorify" himself that glory would be nothing (v. 54). But the important point, the point that his opponents were missing, was that it is the Father who glorifies Jesus.

Notice that Jesus sees his own relationship to God as very different from that of his antagonists, when he speaks of "my Father . . . of whom you say that he is our God." He enjoyed such a close personal relationship to him that he could speak of him as "my Father." They could not and did not; they called him "God." The manuscripts are divided, some reading "our" God and some "your" God; but it is the noun and not the adjective that is important. Where Jesus found the intimate relationship expressed in the word *Father* they were more at a distance.

But even when they called him their God they were not being accurate. They did indeed call him God, and it was their proud boast that there is only one God and that he was their God. They were sure that they had a relationship to the one God closer by far than that of any other nation on earth. It was a point of national pride as well as of religious exclusiveness.

And in this they were wrong. "You do not know him," Jesus says (v. 55). Far from having a good relationship to the one God, they did not even know him. They were self-deceived and could not grasp what was really the situation.

They remind me of a teacher in a school whose pupils almost all came from very wealthy homes. The teacher tried to help them see the problems of people who were in a very different situation from their own. One day she asked them to write an essay on the subject "A Poor Family." It would make them think hard, she thought, of how the other half lives. One child wrinkled his brow and began: "Once there was a very poor family. The father was poor, the mother was poor, the children were poor." Then really entering into the spirit of the thing he went on, "The butler was poor, the chauffeur was poor, the maids were poor, the gardener was poor. . . ." The child clearly had no conception whatever of what poverty means.

And these Jews had no conception whatever of who God is. They had their own pet ideas about God and they stuck firmly by them. They did not allow the facts to intrude on their beautiful illusion. They claimed to know God but had no real knowledge of him at all. Jesus was in a different position. He really did know God, and he points out here that if he were to deny that (and take up a position like theirs), he would be a liar, as they are. "But," he says, "I do know him and I keep his word" (v. 55). That is a truth insisted on throughout this Gospel. Indeed, the whole gospel is written out of the conviction that God had acted in Christ for the world's salvation and nothing matters alongside this.

Abraham

The Jews had brought Abraham into the conversation earlier (v. 52). Jesus did not follow that up straightaway, but now he returns to the great patriarch and says some strange words: "Abraham, your father, rejoiced to see my day, and he saw it and was glad" (v. 56). By saying "your father" Jesus is perhaps indicating that the Jews ought to behave differently. If they really were the true children of Abraham, they would act towards Jesus in a way very different from the way they were behaving. They would welcome him as Abraham did.

There are two specially difficult problems about what Jesus said: the meaning of Abraham's rejoicing and the meaning of Jesus' "day." The "day" of Jesus in the New Testament often is clearly the great day when Jesus will return in glory to end this whole world order and to bring in God's new order (e.g., Phil. 1:10; 2:16). But such a meaning does not suit the context here as well as the view that it is Jesus' first coming that is in mind, his coming to make atonement and to open the way to salvation for sinners. That was the critical thing in the working out of salvation. Abraham rejoiced at the coming of Jesus to be our Savior.

When did Abraham rejoice at this day? Jesus is not saying that Abraham is rejoicing now in heaven, but that he "rejoiced." It is a past event, and it is not easy to see when it could have been. We may get a little help if we consider some of the things the Rabbis said about Abraham. Take, for example, the way they understood some words uttered on the occasion of the great patriarch's first appearance in Genesis. God said to him (among other things): ". . . all peoples on earth will be blessed through you" (Gen. 12:3). The Rabbis took this as a prophecy of the coming of the Messiah and held that Abraham rejoiced at this prospect. Another passage they saw as messianic was the vision narrated in Genesis 15. Here Abraham is told that his descendants will be as numerous as the stars in heaven (v. 5), and subsequently God made a solemn covenant with him (v. 18). The Rabbis understood this passage, too, as messianic and a cause for joy.

A third relevant passage is that in which God promised Abraham that he and Sarah, his wife, would have a child. The old couple were incredulous and both laughed at the prospect, Abraham as told in Genesis 17:17 and Sarah in Genesis 18:12. Curiously the Rabbis interpreted Abraham's laughter not as an incredulous reaction, but as joy at the prospect of having a child by Sarah. That is an incredible piece of exegesis; they did not really take notice of what the words meant.

People sometimes miss the point, and some statements must be interpreted with great care. I like the story of a man who worked for a great film actress who was somewhat temperamental and a great trial to those unfortunate enough to have to work with her. She demanded that they agree with her in everything and was quite put out if they did not. But she liked to put on a good face with the press and at an interview one day said, among other things, "I always have great respect for those who differ from me." These words were relayed to the man we are speaking of, and he was asked his opinion. He replied, "Sure. So I differ from her and she respects me. But where do I get my next job?" We are left feeling that the man did not put the same interpretation on the words as the actress did.

The lady's words were all right, but they did not correspond to reality. It is something like that with the rabbinic interpretation. The view sounds attractive, but it is not the meaning of Scripture.

We should think of yet another rabbinic interpretation, this time of Genesis 24:1, where the New International Version tells us that Abraham "was now old and well advanced in years." More literally this last expression means "gone into the days," and our translators have simply said this in the way English speakers would naturally express it. But it is possible to understand "gone into the days" in more ways than one, and the Rabbis took it to mean that Abraham, being an inspired man, was able to go in thought through all the days up to the coming of the Messiah. Once again we may feel compelled to conclude that this is not exegesis. This is not what the passage means. The rabbinic interpretation tells us little about the meaning of Genesis, but much about the way the Rabbis thought.

But it helps us to see the force of what Jesus was saying to the Jews. They had brought up Abraham. Very well, let us think about Abraham, Jesus is saying. From their understanding of a number of passages the

Jews were ready to say that Abraham rejoiced. Jesus is saying that Abraham's joy was real enough, and that it concerned the Messiah, as Jewish tradition held. The things that were taking place before his opponents' very eyes were the things at which Abraham rejoiced. He looked for the coming of God's Messiah and it was this that made him happy. But God's Messiah was now before them; if they really accepted what Abraham was saying, they would rejoice with him at the presence of the Messiah.

"Before Abraham Was—"

The Jews scarcely look at the claim that Abraham *rejoiced;* they are preoccupied with the thought that *Abraham* rejoiced. They are quite prepared to agree that Abraham looked for the coming of the Messiah, but they could not for one moment countenance any view that there was a connection between Abraham and Jesus. So they seize on the question of age. "You are not yet fifty years old," they say to Jesus, which leads us to wonder why they fixed on this figure. Luke tells us that when Jesus began his ministry he was about age thirty (Luke 3:23). Nobody tells us how long the ministry lasted, but it is usually accepted that it covered a span of no more than about three years. Of course a man who was in his early thirties is "not yet fifty," but that is not the way he would usually be described. But fifty was the age when the Levites were considered to have finished their life's work (Num. 4:3), and it may be that they are saying, "You are far too young to have seen Abraham. He lived a long time ago and you have not even completed a normal working life!" Or it may be that they were simply making every allowance without seriously estimating the actual age of Jesus.

They are saying that when you add on every possible year you can think of there is no way of taking Jesus' past back nearly far enough for Abraham to have seen him. Actually, considering the way the Rabbis interpreted the passages we were looking at, this was not strictly necessary. When they said that Abraham had gone into all the days they did not mean that the Messiah had actually been alive at the time of Abraham's vision. They meant that the patriarch had seen the Messiah prophetically. But these Jews were not trying to make allowances for Jesus. They were trying to condemn him; a connection with Abraham looked like an outrageous claim, and that is the way they saw it.

Jesus quite realizes that this was the way what he had said appeared to them. But he makes no attempt to modify it or to make it more acceptable in any way. Instead he introduces his words with the solemn "Truly, truly." What he is about to say is very solemn and very important. Then he says, "Before Abraham was, I AM" (v. 58). This is emphatic speech in the style of deity, which we have seen Jesus using before. There is a claim to deity in the form of words he uses and there is a claim to deity in the meaning we must give them. Jesus claims to have existed not only in the time of Abraham (who could thus have seen him and rejoiced), but before that time. Jesus' "I AM" is timeless. He existed long before Abraham. We should probably understand the words to mean that he has always existed. This is a tremendous claim.

It was a claim that outraged his hearers. To them it was nothing less than blasphemy. In the face of that claim there are only two possibilities. We may accept it and open our hearts to Jesus so that he becomes our Lord and we live to do his will. Or we will reject him. There is no middle course. And if we reject him, we may well take action against him and that was what these Jews did. "They took up stones to throw them at him" (v. 59). Stoning was the Jewish punishment for blasphemy, and these people did not wait for the verdict of some court. Had they not heard him themselves? They saw no reason to delay but attempted to carry out an execution in the traditional style.

But they could not do it. Jesus "was hidden," which may mean that he hid from them in some way. Or the passive may be taken with full seriousness and we then see in it the thought that the Father hid him so that these evil people could not carry out their plan. The will of God is done. Jesus would die on the cross, but it would be in God's good time. There would be no precipitate execution.

Let us finish this meditation with some words from Augustine, a great Christian from an earlier age: "As man, He fled from the stones; but woe to those from whose stony hearts God has fled."

43

Sight to the Blind

And as he passed by he saw a man blind from birth. And his disciples asked him, "Rabbi, who sinned, this man or his parents, that he was born blind?" Jesus replied, "Neither did this man sin nor his parents, but (it happened) so that the works of God might be made manifest in him. We must work the works of him who sent me while it is day; night comes when no one can work. As long as I am in the world I am the light of the world." When he had said these things he spat on the ground and made clay of the spittle, he smeared his clay on his eyes and said to him, "Go, wash in the pool of Siloam (which interpreted means 'Sent')." He went off and washed and came seeing (John 9:1–7).

During the course of the discussions that followed this healing the formerly blind man said, "From of old it was never heard that anyone opened the eyes of a man born blind" (v. 32), and as far as we know the man was accurate. There is no example of the giving of sight to any blind person (let alone one born blind) throughout the entire Old Testament. And in the New there is no example of any of Jesus' followers being instrumental in bringing about such a miracle. As near as we come to it is the occasion when Ananias laid hands on Saul and prayed, with the result that the temporary blindness that followed his vision on the Damascus Road gave way to normal sight. But this is nothing like the miracle that Jesus did on the man who had never seen throughout his entire life.

It is all the more interesting that there are more accounts of the giving of sight to the blind in Jesus' ministry than of any other form of healing. It is never said why this should be so, but perhaps we should think here of the Old Testament prophecies that link the giving of sight to the blind with the activity of the Messiah. "In that day," writes Isaiah, "the deaf will hear the words of the scroll, and out of gloom and darkness the eyes of the blind will see" (Isa. 29:18). And again we read, "Then will the eyes of the blind be opened . . ." (Isa. 35:5), while God says of the Servant of the Lord, "I will . . . make you to be . . . a light for the Gentiles, to open eyes that are blind . . ." (Isa. 42:6–7). There are passages, too, where it is said that "the LORD gives sight to the blind" (Ps. 146:8; see also Exod. 4:11), We should probably understand the writers of our Gospels to be telling us that the giving of sight to the blind shows us Jesus fulfilling messianic prophecies and doing things that God alone can do.

The Problem of Suffering

John introduces this story by saying that Jesus "passed by" but does not say what or where or whom he passed by. Evidently he did not think it important to place the story exactly in a chronological sequence or to tell us precisely where the incident took place. He simply says that Jesus saw a man "blind from birth" (v. 1). That was the important thing. Evidently it was well known that this man had been blind from birth, for John does not mention any discussion of the topic nor does he say that anyone told Jesus or the disciples this fact. It is assumed that they all knew and John takes the story from this point. And, of course, a blind man would be a beggar; as such his story would tend to be known and he would probably be found in a regular spot where pious and generous citizens would be likely to give him money.

The disciples address Jesus as "Rabbi" (v. 1); the word means "my great one" (like the French *monsieur*). Theoretically it might have been used of people in a wide variety of occupations but in practice was confined to teachers, and that is its meaning here. "Teacher," they say, "who sinned?" They do not argue the point as though there was any doubt about it. The man had been blind all his life. Therefore, they reasoned, someone had committed a terrible sin.

There is a rabbinic saying, "There is no death without sin, and there is no suffering without iniquity" (the Rabbis held that this was proved by two texts from Scripture, Ezek. 18:20 and Ps. 89:32). Evidently this view was widely held and the disciples assume it without question. There had to be sin somewhere behind the man's blindness. For the disciples the question was not whether it was sin that had brought about this terrible affliction, but rather "Whose sin was it?"

Never to have seen is a frightful hardship. It deprived this man of much that is valuable and enjoyable in life and meant that the only occupation that had ever been open to him was that of a beggar. In those days there was no other option. Why had such a punishment been inflicted on him? Was it due to some sin of his own? It was not easy to see how this could be. What sin could a person commit before being born that was so dreadful that its punishment was lifelong blindness? But if the man had not committed the sin himself, his parents must have been responsible, and it was not easy for the disciples to see what they could possibly have done that would have brought this punishment not on them but on their son. It was all very puzzling.

Actually it was not beyond the ingenuity of the Rabbis to find an answer. The sin might well have been that of the man himself, as they saw it. Some of them held that the soul existed before it came into the body. Thus, in the apocryphal book *The Wisdom of Solomon,* the author says that "a good soul fell to my lot; or rather, being good, I entered an undefiled body" (8:19–20). Since that author claims that he was good before he entered the body, it is clear that the possibility had to be allowed that other people were bad before they began their lives on earth. The view was apparently not widely held, but certainly some people thought that way. Thus the man might have sinned before he came to earth. But could he have sinned so greatly that he would merit the punishment he had received?

More common was the thought that children might sin in the womb. We read in Scripture that when Rebekah was pregnant with twins "the babies jostled each other within her" (Gen. 25:22). This opened up the possibility that unborn babies were active and could thus do what was wrong as well as what was right. So prenatal sin was thought to be quite possible. Only, in this case, it seemed that a very great punishment was being inflicted for what could scarcely be a very great sin.

That left the possibility that it may have been the parents who sinned. One Rabbi held that a man should not gaze at a woman, "and he who looks even at a woman's heel will beget degenerate children," while another maintained that this was true of a man's own wife during menstruation. Yet another held that if anyone who "has had a blood-letting has marital intercourse, he will have epileptic children." There are many such sayings, and it is clear that the Rabbis were firmly of the conviction that it was quite common to have the sins of the parents punished by various defects in the children, defects for which the children would have to suffer all their lives.

So the disciples were not manufacturing an imaginary problem. It is clear that among the religious teachers of the Jews there were some who thought a person might well be punished for sins he had committed before birth, and there were some who held that even very serious afflictions might be the punishment of parental sins. So this blind man presented them with a problem. It was not easy to see how he could have sinned before birth a sin serious enough to merit such a heavy punishment. Nor could they see why the heavenly Father of whom Jesus had taught them so much would punish a man in this terrible fashion for the sins of someone else. But in their culture these seemed the only possibilities. So they ask Jesus. Whose sin was it?

The Works of God

Jesus immediately dismissed both possibilities (v. 3). There are still mysteries about the afflictions that trouble us in this life, but we must not seek the answers along the lines that the disciples were pursuing. Jesus did not say that sickness and the like are never the consequence of sin. In a previous incident he said to the man he had cured of lameness, "Sin no longer, lest something worse happen to you" (5:14). Sin can have damaging consequences. But it is a great mistake to think that all our afflictions and illnesses are due to sin.

This blindness, Jesus said, was "so that the works of God might be made manifest in him." I do not think that Jesus means that the man was made to go through all his life up to this point without ever having been able to see, simply in order that Jesus might effect a cure and thus manifest "the works of God." Rather he is saying that the blindness is something in and through which God's "works" are manifest.

It is important that we recognize that God's hand is in all our afflictions as well as in those good things that we recognize as his blessings. Christians are not shielded from the hardships and difficulties of life so that they are freed from the afflictions that trouble other people. On the contrary. They live on the same terms as do other people; they have the same kind of troubles, illnesses, accidents, and the like. There are some differences; perhaps a Christian, to take an example at random, is not very likely to find himself incapacitated as the result of driving a car while he was drunk. But, setting such consequential sufferings apart, Christians live their lives with the same kind of problems as other people have.

The difference is that, as God's children, Christians look to God for the grace to see them through. In their troubles they manifest the fact that, as Paul found out, God's grace is always sufficient and that his power "is made perfect in weakness" (2 Cor. 12:9). They do not complain bitterly at every trial, for they know that the heavenly Father has his purpose in everything that happens in life.

And, of course, sometimes "the works of God" are made manifest in the removal of an affliction. So it is in this case. What God had done through the man's blindness in past days we do not know. But we do know that the removal of that affliction was a manifestation of the divine power and resulted in both physical and spiritual blessing to the man.

That the works of God are made manifest has its consequences for the people of God: "We must," said Jesus, "work the works of him who sent me" (v. 4). God chooses to do his mighty works through those on earth, at least as a general rule. He can do mighty miracles without human participation, but normally he chooses to let his people have a part in the great works he is doing. So now. It is not certain whether Jesus said "we must work" or "I must work"; some of the manuscripts have one reading, some the other. But "I must work" is the reading of most of the later manuscripts, while the earlier ones for the most part have "we must work." Scribes would be tempted to alter "we must work" to "I must work" because Jesus immediately goes on to refer to the time while "I am in the world"; with those words to follow it would be easy for scribes to reason that "we must work" must be wrong. So most scholars accept "we must work" as the true reading and think of "I must work" as a scribal alteration.

That means that Jesus was associating his people with himself in this obligation. He did the miracle himself, of course, though even here we should bear in mind that Jesus did not simply speak a word of power as he often did in his healing miracles. He put clay on the man's eyes and told him to go and wash in Siloam. The man was given a part to play. But in general God calls his people to work with him when he does his mighty works. We are given a great privilege, which Paul expresses by saying that we are God's "fellow-workers" (1 Cor. 3:9). There is a dignity about Christian service, a dignity such as attaches to nothing else on earth.

Notice further that Jesus says that we "must" work. The term means that there is a compelling necessity about this. He is not saying that it would be a good idea for us to do some work for God. He is saying that it is necessary that we do this work. Salvation by God's grace is not an invitation to spiritual laziness. The fact that we do nothing to merit our salvation should not lead us to reason that it does not matter what we do with our lives. Rather it should impel us to do the best we can in living out what salvation means. It should motivate us to do the works of God "while it is day."

We might expect that after "we must work" we would have a reference to "him who sent us" (which indeed we find in some manuscripts; the scribes were apparently uneasy with the change from "we" to "me" and while some altered "we" to the singular, others altered "me" to the plural). But very few scholars doubt that "me" is correct here. John makes a great deal of the fact that the Father sent the Son. It was the sending of the Son that altered everything. Jesus' death on the cross is the great central fact. It brings us salvation and it reveals to us the magnitude of God's love. So when Jesus is speaking about the work of God that his followers must work he links it with the mission on which he had come. All Christian work is connected in one way or another with the fact that the Father sent the Son.

The Light of the World

Jesus says that we all must work "while it is day"; he contrasts the day with the night that is coming, when "no one can work." He does not define the day and the night here, but we must surely see them as the time while we have the opportunity of working and the time when work is done. In Jesus' own case there is the approach of the crucifixion, when his earthly work would be done. There is a sense in which it was indeed "night" when Jesus died, and this is symbolized in the darkness that the Synoptists tell us was over all the land while he was on the cross (Matt. 27:45; Mark 15:33; Luke 23:44). All the work that Jesus was sent to accomplish had to be done before the "night"; after the cross there was none of the earthly life left in which to do anything.

In the case of the servants of Christ there is an equivalent. It is true of us, as it was of him, that when our earthly life is done our earthly work is done. We must not put off doing service until it is too late. We must also bear in mind that for particular pieces of service there is an earlier "night"; before our lives are over the opportunity for doing them will have gone. In other words, opportunity must be grasped while it is there; every opportunity passes away sooner or later and if we miss it we cannot bring it back.

With this encouragement to get on with the work we are given to do, Jesus links the words: "As long as I am in the world I am the light of the world" (v. 5). These words bring out the shortness of the incarnation. The time when Jesus was in the world was definitely limited and, therefore, he must act decisively. And throughout that time he was "the light of the world." Of course he still is and always will be. But in a special sense he was light to the world during the days of his life, and it is in that sense that he now says, "I am the light of the world." As long as he lived here on earth it was his function to be light to the dwellers on earth.

The Giving of Sight

Jesus proceeded to give sight to the blind man. It is interesting that John says nothing about any initiative from the man himself. He did not ask for sight, for example. Nor is there any conversation with him as there was with the lame man in chapter 5. John says nothing about whether the man had faith in Jesus or not, or even whether he knew who Jesus was. We are probably right in thinking that he had no faith as yet, because at the end of the incident John records Jesus as asking him whether he believed on the Son of man, only to have the man ask, "Who is he?" (vv. 35–36). It seems that he became a believer only after the miracle. It is also to be noted that on this occasion Jesus invited the man's cooperation. Just as he had said to the lame man, "Get up, pick up your pallet and walk" (5:8), so he could have said to this man, "Open your eyes and see." But he did not. He asked him to do something.

Jesus spat on the ground and made a little bit of clay. Then he smeared the clay on the eyes of the blind man. The ancient world thought highly of the curative values of spittle, but it is impossible to think that it was spittle itself as a medical method that brought about the cure. Jesus healed many people without resort to such means (though Mark tells us that he used spittle on two other occasions: Mark 7:33; 8:23). It is probable that Jesus used spittle on this occasion because of the way the man himself would view it; it may have been a help to him to have this method used in his own case.

Having put the clay on the man's eyes, Jesus sent him off to the pool of Siloam and told him to wash (v. 7). John explains the meaning of Siloam as "Sent." King Hezekiah had a tunnel dug from the Virgin's Fountain (which was outside the city) to this pool to bring a water supply into the city, so that the water was "sent" along by this tunnel. The name properly belongs to the conduit but was given to the pool and that at quite an early date (Neh. 3:15; Isa. 8:6). John probably includes an explanation of the meaning of the name because of the large place he gives to the concept of Jesus as having been "sent" by the Father. Now a blind man is cured by means of the "sent," basically by Jesus but in a secondary manner by the pool. The word for "pool" is connected with the verb "to swim"; it was quite a large pool, not some ornamental pond.

The man did as Jesus told him. He went off to the pool and washed and "came seeing." He found that he had received the gift of sight. "The light of the world" was meaningful to him.

44

Friends and Pharisees

The neighbors, then, and those who formerly had seen him that he was a beggar said, "Is not this the man who sat and begged?" Others said, "No, but he is like him." He said, "I am he." They said to him therefore, "How were your eyes opened?" He replied, "The man called Jesus made clay and smeared it on my eyes and said to me, 'Go to Siloam and wash.' So I went off and when I had washed I saw." And they said to him, "Where is he?" He says, "I do not know."

They bring the formerly blind man to the Pharisees. Now it was the Sabbath on the day when Jesus made clay and opened his eyes. Therefore the Pharisees too asked him how he received his sight. He said to them, "He put clay on my eyes and I washed and I see." So some of the Pharisees said, "This man is not from God because he does not keep the Sabbath." But others said, "How can a man that is a sinner do such signs?" and there was a division among them. So they said to the blind man again, "What do you say about him, because he opened your eyes?" And he said, "He is a prophet."

The Jews did not believe about him that he was blind and had received sight until they called the parents of him who had received sight. And they asked them, "Is this your son, of whom you say that he was born blind? How therefore does he now see?" So his parents replied saying, "We know that this is our son and that he was born blind. But how he now sees we do not know, or who opened his eyes we do not know. Ask him, he is of age; he will speak for himself." His parents said these things because they were afraid of the Jews, for the Jews had already agreed that if anyone should confess him to be the

Christ he should be put out of the synagogue. For this reason his parents said, "He is of age; ask him."

So a second time they called the man who was blind and said to him, "Give glory to God; we know that this man is a sinner." He therefore answered, "Whether he is a sinner I do not know. One thing I know, that I was blind, now I see." They said to him therefore, "What did he do to you? How did he open your eyes?" He answered them, "I told you already and you did not listen; why do you want to hear it again? You don't wish to become his disciples, too, do you?" And they abused him and said, "You are a disciple of that fellow, but we are Moses' disciples. We know that God spoke to Moses, but as for this man, we don't know where he is from." The man answered them saying, "Why in this is the marvelous thing that you do not know where he is from and yet he opened my eyes! We know that God does not hear sinners but if anyone is devout and does his will, him he hears. From of old it was never heard that anyone opened the eyes of a man born blind; if this man were not from God he could do nothing at all." They answered him saying, "You were altogether born in sins and are you teaching us?" And they threw him out (John 9:8–34).

The man born blind doubtless was a very happy man as he exulted in his new gift of sight. But it was not long before he found himself in conflict with some of the highest in the land—a most unexpected result of what he must have seen as the most wonderful thing that had happened to him in all his life. The inquisition the Pharisees carried out when it was all reported to them shows the man as a sturdy character, one who would not be stampeded by the opposition of those in authority but was ready to give a good account of himself as he stood by the facts of the situation. He knew what had happened and was not going to let himself be browbeaten into a criticism of the healer who had given him the wonderful gift of sight.

John begins with a paragraph in which he tells of the man's reception by his friends and neighbors (vv. 8–12). He was obviously sighted, a fact that caused a division of opinion among those who saw him. He was recognizably the same man, and that was what impressed some who saw him. But blind men do not see, and that was what impressed others. The man was able to resolve that problem and he announced his identity.

That raised the question "How were your eyes opened?" (v. 10) to which he gave a concise answer, explaining how Jesus had healed him.

But to the question "Where is he?" he could reply only "I do not know" (v. 12). He had left Jesus in response to the command to go off to the pool of Siloam, and when he found that he could see he had evidently gone off home straightaway. He had had no opportunity for knowing where Jesus was.

The Sabbath

The excited group brought the man to the Pharisees (v. 13). John does not say why they did this, nor when. It may have been a spontaneous, immediate reaction. But from the subsequent conversation it seems more likely that it was some time later. It is interesting that they brought the man to the Pharisees, not to the priests or any official body. But in popular esteem it was the Pharisees who were the religious experts and, in any case, many of them were members of the Sanhedrin. They were prominent in the life of the nation and evidently were regarded at least by this little group of ordinary people as the kind of leading people who could give a decision on matters that troubled them.

John does not tell us what they said when they came to the Pharisees. But the giving of sight took place on the Sabbath, and the subsequent discussion shows that it was this that troubled the religious leaders and presumably also some of the people who brought the man before them. It may be that it was not so much the cure in itself as the cure on the Sabbath on which they wanted the verdict of the learned Pharisees. In any case it was the Sabbath that loomed large, and John now tells us that it was on that day that the cure took place (v. 14).

Throughout this section of the Gospel the Sabbath is stressed. The healing of the lame man took place on the Sabbath (5:1–18), as, according to some manuscripts, did the teaching in the synagogue at Capernaum (6:59). At the Feast of Tabernacles there was a discussion about the bearing on Sabbath observance of the regulation that circumcision be carried out on that day (7:22–23), and now we have a further work of healing on the holy day. Clearly the right use of the Sabbath formed a large part of Jesus' conflict with the authorities in Jerusalem. They saw the day as one on which not the slightest risk should be taken of doing anything that profaned its holiness. Accordingly they ringed it about with a multitude of restrictions, with the praiseworthy intention of bringing glory to God but with the unfortunate practical result of making the Sabbath a burden.

Jesus called people back to an understanding of what God meant when he called on people to keep the day holy. It was wrong to see God as simply calling for abstention from all sorts of work. This misunderstanding led the Pharisees and others into a close examination of exactly what constituted work (and which accordingly could not be done) and what could be seen as not coming under the heading "work" (and thus was permissible). God created everything in six days and rested on the seventh, and this was the basis of the Sabbath. But his "rest" did not mean cessation from all activity. If God did not continually sustain his creation on the Sabbath it would cease to exist. It was therefore proper for people to do things on the Sabbath that would bring honor to God, things like circumcising a child, or healing a blind or lame man.

It was this failure to understand the ways of God that led the Pharisees into their bitter and continuous hostility to Jesus. They saw him as giving teaching that cut at the heart of service to God as they understood it. He saw them as blind to what God was saying to them. Throughout this part of his Gospel John is emphasizing the importance of the right use of the Sabbath as opposed to the way the Pharisees observed it.

Signs and Sinners

The Pharisees began quite properly by asking the man what had happened (v. 15). They had not been there at the time and wanted him to tell them exactly what had occurred. We have already seen that the man had a gift for saying things concisely, and once again we have a very short but very clear account of the miracle.

Immediately the more hidebound of the Pharisees trotted out their doctrinaire verdict. Their views on the Sabbath were clear, and equally clear was it that what Jesus had done did not fit in with those views. Therefore, reasoned this group, Jesus "is not from God" (v. 16). If he did not keep the Sabbath according to their rules, how could he be?

They were not prepared for anything outside their normal approach. I am reminded that it is said that during his time as a recluse Howard Hughes would often demand the same meal day after day. At one time he ate two scoops of banana-nut ice cream at every meal. There was consternation among his staff when they learned that the manufacturer had decided to discontinue the line. But they got in touch with him and persuaded him to make a special batch. As 1,325 liters was the smallest amount he would make, they felt that they were well provided for, for quite some time. But when they served the millionaire his next meal he said, "That's fine ice cream, but it's time I changed. From now on I want French vanilla."

Like the aides of Howard Hughes these Pharisees were prepared for what could be expected. But something outside the normal did not fit into their rules, and they could not recognize it as anything other than wrong.

But that was not the only opinion. Others asked, "How can a man that is a sinner do such signs?" These men were impressed by the miracle. They recognized that Jesus had given sight to a man born blind, and they saw that this called for a mighty divine intervention. No quack or charlatan could call forth the power of God in this way. Sabbath rules or no Sabbath rules, for them this was clear evidence that Jesus was not the sinner their comrades claimed he was.

We very often overlook this section of Pharisaism. The Pharisaic system was such that it all too easily degenerated into a keeping of rules, and that meant a process of defining with the greatest precision what constituted a fulfillment of the rules and what constituted a breach. With a great variety of exceptions open to those who were learned in these definitions, it was all too easy to give attention to the letter rather than the spirit, and thus for us Pharisaism has become synonymous with hypocrisy. But it is well to remember that there was another side to Pharisaism. There were Pharisees who were more open-minded and who were genuinely pious people. While those who opposed Jesus received the emphasis in the Gospels, there were those who agreed with him, and we should not forget that in the early church there were Pharisees who believed and who were heard in the councils of the church (Acts 15:5).

So on this occasion there were some who saw that it was simply not possible for a sinner to do "such signs." It was, of course, possible for Satan to disguise himself as an angel of light, and they were not dismissing the possibility of the evil one's deceit. But they were talking about "signs," about mighty works that taught people about God and his ways and brought them near to God. Miracles like that are not possible for evil people. And it was miracles like that that Jesus kept doing.

The result was division. Neither group could accept the position of the other. So they called the blind man into the discussion again. He had told them what had happened. Now they wanted to know what he thought about Jesus (v. 17). Normally these religious experts would never have dreamed of asking an opinion about a religious teacher from a beggar. It shows us how perplexed and divided they were that they should ask such a thing of such a man.

Progress and Regress

The man's instant response was "He is a prophet" (v. 17). We may feel that this is inadequate, but we should bear in mind that it was probably the highest religious title that the man was able to give at that instant. He was no theologian; he had lived all his life in the world of darkness and had known no occupation other than that of a beggar. So he could not be expected to know all about Jesus from the very brief contact he had had with him.

One of the intriguing things about this chapter is the way the blind beggar grew in understanding, while at the same time the Pharisees with all their advantages became progressively more limited in their understanding of Jesus. Evidently the blind man was quite intelligent and was a man of character. The result was that he came to see more and more of who and what Jesus was.

The blind man's first description of Jesus was "the man called Jesus" (v. 11). By now he has gone on to see him as a prophet. During subsequent discussions he came to see that he was a leader, one whom it was well to follow, and he spoke of disciples (v. 27). Toward the end he says that Jesus could not do what he does if he were not "from God" (v. 33). This means, since Jesus does in fact do these things, that he *is* "from God." Finally, when Jesus seeks him out, he comes to see him as the Son of man, as Lord, and as one who may fitly be worshiped (vv. 35–38). It is an interesting spiritual progression.

But the Pharisees went the other way. They started with the conviction that Jesus was "not from God" (v. 16), then went on to question the reality of the miracle he had done (v. 18). They declared their certainty that he was a sinner (v. 24) and made statements arising from this that showed them to be ignorant in matters spiritual (v. 29). Finally they were shown to be both blind and sinful (v. 41).

People do not stand still. As we go through life we either make progress in spiritual things or we slip back. The two parties in this discussion press an important lesson on us.

The Blind Man's Parents

For some reason John drops his references to "the Pharisees" (they are mentioned specifically again only in v. 40). He reverts to the name he usually used for Jewish leaders in opposition to Jesus, "the Jews," but we need not think that anyone other than the Pharisees mentioned in the earlier part of the chapter are in mind. They could not believe that Jesus had worked such a striking miracle and looked at ways of discrediting the report.

They began with the parents of the man. They summoned them to the discussion and asked whether this sighted person was their son and, if so, how he had received sight (v. 19). We have already seen that the formerly blind man was ready to stand up to the Pharisees, but this was not true of his parents. Evidently they were humble people and did not want to come into conflict with those in high places. So they are prepared to identify their son and to attest the fact that he was born blind (v. 20). But they will not go beyond that. They were not there when the cure took place and thus could not testify of their own knowledge that it was Jesus who had given him sight. So they say, "But how he now sees we do not know."

They could scarcely be blamed for this. It was no more than the truth. But they went on to say that the Pharisees should direct their questions to the man himself. They said, ". . . he is of age; he will speak for himself" (v. 21). It is clear that they discerned danger in this inquiry. The leaders were clearly displeased with their son. He might be punished severely. They wanted to make sure that whatever happened, they were safe. So they put all the responsibility on their son.

John adds a little explanation (vv. 22–23). The Jews had agreed to excommunicate anyone who confessed Jesus to be the Christ. Some writers go into detail as to what this meant, while others deny that any form of excommunication existed at this time. Both extremes seem to be wrong. Excommunication in some form is as old as the time of Ezra (Ezra 10:8), though little is known of precisely what this involved at the time of Jesus or of just how it was carried out. But the withdrawal of any synagogue privileges would be a serious matter to anyone from such a religious community as the Jews of that day, so it is not surprising that the man's parents did not want to incur the punishment. That must be said, but it is still surprising that they did not give more support to their own son in his difficulties just as he was beginning to find his way in the sighted world.

Give Glory to God

Not being able to make much progress with the parents, the Pharisees went back to questioning the man himself. This time they began with "Give glory to God" (v. 24), the precise bearing of which is not clear. They may mean, "You have been lying. We know that. This man Jesus did not give you sight. You have done wrong in saying so. Now we invite you to leave your sinful path and do what is right. Give glory to God and tell us the truth" (Joshua made a somewhat similar plea to Achan, Josh. 7:19).

Another way of taking their words is to see them as reasoning that Jesus did not do the work of healing. All he did was put clay on the man's eyes. If there was healing, then it was God who did it and all the glory should be given to him.

They reinforce their exhortation by informing the man that they know that Jesus is a sinner. Their "we" is emphatic; whatever be the case with ignorant people like blind beggars, these religious experts have knowledge and they lay it down categorically that "this man is a sinner."

But the former blind beggar is not a man who can be easily moved from a position he knows to be right. He does not know anything about Jesus and thus does not know whether or not he is a sinner. But he has one important certainty: "I was blind, now I see" (v. 25). Nobody is going to shake a man out of a certainty like that. And, as it was Jesus who gave him his sight, nobody is going to make him take sides against Jesus.

All this must have been quite unexpected. The Pharisees did not usually discuss religious matters with common people like a beggar, and when they did they expected that what they said would be accepted without question. It was very unusual to have anyone react like this man.

I am reminded of a little old lady who went into a shoe shop and asked for a pair of shoes with platform soles. This was high fashion at the time, and the little old lady looked a long way from being glamorous. The assistant, however, did not argue. She produced a number of platform soles and eventually sold the most stylish of them all, with platform soles twelve centimeters high. As she was wrapping them she asked, "Are you buying these for some special occasion?" "Good heavens, no," said the little old lady. "They're for when I do my washing. I'm not tall and the sheets touch the ground when I'm trying to get them onto the clothesline. Now I'll be high enough to keep them out of the dirt."

It was a quite unexpected reaction (and an unexpected use for high-fashion shoes). So with the blind man. The Pharisees did not quite know how to proceed. So they went back to the beginning: "What did he do to you? How did he open your eyes?" (v. 26).

But the man wanted nothing to do with going over the story again. He reminded them that he had told them all this already. And perhaps with a mischievous twinkle in his eye he asked whether they wanted to become Jesus' disciples, too (v. 27). The way he put his question shows that he expected a negative answer. He knew that this kind of person was not going to become a disciple, but it was fun suggesting it. We should notice his "too." He is already counting himself as a disciple of Jesus.

Disciples of Moses

The Pharisees clearly are angry. They take up this mention of discipleship and distance themselves from the blind man. They use emphatic pronouns to say, "*You* are a disciple of that fellow, but *we* are Moses' disciples" (v. 28), and speak contemptuously of Jesus. They want there to be no doubt of their repudiation of the blind man and also of Jesus. They clinch their position (so they think) with the assertion that God spoke to Moses but that they have no knowledge of Jesus' origin (v. 29).

The formerly blind man comes up with an interesting piece of reasoning. He begins by referring to "the" marvelous thing: more astonishing even than his miraculous cure is the ignorance of the Pharisees in the face of convincing evidence. He marshals his arguments: (1) Jesus opened his eyes; (2) God does not hear sinners (they had said, "We know that God spoke to Moses" and he retorts with another "we know," this one referring to God's refusal to bless sinners); (3) God hears the devout who do his will; (4) In all the history of the world no one has opened the eyes of a blind man; and (5) If Jesus were not from God he would be powerless.

It is a convincing case and all the more remarkable in coming from a man who could have had little experience in this kind of discussion. But the Pharisees took absolutely no notice. Their minds were made up and they refused to receive enlightenment from one who was "altogether born in sins" (v. 34). They had no answer to what the man said and took refuge in getting rid of him. To the end they resisted the light.

45

Faith in the Son of Man

Jesus heard that the Pharisees had thrown him out and when he had found him he said, "Do you believe in the Son of man?" That man replied, "And who is he, sir, that I may believe in him?" Jesus said to him, "You have both seen him and it is he who is talking with you." And he said, "Lord, I believe"; and he worshiped him.

And Jesus said, "For judgment I came into this world, so that those who do not see might see and those who see might become blind. Some of the Pharisees who were with him heard these things and they said to him, "We're not blind, are we?" Jesus said to them, "If you were blind, you would not have sin; now you say, 'We see'; your sin remains" (John 9:35–41).

The giving of sight to the man born blind must have caused a great deal of interest. People would have taken notice, too, of the attitude of the Pharisees. There is no suggestion that the proceedings we were looking at in our last study took place in secret. The Pharisees evidently interrogated the man quite openly and it would be common knowledge that in the end they had "thrown him out," whether this means something like excommunication or simply exclusion from their assembly. By no stretch of the imagination could it be called a friendly act, and all Jerusalem would know that the Pharisees, while unable to deny that a most unusual miracle of healing had taken place, had rejected the man. What they did about the minority of their own group who had spoken up on his behalf (v. 16) we do not know. They may have censured them or they may have ignored them. What we know is that the Pharisees did not act in accordance with the views of that minority.

Since it was common knowledge that the man had been rejected, Jesus sought him out. It is interesting that John says simply "when he had found him" (v. 35); John evidently felt that it was not necessary to tell his readers that Jesus looked for him. He was a person who had been helped by Jesus and then had been subjected to some form of persecution by the religious establishment. John knew Jesus well enough to know that his Lord would never desert a person in such a situation. He would certainly look for him and support him and do whatever needed to be done for him. So he says no more than "when he had found him." We are probably to understand that Jesus did not conduct a perfunctory search. The man was in some difficulty. Therefore Jesus continued looking until he found him.

Faith

Then he asked him the question "Do you believe in the Son of man?" This is the first time faith has been mentioned in connection with this miracle. (In v. 18 the verb *believe* is used as we are told that the Jews did not believe that the man had been born blind and had received sight until they spoke with his parents; but this is clearly something quite different from faith in the sense in which Jesus is using the term.) In the synoptic Gospels we often find Jesus saying, "Your faith has saved you," or the like. We tend to get the idea that faith was the necessary prerequisite to healing: no faith, no healing!

But that does not seem to be the correct way of understanding it. The divine Son of God is not dependent on people's help before he can do mighty works. We have seen that he once cured a man who had been lame for thirty-eight years and who did not even know Jesus' name (5:1–18). There was no possibility of faith there. Jesus commonly responded to faith, but there was no absolute necessity for it.

In the ancient world there were religious "quacks" who managed to get quite a good living by demonstrating "miracles" of some sort. At this distance in time it is not possible to say exactly what it was that they did, but we know from experience in our own days that any good conjurer can do things that to the uninitiated look suspiciously like miracles. We cannot understand them and we just marvel. It appears to have been something like this in the first century. People could not explain how these "miracle workers" did their act, and they responded with some form of veneration (and, of course, financial assistance).

Now Jesus was not that sort of "miracle worker." He did not work spectacular but purposeless miracles. Mark tells us that when Jesus went back to Nazareth he "could do no mighty work there" and that "he was astonished at their unbelief" (Mark 6:5–6). Luke says that in his synagogue sermon in that village Jesus recognized that they wanted him to do miracles like they had heard he had done in Capernaum (Luke 4:23). These people were not humbly looking for the presence and the power of God. They wanted no more than what we want when we see a good conjurer at work. To gratify that desire and class himself among the "miracle workers" was quite impossible for Jesus. He "could not" do that kind of miracle. This does not mean that he lacked the power. Of course not. Even in Nazareth he healed a few sick people (Mark 6:5).

The impossibility lay in the kind of person he was and the kind of work he had come to do. Being the kind of person he was, and having come to do the will of God as he did, he could not do the kind of "miracle" that would brand him as a publicity-seeker.

But where there was faith, where people believed in him, there was not that possibility of misunderstanding. So it was in such an atmosphere that Jesus did most of his miracles.

The blind man of whom we have been reading seems not to have been a believer. At any rate he did not know who "the Son of man" was and this was Jesus' favorite way of referring to himself. But he had a spiritual need as well as a physical one, so Jesus came to him with a question about believing. In some of our earlier studies we have seen that John has a number of ways of expressing what "believing" means. Here he uses the construction that means wholehearted faith, literally "believing into," the faith that makes the believer one with Christ. John later has a good deal about "abiding in" Christ, and the faith of which he writes here has that flavor. Jesus asks whether the man has that kind of faith.

The Son of Man

He does not ask, "Do you believe in me?" but "Do you believe in the Son of man?" Jesus mostly called himself "the Son of man," an expression that is used in all four Gospels and is always used by Jesus himself. There is only one passage in the whole New Testament where anybody else used the expression and that is when Stephen said that he saw the heavens opened and "the Son of man" standing at God's right hand (Acts 7:56). It was Jesus' own way of referring to himself.

Most scholars agree that when he used this term Jesus was referring back to the vision in Daniel 7, where "one like a son of man" came with the clouds of heaven, was brought into the presence of "the Ancient of

Days," and "was given authority, glory and sovereign power" (Dan. 7:13–14). It was not an accepted name for the Messiah, and thus when Jesus used it people would not think that he was claiming messianic status. Of course, when they came to know him they would recall the passage in Daniel and see in it a fullness of meaning.

Jesus commonly used this expression, it would seem, as a way of both asserting and concealing his messiahship. It asserted it, for that was what the term meant in Daniel 7. It also concealed it, for this was not the way the passage was normally interpreted. What would the formerly blind man understand by the term? It is impossible to say.

A New Believer

But he knew the voice of Jesus. Never in all his life would he forget the voice that had told him to go and wash in Siloam! And, from the way Jesus put it, it was obvious that he looked for people to "believe in the Son of man." And, if Jesus wanted it, the formerly blind man was willing to believe in that Son of man. But there was a problem. Throughout his discussion with the Pharisees it had become abundantly clear that this man was fundamentally honest and was not now going to profess faith in someone he did not know. He was willing, but he needed more information. So he asked, "And who is he, sir, that I may believe in him?" (v. 36).

He addresses Jesus as "sir." This is the translation of the Greek word *kurios,* which has several meanings. It may denote the owner of a vineyard (Matt. 20:8) or other property. It may mean someone in high authority, and Festus uses it when he speaks of writing to his "lord" (the emperor) about Paul (Acts 25:26). It was used commonly of anyone in high place, but it was also frequently employed as a form of address in polite society. In this it was not unlike the English word *Sir*. This is a very common form of polite address, but in England it is also a way of designating a knight.

So the healed man's "sir" is here probably no more than this polite way of speaking. He is willing to go along with what Jesus is suggesting, providing that he understands it a little better. But he as yet does not know enough to understand that it is Jesus who is "the Son of man" and that he is far more than just a man. He asks for information "that" (his word means "in order that") he may believe. There is purpose in the way he puts this.

Jesus says, "You have both seen him and it is he who is talking with you" (v. 37). This self-disclosure is decisive for the man. John Marsh puts it this way:

> . . . in the pause between one sentence and the next, it is almost possible to see the once blind man take a new look at his interrogator, and see precisely the same phenomena as he had seen before, as even his previous questioners had seen as they looked on Jesus—face, hair, clothes, hands, gestures all the same, and like those of any other man—and yet! Yet now, with power of sight given to him by Jesus in a humanity that was a new creation, he can see beyond or through the phenomena that are but signs and symbols to the reality inherent in them. . . .

The words of Jesus have brought a new enlightenment. He sees now something that he had not seen before.

The result is seen in both words and action: "And he said, 'Lord, I believe'; and he worshiped him" (v. 38). He uses the same word *kurios* that he had used before. But then he did not know Jesus for what he was and had surely used the term in nothing but a normal, polite way. But now he uses it with fuller meaning, and we must translate "Lord" to bring this out. Where before he saw Jesus as an honored acquaintance, the leap of faith enabled him now to see him as Lord. What form his worship took John does not say. It does not matter. What matters is that it was worship, and this enables us to know that the man had entered into a satisfying relationship with his new Lord. He was a believer. He does not say, "I believe in you." He lets "believe" stand by itself. It is of course the case that it is Jesus in whom he believes, but he speaks simply of believing. He had become a man of faith.

Judgment

John does not say whether the dialogue of this final paragraph (vv. 39–41) took place right then or whether it was somewhat later. A later time seems more likely, because Jesus would surely not have had the conversation that led the formerly blind man to faith in the presence of hostile witnesses. It seems best to hold that John has added at this point a short conversation that arose out of the miracle and its results.

It is somewhat startling to find Jesus saying that he came into this world "for judgment" (v. 39), especially since at an earlier time he said that God did not send him into the world to judge it (3:17). But the offer of salvation necessarily means judgment. What are we to say about those who reject God's offer of salvation and go their own careless way? The fact that they have rejected God's good gift means in itself that they have pronounced their own judgment; they have chosen to be lost, to be condemned. It is not the purpose of the shining of the sun to cast shadows. But where the sun shines on opaque objects, shadows are inevitable. It is not the purpose of the coming of the Son of God to bring condemnation. But when his offered salvation is rejected, condemnation is inevitable.

Jesus explains this in two ways. First, he came "so that those who do not see might see." This presents us with no problems. We have had an excellent example of what Jesus means in the man who had been healed first of physical blindness and then, more importantly, of spiritual blindness. He had really entered into light.

But Jesus also says that he came "so that . . . those who see might become blind." This is a difficult saying. But both the words themselves and also the subsequent conversation indicate that Jesus is speaking of people like the Pharisees, people who claimed to be religiously enlightened but were not. He is saying that he came to expose the sham and show these people for the blind folk they really were. The way of salvation is not that of religious pretension, outward conformity to a series of rules, pride in one's own standing before God, and all the rest of what made up the Pharisaic system.

It is not only the Christians who were critical of the Pharisees. Some of the Rabbis were very conscious of the faults of these people. The Rabbis could say, "There are seven types of Pharisees," and go on to describe them. The first type is the Pharisee who is circumcised from an unworthy motive; the second, they said, walks with exaggerated humility; the third is so anxious to avoid looking at women that he keeps knocking his head against walls; the fourth is the "pestle" Pharisee—he is bowed like a pestle in a mortar (in ostentatious humility); the fifth keeps saying, "What further duty may I perform?" (implying that he has fulfilled every obligation); the sixth is the Pharisee because he loves rewards; and the seventh is the Pharisee because he fears punishment. It is obvious that those outside the Pharisaic party were well aware of their faults.

There were Pharisees with Jesus at this time. These may have been some of the Pharisees who believed in him, but the subsequent conversation makes that unlikely. It is much more probable that these were typical Pharisaic critics of what Jesus was doing and teaching. Such people had to be near him to find out what he was saying; secondhand reports tend to be unreliable!

These people took up the word *blind* that Jesus had just used and asked whether they were blind in this sense (v. 40). They put their question in a form that expects the answer "No." Whoever might be spiritually blind, they were sure it was not such religious people as they. Surely no one in his right mind would suspect them of a religious defect like this?

People have a way of being blind to their own defects even if they are very conscious of those of other people. I like the story of the district council clerk in a certain English town who decided that the municipality was run far too inefficiently. He met waste and bungling every day and was very conscious of the unnecessary expenditure the council was incurring. So he persuaded the councilors to hire some efficiency experts to look into the problem and make recommendations. The experts did their task faithfully. They looked into everything and did a thorough survey. Then they reported that the most expedient saving would be made by firing the district clerk.

These Pharisees were a bit like that district council clerk. They could discern faults in all the people around them but did not realize their own shortcomings. So they ask their question of Jesus out of an attitude of conscious rectitude: "We're not blind, are we?"

Jesus' reply must have been totally unexpected. They would have been ready for him to say, "Of course you are blind!" or even (perhaps) to agree with them that they were not. But he says that their claim to sight puts them in the wrong (v. 41). There is one kind of spiritual blindness that is not blameworthy, the blindness, for example, of a person in a primitive society who has never heard of Jesus and knows nothing of the way of salvation. Such a person is not a sinner in the sense of rebelling against the commandments of God. He will have other sins, but his blindness means that his sins are not sins against the light, since his eyes have not yet been opened.

But people who have been brought up to know that God has revealed himself and that this revelation is recorded in Holy Scriptures are not in the same position. They know what God has revealed. They say, "We see," and therefore, Jesus says, their sin remains. The Pharisees were apt to appeal to the Law, both as a means of justifying what they were doing and as a means of condemning Jesus. But their very appeal to the Law of God took away every possibility of saying, "We know no better." They did know better. They knew the Law of God.

It is, of course, easy to condemn the Pharisees, but in doing so we run the danger of repeating their sin. Light shows us our own shortcomings and gives encouragement to us to seek forgiveness and amendment. To use it instead as a means of congratulating ourselves that we are not as other people is simply to repeat the sin of the Pharisees. Light demands of us a better attitude than that.

46

The Sheep and the Door

"Truly, truly, I tell you he that does not enter the courtyard of the sheep through the door, but comes up some other way, that man is a thief and a robber. But he who enters through the door is the sheep's shepherd. To him the doorkeeper opens; and the sheep hear his voice and he calls his own sheep by name and leads them out. Whenever he puts all his sheep out he goes in front of them and the sheep follow him because they know his voice. They will not follow a stranger but will run away from him, because they do not know the voice of strangers." Jesus spoke this parable to them but they did not understand the things he was saying to them.

So Jesus said to them again, "Truly, truly, I tell you that I am the door of the sheep. All who came before me are thieves and robbers, but the sheep did not listen to them. I am the door; if anyone enters through me he will be saved; he will go in and out and find pasture. The thief comes only in order to steal and kill and destroy. I came so that they may have life and have it abundantly" (John 10:1–10).

Sheep are peculiarly helpless animals. They have little in the way of offensive mechanisms, so they cannot fight with attackers with any hope of success. Their association with humans, bred into them over many generations, means that they are dependent animals. Unlike goats (who can look after themselves much better), they are not good foragers; unless they are brought to the place where the pastures are they are in trouble. They are not good at seeking out water either. Early in my ministry I had an extensive parish in the Australian outback and I recall one sheep station where I used to drive through a paddock measuring ten miles by ten miles. The men on the station told me that when they put a flock of sheep (a "mob" they called it) into such a paddock, for some days they had to come out and drive the animals to the water troughs. There was no shortage of water in the troughs. But, left to themselves, the animals did not know how to find it. (Does not the Shepherd Psalm say "he leads me beside quiet waters" [Ps. 23:2]?). After a while, of course, they learned where the water was. But they had to be taught.

Sheep can be incredibly stupid. I have seen sheep moving along when one thought he saw an obstacle and jumped over it. Those that followed leaped over the same imaginary obstacle at the same place. Again, there may be difficulty in getting sheep through a gate. Apparently they wonder what perils may lurk on the other side. So they will mill round in a mob and refuse to go through. But, after the drover pushes one or two through, the rest follow without any trouble. They can be exasperating.

The helplessness of sheep and their complete subservience to their shepherds has led to sheep imagery being used at many times and in many places. Rulers have often seen themselves in the capacity of "shepherd," and people have often longed for a real "shepherd" so that their needs for leadership and sustenance might be met. We find this often in the Old Testament. The outstanding example, of course, is the great psalm that begins "The Lord is my shepherd, I shall lack nothing" (Ps. 23:1). But there are also passages in which the shepherd imagery is applied to human shepherds, often, alas, to bewail their failures.

Thus "Israel's watchmen" are castigated for a number of reasons, culminating in the words: "They are shepherds who lack understanding; they all turn to their own way, each seeks his own gain. 'Come,' each one cries, 'let me get wine! Let us drink our fill of beer! And tomorrow will be like today, or even far better'" (Isa. 56:10–12). There is a powerful denunciation of Israel's shepherds in Ezekiel 34, where we read: "Woe to the shepherds of Israel who only take care of themselves! Should not shepherds take care of the flock?" (v. 2). The prophet goes on to show how those in places of responsibility in Israel had signally failed to fulfill their vocation as shepherds.

Jesus' words about "the Good Shepherd" are to be understood against this background. All too often those in the position of "shepherd" to the people of God were interested only in their own welfare, not in that of the flock. But God knew what they were doing and God said, "I will save my flock, and they will no longer be plundered. I will judge between one sheep and another. I will place over them one shepherd, my servant David, and he will tend them; he will tend them and be their shepherd" (Ezek. 34:22–23). It is this shepherd of whom Jesus speaks in John 10.

Both Matthew and Luke record a parable about the shepherd who was not content with the ninety-nine sheep in the fold, but went out into the wilderness to search for the one that was lost and bring it back (Matt. 18:12–14; Luke 15:3–7). It is a wonderful picture of God's love and care for his own and marks a significant advance on the Judaism of the day. Among the Jews it was accepted that if a sinner repents, God will receive him, but there is nothing corresponding to this thought of a God who loves so much that he goes out looking for the lost and brings them home.

It is clear, then, that Jesus used the shepherd imagery more than once and to teach different lessons. But perhaps nowhere does he do this as powerfully as in this passage where we read of the Good Shepherd, the one who lays down his life so that the sheep may live.

The Door

Jesus begins this discourse with his solemn "Truly, truly" (v. 1), which emphasizes that what follows is important and is to be taken with full seriousness. He distinguishes between the person who enters a courtyard through the proper door and one who climbs over the fence. The word Jesus uses is *aule,* which properly means a courtyard and is used, for example, of the courtyard at the high priest's house (Matt. 26:3; Mark 14:54, etc.). Here he may mean that sheep were kept in the courtyard of a house (which makes a lot of sense—why waste a courtyard?). Or he may use the word that properly means a courtyard round a house for a structure that was similar but was erected in the wilderness where the sheep grazed and was used to keep them safe at night. There were wild animals in Palestine at that time and sheep could not safely be left in the pastures overnight. So they were herded into enclosures. It is either one of these enclosures or a courtyard round a house of which Jesus is speaking.

He says that you can tell a man's business by the way he gets into such an enclosure. If he does not use the door, but climbs over the fence (or wall), he has no right to be there. The manner of his entrance shows what kind of person he is. Jesus calls him "a thief and a robber." These two words for dishonesty can be distinguished. The word for "thief" is *kleptes* (from which we get our "kleptomaniac"), which properly means a petty thief. It is used, for example, of Judas Iscariot, who took money from the common stock of the little group round Jesus (12:6). The "robber" is *lestes,* which strictly means a brigand; it points to a member of a robber band, a much more interesting character. The word is used of Barabbas (18:40). In this place there is probably no great difference in mind. Jesus simply uses two different words for a dishonest person to make his point that the manner of entrance points to someone who has no business being there.

But the man who "enters through the door" is a different kind of person altogether (v. 2). The fact that he comes through the door shows that he has the right to be there. He is the shepherd, one who stands in a relationship to the sheep such as nobody else does. His open manner of entry shows that he has legitimate business there and that he has no need to be furtive.

This is shown also by the fact that the "doorkeeper" opens to him (v. 3). A small flock in a small sheepfold would not need such an official, but if the courtyard was a large one and if there were several flocks of sheep in it, such a person would perform a useful function. That is apparently what is in mind here, for Jesus goes on to speak of the sheep as hearing the voice of their shepherd.

Perhaps we should notice here a little grammatical point about the way John uses the Greek verb for "to hear." When it is used of hearing a person he uses one construction (the genitive case), and when it is used of a sound (for example, a voice or a cry) he uses another (the accusative). But sometimes John uses the usual construction for a person when he is referring to a voice, and each time he means not only that the voice is heard, but that it is heard with understanding and acceptance. That is what he has here. The sheep not only hear the sound of the shepherd's voice; they understand that it is their shepherd (and not someone else) and they respond to it.

The shepherd "calls his own sheep by name," which is something a modern Australian finds hard to understand. In my country flocks of sheep tend to be large. I recall seeing a few drovers move a flock of over five thousand. I don't know that it was particularly large; I simply mention it as one I have seen. When you are talking about numbers like that it is impossible to think of the sheep as individuals. They simply belong to a huge undifferentiated mass. But a Palestinian shepherd would have a small flock, maybe twenty or thirty, or perhaps a hundred. Nathan spoke of a flock whose number was the irreducible minimum: "one little ewe lamb" (2 Sam. 12:3). In small flocks individual sheep could be recognized and the shepherd could call them "by name."

But the emphasis here is not so much on the individual sheep as on the individual shepherd. Travelers tell of modern-time Palestinian shepherds whose flocks have been brought together (perhaps for shelter overnight). Then in the morning the sheep have been separated when one and then another of the shepherds gives his own call. The sheep recognize the voice and respond to it.

When such a shepherd moves his sheep he does not drive them but leads them (v. 4). Even in modern times this happens. I have seen a flock being moved in Palestine in this way. The shepherd went on ahead, and the sheep followed him. (In this case he prudently had a rear guard; an assistant followed the last of the sheep to make sure they did not stray! I have no idea how common that is.) The reason given here is that "they know his voice." The reassuring voice of their own shepherd keeps them in line.

But an alien voice is different: "They will not follow a stranger" (v. 5). Presumably from time to time a dishonest stranger would try to get sheep to follow him, but, says Jesus, they will not go. On the contrary, they will run away, for they do not know his voice. It is not simply any voice, but the voice of their own shepherd that they follow.

John rounds off this section by saying that Jesus spoke this "parable" (v. 6), but his word is not that used for "parable" in the well-known stories in the synoptic Gospels (*parabole,* a word not found in John). The word here (*paroimia,* not used in the other Gospels) is often used of a short, pithy saying like a proverb. But it is not easy to find a difference between them. The passage here is not quite the same as the parables in the Synoptics, but it is more like them than like a proverb, so I have translated it "parable." However we translate, John is speaking of an illustration Jesus used as he taught the people. "But," John adds, "they did not understand the things he was saying to them."

The Door

I like the story of Dr. Andrews, who was giving a public lecture on his explorations in Mongolia and referred on a number of occasions to the "Gobi desert." An expert in the field rebuked him afterwards for using the redundant expression. "Gobi means 'desert,'" he said. "You should not say 'Gobi desert.'" "Well," replied Dr. Andrews, "you know that and I know that. But few of my audience are fluent in Mongolian. I address them in language they will understand."

The good teacher accepts the limitations of his audience. That is what Jesus does here. The people do not understand. Very well. He puts it another way. Again there is the solemn "Truly, truly." This is important and is to be taken seriously. He makes clear the application to himself: "I am the door of the sheep," he says (v. 7). What he has been saying is not just so much instruction in animal husbandry. He is teaching spiritual truth.

"Door" is used figuratively elsewhere in the New Testament, as when Jesus speaks of entering the narrow door (Luke 13:24), or when we read of the "door of faith" that God opened to the Gentiles (Acts 14:27). But this is the only passage in which Jesus is himself spoken of as "the door." Elsewhere he is said to be like a ladder connecting earth and heaven (1:51) or "the way" (14:6). These are similar thoughts, but Jesus calls himself "the door" only here. The expression "of the sheep" is unusual in such a connection, but it probably means the door by which the sheep enter. There is something exclusive about "the door." Jesus is not suggesting that there are several doors to salvation and that he is but one. He says that he is "the" door. We are not to think of many ways of coming to God. Jesus is saying that he is the one way, the door by which all the sheep enter.

Thieves and Robbers

Jesus goes on to speak of those who preceded him, and he speaks of them all as "thieves and robbers" (v. 8). This presents us with something of a problem. He has already spoken of people who get into the sheepfold other than by the door with the use of just these words (v. 1), and this is probably part of the same imagery. The people who enter the sheepfold by climbing over the wall are up to no good and are seeking their own profit rather than the welfare of the flock. But who are they? Those "who came before" Jesus, if taken strictly, would refer to teachers of Old Testament days and those between the Testaments. But Jesus always speaks respectfully of Old Testament teachers, as when he said that Moses wrote of him (5:46) or that Abraham rejoiced to see his day (8:56).

In any case we should notice that he says that these predecessors "are" thieves and robbers, not "were." We should take "before me" as part of the general picture of the fold and not as indicating strict chronology. The thieves and robbers are surely people of Jesus' own day. They may have been teaching before he started his mission, but it is their error and their motives rather than the precise time of their appearance that are important. Some think of revolutionary leaders like Theudas or Judas the Galilean (Acts 5:36, 37), but there seems no reason why Jesus should be referring to men of violence like these. Others think of the Teacher of Righteousness of the Qumran scrolls, but Jesus does not seem ever to refer specifically to the men of this community, and it is hard to see a reference to one or more of them here. It is much more likely that he is referring to the Jewish teachers in general, those who so consistently opposed him and refused to recognize that he had come from God. Jesus is saying that they are dishonest leaders and are not to be followed.

Abundant Life

Jesus repeats the words "I am the door" (v. 9), this time without the addition "of the sheep." It is Jesus' function that is of central importance and it is this that stands out. Anyone who goes through this door enters salvation. John does not use the verb *to save* very often (six times in all), certainly not nearly as often as the other Gospel writers (Matthew has it fifteen times, Mark fifteen times, and Luke seventeen times with another thirteen in Acts). Nor does he use it in the same way. The others often use the verb for the healings Jesus performed, but John does not use it in that way. For John it denotes much the same as eternal life (the two are linked in 3:16–17). It seems that Jesus is here giving expression to a thought we find often in this Gospel, namely that the way to eternal life is through Jesus. That means a lot to John and he brings it out in all sorts of ways.

The saved person, the one who enters through Jesus, will have real freedom ("he will go in and out"). Other ways of life are restricted in one way or another. Sin is always a limiting factor. But Christ brings us a genuine and complete liberty. With that he links "and find pasture." This is not defined, but it surely refers to spiritual nourishment. Just as a sheep finds all its needs met when it is securely in the fold with a caring shepherd, so the sinner will find all the nourishment his soul needs when he enters life eternal through Jesus.

This is a contrast with the teachers whom Jesus is castigating. "The thief," he says, "comes only in order to steal and kill and destroy" (v. 10). The verb translated "kill" seems to mean either kill for sacrifice, or kill for food, the second meaning developing naturally enough from the first, for in a sacrifice part of the victim was usually eaten by the worshipers. Here we probably have the second meaning, so that the three possibilities are "steal," "kill for food," and "destroy." None is very attractive from the point of view of the sheep, and the combination brings out the thought that the false teachers are interested in getting what they can out of the people they teach and that in the end their pupils must suffer loss.

Jesus, by contrast, is not interested in any personal profit. He came "so that they may have life." Right through this Gospel there is this thought: Jesus came into this world in order that he might make eternal life available for those who trust him. In due course he would die on the cross to put away their sins and to open wide for them the way into life. And this life is wonderful. Jesus speaks of believers having it "abundantly." Put negatively, there is nothing cramped and limiting about the life Christ gives. Believers have an "abundant" life. (How, I wonder, have Christians so often given the impression that the life they live is a negative affair, full of occasions when they must say, "Christians must not do this," "Christians never do that," and lacking in sheer enjoyment?)

The Christian life is an exuberant affair, full of the joy of the Lord and the power of the Holy Spirit. The early-church Fathers often thought that it is life in the world to come that is meant. True, that is an abundant life. But surely those Fathers had missed the wonderful thing Jesus is saying here. Not only does he give believers the best of things in the life to come; he also gives them the best of things here and now. There are difficulties and troubles for the believer. Sure. That, in the modern phrase, is part of the deal. But the wonderful joy that comes from constant fellowship with the Lord far outweighs any such inconveniences. The life Christ gives is the abundant life.

47

The Good Shepherd

"I am the Good Shepherd; the Good Shepherd lays down his life for the sheep. The hired man (and one who is not a shepherd), whose own the sheep are not, sees the wolf coming and leaves the sheep and runs away—and the wolf seizes them and scatters them—because he is a hired man and he does not care about the sheep.

"I am the Good Shepherd and I know my own and my own know me, even as the Father knows me and I know the Father; and I lay down my life for the sheep. And other sheep I have which are not of this fold; I must bring them too and they will hear my voice and there will be one flock, one shepherd.

"For this reason the Father loves me that I lay down my life for the sheep so that I may take it again. Nobody took it away from me, but I lay it down of myself. I have authority to lay it down and I have authority to take it again. This commandment I received from my Father."

There was again a division among the Jews on account of these words. Many of them were saying, "He has a demon and is mad. Why are you listening to him?" Others were saying, "These words are not those of a demoniac; does a demon open the eyes of blind people?" (John 10:11–21).

When Jesus called himself "the Good Shepherd" he used a title that has meant much to Christians through the centuries. It makes a universal appeal. Even people who are strangers to pastoral pursuits and have never seen a sheep (or a shepherd) in their lives find this an attractive title and respond to it. It is a title that emphasizes Jesus' care for his own. We saw in our last study that sheep need a good deal of care; left to themselves they are apt to fare badly. They do not seem well equipped to face life's hardships and need a shepherd to lead them to pasture and to water and to defend them against life's dangers. So when Jesus speaks of himself as the Good Shepherd he is saying that he will provide for all the needs of those who are his sheep. Life often finds us at our wit's end, but if we belong to Jesus we may confidently look to him to lead us in the way in which we should go. He will see that we get all that we need (though not necessarily all that we want!).

There is another implied claim in this statement. As we saw when we were thinking of words like "I am the bread of life" and "I am the door," the "I AM" is the language of deity. It is not the normal way people would say these things, but the way God would say them. So, in claiming to be the Good Shepherd in this way, Jesus is using the language of deity. He is more than just a man, and this is involved in his claim to be the Good Shepherd and to do what the Good Shepherd does.

We may notice an interesting point that arises from the fact that Jesus uses the word *kalos* for "good." Greek has a number of words that may convey the idea of goodness and very often they do not differ greatly. But Abbott-Smith's lexicon informs us that while *agathos* points to "inner excellence" and *dikaios* refers to the person "who merely measures up to a high standard of rectitude," *kalos* "properly refers to goodliness as manifested in form." In other words it refers to what is beautiful as well as what is good (we have taken this over into our language; we speak of beautiful handwriting as "calligraphy" while "callisthenics" combines strength with beauty). E. V. Rieu, a classical Greek scholar, some years ago produced a translation of the Gospels and here has "I am the shepherd, the Shepherd Beautiful," which brings out this aspect of what Jesus was saying. I see no reason for departing from the usual translation, "the Good Shepherd," but we should bear in mind the point made by William Temple that "it is possible to be morally upright repulsively!" There was something attractive about Jesus' goodness, a point we should bear in mind as we seek to serve him.

The Death of the Shepherd

Jesus might have gone on to quite a lot of things that a good shepherd does for his sheep. As we saw in our last study, a shepherd can be a very busy person, for the sheep are so helpless that he must look to all their needs. But, interestingly, Jesus passes over all that and goes straight to one unexpected thing: "the Good Shepherd lays down his life for the sheep."

A shepherd's life had its dangers, and we must not overlook the fact that in biblical Palestine there were wild animals, some of which have since died out. David mentions his fights with a lion and with a bear while he was looking after sheep (1 Sam. 17:34–36; cf. Isa. 31:4) and Amos speaks of the shepherd who rescued two legs or a piece of an ear from a lion's mouth (Amos 3:12). At an earlier time Jacob said, "I did not bring you animals torn by wild beasts; I bore the loss myself . . ." (Gen. 31:39), which brings before us another aspect of the shepherd's life.

It is plain enough that dangers could arise for the shepherd at any time. But the Palestinian shepherd did not reckon on dying; he thought he would survive. The job had its dangers, certainly. But men have never been deterred from jobs simply because there are dangers (as we can see from modern life as well as any other). Men always think that there are ways of dealing with the danger and never expect the dire results to follow for them—it is always other people who get caught! So with the shepherd in antiquity. Allowing for the fact that there would be problems as he looked after the sheep, he thought he could cope; otherwise he would not be a shepherd. He knew that there was the possibility that he would be wounded or even die, but he knew the resources he had and was optimistic. No man willingly dies for animals like sheep.

But the one thing Jesus says he will do for people in his capacity as Shepherd is die for them. That for him was the central thing. He had come to bring salvation, and that meant death on behalf of his sheep.

A Palestinian shepherd might sometimes die in the exercise of his duty as a shepherd, but that was always a mishap, something that occurred as a result of some miscalculation. If he was thinking of the welfare of his sheep, the shepherd thought of what he could do by his life, not of what he could do by his death. Jesus' attitude was quite different. He put his death in the forefront. That is what the Good Shepherd would do.

The Hired Help and the Wolf

Jesus contrasts the attitude of the hired help (v. 12). The man who does not own the sheep and who simply looks after them for pay is different from a true shepherd. As I have said, even a true shepherd will not willingly die for sheep, but he will certainly run into danger for them and put up a fight for them. But the man whose interest is in his pay rather than the sheep in his care will think of his own skin and take no risks.

When he sees the wolf coming he simply runs away. Actually he is wrong in doing that, for according to the Mishnah he is required to defend the sheep against one wolf. But, continues the regulation, "two wolves count as unavoidable accident." A man who was simply a hired shepherd was not expected to cope with more than one wolf; there was a limit to what could be asked of such a person. And Jesus' words show that the hired man might well do less than he was supposed to, rather than more. That one wolf could do considerable damage to the flock. Quite apart from the sheep that he seized and ate, his coming would scatter the remainder, and in due course they would have to be found and brought back.

The hired man runs because of what he is—a man who is interested in his pay (v. 13). Jesus does not mean that there were no paid shepherds who did more than this. Of course there were. But typically the hired man did less than the shepherd who owned the sheep. And Jesus is saying that this arises from the nature of the case: the man whose interest is in pay will always react differently from the man whose interest is in sheep.

One Flock and One Shepherd

Jesus repeats his words, "I am the Good Shepherd," and this time adds "I know my own and my own know me" (v. 14). We saw in our last study that the Palestinian shepherd of Jesus' day commonly knew his sheep very well, and they knew him so well that they would respond to his call and follow him, while they would not respond to the call of other people (v. 5). There is a difference between those who are genuinely the sheep of a given shepherd and those who are not.

Genuineness is important over a wide range of life. I like the notice I read about that is supposed to hang in one of the museums given over to memorabilia of the Wild West. The notice is reputed to say: "We do not have the gun that killed Billy the Kid. Two other museums have it." The museum asserted its own rectitude and its own regard for what is genuine, though it did not find this universal in its competitors.

Genuineness matters when we are talking about the sheep of Jesus' flock. It is not what we say that matters, but what is really the case. Jesus sees through shams and knows exactly who really belong to his flock and who do not. He goes on to liken the mutual knowledge between him and his sheep to that between him and his Father (v. 15). There is no possibility of mistake in that knowledge. The Father and the Son know each other intimately. Jesus is saying that the mutual knowledge of the Good Shepherd and the sheep is something like that. I do not think that he means that the sheep know the Shepherd as well as the Son knows the Father. We are all prone to mistakes, though he is not. It is the reciprocal knowledge that Jesus is stressing. It is not only that Jesus knows us, but that we know him, and it is this that is likened to the fact that the Father and the Son know each other.

It is significant that Jesus goes on to say again, "I lay down my life for the sheep." This is the characteristic thing and he leaves his hearers in no doubt of its importance. The teaching of Jesus is wonderful and his people have been grateful for it through the centuries, but it is not the teaching that is of central importance. It is the atoning death, the death "for" the sheep.

And this has meaning, not only for the few people that had so far followed Jesus. He goes on to speak of "other sheep" not of the "fold" of Judaism (v. 16). In all four Gospels there is mostly a concentration on the people who were with Jesus at the time, as we might expect. But now and then there are glimpses of the wider application of the gospel and we have one here. The death of Jesus would be for people everywhere, not only for those in Palestine who had so far heard his voice and followed him.

Notice that he says "I *must* bring them too." There is the thought of a compelling necessity. He had come on a mission of salvation, which meant dying for sinners. It also meant that those sinners must be informed of what had happend and invited to put their trust in the crucified Savior. In other words, he *must* bring them. That was in the divine plan and in due course it would inevitably come about.

These "other sheep" would be on the same footing as those already in the fold. "They will hear my voice," Jesus says, which means that they will be in the same intimate relationship to the Shepherd as those who were already following him. There were those in the early church who apparently thought that the Jews had a privileged position in the church. When Gentiles were converted such people wanted them circumcised and made full members of Judaism. But Jesus is saying no such thing. For him the important thing was that these sheep would hear his voice.

And when they do "there will be one flock, one shepherd." There is a play on words in the Greek, which we cannot easily reproduce in English: one *poimne,* one *poimen*. The important thing is that the two go together. The unity that links all believers is not due to their coming from any particular nation, to their being the same kind of "religious" people, to their position in society, to natural affinity, or anything of the sort. It is a unity that arises because of their relationship to the one Shepherd who "brings" them all.

Authority to Die and Authority to Rise

Jesus goes back to the thought of his death (which, of course, is what would make them all members of the one flock). He says that the Father loves him for it (v. 17). This does not mean that the Father did not love him until he died for people. The Father always loved the Son. Jesus is saying that this love was connected with the cross. His death for sinners was an expression of the love of the Father as well as that of the Son (cf. 3:16). We should never think of the cross as though it meant that the love of the Son was triumphing over the wrath of the Father. That is not the way of it at all. The love of the Father and the love of the Son were both there, and the Father loved the Son because of his death for sinners.

Sometimes, when people have been married for many years or have been friends for many years (or both!), one will do something that wins the approval of the other and will get the response "I love you for that!" The love was there before the deed. But the deed calls forth the love yet once more.

And on this occasion the deed was the laying down of the life. Throughout this passage this is brought out repeatedly. It is central to the teaching of this Gospel and indeed central to Christianity. John will not let us miss it and he keeps recording words that bring it out. Perhaps in part at least this is because God does not act as we do. It is natural for people to try to avoid hardship and to take the easiest way. We do it constantly.

There was a time in World War II when the American army launched a strong attack and drove back the central part of the enemy line quite a distance. But then the enemy counterattacked and the Americans were in danger of being completely surrounded. In this emergency everyone was pressed into service. Even those whose normal duties were routine office work found themselves called up into defense. One pusher of typewriters found himself instructed to dig foxholes in very hard ground. He was making heavy weather of it, so made a suggestion to his superior officer: "Sir, wouldn't it be better if we attacked and made *them* dig the foxholes?"

That corresponds to something deep down in the heart of most of us. We don't want to do the hard things and like to discover some easy way round. But we must not read our own attitudes into the way our salvation was brought about. The road to Calvary would be hard, but the Good Shepherd would tread it resolutely. So Jesus says that he will lay down his life "for the sheep" and do this "so that I may take it again." "So that" indicates purpose. We are to see the resurrection as in mind long before the death took place on the cross. Jesus is saying that his attitude to life and to death is different from ours. He will go to death, but it will be a voluntary act and he will rise in due course triumphant over death.

He makes this clear by saying, "Nobody took it away from me" (v. 18). It was true that in due course people like Judas, the Jewish high priestly party, and the Romans, especially Pilate, would all play their part. But if Jesus had not allowed them to put him to death, he would not have been killed. He is supreme over life and death. So he repeats that he lays his life down of himself. Many manuscripts read "Nobody takes it away from me," and this may well be the right reading. But it corresponds to what we would expect and looks like a scribal "correction" to make an easier reading. I think that this Gospel text did read "took" and that Jesus is regarding his death as so certain that he can speak of it as already accomplished.

He makes clear his lordship over life and death by saying that he has authority to lay down his life and to take it again. The repetition of "authority" gives the word some emphasis (as is the case when Pilate repeats the same word later in this Gospel, 19:10). Some translations prefer the word *power* but that is not the meaning of Jesus' word. It is true that he has power over death, but it is also true that this is not simply naked power. Being the Son of God, he has the right to die and to rise, and it is of right rather than of power that Jesus is speaking.

He concludes this part of his address by saying that he has received a command from the Father. Once again we have the typical teaching in this Gospel that the Father and the Son are at one in this matter of salvation. There is no division in the Godhead.

Division

But there was "division" among the hearers (v. 19). Some were for Jesus and some against. Those against were saying, "He has a demon and is mad." The accusation that he had a demon was made before (7:20; 8:48, 52); indeed, in this Gospel the only times demon-possession is mentioned is when this accusation is being made or refuted. Apparently these people saw demon-possession and madness as much the same thing, though elsewhere the two seem to be distinguished. Thus Matthew tells of an occasion when people brought to Jesus for healing "demon-possessed and lunatics" (Matt. 4:24; some translations have "epileptics" instead of "lunatics," but Phillips is surely right when he renders "the insane"; *The Living Bible* also has "insane"). The separate mention of the two groups shows that they were different; the demon-possessed and the insane were not the same. But these determined opponents of Jesus are refusing to take him seriously. They are convinced that he is in error and simply throw out accusations: "he has a demon" and "he is mad." They produce no reason for what they are saying and indeed they could not.

But others are more balanced. They have listened to what Jesus said and are clear that words such as Jesus has spoken are not the words of a demoniac (v. 21). And it was not only the things he said. What about his deeds? Can a demoniac open the eyes of the blind? They find both his words and his deeds convincing.

The contrast between the two groups is instructive. We find such division again and again in the history of the human race. Where people are blinded by prejudice they will always find some "reason" for rejecting Jesus: demoniac, madman, anything will do. But where people listen to what he says and where they take notice of what he does there is always a different verdict.

48

"I and the Father Are One"

Then it was the Feast of the Dedication in Jerusalem. It was winter and Jesus was walking in the temple in Solomon's colonnade. The Jews stood around him and asked him, "How long are you going to keep us in suspense? If you are the Christ, tell us plainly." Jesus answered them, "I told you and you do not believe. The works that I am doing in my Father's name, these bear witness about me. But you do not believe because you are not of my sheep. My sheep hear my voice and I know them and they follow me, and I give them life eternal. They will never perish and no one will snatch them out of my hand. What my Father has given me is greater than all and no one can snatch them out of my Father's hand. I and the Father are one" (John 10:22–30).

John moves to the Feast of the Dedication, an eight-day festival that began on 25th Chisleu, which means somewhere in November–December in our calendar (the Jews had a lunar calendar, not a solar year like ours, and thus a given day on the one calendar will not always fall on any one given day in the other). It was an important feast, for it commemorated the last great deliverance the Jews had known.

There was a time when Antiochus Epiphanes, the king of Syria, conquered Palestine. This king set out to make Hellenistic culture a unifying bond, which he thought would unite the diverse peoples in his empire. Among other things this meant imposing the same heathen religion on them all, and the Jews were not allowed to continue their characteristic religious practices. Thus they were forbidden to circumcise their children, to observe the Sabbath, and to do many other things that they valued highly in connection with their religion. They were required to offer sacrifice to heathen gods. There were, of course, some people who conformed to the Syrian edicts, not only because they were told to, but also out of a desire to be up with the latest fashions: Hellenism was the "in" thing. Others did so from fear.

But it was a time of indescribable horror for those who took their religion seriously. There were pious and patriotic people who would not do what Antiochus required of them at any price. This led to the Maccabean rebellion, which started in a very small way but in the end was successful in liberating the Jewish people, giving them rulers of their own and the right to worship according to the teachings of the Bible. There came the great day when the Jewish warriors liberated Jerusalem and the heathen altar that had been set up in the temple was removed. There was a joyous celebration as the temple was restored and rededicated, and this wonderful event was commemorated in an eight-day festival that was held each year. This was the Feast of the Dedication of which John writes. It was a feast that reminded everybody of the way God had delivered the people out of a situation that had seemed hopeless, and this must have been an encouragement to those who looked and longed for the day when they would be delivered from the Romans.

It was not necessary for John to mention the time. But he has a habit of referring to the Jewish feasts, and he mentions more of them and mentions them more often than do any of the other Gospel writers. It seems that he sees Jesus as the fulfillment of all that the feasts symbolized. If that is the reason he mentions this one, it will surely be to make the point that the hopes that people had of freedom, hopes that centered on resistance movements and leaders like Barabbas, would be filled in Jesus and in him alone. He would bring deliverance from sin and thus a liberty far more significant than any that warriors could envisage, let alone accomplish.

Jesus was in Solomon's colonnade (v. 23). This was a structure with a roof supported on pillars. It would have given some protection in the winter weather and would have been open to the sun if it was shining. It was a very old structure, and the people in general thought it had been built by Solomon, though that was not very likely. But evidently it was a pleasant place to be on a winter's day.

Suspense

"The Jews" (John's way of referring to Jewish people, especially those in leading positions, who were hostile to Jesus) surrounded Jesus

(v. 24). Phillips translates "The Jews closed in on Him," which brings out the truth that they had no friendly intent. By surrounding him they apparently thought that they could compel Jesus to give them the answer they were looking for. I have translated the question they put to him as "How long are you going to keep us in suspense?" and it is not easy to find an alternative. But it is not certain that this is what they meant.

The words John records mean "How long do you lift up our soul?" The usual translation takes this to mean that Jesus' teaching was such that his hearers' "soul" was disturbed, raised from its resting place so to speak, and not given a new one. It is this that enables us to translate "keep us in suspense." This may be the correct way of understanding it.

If so, at least they were honest in confessing their ignorance. People are not always like that. There is the story of a wife who asked her husband, "What makes the stock market go up and down?" There was a thoughtful silence, then the reply, "There are several factors like inflationary pressures, fiscal instability and, of course, political pressures and national imbalance." The wife thought about this for a moment, then said, "If you don't know, why don't you just say so?"

Unlike the man in the story, the Jews may have been honestly admitting that they did not know what Jesus' teaching meant. But their words could be understood in other ways. To "lift the soul" might mean that the soul is set adrift, so to speak. The words could mean that the hearers felt that Jesus was upsetting their cherished beliefs without giving them any satisfactory alternative. "Why do you trouble us?" would give credence to this view.

The Christ

We should also bear in mind that the word for "soul" also means "life," and the question might mean "Why are you taking our life away?" This view would be supported by the fact that nobody doubts that Jesus was talking about death when he used the same verb together with a reference to the same noun no farther away than verse 18 (where "it" refers to "life" in v. 17). In that passage Jesus was referring to his life being taken away, and it is quite possible that the Jews have a similar meaning here. A little later Caiaphas was to say that if they left Jesus alone they would be destroyed; the Romans would come and take away their place and their nation (11:48). The Jews may have had a dim perception that Jesus' teaching meant the end of things as they knew them. To accept and act on his teaching, they may have thought, would be to put an end to Judaism as they knew it. It would be to destroy their whole way of life. "Is this what you are trying to do?" they may be asking. They want to be clear on Jesus' program.

Their supplementary request is easier to understand: "If you are the Christ, tell us plainly." But it was not an easy question to answer because there were different ideas of what "the Christ" meant. To follow the thought of the last paragraph for a moment, Jesus has just been envisaging followers from outside the fold of Judaism (v. 16), and he had earlier raised the possibility that his Jewish hearers might die in their sins (8:21, 24). Does this mean that being the Christ means putting no difference between Jew and Gentile when we stand before God? That some Gentiles must be brought into the fold? That some Jews will die in their sins and therefore be excluded? What sort of Messiah is this? Most Jews of the day did not think that the Messiah would treat the Gentiles with favor and judge the Jews in this way. They usually saw the Messiah as a Jewish deliverer of some sort. Many thought he would be a warrior who would raise an army and drive the Romans out of the land. Had not the Maccabean warriors done just that to a very mighty conqueror at the time they were commemorating in the Feast of the Dedication they were even then observing?

The Works Bear Witness

With different ideas of messiahship in circulation, obviously the question the Jews asked was not easy to answer. They asked Jesus to answer "plainly"; clearly they wanted a straight "Yes" or "No." But because the meaning of "Messiah" was understood in so many different ways it was impossible to give the short, clear answer they looked for. Even so, Jesus' reply must have been completely unexpected: "I told you" (v. 25). John has not recorded any plain statement that Jesus has made to the Jews on this subject. He has informed us that Jesus told the woman of Samaria that he was the Messiah (4:26). Again, although that term is not used, we might well think that it was the meaning of what he said to the man born blind (9:35–38). From the beginning, at least some of his followers had recognized that he was the Messiah (1:41). But John has not told us of any occasion when Jesus has used the word of himself when he was talking to the Jews generally.

Jesus may mean that his teaching had been plain enough. After all, there was a group of people around him who followed him as the Messiah. They were in no doubt about it, and the Jews had access to the same teaching as they did. If they had really wanted to know whether or not Jesus was the Messiah, they had before them the kind of teaching that would have told them. The trouble was not that they had not been told enough; the trouble was that they had not given attention enough.

Or Jesus may mean that some of the things he had said to them and to which they had taken exception were plain enough. For example, he had said, "Before Abraham was, I AM" (8:58). On that occasion they had taken up stones to stone him. They had a clear enough answer. On an earlier occasion they had recognized that the way Jesus spoke of God as his Father was in fact a way of "making himself equal to God" (5:18). They had heard enough and understood enough to have an answer to their question if they really and sincerely wanted one.

Jesus draws attention to "the works" that, he says, "I am doing in my Father's name." He had done a series of miracles such that no mere man could have accomplished them. And, as we have seen before, in this Gospel Jesus often calls his miracles "works," a term that applies also to his non-miraculous deeds. The word is wide enough to include his whole manner of life as well as the astonishing miracles he did. He is inviting his questioners to contemplate the kind of person he was and the kind of deeds he did. There was their answer.

"My Sheep"

But they did not believe (v. 26). The word "you" is emphatic: it puts them in strong contrast with other people who did believe. This Gospel has recorded many examples of people who came to believe, and John is constantly using this verb, "believe." Jesus is making it clear that it was lack of faith, not lack of evidence, that led to these questioners being uncertain. They cannot in all honesty complain that there was not enough evidence. There was evidence that convinced other people. Why not them?

Jesus gives an answer to that: "you are not of my sheep." These words link this conversation with the discourse earlier in the chapter. The sheep who belong to a particular shepherd hear his voice and respond to it, but those who belong to another shepherd do not. These Jews are showing quite plainly by their attitude and their questions that they do not belong to the flock of which Jesus was the Good Shepherd, the Messiah. Of course they could not recognize him as their Messiah when they followed all sorts of other shepherds.

"My sheep hear my voice" (v. 27). It is still the case that those who are Christ's hear his voice in all the circumstances of life, while those who are not his do not. For them life is simply a succession of haphazard happenings with no meaning and no pattern. For Christ's sheep there is always the thought of the Good Shepherd, who gave his life for them and who constantly leads them into the places where they should go. His voice gives meaning to all of life.

We might have expected him to go on with "and they know me." That was what happened with flocks of sheep and their shepherds. The sheep hear the voice of their own shepherd; they know that voice and they respond to it. But, instead of saying that the sheep know him, Jesus says that he knows the sheep. He is moving on to the thought of the security of his sheep, and it is more important in this connection that he knows them than that they know him. His knowledge of them is part of his watching over them and providing for their every need.

"They follow me," Jesus goes on. He has referred to this in the realm of the ordinary Palestinian shepherd and his sheep. When that shepherd calls his sheep there are results. The sheep know his call and follow the shepherd when they hear it. This has its equivalent with the people who hear Jesus' call. If they really are his sheep, they will certainly respond and will follow him as the disciples had done.

Security

Jesus moves from the illustration taken from pastoral life to the facts of spiritual life. He says that he gives "life eternal" to those who follow him (v. 28). As we have seen in previous studies, this expression means the kind of life that is appropriate to the age to come, when this world has ceased and Christ has returned to bring in the final state of affairs. That life does not end and thus may be called "everlasting." But its real characteristic is not this but the fact that it is the kind of life people will enjoy in the final shape of things. It is the quality of this life rather than its quantity that is the significant thing.

That said, it seems that in the present passage there is some emphasis on the "everlasting" aspect. Jesus goes on to say that those who receive this life "will never perish." His verb points to the ultimate disaster. The German scholar A. Oepke says that this verb means "definitive destruction, not merely in the sense of the extinction of physical existence, but rather of an eternal plunge into Hades and a hopeless destiny of death in the depiction of which such terms as wrath, anger, affliction and distress are used." We should be clear that perishing is a terrible fate and to be delivered from it is a priceless gift. Oepke also says that this idea is not found in the apocryphal writings, nor in those of the Rabbis. This is distinctive of Christianity. People often think of Christians as being sure that the life after this is one of joy and bliss. So it is for those who are Christ's sheep, but we should be clear that his salvation is from real peril, real disaster, and that Jesus made this clearer than did contemporary teachers.

Jesus further brings out his people's security by saying that "no one will snatch them out of my hand." The verb *to snatch* is often used of violent activity, but no matter how strong the force arrayed against us, Jesus says, it will not be enough to snatch us out of his hand. Christians have always found it an immensely encouraging thought that our eternal security does not depend on our own ability to retain a hold on Christ, but on the fact that he holds us within his strong hand. This is real security.

Our earthly securities are often all too fallible. I like the story I picked up somewhere of a bomber crew during World War II. On a raid over enemy territory they ran into heavy flak and were hit a number of times. There was a problem with steering, and the pilot asked the rear gunner if there had been a hit at the rear of the plane. The gunner replied, "There's a three by five hole in the left horizontal stabilizer and elevator." He added an anxious query, "Will we be able to make it home?" "No sweat," the pilot assured him. Eventually they made it, though as they landed the plane skidded and skewed alarmingly. When they got out and the pilot viewed the damage he exploded: "When you said three by five I thought you meant inches, not feet!" "I thought you might have gotten that impression," said the gunner, "but you were busy with the aircraft and I didn't want to bother you with details."

A good deal of our earthly security is like that: it is far from being as secure as we imagine. Sometimes things turn out all right for us and sometimes they don't. We learn that uncertainty and trouble are part of this life. But the wonderful thing about eternal life is that it is absolutely secure. Jesus holds his people in his own firm grasp, and they can trust his assurance that they will never perish.

The manuscripts differ a little about the text of verse 29. Some have "My Father, who has given them to me, is greater than all" and there are other readings. It seems likely that the true text is as I have translated and that the scribes made small alterations to make the reading more acceptable. It is, of course, true that the Father is greater than all, and in the absolute sense that must be accepted. But it seems that what Jesus is saying here is that, among things and people here on earth, the church ("what my Father has given me") is the greatest. This is not due to the wonderful excellence of church members, because they are but sinners. What makes them so great is what God has done in them. They are sinners, indeed, but forgiven sinners, sinners whom God has transformed and to whom he has given of his Holy Spirit. They are those through whom he does much of his work on earth and those he will keep eternally.

Since these transformed sinners are so much involved in what God is doing in the world, it is not surprising that Jesus says that "no one can snatch them out of my Father's hand." This is similar to the statement about himself in verse 28, but it is not the same. Jesus has said that no one "will" snatch them from his hand. Now he says that no one "can" snatch them from the Father's hand. Here is a reference to the power of the Almighty Father. He is so strong that the sheep need never fear. Nobody has the power to take them from the hand of the Father. The two thoughts, that nobody will snatch them from the Son's hand and nobody can snatch them from the Father's hand, combine to give us the strongest assurance of our security throughout all time and all eternity.

The Unity of the Father and the Son

"I and the Father are one" (v. 30) is a statement whose full meaning is beyond us. We can say that in the Greek "one" is neuter, not masculine: "one thing" and not "one person." Jesus is affirming a deep, basic unity, but he is not saying that the two are identical. Some point out that later in this Gospel we have Jesus' prayer that his followers may be one as he and the Father are one (17:11, 21). They suggest that the unity that binds Christians is a unity of love and it is this that binds the Son to the Father. There is truth here, of course, for there is a bond of love between the two, but it is not easy to think that this is all there is to it. C. K. Barrett remarks, ". . . the oneness of Father and Son is a oneness of love and obedience even while it is a oneness of essence." We need something like this for a full understanding.

It is true that there is a unity of love. It is also true that there is a unity that proceeds from Jesus' constant obedience to the Father. A further aspect of unity consists in the fact that Jesus is the perfect revelation of the Father (1:18), and there is a unity between the Son who reveals the Father and the Father he reveals.

But, as Barrett says, there is also "a oneness of essence." What that means we cannot understand here and now and perhaps shall never understand it. We are created beings and we are talking about the Creator. But we can know that there is such a unity of being between these two as exists nowhere in all creation. And in the context that is a reassuring and encouraging thought, for Jesus has been speaking about what the Father does and specifically about what he does in keeping us safe within the fold. There is no division between these two over the keeping of their people secure.

49

Unbelief—and Faith

The Jews again brought stones in order to stone him. Jesus answered them, "I have shown you many good works from my Father; on account of which of them are you stoning me?" The Jews answered him, "We are not stoning you for a good work but for blasphemy, and because you, being a man, make yourself God." Jesus answered them, "Is it not written in your law, 'I said, "You are gods"'? If he called them gods to whom the word of God came, and the Scripture cannot be broken, do you say of him whom the Father sanctified and sent into the world 'You are blaspheming' because I said 'I am the Son of God'? If I do not do the works of my Father do not believe me. But if I do, even if you do not believe me believe the works so that you may come to know and keep on knowing that the Father is in me and I am in the Father." Therefore they were trying again to arrest him, and he went off out of their hand.

And he went away beyond the Jordan back to the place where John had been baptizing at first and he stayed there. And many came to him and said, "John did no sign, but all things that John said about this man were true." And many believed on him there (John 10:31–42).

Jesus had just made his great assertion, "I and the Father are one" (v. 30). This has brought enlightenment, comfort, and inspiration to Christians through the centuries, but for those Jews it was an incredibly wicked thing to say. They regarded it as blasphemy and were so incensed that they got ready to stone Jesus. In this way they were being as wicked as they claimed Jesus was, because they were preparing to kill a man without giving him the opportunity of defending himself. They were setting aside all due process and taking the law into their own hands. It is a measure of their anger and of their abhorrence of what they saw as blasphemy that they should be ready to engage in a lynching.

There were actually a few offenses for which action of this kind was encouraged. If a man stole a sacred vessel, for example, we read in the Mishnah that "the zealots may fall upon him." There is no indication of a trial. This is the case also when a priest served at the altar in a state of uncleanness. This was seen as a very horrible thing, cutting at the heart of much of the Jewish understanding of the way to approach God. In this case the Mishnah tells us that his brother priests did not bring him to the court. Instead, "The young men among the priests took him outside the Temple Court and split open his brain with clubs." It was a horrible offense and brought a horrible punishment. So the action of the crowd on this occasion cannot be said to lack precedents of a sort. But it was still illegal. On their own understanding of the law they should not have done it.

The Jews had tried to stone Jesus before (8:59), which is the point of John's "again." The word I have translated "brought" really means "carried"; there would have been no stones lying round in Solomon's colonnade, and they would have had to go elsewhere to get them. So they found stones and brought them back. One would not have expected a stoning in such a place, but evidently the Jews were so angry that they did not stop to think about such a thing. It was there that Jesus had committed the offense, they may have reasoned, and it was there that he would suffer the penalty for it. They may even have thrown a few stones, for they say, "We are stoning you," not "We are going to stone you" (v. 33). But clearly the stoning did not get far. Jesus spoke to them and they got caught up in further discussion.

Jesus responded to the attempt by drawing attention to his deeds (v. 32). He reminded them that he had done "many good works" and asked for which they were stoning him. In this Gospel the word "works" is the one Jesus usually used when talking about his miracles, so he may well be drawing their attention to the fact that he had accomplished many great deeds that were quite beyond the power of men. Should they stone someone who had done such unusual deeds? But since the word is broad enough to cover the non-miraculous, Jesus may well be drawing attention to his whole manner of life. He had once asked them, "Which of you convicts me of sin?" (8:46), and no one had responded. Should they stone a man who lived a life they could not fault?

Those good works, Jesus says, were "from my Father." It is consistent with his whole approach throughout this Gospel that he does not ascribe the "good works" (whether miraculous or non-miraculous) to himself. He is not speaking of his own unaided achievement. He is speaking of what the Father was doing through him. He has earlier spoken of his works as the works the Father gave him to do (5:36), and in the upper room he would in due course say "the Father dwelling in me does his works" (14:10). He has just said that he and the Father are one (v. 30), and it follows that the works he is doing are in a very meaningful sense the Father's works. They are not to be understood apart from the Father.

Perhaps we should notice also that the word Jesus uses for "which" is not the normal relative pronoun, but a word that has the notion of quality about it. It is often translated as "what kind of." The kind of works Jesus did, the quality apparent in them, showed to discerning people something of their origin. The works were not the kind of works anyone could do. There was a quality in them that showed their divine origin.

Blasphemy

The Jews deny that they are stoning him for anything good. The reason, they say, is "blasphemy," and they explain this in the words "you, being a man, make yourself God" (v. 33). It is sometimes objected that these words cannot be authentic, because blasphemy as the Jews defined it meant that a person had pronounced the divine name in what he said about God. Jesus had not done this, so whatever he had done, it was not blasphemy. It is not necessary to take this seriously. It is true that blasphemy was narrowly defined in the Mishnah, but this represents a development of Pharisaic thought and it may not have been defined as early as this. In any case the Pharisaic view was not the only one in Judaism and there was a wider view of what constituted blasphemy. Whatever the basis in law, these people were angry. For them what Jesus had said was blasphemous and they were not going to be deterred by legal hairsplitting.

They had discerned accurately enough the thrust of Jesus' teaching. They recognized that what he was saying was not the kind of thing that any mere man, one who was no more than a created being, could legitimately say. That for them was enough. The man was a blasphemer and must suffer the fate of blasphemers.

There is a nice piece of Johannine irony here. "You, being a man, make yourself God," they say. But John knows, as do his informed readers, that the real truth is something like the opposite: he, being God, made himself man! John does not dwell on the thought, but as he has brought it out throughout his Gospel he could trust his readers to see it.

"The Scripture Cannot Be Broken"

Jesus' reply was to direct their attention to a passage of Scripture that he speaks of as "your law" (v. 34). The passage he quotes is from the Psalms, which strictly speaking was not in the law. "The Law" as the Jews understood it was the books from Genesis to Deuteronomy. These books they saw as Scripture par excellence; they excelled all else and to these books they gave special honor. But sometimes they extended the name that strictly meant these five books so as to include all of Scripture and that is what Jesus is doing here.

He speaks of "your" law. This does not mean that he himself repudiates it. On the contrary, he recognized all Scripture as being God's word and he goes on to say that it "cannot be broken" (v. 35). But it was Scripture on which the Jews based their position. When they opposed Jesus they did so because they could not reconcile what he was saying and doing with what they understood Scripture to teach. Consistently Jesus points out that if they really understood what the writings to which they gave so much honor were saying, they would recognize that he has been sent from the Father. Here he is saying something like: "This is not merely what I am saying. It is what the Scripture that you praise so highly is saying."

The passage Jesus quotes is from Psalm 82:6. This psalm is one that deals with the problem of unjust judges. "How long will you defend the unjust and show partiality to the wicked?" asks the psalmist and then goes on to urge them to defend the weak and uphold the rights of the poor (vv. 2–3). The words Jesus quotes use the word *gods* of these people and thus bring out their very great dignity. Judges have a great responsibility and are to be seen as very significant people. "Gods" though they were, the psalm goes on, they would "die like mere men"; they would "fall like every other ruler" (v. 7).

The point Jesus is making is that the word of which the Jews were complaining was used of the judges in the Scriptures they recognized and to which they gave such honor. How, then, could they complain when it was used of "him whom the Father sanctified and sent into the world"? If it was rightly used of the judges of old, how much more did it apply to Jesus?

He speaks of himself as "sanctified," a word used again in this Gospel only in 17:17, 19. In the great prayer in the upper room Jesus prays that the Father will sanctify his disciples and goes on to say that for their sake he sanctifies himself. His sanctification of himself clearly means his setting of himself apart to die for sinners. It is a word with solemn overtones. It suits the context of the Feast of the Dedication (when the people remembered the sanctification of the temple) that Jesus should speak of himself as "sanctified." What the feast symbolized was fully accomplished in Jesus. With this is joined the thought of mission, a concept we have seen again and again and which is very characteristic of this book. John will not let his readers forget that Jesus was sent by the Father.

This passage is sometimes misinterpreted as though Jesus was simply classing himself with men in general. He appeals to the psalm that speaks of men as "gods," so runs the reasoning, and thus justifies his speaking of himself as Son of God. He is "god" in the same sense as others. But this is not taking seriously enough what Jesus actually says. He is arguing from the less to the greater. If the word *god* could be used of people who were no more than judges, how much more could it be used of one with greater dignity, greater importance and significance than any mere judge, one "whom the Father sanctified and sent into the world"? He is not placing himself on a level with men, but setting himself apart from them.

The justification of his appeal to Scripture is "the Scripture cannot be broken." This is important for our understanding of the Bible. Notice that Jesus' argument depends on the exact word used. The psalmist could have used any one of a number of words for "judge" to make his point. After all, there are several ways of bringing out the dignity of important people like judges. Had any one of these ways been used, Jesus could not have used the passage in the way he did. Everything depends on the fact that it was the word *gods* that the psalmist used. But it is with respect to this passage from the Psalms that Jesus says that "the Scripture cannot be broken." It is a strong affirmation of the reliability of the Bible.

The Father's Works

Jesus refers to his having said, "I am the Son of God," although John has not recorded a claim made in just these words. Jesus may mean that this is the thrust of what he has said. After all, he has called himself "the Son" on a number of occasions (e.g., 5:19; 6:40) and once, "the Son of God" (5:25), and he has used language that shows that there was a special relationship between him and the Father (5:19–20). It may be, too, that this is Jesus' way of answering the charge the Jews had made against him (v. 33). The Jews did not understand the relationship existing between him and the heavenly Father. If they had understood this, they would have seen both the truth and the error of what they had said. There was truth, because Jesus was claiming to be divine. But there was also grievous error, because he was not "making" himself God. He did no more than accept the facts as they were. He could not deny his essential nature, but that did not mean that he was "making" himself anything. He was simply accepting the facts that he was who he was and that he had been sent by God on a mission to this earth. That meant that he was not to be put in the same category as his opponents. They were simply refusing to face the facts and because of this were imagining blasphemy when there was no blasphemy.

Jesus accordingly invites his opponents to face the test of "works." His life was an open book; they could see as well as anyone the things that Jesus did so habitually. He invites them not to believe him if the things he did were not "the works" of his Father" (v. 37). It was basic to the Jewish position that people should live lives in accordance with the commandments of God; they should do the service (the works) of God continually. Well, then, let them see what Jesus was doing. His whole life was a life of service, service of God and service of mankind.

The works he did were very important. Jesus goes on to say that even if they did not believe the things he taught, they ought to believe the evidence of "the works" (v. 38; actually he says "believe the works"). They might conceivably find some of Jesus' teaching incredible, not because it was in error but because nothing in their experience had prepared them for teaching that came so directly from God. But the things Jesus did were another matter entirely. When he healed the sick, when he gave sight to the blind or enabled the lame to walk, when he was found constantly doing the service of God, then that was evidence that they could believe and ought to believe. It did not need a degree from the rabbinical schools to enable them to say that the person who did these things was a good man, to say the least. Their refusal to face the test posed to them by the life of Jesus was their condemnation. The works could have been the means of bringing home to them important truths about both Jesus and the Father.

He goes on to speak about knowledge. Most translations have two different verbs for "knowing" (e.g., NIV: "that you may learn and understand"). Actually John uses the same verb both times but in different tenses. On the first occasion he has the aorist, which has a meaning like "come to know," "begin to know" (and which is the basis of NIV's "learn"). The second time the tense is present continuous, with the meaning "keep on knowing." It is not enough to have a brilliant flash of insight and then let the knowledge gained fade away. It is important both to come to know things about Jesus and about the Father and also to keep on knowing these things, to retain them in our memory. If they had really considered what his works taught them, they would have enlightenment and abiding knowledge.

And that knowledge concerned the mutual indwelling of Jesus and the Father. That is a truth that runs through this Gospel and we find it taught over and over. It was of central importance, and Jesus is saying that if his enemies had considered what his life was teaching them, they would find this truth.

But they did not. Their only response was to try to arrest Jesus again (v. 39; at least that was a small improvement on trying to stone him!). The tense of John's verb implies that they kept trying, though he does not tell us in what the persistence consisted. But Jesus escaped. How he did it John does not say. For him that was not important. What mattered was that Jesus was steadily moving on towards his "hour." When that time came he would die to bring salvation to the world (3:16). Until that time came no enemy could destroy him. They could plot and rage as they liked; they could not overthrow the plan of God.

The Witness of John the Baptist

Probably because of the hostility that this incident revealed, Jesus went away to the other side of the Jordan (v. 40). There is an ambiguity here, arising from the fact that there is a Greek word that may mean either "again" or "back." Many translations have "again" here, but it seems more likely that John is telling us that Jesus went back to the place where he had had his early ministry, "the place where John had been baptizing at first." We should not understand this withdrawal as due to fear. Jesus was quite ready to die, and in due course he would die for our salvation. But he would die at the right time in the purposes of God. It would be at his choosing, not that of his enemies. Clearly those enemies were angry and were ready to take extreme action. So Jesus removed himself from the possibility of trouble until the right time had come.

In the first chapter of this Gospel we read of John the Baptist's testimony to Jesus and of how Jesus first met some of his disciples. There must have been some very happy memories for both Jesus and the disciples when they went back to where this had happened.

John the Baptist was well remembered in those parts. He had called for people to repent and be baptized, and it is this for which we often remember him. But in this Gospel the one thing the Baptist did was to bear his witness to Jesus. The Fourth Evangelist says nothing about the things John the Baptist did and not very much about what he said. The one thing he is interested in is the Baptist's testimony to Jesus, and that he makes very clear. Now we find that the people in this area remembered that testimony, too. The Baptist had been so forthright in his witness that his hearers knew well that one greater than he would come. They looked forward to that greater one and now that he was among them they welcomed him. John had left them eager to find out about Jesus.

I am reminded of a story about a ringing telephone. A harried housewife picked it up and shouted, "Sorry, I can't talk now. Our white mouse is loose in the kitchen and I have to catch him before the cat does." She left the receiver dangling, and sundry strange noises filtered through for the next five minutes or so. Then she took up the phone and heard a strange voice say, "Excuse me, lady, I know I have a wrong number. But I just had to find out. Who got the mouse?" The housewife's speech had not been brilliant, but it left the hearer eager to find out what happened. It was a bit like that with John the Baptist. He spoke about Jesus in such a way that his hearers wanted to find out about him. And when Jesus came among them they did.

So they said, "John did no sign, but all things that John said about this man were true" (v. 41). "Sign," of course, is used in the sense "miracle." The Baptist had been a witness, a forerunner. He disclaimed being the bridegroom and said he was simply the friend of the bridegroom (3:29). He did not do spectacular things like the miracles Jesus did.

But he did bear his witness. And now that they met Jesus the people could see that what John had said was quite true. They in turn bear their witness to the truth of what the Baptist had said. The result was that "many believed on him there" (v. 42).

There is an important lesson for all Christian workers here. It is not easy to be the servant of God in days like these. In all our Christian organizations and in all our Christian churches there are great demands on those who serve Christ. The need is tremendous, and the resources always seem too limited for us to accomplish what we would like to do. Whenever a new pastor is appointed, or the secretary or president of an organization, or the leader of a youth group, we expect miracles of that person. Perhaps in a few cases our verdict is that some small miracle has occurred. But that is very rare. And it does not matter. What matters is that we so live and so speak as to bring people to Jesus.

We will probably never be able to do the miracles people expect of us. But at the end of the day it will not matter much whether we can walk on water. It will matter everything, however, that people should be able to say of us, "All things that John [or whatever our name is] said about Jesus were true."

50

"Lazarus Is Dead"

Now there was a man who was sick, Lazarus from Bethany, of the village of Mary and her sister Martha. Now it was Mary who anointed the Lord with perfume and wiped his feet with her hair whose brother Lazarus was sick. The sisters therefore sent to him saying, "Lord, look, the man you love is sick." When Jesus heard this he said, "This sickness is not to death but for the glory of God, so that the Son of God may be glorified through it." Now Jesus loved Martha and her sister and Lazarus. When then he heard that he was sick he stayed in the place where he was for two days. Then after that he says to the disciples, "Let us go to Judea again." The disciples say to him, "Rabbi, just now the Jews were trying to stone you, and are you going there again?" Jesus replied, "Are there not twelve hours in a day? If anyone walks in the day he does not stumble because he sees this world's light. But if anyone walks in the night he stumbles, because the light is not in him." These things he said, and after this he says to them, "Lazarus our friend has fallen asleep, but I am going to wake him up." So the disciples said to him, "Lord, if he has fallen asleep he will be healed." But Jesus had spoken about his death. But they thought that he was speaking about resting in sleep. Therefore Jesus then said to them plainly, "Lazarus is dead, and I am glad for your sake that I was not there, so that you may believe. But let us go to him." So Thomas who was called "Twin" said to his fellow-disciples, "Let us go, too, so that we may die with him" (John 11:1–16).

The story of the raising of Lazarus from the dead is told only in this Gospel, and this leads some people to doubt whether it happened. They point out that according to John it took place quite close to Jerusalem, that it was witnessed by a large crowd of people, some of whom speedily told the authorities in the city what had happened (v. 46), and that this set in motion the series of events that brought about the death of Jesus. It was thus a very significant action and took place in a blaze of publicity. If it had happened, the doubters argue, the writers of the other Gospels must have known about it, and if they knew about it they must have included it. Since it was a stupendous miracle, they say, it is impossible to hold that they would not have thought it worth including in their narratives.

But there is more to be said than that. First, it is not certain that the other writers would have known about it. The traditional view is that it is Peter's story that lies behind the Second Gospel, and it is not certain that Peter was there when Lazarus was raised. He is not mentioned in this Gospel between 6:68 and 13:6, in Matthew between 19:27 and 26:33, or in Luke between 18:28 and 22:8. In Mark the gap is shorter (as we would expect if Peter's reminiscences are the basis), but Peter does not appear between 10:28 and 11:21. As far as I can see, there is nothing against the view that Peter was not with the little band at this time and that he rejoined them just before Passover. If something like this was the case, the story is not in Mark because Peter did not see it, and its absence from Matthew is probably due to the fact that Matthew appears to be following Mark at this stage of his book. Luke is not giving us a complete account of all that happened; anyway, he has his own story of a raising from the dead when he tells of the restoration to life of the son of the widow of Nain. We should also remember that none of the first three Gospels has any of the miracles Jesus did in Jerusalem; they concentrate their stories of miracles in the Galilean mission.

It is also possible that the story did not seem quite as outstanding to first-century people as it does to us. E. M. Sidebottom has said, ". . . it must be remembered that in the world of those days tales of marvels and omens, rivers running blood and stones gushing out water were of everyday occurrence. . . . The 'tremendous miracle' of the raising of a dead man would not be such a sensation to a first-century writer as to necessitate its inclusion by Mark; Luke's widow of Nain and her son are tucked away into a corner." We cannot say that if the other writers knew the story they would have felt compelled to include it, though they would no doubt have regarded it as a splendid miracle.

The Sickness of Lazarus

This story is quite separate from the preceding one, and John begins by introducing the people who are to feature in it. First there is Lazarus.

The name is a shortened form of Eleazar, a name we meet in the Old Testament, notably as the name of one of the sons of Aaron (Exod. 6:23, 25, etc.). It means "God has helped." Lazarus is described as "a man who was sick," though the nature of his sickness is not told us either here or elsewhere. That it was very serious is clear from the fact that Lazarus died from it, but we know nothing of the nature of the ailment. Curiously, John tells us that Lazarus was from the same village as Mary and Martha but does not at first speak of their relationship. That comes in verse 2, where we find that he was their brother.

The little family lived in Bethany, a village within easy walking distance of Jerusalem. We read of Martha and Mary in Luke 10:38ff., which may imply they were living in Galilee. If so, they changed their residence in the meantime. But, as the passage occurs in Luke's long section about Jesus' journey to Jerusalem, they may well have been living at Bethany all the time. Martha was apparently the hostess in the Lukan story, from which it has been deduced that she was the elder sister. If so, it is curious that it is Mary who is mentioned first in this place (v. 2). It would seem that Mary was the better known in the early church, so John speaks of her first. And it is this that will explain the fact that Mary is described with reference to her anointing of Jesus, though John does not give an account of this until the next chapter. Evidently the story was well known in the church and John could allude to it as showing which Mary he had in mind.

The sisters sent a message to Jesus (v. 3). They did not ask him for help; they did not ask him to come to them. In fact they asked for nothing; they simply informed him of the situation. They were certainly aware that Jesus would be in great danger if he were to come into their part of the country. In the preceding chapter John has described an attempt made by the Jerusalem Jews to stone Jesus, and the Lord's withdrawal to Trans-Jordan was clearly undertaken in order to remove the possibility of further attempts of this kind. So the sisters did not ask Jesus to put himself into danger. But Lazarus was his friend. It would not do to let Jesus remain in ignorance of his friend's serious illness. And the words are an implied plea for help. They specify nothing, but the sisters knew that Jesus was a very resourceful person and it was enough to let him know that the family was in need. He would surely do something!

Interestingly, they do not name the sick man nor refer to him as their brother. They speak of "the man you love." The Gospels make it clear that Jesus loved all sorts of people; he certainly did not restrict his love to a narrow circle. He was a loving person, and it would be expected that he would love anyone. But the way the sisters speak shows that he had a special affection for Lazarus. A little later in this Gospel we will read of a person described as "the disciple whom Jesus loved" (13:23; 19:26; etc.). A few have thought that this man was identical with Lazarus, but it seems better to think of two different people, and most agree that the Beloved Disciple was John.

Two Days

The message of the sisters as we have it said nothing about Lazarus being in danger of dying. Perhaps more was included than what is reported; in any case the messengers would have known the situation and would have spoken about it at greater length than their very succinct message. Or Jesus may have deduced the danger without its being explicitly mentioned to him. Whichever way it was, he began by denying that the sickness was "to death" (v. 4). We should not understand this as meaning that Lazarus would not die, for a little later Jesus said plainly that Lazarus was dead (v. 14). John uses here an unusual Greek construction that has a meaning like "with a view to death." Jesus is saying that the ultimate end of Lazarus's sickness would not be death. It would be "the glory of God," and this is further explained as "so that the Son of God may be glorified through it." The glory of the Father and the glory of the Son are one: when one is glorified so is the other.

In an earlier volume in this series we noticed that in John "glory" often has a meaning far from splendor and majesty and is to be seen in lowly service. True glory is seen when someone who is not compelled to do so takes a place of lowliness and does service to others. Especially is this the case with the cross, for there we see the sinless Son of God laying down his perfect life for sinners. Perhaps there is something of this here, too. Obviously the raising of Lazarus meant something glorious in the way we normally use the term. But it also began a chain of events that would lead in time to the cross (see v. 50). So there is something of "humble glory" here, too.

John is going to tell us that Jesus did not move immediately. He forestalls any possible criticism that this shows a lack of affection for the man called his friend by a statement of Jesus' love for the family (v. 5). He says first that Jesus loved Martha. It seems as though Martha was the elder sister, so it would be natural to mention her first, though that was not the case in verse 1. This time Mary is not named but simply characterized by her relationship to Martha. The mention of each of the persons separately is probably to show that Jesus loved each one; it was not only that he had an affection for the family as a whole, but that he loved each of the people in it, each as an individual person.

Having made that clear, John goes on to say that Jesus stayed where he was for two days (v. 6). This is very unexpected. We would have anticipated that Jesus would take immediate action to help his friends. We should perhaps notice that in two previous incidents Jesus was urged to do things that he did not do as and when people asked him to do them, but rather did them in due course. This was the case when his mother spoke to him at the marriage in Cana (ch. 2) and again when his brothers told him to go up to Jerusalem at the Feast of Tabernacles (ch. 7). In all three cases, it seems, Jesus waited for the proper moment. He acted in accordance with the will of God rather than in accordance with the suggestions people might make. He acted in God's good time, not at the time that human wisdom deemed best.

Some have said that the delay was in order to make certain that Lazarus was dead. Jesus was to do a miracle, they suggest, and it would be a greater miracle if he raised a man from death than if he cured a sickness. This kind of reasoning is surely quite wrong. It is impossible to think that Jesus would deliberately allow his friends to go through the trauma of bereavement simply in order to do a greater rather than a smaller miracle. That is not the way the Jesus of the Gospels acts.

This view moreover does not reckon with the fact that when Jesus finally got to Bethany Lazarus had been dead four days (vv. 17, 39). It would have taken the messengers a day to walk from Bethany to the region beyond the Jordan where Jesus was (10:40), there were the two days after this that Jesus remained there, and it would have taken him and his companions yet another day for their journey to Bethany. It is clear that Lazarus must have been dead by the time the messengers reached Jesus, as indeed Jesus said he was (v. 14). There is no question of delaying until Lazarus should die. He was dead when Jesus got the message, and the delay was due to some other cause. Jesus simply waited for the right time.

Walking in the Day or the Night

After the two days Jesus invites the disciples to go with him to Judea (v. 7). John often uses the present tense as he does here; perhaps it gives greater vividness. He does not keep it up, for after another present in verse 8 we have the past tense in verse 9. Such changes are a mark of John's style. Notice that the disciples address Jesus as "Rabbi" (v. 8). He had not been through the rabbinical schools, but the word means "my great one" and was used in the sense of "teacher." And, of course, for the disciples Jesus was just that. They remind Jesus of the danger of going into Judea. It was there that "the Jews," the leading Jews who were strongly opposed to Jesus, had tried to stone him. It seemed to them foolish to run into danger like this.

Jesus reminds them that there are twelve hours in a day (v. 9). It was the Jewish custom (and that of many other people) to divide the hours of daylight into twelve parts, so that an hour was the twelfth of a day (or, of course, of a night, for a similar division was made of the hours of darkness). This meant that an hour of the day was longer in the summer than in the winter. But all the year round there were twelve hours in the day. "Twelve hours" stood for the whole day. This will mean more than one thing. It will mean that there is time enough for everything that needs to be done. There is no need for fuss or for undue haste. During those hours disciples can do all that needs to be done. It is a lesson we may well take to ourselves. In our modern society we are so often concerned about all the things we want to do. "If I only had more time!" we say. What do we mean? We have all the time there is; there is no "more time." Jesus is saying that each day gives all the time that is needed for the duties of that day.

But if there are twelve hours in a day, there are no more than twelve hours. There is time for all that God wants us to do, but there is no time to waste. The thought is not unlike that in 9:4, where Jesus reminded the disciples that it is important to do God's work while we have the opportunity. We must be active about the business God has committed to us. Jesus brings this out with the metaphor of walking. If anyone walks in the daylight he does not stumble over obstacles hidden in the dark. There is a contrast with walking "in the night" (v. 10). The person who walks with no light to guide him is very apt to stumble.

We might have expected Jesus to say that such a person stumbles because he is not in the light, but he says "because the light is not in him." It is true that to walk in darkness is to invite trouble and that it inevitably means stumbling over whatever obstacles there are in the way. But the darkness within a person is more significant than the darkness outside. Anyone who has not opened his heart to the light brought by Jesus, the Light of the World (8:12; 9:5), necessarily walks through life in an impenetrable darkness. And that means many a moral and spiritual stumble. There is no darkness like the darkness in the soul.

Death and Sleep

Now Jesus returns to the subject that must have been in everyone's mind, the problem of the sickness of his friend Lazarus. The Lord's purpose in going to Judea would be to wake Lazarus out of the sleep into which he had fallen (v. 11). Jesus speaks first of Lazarus as having "fallen asleep," which does not mean that he was mistaken about his friend's condition, for a little later he says plainly that Lazarus is dead (v. 14).

But Jesus has transformed death for the believer. For the one whose trust is in Jesus, death is no more than sleep.

This is an important distinctive of New Testament Christianity. For the ancient world, death was a horror, the end of everything. People might have the thought of the existence of the "shades" in Hades, but this was no full-blooded form of life, but a dreary and shadowy affair, the end of all living worth the name. The inscriptions on the tombs of antiquity may be impressive in their use of costly materials, but, rich as they are, they are full of hopelessness. By contrast, the roughly scratched inscriptions in the catacombs where Christians were buried abound in hope, the sure and certain hope of resurrection in Christ. The New Testament does not speak of the followers of Jesus as dying; they simply fall asleep. In contrast, Jesus' death is not called sleep. He underwent the full horror that is death and in doing so transformed death, so that for his followers it is no more than sleep.

The disciples misunderstand the reference to sleep and think that if he is sleeping Lazarus is on the road to recovery (v. 12). So Jesus enlightens them and says plainly, "Lazarus is dead" (v. 14). He immediately adds, "and I am glad for your sake that I was not there" (v. 15). It was better for them that Lazarus should die, and Jesus connects this with their faith. Of course, in some measure they were believers. Had they not left home and friends and jobs to be with him? Had they not committed their all to being his followers? But faith can grow. Faith can enlarge. Faith can go from strength to strength. Jesus is saying that what is to happen will enable them to grow in faith, to believe more fully and more firmly.

Thomas becomes the spokesman for the little band. John tells us that he was called "Twin" (v. 16). Since there were not as many names in a first-century community as with us, it would seem that when twins were born people sometimes had a problem. They had a name ready for one of the two, but what about the other? Well, sometimes they simply called him "Twin." Some translations have "Didymus" here, but this is simply the Greek word for "Twin." Actually "Thomas" is our form of a Hebrew word that also means "Twin." Thomas may have had a real name of his own, but if so it is not recorded. As far as we know, either in Hebrew or in Greek, he was called simply "Twin."

We usually remember Thomas as "the doubter." He was absent when Jesus first appeared to the disciples after the resurrection and refused to believe them when they said that they had seen the Lord. He needed the evidence of his own eyes before he would believe. But we should also bear in mind that Thomas was a courageous man. At this point in the Gospel narrative it is clear that all the disciples believed that if Jesus were to go into Judea he would die. And they were right. He went there and he died. Faced with this, it was Thomas who said, "Let us go, too, so that we may die with him."

Let us remember Thomas as the man who at least on one occasion looked danger in the face and chose death with Jesus rather than life without him.

51

The Resurrection and the Life

When Jesus came then he found that (Lazarus) had already been in the tomb for four days. Now Bethany was near Jerusalem, about fifteen stadia away and many of the Jews had come to Martha and Mary to comfort them over their brother. Martha therefore when she heard that Jesus was coming went to meet him but Mary was sitting in the house. So Martha said to Jesus, "Lord, if you had been here my brother would not have died. But even now I know that whatever you ask God, God will give you." Jesus says to her, "Your brother will rise again." Martha says to him, "I know that he will rise again in the resurrection at the last day." Jesus said to her, "I am the resurrection and the life; he who believes in me will live even if he dies, and everyone who lives and believes in me will never die. Do you believe this?" She says to him, "Yes, Lord. I have believed that you are the Christ, the Son of God, he who comes into the world" (John 11:17–27).

John tells us nothing about the journey or anything that happened on it. He moves from Jesus' invitation to the disciples to go with him to Bethany, and Thomas's pessimism about the outcome, to the arrival. He tells us that when the little band got there Lazarus had been buried for four days. There was a Jewish belief that when anyone died the soul of the dead person lingered in the vicinity of the body for three days. But by the fourth day the soul had left, which meant that there was no longer any possibility that the soul would reenter the body and a recovery take place. Four days of death meant that the person was dead and would stay dead. Every last hope had gone.

John proceeds to locate Bethany for the reader who was not well informed about the geography of Palestine: it was about fifteen stadia away (v. 18). A stadion was 606¾ feet, so that fifteen of them came to a little less than two miles, or about three kilometers. This was a comfortable walking distance. It was not necessary to mention Jerusalem in telling the story of how Lazarus was brought back from the dead; wherever Bethany was, that story remained the same. But basically John is telling us of the way Jesus came to die for our salvation, a critical event that took place at Jerusalem, and the mention of the capital lets the reader see that Jesus was now very close to the city where the climax of the whole narrative would take place.

That Bethany was close to Jerusalem meant also that it was possible for "many of the Jews" to come and comfort the sorrowing sisters (v. 19). Among the Jews of that time the comforting of mourners was a work of piety that was highly regarded. There was a threefold division of the time of mourning: the first three days were days of weeping, the next four were still days of heavy mourning, while lighter mourning lasted for the remainder of thirty days. During the first week, the time of heavy mourning, visitors constantly came to the house to console the family. John is thus telling us that Jews from Jerusalem were following the normal pious practice and consoling the bereaved family. John says that they "had come"; evidently they were not dropping in for a perfunctory visit but were staying for a lengthy time, as befitted serious comforters. The use of the term "the Jews" is interesting, for in this Gospel it usually denotes those who were hostile to Jesus. Even his enemies, it would seem, came to bring comfort to this family that was so dear to him. Their hostility to Jesus did not stop them from doing their pious duty to Martha and Mary.

Martha Meets Jesus

It is perhaps typical of the two sisters that when the news came of Jesus' approach it was Martha who went out to meet him, while Mary stayed quietly where she was. John does not say that Jesus called for Martha, though this is not decisive, for clearly he called Mary (v. 28) though no call is recorded. But it seems likely that when Martha heard of Jesus' approach she simply went out. She was the hostess; the sisters had sent a message to Jesus, so it was natural for Martha to go to welcome this most important guest.

Martha begins with an expression of confidence in Jesus: "Lord, if you had been here my brother would not have died" (v. 21). There is assurance here: Martha knew something of the power of Jesus. There is also regret: when he was so greatly needed he was not there. But there is no word of rebuke. Clearly, from the times given, Lazarus must have died before the message reached Jesus, and Martha is not saying, "You should have come earlier." Probably she is repeating something that she and Mary had said over and over, "If only Jesus were here—"

Martha goes on to express confidence that God would give Jesus whatever he asked (v. 22). This looks as though she had some thought of a raising from the dead, but this is ruled out by her later words when she strongly objected to the opening of the tomb (v. 39). She is probably saying something like "If you had been here my brother would not have died, for I know that God gives you what you ask. Even though he has died, I know that."

Jesus directs Martha's thoughts to the certainty of Lazarus's resurrection (v. 23), but Martha understands this in terms of the general resurrection "at the last day" (v. 24). This leads on to one of the great declarations in this Gospel, as Jesus says, "I am the resurrection and the life" (v. 25). Jesus does not say that he brings about resurrection and gives life: he says that he *is* both resurrection and life, so closely are they linked to his person. "Resurrection" is not a common concept in this Gospel (outside this passage it occurs only in 5:29), but "life" is one of John's great themes. In his opening words he tells us that "life" is in the Word (1:4), and he keeps coming back to the theme. We read once more of Jesus *being* the life, when in the Upper Room he said, "I am the way, and the truth, and the life," adding "no one comes to the Father but through me" (14:6). Life is connected with Jesus in the closest possible fashion. The Father, John says, "has life in himself" and has given to the Son "to have life in himself" (5:26). In these words the life of the Father and of the Son is distinguished from all other life. This means that the divine life is of a different quality from ours. We are alive, but everything would go on in much the same fashion if any one of us were not alive. Not so with God. It is not that he happens to be alive, but that his life is a necessary life and the source of all other life.

That has consequences. Jesus goes on to say that anyone who believes in him "will live even if he dies" and moreover that "everyone who lives and believes" in him "will never die" (v. 26). Faith in Christ brings the believer into vital contact with life and the source of life; it gives the believer life, a life that death cannot touch. "Even if he dies" the death that is the end of all life here on earth, he "will live." If he lives and believes in Jesus, he "will never die." These are ways of saying that death, that physical death that is the end of all earthly life, has no power against the life that Jesus gives. The believer faces physical death along with the rest of the race. But for others death is the end of everything; it is the final tragedy. For the believer it is the gateway into life, that life that is alone worthy of the name. When Jesus goes on to say that "everyone who lives and believes in me will never die," he is saying that the life he brings is superior to death. He is not saying that the believer will never pass through the gateway we call death, but rather that the life he gives continues through that death. Death cannot blot out life, not the life that Jesus gives.

A Woman of Faith

Jesus finishes with "Do you believe this?" (v. 26). His teaching about resurrection and life is not simply an interesting piece of information about matters beyond our ken. It is a challenge to faith. When anyone sees that Jesus is the resurrection and the life, he is challenged to do something about it. He cannot regard this as a curious piece of knowledge to be put away safely in some file of comparative religion. He may take it seriously, in which case he responds to it with a wholehearted faith. He puts his trust in Christ and receives that gift of life that means that he will never die in any meaningful sense. Or he may reject it and withhold faith, in which case he numbers himself among those who do not know life and never will.

It is said that C. H. Spurgeon once visited Trinity College, Cambridge, and that in the library he was shown the bust of Byron. The librarian stood him in a certain place and Spurgeon exclaimed, "What an intellectual countenance! What a grand genius!" The librarian moved him to another spot and when Spurgeon looked at it again he cried, "What a demon! There is a man who could defy the Deity!" The sculptor had evidently managed to bring out two contradictory aspects of Byron's character. There may have been that in Byron (as there is in everyone) that points to what is good and useful, but there was also in Byron (as there is in everyone) that which is evil. Christ challenges people to abandon their trust in that part of them that they see as good (which is always balanced by the evil that is in their hearts) and to look to him for that life that is life indeed. This was a challenge that Martha could not avoid and that we cannot avoid. To all of us the question comes: "Do you believe this?" It is the most important question we ever face.

And Martha was not found wanting when she was confronted with that question. We should bear this in mind when we think of Martha, since she has had a bad press. It is common among Christians always to think of Martha as the lady who was cumbered about with much serving, while her sister sat at Jesus' feet and absorbed his teaching. We remember Jesus' gentle rebuke and his declaration that but one thing is needful and that Mary had chosen the good part (Luke 10:41–42). But, with all her faults, Martha could learn and she did learn. She was a woman of faith, a faith that she affirmed immediately when Jesus posed his question (v. 27). It is worth bearing in mind that no such clear declaration of faith in Jesus had been recorded from anyone hitherto (and, while no one surely would wish to denigrate Mary, no such declaration is ever recorded as coming from her). It is also worth noticing that this declaration is made in much the same terms as those John uses when he is telling us why he wrote this Gospel (20:31). Martha had the kind of faith that John longed to see in all the readers of his book.

Let us look at what Martha said. First there is the affirmative answer: "Yes, Lord" (v. 27). Jesus asked her a question; Martha answered it firmly. Then she went on to expand and explain something of what it meant to her to believe. She said, "I have believed," where her use of the perfect tense indicates a firm and continuing commitment. The perfect is normally used of something that happened in the past in such a way that it continues into the present. Martha's faith is not a novelty. At some unspecified time in the past, she put her trust in Jesus and that is where it remained. Many translations read, "I believe," and this brings out the present reality that is also implied in what Martha said.

Her faith has content, for she says, "I have believed that. . . ." She has more than the vague trust that hopes for the best. For Martha, faith begins with the conviction that Jesus is "the Christ," the Messiah of Jewish expectation. The Old Testament does not use this expression very often, but the thought that in due time God would send a Great One is found in many places. In the first century of our era many Jews were looking with eager longing for the coming of this Messiah, and Martha declares her conviction that he has come and that it is Jesus who is the Messiah.

She further explains that he is "the Son of God." This is an expression that could mean much or little. Thus God said of Solomon, "he will be my son" (2 Sam. 7:14; see also 1 Chron. 17:13; 22:10; 28:6). But, while the term could be used of a mere man in this way, it could also be used of one who stood in a special relationship to God, as when the archangel Gabriel told the Virgin Mary that he who would be born of her would be called holy and "the Son of God" (Luke 1:35). It is in this special sense that Martha affirms her faith. Perhaps we should notice that in some parts of the New Testament the term *son* is applied to those who have entered the heavenly family and can call God "our Father" (e.g., Rom. 8:14). But John never has this use. He will refer to believers as "children of God" (1:12), but he reserves the term *son* for Christ. When he records Martha's confession, then, he does so in terms that imply that Jesus was "Son of God" in a way no one else is.

Martha further speaks of Jesus as "he who comes into the world." This is not a recognized way of referring to the Messiah, but it seems clear that Martha means "the Messiah" when she uses the expression. One thing the Messiah would do would be to come from his previous place outside this world into this world, and accordingly the words are another way of saying that Jesus is very special. He is close to God and he came into this world from his place with the Father. His coming into the world is different from that of the human race in general.

At the Tomb

When she had said this she went off and called Mary her sister secretly saying, "The Teacher is here and he is calling you." When she heard this she rose quickly and went to him. Now Jesus had not yet come into the village, but was still in the place where Martha met him. The Jews who were with her in the house and were consoling her, when they saw that Mary got up quickly and went out, followed her thinking that she was going out to the tomb to wail there. Mary then, when she came to the place where Jesus was and saw him, fell at his feet, saying to him, "Lord, if you had been here my brother would not have died." When Jesus saw her wailing and the Jews who had come with her wailing he was deeply moved in spirit and troubled himself and said, "Where have you put him?" They say to him, "Lord, come and see." Jesus wept. The Jews therefore said, "Look, how he loved him." But some of them said, "Could not this man, who opened the eyes of the blind man, do something so that this man would not die?" (John 11:28–37).

Martha went off and called Mary (v. 28). John does not record any words of Jesus that say that he wanted Mary to come to him, but clearly John is not telling us everything that happened. Martha simply told Mary that Jesus was calling her, and Mary got up quickly and went off (v. 29). John explains that Jesus had not yet come into the village, but was in the place where Martha met him (v. 30). Evidently he had stopped a little way short of the village so that he could have a quiet word with the sisters away from the crowd of consolers. So Mary went off to meet him in this place. But she did not come alone. There were evidently quite a few people in the house trying to bring comfort to the bereaved family. Interestingly, when Martha went out she was apparently able to go by herself. This strong and bustling character was perhaps thought not to be in such need of comfort as was Mary. For whatever reason, the crowd of consolers stayed behind when Martha left the house but went out with Mary when she went to meet Jesus (v. 31). They had no idea that she was going to see the Master but thought she was going to the tomb to wail there, a statement that gives us an insight into the kind of thing that was expected during a first-century Jewish time of mourning. Many translations say that the Jews thought that Mary had gone to "weep," but the verb John uses does not mean a quiet shedding of tears but a noisy expression of grief, a wailing. A standard lexicon gives the meaning of the verb as "*cry, wail, lament,* or any loud expression of pain or sorrow."

Mary's first words to Jesus are the very words that Martha had used (v. 32), strengthening our conviction that these were words that the sisters had used frequently during the days leading up to the death of Lazarus. John does not follow this up. Evidently there were no striking words from Mary as there were from Martha, and the writer goes straight on to Jesus' reaction to what he was seeing. Mary apparently had started to wail and the Jews joined in with her (v. 33). There must have been a dreadful din, with all these people giving utterance to a noisy expression of their sorrow at the death of Lazarus.

Jesus was deeply moved at the sight. John makes use of a very unusual verb to describe his feelings. It is used elsewhere in the New Testament only in verse 38; Matthew 9:30; Mark 1:43 and 14:5. Outside the New Testament it is used of such things as the snorting of horses. It clearly denotes a deep emotion and on occasion means "to be angry," a meaning some people find here. If it is understood in this way, the anger will be directed at death, though some think Jesus was angry with the crowd who so misunderstood both what death is and what the power of Jesus is. But it seems more likely that John wants us to see that Jesus was deeply moved at the attitude of the mourners than that he was angry. The crowd did misunderstand Jesus and his power over death, but it is surely deep sorrow rather than anger that Jesus felt towards them. That this is the right understanding seems clear from the addition that he "troubled himself," another expression for deep perturbation of spirit.

Jesus asked where Lazarus was buried (v. 34), and the people invite him to come and see. John tells us that Jesus wept (v. 35), his verb being not that for loud wailing, which has been used of Mary and the crowd of Jews, but one that points to a quiet shedding of tears. This is further evidence of the depth of feeling Jesus had in the presence of these people, who had so little understanding of what he could do in the face of death.

The people took the tears as evidence of Jesus' love for Lazarus (v. 36). There is no doubt about that love (vv. 3, 5), but Jesus knew that he would raise Lazarus, so we should not think that his tears arose from grief for a loved one. Another idea in the crowd surfaces with the suggestion that surely the healer who had given sight to the blind man (ch. 9) should have been able to prevent his friend from dying. John does not stop to comment on either of these ideas.

Lazarus Brought to Life

Jesus therefore deeply moved within himself again comes to the tomb. Now it was a cave and a stone was lying on it. Jesus says, "Take the stone off." Martha, the sister of the man who had died, says to him, "Lord, already there is a smell for it is the fourth day." Jesus says to her, "Did I not tell you that if you believe you will see the glory of God?" So they took away the stone. Jesus lifted up his eyes and said, "Father, I thank you that you have heard me. And I knew that you always hear me. But I spoke on account of the crowd standing round so that they may believe that you sent me." And when he had said these things he shouted in a loud voice, "Lazarus, here, outside." The dead man came out bound feet and hands with grave clothes and his face was covered with a cloth. Jesus says to them, "Loose him and let him go" (John 11:38–44).

The scene moves to the tomb, and John speaks of Jesus as again beingly deeply moved (v. 38). We are not to think that the Savior approached this climax in a spirit of untroubled calm. He was deeply moved throughout. John adds the information that the burial place was a cave with a stone on it. This may mean that it was an opening in the ground with the stone lying right on top of it, but in view of the fact that Lazarus later came out of it himself, despite the handicap of being bound up in grave clothes, it seems more likely that it was a horizontal cave with the stone against the mouth of it.

Jesus told them to take the stone away, which provoked a reaction from Martha (v. 39). She reminded Jesus that Lazarus had been dead for four days, so that decay must already have set in. To open the tomb would be most unpleasant for everybody. But Jesus reminds Martha of a previous saying of his "that if you believe you will see the glory of God" (v. 40). There is a problem in that this saying is not recorded anywhere. Jesus has spoken about the glory of God (v. 4), but Martha was not there on that occasion. He has spoken about believing and death, but there is no mention of glory (vv. 25–26). We should probably understand that the words were spoken on an occasion that is not recorded. We have already noticed that John is not giving a complete account of everything that was said and done. In any case, what is important is not that we can recognize the words but that Martha could. They were enough to convince her that what Jesus said should be done. So they rolled the stone away.

Jesus prayed. His prayer expresses his confidence that the Father always heard him and adds that he has spoken on account of the crowd (vv. 41–42). They did not know that the Father always heard him, but they were about to receive a demonstration of the truth of this fact. Then Jesus called Lazarus out (v. 43). His language is somewhat unusual: "Lazarus, here, outside," with the meaning "Come here, come out." The result was that Lazarus came out bound as he was in the grave clothes (v. 44). John specifically mentions the bindings on the feet and the hands, which must have meant that Lazarus hobbled out rather than sprang forth. Then Jesus told the people to loose him.

Through the centuries this story has brought comfort to the people of God as they contemplate death. It is not that they expect the miracle to be repeated. It has not been. But it shows that our Lord stands in a relationship to death very different from that of our powerlessness. Knowing that he has power over death and that those who believe in him will never know the full horror of death (vv. 25–26) gives believers confidence and calm in the face of their last enemy. That enemy has been decisively conquered.

52

"One Man Should Die"

Therefore many of the Jews, those who had gone to Mary and had seen what he did, believed in him. But some of them went off to the Pharisees and told them what Jesus had done. The high priests and the Pharisees therefore gathered a Sanhedrin and said, "What are we doing? For this man is doing many signs. If we let him alone like this everyone will believe in him, and the Romans will come and take away both our place and nation." But one of them, Caiaphas, being high priest that year, said to them, "You don't know anything, nor do you work it out that it is expedient for you that one man should die for the people and not that all the nation should perish." This he did not say of himself, but being high priest that year he prophesied that Jesus would die for the nation and not for the nation only, but that he should gather together into one the children of God who were scattered abroad. From that day then they took counsel to kill him.

Therefore Jesus no longer walked among the Jews, but went away from there into the region near the wilderness, to a town called Ephraim, and he stayed there with the disciples (John 11:45–54).

The raising of Lazarus from the dead caused a great stir. It was an exciting happening, so it caught people's interest and many were talking about it. As always, when people realized what Jesus was doing there was division. Some enthusiastically supported him and some just as enthusiastically opposed him. There are some things in life about which it is possible to be neutral and others about which this is not possible. Thus, if our neighbor is painting his house, it is possible to say, "I don't care whether he paints it white or brown; I am neutral on the issue." But if we see a big bully hitting a little chap, we cannot retain a decent and respectable neutrality. There may be little that we can do about it (the bully may be bigger and stronger than we are and have powerful allies as well). But if we do nothing, our actions are then saying (whatever our words may be), "As far as I am concerned he can go his hardest." It is not possible to be neutral about moral issues.

The raising of Lazarus was one of these "no neutrality" issues. To bring a man back from the dead is no common happening, and the way Jesus did it, by calling on the heavenly Father, was clear evidence that this was a divine intervention. Those who saw it had to take sides. They might recognize the divine visitation and rejoice to support Jesus. Or their prejudices might be such that they fail to see that God was at work and simply oppose Jesus all the more.

John proceeds to describe the two reactions and begins with the reaction of faith. He speaks of "many of the Jews" (v. 45), so he is concerned with a large number. As we have seen in our earlier studies, John mostly uses the expression "the Jews" for the enemies of Jesus, especially those in high places, but that is not the way he is using the term here. There may be a hint that these people had once been opposed to Jesus, but if so they had ceased to take up such a position. They were not local people, for they "had gone to Mary," so we should probably think of people from Jerusalem, the place where there was so much opposition to Jesus from those in places of leadership.

Interestingly, John says that they had come "to Mary." Martha had also been bereaved, and it is Martha who is more prominent throughout this story, but it was "to Mary" that these people came. It may be that Mary is the only one mentioned because she was better known among John's readers. Or it may be that she was more emotional and not as resilient as Martha and thus was more in need of help from others. From all that we know of the two sisters, it would seem that Martha was a competent and busy lady, and people like this do not seem to need consoling as much as quieter and more retiring persons. For whatever reason, John tells us that the Jews in question had come to Mary.

But, having come, they saw what Jesus did. There is an interesting division among the manuscripts that is not easy to bring out in English. Some manuscripts have the singular, which means that the people saw the raising of Lazarus, while others have the plural—they saw "the things Jesus did," i.e., they saw lots of things he did. The plural is certainly found in the next verse, and it may well be that some scribes altered an original singular here in order to tidy up the story, as they saw it. While these Jews may well have seen other things that Jesus did, it would seem that at this point John is speaking of this one outstanding happening. Whatever else they had seen, it was what Jesus had done with Lazarus that brought conviction and faith to these people.

So John tells us that they "believed in him," and the construction he uses makes it clear that this was a genuine faith: they really came to trust in Jesus. They came on the basis of the miracle. In this Gospel, while faith that depends on the miracles Jesus did is not the highest kind of faith, it is better than no faith at all, and Jesus accepts it. John is telling us that these people started out to do a good work in consoling the bereaved, found themselves face to face with a stupendous work of God, and came as a result into the blessing of faith. John is writing his Gospel in order that people may come to believe (20:31), so that the reaction of these people is the kind of reaction he is looking for from his readers generally.

Unbelief

But the reaction of faith was not the only reaction to the raising of Lazarus; there was also the reaction of unbelief, though John does not use exactly this expression. But he says that some of the Jews "went off to the Pharisees and told them what Jesus had done" (v. 46). The Pharisees were known to be opposed to Jesus; in all four Gospels they are the people who were most consistently hostile to the Lord. So going off with the story to the Pharisees, of all people, is a clear indication that this group was not impressed by the miracle. They may have been there when Jesus raised Lazarus, though the way John puts it seems to imply that all those Jews who were there believed. It was "some of the Jews" rather than "some of those who had been there" who went off to the Pharisees. Clearly they knew what had happened, yet they did not believe. They simply went off to Jesus' known enemies with the story and with more. "What" is plural here, so clearly they spoke about many things that Jesus had done. We should see that when people do not want to believe they will always find a way of discounting even the strongest evidence. It is so to this day. Most people, at any rate in Western countries, are inclined to think that the church is not doing well, that it is declining in membership and influence, and that this somehow justifies those who do not believe. They cheerfully ignore what is happening in the worldwide church and completely overlook the fact that there are more Christians in the world today than there have ever been. The reaction of unbelief is always to ignore the power of God, even if it is at work before one's very eyes.

Now the Pharisees were a religious party. They spent a lot of time studying Scripture and were known for their public display of piety. They were certainly not backward in letting people know that they were the religious experts and that they put into practice what they learned from the Bible. They were sure that they had the right understanding of Scripture and rejected anyone who saw things differently. That brought them into conflict with Jesus, for he refused to accept their superficial understanding of the sacred text. So the Pharisees were found consistently in opposition to Jesus.

Being a religious rather than a political party, the Pharisees' power to act was limited, so they joined with the "high priests" (v. 47). There was, of course, only one "high priest" and he combined religious and political functions. Through the years it was the high priest who had come to be the nation's leader in the wonderful days of independence in the Maccabean period and also in the less wonderful days of being ruled by the Romans. What political power the Jews still possessed was exercised through the high priest, in conjunction, of course, with the Sanhedrin (i.e., "the Council"). Because the high priest was a political figure, the Romans were very interested in having a man in that position who would be ready to cooperate with them. When a high priest did not suit them they simply deposed him and appointed another. This was not according to Jewish law (the high priest was appointed for life) but there was little the Jews could do about it. They had to accept the political realities, and the reality was that the actual rulers were the Romans. So there was the high priest actually in office (who at this time was Caiaphas), and there were others who had once been high priests but were so no longer. It seems that all were still called "high priest," hence the use of the plural. The term may even have been extended to include others of the high priestly families. But certainly there was quite a group of people known by this name, and it was to this group that the Pharisees went.

It is a little mark of accuracy that all four of our Gospels make it clear that throughout Jesus' public ministry the chief opposition came from the Pharisees, but in the events leading to the crucifixion the leaders were the high priestly party. During his time of teaching and healing, the Pharisees with their interest in religion watched Jesus closely and opposed him strongly, whereas the high priests and their cronies seem to have taken little notice of him. With their political interests they would not have been greatly concerned about new religious teachings until they impinged on those interests. But in the end the Pharisees with their lack of political power faded from the picture, while the high priests, seeing their interests threatened, took the lead. At this point in John's story we see the changeover beginning. The Pharisees combine with the high priests to call a council and we hear little of them after this.

It is not certain whether the gathering was a meeting of the official Sanhedrin or whether what was gathered was "a" sanhedrin, a council (which is what the word *sanhedrin* means). This is the only place in the New Testament where the word occurs in the singular without being prefixed by the definite article; every other instance says "the" Sanhedrin, this says "a" sanhedrin (sometimes the word is found in the plural, meaning "councils," such as in Matt. 10:17; Mark 13:9). That it was an unofficial gathering seems indicated also by the fact that Caiaphas is called simply "one of them" (v. 49); in "the" Sanhedrin he would be the president, not simply one of them. On the whole it seems probable that John is talking about an unofficial gathering called to consider what should be done in the light of the kind of thing Jesus had been doing and now his raising of Lazarus.

So the gathering reviewed the situation. Some translations have them beginning with "What shall we do?" or the like, but this is not correct. At this point they are not asking for a course of action but wondering where all their efforts were getting them. They ask, "What are we doing?" (v. 47), with the implication "We're getting nowhere fast!" It is interesting that they do not contest the reality of the miracles: "For this man is doing many signs," they say. They could recognize that Jesus did not do just one or two, but *many* miracles; yet they did not reflect on what that should teach them. Unbelief can mean a complete failure to reckon with the facts. Though these people recognized that Jesus did a multitude of signs, nevertheless they pressed on with their opposition.

It was not only that they saw the signs taking place; they saw the effects: people were believing in Jesus (like "the Jews" in v. 45). They express the fear that if they do nothing, the Jesus movement will grow and "everyone will believe in him" (v. 48). Clearly the number of those who gave their allegiance to Jesus was growing and had the potential to grow further.

The effect of that, they thought, would be strong action on the part of the Romans. Above all things, the Romans looked for stability in their empire, and did not want the subject peoples to engage in seditious and dangerous movements. Though they let people alone if there was nothing much happening, they could intervene in strength if the peace was disturbed. On this occasion the gathering feared that the Romans would "take away both our place and nation." It seems likely that the "place" means the temple (as it seems to do in Acts 6:13–14; 21:28), though some have held that it means the city of Jerusalem and others the land of Palestine. Each of these could be qualified with the adjective "holy," but the temple seems more likely. In any case, if the Romans intervened none would be safe. The leaders scented a danger to their position and they wanted none of it.

An Unconscious Prophecy

Now John singles out Caiaphas, whom he describes both as "one of them" and as "high priest that year" (v. 49). "One of them" locates him in this group of haters of Jesus and, as we noticed before, perhaps shows that the meeting was not official; if it were, Caiaphas would not be simply one of those gathered together but the president. "High priest that year" is to be understood as "high priest in that fateful year," or "high priest in that year in which God acted so decisively for the salvation of the world." Some have taken this to mean that the high priesthood was held only for one year, so that the author meant that this was Caiaphas's year. Since it is clear that the high priesthood was not an annual office, this is taken to mean that the author of this Gospel did not know much about Palestine. But John's whole Gospel shows that he was well informed about the land and the people and their customs. It is incredible that the man who wrote this Gospel should have been in ignorance of the fact that the office of high priest was for life. But throughout the Gospel there are references to the "hour" of Jesus or his "time," as John makes it clear that everything moves forward steadily to the cross. Here he is saying that Caiaphas had his part to play in the unfolding of the critical events.

The ruling classes, including the high priestly families, were for the most part Sadducees, and the historian Josephus says of this party: "The Sadducees . . . are, even among themselves, rather boorish in their behaviour, and in their intercourse with their peers are as rude as to aliens." There was nothing of the consideration for other people that shines through in a story I heard somewhere about Katharine Hepburn. In one film she was acting with two small boys who were understandably nervous at being on camera with her. But she succeeded in putting them at ease. We see something of how she did it from this example. On one occasion when one of the boys fluffed his lines, the great actress immediately said, "My fault, my fault." The boy asked, "How could it be your fault? I forgot the line." "But I delivered *my* line too fast," said Miss Hepburn. "That made you forget." This kind of understanding and consideration was apparently very scarce among the Sadducees. Since rudeness was the general rule, Caiaphas was in character in beginning with "You don't know anything." He was conscious of his superiority and made that clear.

Caiaphas went on to comment on their inability to work out a solution to their problem. (His verb is one often used of reckoning up accounts. "You can't work it out for yourselves" is the thrust of what he is saying.) Then he cynically gave his solution: ". . . that one man should die for the people and not that all the nation should perish" (v. 50). There is no doubt that Caiaphas meant by this that he was not going to be bothered by questions of justice or morals. He says, "it is expedient," not, "it is right." It did not matter whether or not Jesus was guilty of a crime; the solution to the problem posed by his growing popularity was to have him killed. If he was put out of the way, there would be no problem; the nation would be saved.

John goes on to point to the truth in these words, a truth deeper by far than Caiaphas recognized and one that neither he nor those to whom he spoke could possibly understand. Caiaphas was not a religious man (even though he held the office of high priest) but an unprincipled politician. He was not trying to speak the truth in the sight of God. But he did hold high ecclesiastical office, and God spoke through him. John says that he "prophesied" (v. 51). God used him to enunciate a truth that was greater and more significant than Caiaphas ever dreamed. Jesus would die for the nation, but he would do more than that. He would die for all God's children and gather them "into one" (v. 52). Scattered abroad through the world they might be, but the atoning death of Jesus would form a bond of unity. To this day those who have been saved through Christ's death are one with each other in a way that surpasses all merely human unities. The words of Caiaphas express a most important truth, little though he realized it. All he saw was an excellent though immoral plan, and it carried the day. From that day they plotted Jesus' death (v. 53).

So Jesus went off into the country near the wilderness. The actual site of "Ephraim" (v. 54) is not known for certain, but most incline to identify it with El-Tayibeh. If this is correct it was not so very far from Jerusalem (about fifteen miles). This means that Jesus was in a sufficiently obscure place to be secure from his enemies but also close enough to go up to Jerusalem when he was good and ready. What John makes clear is that Jesus would die for his people, but that he would do this in his own good time, not when his enemies planned. So he withdrew until the right time came.

53

The Anointing at Bethany

Jesus, therefore, six days before the Passover came to Bethany, where Lazarus was whom Jesus had raised from the dead. So they made him a dinner there and Martha was serving, but Lazarus was one of those who reclined with him. Mary then having taken a pound of perfume, very costly pistic nard, anointed Jesus' feet and wiped his feet with her hair; and the house was filled with the fragrance of the perfume. Judas Iscariot, one of his disciples, who was going to betray him, says, "Why was not this perfume sold for more than three hundred denarii and given to poor people?" He said this not because he cared about the poor but because he was a thief and, having the money-box, carried off what was put in it. Jesus said therefore, "Let her alone, that she may keep it for the day of my burying. For the poor you have with you always, but me you do not have always" (John 12:1–8).

Each of our four Gospels has a story about an anointing of Jesus by a woman, and there have been some scholars who hold that all four refer to the same incident. There can be little doubt that Matthew (26:6–13) and Mark (14:3–9) are telling the same story as John, but Luke (7:36–50) surely has a different incident. His story took place earlier in Jesus' ministry, and it was in Galilee not in Bethany and in the house of a Pharisee. Luke tells us that the woman was "a sinner," that her tears rained down on Jesus' feet, that she wiped them with her hair and anointed them. The use of the hair and the anointing of the feet are found in both Luke and John, but there are too many differences for us to take seriously the suggestion that it is the same incident in both Gospels. There is no reason for thinking that Mary would be described as "a sinner," and the time and place are different, as is the conversation that followed the anointing. We should think of two incidents with some things in common.

The "therefore" that links this incident to the preceding narrative is important (v. 1). At the end of the previous chapter John has told his readers that the high priests and the Pharisees had given orders that anyone who knew where Jesus was should declare it so that they could arrest him. At the time Jesus was safely installed in the little town of Ephraim (11:54), and this it would seem was enough of a backwater and sufficiently far from Jerusalem for his whereabouts to remain unknown to his enemies. But Jesus had not come to earth to live the life of a hermit; he had come to die to put away the sins of his people. This did not mean that his enemies could arrest and kill him at any time they chose. He was in the hands of his heavenly Father and would die at the time the Father chose, not at the time his enemies would like to execute him. Until that time he was safe and they could not find him. But now, John is saying, the time for Jesus' sacrificial death was approaching, and therefore he came out of his wilderness retreat and came to Bethany.

As he often does, John gives us a precise note of time: this happened "six days before the Passover." We have seen in our earlier studies that John has a great interest in the Jewish feasts and specifically in the Passover. He has mentioned two earlier Passovers (2:13, 23; 6:4), and this third one, the one at the time of the crucifixion, he speaks of often (11:55; 12:1; 13:1; 18:28, 39; 19:14). John never says why he speaks of the Jewish feasts so much more frequently than any of the other Gospel writers does, but it seems clear that he thinks that Jesus fulfilled perfectly all that the feasts pointed to. The Passover was a time when the Jews looked back to the striking events in which God delivered his people from their bondage in Egypt and brought them out to be free. As they offered their lamb or kid in sacrifice, they remembered the sacrifice made in those earlier days, when the blood of the slain victim was put on the doorposts and the lintel and those under the blood were kept safe. And John is thinking of that Lamb of God whose blood was about to be shed so that sins would be forgiven and those under the blood would be kept safe. The Passover was a little picture of one aspect of Christ's saving work, and its mention throughout the closing chapters of this Gospel brings that out.

John not only gives us the time of this incident but also the place. Jesus came to Bethany, which John has already told us was near

Jerusalem (11:18). This time he says it was the place where Lazarus was and adds a reference to the raising of that man from the dead. Clearly that miracle had made a very big impression and it was enough to say that Lazarus was there. John might have mentioned Mary or Martha, but it was enough for him to refer to Lazarus. It is the miracle that is in mind.

So, when Jesus came to their little village, they put on a dinner for him (v. 2). The word John uses *(deipnon)* can be used of a meal at any time of the day, but in the New Testament it seems always to refer to the main meal of the day, usually held in the evening, so "dinner" is a suitable word for it. Martha, we read, "was serving," which is quite in character with what we find her doing in an earlier incident (Luke 10:40). But there is a difference. In that earlier incident, with apparently quite a small group in the home, Martha was troubled about the serving. On this occasion there would have been Jesus and all his disciples, Mary, Martha, Lazarus, and probably other guests (which seems implied in "they made him a dinner"). It was quite a sizable dinner party but, as Campbell Morgan reminds us, "there is not a word here about being distracted. Martha had learned something on that sad, dark day. . . . Her service had not ceased, but some secret had been learned, which kept her from distraction." John has already let us see something of the faith of Martha (11:27), and it is good to see also that she had learned something of the spirit in which she should serve.

Lazarus, we are told, was one of those who reclined with Jesus. People did not sit at table for a meal in those days. It seems that their table was normally somewhat lower than ours and people reclined on couches. Normally they leaned on their left elbow with the head toward the table, the feet away from it, and the right hand free to use in picking up food. That Lazarus is mentioned in this way seems to mean that the meal was not in his own home. If it had been, he would have been the host, and his presence among the guests would not be the sort of thing to be commented on. He appears to be a guest, as was Jesus.

The Anointing

Now Mary comes on the scene (v. 3). She had "a pound of perfume," which was a fairly considerable amount. The word John uses (*litra* = the Roman *libra*) indicates a weight of about 12 ounces or nearly 330 grams. The word *ointment* has traditionally been used for what she brought. But this is not ideal; as we use the term, it applies to a substance that is smeared rather than poured. "Perfume" is not an ideal translation either, for we use it of a substance that is sprinkled or dabbed on rather than poured. The word refers to a perfumed oil, and such fragrances were much used in first-century Palestine. "Perfume" is at any rate part of the meaning, and if we realize that it was not as concentrated as the perfumes with which we are familiar it will probably do.

If we ask, "Precisely what was it that Mary used?" we will find difficulty in coming up with the answer. The noun is no great problem. It refers to a plant called nard, and from that it came to be used of the perfumed oil derived from that plant. It is the adjective *pistike* (which I have simply transliterated) that is difficult. Since the Greek word is not unlike that for "faith" some scholars think we should understand it to mean "faithful," "trustworthy," which might give the meaning "pure" (which a good number of modern translations adopt). It would seem that nard was all too often mixed with some inferior oil, which made it go farther and increased the merchant's profit. If "pure" is the meaning it will point to nard that had not been diluted in any way. Another view is that the word derives from the pistachio tree. Or it may be a place name (as Augustine, one of the very early commentators, thought). It may even be a trade name whose significance is now lost. With the evidence available to us we cannot be certain, but it seems to me that there is most to be said for the last suggestion. In any case, John tells us that this unguent was "very costly"; clearly it was not the kind of thing that everybody had somewhere about the house and that would be used on any occasion of rejoicing. This was very special, an oil that had cost a great deal and would be used only on some great occasion.

What was striking and unusual about Mary's action was that she anointed Jesus' feet. It was the head that was normally anointed (cf. Jesus' words to Simon the Pharisee, "you did not anoint my head with oil" [Luke 7:46]). To pour any unguent on the feet was extraordinary, even more so with an expensive one. We should probably understand the action as an expression of deep devotion and complete humility. Since people did not wear socks or stockings in ancient Palestine, their feet inevitably got dirty as they walked about the dusty paths with open sandals. It was a normal courtesy to provide water for the feet to be washed when guests came into one's house (and a breach of hospitality when water was not provided [Luke 7:44]). But actually attending to the feet was considered a menial task, fit for a slave. When John the Baptist said that he was not worthy to loose the sandal of the Messiah, he was taking the lowliest possible place (1:27). And a little later in this Gospel we will read of Jesus' washing the feet of the disciples (ch. 13). This is more than a lesson in humility, but it is certainly that, too. The disciples evidently saw the task as too degrading and thus did not undertake it. They were rebuked by Jesus' action.

Mary, then, was expressing something of the greatness she saw in Jesus and of the smallness of her own station by pouring the oil on his feet. This was carried on by her use of her hair to wipe it off. That she wiped it off at all is curious. Why put it on if she was going to wipe it off? In the incident in Luke 7 the sinner wiped the tears off Jesus' feet before pouring on the oil, and that is understandable. We are left to guess at the reason for what Mary did. But there is no question that the use of the hair was completely unexpected. A respectable Jewish lady never unbound her hair in public. We see something of the disgrace involved in that when a woman was accused of adultery the priest was required to loosen her hair (Num. 5:18). I like the story that is related of a certain pious Jewish woman who had seven sons, all of whom were high priest in due course. She was asked how she obtained this singular honor and replied, "The rafters of my house never saw the hairs of my head." Even indoors she kept her head covered.

But Mary was not concerned with what people might think. She was caught up in her love and devotion to her Lord and acted completely spontaneously. It may have been a scandalous thing to attend to Jesus' feet, but she did so. John speaks of the feet twice: Mary poured the unguent on his feet and wiped the feet with her hair. It was not necessary to repeat the noun, and the fact that John does so may mean that he is putting some emphasis on the truth that it was the *feet* of Jesus she was tending. She was certainly taking a lowly place.

John goes on to say that the fragrance of the perfume filled the house. This is a small detail that is not necessary for the telling of the story. It reads like something that was lodged in the memory of someone who was there, the kind of small detail that an eyewitness will recall in narrating an event. It is possible that it is more. One of the sayings of the rabbis was "(The scent of) good oil is diffused from the bed-chamber to the dining-hall while a good name is diffused from one end of the world to the other." If John is making a similar transition from fragrance to a spreading throughout the world, he may be saying in his own way what Jesus said in these words: "Wherever the gospel is preached throughout the world, what she has done will also be told, in memory of her" (Mark 14:9). Hoskyns comments, "The action of Mary is of universal significance, and its odour permeates the Church and reaches the extremities of the world" (he cites a number of the early Fathers for this thought).

Give It to the Poor

But not everyone there saw Mary's action as a beautiful gesture. Judas was there and he did not. John describes this man in two ways: he was one of Jesus' disciples, and he was going to betray his Lord in due course (v. 4). It is interesting that none of the writers of our Gospels ever utters harsh words of criticism of Judas; they content themselves with the facts. A verse or two later John tells us that Judas was a thief, but this is also a recording of fact. John never says "that villain, Judas" or "that evil man" or the like. The worst he does is to link the facts that Judas was a disciple and that he was the betrayer. It was a terrible thing that one who was so close to Jesus should in the end betray him to his enemies.

Judas then asked why the perfume had not been sold and the proceeds given to the poor. That it was very costly has already been said (v. 3) and that it would have fetched three hundred denarii shows this. It is very difficult to translate biblical currency into its modern equivalent, but a denarius was the wage paid to a laborer for a day's work (as we see from Matt. 20:2). Remembering that no work was done on the Sabbath, three hundred denarii amounts to about a year's wages, so it was a significant amount. Judas pays no attention to the fact that the perfume did not belong to the little band. They had no authority to discuss what should be done with it. His speaking up under these circumstances shows something of his disappointment.

John now acquaints us with two important facts. One is that Judas was the treasurer of the little band, for he had the "money-box"; the other is that he was dishonest (v. 6). A small point is that the word for "money-box" is often translated as "money-bag," but this is probably in error. The word means "a little box" and was used initially for the box in which a musician carried the mouthpiece of a flute. It came to be used for any small box, but both here and in 13:29 (the only places where it is used in the New Testament) it is used of a money-box.

More important is the fact that Judas was a thief. Some hold that this is an invention of John's to discredit Judas, and they point to the fact that there is nothing else in all the four Gospels to Judas's discredit before the betrayal. This is so, but it means no more than that Judas was able to cover his thefts very well; nobody suspected him. John's statement may be held to be supported by the fact that in Matthew and in Mark it was after this incident that Judas went off to the high priests and agreed to hand Jesus over to them. Matthew tells us that his approach was with the words "What are you willing to give me if I hand him over to you?" (Matt. 26:15). Plainly he is just as clear as John that disappointed avarice weighed heavily with Judas.

"Let Her Alone"

It was Jesus who answered, and he began with "Let her alone" (v. 7); there was no reason for Judas or anyone else to question what Mary had done. The unguent had been hers, and it was her right to do what she wanted to with it. Let the critics mind their own business.

Interestingly, Jesus goes on to connect what Mary has done with his burial. Anointing was connected with festivity and social life, not with burial customs, so the words are unexpected. Perhaps they show us how much the thought of his death was in Jesus' mind at this time. He was approaching the climax of his work on earth and that meant dying for his people. So he interpreted this beautiful action in terms of his death.

It is not easy to see the exact force of Mary's keeping the unguent for the day of Jesus' burying, for Mary had just done the opposite of keeping it. She had poured it out. Some scholars think that she did not pour it all out; they assume that she retained some and that Jesus is saying that this remainder would be used for his burying. But it is not easy to see this in the words John uses. We have no reason for thinking that only part of the unguent had been poured out. The understanding we get from the narrative is that Mary had wholeheartedly given it all for Jesus.

A better interpretation of the words is to see them as pointing to the truth that Mary had a clearer understanding of what was going on than did the others. All the evidence we have is that this lady, who had "chosen the good part" (Luke 10:42), was a deeply spiritual person, one who was not likely to be misled by outward circumstances. It would seem that, while she did not realize all that was about to take place, she did realize that Jesus' work on earth was coming to its climax and that his death was not far away. Her action then was a kind of celebration of the life Jesus had lived and the death he would die. At the very least it was a costly gesture that proceeded from a deep faith in Jesus. Perhaps also, writing at a later time, John has recorded these words because they show that Mary's action, rightly understood, was a celebration of the death of Jesus. That could not be seen by all the participants at the time, but it was plain enough to John when he wrote his Gospel.

Jesus goes on to point out that the poor are always with us, contrasting that truth with the fact that his stay on earth was limited in time (v. 8). The sentence structure puts "the poor" and also "me" in emphatic positions. Jesus is, of course, not saying that his followers can constantly put off doing good to the poor. On the contrary, his teaching makes it clear that the poor are important and that his followers must always have a deep concern for them. But these words also make it clear that concern for the poor is not to override all other considerations at all times. His time on earth was limited, and those who wanted to do the kind of service that Mary had just done had to take the opportunity while it was there.

54

The Triumphal Entry

The great crowd of the Jews knew therefore that he was there and they came not on account of Jesus only but so that they might also see Lazarus whom he raised from the dead. Now the high priests took counsel that they should kill Lazarus too because many of the Jews were going away because of him and were believing in Jesus.

The next day the great crowd, which had come to the feast when they heard that Jesus was coming into Jerusalem, took palm branches and went out to meet him, and they cried out "Hosanna; blessed is he who comes in the name of the Lord, even the king of Israel." Now Jesus, having found a little ass, sat on it as it is written, "Don't be afraid, daughter of Zion; look, your king is coming, sitting on an ass's colt."

These things then his disciples did not know at first, but when Jesus had been glorified then they remembered that these things had been written about him and they had done these things to him. Therefore the crowd that was with him when he called Lazarus from the tomb and raised him from the dead bore witness. For this reason too the crowd met him because they had heard that he had done this sign. The Pharisees therefore said to themselves, "You see that you are nothing profited; look, the world has gone off after him" (John 12:9–19).

John has told the story of Mary's anointing of Jesus, but he does not forget that just before that he had spoken of Jesus' raising of

Lazarus from the dead. Not unnaturally that stupendous miracle had created a profound impression, and John talks about "the great crowd of the Jews" as knowing about it (v. 9). As we have noticed in previous studies, he normally uses the expression "the Jews" for the enemies of Jesus and particularly those in Jerusalem, so we should understand him to mean here that a great number of the people of Jerusalem heard about this miracle. That would be very natural, as Bethany was quite close to the capital city (in 11:18 we learned that it was about three kilometers from Jerusalem, less than two miles). And that would be why they "came". Bethany was within comfortable walking distance for people who walked as much as they generally did in those days (though many twentieth-century city-dwellers might not be so comfortable at such a walk!).

They came "on account of Jesus." It had been known that the authorities were not pleased with Jesus and that he had been out of circulation (in the region on the other side of the River Jordan [10:40]). But now he had left those remote places and had come to Bethany. The crowd was interested. Many wanted to see and hear him, so they went off to the little village.

But they came also because of Lazarus. They had heard that the tremendous miracle of the raising of a man from the dead had taken place, and they wanted to see Lazarus, too. After all, it is not every day that we have the chance of seeing someone who has died and then been brought back from the grave! It was an opportunity not to be missed. Clearly the raising of Lazarus had made a deep impression on many people, and there was the possibility that no small number would be moved to become followers of the mighty prophet who had done this wonderful miracle.

That did not suit the governing authorities. We have already seen that their reaction to the raising of Lazarus was not an open-minded one. They recognized the reality of the miracle and, indeed, of the many miracles that Jesus did (11:47), but instead of that leading them to faith it only spurred them on to more vigorous opposition. It led them to a determination to kill Jesus when they had a suitable opportunity (11:53). The rising interest among the Jerusalemites in Jesus and in Lazarus spurred on the authorities to take the sort of action that they thought would surely end all this. They would kill Lazarus (v. 10)!

In a way it was an astonishing decision. Lazarus had died once and now there he was, alive again. If Jesus had raised him once he could surely do it again, and there seems no point in trying to end the problem by putting Lazarus back where he had been before. But we should not overlook the importance of "too." They had already decided to kill Jesus, and now they wanted to add another to their murders. If they killed

Jesus he would not be raising anybody from the dead, and if they killed Lazarus as well there would be no living evidence of Jesus' power over death, at any rate near Jerusalem. (There would also be the son of the widow of Nain and the daughter of Jairus [Luke 7:11–17; 8:40–56], but these were a long way away and perhaps such raisings among humble rustic folk were not even known among the superior citizens of the capital.) So they plotted a second evil deed to put alongside their determination to kill Jesus.

It is worth stopping for a moment to reflect that evil has a way of growing. When anyone plans an evil course it usually happens that this course cannot be successful without picking up more evil along the way. One lie leads to another to cover up the first. Violence leads to more violence, sometimes by way of reprisal, sometimes as the inevitable second step after the first violent act. Dishonesty leads to more dishonesty, as when a theft is followed by the disposal of the proceeds of the robbery. It is one of the problems of our troubled modern world that this truth is so little realized. People are so set on getting their own way that they do not shrink from employing evil means to accomplish their purposes. Then they are surprised to find that their evil deeds are simply the stepping-stones to more evil deeds, and in the end the situation is worse than when they started. There is ample room for the followers of Jesus to take a firm stand on the importance of doing what is right.

The high priests and their allies were troubled because "many" of the Jews were being affected (v. 11). We have no way of knowing just how large the number was, but we can well imagine that it must have been considerable. John tells us that they were "going away," which in this context will mean not simply going off to Bethany, but going away from their allegiance. While the verb John uses has a wide meaning (as does the English "go away"), he has already used it of those casual disciples who were deterred by Jesus' "hard sayings" in the synagogue sermon at Capernaum. They left Jesus, which led him to put a question to the Twelve: "You won't go away, too, will you?" (6:67). The Twelve, of course, did not "go away," but it is the same verb John uses here of these Jews who were going away from their previous allegiance to the priests and the other authorities in Jerusalem.

But their action was not simply the negative one of leaving the Jerusalem leaders. They "were believing in Jesus." This is John's way of indicating the essence of being Christian. He wrote his whole Gospel in order that people might come to believe (20:31), and it was this that these people were doing. John is describing happenings in those last days before the enemies of his Lord would succeed in putting him to death, and he is making it clear that the evil they were planning was not the only thing that was happening. Even then, in the shadow of the betrayal and the killing of Jesus, people were believing in him. The purposes of God are not overthrown by men.

Palm Branches and Hosannas

Having described the attitude and the plans of the enemies of Jesus, John now takes up the narrative again and tells us what happened on the day after the anointing (v. 12). He speaks of "the great crowd," but this is not the same crowd spoken of in the earlier verses. That crowd was made up of Jerusalemites who went out to Bethany; this one was mostly pilgrims come up for the feast. There is no reason for denying that some people may have been included in both crowds, but essentially this crowd is the group of pilgrims who had come to Jerusalem to celebrate the Passover. There must have been included in its number many Galileans who had seen and heard Jesus during the years of his ministry in their region and who had some enthusiasm for his cause. It is often said that crowds are fickle; the same people who welcomed Jesus on Palm Sunday with their Hosannas were ready to cry "Crucify him" on Good Friday. There may well have been some who were in both groups, but it makes more sense to see the Palm Sunday crowd as mostly pilgrims from places like Galilee and the Good Friday crowd as basically the Jerusalem mob.

The crowd of pilgrims could have been very large. Josephus, the first-century Jewish historian, says that 2,700,000 people came up to Jerusalem for the Passover. Most authorities agree that this figure is too large; Jerusalem was not big enough to take in so many, and Josephus was prone to exaggeration on occasion. One modern authority has worked out that there would most likely have been about 150,000 pilgrims. Whether either of these estimates is correct, or whether we should think of some other figure, it is clear that there were large numbers of people in Jerusalem at this time. There is no way of knowing how many went out to meet Jesus but clearly it was a large number.

The people took "palm branches" (v. 13), on which John puts some emphasis, for he actually says something like "palm branches of palm trees." This is a detail we know from this Gospel only; the others speak of the general enthusiasm and of people spreading garments on the road. They even speak of branches from the trees but do not say which sort of trees. John's insistence that they used palms raises the question of where they got them. Since Jerusalem stood on a hill, it is thought that palms would not grow there (Jericho was called "the city of palms," which seems to mean that palms did not grow everywhere). It has been suggested, however, that it was quite warm in some of the valleys near Jerusalem and that palms could be obtained there. And, of course, it is possible that the palm branches were brought in from elsewhere. Wherever they came from, palm branches were certainly used in Jerusalem on occasions of celebration, for example at the Feast of Tabernacles. They were also used at times of national rejoicing, as we find from references in the books of Maccabees. By bringing out this point, John is making it clear that the people who greeted Jesus regarded this as a great occasion. It seems that they were greeting him as the Messiah.

They also cried "Hosanna," which unfortunately is of uncertain meaning. It is a transliteration of a Hebrew expression that means "Save now"; it is used in Psalm 118:25, where the New International Version reads "O Lord, save us. . . ." It came to be used in Jewish worship, for which, of course, it is obviously suitable. But the Greek expression found here is not attested before the Gospels, and it was apparently the Christians who made use of it (it is not found, for example, in the Greek translation of the Old Testament). The puzzle for us is why an expression that in form is a petition for deliverance should be used at a time when we look for an acclamation. It is possibly a prayer addressed to Jesus as the Messiah. That would account for the petition but scarcely fits the addition "in the highest," which we find in Matthew and in Mark. Or it may be a petition to God to save his Messiah (like the royalist "God save the king").

Perhaps the best suggestion is one ascribed to Augustine, namely that it no longer had a precise meaning but was a general expression indicating "rather a state of mind than having any positive significance." In modern times we might draw attention to the fact that when someone calls for "three cheers" we shout "Hooray" with the best of them, though most of us would be hard put to say precisely what this word means. Indeed, the *Shorter Oxford English Dictionary* can do no better than tell us that it is a "later substitute for HUZZA" (which it sees as apparently a mere exclamation), though it does give us the information that "The form *hurrah* is literary and dignified; the popular form is *hooray.*" Perhaps it was something like that with "Hosanna" in first-century Palestine. It indicated enthusiasm and joy without being specific. The crowd was showing its regard for Jesus with an enthusiastic shout.

"Blessed is he who comes in the name of the Lord" is a quotation from Psalm 118:26 (though the Hebrew of that passage seems to mean "Blessed in the name of the Lord is he that comes"). "He who comes" or "he who is to come" was apparently a messianic title. It occurs a number of times in the Gospels (e.g., Matt. 11:3; Mark 11:9; Luke 7:19–20; John 11:27) but very rarely in the other New Testament writings. It seems that we should understand it as a title of the Messiah that was not used very widely and was speedily dropped by the Christians. But the crowd understood it and used it to express their appreciation of who Jesus was and what he had done.

They added "even the king of Israel," which puts the messianic meaning beyond doubt. These words do not occur in the words of Psalm 118 but are the crowd's own addition. In his first chapter John has told us that Nathanael used the same expression when he first met Jesus (1:49), and now we have it again. Though he lived in poverty and rejection, Jesus really was the king; John brings this out with some emphasis, especially in his narrative of the trial and crucifixion of Jesus. Here we simply notice that the crowd saw this aspect of Jesus' messiahship and cried out the words as they greeted him.

A King on an Ass

There is a difference between this narrative and the way the other writers of Gospels tell of the ass. The others speak of Jesus as having sent two of his disciples to get the ass, and the animal is thus in the narrative from the begnning (e.g., Mark 11:1–3). John puts his emphasis on the palms and the Hosannas, though he is making the same point in his own way, namely that Jesus came into Jerusalem as a king. Now he turns to the ass (v. 14). He does not tell us in detail, as the others do, how the ass became available; in fact he says no more than "having found" it. (This, of course, is not in contradiction to the account in the other Gospels; John simply says nothing about the animal until Jesus secured it.) John's word is a diminutive and I have translated it "little ass," though we should bear in mind that sometimes the diminutive form was used without any real emphasis on small size. The word does not tell us conclusively how big the donkey was, but the probability is that it was small.

The significance of the ass is brought out by a quotation from Zechariah 9:9, which speaks of the king as coming to the "daughter of Zion" (which is a way of referring to all the people of Jerusalem) riding on an ass. We should not miss the point that the comfort represented by "daughter of Zion" is not indiscriminate, but refers to a definite group. I am reminded of an old lady who lost some jewelry. The gems, however, were insured, so she happily collected what was due. Some time later her insurance company was intrigued to get a letter in which she informed them that she had found the lost jewelry on which they had paid. "I did not think it was fair to keep both," the lady went on, "so I have sent the money to the Red Cross." Doubtless she speedily discovered that the insurance people did not fancy being beneficiaries of the Red Cross.

The king of whom the prophet wrote was not bringing good news to everyone. He was coming to the "daughter of Zion," and it was for her that he was the agent of God's blessing. The prophet tells us that he would be riding on an ass. This perhaps does not matter greatly to us, but to first-century Jews it marked out Jesus as king and as having a distinctive kind of kingship. The point is that a king would not normally ride on an ass; it was known to happen but was not common. A king would be a martial figure; he would march in proudly at the head of his troops or more probably ride on a magnificent war-horse. But he would not use an ass. An ass was the animal used by a peaceable civilian, a merchant, or a priest.

So the choice of animal not only fulfilled the prophecy but told the perceptive observer something about Jesus' way of being king. He was not to be a royal ruler like the kings with whom the people of Jerusalem were familiar. He would indeed be a royal ruler but not one who saw glory in war and conquest. He would be "king of peace" (cf. Heb. 7:2). Paul brings out powerfully the way Jesus made peace between heaven and earth, a peace that meant peace between people of groups that were naturally hostile to one another (Eph. 2). We are to see, then, both the fact of Jesus' kingship and its distinctive nature as concerned with peace.

The Disciples

We have been looking at something of what it meant to Jesus to be "king of peace," but John makes it clear that the disciples did not understand all this at this time (v. 16). From our perspective on this side of the cross and after centuries in which the people of God have seen the way Jesus works out his kingship, we all too readily think that the disciples must have known all this from the very first. But, of course, they did not. To the end it seems they thought that Jesus would bring in an earthly kingdom; there is no doubt that the cross took them very much by surprise and shattered them. So, while John records what happened on that first Palm Sunday and lets us see something of how Scripture was fulfilled, he does not mean that all this was clear to the disciples at the time it occurred. They were there and they remembered what happened. John could write down what they remembered. But he now makes it clear that they did not understand it at the time.

They did not understand it until Jesus was "glorified." As we have seen in earlier studies, this is the way John often refers to the crucifixion. For this writer, true glory is not seen in the pomp and show that earthly rulers so often favor. It is seen in lowly service. When someone who need not take the lowly place nevertheless does so and serves the needs of others, that is real glory. Supremely do we see what glory is when we see the Son of God crucified to put away our sins. John is saying that it was only when the meaning of the cross had become clear to them that the meaning of ever so many other things became clear. It was when the saving work of Christ had been accomplished that the disciples began to understand the real meaning of the scriptural passages that referred to Jesus.

It is interesting that included in this later understanding is that "they had done these things to him." "They" in this expression means the disciples. It was only after the crucifixion that they saw the significance of what they themselves had done. They had joined in the enthusiasm, and some of them had been intimately concerned with obtaining the donkey. But they did not understand it all. Only after the cross could they see what it all meant. And, of course, those to whom the cross meant nothing never did come to this place of understanding. Some scholars see a contradiction here. The disciples did not understand, they say, and yet the multitude greeted Jesus as king. But this is a shallow approach to what John is saying. Of course the multitude greeted Jesus as king, but what did they understand by "king"? Certainly nothing like the understanding the disciples had after the crucifixion. Anyone could understand "king" after a fashion. It is the real meaning of what Jesus was and did that the disciples would understand in due course.

The Crowd and the Pharisees

John rounds off this part of his narrative with a contrast between the crowds and the Pharisees. He has inserted a little explanation of the way the disciples came to understand the significance of what was happening, including the things that they themselves had done, and now he links up what follows with the preceding narrative. Jesus rode into Jerusalem in fulfillment of the prophecy of Zechariah, *therefore* the people who had been there when Lazarus was raised kept bearing their witness (v. 17). The verb comes first in the sentence for emphasis, and the tense points to continuing action; the continuing witness of the crowd was important for John. We can understand the Greek as meaning that the crowd was bearing witness to two facts: (a) that Jesus called Lazarus from the tomb, and (b) that he raised him from the dead. Alternatively it means that the people were with Jesus when he did these two things. John is stressing the importance of both; that solemn call mattered as well as the fact that Lazarus rose.

It would seem that there were two groups of people, perhaps the one lot coming into the city with Jesus and the other coming out to meet them. John now switches to the crowd coming out (v. 18). Again the raising of Lazarus was important; they were coming out because they had heard of what Jesus had done. Evidently they had heard that it was the Jesus who had raised Lazarus who was coming into their city, and accordingly they went out to meet him. Nothing is said about their attitude, but the general impression is one of friendliness. At least they were interested enough to want to see the person who had done *this sign.*

But Jesus' enemies were there, too. The Pharisees saw what was going on and were displeased (v. 19). They spoke pessimistically of "the world" as going after Jesus and assured one another accordingly that they were getting nowhere ("nothing profited"). We should probably see this as another of John's statements with a double meaning. The Pharisees were concerned that some people from Jerusalem were going after Jesus, but the way they express their concern has a fuller meaning for John. In another and much more important sense the world was going after Jesus. The church when John wrote was no insignificant Jewish sect but a great group of people from many lands. Truly "the world" was coming to know its Savior.

55

"But If It Dies . . ."

Now there were some Greeks among those who were going up to worship at the feast. These then came to Philip (who was from Bethsaida of Galilee) and asked him, "Sir, we want to see Jesus." Philip comes and tells Andrew; Andrew and Philip come and tell Jesus. And Jesus answers them saying, "The hour has come that the Son of man be glorified. Truly, truly I say to you, unless the grain of wheat falls into the ground and dies it remains alone by itself. But if it dies it bears much fruit. He who loves his life loses it, and he who hates his life in this world will keep it to life eternal. If anyone serves me let him follow me and where I am there also will my servant be. If anyone serves me my Father will honor him" (John 12:20–26).

We would like to know more about these Greeks. John is the only one of our Gospel writers who mentions them, and he tells us no more than the bare minimum. First, he says that they were Greeks who came to worship (v. 20), but he does not say why. We naturally understand "Greeks" to mean people of Greek nationality, but the term could be used for Gentiles in general, in distinction from Jews (Acts 14:1) and even for cultured people over against barbarians (Rom. 1:14). But, in this context, people of Greek nationality seems the likely meaning. Clearly these Greeks were attracted to the way the Jews worshiped God (otherwise they would not have come). But were they proselytes or simply devout people? John does not say.

Proselytes were full converts. They were people who were so attracted to Judaism that they forsook whatever their religion had previously been and became full members of the Jewish faith. The males in the family were circumcised, and all the members, female as well as male, were baptized. Jewish attitudes toward proselytes varied. Some Jews welcomed them, while others were somewhat suspicious and apparently felt that at heart these people remained what they had been before. There seems to have been a greater readiness to accept them in the Judaism of the Dispersion (i.e., Jews living outside Palestine), while those in the home country tended to take a harder line. But converts were full members of Judaism and were entitled to be treated as such.

There were other Gentiles who did not become proselytes but were interested in some of the things the Jews taught. These people were dissatisfied with the multiplicity of gods and goddesses in the Greek and Roman religions and in the very doubtful morality set out in the colorful stories that were told about these deities, a morality that all too easily became characteristic of their worshipers. They were attracted by the monotheism that the Jews held so firmly and by the lofty morality that accompanied it. At the same time they were repelled by the Jewish ritual requirements—circumcision, food regulations, and the like—so they did not wish to become full members of Judaism. These people were called by some such name as "God-fearers" or "devout." Though they tended to attach themselves loosely to Judaism and would worship in the synagogues, they did not become full Jews. We read of such people in a number of places in Acts, and it seems that many of the early converts to Christianity came from among them.

Outside Palestine such people were often welcomed by the Jews, while those in Palestine tended to be more strict. The Jewish historian Josephus tells of the conversion to Judaism of Izates, King of Adiabene. A merchant named Ananias taught this king to worship the true God, but Izates was not circumcised. Indeed, Ananias strongly advised the king not to undergo this rite, for if it were known that he had become a full convert to Judaism, there might well be disaffection among his subjects. Ananias also thought that he himself would be punished for instructing the king in "unseemly practices" if circumcision took place. He argued that it was more important to be a devout worshiper of God than to undergo circumcision, and the king agreed. But later a Palestinian Jew called Eleazar told the king that he was guilty of the greatest offense against the Law and thus against God. He urged him not only to read the Law but to do what is commanded in it. "How long will you continue to be uncircumcised?" he asked and went on, "If you have not yet read the law concerning this matter, read it now, so that you may know what an impiety it is that you commit." The king was persuaded and had himself circumcised forthwith.

There was thus a difference of opinion. The Talmud records that Rabbi Joshua held that baptism was enough to make a man a proper proselyte (*Yebamoth* 46a), but Palestinians generally thought that circumcision was indispensable. Jews who lived in the Dispersion, being constantly caught up in the Gentile way of life and coming into contact with the best as well as the worst Gentile thinking, tended to be less strict than those in Palestine.

John does not say whether these Greeks were proselytes or simply God-fearers. It seems probable that we should understand them to be God-fearers, for it is unlikely that they would be called simply "Greeks" if they in fact were full members of the Jewish religion. Like many others—Jews, proselytes, and God-fearers—they came up to worship at the feast. It was not necessary to be a proselyte to come to worship in Jerusalem at a feast, for we read of the Ethiopian eunuch that he came to the holy city for that purpose (Acts 8:27), and a eunuch could not be a proselyte. It was customary for people to come from far and wide at the great festivals; anyone who could make it to Jerusalem at Passover would do so. We should add that the fact that they were called "Greeks" does not mean that they lived in Greece. There were Greeks in all sorts of places; for example, many lived in Decapolis (mentioned in Matt. 4:25; Mark 5:20; 7:31).

"We Want to See Jesus"

These Greeks wanted to "see Jesus," which, of course, means more than simply catch sight of him. They wanted to meet him, to talk with him, to benefit from his teaching. Anyone could "see" Jesus by simply standing in places where he would come. These Greeks plainly wanted more, so they came to Philip (v. 21). It is not clear why they chose this man, though it has been suggested that his Greek name had something to do with it. This is possible but not decisive, for "Andrew" is also a Greek name. In any case, there were many Jews who had a Greek name as well as a Jewish name. Greek was the language spoken all over the Roman Empire, and it seems that the use of a Greek name helped identify people wherever they went. So people would often have a Greek name as well as their own Jewish name.

In earlier studies we saw that Philip was not the most resourceful of Jesus' disciples (1:43–46; also 6:5–7), and it seems clear that on this occasion he did not know what to do. Could he possibly bring Greeks to Jesus? All Jesus' ministry had been in Palestine and very rarely had he had contact with non-Jews (John does tell us of one such occasion, when

Jesus spoke to the woman of Samaria, [ch. 4], but this was distinctly exceptional). Religious Jews generally in Judea were inclined to be suspicious of foreigners. So Philip was hesitant. On the other hand, could he possibly refuse? Jesus had received all kinds of people, tax collectors and sinners, people of bad reputation as well as good. Would he not want to receive these people, too? Philip apparently was perplexed. So he consulted Andrew (v. 22).

Andrew would have been in no doubt. Every time we meet him in this Gospel he is bringing someone to Jesus (cf. 1:41–42; 6:8–9). Obviously, for him, that was always the right thing to do. So now he joins with his friend Philip and comes to tell Jesus that these foreigners wanted to see him. John does not actually tell us that the two apostles brought the Greeks to Jesus, but this seems implied.

"The Hour Has Come"

We would have expected John to tell us something of what Jesus said to these Greeks, but there is not a word. Indeed, as we have just noticed, it is not even completely certain that they did in fact see Jesus.

Life often takes surprising twists. It is said that a spiritualist once wrote to Dr. Charles Mayo and said, "Ever since your late great father passed over, he has been my doctor. What do you say to that?" Well, what do you say in such circumstances? I suppose each of us would have his own approach. Dr. Charles Mayo is said to have replied, "Fine. Please estimate what my father's services have been worth and send the check to me." This must have been a most unexpected reaction to the spiritualist as well as to us!

Similarly, in John's narrative what takes place is unexpected. Jesus does not say a word *about* the Greeks or possibly even *to* them. We must, however, bear in mind that John is not giving us a full account of everything that happened, and it may well be that Jesus had a long conversation with these people. If so, what he said did not fit into John's plan for his Gospel, so he did not record it. What he did make clear is that the coming of the Greeks in some way signaled to the Lord the fact that the climax of his work on earth was at hand.

Jesus' immediate reaction is to say, "The hour has come that the Son of man be glorified" (v. 23). Throughout this Gospel there is a series of references to Jesus' "hour" or "time." They begin in the story of the wedding in Cana, when Jesus says, "My hour has not yet come" (2:4). This "hour" or "time" was noted again as *not* having come in 7:6, 8 and 8:20. But now, with the cross so near, Jesus says "The hour has come" (which is repeated in one way or another in 12:27; 13:1; 16:32; 17:1). John nowhere draws attention to this series of statements, but their occurrence is an impressive witness to the steady unfolding of the purpose of God. What had been planned would in due course take place, and Jesus had come for a specific "hour."

"The Son of man" is Jesus' most frequent way of referring to himself. It occurs in all four Gospels and in all the strata that scholars find in their study of these Gospels. It is used by Jesus about eighty times, but nobody else in any of the Gospels ever uses it (except the crowd who ask, "Who is this Son of man?" [12:34], and as this is a response to Jesus' use of the term it scarcely counts as an exception). Jesus uses it in connection with his mission, and that will be the point of it here. Jesus recognizes in the coming of the Greeks the embodiment of the truth that the gospel is the gospel for the whole world. And that gospel, of course, centers on the cross.

The cross is meant when Jesus speaks of his being glorified. In this Gospel real glory does not consist of majesty and splendor; it consists of lowly service. And the supreme example of lowly service is Jesus' death on the cross for sinners. He was supreme in heaven. There was no compulsion for him to come to earth and die. But in order to save sinners that is what he chose to do, and John sees real glory in that. So now, when Jesus says that he will "be glorified," he means that he will be crucified. In that way his real glory will be revealed.

The Grain of Wheat

Now comes another solemn statement introduced by "Truly, truly" (v. 24). This emphatic mode of speech is found throughout this Gospel (the Synoptists use the single "Truly"). It is always used by Jesus and it introduces a saying that is important and is to be taken with the utmost seriousness. On this occasion the saying concerns the agricultural process. "The" with "grain" is a way of making the statement universal: it means grains of wheat in general. Jesus points to what is obvious in farming, that unless the seed is planted in the ground there will be no crop. The more literally minded may object that the wheat does not really die: there is life in it and this becomes apparent when it is sown in favorable conditions. But this is pedantic. The grain certainly dies as grain, for what emerges is not grain but a plant. This, of course, is the point of what Jesus is saying. When he calls on his followers to die in order that they may live, he is saying that they are to die to a whole way of life and in that way will rise to a totally new life. The death of the old is the necessary prelude to the new life.

The Jewish teachers sometimes made something of the same approach. Thus the Talmud records a decision given by Rabbi Meir to the question of whether the dead will rise clothed or naked at the general resurrection: "Thou mayest deduce by an *a fortiori* argument [the answer] from a wheat grain: if a grain of wheat, which is buried naked, sprouteth forth in many robes, how much more so the righteous, who are buried in their raiment!" (*Sanhedrin* 90b). This is, of course, quite different from the point that Jesus is making. I am simply drawing attention to the fact that an appeal to the processes of plant growth was quite natural for people who lived so much closer to the land than most of us do in the twentieth century. When Jesus spoke of what happens to the wheat grain, he was speaking in a way that would bring his point home to his hearers with some emphasis.

The wheat that is not put into the ground and buried remains *alone by itself.* The repetition hammers in the point. Those who seek to serve God without knowing the death to the old, selfish way of life are left with the self they so much wanted to preserve, with that self and no more. It will be alone. It will be by itself. Someone has said that miserable people are nearly always selfish, and there is an important truth there. If we concentrate on our own aims, our own life, we cut ourselves off from all that is beyond us. The selfish person, simply because he *is* a selfish person, cuts himself off from all the joys of unselfishness. "A man wrapped up in himself makes a very small parcel."

The fruitful way of life always involves a death. This is true in much more than spiritual life. Anyone who wishes to excel must make a hard decision to cut himself off from a great deal that other people do. There is the time of training for whatever course is chosen, there is the mastering of a discipline or a technique. Be it art or business or sport or scholarship or any other useful branch of human endeavor, the way to effectiveness is through a death of some sort.

But Jesus is concerned with the spiritual development of his followers. He is saying that as long as we insist on retaining a firm grasp on our own petty ambitions, we cut ourselves off from the real life he is offering us. The taking up of our cross (Luke 9:23) is always a painful business, but it is a fundamental necessity if we are serious about Christian service. No death, no life. But where there is such a death there is fullness of life. The history of the Christian church is full of examples of people who, in response to the call of God, have "buried" themselves (as the world puts it) in obscure places where the world sees no scope for their talents, and then by God's grace have done extraordinary things.

The same truth is put in another way. The person who loves his life by that very fact loses it (v. 25; there is similar teaching in Mark 8:35 and the parallel passages). Jesus goes on to speak of hating his life, which must be understood carefully. Among the Hebrews "hate" was sometimes used in the sense of "love less." For example, Luke records one saying of Jesus: "No household servant can serve two masters; for either he will hate the one and love the other . . ." (Luke 16:13) and another beginning "If anyone comes to me and does not hate his father and mother and wife and children and brothers and sisters, yes and his own life too, he cannot be my disciple" (Luke 14:26). Obviously, Jesus was not saying that his follower must literally hate his closest relatives. His point is that allegiance to the cause of God in Christ must be such as to outweigh all other allegiances. Alongside the love for God, all other loves must look like hate. So here he is saying that his follower must not prize his life but be ready to lose it. Indeed, in the sense that all is well lost for Christ's sake, he does in fact lose it.

And in this way he keeps his life "to life eternal." The possession of eternal life is incompatible with selfishness. Jesus is saying that those who will live with him in eternity count all well lost for him here and now. Once again we have the thought that the service of Christ is a wholehearted affair. Unless we are ready to die to the old way, we do not enter the new. Unless we hate the life that is only the life of this world, we do not know what that life is that lasts through eternity.

Service and Reward

From dying and loving we move on to service and the reward of service. This does not mean that we have brought back the selfish motive, for Jesus is speaking of a service that is selfless. The way of service, he says, is that of following him (v. 26). There is some emphasis on "me." Whatever may be the case with serving others, such as Caesar or the Jewish state or local religious leaders or anyone earthly, the service of Jesus means following Jesus. The servant is not expected to renounce his Lord by launching out into avenues of service that contradict all that his Lord stood for. To serve him is to follow him.

Then Jesus moves on to the thought of reward. People have some curious ideas of what heaven means. I was interested to read that Catherine Bowen once got a letter from a fan who wrote: "You said if you died you would know you were in heaven if Mozart came up and said, 'I have written 258 new string quartets and we badly need a second fiddle. So glad you're here!' Well, if you get there first please mention me for the cello position if not already filled. I'll practise all I can." Doubtless, people other than musicians would have other ideas about what heaven means.

It is interesting that Jesus says no more than "where I am there also will my servant be." But what more could the servant really want? A. M. Hunter has written, "It has been said that *follow me* is the whole of a Christian's duty, as to *be* where Christ is is the whole of his reward." It is fellowship with Christ throughout all eternity that is the most significant part of the Christian's reward. Indeed, to know God and Jesus Christ *is* eternal life (17:3).

And that is probably meant also when Jesus says that the Father will *honor* anyone who serves Christ. There is no final separation of Father and Son, and to know the one is to know the other. To be honored by one is to be honored by the other. And the essence of it all is fellowship. What a magnificent prospect is held out before the servant of Christ!

56

"Lifted Up Was He to Die"

"Now is my soul troubled, and what shall I say? 'Father, save me from this hour'? But for this reason I came to this hour. Father, glorify your name." There came therefore a voice out of heaven, "I have both glorified it and I will glorify it again." So the crowd who stood and heard said it had thundered. Others said, "An angel has spoken to him." Jesus answered saying, "This voice did not come for my sake but for your sake. Now is the judgment of this world, now will the ruler of this world be thrown out. And I, if I be lifted up from the earth, will draw all people to me." He said this, signifying by what death he would die. Therefore the crowd answered him, "We have heard from the law that the Christ abides for ever so how do you say that the Son of man must be lifted up? Who is this Son of man?" Jesus therefore said to them, "For a little while the light is still with you. Walk as you have the light so that darkness does not overcome you; he who walks in the darkness does not know where he is going. As you have the light believe in the light so that you may become sons of light" (John 12:27–36).

We saw in our last study that when the Greeks came wanting to see him, Jesus recognized that the climax of his mission was at hand. This meant going to the cross, and it is this that is before him when he says, "Now is my soul troubled." In reporting this, John employs a rather picturesque verb, one used of things being shaken together or of water being agitated, so it points to something more than a mild disturbance. The New English Bible translates here "my soul is in turmoil." While Jesus went forward resolutely to suffer for us all, we ought not to think that it was easy for him. To undergo the death on the cross in which he bore the sin of the world was a grim prospect for the sinless Son of God, and it is this to which John is drawing our attention. We should be clear, though, that being troubled is not the same thing as being afraid. John does not mean that Jesus expressed fear; that would be quite out of character. The verb means being disturbed rather than being afraid.

In the other Gospels we read of Jesus' agony in Gethsemane. There, Luke tells us, Jesus was in such deep emotion that as he prayed his sweat was like great drops of blood falling down to the ground (Luke 22:44). John does not tell us of the agony in the Garden, but we should probably see this passage as his equivalent. He was just as sure as the Synoptists that Jesus suffered in his spirit as he contemplated his coming death, but John characteristically makes the point in his own way.

Jesus could see then that his death was approaching. The coming of the Greeks brought home to him in some way the truth that the salvation of the world was at stake and that he was approaching the decisive moment. But the death in which he was to be "numbered with transgressors [or, lawless people]" (Luke 22:37) was a terrible prospect. So Jesus asks, "What shall I say?" and then looks at a possible prayer: "Father, save me from this hour." Some understand this to be a real prayer; for example, it appears as such in the New English Bible. If it is a real prayer it should probably be understood in the sense of "Father, keep me safe through this hour" (i.e., "bring me safely out of this trouble," not "save me from entering into it"). It is true that Jesus prayed in Gethsemane, "My Father, if it be possible, let this cup pass from me" (and immediately added, "Nevertheless not as I will but as you do," Matt. 26:39). But John is not describing what happened in Gethsemane but another occasion, and on this occasion the language used shows not that Jesus prayed that he might not undergo death, but that he simply looked at that as a possible prayer.

When he contemplates this possible prayer, Jesus immediately responds, "But for this reason I came to this hour." The prayer is impossible because the whole purpose of his coming to earth was to fulfill all that "this hour" meant. John has made it very clear with his references to the "time" of Jesus or the "hour" of Jesus that he moved steadily forward to that time. The purpose of his being on earth was that he might secure the world's salvation and this would be by his atoning death.

So Jesus prays his real prayer: "Father, glorify your name" (v. 28). Throughout this Gospel we have had occasion to notice the frequent use of the term *glory.* (John uses the noun eighteen times and the verb *glorify* twenty-three times.) And we have seen that he uses it in a distinctive way. He does not see real glory in terms of pomp and majesty, but as humble service, and the supreme example of glory is in the lowly service we see at the cross. It seems that it is this that is in mind at this point. The tense of the verb indicates that it is not so much a continuing process of glory for which Jesus prays (it is not "keep on glorifying") as a single act. And, of course, at this point of time the single act can scarcely be anything other than the cross. That would be the place where the greatest possible piece of service would be accomplished for the greatest possible number of people by the greatest possible person of all.

The word *name* was, of course, used in the first century in a way different from our use. In some way it summed up all that the person who bore it meant. Here "glorify your name" means "glorify yourself"; the usage is not unlike that in the Lord's Prayer: "May your name be hallowed" (Matt. 6:9). It is a way of referring to all that the Father is and means and, in this context especially, to the Father's saving love.

In the New Testament there are many examples of prayer, but few where the answer is as immediate and as obvious as on this occasion. There came a voice from heaven, which assured Jesus that God had already glorified his name and that he would do this again. That he would do it again we may readily understand as a further reference to the saving act at the cross.

But it is not easy to see the meaning of "I have already glorified it." Some suggest that it is a reference to the transfiguration, but John does not record that incident, so it is very unlikely that he would tell us of a prayer that had to be understood in that way. It is much more likely that this refers to the whole of the life of Jesus. Throughout his entire life, and especially in his public ministry, Jesus was bringing glory to the Father. He never appeared at the center of the world's stage but spent his whole life in what people would see as a backwater. He was not at the hub of civilization, in Rome or even in Athens, but in Judea. And in Judea most of the time he was not in Jerusalem, the capital, but in places like Capernaum, small provincial towns. This is not the kind of life that worldly people, or for that matter religious people, would associate with the coming of the Son of God. It is natural for people to think of God in terms of greatness and glory and to associate that with the most important places on earth. Not so did God act. In his lowliness Jesus was doing the glorious will of God and turning away from human praise. John sees glory in the continuing lowly service in obscure and poverty-stricken places.

The World's Judgment

The voice from heaven evidently was audible in the sense that the people near Jesus heard a sound. But, while he understood what the Father was saying, they did not. Some of the crowd gave their verdict that it had been thunder (v. 29), so it must have been a very loud noise.

But others thought of an angel's voice rather than thunder. It is not clear why they thought this, but presumably an angel would speak loudly and they evidently discerned that there was something more significant than a peal of thunder. As Jesus had just been praying, what would be more natural than that there had been a heavenly response in the form of words from an angelic messenger?

Surprisingly, Jesus tells his hearers that the voice had come not so much for his sake as for theirs (v. 30). John tells us that he "answered" them, though he does not record any question. He probably means that Jesus answered their incomprehension. Both those who had spoken of thunder and those who had referred to the voice of an angel had been wrong. Jesus spoke in order to put them both right. What they had heard had been a voice, but, while the words had been addressed to him, the voice had been for their sakes. Jesus lived in constant communion with the Father and did not need some audible voice to be sure that the Father had heard and was answering his prayer. But they did not live close to the Father and needed all the aids they could get.

One question inevitably arises: If the voice was for their sakes why did they not understand it? They did not even realize that what they heard was the voice of God; they thought they were hearing thunder or an angel. The answer is not easy, but perhaps we are not wrong if we say that it was their spiritual deafness that created the problem. They were so sure that they were right in their entrenched ideas, so sure that Jesus was a heretic, that when God spoke they did not know what was happening. It always takes some degree of spiritual perception to hear what God is saying. That is important for us all to realize. We do not hear the voice of God speaking in the way he spoke in this incident, but he still speaks. And if we are entrenched in our own prejudices, as these people were, we will no more understand what he is saying than they did.

"Now is the judgment of this world," Jesus went on (v. 31), a saying that is probably to be understood on more than one level. It follows on from what has just been said about the spiritual incapacity of the crowd. That judgment is a present reality is part of the teaching of this Gospel, and the crowd's inability to hear the voice of God is part of their judgment. We should be clear that God always wills to bless us, and if we are not experiencing the blessing of God that is because in one way or another we refuse to receive it. Our failure to receive the blessing is a judgment on our refusal. So often it seems to us that the sins we do are very small and of no great consequence, but this fails to reckon with the fact that every sin in some measure cuts us off from God. The prophet of old said to the people of God "your iniquities have separated you from your God; your sins have hidden his face from you . . ." (Isa. 59:2). There is a continuing judgment on all sin, and we shut our eyes to reality unless we perceive that.

But it is probable that Jesus means more than this. Jesus speaks not only of the judgment of this world but also of the throwing out of "the ruler of this world." This expression is a way of referring to Satan, which we see again in 14:30; 16:11 (cf. 2 Cor. 4:4; Eph. 2:2 and 6:12). From one point of view the cross was the defeat of the evil one, and that is here seen as judgment. We should not miss the point that Jesus goes on to speak of his being "lifted up" (v. 32), and being "thrown out" is the very opposite. Just as the cross means the exaltation of Jesus, so does it mean the overthrow of Satan. It is also the case that the people of Jerusalem came under judgment by their attitude to Jesus when he was accused before Pilate and eventually slain. They condemned themselves by their share in bringing about the crucifixion.

Thus we see that judgment is a grim reality and one that may be seen on a variety of levels. The final judgment at the last day is referred to in many parts of the New Testament, including this Gospel (see 5:28–29), and we are all familiar with the thought that there will be such a judgment. But we do not realize as much as we should that judgment also takes place here and now in a variety of ways. It is well that those who profess to serve the living God do not place themselves under condemnation.

"Lifted Up from the Earth"

Jesus contrasts himself with "the ruler of this world" by using the emphatic pronoun *I* (v. 32). His "And I" separates this from the rest of the sentence and shows us that what will happen to Jesus is very different from what will happen to the evil one. Then, for the third time in this Gospel, we read of Jesus being "lifted up" (see 3:14; 8:28). This is not a common way of referring to crucifixion, but it is intelligible; Jesus' hearers would get the point. John probably means his readers to see something else, something that arises from the fact that the verb is mostly used for something quite different, something that we might express by the word *exalt*. It is used of Jesus' exaltation to heaven at the end of his work on earth (Acts 2:33; 5:31), which is a far more usual way of employing the verb. It is also used of people being exalted (James 4:10; 1 Peter 5:6), of the person who exalts himself (Matt. 23:12), and in other ways.

So, when it is used of Jesus being lifted up on the cross, there is probably something of the flavor of exaltation about it. We saw a moment ago that the use of "glory" in this Gospel is unusual in that it conveys the idea of the lowly service that is the real glory. There is something of that thought here. It was on the cross that Jesus performed the lowly service of undergoing the painful and shameful death of crucifixion. To the people of the day it would have seemed the end of Jesus, an end that emphasizes disgrace. But to those who could see more deeply into the realities of the situation it was the exaltation of the Son of God. We should not miss the fact that the expression combines the ideas of death by crucifixion and of exaltation.

John adds that Jesus put it this way, "signifying by what death he would die" (v. 33). The verb was so often used of exaltation that there was the possibility of misunderstanding; readers might not realize that it was being lifted up on a cross that was meant. But this death was so important to John that the reference to it must not be allowed to go unnoticed. So he puts in these few words that enable us to get the picture.

"Who Is This Son of Man?"

What John has just written is full of meaning to the followers of Jesus, but it puzzled the members of the crowd. They express their view with some emphasis and, just as Jesus had used the emphatic pronoun *I*, they now use an emphatic pronoun of their own: "we" (v. 34). "Whatever *you* may say" is apparently the line of their reasoning, "*we* have heard . . ." and what they had heard they could not square with what Jesus had said. As we saw earlier, they lacked spiritual perception, so perhaps this is not surprising. But they in turn puzzle us, for they say, "We have heard from the law that the Christ abides for ever" (v. 34), and it is not easy to see what passage they have in mind. Bear in mind that for them "the law" meant the first five books of our Old Testament: Genesis to Deuteronomy. It is not easy to see anything in those books that indicates that the Christ, the Messiah, will never die.

It may be that the people had in mind some such passage as Psalm 89:36, which says that God has sworn "that his [i.e., David's] line will continue forever and his throne endure before me like the sun" (cf. also Ps. 110:4; Isa. 9:7; Dan. 7:14). The trouble is that none of the passages suggested are from the Law. Perhaps the people are using the term *law* very generally, meaning Scripture as a whole. But, even so, it is not easy to find a passage in any part of the Old Testament that says in set terms that the Messiah "abides for ever." However, they clearly thought that this was good scriptural teaching, and this was the basis for their puzzlement at what Jesus had just said.

They understood the reference to being "lifted up." They have an emphatic *"you"* to offset their emphatic *"we"* as they ask how Jesus can say that the Son of man must be lifted up. This is an interesting way of putting it because Jesus did not use the expression "the Son of man" on this occasion. But he did use it about himself often (and indeed did so on both the earlier occasions when he spoke of being "lifted up" [3:14; 8:28]), so they are giving the sense of it even if they do not quote him exactly. They proceed to ask, "Who is this Son of man?" They may be asking whether the Son of man is to be equated with the Messiah. They had said that the Messiah would not die and are perhaps asking whether in the light of that "the Son of man" was someone other than the Messiah. It is difficult to be sure. But what is abundantly clear is that to the end the Jerusalem mob remains confused and puzzled about spiritual things. We may perhaps infer that they had no real commitment to the truth and that therefore they could not recognize what God was saying to them through the Messiah.

The Light and the Darkness

We return to one of the great themes of this Gospel when Jesus replies in terms of light and darkness (v. 35). We should not pass over his "therefore," since what he says arises out of their parlous spiritual state. He warns them that the light is still with them, but this is something that will not last much longer. There is a sense of urgency about it all. Had they but known it, they had the greatest opportunity in all their lives, an opportunity that every subsequent generation of Christians would like to have had for itself. But so far they had failed to respond to the light.

"Walk as you have the light," Jesus says. Many translations have "Walk while you have the light" (e.g., RSV), a rendering that depends on giving to the conjunction a meaning it mostly does not have. But this is a possible understanding; if it be accepted, Jesus is saying that they should make use of their opportunity while it is still there. But it seems better to take it in its normal sense of "as" to give the meaning of "walk according to the light you have." They are being urged not to shut their eyes to what God is doing in their very presence. It is well that we take good heed to this and apply it to our own very different situation.

There is an urgency that is brought out in the words "so that darkness does not overcome [or "overtake"] you." The verb may be used in either sense, and many translations prefer to carry the imagery through with "overtake." In that case, Jesus is appealing to the fact that night follows day inexorably, and that it is important accordingly to act while the opportunity is still there. But in this Gospel there is often the thought that light and darkness are in conflict, and it is not unlikely that we should understand the words to mean that they should take their part in this great conflict (cf. 1:5). To walk in darkness is to be ignorant of where one is going. Illumination is important for every traveler, and Jesus is saying that this is true of the person traveling through life.

We expect the exhortation to continue with a further reference to walking, but instead we have "As you have the light believe in the light" (v. 36). The same spiritual truth is being hammered in but from a different angle. Jesus is the light, and it is important to walk steadfastly in the light he sheds on our way. But it is important also to believe in him, and it is this for which he calls as this part of his teaching comes to an end. It is in this way that people become "sons of light," i.e., people characterized by light, people who habitually reject the darkness and live in the light.

57

Why Don't People Believe?

Although he had done so many signs before them they did not believe in him so that the word of Isaiah the prophet might be fulfilled which he spoke: "Lord, who believed our message? And to whom has the arm of the Lord been revealed?" For this reason they could not believe because again Isaiah said: "He has blinded their eyes and hardened their heart lest they should see with their eyes and understand with their heart and should turn and I should heal them." These things Isaiah said because he saw his glory, and he spoke about him. Nevertheless many of the rulers believed in him, but because of the Pharisees they did not acknowledge it lest they should be put out of the synagogue. For they loved the praise of men rather than the praise of God.

But Jesus cried out and said, "He who believes in me does not believe in me but in him who sent me, and he who sees me sees him who sent me. I, light, have come into the world in order that everyone who believes in me should not remain in the darkness. And if anyone hears my words and does not keep them I do not judge him, for I did not come to judge the world but to save the world. He who despises me and does not receive my words has one that judges him. The word that I spoke, that will judge him on the last day, for I did not speak on my own initiative but the Father who sent me himself gave me commandment what I should say and what I should speak. And I know that his commandment is life eternal. The things therefore that I say I say according as the Father has spoken to me" (John 12:37–50).

The public ministry of Jesus is over. John still has a good deal to tell us, but it is about what Jesus said in the Upper Room to the little circle of his close followers and about the death Jesus would die to bring salvation to believers and about the resurrection and what followed. He has finished his story of the way Jesus moved among the people, teaching them how they could come to know the Father and how they should live in his service.

Not very many people have accepted what Jesus said. There are some who did, the Twelve and some other close followers. But on the whole the nation that saw itself as the people of God did not. That posed a very difficult question for the earliest Christians: "Why did the people of God not accept God's Messiah when he came?" We perhaps do not realize what a puzzle this was to them. We stand at the other end of centuries of the history of the Christian church, and we take it for granted that most believers will be Gentiles. We thankfully recognize that there are Jews in the church and rejoice to have fellowship with them, but for us the thought that the church is mostly Gentile does not have to be spelled out. We take that for granted.

The first Christians, however, found this a very difficult problem, as we see for example from Paul's discussion in Romans 9–11. Paul could not understand why his own people, that people who had received so many blessings from God through the centuries, should have turned its back on the salvation the Christ had come to offer them. Each of the writers of the Gospels had to face the problem in one way or another.

There are two principal points that are made in the answers given to this problem. The first is that God is supreme and that he works out his purpose. He willed that salvation should go to people of all nations, and when the Jews refused the gospel the natural thing for the first messengers was to go to the Gentiles. Had the Jews responded, these messengers may well have continued to preach to the Jews, but the Jewish rejection of them and their message compelled them to fulfill the will of God and go to the Gentile peoples. The Jewish rejection of the gospel thus led to the preaching to the Gentiles, and in this we can see the working out of the purpose of God. The other point made is that there was no compulsion on the Jews to reject the Christ. They themselves chose to do this. Thus divine purpose and human responsibility come together at this point. John brings out both these points in succession.

The Prophet Isaiah

Throughout his Gospel John has drawn attention to the miracles that Jesus did, and one of his favorite ways of referring to them has been to call them "signs." They are not simply works of power; they are full of meaning. The person who has spiritual insight will see that God is acting in these deeds and that he is teaching people important truths.

John now reminds his readers of those "signs" (v. 37) and reminds them that there had been many signs. He has given no more than a selection from a very large number (as he makes plain later, in 20:30–31). Since God had done such great things in their very midst, it might have been expected that they would respond with joy. But they did not. "They did not believe in him," John sorrowfully reports. This is the supreme tragedy. John's whole Gospel was written so that people would come to believe (20:31), and the fact that those who saw the signs for the most part did not come to faith means that they were setting themselves into opposition with the God they professed to serve.

But to John it is clear that this did not mean that God was defeated. Those people from Galilee and Judea might fancy that they were too wise in the ways of God to bother with Jesus, but the purpose of God was not going to be overthrown by such spiritual silliness. God had his purpose and he would work it out in his own way. John proceeds to draw attention to Isaiah the prophet, one whom the Jews would recognize as a man who spoke from God. Isaiah spoke words that had relevance to the present situation and John quotes them (v. 38).

"Lord, who believed our message?" Isaiah had asked so many centuries before. The rejection of the messengers of God was no new thing; it had happened again and again. Stephen asked the Jews who sat in judgment on him, "Which of the prophets did your fathers not persecute? They killed those who spoke beforehand about the coming of the Righteous One of whom you now have become the betrayers and murderers" (Acts 7:52). It is a sad fact that prophets have rarely been popular. Though the Jewish nation recognized that the prophets as a group were people whom God had sent to them, and though they revered the writings of the prophets and read them in their worship, Sabbath by Sabbath, when the prophets actually appeared their message had not been accepted.

This is, of course, still the case. In our day Jesus is widely revered as a great religious teacher, but even in nominally Christian lands many people take little or no notice of what he said. Christians proclaim the gospel without seeing the results they would like to see. Communities are saturated with the spirit of selfishness, violence abounds, kindness and courtesy are lost arts. We are tempted to think of this generation as worse than any other. And so it might be. Never having lived in any other generation, I do not know. But I do know that those who take the Bible seriously should not be surprised at the sinfulness of people. "Who believed our message?" is a question that has always been on the lips of the faithful messengers of God. The "arm of the Lord" has always been at work, and God has done mighty things in every generation. For those who have eyes to see there are mighty things done in our own day. But most people have never recognized this. They did not in Isaiah's day, and they do not in our own.

Blind Eyes and Hard Hearts

John emphasizes the importance of the sovereignty of God with a further quotation. "They could not believe," he says (v. 39) and proceeds to words of Isaiah that speak of God as blinding their eyes and hardening their hearts (v. 40). There is a great mystery involved here, and it is unlikely that we will penetrate it to the full. But we can see, as J. O. F. Murray puts it, "that it is by God's appointment that if His word does not quicken, it must deaden." Sinners never defeat the purpose of God. They may rebel against God and defy God. They may proclaim that they care nothing for his will and that they are determined to live completely for their own happiness. But none of all this affects the fact that God is a great God and that he works out his purpose in the sin that people commit as well as in the good that they may accomplish. Sinners are blind and their hearts are hard and they think that in these things they are independent of God. Isaiah says that they are not. They have rejected the gracious invitation of God, and it is God, none less, who has decreed that those who act in this way have their eyes blinded and their hearts hardened.

It is interesting and significant that, even in these words that speak of blindness and hardness, the prophet goes on to thoughts of understanding and healing. Though evil people turn away from the good that God offers them, it is still good. An evil generation goes its own sinful way with the resulting chaos and unhappiness, but it is still true that it is understanding and healing that God offers.

The people of his day were blind and hard, but not so Isaiah. John goes on to the truth that the reason Isaiah spoke in this way was that "he saw his glory, and he spoke about him" (v. 41). These words may refer to the glory that the young prophet saw when he had his vision in the temple and heard the seraphim say: "the whole earth is full of his glory" (Isa. 6:3). But John is also saying that Isaiah looked forward to the coming in due time of the Son of God. It may well be that the complex idea of glory that we have already seen in this gospel is to be discerned here also, the idea that true glory is to be seen not in majesty and splendor but in lowly service. For Isaiah speaks not only of glory in the temple but of one who was "despised and rejected by men, a man of sorrows, and familiar with suffering . . ." (Isa. 53:3), one of whom it could be said ". . . the punishment that brought us peace was upon him, and by his wounds we are healed" (Isa. 53:5). "He spoke about him" means that he spoke about Jesus as well as that he spoke about God.

Scared Believers

There was, then, prophetic warrant for recognizing the glory of God in Jesus the Savior. While John records his understanding of the way the purpose of God worked out, even in the rejection of Jesus according to the prophetic word, he wants his readers to understand that the rejection was not the only attitude. There were some who had enough spiritual insight to recognize that Jesus was indeed the one in whom they should believe and who did just that (v. 42). There were some of "the rulers" who believed, but John does not explain exactly who these people were. His word is a general one for people in authority and might apply to anyone who exercised a ruling function.

We should think of Nicodemus, who came to Jesus at first by night (3:1–2) and who later made a tentative defense of Jesus (7:50–51). And there was Joseph of Arimathea, who looked after the burial of Jesus (19:38–42). Neither of these men wholeheartedly identified himself with Jesus during his lifetime, though subsequent events showed that their faith was genuine. John is saying now that there were others from the ruling group who believed in Jesus but did nothing about it. The Pharisees were explicit in their opposition to the Savior and were ready to put out of the synagogue anybody who openly allied himself with Jesus. The synagogue was the center of community life, being a school and a place where Jewish affairs were discussed and set forward, as well as being a place of worship. So to be excluded from it was a heavy punishment, and many were not prepared to undergo that.

Their condemnation was that they thought more of what people would say about them than what God would say (v. 43). In this verse I have translated the word that normally means "glory" as "praise," for that is what the context seems to demand. But we should not overlook the fact that it is the word that was translated "glory" in verse 41. The real glory is that which God recognizes and not that which the Pharisees approve. John is saying that those who follow the Christ must be concerned first and foremost with God and his glory, not with what people like the Pharisees may think and do.

Light in the World

John does not say when it was that Jesus spoke these words, but he clearly includes them here as being a fitting close to the public ministry that Jesus has exercised. They are a ringing challenge to believe, coupled with a strong affirmation of Jesus' unity with the Father.

"But" (v. 44) sets what follows as a contrast to what has just been said. There were those who said nothing about their real beliefs and kept them hidden. In contrast Jesus spoke boldly and loudly. He makes the point that we have seen often in this Gospel, that he has a very close unity with the Father. To believe in him, he now says, is not to believe simply in a man from Galilee, and to see him is not simply to see a first-century Jew. He was indeed a first-century Jew from Galilee, but if we see no more than that we are missing what matters. It is God, no less, who has "sent" Jesus, and the divine sending puts everything Jesus says and does into a new dimension. The mission (being "sent") of Jesus is a divine mission, so that those who respond to him are responding to God. To believe in Jesus is to believe in God, a truth that our generation does not always appreciate as it should. When Christians proclaim the gospel and invite people to believe in the Lord Jesus Christ for salvation, they are not reproducing some merely first-century Jewish ideas. They are inviting people to put their trust in God.

Now we have the thoughts of light and darkness again (v. 46). This is a recurring theme throughout John's Gospel, and Jesus speaks of himself as "light." His "I" is emphatic; whatever be the case with other teachers, they may know that Jesus is different. He is light. Earlier he had spoken of himself as "the light of the world" (8:12; 9:5), and it may be much the same thought here. But the construction is different, and "I" and "light" are set alongside one another. It may be that we should understand the words to mean "I have come as light" (as several translations run). Whichever way we take it, Jesus is saying that he is the light and is reminding his hearers that there is a continuing conflict between light and darkness. But people need not continue in darkness. They cannot, it is true, defeat darkness in their own strength, but if they believe in Christ they are delivered from it. Jesus is offering them a way out of the darkness. If they remain in darkness it is not because there is no better way or because they do not know of the better way. They may, in fact, not know of that way, but they have been told about it. Indeed, when they were brought into contact with Jesus they were brought into contact with the light. But to shut one's eyes to the light is a sure and certain way of remaining in the darkness.

Judgment

Jesus is saying that he came to deliver people from the plight into which their sins have placed them. He came as light in order to deliver people from darkness, not to shut them up to darkness. To remain in darkness is a form of judgment, but he makes it clear that he did not come in order that those who reject him might be the more strongly condemned. There are people who hear his words and do not keep them (v. 47), and these people are certainly condemned. But that is because whenever salvation is offered there is also the possibility that people may reject the good gift. The very offer of salvation pronounces a judgment on those who do not receive it. Now, in his summing up, Jesus makes it clear that he does not judge people. The purpose of his coming was salvation, not judgment (cf. 3:17–18). People may in fact bring down judgment on themselves, but that is their doing, not his. Jesus' purpose was to offer them salvation.

It is a sobering thought that there were people who despised the Son of God when he was here on earth. Puny, insignificant people took it upon themselves to look down on the sinless Son of God. And, of course, our studies are useless unless we see that the possibility is with us still. There are always those who are so sure of the rightness of their thinking and their living that they look down on the Man from Galilee and sit in judgment on his teaching.

Jesus now refers to those people, those who despise him and reject his words, and assures them that they will certainly be judged, even though it will not be Jesus who does the judging (v. 48). But the word that he spoke, the teaching he gave about the Father and about sin and about believing in him, that will judge them. There is, of course, a sense in which Jesus is himself the judge (5:28–29). But that is in the sense that it is their attitude toward Jesus that is finally decisive, not in the sense that he sought their condemnation. We have that truth now in the saying that it is his "word" that will be their judge on the last great day. They will then have no excuse. They will not be able to say, "We did not know how to be saved." Of course they knew how to be saved. Jesus had told them. His word will rise up against them. The fact that they chose to reject his teaching will not save them. It will condemn them, because it will show that when they were confronted with the message from God himself, they turned away from it in the belief that they knew better. That will be their condemnation.

We are back on the teaching that the Father and the Son are one. Jesus' teaching was not of purely human origin. There was, of course, a human aspect to it. It was given in the language of first-century Galilee and Judea and expressed in accordance with the thought forms and conventions of the day. But it was teaching that originated with God the Father (v. 49). That was why rejecting it was (and is) so serious. It was God the Father who commanded Jesus to speak as he did.

This leads right on to the thought of eternal life (v. 50). Just as Jesus did not come to bring judgment on people, so God did not give him a commandment in order to secure the condemnation of sinners. It was life eternal that was the Father's object in sending his Son. There is life eternal in believing on the Son as he invited people to do. And the reason is that the things he says he says "according as the Father has spoken" to him. It is significant that the very last words recorded in this Gospel in Jesus' public ministry is this statement, that what he has said he has said in accordance with the Father's command. It is this that made them so solemn and so significant for Jesus' hearers.

And it is this that makes them so solemn and so significant for us.

58

Washing the Disciples' Feet

Before the feast of the Passover Jesus, knowing that the hour had come for him to go out of this world to the Father, having loved his own who were in the world he loved them to the end. And during supper (the devil having made up his mind that Judas the son of Simon Iscariot should betray him), knowing that the Father had given all things into his hands and that he had come out from God and was going to God, he rises from the supper, puts aside his garments, took a towel and girded himself. Then he pours water into the basin and began to wash the disciples' feet and wipe them with the towel with which he was girded. He comes, then, to Simon Peter. He says to him, "Lord, are you washing my feet?" Jesus answered him saying, "What I am doing you do not know now, but you will know afterwards." Peter says to him, "You will certainly not wash my feet, not for ever." Jesus answered him, "If I do not wash you you have no part with me." Simon Peter says to him, "Lord, not my feet only but also my hands and my head." Jesus says to him, "He that is bathed has no need except to wash his feet, but he is altogether clean. And you are clean, but not all." For he knew who was betraying him; for this reason he said, "You are not all clean."

When then he had washed their feet, he took his garments and reclined again and said to them, "Do you know what I have done to you? You call me 'The Teacher' and 'The Lord' and you say well, for I am. If then I, your Lord and Teacher, have washed your feet you also ought to wash one another's feet. For I have given you an example that as I have done to you so you should do. Truly, truly I tell you, a slave is not greater than his owner, nor a messenger greater than him who sent him. If you know these things you are blessed if you do them" (John 13:1–17).

It is clear that for John the death of Jesus occupied the central place. He has referred to Jesus' "hour" or his "time" on a number of occasions during his account of the public ministry of our Lord to let us know that everything moves on to this climax, and his arrangement of his Gospel gives twelve chapters to the whole of the life of Jesus up to the eve of the crucifixion and nine to the last night of his life, together with the death and resurrection narratives. It is obvious where the emphasis lies. John will not let his reader miss what is the very central thing.

He gives us a time note for the next stage of his narrative, locating it before the Passover (v. 1). We have seen that John has a great interest in the Jewish feasts, and particularly in the Passover, which he mentions a number of times and with reference to at least three Passovers. One of the truths he will bring out a little later is that in his death Jesus accomplished all that the Passover symbolized. But here he simply uses the Passover as a time note. What he is about to narrate took place before the Passover.

John goes on to another note he has stressed, namely Jesus' control of events. He is about to tell us how Jesus was betrayed, arrested, tried, and crucified. It might well appear to the casual observer that the Man from Galilee was overtaken by the swift march of events and overwhelmed by superior force. But that is not the way John sees it. His story is about one who is supremely the master of events and whose sovereignty is nowhere clearer than in those happenings in which he came to be crucified. So now, as he begins to tell us what led up to the death of Jesus, he says that Jesus knew it was time for him to leave this world. John does not say "time for him to die" or anything like that. He says that "the hour had come for him to go out of this world to the Father." Here "the hour" links up with several references in the earlier part of the Gospel, "go out" reads like someone going on a journey rather than being arrested and executed, and "to the Father" brings out the wonderful destination that lay before him. This is no feeble loser, but the strong Son of God, fulfilling that for which he came into the world.

It is typical of John that he goes on to speak of Jesus' love. The cross, above all things, shows us the greatness of that love, and it is fitting that as he comes to his climax there should be a strong emphasis on love. Whereas in chapters 1–12 John has used the noun *love* and the verb *to love* nine times, he has them thirty times in chapters 13–17. Love is a dominant theme in the story of what went on in the Upper Room. Now John tells us that Jesus loved "his own who were in the world"; they belong to him no matter what, but they are still subject to all the trials and troubles that this world brings. They should not forget that Jesus loves them, even though they suffer constantly what Shakespeare calls "the slings and arrows of outrageous fortune." We may not understand why we are subject to the trials we experience, but we can understand that through them all we are the objects of the love of our Lord. John says "he loved them to the end," where we might translate, as Rieu does, "now he showed how utterly he loved them." The one expression sometimes means "to the end" and sometimes "utterly." Both are true and it may well be that John wants us to see them both.

There are some slight differences in the manuscripts at this point (v. 2), and they affect the way we are to understand the passage. But it seems that the best text tells us that it was "during supper" that Jesus took action (some manuscripts have "supper being ended," as KJV). The word for "supper" is that which means the main meal of the day, usually a meal in the evening. That Jesus should move during the meal itself was most unusual. People had their feet washed when they came to a house, not during the course of a meal. To wash them at such a point was to draw attention to the action and mark it as unusual and significant. The disciples would never forget it.

Most translations go on to say that the devil had put it into the heart of Judas to betray Jesus, and this may be the way to take it. But the Greek of the best manuscripts means something like "the devil already having put into the heart that Judas son of Simon Iscariot should betray him." Some manuscripts do indeed read "the heart of Judas," but this is probably not the right reading. "The devil having put into the heart" means "the devil having made up his mind" (the heart was seen as the center of thought, not only of the emotions as with us). John is telling us that the evil one had his place in bringing about the crucifixion. God is able to use even Satan to effect his purpose.

Washing the Feet

John is beginning his crucifixion narrative and will shortly tell us of Judas' slipping out to betray Jesus. We might expect something like "Jesus knew what Judas would do" or some indication of the greatness of the peril in which Jesus found himself. In the eyes of contemporary rulers Jesus was unimportant, and anyway he would be killed within a matter of hours. It is accordingly an audacious statement that at this moment Jesus knew "that the Father had given all things into his hands" (v. 3). All things! From the standpoint of this world Jesus was staring disaster in the face. He was about to be killed and his few followers were about to desert him for fear of the enemy. But Jesus knew that the Father had given him "all things." The heavenly perspective is not that of earth. We see this also in the further statement that "he had come out from God"; even in this trying moment there was not the slightest doubt of his heavenly origin. He was not a reformer from Nazareth trying to impose a Galilean perspective on the leaders in Judea. He had come from God to execute a divine plan. Now that plan was about to come to its consummation, so he "was going to God." This is a sublime statement of the difference between the worldly and the heavenly ways of viewing things.

At a meal in those days people did not sit on chairs (a slave might sit for a meal but not a free person!), but reclined on couches. A couch would hold three persons, and each would lean on the left elbow with the head towards the table and the feet away from it. We find now that Jesus got up from his place at table and prepared to wash the disciples' feet (v. 4). The washing of people's feet would normally have been done earlier. There were few paved roads, and people had no equivalent of our socks or stockings; they simply wore open sandals on their feet. As they walked on dusty roads it was inevitable that their feet would become dirty (and, if it was at all hot, smelly as well). It was thus a courtesy usually extended to guests to have a slave wash their feet when they arrived at a house. Clearly on this occasion there was no slave, and if feet were to be washed it would have to be one of the little band who did it. But who wants to perform a menial task like washing dirty, smelly feet? Clearly everyone had quietly by-passed the task, hoping that someone else would do it. But nobody did, and now Jesus drew attention to the oversight by doing it himself.

He "rises from the supper" (the present tense makes it all so very vivid) and puts off his garments (which would get in the way in such a task). John may mean that he divested himself of his outer robe, but it is perhaps more likely that Jesus stripped to his loincloth (like a slave). He "girded himself," which means that he put a long towel around his waist in such a way that the end of it was free to be used in wiping the feet. A minor point is the meaning of the word I have translated "basin" and which occurs nowhere before this passage. It is thus not a well-known word and we can say for certain only that it has something to do with washing. It may be a basin, but it is also possible that it means a jug. People would not wash in a basin like we might but would use a jug to pour water over the feet and then catch it in a basin. The word could mean either implement, but perhaps "basin" is more likely. Jesus then began to wash the disciples' feet and to dry them with the towel.

"Not Me, Lord"

Apparently nobody said anything until Jesus reached Peter. The disciples would all have been disturbed and ashamed, so they said nothing. There was a deadly hush. But Peter was not going to stand for this sort of thing, so when his turn came he remonstrated with Jesus (v. 6).

Jesus' reply was "What I am doing you do not know now, but you will know afterwards" (v. 7). We do well to reflect on this. Peter saw only that the one he revered as Lord and Master was taking the place of a slave to serve him, and he did not like it; it was not the way Peter wanted to have things done. So he objected. It is easy for the Lord's servant to take up such an attitude, and we all do this from time to time. But God's purposes are worked out despite our blindness. At any given time it is likely that we do not know what God is doing, though if we look back we can say with the hymn writer, "All the way my Savior leads me." It is well accordingly that we learn to trust where we cannot see.

But Peter was probably too deeply stirred to take much notice of what Jesus was saying. He was preoccupied with the fact that Jesus proposed to wash his feet, and he did not see this as at all fitting. So he says very emphatically, "You will certainly not wash my feet" and adds "for ever" (v. 8) to show that he is not referring only to the present moment. He knows his place and he will stay in it "for ever." There is humility here that we cannot but admire. But there is also stubbornness that we cannot but deplore.

Jesus' response is "If I do not wash you you have no part with me." We are moving now into some understanding of the meaning of the symbolism in Jesus' action. Obviously he did not mean that nothing mattered other than the washing of the feet at that particular meal. We cannot think that if Peter had his feet washed on that one occasion he belonged to Jesus forever. It was what the washing of the feet symbolized that mattered. Jesus was about to die, to die the atoning death that meant cleansing for his people. There is no other way of being Christ's than in receiving the cleansing he died to bring. If he does not wash us in this way, we have no part with him. The washing of the feet of the disciples was a parable in action. It is only in accepting the truth that we cannot secure our salvation by our own effort, but that Christ can cleanse all who trust him, that we are freed from our sin and brought into Christ's salvation.

Now Peter certainly did not want to be excluded from those who belong to Christ. His response is characteristic: "Lord" (he takes the lowly place) "not my feet only but also my hands and my head" (v. 9). If Jesus is going to do the thing, let it be done wholeheartedly. So Peter suggests not a mere washing of the feet but of other parts of the body as well. There is genuine humility here, but there is also pride. Peter is still not accepting Jesus' way but laying down his own terms. This is not something at which we can take up a knowing and condescending attitude, as though we are better than Peter was. Is it not the case that we are all prone to tell God the way in which we propose to serve him? To accept God's way is often to do things we would rather not do, and we are adept at finding reasons for doing the "better" things of which we approve.

Jesus takes up the imagery of the situation in which they found themselves. The person who is going out to a meal has a bath before leaving home. It is true that he will pick up dirt and defilement along the dusty way, but if his feet are washed when he arrives he will be "altogether clean" (v. 10). Jesus is giving some teaching that they will presently understand in connection with his death. That death will be like the bath: it will cleanse them wholly. But life is a difficult affair, and from time to time they will pick up defilement from the evil world in which they live. Then they will need to come back to their Lord for cleansing. Some commentators see a parallel in our use of baptism and holy communion. We are baptized once and for all, but we come to communion over and over.

Jesus is confident of the little band and knows that they are "clean." But he knows also that there is a traitor among them, so he adds "but not all." Judas could not be included among those who were cleansed by Christ; he did not respond with heart and soul to Jesus' offer of cleansing. So, although he was numbered with the Twelve, he was not part of them in any meaningful sense. We should notice John's emphasis on the fact that throughout his passion narrative Jesus was always in command of the situation, even though appearances might indicate otherwise. He was going to die for the sins of the world, and all the movements of friend and foe did but set forward his purpose. So now John makes it clear that Jesus was not going to be overtaken with surprise when it was revealed that there was a traitor in the ranks: "For he knew who was betraying him" (v. 11).

The Meaning of It All

Jesus washed the feet of all of them (v. 12), evidently including Judas. Knowing what he did about the traitor, this is evidence of a deep love and compassion for sinners that we should not pass by too quickly. Even Judas was the recipient of Jesus' loving service. Then Jesus took his clothes again and resumed his place. He proceeded to make the disciples think about what had happened. The washing of the disciples' feet was a very meaningful action. It is often pointed out that it was a lesson in humility and this, of course, is both true and important. Pride is never a Christian virtue, and Jesus set the example that he wishes us to follow.

But we must not see this as all that the footwashing meant. The incident took place in the shadow of the cross, and the words that are used for Jesus' laying aside his garments and taking them again are the same as those used of his laying down his life and taking it again in the teaching about the Good Shepherd (10:17). Again, if what was happening was only a lesson in humility, then Jesus' conversation with Peter misses the whole point. Jesus does not speak of being proud and humble, but of cleansing, that cleansing that he would effect, and of belonging to him. We must see this story first and foremost as a way of setting out in actions the truth that Christ brings cleansing and that no one else does. A. M. Hunter says that the "deeper meaning" of this incident "is that there is no place in his fellowship for those who have not been cleansed by his atoning death. The episode dramatically symbolizes the truth enunciated in 1 John 1:7, 'We are being cleansed from every sin by the blood of Jesus.'"

Jesus invites his followers to think about what he has done (v. 12). This makes it clear that his action was not simply a way of overcoming a minor social embarrassment. It was meaningful, and the disciples should think about it. I have translated his opening as a question, and so it may well be. But it could be understood as an imperative: "Know [or understand] what I have done to you." Either way, the disciples are reminded that they habitually think of Jesus as their Teacher and as their Lord (v. 13). "Teacher" was equivalent to "Rabbi" and shows that they saw him as the one who would give them instruction. In a day when not many people owned books a teacher was a very significant person, and it was important for the little band that they could look to Jesus for authoritative instruction in the things of God.

They also called him "Lord," and this was not nearly so usual. The term was used of a variety of lordships, such as that of the owner of slaves or property, or a person in high position (like the "lord" in a country like England). It could be a title of respect, used for example of the head of a family or the master of a house. But it was also employed by religious people to designate the god they worshiped, and we find it used of the emperor when the Romans began to see him as divine. It was used of the true God by those who had learned of him from the Old Testament. So to call Jesus "Lord" might mean much or little; the disciples might simply be using a title of respect or they might be thinking of Jesus in the highest terms open to them. This was certainly the way they used it after the resurrection (cf. 20:28), but it is not clear just how full a content they gave it at this time. But we are surely not wrong in seeing it as an exalted title. Jesus accepts both titles ("for I am").

He really was their leader. In earthly leaderships there is often a lack. I have read of Maurice Ravel that, though he was a fine composer, he was not a great conductor. It happened that one day he was to conduct an orchestra as they played his *Bolero.* One of the musicians, anxious to please, said to him, "Maestro, I'll keep my eyes on you all the time!" "Don't do that," Ravel replied. "Just play with your usual rhythm and I'll try to go along with you." Now that is no way for a leader to behave. A leader is to lead, even if he should at the same time take notice of the way his subordinates think and act.

Jesus cared for his disciples, but he left no doubt that he was their leader and that he expected them to follow. These words lead to a demand that the disciples follow the example he had set them. It is not clear whether we should understand the words of verse 14 as "If I have washed your feet *because* I am your Lord and Master" or "If I have washed your feet *although* I am your Lord and Master." Either makes good sense and brings out an important truth. Perhaps, as often in this Gospel, the double meaning is intended and we should appropriate both aspects. It is certainly true that among Christians being in a high place does not absolve from lowly service; heads of denominations are people who should perform lowly service. It is also true that this arises precisely because lowly service is a function of leadership as Christians know it. "You also ought to wash one another's feet," Jesus says, where his *you* is emphatic. They are not spectators in the business of serving the Lord Christ, but participants. It is important accordingly that they take to heart what Jesus has done and apply it to their own circumstances. This is not particularly easy, and Temple makes the point that "We would gladly wash the feet of our Divine Lord; but He disconcertingly insists on washing ours, and bids us wash our neighbour's feet." But it is in lowly service of other people that the genuineness of our Christian profession is brought out. And Jesus goes on to say that what he has done he has done as an example to them (v. 15). Again there is emphasis on *you;* this is something that is relevant to every Christian and we must not think that Jesus is talking about someone else.

We must not think or act as though we were greater than Christ. As we have seen elsewhere, "Truly, truly I tell you" (v. 16) is Jesus' way of drawing attention to what follows as something specially important or emphatic. The slave, Jesus says, is not greater than his owner (the word is that which I translated "Lord" in vv. 13–14). The "messenger" is the word usually translated "apostle" in the New Testament. Apostles were people sent with a message and that, of course, is their Christian signification. Christian apostles did many things, but essentially they brought the gospel message to those to whom they were sent. There is a reminder of their function here. They were Jesus' apostles. He would send them out in the not-too-distant future to proclaim his message. Let them remember that this does not give them a position in some way above that of Jesus. The giver of the message is superior to the messenger.

This section finishes with a blessing on those who not only "know these things" but who "do them" (v. 17). In our modern world, with all its emphasis on education and on knowledge, there is always a tendency to be content with the acquisition of knowledge. For the Christian that is not enough. For the Christian the important thing is to act on what we know. And this part of John's Gospel has taught us to know that lowly service is that to which we are called.

59

Betrayal

"I am not speaking about all of you; I know whom I have chosen, but, in order that the Scripture may be fulfilled 'He who eats my bread has lifted up his heel against me'—. Now I am telling you before it happens so that when it happens you may believe that I am. Truly, truly I tell you, he who receives whomever I shall send receives me and he who receives me receives him who sent me."

When Jesus had said these things he was troubled in spirit and he testified in these words, "Truly, truly I tell you that one of you will betray me." The disciples looked at one another, perplexed about whom he was speaking. Now there was reclining on Jesus' breast one of his disciples whom Jesus loved; Simon Peter accordingly makes signs to this man to inquire who it was about whom he was speaking. So that man leant back, as he was, on Jesus' breast and says to him, "Lord, who is it?" Jesus replies, "It is that man for whom I shall dip the bread and give it to him." So he dipped the bread and gives it to Judas, son of Simon Iscariot. And after the bread Satan then entered that man. So Jesus says to him, "What you are doing do more quickly." None of those reclining at table knew for what reason he said this to him, for some thought that since Judas had the money-box Jesus was saying to him, "Buy what we need for the feast," or that he should give something to the poor. Having received the bread that man went out straight away. Now it was night (John 13:18–30).

None of the Twelve comes out of the passion narrative very well. At the critical moment they all abandoned Jesus and ran away

(Mark 14:50), but none appears in a worse light than Judas, for he did more than adopt the negative attitude of running away: he actively betrayed Jesus into the hands of his enemies. He must have had some idealism earlier on or he would not have joined the little band of Jesus' followers. But evidently he had become disillusioned for some reason. It has been conjectured that this was because Jesus made no attempt to overthrow his enemies or, taking a very different line, because of Jesus' association with the wrong kind of people, tax collectors and sinners. Some have thought that Judas really was fanatically loyal and that the betrayal was not with a view to having Jesus executed, but rather was an attempt to put him in a position where he would have to put forth his power and take decisive action against his foes. This, however, is a romantic notion not borne out by any of the facts known to us. John has told us that Judas was dishonest (12:6), and disappointed avarice must have played some part in it all. Thirty pieces of silver is so small an amount, however, that it is unlikely that this was the whole story.

We have no way of knowing for sure why Judas did what he did. None of the Gospel writers goes into that question, and all the suggestions made in modern times are conjectures. Probably Judas had mixed motives, some of which may possibly have been creditable. But all that we know for certain is that the desire to make some gain for himself was one of his aims. None of the Gospel writers is trying to give us a full account of the man and his motives. What they are concerned with is what happened. They tell us the facts and leave us to draw our own conclusions.

John tells us of the betrayal right after the footwashing. He goes from the attitude that Jesus looks for from his followers (a readiness to perform lowly service) to the very opposite (a desire to have one's own way and make one's own profit). And he begins by drawing attention to a fact he has brought out throughout his narrative, namely that God has his great purpose and he works it out despite what people may do, even evil people. Jesus has said that those who follow the example he set in washing the disciples' feet are blessed (v. 17); now he says that he was not speaking about them all (v. 18). He goes on to his knowledge of those who are his own. The divine choice is important throughout the New Testament, and Jesus says here, "I know whom I have chosen." He was not deceived by the machinations of Judas or, for that matter, by the inconsistencies of Peter. He knew the fundamental baseness of the one and the fundamental loyalty of the other. No, it was not that the situation was in any way getting out of hand. Jesus knew the Twelve and knew that the plan of God would be worked out through them. He saw the betrayal as foretold in Scripture, which meant that inevitably it must happen. Judas was not in control of the situation, but God was working out his plan, a plan in which Judas simply played his part. This does not mean that in some way Judas was compelled to be a villain. Rather, being the kind of man he was, he would do what he saw as best for himself in the situation in which he found himself. And Jesus is saying that this was known to God and that God used it in working out his purpose.

The passage Jesus quotes is from Psalm 41:9. The eating of bread together points to fellowship and friendship. Easterners took very seriously the implications of sharing meals together. This meant peace and harmony and made hostile actions against those with whom one had eaten especially horrible. To lift up the heel against someone may be taken from the action of a horse as it prepares to kick. Or it may have something to do with shaking the dust off one's feet in leaving a hostile town (Luke 9:5; 10:11). Whatever the precise significance, it surely points to a hostile act and a hostile act, moreover, coming from someone who ought to be behaving with friendship.

Jesus might well have simply gone through what lay ahead of him and done no more than let the events unfold. But even in these dark hours for him he bore in mind the disciples and the bewilderment and loss they would so soon be feeling. He took thought for them and therefore told them of the betrayal at this point. They might not understand all that it meant then and there, but at some later time it would be a help to them. When they reflected on the events now beginning they would recall that Jesus had foretold the betrayal and would, as he says, "believe that I am" (v. 19). He was in control and simply went ahead on the path of obedience to his Father. We have seen the mysterious "I am" before and noted that this expression contains an implied claim to being greater than any man. It is the language of deity, and this evidence of Jesus' foreknowledge would in due course strengthen their conviction that he shared in the nature of God.

This is further brought out with the statement that to receive anyone that Jesus sends is to receive him, and to receive him is to receive no less than the One who sent him, the Father (v. 20). The fact that Jesus had been sent by the Father runs through and through this Gospel. And the truth that he was on a divine mission meant that people who received him were brought close to the heavenly Father. It is, of course, still the case that the way to fellowship with the Father is to receive the Son.

Betrayal Foretold

Up to this point Jesus has spoken of opposition that would come from one who should be a friend, but he has not said what form that opposition would take. Now he makes it plain. John tells us first that Jesus was "troubled in spirit" (v. 21). This verb has been used of Jesus before (11:33; 12:27); it points to a deep emotional experience and reminds us of the cost to our Lord of going through those events that were to bring us salvation. Although he knew that Judas was going to betray him, he was not unmoved by the prospect. It troubled him deeply and we should not overlook this part of the cost of Jesus' saving work.

John says that Jesus "testified." The verb is a common one in this Gospel, but it mostly refers to the testimony that people bore to Jesus, not to any testimony that he himself bore. Its use here shows that the following statement is important. It is not to be taken lightly. This is further brought out in Jesus' opening words, "Truly, truly." Remember that we have seen this expression throughout this Gospel and noticed that it always puts emphasis on the words that follow. Jesus is about to make not a trivial statement about something unimportant, but a significant pronouncement.

The statement is "One of you will betray me." Jesus leaves it quite general, giving no indication of which one it would be nor of exactly what betrayal means. Since we read the statement with our knowledge of what Judas did, it immediately brings before our minds the thought of the thirty pieces of silver and of the handing over of Jesus to the arresting soldiers. But betrayal can mean being false in lesser ways than that. So, though the statement shows that there was trouble coming, it does not tell the disciples exactly what form that trouble would take.

In any case their minds did not fasten on that. John tells us that they looked at each other and that they were "perplexed about whom he was speaking" (v. 22). They did not at this time wonder what form the betrayal would take. They were concerned about which of them would do such a dreadful thing. Clearly they had no suspicion of Judas. Right up till this time he had evidently covered his tracks very well, and nobody had reason to suspect that he was working against Jesus. But then nobody had reason to suspect anyone else either. It was all very puzzling.

In the other Gospels we find that they asked, "Lord, is it I?" (Matt. 26:22; Mark 14:19). This means that they probably thought that the betrayal would be inadvertent. No one would be asking whether he would willfully and deliberately betray his Lord. Each would be the first to know that about himself. But their questions opened the possibility that somehow one of them would say or do something that would bring harm to Jesus.

Seating Arrangements

To follow the next part of the narrative it is necessary to know something of the way people ate their meals in first-century Palestine. We do not have complete information, but—presuming that things did not change much over the years—some of the later references may help. People did not sit at the table, as we take for granted, but reclined on couches with their heads towards the table and their feet away from it. The couches were arranged round the table in the form of a U, with the principal couch at the junction of the two arms. Usually each couch held three persons (they were called *triklinia*). The host would recline on a couch at the head of the table, with the most honored guest on his left (or behind him) and the next on his right (or in front of him). Each diner would recline on his left elbow and use his right hand to take food.

On this occasion John was clearly the one on Jesus' right, and it could be said that he reclined on Jesus' breast. We can only guess at the places of the others, but it is obvious that Peter was some distance away, for he had to make signs to John. Equally clearly, Judas was not far from Jesus, for the Master could dip some bread in the common dish and hand it to him. It is possible that Judas (the treasurer of the little band) was in the place of highest honor and that this was something in the nature of a final appeal to him. There is, of course, no way of being sure of this, but it is an attractive possibility.

The Beloved Disciple

John proceeds to refer to "one of his disciples whom Jesus loved" (v. 23). This description is given a number of times in this Gospel (19:26; 21:7, 20; and with the change of the verb from *agapao* to *phileo* in 20:2). He is never named, and some scholars think that he was Lazarus, on the grounds that we are told that Jesus loved that man (11:3, 5, 36). This must remain a possibility, but it is not easy to see that Lazarus is meant each time the disciple whom Jesus loved is mentioned. This same disciple is included in the fishing party in 21:2, and there we have the names of Peter, Thomas, Nathanael, and the sons of Zebedee. He was certainly not Peter, for in the present passage Peter was beckoning to him. There is no reason for equating him with Thomas or Nathanael, which leaves us with the sons of Zebedee or the two unnamed disciples. James the son of Zebedee was martyred early (Acts 12:2), and as the Beloved Disciple clearly lived for a long time (21:20–23) this rules him out. We are left with John or one of the unnamed disciples.

While it is not impossible to rule them out altogether, there are some indications that John is meant. The Beloved Disciple is linked with Peter (e.g., 20:2), and Peter and John are mentioned together on a number of occasions (as Acts 3:1; 4:13; Gal. 2:9). There is also the curious fact that the apostle John is not mentioned by name anywhere in this Gospel, though the other three Gospels show that he was an important member of the apostolic band. With this we should take the fact that the writer of this Gospel calls John the Baptist simply "John," although he is careful to distinguish the names of other people who might be confused with one another (e.g., 14:22). It would be natural for John the apostle to speak of the Baptist simply as "John," but anyone else would surely want to indicate which John he had in mind. All this comes short of absolute proof, but it is clear that it is very likely that the apostle John was the Beloved Disciple. That is the way the evidence points.

Who Is It?

The Beloved Disciple, then, was reclining on Jesus' breast and Peter was some distance away. He made signs to the Beloved Disciple that he should ask Jesus who the traitor was (v. 24). The narrative is very vivid, the present tense John uses bringing the scene before the reader's eyes. So John leaned back and asked Jesus, "Lord, who is it?" (v. 25). It would have been possible for Jesus to have whispered the name, but he chose to indicate the person by an action. He said that he would pass on to him a piece of bread that he would first dip in the common dish. This conversation must have taken place quietly, for there is no indication that any of the others in the group overheard any of it. But it meant that John would speedily come to know the identity of the betrayer.

Up till now I have spoken of Jesus as saying he would dip some bread in the dish, but perhaps we should notice that John does not tell us exactly what would be dipped. The word he uses is a diminutive with a meaning like "a little bit," "a morsel" *(psomion).* It is used four times in this account and nowhere else in the New Testament. Some scholars think that it referred to a small piece of meat, for bread would be at the disposal of them all. But this is scarcely conclusive, for as far as we know so would the meat be. We should probably understand it as a small piece of bread. From this narrative it seems to be a mark of honor (in which case nobody other than John would have any idea that Jesus was using it as a sign). But there does not appear to be any evidence that this was a normal procedure or that giving such a piece of food was regarded as a compliment. One scholar holds that it was a warning for Judas, but how he would know it was a warning and what he was being warned of are not clear. All that we know for sure is that it was Jesus' way of marking Judas out to John as the traitor. Notice the careful way he is described, "Judas, son of Simon Iscariot." John leaves us in no doubt as to who is meant.

Satan

John has previously told us that the devil had made up his mind that Judas would betray Jesus (v. 2). Now that the betrayal is imminent he tells us that Satan "entered" Judas (v. 27). The betrayal was the work of a sinful man; we should be clear on that. But it was also the work of Satan. Satan cooperated with human weakness to do what he wanted, and what he wanted was to oppose Jesus. And we should never forget that God is able to use the worst deeds of sinful people and of the evil one himself to bring about his good and perfect will. So here we see the sin of Judas and the sin of Satan and the purpose of God to bring salvation, all at work at the same time.

Jesus told Judas to get on with what he was about to do. He had come to die for the sins of the world and now that the climax was approaching he wanted no delay. Translations usually tell us that Jesus told Judas to act "quickly" and this may be what is meant. But the word used is a comparative and strictly means "more quickly." It is true that it is often used in the sense "quickly," but on this occasion perhaps we should take it in the strict sense. Judas was going to betray Jesus and probably had his own timetable for the process. But it was Jesus, not Judas, who would determine when it would all take place. So he gives instructions to Judas to move more quickly.

Jesus' words to Judas said nothing about betrayal, and John tells us that those at table did not understand what was going on (v. 28). It would have seemed to the apostles quite impossible that Jesus would actually encourage the work of betrayal, and it probably never entered their heads that Judas was about to engage in any such mission. John tells us that their thoughts centered round the fact that Judas had the money-box and that accordingly they thought that Jesus was talking to him about some financial matter (v. 29). They thought that perhaps there was some purchase to be made for the feast or a gift to be given to the poor (it is not without interest that even so poor a group as Jesus and his little band took it for granted that money would be given to those who were poorer).

So Judas immediately "went out" (v. 30). Whether or not he knew the significance of the bread, Jesus' words to the whole group about betrayal and his instruction to Judas to act more quickly showed plainly that Jesus was aware of the plan to betray him. After this Judas would not delay his departure one minute beyond what was necessary. Who could tell what would happen to him if the disciples came to understand fully what Jesus was saying? It was best on all counts to move as quickly as possible.

"Now it was night," John says. This is the recollection of someone who was there. John remembered the darkness into which Judas went. And he surely means his readers to realize that this darkness was more than physical. There was black, grim darkness in the soul of Judas Iscariot.

60

A New Commandment

So when he had gone out Jesus says, "Now has the Son of man been glorified and God has been glorified in him. (If God has been glorified in him) God will also glorify him in himself and he will glorify him straight away. Little children, I am with you for a little while yet. You will look for me and as I told the Jews 'Where I am going you cannot come' so now I tell you. A new commandment I give you, that you love one another; that you love one another just as I have loved you. In this all will know that you are my disciples if you have love among yourselves." Simon Peter says to him, "Lord, where are you going?" Jesus answered him, "Where I am going you cannot follow me now, but you will follow later." Peter says to him, "Lord, why cannot I follow you now? I will lay down my life for you!" Jesus replies, "You will lay down your life for me? Truly, truly I tell you, the rooster will not crow until you deny me three times" (John 13:31–38).

The traitor went out from the little band. This meant two things at least: (1) the genuinely evil element had gone out from among them, and (2) with the betrayal the train of events that would bring about the death of Jesus on Calvary had been set in motion. The disciples, of course, did not know this, but Jesus did. And it opened the way for him to begin his last session of teaching with those who were closest to him. The long discourse in the Upper Room is a particularly important part of Jesus' teaching, and a part that we owe to John. The other Gospels have a much shorter account of what went on in the Upper Room and certainly nothing like what John tells us.

We may perhaps notice that there is a new emphasis in these chapters on certain aspects of Jesus' teaching. John has used the noun *love* only once in his Gospel up to now, but in the Upper Room he has it six times; he has used the corresponding verb seven times but now twenty-four times. Clearly in this last piece of teaching Jesus makes it plain that love is of the first importance.

Another part of the Christian way to be given prominence is joy. Up till now John has used the word *joy* only twice (in the one verse, 3:29), but now, with the cross staring him in the face, Jesus uses the word seven times. The cross meant suffering and sorrow; we must not minimize this. But it also meant joy, for nothing can bring joy like the forgiveness of our sins. Joy is a significant note to be struck in the shadow of the cross.

C. H. Dodd has pointed out that in these chapters there are frequent references to "going" and "coming," and that in fact in the section 13:31—14:31 the longest stretch without a reference to this is only five verses. Now the "going" and "coming" in question are Jesus' going away in death and his coming back in resurrection, so that we see how dominant this thought is in this part of Jesus' discourse. We may well reflect that it is this going away in death that shows us what love means. Apart from that, love would not have its full Christian meaning, for it shows us clearly that Christ's love is a love for sinners and a love that pays the supreme price. We should also reflect that it is the death and resurrection of Christ that brings his followers their great joy. It is the fact that Jesus has put away sin and overcome death that brings the fullest joy to his followers.

Glory

Jesus begins with the note of glory (and expresses it in a very complicated sentence!). We have seen in previous studies that in this Gospel there is a very unusual understanding of "glory." It is not so much a display of majesty and splendor (though now and then it is just that) as the doing of humble service. When someone who could rightfully claim an eminent place forsakes that eminence to do a piece of lowly service, that is true glory. It fits in with this understanding of glory that Jesus, contemplating the cross, says, "Now has the Son of man been glorified" (v. 31). In this Gospel, as in the others, "the Son of man" is Jesus' favorite self-designation, so clearly he is referring here to himself. He uses the past tense in the verb "glorified," which means that he sees the cross as so certain that he can speak of it as over. It has been determined by God: it will assuredly come to pass. And when it comes to pass it will be the supreme manifestation of glory.

But the cross is not only a glorifying of Jesus: it is also a glorifying of the Father. We ought never to separate what the Father and the Son are doing in the bringing about of our salvation. We should not think of Jesus as bringing about the atoning act completely by himself and in isolation from the Father. It was the love of the Father that brought about the cross (3:16; Rom. 5:8). It was God in Christ who was reconciling the world to himself (2 Cor. 5:19). It is the Father who has blessed us in Christ, having chosen us before the foundation of the world (Eph. 1:3–4). We should never forget that our salvation was brought about by none less than God himself. He did it in and through Christ, to be sure. But it is God's salvation nonetheless.

There is some doubt as to whether we should read the words in parentheses at the beginning of verse 32. Some good manuscripts have them and other good manuscripts do not. It is not impossible that they were omitted by some scribes who found the passage too complicated if they were accepted. We should probably accept them. The "if" with which they begin does not indicate any doubt. The Greek construction has the meaning "if [as is the case]. . . ." It is not an easy passage to understand, but it seems that Jesus is looking right through the passion to the resurrection and to his restoration to his place in heaven. He is saying that the Father will be glorified in the cross and that he will glorify the Son when he raises him from the dead. And all this, Jesus is saying, will happen "straight away" (v. 32). He is not talking about what will take place on some distant day, but of what will happen in the immediate future.

Jesus is, then, saying four things:

1. He, the Son of man, is glorified in the cross.
2. The Father is also glorified in the cross.
3. The Father will glorify the Son in raising him and bringing him to heaven.
4. There will be no delay.

"Where You Cannot Come"

But all this will be dreadfully difficult for the disciples to follow as the events unfold. They will be caught up in the horror of what they can see only as disaster. It will be all too easy for them to miss the glory and see only the tragedy. Jesus' concern for them comes out in a further reassurance. He addresses them as "little children" (v. 33), using a tender word (found only here in the Gospels). He loves them and cares for them. It will all happen so soon, for he will be with them only for "a little while yet," and at that moment they could have no notion of how short the "little while" would be.

Jesus repeats to them some words he had used to the Jews (7:33–34; 8:21–22). In this Gospel sayings are not often repeated exactly—there is usually some small change. But the words of 8:21–22 are now repeated exactly. This is the only place I have been able to find in this Gospel where we have exactly the same words in three occurrences of an expression. John evidently saw significance in the words. The cross would mean a separation of Jesus from his friends, just as earlier he had said it would separate him from his enemies. And neither friend nor foe could cross that gap.

Love One Another

"A new commandment," Jesus says, putting the words into a prominent position (v. 34). This is the one place in this Gospel where Jesus uses this word for "new" (it is used also in 19:41 of the "new" tomb in which he was laid). There is another Greek word for "new" that means "recent," whereas this word has about it the notion of "fresh." It is not so much that the commandment has not been given before as that it has a different quality about it, a quality of freshness that differentiates it from any other. The commandment to love was not, of course, in itself a novelty. There was a very old commandment that we should love our neighbor as ourselves (Lev. 19:18). But this commandment is that we should love each other as Jesus loved us.

"Just as I have loved you" is what makes this commandment "new." There had never been a situation in which the sinless Son of God had laid down his life for sinners. Those to whom he was speaking had a quarrel in that very Upper Room as to which of them would be the greatest (Luke 22:24). Soon Jesus would be arrested, and at the critical moment every one of them would run away and leave him to his captors (Mark 14:50). They cannot be picked out as supreme examples of shining virtue. They were sinful men, with the shortcomings that are typical of sinful men. Yet Jesus loved them, loved them so deeply that he was about to go to the cross for them.

And it is love like this that he looks for from them. They are to love as he loved. They are to be loving people and love others despite their demerits. It is natural for us to love those we find attractive. There is no difficulty in this. The world does it all the time. But Jesus is not looking for a worldly attitude from his followers. He is looking for them to be transformed by his love so that they would be loving people. They would love because of what they are through Christ, not because of what the people they love are.

The world does not know a love like this. The world has its own ways of looking at love. I have read somewhere that Lady Cunard was given to asking embarrassing questions and that she once asked Lord Wavell (who did not like talking about things like love), "What do you think about love?" Wavell replied, "Love is like a cigar. If it goes out you can light it again, but it's never the same." Now I know nothing about cigars and the difference between lighting them a first and a second time. But I know that Jesus was not talking about a love that can go out and be rekindled like that. The world knows of attractions that fade and die or fade and come again. But Jesus is not talking about attraction. He is talking about love. And the love that he looks to see in his followers is a love that is the natural outflow from transformed lives. When anyone comes to be in Christ a veritable "new creation" has taken place (2 Cor. 5:17). And a very significant part of this new creation is that the believer loves with a love like that of Christ, not the love for the attractive that is so characteristic of the world.

The world's love is false in other ways. It can be largely a sham. I have read of a clever but unscrupulous author who informed his writing friends that it is a good idea to dedicate a book in words like these: "To the one I love and who knows it." This, he said, costs nothing and invariably gives pleasure to half a dozen people! That love costs nothing and is worth precisely what it costs. But believers should beware of taking their standards from the world's love. That will only lead us astray. We are to love as Jesus loved, with a deep and genuine concern for others and with their best welfare at heart.

Jesus repeats his commandment that they love; it is very important. Then he goes on to say that it is to be the distinguishing mark of believers (v. 35). And it was. Tertullian, who lived towards the end of the second century, said that the heathen said of believers, "Behold, how these Christians love one another!" Minucius Felix reports the comment of a heathen called Caecilius: "They love one another almost before they know one another." This worldly-wise heathen looked down on the Christians. Believers did not have the sense to test out new acquaintances to see whether or not they were the right kind of people before they would give affection. They welcomed people with love! How stupid! Caecilius found this plain ridiculous.

The heathen, of course, were prejudiced against the Christians. They did not like them at all and were ready to spread any slander about them. They ridiculed and opposed them. They put them in jail and executed them. But they were compelled to pay their grudging tribute to Christian love. It was undeniable.

Perhaps even more significant is the unintended tribute paid to the Christians by Lucian of Samosata. This writer was scornful of the Christians and had no good thing to say about them. But he tells a story of a certain confidence trickster named Peregrinus, who at one time in his career came across the Christians. He joined up with them because of their well-known penchant for helping one another. Lucian comments, "If any charlatan and trickster, able to profit by occasion, comes among them, he quickly acquires sudden wealth by imposing upon simple folk." Lucian marveled at their stupidity, we at their sacrificial love.

Such references ought to make modern Christians think hard. There are not many places in our busy, materialistic world where we believers so live as to compel the heathen to bear their testimony to the love we have for one another. On the contrary, they often accuse us of bickering among ourselves, of hardness, of indulging in petty criticisms of one another, of backbiting, of intolerance. I am aware, of course, that so often such comments proceed from people who take no trouble to ascertain the facts and who have their own deep-seated reasons for criticizing Christians. But it wasn't much different in the early centuries. And the fact is that the Christians then were able to give the impression that they loved one another. The same command that was addressed to them applies to us, too. And it is just as true in the twentieth century as in the first that "they will know that we are Christians by our love." Modern Christians should give serious thought to the importance of love for one another.

Peter's Denials Prophesied

It is interesting that Peter passes over Jesus' words about love and fastens on those about his departure. Perhaps he thought the responsibility of loving one another was so obvious and so well carried out that it did not need emphasis. Perhaps he took no notice of the quarrel among them as to which would be the greatest. Perhaps he preferred to follow up what was mysterious rather than what was challenging. So he asked Jesus, "Lord, where are you going?" (v. 36).

Jesus does not answer in the way Peter no doubt wanted. He gives no destination but repeats the words of verse 33 in another form. There are some differences. In the earlier passage the pronoun was plural, applying to all the disciples, whereas on this occasion it is singular; Jesus is speaking of what applies to Peter in particular. In the earlier statement the pronouns "I" and "you" were both emphatic; they stood in contrast to one another. Here there is no such strong contrast. This time Jesus includes the word *now,* whereas it was absent from the earlier statement. It puts an emphasis on the present circumstances. Whatever will be the case in other circumstances, *now* Peter cannot follow. But he is told that he will follow in due course. We reflect that, if tradition is to be believed, in the end Peter laid down his life for his Lord. But that was years away in time and infinitely distant in terms of Christian experience.

At this point Peter is more interested in the mysterious journey that Jesus is about to undergo and from which he is excluded. He asks, "Why cannot I follow you now?" (v. 37). Peter was used to journeying up and down Palestine with Jesus, and he probably had in mind another journey of the same kind. It simply did not make sense to him that he *could not follow.* He had followed Jesus throughout the years of the public ministry. Then why not on this journey?

Perhaps Jesus foresees danger and wants to exclude his servant from potential trouble? Peter wants none of that. So he says, "I will lay down my life for you!" And indeed on one trying day in the years ahead Peter would do just that. But that would be another Peter, a Peter who was not nearly so assured of his own capacities and his own courage, a Peter who had entered more fully into an understanding of the ways of his Lord, a Peter who had been disciplined and prepared through years of serving others as he served his Lord.

The words Peter now uses remind us of the words used of the Good Shepherd (10:11). It may be that John wants us to see that Peter is claiming something that properly belongs to Jesus. It was not Peter but Jesus who would die for others. In fact John may have it in mind that there were two ways in which Peter was in error. First, he was talking about his own death and saying that he was quite ready to die for Jesus. Events were about to show that he was quite wrong about this. When the crunch came he was not ready to die; he ran away with the others and went further by denying his Lord. Second, it was Jesus who was about to die. Peter clearly had his mind set on an ordinary journey of some sort. But Jesus was about to lay down his life for sinners.

Jesus took up Peter's words. "You will lay down your life for me?" (v. 38) queries Peter's statement. There was, of course, truth as well as error in what Peter said. His use of the sword in the Garden shows that there were circumstances in which this apostle was ready to risk all for Christ. But he did not have the courage to stand by his Master when all was lost. Then Peter would become like the rest and run away. Jesus proceeds to prophesy that before the rooster crows Peter will three times deny him.

The prediction evidently shocked Peter, for he took no further part in the discussions in the Upper Room (we next hear of him in 18:10). It was incredible to him that he would fail Jesus in this way. But he did. We are warned that we should not let our optimistic estimate of our human capabilities be our guide. Christians, above all people, should be conscious of their weakness and of their constant need for divine help. All that we have and all that we are we owe to our Lord. It is well accordingly that we be not boastful, but rather that we humbly rely on him for the grace we need in times of trial.

61

Christ, the Way

"Let not your heart be troubled; believe in God, believe in me too. In my Father's house there are many dwelling-places (if it were not so I would have told you), for I go to prepare a place for you. And if I go and prepare a place for you I am coming again and I will receive you to myself, so that where I am you may be too. And you know the way where I am going." Thomas says to him, "Lord, we don't know where you are going; how can we know the way?" Jesus says to him, "I am the way and the truth and the life; nobody comes to the Father except through me. If you had known me, you would have known my Father. But from now you know him and you have seen him" (John 14:1–7).

We take Jesus' words "Let not your heart be troubled" too calmly. All too readily we assume that they are addressed to people in much the same position as we are, and that Jesus meant that in the ordinary trials of an ordinary life we should not easily give way to depression. But, as we read them in John, the words were spoken to a little group of confused men. For Jesus they had left all they had: homes, friends, occupations, everything. And he had just told them that he was going to leave them and that they could not follow him where he was going (13:33). Peter had asked him where he was going and had been told that before cockcrow he would deny Jesus three times (13:36–38). What did it all mean? Obviously some very serious trouble lay ahead of them and that in the immediate future; Jesus was not referring to some remote and distant trial. And in that situation Jesus was saying, "Let not your heart be troubled."

"The heart" was a way of referring to the whole of the inner states—thoughts, feelings, and will—and not just of the emotions, as it usually is with us. Jesus was referring to deep disturbance. And the way he expresses his imperative would naturally be understood in the sense of "Stop letting your heart be troubled," not "Don't let your heart start being troubled." In other words, he was recognizing that they were in fact troubled at heart and was urging them not to continue in that state.

Trust

Why not? Did they not have good reason? Perhaps. But the thing that mattered more than the impending disaster was that they had someone in whom they could trust, and Jesus calls on them to exercise faith. If they really trusted God and Christ, then they would not be in such deep distress.

There is more than one way of understanding the words about believing. This is brought about by the facts that the imperative ("believe") and the indicative ("you believe") are identical in Greek and further that there was practically no punctuation in the earliest manuscripts. We could translate with two imperatives as I have done, or we could have two indicatives: "You believe in God and you also believe in me." Or there could be one of each: "You believe in God, believe in me too" or "Believe in God, you also believe in me." Then there is punctuation. We could have a question or two: "Do you believe in God? And do you believe in me?" "Do you believe in God? Believe in me, too," or "You believe in God; do you believe in me, too?"

We could carry this further by using commas and a dash or two. I think some translations are ruled out in that they imply that believing in God is something quite different from believing in Christ, whereas in this Gospel they go together. It seems to me that the best way of taking the words is to understand them both as imperatives, but certainly other ways of understanding them are quite possible. It is not impossible that John wants us to see more than one of these ways—he often uses language that can be taken in more ways than one and seems to want his readers to accept the multiple meanings.

But, however we translate, the main point is that Jesus is telling the disciples that in the troubles that lie ahead they must put their trust in their heavenly Father and in him. Trust in the one implies trust in the other, and it is this trust that will sustain them, no matter what their difficulties. Their own strength will not be sufficient, but divine aid will be given them. They can trust God to see them through.

"In My Father's House . . ."

Jesus looks to triumph rather than to tribulation (v. 2). Traditionally his words have been understood to refer to the "many mansions" in heaven. The Greek word translated in the King James Version as "mansions" is found only here and in verse 23 in the New Testament. It is connected with the verb that means "to abide, dwell," which is used quite often in chapter 15. It points to places to stay. The translation "mansions" is due to the fact that when Jerome translated the New Testament into Latin he used the word *mansiones* at this point, and the King James translators used the English word that came closest to that. But the Latin word means "lodging-places"; it refers to places to stay and not to elaborate houses.

Some people emphasize the temporary character they see implied in the idea of places to stay and hold that Jesus is talking about God's provision for us as we make our way through this life. There are many places for rest and spiritual refreshment, and we should make use of them all. This is true, of course, but it does not appear to be what Jesus is saying. "My Father's house" would be a curious description of this world; further, it is not easy to think of stages on a journey as being found within a house. It is much better to see "my Father's house" as referring to heaven and to understand Jesus to mean that in heaven there is room for all; there are "many" places to dwell.

"If it were not so I would have told you" emphasizes the point. If there were any real cause for concern about God's provision for his people, Jesus' whole teaching would have been very different. These words bring comfort and assurance to the troubled. It seems to me that they are best taken as a parenthesis, and I have translated them that way. But perhaps we should notice that it is possible to see them instead as a question closely linking them with the words that follow: "If it were not so would I have told you that I go to prepare a place for you?" But this raises a problem, for Jesus has not so far told them that he is going to prepare a place for them. Of course, it is possible to say that this is part of his unrecorded teaching (cf. 21:25). But we should not appeal to what has not been written if there is a better way of taking the words, and that seems to be the case here. Jesus is assuring his followers that they have every reason for trust. They know him and if there were not the dwelling-places in heaven of which he now speaks, his whole teaching would have been different.

"I Will Come Again"

Jesus adds, "I go to prepare a place for you." We have an advantage over the Twelve in the Upper Room in that we know, as they did not, that

Jesus' earthly ministry was at an end. Within hours he would die to put away sin and would not come back to resume the kind of life they had known with him. So we know that his going to "prepare a place" does not refer to finding an earthly dwelling of any sort. He may be referring in an unusual way to the cross; his death for sinners would be the means of making it possible for them to enter heaven in due course. If the meaning is that he will prepare in heaven a place for each of his followers, then the words refer to some activity that we cannot understand while we are still in this life.

From the thought of going away Jesus proceeds to the certainty of his coming back (v. 3). He repeats that his going is connected with his preparation of a place for them; they are not for one moment to think that he will forget them or that his departure is not concerned with their welfare. And, as certainly as he will go, he will come back. In this Gospel there are not a great number of references to the second coming; John is more concerned with what happened at the first coming. But now and then he reminds his readers that Jesus will certainly come back in due course, and his recording of these words of our Lord shows that he had it in mind. Jesus uses the present tense: "I am coming again," or "I come again." On this tense a standard grammar remarks: "In confident assertions regarding the future, a vivid, realistic present may be used for the future." The second coming is so certain that Jesus can speak of it as present. Let there be no doubt: it will certainly come about.

And Jesus links that coming with the receiving of his people to himself. His tender concern for his own looks through the cross with all its horror, through the resurrection with all its triumph, through the ascension with its sense of the completion of the life of the Incarnate One, through the waiting we already count in centuries, to what matters intensely to his waiting people: "I will receive you to myself." The love of Jesus never loses sight of his people and he looks for the day when, all our trials over, he will receive us.

Jesus goes on ". . . so that where I am you may be too." Both his "I" and his "you" are emphatic, and in the Greek the two pronouns come together: "I and you." The effect is to emphasize the truth that the aim of it all is unclouded fellowship between the Savior and the saved. The construction emphasizes purpose. Jesus is not talking about an aimless sequence of events that somehow in the end will work out all right. Nor is he referring to a strife between good and evil, which as it happens will take place and as it happens with a happy outcome. He is speaking about a firm divine purpose. It is God's plan that Jesus will come back in due course in order that he and his followers may be together in heaven.

We should notice, further, that Jesus gives no description of the heavenly state other than that his followers will be where he is. Through the centuries Christians have made a big deal of harps and crowns, of angels singing round the throne, and so forth. Part of all of this may conceivably be correct. But the one really important thing is that we will be with the Lord. As the hymn writer puts it, "Where Jesus is, 'tis heaven there." Whatever else heaven may hold, the most wonderful part of it will be the fact that we will be with our Lord forever.

The Way

The manuscripts differ at this point. Those behind the King James Version read "And whither I go ye know, and the way ye know" (v. 4), but most scholars agree that it is better to follow the shorter text: "And where I am going you know the way." The shorter expression almost invites scribes to expand it a little, whereas there is no good reason for a scribe to abbreviate the longer version if he had it before him.

Whichever way we take it, Jesus affirms that the disciples know the way. He switches attention from the destination to the path the disciples must tread in order to reach it. He is not announcing some new and very different path that the disciples must take in view of the fact that he is about to be parted from them. Through the years of their association he has been busy teaching them. They ought to know how they should follow him, whether in fact they do so or not. There has been nothing obscure about the instruction he has given them unceasingly. So now he reminds them of it all.

But Thomas is puzzled. There is a certain honesty and determination about this follower of Jesus. Earlier he had urged his fellows to go to Jerusalem with Jesus in order to die with him (11:16). There is, of course, a gloominess about his words, but there is also a determination to face facts and a willingness to be with Jesus in death (which Thomas was not able to keep up when the crunch came). At a later time he would not take the word of the rest of the apostolic band about the resurrection, but laid it down with the utmost firmness that he wanted proof (20:24–25; he could not keep that up either, for the sight of the risen Lord was enough). So now it is not surprising that it is Thomas who says, "Lord, we don't know where you are going," and who asks, "How can we know the way?"

We can understand his perplexity about Jesus' destination. Peter had expressly asked Jesus where he was going (13:36), and the answer had not revealed the destination. Twice Jesus had said that where he was going they could not come (13:33, 36). For Thomas that was an insuperable obstacle. They did not know the destination, so how could they possibly know the way to it?

Though Jesus had not said so, he knew that he was going to the Father (13:3), and in due course he would tell the disciples plainly that this is what would happen (16:5, 10, 17). But at this point it is the way on which he concentrates attention: he says, "I am the way" (v. 6). This is another of the sayings with the emphatic "I am," expressed in the language of deity. Jesus says not simply that he teaches people the way, but that he himself *is* the way. It is a most unusual thing to have a person described as "the way," and not as pointing people to the way or the like. We should bear in mind that Jesus not only taught people the way, but that he was about to die on the cross to put away their sins. In this he was making it possible for people to come to God; in fact, he *was* the way.

With this he joins "and the truth and the life." This is the one place in this Gospel where an "I am" saying has three parts to the predicate (there are two when Jesus says, "I am the resurrection and the life" [11:25], but three are found here only). As we have seen in earlier studies, truth is a very important concept in this Gospel. John knows that there is a good deal of error among the Jewish teachers and indeed some falsehood, as when men like Caiaphas, who were bound by their office to set forward truth and justice, instead perverted that office into a source of political and even financial advancement. But truth points us to that complete honesty that characterized Jesus in all that he said and did. His teaching was the truth, and it pointed his hearers to God. John has made it clear that truth may be a quality of actions as well as of words (3:21), and Jesus' whole life was true: he set forward the truth in all his actions. So it can be said that he is "the truth."

But truth is concerned also with "the truth of the gospel," as Paul puts it (Gal. 2:5). It is this sort of thing that is in mind when Jesus says that those who abide in his word are his disciples; they will know the truth and the truth will set them free (8:31–32). Truth is closely connected with the Christ when John writes that "grace and truth came through Jesus Christ" (1:17) or says that the Word was "full of grace and truth" (1:14). In recording this saying, then, John is reminding his readers that the truth that connects with salvation connects equally with Jesus.

The third thing Jesus says is that he is "the life." He has said this before, when he spoke of being "the resurrection and the life" (11:25). The life that is life indeed is something that he brings, and he alone brings it. There is no eternal life apart from Christ.

We should not miss the courage that this saying demands in the shadow of the cross. In a few hours Jesus would have been killed by people who vigorously opposed the way of God, but he could say, "I am the way." In the face of the approaching victory of evil people whose lies would bring about his death, Jesus could say, "I am the truth." And although his lifeless body would be put in a tomb so soon he could say, "I am the life." There is thus real courage in the declaration. But there is more than courage; there is deep understanding of the ways of God. The apparent victory of evil on that first Good Friday would not spell final triumph. It was illusory, for the real victor on Calvary was the Crucified One.

Knowing the Father

Jesus goes on to the thought of knowing the Father, which was so very important. Later we find that to know God and Jesus Christ is itself life eternal; it is not something that leads to life eternal but it *is* that life (17:3). Jesus says, "If you had known me" (v. 7), where the construction implies that they in fact did *not* know him. Obviously there was a sense in which they did know him. Had they not left all in order to be with him? And had they not spent a matter of years in following him, absorbing his teaching, and seeing the wonderful things he did? Jesus' meaning is not that they were totally ignorant of him, but rather that there were some very important things about him that they did not know, which meant that they did not know his essential being.

And that means that they did not really know the Father, the God they had professed to worship all their lives. The point here is that Jesus had come as the revelation of the Father. It is the Christ, the only-begotten God (1:18), who had shown who and what the Father really is. Apart from Christ's revelation, all knowledge of the Father is defective. The events of the next few hours, with the disciples' complete misunderstanding of the significance of the cross and with the failure of every one of them to stand with Jesus in his hour of trial, were to show that they did not really know Jesus and that accordingly they did not really know God.

But now all was about to change. "From now" points to a different set of circumstances. Jesus does not mean that at that very minute a change was taking place, but he is saying that the present events were the critical ones. Even as he spoke, the betrayal was on the way, and that meant that the action that would bring God's salvation was fairly launched. It would be a few weeks before the disciples came to appreciate the full significance of all this, but the process had already begun and Jesus can speak of it as accomplished. It was what would happen in the next few hours that would eventually bring them into a genuine and deep knowledge of God. In Christ's saving act they would come to know the Father as they had never known him before.

"You know him," Jesus says. We should notice that this goes beyond anything that the holy people of old normally claimed. Just occasionally there is the assertion that people know God (e.g., Ps. 36:10). But this is exceptional. Generally speaking, the knowledge of God was something that people looked forward to and hoped for. Dodd says, "I cannot discover a place where a prophet expressly says that he knows God. Again, while God's knowledge of Israel is confidently proclaimed by the prophets, they rarely affirm that Israel knows God." Jesus brings to those who believe something new and outstanding in religious experience, the real knowledge of God.

He also says, ". . . and you have seen him." This, too, was something new and very different. Barclay can say, "It may well be that to the ancient world this was the most staggering thing that Jesus ever said. To the Greeks God was characteristically *The Invisible.* The Jew would count it as an article of faith that no man has seen God at any time." So Jesus was claiming to give those who believed in him an intimacy with God such as the ancient world knew nothing of. We ought not to think that in words like these Jesus is simply repeating religious commonplaces. He is doing nothing of the sort. He is claiming something far, far greater than anyone else had claimed.

And it has been the experience of the Christian church through the centuries that he has carried out his promise. Those who know Christ really know the Father and have seen him.

62

Help from On High

Philip says to him, "Lord, show us the Father and it is enough for us." Jesus says to him, "For such a long time have I been with you and you do not know me, Philip? He who has seen me has seen the Father. How then do you say, 'Show us the Father'? Do you not believe that I am in the Father and the Father is in me? The words that I speak to you I do not speak of myself; but the Father living in me does his works. Believe me that I am in the Father and the Father is in me; if not, believe on account of the works themselves. Truly, truly I tell you, he who believes in me, the works that I do he will do too, and greater works than these will he do because I go to the Father. And whatever you ask in my name I will do it, so that the Father may be glorified in the Son. If you ask me anything in my name I will do it" (John 14:8–14).

In one way or another the passages that followed Thomas's query about "the way" bring out the relationship of the follower of Jesus to God. It starts with a request Philip makes of Jesus: "Lord, show us the Father and it is enough for us" (v. 8). Philip would have been familiar with the scriptural teaching that in olden times God had sometimes appeared to people on this earth. For example, there was that time when Moses and Aaron and Nadab and Abihu, in company with seventy elders of Israel, had a vision of God (Exod. 24:9–11). There was that other occasion when Moses had prayed, "Now show me your glory" (Exod. 33:18) and had been told that no one can see the face of God and live, but that God would show him his back (Exod. 33:20–23). And, of course, there was that great vision of Isaiah when the prophet saw the Lord "on a throne, high and exalted, and the train of his robe filled the temple" (Isa. 6:1).

It seems that Philip had the idea that Jesus could bring about some such vision and that this would clear away many of their difficulties. That, Philip says, "is enough for us." We have the same verb here as the one Philip used at the feeding of the five thousand when he said, "Two hundred denarii worth of bread would not be enough . . ." (6:7). Philip had then seen an extraordinary miracle, one that should have told him something about Jesus' relationship to the Father. But, though Philip had seen what had happened, he had not seen what it meant. Now, as John records these words, he is perhaps wanting his readers to see that, despite Philip's hopes, a vision of the sort he was asking for would not in fact be enough. The faith Jesus looked for (and still looks for) from his followers is not a faith dependent on visions.

The great truth that is brought out throughout this Gospel Jesus now puts in a sentence: "He who has seen me has seen the Father" (v. 9). Philip had been with Jesus throughout his earthly ministry, from that day when Jesus "found" him (1:43). He had heard Jesus' teaching and seen the way he lived and the wonderful "signs" that he did. And still Jesus could say, ". . . you do not know me." When he goes on to ask, "How then do you say, 'Show us the Father,'" his "you" is emphatic. With all the advantages that Philip had had of being so near to Jesus, he ought to have known more. But before we sit in judgment on Philip it is well that we reflect that despite all that is recorded in the Bible, and despite nearly two thousand years of church history in which God has been active among his people, we still often deserve the same rebuke. We so often show as little faith and as little understanding as Philip did.

The faith for which Jesus looked in his followers is the faith that believes, as he put it, "that I am in the Father and the Father is in me" (v. 10). The great truth in Christianity is that for our salvation none less than God himself came right where we are and did what had to be done, even to the death on the cross. We are not to think of Jesus as simply a wonderful man who knew and taught about the Father. The Father was in him. He was in the Father. It is impossible to know the one and not to know the other. To know the one *is* to know the other. Jesus' question to Philip is expressed in the Greek in such a way as to show that the answer "Yes" is expected. Through the years with Jesus, Philip ought to have come to understand this. Earlier in this Gospel Jesus had even told "the Jews" that on the basis of what they had seen in him they ought to have come to know that the Father was in him and that he was in the Father

(10:38). If this was so with "the Jews," then much more should one like Philip, who had been closer to Jesus and who had seen more, have come to know the reality of his close connection with the Father.

Jesus' Works

Jesus directs Philip's attention to his teaching and reminds him that it was not self-originated. Throughout this Gospel there runs the thought that Jesus' message was not of human origin: it came from God. Jesus can say, "I do not speak of myself," and then go on to speak of the Father as living in him. There is such a close relationship between them that there is no way of separating them.

Interestingly, Jesus moves immediately to the "works" that were manifested in his life. As we have seen in earlier studies, in this Gospel the miracles of Jesus are often seen as "signs"; they are significant happenings. But when Jesus speaks of them they are usually "works"; what to us is sheer miracle is to him no more than a work. Moreover, the term makes it clear that Jesus' life was a unity; he did not do some things as God and then some things as man. "Works" is used both for the miraculous and the non-miraculous. Jesus was no split personality but one in whom Godhead and manhood were harmoniously blended.

He could have spoken of the works he did, but instead he spoke of the works the Father did. Jesus did not, and could not, act in isolation from the Father. When Jesus did something, whether miraculous or not, it could be said that the Father did that thing. So now Jesus says that "the Father living in me does his works." He passes easily from the words to the works. Both alike are a revelation of the Father and neither can be understood without seeing that.

Philip had seen the way Jesus lived and the wonderful things he did. So Jesus calls on him to believe: "Believe me that I am in the Father and the Father is in me" (v. 11). The imperative "believe" is plural in form; this is something that applies not just to Philip but to all. We should notice further that Jesus says, "Believe me that. . . ." In some quarters today it is urged that Christians should drop their dogmatism and proceed on the basis of simple trust in God. All the load of doctrine that the church has acquired through the centuries should be jettisoned, it is urged, and we should all live simply in trust in God. But Jesus was not arguing in that way. While it is, of course, true that trust is basically a very simple affair and that no more than trust in God is sought, yet we should be aware of the fact that faith has content. Christianity is not a faith in faith. It is faith in a God who has revealed himself in Jesus. It is faith that the Father is in Jesus and Jesus is in the Father. Anything less than that is not Christian faith.

If that seems too difficult, Jesus says to Philip, "believe on account of the works themselves." Philip and his friends had seen the wonderful things that Jesus had done. Those "works" should convince them that here was someone who was more than merely a man. He was the One in whom the Father dwelt and as such he was worthy of their fullest trust.

Greater Works

Now comes a further surprising statement. It is introduced by "Truly, truly," once again the prelude to a solemn and perhaps unexpected saying (v. 12). It warns the hearers to take special notice of what follows. Jesus has been drawing attention to the wonderful works he has done, but now he says that the person who believes in him will do the same works and even greater ones. This is a breathtaking promise.

We should not understand this in terms of physical miracles, such as the miracles of healing that Jesus did or his feedings of the multitudes. The term *works* is, of course, large enough to include them, but it goes beyond that; it also applies to the whole of life. And we should notice that the doing of these works is "because I go to the Father"; i.e., they are the result of the completion of Jesus' whole work of salvation. We are justified in seeing a reference to the death he was about to die, to the resurrection, and to the sending of the Holy Spirit that would enable the believers to go forth in their service of God in a strength not their own. It is in this way that they would do their "greater works."

We may profitably ask ourselves, "What work on earth is greater than the salvation of souls?" When a person is healed of a physical complaint that person's life on earth is enriched for a few more years. But when a soul is saved something has happened that lasts through eternity. Jesus is saying that on the basis of his finished work of salvation the church would go forth in the power of the Holy Spirit to bring many, many more people into salvation than Jesus did during the years of his ministry on earth. It is a tremendous privilege that is given to us to live for Christ and to proclaim his message in such a way that people are brought into salvation.

We are not left to ourselves in bringing that to pass. Jesus goes on to speak of the importance of prayer (v. 13), which he describes as asking "in my name." This does not mean that we must end every prayer with something like "in the name of Jesus Christ" or "through Jesus Christ our Lord" (though these are appropriate ways of concluding prayers). Rather we are to bear in mind that in antiquity "the name" in some way summed up and stood for the whole person. The "name" of Jesus, then, points us to the incarnate life of the Son of God, to the atoning death, to the powerful resurrection, and to the sending forth of the messengers of salvation in the strength of the Holy Spirit. Anyone who prays in that "name" can be sure that his prayers will be heard.

And they will be answered. "I will do it," says Jesus. He is not saying that prayer is a kind of magic, a way of getting anything we want. Effective prayer is prayer "in the name" of Jesus, prayer that bears in mind all that Jesus has done for us, prayer that pleads his saving work, prayer that is exercised in order to set forward the work that Jesus came to do. That kind of prayer is not prayer directed toward selfish ends. If we are praying for something we would like but which is not in accordance with all that the "name" stands for, then such prayer is not covered by what Jesus is saying. True prayer is prayer that fits in with the "name."

Jesus does not say that the Father will do it, but that he will do it. He is the answerer of prayer as well as the one whose name is to be pleaded in prayer. In other places it is said that the Father will answer prayer (15:16, etc.), but there is, of course, no contradiction. Jesus has just said that to see him is to see the Father and that they are "in" one another (vv. 9–10). To say that Jesus will answer prayer is to place him with the Father. The two are inseparable, and it does not matter much which of them we say is answering. The main point is that our Christian service is something that can never be done in our own strength. It proceeds only on the basis of what God has done in Christ for our salvation and in the continual help that God gives.

The promise is repeated (v. 14). This is not the addition of some new thing (unless we see this in asking Jesus in his own name) but the repetition of something that is very important. Christian work that is not done in a spirit of prayer is never going to be effective.

The Promise of the Spirit

"If you love me you will keep my commandments and I will ask the Father and he will give you another strengthener so that he may be with you for ever, namely the Spirit of truth whom the world cannot receive because it neither sees him nor knows him. You know him because he dwells with you and will be in you" (John 14:15–17).

Jesus proceeds to bring out something of the importance of the coming of the Holy Spirit (as he does again in v. 26; 15:26; 16:7–15). There is a strong emphasis on the Spirit throughout the remainder of this discourse and, as there has been so little about him through the ministry of Jesus, we may well reflect that the distinctive work of the Spirit takes place on the basis of Jesus' saving work. We may perhaps bring out the point theologically by saying that justification precedes sanctification. We come into a place of forgiveness through Christ's atoning work and go forward in service in the power of the Spirit. It is thus appropriate that as Christ's death is about to take place he gives his followers instructions about the Spirit.

He begins with love (v. 15). Without love, it is not easy to go anywhere in the understanding of the Christian way or in the living out of Christian commitment. It is love that brought our Savior from heaven to live and die for us, and it is love that is the spontaneous response of our hearts to the love we see on the cross. It is love for God and for our fellows that motivates all effective Christian service. And love has consequences. Jesus now says that if the disciples love him they will keep his commandments.

Notice how love and the keeping of the commandments go together. There is a section of the modern church that takes the commandments lightly. Love, such people say, is not concerned with commandments; the keeping of a law code is the very opposite of love. So it is, if the keeping of the law code is thought of as the means of becoming acceptable in the sight of God. But not if the law code is seen as the expression of the love of God. Then the person who loves will keep it, not as a means of acquiring merit or deserving a reward or winning affection, but because that is the way the One who loves us so much and whom we love so much wants us to live. Obeying the commandments is the natural response of real love to the revelation of the will of the One who loves us, as expressed in the commandments he has given.

Jesus is calling on his followers to get involved in the work of God in the world. This is an important part of life. There is a story about Hubert Humphrey in the days when he taught a university class. His lecture on fascism started one day at 4:00 P.M., but when the bell rang at 5:00 his class went right on. At 6:15 they broke for a light dinner but resumed at 6:40. Humphrey kept firing questions at the students and challenging them. They came right back at him and the discussion showed no signs of slackening. By 8:00 P.M. all lights were out except the one in this lecture theater. At 9:40 Humphrey called it off with a final challenge: "Whatever your views, don't just be jeering from the bleachers. Get out and pitch for what you think is the best team. Get involved."

There is something there for Christians. It is easy to sit back and complain about what is going on in the world and in the church. But Jesus did not call his followers to complain. He called them to love and to keep his commandments. That means getting involved. There is no neutrality in the war between good and evil. If we are Christ's we are wholehearted for him. We are active in the war between right and wrong.

In this situation, with disciples loving Christ and keeping his commandments, Jesus says that he will pray to the Father on their behalf and that he will give them "another strengthener" (v. 16). It is not easy to see how to translate the Greek word *parakletos* (which I have rendered "strengthener") because we have no real equivalent. The word literally means something like "called to the side of" and was used sometimes of the person called to help someone accused in a court of law. In such a context it meant the counsel for the defense, the advocate, and the term is used with that meaning in its only New Testament occurrence outside these chapters of John, namely 1 John 2:1: ". . . if anyone sins, we have an Advocate with the Father, Jesus Christ the righteous." The early Greek Fathers seem generally to have taken the word in this Gospel to mean "consoler," or "comforter," but no good reason ever appears to have been given for this.

The word appears to be used in the sense of a "helper," often with the notion of a helper at court. There is a certain legal air about it: "a friend at court." But it is used in too many places where it can scarcely be legal for that to be regarded as essential in a translation. In the present passage the Spirit is thought of as someone who would be constantly with the disciples but not with the world, and this is said in a context where they are to keep Christ's commandments. It seems reasonably clear that the Spirit is to aid them in this and thus be their "strengthener."

The word is used in this Gospel always of the Holy Spirit and always in words of Jesus (v. 26; 15:26; 16:7). The things the Paraclete is said to do are all somewhere or other assigned to Jesus, such as teaching the disciples (v. 26), being in them and with them (v. 20; 15:4f.), and bearing witness (8:14), so there is point in his calling the Spirit "another." The Spirit is another like himself.

Jesus says here that he will ask the Father, and the Father will give the Spirit. A little later he says that the Father will "send" the Spirit in Christ's name (v. 26). Again Jesus says that he will "send" the Spirit from the Father (15:26) and that he will "send" him (16:7). We should probably not look for hard-and-fast distinctions here. It is plain enough that the Spirit is connected with both the Father and the Son and that both the Father and the Son are involved in sending the Spirit to help the followers of Jesus. In any case, the way the various persons of the Godhead are related to one another is beyond our understanding. We should simply understand that all three are to be thought of in the way divine help is provided for the followers of Jesus.

The first thing Jesus says about the Spirit is that he will be with the disciples "for ever." He has told the disciples that he himself will shortly go away (13:33; 14:3). That visible presence of their Master on which they had relied so heavily is about to be taken from them. But that does not mean that they will be deserted, for "another strengthener" will be with them in such a way that he will never be taken from them. There is encouragement and inspiration in such a message.

The Spirit of Truth

Jesus goes on to call the strengthener "the Spirit of truth" (v. 17), a name that will recur (15:26; 16:13). The title is found very occasionally in Jewish writings, notably in the Dead Sea Scrolls. But though the name is the same, the meaning is different. In the Scrolls there are two spirits that strive for the mastery of all people, the spirit of truth and the spirit of error. The two spirits are apparently fairly evenly matched, and the struggle goes on. The men of Qumran trusted that in the end the forces of truth would prevail and that the spirit of truth would thus prove to be stronger.

But Jesus is not talking about a spirit like other spirits but about a Spirit like himself. The idea of "the Spirit of truth" as linked with Godhead in the way Jesus uses it is an idea that is not found elsewhere. The terminology is the same as that found in some Jewish writings, but the idea conveyed is very different.

Jesus has said that the Spirit will come to help the disciples. Now he says that the world cannot receive the Spirit: not only "will not" but "cannot." There is an incompatibility here. The world does not see the Spirit. The world does not know the Spirit. The world's interests are in other areas than the Spirit and thus the world shuts itself off from the reception of the Spirit. It is not that a hardhearted God shuts off his best gifts from many of the people who live on the earth. They shut themselves off. They are not interested in the Spirit or the things of the Spirit.

But it is different with the disciples. They know the Spirit. They do not just know about him, but they know him. The reason? "He dwells with you and will be in you." There has been some discussion about whether Jesus means that the Spirit will be in the church or in individual believers, but this seems misguided. Both are true. The Spirit is in the church in a way he is not in the world, and he is in believers in a way he is not in the worldly. We must neglect neither way of understanding the words.

63

Going to the Father

"I will not leave you desolate, I am coming to you. Yet a little while and the world sees me no more, but you see me. Because I live, you will live too. In that day you will know that I am in my Father and you in me and I in you. He who has my commandments and keeps them, he it is who loves me; and he who loves me will be loved by my Father and I will love him and manifest myself to him." Judas, not Iscariot, says to him, "Lord, what has happened that you will manifest yourself to us and not to the world?" Jesus answered him saying, "If anyone loves me he will keep my word and my Father will love him, and we will come to him and make our dwelling with him. He who does not love me does not keep my teachings and the teaching which you hear is not mine but that of the Father who sent me.

"These things I have spoken to you while I still remain with you. But the Paraclete, the Holy Spirit whom the Father will send in my name, he will teach you all things and remind you of all the things that I said to you. Peace I leave with you, my peace I give you; not as the world gives do I give to you. Let not your heart be troubled, neither let it be cowardly. You heard that I said to you 'I am going away and I am coming back to you.' If you loved me you would rejoice because I am going to the Father, for the Father is greater than I. And now I have told you before it happens, so that when it does happen you will believe. No longer shall I speak much with you, for the ruler of the world is coming. And in me he has nothing at all, but so that the world may know that I love the Father, even as the Father has commanded me, so I do. Get up, let us go off" (John 14:18–31).

Jesus has spoken about the Holy Spirit, the Paraclete, whom the Father would send in response to his prayer (vv. 16–17). Now he says that he will not leave his people "desolate" (v. 18). The word really means "orphans" (our word *orphan* is practically this Greek word, *orphanos;* it is used in the literal sense in James 1:27). It is a "family" word, a word that brings out something of the love that bound the apostolic band together and united them with Christ. He knew that without him they would be a group of "orphans," leaderless in the world. But, while in their dismay at the events that were about to befall them they might feel that this was the situation, this would not be a true account. When their Master hung on a cross they might well feel themselves as alone in the world as helpless orphans. But that would not be the last of it. He would surely come back to them. Some scholars take this to be a reference to his coming in the person of the Holy Spirit. There is a truth in this, but it seems more likely that at this point Jesus is referring to the post-resurrection appearances. It was these appearances that would convince the disciples that they were not alone. Jesus himself was coming to them. There is, of course, a further and a fuller meaning, that he will come back at the second coming, but it is not this on which the emphasis falls here. Jesus is assuring his close followers that they will not be left like orphans in the world, for they will see him.

Events are moving rapidly, and Jesus speaks of "a little while" after which the world will no longer see him (v. 19). He uses the present tense, which makes it more vivid. The people of "the world" had had their opportunity of seeing Jesus as he moved among them during the days of his earthly ministry. They had seen what he did, his manner of life and his miracles. They had heard what he said, his wonderful teaching about this world and the next. They had been challenged to believe but had remained faithless. Now they see Jesus no more. Their day of opportunity has gone.

Jesus marks the contrast between the world and the disciples, when he uses the emphatic pronoun: *you* in opposition to the world. In a meaningful sense the world never had seen Jesus; it had discerned the man Jesus as he moved about, but it had never seen by faith that here was the Son of God. The disciples were different; they were not caught up in the same error. They had seen Jesus and were still seeing him; they recognized that God was in him in a special way and that he was the one who drew them to the Father. In that sense they would not cease to see him, and Jesus uses the present tense when he speaks of them: "you see me," not "you will see me." There is a future aspect of their relationship and it is not unimportant. But here he dwells on the fact that they see him as he is and this is not something that would ever be taken away from them, not even in the dark days immediately ahead when their faith would be so sorely tested.

This is, of course, one of the precious things Jesus gives to all his followers in all the ages. Like the apostles of old, we too have our dark days, the days when our faith seems to fail. But through it all we have the sure and certain knowledge of Jesus. We see him as he is. And, no matter how difficult our circumstances nor what our feelings may be, we *know* accordingly that he is with us and will be with us, no matter how sore the trial. To have the vision of Jesus as he is is a great and wonderful blessing.

Christ's Life and Ours

Jesus moves to the thought of life. "Because I live," he says, "you will live too." Both "I" and "you" are emphatic. It is because Jesus lives, not because of anyone else's life, that they will live, too. And it is they who would live, not people like Caiaphas or Pilate or any of those others who seemed so important to the people of the day. Jesus is not speaking of a universal salvation that will take place by some natural process and extend to everybody. He is speaking of a salvation that depends on him and the particular kind of life he lives. And it is a life given to those who put their trust in him, not to the community at large.

Their life is bound up with his. It is interesting that as Jesus faces the cross he says, "I live." His "I" is emphatic. He is not uttering a commonplace, something that applies to everybody. He is different, and what he is saying he is saying because he is different. It is, of course, the great, central truth that his life is not like ours. It may appear to have been taken away in the crucifixion, but that is no more than appearance. He is "the Prince of life" (Acts 3:15); it was not possible for death to hold him (Acts 2:24). The whole New Testament depicts him as supreme over death and all that death means. That "he lives" is the great fundamental truth about life. His death on the cross was followed by the resurrection because he was that kind of person.

And his life, that life that persisted through death and was manifested in the resurrection, meant life for his followers. Again there is the emphatic pronoun: *you* will live, *you* who have put your trust in me, *you* will live. Sometimes the New Testament writers speak of Jesus' death rather than his life as bringing life to his people (Rom. 5:10; 2 Cor. 5:15), but the thought is much the same. They are all saying that the central event in bringing about our salvation was the death of Christ on the cross, which led to the resurrection. His life was such that inevitably it triumphed over death and in the process brought life, real life, to those who trust him.

"In that day," Jesus goes on, "you will know that I am in my Father" (v. 20). He does not say explicitly which day that is, but in the context it must refer to the day of his resurrection. It was this that would bring enlightenment to them and enable them to see all things from a new perspective. They must have had some idea of Jesus' closeness to the Father from what they had learned throughout his earthly ministry. But they had still to learn how close the Son was to the Father, and the resurrection would in due course bring them enlightenment. They would know not simply that there was a power resident in Jesus that was superior to the power of death, but that he was "in the Father." It was his relationship to the Father that would bring about the resurrection.

This had consequences for them. We might have expected that Jesus would go on to say after "I am in my Father" that "my Father is in me." That is true and it is an important truth. But instead Jesus says "you in me and I in you." The mutual indwelling of the Father and the Son is a wonderful truth about the Godhead. And the mutual indwelling of the Savior and the saved is a wonderful truth about salvation.

Love and Love's Manifestation

It is perhaps unexpected that from this wonderful truth of the gift of life, the gift that means that Christ lives in his people and they live in him, Jesus moves on to the commandments (v. 21). These days any emphasis on the commandments is bound to run into criticism. We are warned against thinking that obedience to a set of rules has anything to do with Christianity and are urged to put all our emphasis on love. Now nothing should be said to minimize the significance of love. In a Christian context how could it? But we should not overlook the fact that, as he has done before (v. 15), Jesus links love with the keeping of his commandments. It is, of course, true that it is possible to cultivate a hard, legalistic mentality that puts all its emphasis on conformity to a written code and cares for nothing else if only the outward letter of the law has been kept. But people who develop this outlook know nothing of the sacrificial love that is at the heart of Christianity.

It is also true, though, that those who really love, those who have steadily looked at Calvary and seen what sacrificial love really is and have responded with all their heart, those people have a special regard for the commandments. They see them not as a harsh set of external requirements, but as the guidance needed by weak and imperfect people as they respond in love to the wonderful love of Christ. It may be that we should see the expression "has my commandments" as full of meaning. This is a very uncommon way of speaking about commandments;

mostly there are references to "keeping" the commandments or "obeying" them or even "loving" them. But to "have" them is a very unusual way of talking about them. Jesus does not explain it further, but he seems to mean that there are some people who make the commandments their own. They take them into their inner being, they meditate on them, and by God's grace they make a determined attempt to live them out.

It is the person who keeps the commandments who loves Christ. When someone claims to be a Christian but takes no notice of what Christ has commanded his followers to do, there is something hollow about his profession. Real Christianity is not like that. To love Christ means to keep his commandments. Do not all those who love anyone delight to do what they know is pleasing to the one they love?

These people, Jesus says, are the ones who really love him. And there are consequences. They will be loved by the Father and by Jesus himself as well. There is a little problem here for some, because elsewhere we read that God loves the world (3:16), that "God is love" (1 John 4:8, 16), and that God shows his love in the death of Christ for sinners (Rom. 5:8). Do not such passages mean that God loves everyone? What is the meaning, then, of saying that God loves those that love Jesus? But the problem does not seem to be insoluble. It is God's nature to love, and he loves all that he has made. But God is good and has a special love for those who turn away from evil and respond to his love. It is this that Jesus is speaking of at this point. When people respond to what God has done in Christ, when they turn from their sin and in faith commit themselves to him who died for them, when they love him and keep his commandments, all this does not go unnoticed. God does not treat such people with indifference. He loves them. And Christ loves them.

Christ Manifests Himself

Christ not only loves the person who responds in the way he has just outlined, but he says, "I will . . . manifest myself to him." The verb is a rather unusual one (it is used only here and in the next verse in this Gospel), and Jesus does not explain in detail what he means by it. But the term is used elsewhere for Moses' desire for a visible manifestation of God (Exod. 33:13); outside the Bible it is sometimes used of God's making himself known to people who trust him (it is used in this way in the book called "The Wisdom of Solomon" [1:2]). Clearly, Jesus means that part of his response to the genuine love of disciples is to make himself real to them. It is not easy to put this into words, but those who have experienced the love of Christ know what he means.

But, at the time the words were spoken, there was at least one disciple who did not understand them. He was called Judas, and John expressly tells us that this is not Judas Iscariot (v. 22). This second Judas is not a prominent member of the apostolic band; for example, he is mentioned here only in this Gospel. Luke includes him in his list of the Twelve when he speaks of "James's Judas" (Luke 6:16; so again in Acts 1:13); this probably means "son of James," though it could possibly mean "brother of James." This Judas, then, did not understand what Jesus meant. He gathered that the Lord was talking about a manifestation that would be real to the disciples but that the world outside would not experience. Judas puts "to us" in a prominent position and has an emphatic negative when he says "not to the world." How can this be? He wants to be clear.

Uncertainty can lead to trouble. I am reminded of a story from the Vietnam War. An army major approaching an outpost was disturbed that there was no challenge. When he was within ten feet a GI came out with no helmet on his head and carrying no weapon. The major, highly displeased at this lack of appreciation of the dangers of the warfare in which they were engaged, barked, "Don't you challenge anyone approaching your bunker?" "Yes, sir, we do," replied the GI, "but we thought you were the coffee man. Last time we challenged him and he dropped the lot!" Like the men in Vietnam we can be in trouble when we are unaware of what is going on (and who it is that is approaching). Judas shows his appreciation of the problems of uncertainty and tries to get the matter clarified.

The answer comes in terms of love (v. 23). Judas may not know exactly what will befall him and his comrades, but he does know that he is required to live in love. We have just seen that those who love Christ keep his commandments, and there is something similar here. Jesus does not answer Judas's question in the way that apostle probably wanted it answered. But he points out that love and obedience are all we need to know. Anyone who loves Jesus will keep his "word," which here stands for his teaching (as in 8:51; cf. 17:6). We are reminded that there are many things about the difficulties of living for Christ in the world that we do not know and cannot know. But that is not important. What is important is that we love Christ and keep his word.

When we do we experience the love of God. This is the truth we saw earlier in this study. It is not that we merit the love of God. We can never do that. But the love that is being so constantly showered on us becomes more apparent to us and, of course, it is also the case that God responds to our love with his love.

There is more. When we live in love in this way, we live in constant fellowship with God. "We will come to him," Jesus says, "and make our dwelling with him." To live in hatred and strife is to shut God out, but to live in love is to invite him in. And both the Father and the Son respond to the loving invitation. The word I have translated "dwelling" here is the one used in 14:2 (where I rendered it "dwelling-places"). These are the only two places in the whole New Testament where this word is found. It points to something lasting; it is not a temporary lodging but a permanent dwelling. God is love, and it is natural that he makes his dwelling with people whose lives are full of love.

But the opposite of that is also true, and Jesus goes on to point out that the person who does not love him is not concerned to keep his teaching (v. 24). Just as obedience and conformity to Jesus' teaching is the inevitable consequence of love, so a neglect of that teaching is the inevitable consequence of a lack of love.

Jesus brings out the seriousness of this neglect by reminding Judas that the teaching Jesus gives is not that simply of the Man from Nazareth. It is in one sense his, but in another and a very important sense it is the teaching given to him by the Father who sent him into the world. Those who heard Jesus in first-century Palestine and did not respond neglected this divinely given teaching at their peril. And those who hear that teaching in our very different twentieth-century world neglect it at their peril, too.

The Holy Spirit

This is Jesus' last connected section of teaching with his disciples before he goes to the cross. They do not know this, but he speaks of still remaining with them (v. 25), which shows that it is very much in his mind. "These things I have shown to you" is a form of words that is found seven times in the discourse in the Upper Room and nowhere else in this Gospel. The verb is in the perfect tense, which points to the permanent importance of what Jesus has said. This is true of all his teaching, but the probability is that this expression applies particularly to the words spoken in the Upper Room. There is a special solemnity about these last words of Jesus to his disciples, and there can be no doubt that he used this last occasion for teaching as a time for stressing what is particularly important.

What was to be of critical importance for the disciples in the days ahead was the presence of the Holy Spirit with them, and Jesus turns his attention once more to the Spirit. He calls him "the Paraclete," that term for which there is no precise English equivalent and which has about it the thought of a friend at court and of helping and strengthening.

He goes on to refer to the Spirit as "the Holy Spirit." It is significant that Jesus uses this way of describing him; he does not say "the mighty Spirit," "the wise Spirit," "the guiding Spirit," "the exciting Spirit," or any such thing. While the Spirit does many things and can be thought of in so many ways, the way in which he is usually described in the New Testament is that which Jesus uses here: "the Holy Spirit." What matters most is his character as holy. Christians still speak of the Spirit in this way, but it is worth noticing that it is not perhaps the most obvious way of naming him. These days we are all conscious of the many "gifts" the Spirit gives to believers, and it is perhaps surprising (but true to Scripture) that we do not usually characterize him with reference to those gifts but with reference to holiness.

Here we find that the Father is the One who will send the Spirit and will send him in the name of the Son. As we saw in an earlier study, there is a variety of ways in which the mission of the Spirit is described, but the effect of them all is to see both the Father and the Son as concerned with it. The Spirit is to do two things: (1) teach "all things," and (2) remind the disciples of all that Jesus had told them. The first expression conveys the thought that whatever the disciples need to know as they go about their task of serving God the Spirit will teach them. It is still the case that the church is effective only when it is following the leading of the Spirit and going forward in the strength the Spirit supplies.

The second expression underlines the importance of the teaching of Jesus. It is his teaching that is normative for Christians to this day. It is not the case that in every generation something new is evolved that replaces what is outmoded, so that the church goes on forever changing. The teaching of Jesus is the foundational teaching of the church. We do well to be grateful to those who in every age are able to discern the leading of the Spirit and to do what is necessary to set forward the divine purpose. But none of this replaces the teaching of Jesus. That, as we have been reminded in this passage, comes from the Father. We have no license to modify it. We have only to proclaim it.

Peace

Jesus turns to the thought of the peace he would give his followers (v. 27). With us today, peace is a negative concept, the absence of war. But among the Hebrews it was positive, the presence of the blessing of God on the well-rounded life. One element in this life is the absence of war (the Hebrews were one of the very few races whose great men were not warriors, but men of peace, lawgivers, prophets, and the like). So sometimes the Hebrew for "peace" is used in much the same way as we would use the term. But characteristically it is a more comprehensive term. And this deep peace, Jesus says, he gives to his own. This is unlike the peace the world gives from time to time, for it is a peace that sustains God's people even in the middle of the worst troubles. Jesus does not promise to keep the disciples from trouble, but to give them peace, whatever the world does to them. So, kept by his peace, they should not be troubled or afraid, no matter how great the difficulties in which they find themselves.

That is important as Jesus contemplates his going to the Father. This, he says, should cause them to rejoice (v. 28). In fact, when he went to the Father they were most unhappy, but that was because they were lacking in understanding. Instead of seeing Jesus go to the Father, they saw the death of their leader and the disappointment of their worldly hopes. But their failure to understand did not alter the reality of the situation. Jesus was not destroyed on the cross. He was simply going to be with the Father, who is greater than the incarnate Christ. That is matter for rejoicing.

The End Is Approaching

Jesus' concern for his own comes out in his telling them these things before they happen. Then, when it all turns out as he said it would, "you will believe" (v. 29; cf. 13:19). The cross will be a tremendous shock to them all, but Jesus gives them information that will be a source of encouragement to them in the days ahead. They will come to see that it all happened as he said it would.

The end is near, and Jesus will not speak much more with them (v. 30). "The ruler of the world" is a designation of Satan; it is in this world that he holds sway, and it is part of Jesus' work to defeat him. But that is on the cross. At the moment of speaking it is as "the ruler of the world" that the evil one comes. But he "has nothing at all" in Jesus, for Jesus has no sin. There is nothing in him that Satan can take hold of. The cross will take place indeed, but this will not be because Satan has won a victory. Rather, the victory will be with love, and again Jesus speaks of the cross as a demonstration of love. This time he says that it will make it clear to the world that he loves the Father. In loyalty to the Father he would go to the cross, and thus his love would be quite plain.

64

The Vine and Its Fruit

"I am the true vine and my Father is the vinedresser. Every branch in me that does not bear fruit he takes away and every branch that bears fruit he cleanses so that it will bear more fruit. Already you are clean because of the word that I have spoken to you. Remain in me, and I in you. As the branch cannot bear fruit by itself unless it remains in the vine so neither can you unless you remain in me. I am the vine, you are the branches. He who remains in me and I in him, this person bears a lot of fruit, for apart from me you can do nothing. If anyone does not remain in me, he is thrown out like the branch, and it is withered and they gather them and throw them into the fire and they are burned. If you remain in me and my words remain in you, ask what you will and it will be done for you. In this has my Father been glorified that you bear much fruit and be my disciples. Just as the Father has loved me I also have loved you; remain in my love. If you keep my commandments you will remain in my love, just as I have kept my Father's commandments and remain in his love. These things I have spoken to you so that my joy might be in you and your joy might be filled full" (John 15:1–11).

The imagery of the vine and its fruit is perhaps unexpected, for the vine was used as a symbol for Israel rather than for an individual, be he the Messiah or anyone else (see Ps. 80:8–16: Isa. 5:1–7; and other passages). It did not suit the ideas that were current about the Messiah, ideas that saw him as a conqueror or a political figure. But, with Jesus' determination to give himself in order to bring salvation to his people, it was another matter. The vine imagery brought out important truths. As William Temple put it: ". . . the vine lives to give its lifeblood. Its flower is small, its fruit abundant; and when that fruit is mature and the vine has for a moment become glorious, the treasure of the grapes is torn down and the vine is cut back to the stem and next year blooms again,

> Not bitter for the torment undergone,
> Nor barren for the fulness yielded up."

(The last lines are from a poem by Mrs. Hamilton King.) Precisely what made the vine unsuitable as an illustration of what the run-of-the-mill claimants to being the Messiah saw as the essence of their function was that which made it suitable for Jesus. He would bring salvation to others at cost to himself.

Jesus speaks of himself as the "true" vine, which marks a contrast between him and others. When the vine imagery is used in the Old Testament it is mostly used of Israel, as we have seen; further, it is used of Israel in its sinfulness rather than its fruitfulness. Thus the prophet can say: "Israel was a spreading vine; he brought forth fruit for himself. As his fruit increased, he built more altars; as his land prospered, he adorned his sacred stones. Their heart is deceitful, and now they must bear their guilt . . ." (Hos. 10:1–2). Here Hosea sees the nation as concerned not to bring forth the fruit that brings good to others, as God would have the people do, but as concerned with fruit "for himself." It is not in this way that real fruitfulness is achieved.

Jesus, by contrast, was and is the true vine. His whole life was a ministry, a service of others. And it was about to culminate in a death that would bring untold blessing to those for whom he died. There is nothing of self-seeking anywhere, but rather a deep concern for the well-being of needy sinners. He would be the source of rich and deep blessing for others.

The Vinedresser

But while the passage brings out something of Jesus' deep concern for his people and his readiness to die for them, there are other truths that he stresses here, notably the importance that the "branches" of the vine bear fruit. He speaks of the Father as "the vinedresser," where the Greek term *(georgos)* really means a "farmer." The word basically means someone who works the land or tills the soil and thus is the right term for a farmer or a gardener (which is the rendering adopted here by several translators). But in this context it means someone who works with vines, not someone engaged in general farming, so "vinedresser" seems right.

Now an important part of looking after a vine is pruning. Left to itself, a grape vine will tend to produce large quantities of foliage, and this tendency must be checked if maximum fruitfulness is to be attained. So the vinedresser will do a good deal of pruning in order to encourage fruitfulness. There is a parallel in spiritual things, and Jesus says that the Father "takes away" barren branches and that he "cleanses" those that bear fruit so that they will bear more fruit (v. 2). We should be clear that Jesus is here referring to conditions of fruitfulness, not to eternal salvation. We should not understand the passage to mean that God will remove from the number of the saved those who are not fruitful. Eternal security is not being discussed here (see, rather, 10:28–29). Jesus is talking about the saved and about what will happen in order that they may be the most effective servants they can be. For that, he says, it will be necessary for some judicious pruning to take place. We never become the best servants of God by simply letting our natural impulses have full rein. It may be necessary to discipline activities that we would much prefer to indulge in. Jesus is saying that the Father will do what is necessary.

This points to what may be uncomfortable. We would all prefer to go our own way without being brought into line. When God takes away something we like we feel pain. What Jesus is saying is that this is part of a process that leads to maximum fruitfulness in our lives and that apart from this process we do not attain maximum fruitfulness.

There may be something analogous to this in human activities, but our efforts at bringing to pass what we see as desirable have something of the "hit or miss" approach about them. I like the story of the British officer who was confronted by a new East German border guard at Checkpoint Charlie in Berlin. The new man was a very obnoxious person who seemed to go out of his way to make things difficult for Westerners passing through the checkpoint. He held up people on technicalities, let the barrier fall on a car, and generally was unhelpful. There was a good deal of resentment. But the officer of whom I am speaking did not protest. Instead, when he was in conversation with an East German officer, he took the opportunity of praising the new guard highly. With scant regard for the truth, he spoke of how wonderful it was for the West to have such a helpful and cooperative person to work with. He stressed the man's pleasant personality and his obvious interest in promoting understanding between East and West. Within two days the new guard had been posted elsewhere!

There is guile and hypocrisy in the story, and there is in the end a highly desirable result. But with the world's weapons this kind of thing is unpredictable. Sometimes the end result is good, sometimes it is bad. What Jesus is saying is that God's disciplining of his people is done with a surety of touch. We may not like his discipline, but his removal from our lives of what will hinder fruitfulness is always essential. It is well that we recognize this and respond to the divine discipline with thankfulness.

Jesus does not say what the "fruit" that we should bear is. But elsewhere in the New Testament it tends to be qualities of Christian character (see Matt. 3:8; 7:20; Rom. 6:22; Gal. 5:22; Eph. 5:9; etc.). We should probably see this as the meaning here, though some believers think it is to be understood as bringing others to know Christ. We need not think that this is excluded, and it is an important part of fruitfulness. But it is not the whole of it, and here Jesus seems to be referring to a wider fruitfulness than evangelism.

Most translations use the word *branch* here, and I have gone along with that, though with some misgiving. The word denotes rather a vine cane, a slender outgrowth without the firmness that we associate with a branch. But nothing much seems to depend on the distinction, so I have gone along with the usual way of rendering the word.

Cleansing

Another word posing a problem in translation is the one I have rendered "cleanses" and which the Good News Bible translates as "prunes." Others have "trims clean," and this may help us with the sense. The point is that the verb does mean "cleanse" and is related to the adjective rendered "clean" in verse 3; such a translation as "prunes" misses this connection.

The point of all this is that a process of cleansing is necessary if there is to be fruit in Christian lives. It is not only a matter of taking something away; it is a matter of taking something evil away. God's pruning activity in the lives of believers is not concerned with growth as such, but with growth in all that is good. The other side of this coin is a doing away with all that is evil, and it is this process of which Jesus is speaking. As we seek to live out our Christian lives we will inevitably find God's activity in pruning. There are things in our lives that ought not to be there, and it is part of the way that God deals with us that he takes them away. This may be painful, but it is necessary.

Jesus proceeds to tell the disciples that already they are clean "because of the word that I have spoken to you" (v. 3). The teaching of Jesus is such as to bring to their notice things that need to be put right and to lead them to do this. There is a sense in which their cleansing has already taken place: to become a disciple is to undergo a once-for-all cleansing at the hand of Christ and decisively to leave the world and its fancied securities. There is another sense in which the cleansing is an ongoing process. But it is the former with which Jesus is concerned at this point. Our study of Scripture, and specifically of the word of Jesus, is important, for it is this that is normally the agent for our cleansing.

The Vine and the Branches

It is one of the very obvious things about pruning that the part that is cut off cannot bear fruit: vital contact with the vine is essential for fruit-bearing. When a branch is pruned part of it is removed. The part that will bear fruit is the part that remains in living contact with the vine, not the part that is taken away. Jesus makes this the point of an appeal to the disciples to "remain" in him, with which he links his "remaining" in them (v. 4). This mutual indwelling or abiding is an important part of the Christian life. Paul has a good deal to say about being "in Christ," and this is the Johannine equivalent. All these ways of putting it express the truth that believers, left to themselves, are unable to accomplish any significant spiritual achievement. We may speak of living close to Christ, but the Savior makes it even closer than that. We are to be "in" him and he is to be "in" us. Without that continual and close contact our lives will always be unfruitful.

"I am the vine" (v. 5) is the last of the great "I am" sayings of this Gospel. Like the others, it is in the style of deity and expresses something of Jesus' great claim for himself. Only one who is supremely great can fulfill what is implied in being the vine of which all Christians are no more than branches. Just as his "I" is emphatic, so is it with his "you." Jesus is not speaking of people in general, but of those who had committed themselves to him and who had been "cleansed" by his word (v. 3). The words express at one and the same time the difference between Christ and his followers and their closeness. And it underlines the truth he is pointing out that fruitfulness depends on living contact with him. The vine cane severed from the vine will bear no fruit.

But Jesus does not remain with the negative. He goes on to say, "He who remains in me and I in him, this person bears a lot of fruit." The normal state of discipleship is one of fruitfulness, and we should be clear about this. Jesus does not look for fruitfulness simply from a few great saints. He expects each one of us to live a fruitful life. And he speaks of a large quantity of fruit. We are not disciples in the sense in which we should be if we are content with the minimum. Jesus expects each of his followers not only to bear fruit, but to bear much fruit.

And this is a reasonable expectation because it depends not on the extent of our talents but on our contact with our Lord. "Apart from me you can do nothing" was true of the original apostles and is true of us. Right through this passage there runs the throught that fruitfulness is impossible apart from Christ, but that it is inevitable if we preserve vital contact with him. Fruitfulness is not something we achieve in the natural energies of the flesh but something that follows naturally enough when we are in Christ.

There is no life apart from Christ, and this is brought out with the grim warning for anyone who "does not remain in me" (v. 6). We should not understand this to mean that Christ will ever cast off anyone who is a genuine disciple. We might take Judas as an example. He had had very close contact with Jesus, had indeed been an honored member of the apostolic band, for he had been entrusted with their financial affairs (12:6). But in the Upper Room Jesus said that this man was not "clean" (13:10–11), using the very word he has just used to characterize his followers (v. 3). Despite outward appearances, Judas was not really a disciple. Such a man "does not remain" in Christ (how could he?), and we should be in no doubt that the ultimate fate of such a person is horrific.

The imagery of the vineyard is brought in to emphasize the point. The barren canes that are cut from the vine wither up and in the end they are gathered, thrown into the fire, and burned. The past tense is used in the verbs "thrown out" and "withered," presumably to emphasize the certainty of it all. There is to be no doubt as to their ultimate fate.

Prayer

Abiding in Christ is important for other reasons than the production of Christian character, the bringing forth of Christian qualities in the life day by day. Jesus now tells his hearers that it is a condition of prevailing prayer. "If you remain in me," he says, bringing out this point of personal relationship, "and my words remain in you," which stresses the importance of being at home in Jesus' teaching, then "ask what you will and it will be done for you" (v. 7). The verb *ask* is an imperative. There are, it is true, some manuscripts that read "you will ask" (and which were followed by the translators of KJV), but most scholars agree that this reading is not as well supported as the imperative. The better manuscripts read "ask"; Jesus is not simply telling the disciples that if they pray certain things will follow. He is encouraging them to pray, indeed, commanding them to pray. We should not think of prayer as an optional activity for Christians who like that sort of thing. It is a necessary part of being followers of Jesus.

A breathtaking promise is attached to prayer like this. Disciples are to ask what they will "and it will be done for you." We should not understand this to mean that prayer is a kind of magic talisman, such that any desires the Christian may have are bound to be gratified. Jesus is talking about prayer that is made by the person who "remains" in him and in whom his "words" (i.e., his teachings) remain. In other words, he is speaking about the person whose life is directed singly towards the doing of the will of God. One who is in this way close to Christ and whose understanding is enlightened by the teaching of Christ will naturally pray the kind of prayer that is in line with the will of God. The result will be answered prayer, and Jesus sees this as an encouragement for the person doing him service.

Jesus returns to fruit-bearing and links that with the essence of discipleship (v. 8). There is an ambiguity about the words, and it is not at all clear which way we should take them. It is plain that Jesus starts this sentence with a reference to the glorifying of God; we glorify God by the bearing of the kind of fruit he has been talking about. When we become the kind of people who are bearing the fruit of Christian character, this brings glory to God, for it is he who brings the fruit into ripeness.

But the question is whether we should supply "so" before "be my disciples." Some hold firmly that we should, in which case we are to understand Jesus to mean that it is in the bringing forth of fruit that we are in fact disciples. Some hold equally firmly that we should not interpose a "so" in this way. They understand the words to mean that we bring glory to God in two ways: in bearing fruit and in being disciples. It is not easy to decide between these two possibilities, but, however we do it, it is clear that Jesus is teaching that discipleship goes on and on. We are not to think of it as something that is over and done with when we turn from our sin and look to Christ for forgiveness. That is the beginning, but the bearing of fruit and the increasing growth in discipleship are important parts of being Christian.

Love and Joy

It is characteristic of this Gospel that we now find a reference to love and a further connection between love and keeping Jesus' commandments (v. 9). Jesus begins with the Father's love for him. That is the foundation of everything. It is only because of the Father's deep love that Jesus' earthly mission takes place. Jesus goes on to say that, in the same way as the Father loves him, he loves the disciples. This is a wonderful and surprising thought, and we should be in no doubt as to the magnitude of Christ's love for his people. His love is no shallow emotion, easily aroused and as easily dispersed. It is a love that proceeds from what he is and is an expression of his innermost being. Jesus leaves no doubt that he loves them and that they should take care that they "remain" in that love. There is a sense, of course, in which it is impossible to stop Christ from loving us. In that sense we need do nothing. But there is another sense in which we can so live and feel and think that we cease to find that love the center of our being. We can turn our thoughts and our attention to the things of this life and be so caught up in that life that we cease to "remain" in that love. As far as it concerns us, we are thereby no longer in love and are cutting ourselves off from some of the blessings that Christ offers us.

Now to love with any depth is to have such a concern for the beloved that we want to do what will please the one we love. Jesus says that this is so with the love of God and with his love (v. 10). He says that he has kept the Father's commandments and abides in the Father's love. He calls on his followers similarly to keep his commandments and abide in his love. If we disregard the things Christ wants us to do, we are not really abiding in his love. We are cutting ourselves off from some of the blessings he offers.

Jesus goes on by bringing in a new note, that of joy (v. 11). Up till this point the word *joy* has occurred in only one verse in this Gospel (3:29). But in the Upper Room it is used seven times. The last night Jesus had with his disciples was certainly a very solemn one, and there is a note of serious purpose running through all that he said to them. But we are in serious error if we think of that evening as a gloomy one. The service of God is a joyous affair and Jesus makes that very clear. The purpose of what he has spoken, he now says, is "so that my joy might be in you." He looks to his followers to have the same joy as he has. They are serving the same God and they should share the same joy. He puts it another way when he goes on "and your joy might be filled full." He does not want their joy to be lacking in the slightest degree.

Perhaps it is worth reflecting again that this is something very different from the world's happiness, which depends on what happens day by day. If those things please us, we are "happy"; if they displease us, we are sad. But joy goes much deeper. It is possible to have an abiding joy even in the midst of troubles and disasters. It is joy, not passing happiness, that Jesus looks for in his followers. He has taught them so that they might have their joy as full as it can possibly be.

65

Love and Hatred

"This is my commandment that you love one another as I have loved you. No one has greater love than this, that one lays down his life for his friends. You are my friends if you do what I command you. No longer do I call you slaves, because the slave does not know what his lord is doing; but I have called you friends because I have made known to you all the things that I heard from my Father. You did not choose me, but I chose you and appointed you so that you might go and bear fruit and that your fruit should remain so that whatever you ask the Father in my name he will give it to you.

"These things I command you, that you love one another. If the world hates you, know that it hated me before it hated you. If you were of the world, the world would love its own; but because you are not of the world, but I chose you out of the world, for this reason the world hates you. Remember the word that I said to you, 'A slave is not greater than his lord.' If they persecuted me, they will persecute you too; if they kept my word, they will keep yours also. But they will do all these things to you for my name's sake because they do not know him that sent me. If I had not come and spoken to them they would not have had sin; but now they have no excuse for their sin. He who hates me hates my Father also. If I had not done among them the works which nobody else did, they would not have had sin; but now they have both seen and hated both me and my Father. But (this happened) so that the word that has been written in their law might be fulfilled. 'They hated me without a cause'" (John 15:12–25).

Love is the greatest thing, and Jesus comes back to it in this part of his discourse. Once again we have an emphasis on the importance of following Jesus' instruction. We have seen several times in our study of this discourse that love and the keeping of commandments are linked. Indeed, Jesus joined them no farther back than verse 10, though we should notice a difference: there he spoke of keeping his "commandments," here of his "commandment." Both ways of looking at it are important. If we consider the plural, we are reminded that we must not pick and choose among Jesus' commandments, keeping the ones of which we approve and neglecting others, either because we do not like them or because we find them too hard. They are all commandments of our Lord, and being his servant means recognizing them all as important. It is very easy to be selective in our obedience, but that is not the Christian way. If Jesus is truly our Lord, then we will see all his commandments as important.

But here we have the singular. While it is true that there are many commandments, it is also true that in the end they all boil down to one—love! If we really understand what love in the Christian sense is, we need no other guide. This is behind a saying of Augustine's, which is often misquoted in modern writings in the form of "Love God and do what you like." What that great man really said was even more shocking: "Love, and do what you like." But we must understand Augustine carefully. He was not saying that if we love we can go happily through life doing good or ill as we choose. He was saying that if we understand what love in the Christian sense is, if we really understand it, then we need no other guide to Christian living.

Love in the Christian sense is not sentimentality; it is not a gushing, emotional indulgence of some loved one. Love is what we see in the cross. It is what Christ showed when he laid down his perfect life for sinners. It is important to bear in mind that it is love *for sinners*. Jesus does not mean the kind of love that we so commonly have in mind when we use the term, a love for someone whom we find supremely attractive (sinners are not attractive to a holy God). Nor is it a love for those bound to us by natural ties, such as family members (God is not bound by natural ties to sinful people). Nor is it the love of friendship, a love drawn out from us by those we find congenial (God does not find sin or those who practice sin congenial). A love for sinners means a love that proceeds from the fact that God *is* love; he loves because it is his nature to love.

And redeemed sinners love because it is their nature to love. Not their old sinful nature, but the result of the "new creation" that takes place when they put their trust in Christ (2 Cor. 5:17). That means a complete transformation. As Paul puts it, "The old things have passed away; look, they have become new!" I imagine that this transformation is never one hundred percent in this life. But every real Christian knows that Christ transforms. And the closer we live to God, the more loving we become. We who are Christians love, but not because it has been our good fortune to come across some highly attractive people. We love because we have become loving people ourselves, people who love because we have been loved, not because of the merits of the people we encounter on our way through life. That is surely what Jesus is saying when he says "love one another as I have loved you." We are not to love in the same way as the world loves, but in the same way as Christ loves.

Friends and Slaves

These words were spoken on the eve of Calvary. Accordingly, when Jesus then said, "No one has greater love than this, that one lays down his life for his friends" (v. 13), this is more than rhetoric. He was about to do just that for the little band before him and for sinners throughout the world and through all the ages. His love is the standard. We are not to estimate our love by the kind of love we see in the world round about us, a love hopelessly caught up in emotions directed towards the attractive. I do not mean that such love is not a real and meaningful part of life. Romantic love, family love, love for friends—all these are wonderful parts of the well-rounded life. But we must be clear that, wonderful as they are, they are not "love" in the sense that Jesus is using the term here. He is talking about the kind of love that persists even though it means death.

He speaks of dying for friends, but this must be understood carefully. It is true that those who were with Jesus in the Upper Room were his friends and that he would die for them. But one of the little band was Judas, who even as Jesus spoke had gone out to betray him. Others had spent time in the Upper Room quarreling about who would be the greatest (Luke 22:24). In Gethsemane, when Jesus would ask the three who were closest to him to watch with him in the hour of his greatest agony, they would simply fall asleep (Mark 14:33f., 37). And when the soldiers came "they all forsook him and fled" (Mark 14:50). It was not his friends' supreme merits that won Christ's love. His love for them was despite their many demerits, for they were sinners, as are all the human race. But, sinners though they were, he loved them. And his love issued in his atoning death, a death for them and for other sinners.

Despite everything, he says that they are friends and reminds them that this means obedience on their part (v. 14). It is impossible to continue as friends with people whom we oppose. Jesus does not mean that a condition of friendship is a servile, boot-licking relationship. The obedience for which he looks is not that. It is rather a recognition that what he says is to be taken with full seriousness, and that seriousness is to be shown in the manner of our living, with due regard to what Jesus wants of us.

There is a difference between a friend and a slave. A slave may be well liked by his master and well treated. But in the end he is a slave, owned and used by the master and not knowing what it is that he is really doing or why he is doing it (v. 15). The slave receives his instructions and goes off to do what he is told. But he is not informed of his master's purpose and is required only to give blind obedience.

On a different level there is a story that illustrates the point. It is said of Henry Ford that he used to call on his executives in their offices when he wanted to confer with them on ways of ironing out problems in the organization. They greatly appreciated his courtesy. He could have summoned them to his office, but instead he called on them. But one day one of his associates said to him, "I wonder that in such a big organization you go out to call on people. Wouldn't it save time if you asked them to call on you?" "No, it would not," said Henry Ford, "When I'm through I can get out of their offices faster than I can get them out of mine!" His executives were not slaves, but they certainly did not know what their master was doing. It was the saving of time, not courtesy to his associates, that dictated his action.

This sort of ignorance runs through much of life. People in high places do not always take those with whom they work into their confidence. But Jesus says that he has "made known" to his followers "all the things that I heard from my Father." This does not, of course, mean that they had become omniscient, but it does mean that they had had a full revelation. All the things that it is good for the servants of God to know they knew. Their lives should respond to that knowledge. We should remember that in the Old Testament we read that Abraham was the friend of God (Isa. 41:8) and that God did not hide from Abraham what he proposed to do (Gen. 18:17). Similarly, God spoke to Moses as to a friend (Exod. 33:11). The disciples had been admitted to a relationship like that. They were not slaves but friends.

Chosen and Appointed

The hand of God was in all this, which brings us to another point, namely that the disciples did not choose Jesus but he chose them (v. 16). This was not the way it was in the schools of the day. A would-be disciple chose the rabbi under whom he wished to study and sought acceptance as one of his followers. But Jesus' disciples did not in the first instance seek him out—he chose them and called them. This idea of election is important throughout the New Testament. It is not always expressed in the same terminology, but the idea that it was God who took the initiative in bringing people to salvation is found in one way or another right through the New Testament.

In a way this is fairly obvious. Sinful people do not want to forsake their sin. It is much too uncomfortable a process and, left to themselves, they will never do it. But all believers have had their equivalent of the Damascus Road. It may not have been as spectacular as Paul's experience, and they may not even be able to pinpoint a particular time and place when it occurred. These things do not matter. What matters is that we have all had our experience of coming to realize that it was God who chose us, not we who chose God. Without that divine initiative we would never have become Christians at all.

God did not only choose the disciples to be saved but "appointed" them, and this, too, points to a universal Christian experience. God does not call any of his children simply to become members of his heavenly family and then spend their time in blissful idleness. He calls us all to service. This, of course, gives a certain dignity to the life of the Christian. No matter how humble our circumstances, how small our abilities, how limited our scope, we are all called to serve. There is always something to be done for God in the place where we find ourselves. And because we (and no one else) are there, we must do it.

Jesus speaks of the importance attaching to "fruit": the disciples were chosen and appointed so that they "might go and bear fruit." We saw in an earlier study that "fruit" probably means the fruit of Christian character (cf. Gal. 5:22f.), though it is not excluded that it may mean the winning of others for Christ. In this place the command to "go" and bear fruit seems to show that winning people is at least partly what is meant. There seems no point in their "going" unless it was to be where people are and to do something about their lostness.

Whichever be the right understanding, Jesus calls on them to bear the kind of fruit that will "remain." He does not look for cometlike Christians, people who flash across the firmament in a brilliant blaze of light and then speedily disappear. It is important that their fruit should remain, whether we are thinking in terms of qualities of character or of converts. It is important that we keep on living lives appropriate to our Christian profession. We cannot be worthwhile Christians by fits and starts. Constancy is an important part of being a Christian.

And when we bring people to Christ it is important that they, too, remain. We should not encourage them to make an outward profession with no inward substance. They should know the kind of commitment that is required of the followers of Christ before they make their own. Perseverance is a most important quality.

Interestingly, all this is to be done "so that whatever you ask the Father in my name he will give it to you." We usually think of things the other way round. We see prevailing prayer as important because it enables us to bear fruit, and, of course, there is truth in this. Unless we do our service of God prayerfully, unless prayer precedes and follows all we do, we need not expect to accomplish anything lasting. But what Jesus says here shows that we ought not to think of prayer as something in the nature of a tool that enables us to do better service. Rather, we do better service in order that we may pray more effectively. It seems that Jesus wants us to see a ministry of prayer as in itself important. We know of a few people who have been great men and women of prayer. We think, perhaps, of a "praying Hyde" and recognize that a person who prays effectively may do great things for God. But mostly we see this in terms of someone else. Prayer, however, is important for each and every one of us. Jesus is here telling his followers that it is important that we should all have set before us the goal of being more effective in our praying.

Love and Hate

We could take verse 17 either with what precedes or with what follows. Many regard it as the conclusion of the preceding paragraph, and they may be right. I rather think it begins a new section with the reminder that the Christian way is the way of love, before Jesus goes on to speak of the world's hatred. That hatred is discerned for what it is over against the background of the love that should characterize Christians.

Jesus repeats a command he has given more than once (v. 17; cf. 13:34; 15:12). It is very important and the repetition underlines this. He introduces it with "these things," which is not what we expect when there is but one thing commanded. The meaning may be that all the commandments Jesus has given in the end amount to this: love one another. Alternatively Jesus may mean that all the varied commandments he has given are for one purpose: to lead the disciples to love each other. A few manuscripts leave out "that," in which case we would have "These things I command you: love one another." This is very forceful if somewhat ungrammatical, and it is adopted by the New English Bible (with a correction of the grammar): "This is my commandment to you: love one another." Whichever way we take it, there can be no doubting the emphasis Jesus is placing on love. That is the supremely important thing for the Christian. It was so in the days of his flesh and it is so still.

From the love of Christians Jesus moves on to the hatred of the world. "If the world hates you . . ." (v. 18) does not throw any doubt on the process. This is a conditional with the meaning "If [as is the case]. . . ." Christians are called on to put their emphasis on love, but as they do this they should not live in some fairyland of their own manufacture, imagining that the world will respond to their love with an answering love. Unless there is a miracle of grace in the hearts of worldly people, they will do nothing of the sort (and if the miracle takes place, they cease, of course, to be "the world"). William Temple remarks that the world "would not hate angels for being angelic; but it does hate men for being Christians. It grudges them their new character; it is tormented by their peace; it is infuriated by their joy." Whether or not Temple is right in his reasons, the fact is that the world typically refuses to be impressed by the love Christians show, and we deceive ourselves if we look for anything other than hatred or at best indifference.

Jesus goes on to point out that the world hated him before it hated his followers. Indeed, it was initially their hatred of Jesus that led worldly people to hate Christians. When they experience the world's hatred it is an encouragement to Christians to reflect that they are sharing their Lord's experience. It is quite something to be called on to share what Jesus underwent.

There is an inevitability about all this. "If you were of the world . . ." Jesus goes on (v. 19), where the construction implies a negative: "If you were (as you are not). . . ." There is a sharp distinction between worldly people and Christians. "Of" here points to origin: "If your essential being originated in the world. . . ." There is, of course, a sense in which Christians do belong to the world. They were born into it in exactly the same way as the worldly, and they grew up seeing exactly the same glitter and tinsel. But they are not worldly people in what matters. "You are not of the world," Jesus says, drawing attention to the fact that that which is distinctive of Christians did not originate in anything in this world. What has happened to them is that Jesus "chose [them] out of the world." Here again we have the wonder of election, the marvel of divine grace. Christians live *in* this world, but their essential being is not *of* this world. They are what they are because of what God has done in them and not on account of any merit or achievement of their own.

Persecution

The believer should not delude himself into thinking that he can do better with the world than his Master could. Jesus reminds his followers that he had earlier said, "The servant is not greater than his lord" (v. 20; cf. 13:16; Matt. 10:24). If, then, the world persecuted Jesus, it is inevitable that it will persecute his followers. They stand for the same truths.

We might have expected him to go on "If they did not keep my word. . . ." As we go through this Gospel we see how over and over again the people who heard Jesus rejected him; certainly those we would regard as "the world" often did this. But Jesus says, "if they kept my word. . . ." While there was widespread rejection of all that Jesus stood for, a rejection that would in the end put him on a cross, it was also the case that there were some people who took heed: they "kept" his word. There were people like the apostles, like Nicodemus, like the woman at the well, like Joseph of Arimathea and others. Jesus remembers this and includes it in his warning. While his followers could not expect to be wildly popular among worldly people, and while they must expect that by and large their message would be rejected by the world, they must also expect that sometimes there would be encouragement. Some worldly people accepted Jesus' message and were changed by the power of God, and some people would accept the message of his followers and be changed by the same power of God. There is warning but there is also encouragement in the words.

There is a reason behind the world's action. The world "will do all these things to you," Jesus says, "for my name's sake" (v. 21). The latter does not mean, as we might expect, "to set forward my purposes" or the like. Rather the reverse. The "name," as elsewhere, stands for the whole person. The people in question will act like this because of their attitude to Jesus. They do not know God (whatever pious expressions they might use). God is "him that sent me." Again we have the thought of mission. That God had manifested himself in Jesus is one of the key thoughts of this Gospel, and we meet it again and again. But these people do not know the God they profess to worship. And, because they do not know God, they do not respect Jesus or his teaching or his sacrificial love. The more closely his followers stick to his teachings, the more certainly the world will reject them.

No Excuse

We are not to think that there was some natural inability on the part of the Jews such that they were guiltless in their rejection of Jesus. They had had the very best of opportunities. The Son of God himself had come and spoken to them (v. 22) and had done in their presence "the works that nobody else did" (v. 24). Had it not been for his presence perhaps they would have been able to say, "We did not know." But they can have no excuse now. What more could be done for people than had been done for them?

Throughout this Gospel it is made plain that the rejection of Jesus is a very serious matter. It is the rejection of God himself, and no one can do this and remain guiltless. In rejecting Jesus the people had rejected God, for there is no way of differentiating between them.

The last words in this section of the Gospel assure the reader that all this does not mean that people had become too strong for God and that matters were now no longer under his control. For John that would be blasphemy and a serious misunderstanding of the facts of the case. God is a great God and he is supreme, no matter what people may say and do. So in the end—when they have rejected Jesus, dispersed his followers, and put him on a cross—they would not have won a notable victory. They would simply have set forward what God had planned. Their very hatred was foretold in Scripture (see Ps. 35:19; 69:4; 109:3). Their evil actions left them blameworthy. But in the end God is not mocked: his purposes come to their appointed conclusion.

66

The Spirit—And the Persecuted

"When the Paraclete comes, whom I will send to you from the Father, the Spirit of truth who proceeds from the Father, he will bear witness about me; and you also bear witness, because you have been with me from the beginning" (John 15:26–27).

For a third time, Jesus refers to the Holy Spirit as "the Paraclete" (v. 26; cf. 14:16, 26), that term that is so difficult to translate and that brings out something of the ideas of "a friend at court" and of strengthening. In the older translations this term was often rendered as "Comforter" (so the KJV), a term we owe to Wycliffe. The derivation of the word may be held to support this (from the Latin *con* ["with"] and *fortis* ["strong"]). It can also be said that the understanding of the word as "comforter" or "consoler" goes back to the early Greek commentators on the text, and what they said must always be treated with respect because they were commenting on a Gospel written in their own language. They had a natural feel for the words that we do not, for we come with a different linguistic approach. But in this case it is difficult to think that they were right. They give no reason for this understanding of the term, and no passage outside John, whether in the Greek Bible or in non-biblical Greek, can be cited in support of the meaning "consoler." Incidentally, the word is used of Jesus in 1 John 2:1; but in its other New Testament occurrences it always refers to the Holy Spirit, and when used of the Spirit it is always used by Jesus.

As we noted in an earlier study, the term is often used in legal contexts, where it can denote someone like the accused's legal representative, his "advocate" or "counsel for the defense." The translation "Advocate" is adopted by the New English Bible, while "Counselor" in the Revised Standard Version has much the same force. Though such an understanding can claim support from Greek writings in general, it does not seem right in John. While it is true that sinners are in danger when they face the judgment of God and that they can do with a capable defender at such a time, it is also true that in this Gospel the word never applies to that time. Rather, it is used of the Spirit's activities now. Again, a legal representative argues *for* his client, but the Spirit argues *with* his client (16:8ff.). He convicts people rather than defends them.

But among the Greeks a *parakletos* was used in a wider sense than is a "legal representative" with us. If you were in trouble in a lawsuit in ancient Greece, it seems that your friends could come to the court and say things like "I was not present at the scene of the crime so did not see what happened. But I know my friend and I know he would not have done it." This is the activity of "a friend at court," though not a legally trained expert to control the defense, and *parakletos* may be used of it.

It seems as though the term has something of this meaning in John. What is in mind is a friend, a helper, one who provides what is needed and may on occasion be a strengthener. There is a legal background to the term, but the main idea here is of providing the help that is needed.

When Jesus says that the Paraclete "comes" he is pointing forward to a much fuller manifestation of the Spirit than people had seen hitherto. The Spirit is spoken of at times in the Old Testament (e.g., Gen. 1:2; Judg. 14:6; Ps. 51:11), and there are references to him during the time of Jesus' ministry (e.g., Mark 1:10; Luke 2:27; 4:1, 18). But the really striking activity of the Spirit begins with the day of Pentecost in Acts 2, and from that time on the Spirit is constantly at work among the people of God, guiding them in the path of service, leading and empowering them. It is to this abundant outpouring of the Spirit that Jesus looks forward.

The Spirit of Truth

Jesus has previously spoken of the Spirit as "the Spirit of truth" (14:17), and he will use the expression again (16:13). It is an important way of looking at the Spirit, and truth is an important concept in this Gospel. We have seen that actions as well as words may be linked with truth (3:21) and that Jesus can say that he himself is the truth (14:6). We are to understand that God is concerned with truth in the deepest sense, not with the half-truths in which people so often delight. We frequently find ourselves in a situation in which to speak and act truly is most uncomfortable. We do not normally care to put ourselves squarely in the place of the liar and the evildoer, but we so easily settle for a halfway position. We should be clear that this is not the Christian way.

The truth that Jesus embodies is absolute truth, and when we declare ourselves to be his people we profess to be on the side of truth. What we find here is that the Spirit of God is as much for the truth as is Jesus. The Spirit who dwells in believers, who is their guide and helper, is a Spirit characterized by truth.

Sent from the Father

Jesus says, "I will send" him and send him "from the Father." There is a variety of ways of looking at the sending of the Spirit, and elsewhere we find that Jesus prays to the Father that he would send the Spirit (14:16). Or it may be said that the Father sends the Spirit in Christ's name (14:26). Again, Jesus can say simply that he will send the Spirit (16:7). From all this it seems that in some way both the Father and the Son are involved in the sending of the Spirit. We ought not to think of division or of compartmentalization within the Godhead. Clearly these various ways of putting it bring out the truth that all three persons of the Godhead take part in bringing to believers the help they need as they seek to do their service of God in this difficult world.

Jesus goes on to refer to the Spirit as one "who proceeds from the Father." This seems reasonably straightforward, even though there are some difficulties. Jesus is surely saying that, when he leaves this earth to go to be with his Father, he will send the Spirit to them, the Spirit who is with the Father. There appears to be some emphasis on the fact that, even though it is Jesus who will send the Spirit, it is from the Father that he will send him. Indeed, it can be said that it is from the Father that the Spirit "proceeds."

This verse has been drawn into profound theological discussions, and historically it was the occasion of the split of the Eastern church (which we often speak of as "the Greek Orthodox Church") from the Western church (the church of Rome). The trouble arose from the way worshipers say the creed. The Nicene Creed was used throughout the church in early days, and it affirmed belief in the Holy Spirit "who proceeds from the Father." In this form it was derived from the verse before us. Theologians were not able to say precisely how the Spirit is related to the other persons in the Godhead, but they felt they were safe enough if they stuck to what is said in Scripture, so they quoted John 15:26 and said he "proceeds from the Father."

An objection might be lodged to what they did, for Jesus is clearly speaking about the Holy Spirit's mission in the church ("I will send . . ."), whereas the theologians were referring to the eternal relationship between the Father and the Spirit. It was not really wise to take words that apply to one temporal activity of the Spirit and apply them to an eternal relationship. But the words certainly emphasize the close relationship between the Father and the Spirit, and that is important. And presumably that is why the Eastern churches find it satisfactory to recite the creed in that form to this day.

But in the West there tended to be an emphasis on the fact that the Spirit is closely connected with the Son as well as with the Father. He could be called "the Spirit of Jesus" (Acts 16:7) or "the Spirit of Christ" (Rom. 8:9), as well as "the Spirit of God" (Rom. 8:9; 1 Cor. 2:14). And it is not just a matter of quoting a few isolated passages. Throughout the New Testament the Spirit is closely associated with Jesus, just as he is with the Father. Indeed, in the passage we are discussing, which says that the Spirit proceeds from the Father, it also says that it is Jesus who sends him. The result of giving emphasis to this aspect of scriptural teaching led the church in the West to recite the creed in the form "proceeds from the Father and the Son." While this was not the wording of the creed in its original form, the form in which it was adopted by the ancient councils of the church, it seemed to the Westerners to express an important truth.

In time the Eastern church demanded that the Westerners use the creed in its proper, ancient form and, indeed, said it would not remain in communion with the Western church if it did not. But the Western church held that—while it was proper to speak of the Spirit as proceeding from the Father (there was no objection to the Easterners continuing their practice)—to remove the reference to the Son, after they had for centuries recited the creed in this way, would be to deny an important piece of New Testament teaching. So bitter was the quarrel that the Eastern church separated from the Western church, and to this day there has been no reconciliation.

The passage at which we are looking has thus had an important influence on the course of church history. We cannot but feel that it is a pity that theologians have been so bitter about a passage that is really not dealing with their subject. Jesus is talking about the mission of the Spirit here on earth, not about his eternal relationship to the Father. It is a warning to us to use Scripture carefully and not to try to make it say something it is not saying.

For us it is important that the Spirit who lives in our hearts comes from both the Father and the Son. There is no division in the Godhead, but God has provided for our need by sending the Spirit to us. It is well, accordingly, that we respond with all our hearts to what the Spirit does for us and in us.

Witness

The mission of the Spirit is described in terms of witness, a concept that means a great deal to John, as we have noted before. He sees witness as borne by the Father (5:31f.) and the Son (8:14, 18) as well as the Spirit. Witness is also borne by Jesus' works (5:36) and by Scripture (5:39). A good deal of emphasis is placed on the witness of the Baptist, who indeed came in order to bear witness (1:7), and there is a variety of other human witness (e.g., 4:39; 12:17). John leaves us in no doubt that he is not telling us of interesting fables he has acquired or made up, but of real happenings to which witness has been borne. And especially is witness borne to Jesus, as it is here.

The witness is first spoken of as that of the Spirit. Human witness is not unimportant, but it pales into insignificance alongside divine witness. When believers go forth with the Christian message they are referring not to something human wisdom has thought up but to that for which there is divine testimony. This is one of the most fundamental of all the things John is saying to his readers.

The basic task of believers is not to do some incredible feat of service, but to bear witness to what God has done. Their witness is joined to that of the Spirit (v. 27). This surely means that the witness we bear is not a purely human achievement. If we set out to do it the way we want and in the terms we choose, we are in danger of perverting the essence of the gospel message. We are to do it looking to the Spirit to be our helper. It is as he prompts us and in the terms he gives us that we are to bear our witness.

"You also bear witness," Jesus says (v. 27), where "you" is emphatic. This is a task that he gives over to his followers, not to the human race in general. And on this occasion he can give as his reason "you have been with me from the beginning." The definitive witness is borne by those who have been with Jesus and have had the opportunity of learning directly from him. All that claims to be Christian teaching must agree with what the apostles testified. The church claims to be "apostolic," and the claim is justified only as far as it teaches what the apostles taught. In our modern environment, with all its cultural differences, there will be many things we must say that are not exactly the way the apostles would have put it in their day. But it is important that the modern church agrees with the apostolic witness. We may use the language that is proper to our own situation, but it must express the truths the apostles were setting forth. "Witness" reminds us that we are testifying to what God has done in Christ, and with all our readiness to adapt to our cultural and social environment this is something we must always bear in mind. It is witness, not inventiveness, that is called for from us.

"Bear witness" here might be imperative or indicative: Jesus may be giving a command or saying what it is that his followers do. There is probably not much difference, for even if we take the words as a statement, there is a command lying behind it. Jesus is making it clear that it is witness that is the significant Christian activity.

Persecutions Will Come

"These things I have spoken to you, so that you will not be trapped. They will put you out of synagogues; indeed an hour is coming when everyone who kills you will think he offers God service. And these things they will do because they have known neither the Father nor me. But I have spoken these things to you so that when the hour comes you may remember them, that I told you. I did not tell you these things at the beginning, because I was with you" (John 16:1–4).

Again Jesus uses the expression "These things I have spoken to you" (v. 1; seven times in this discourse), where the perfect tense gives a sense of permanence and solemnity to the words in question. This final discourse of Jesus to his apostles is of special significance. The verb I have translated "be trapped" is one that is derived from the term for the bait stick of a trap, the stick that triggers a trap when a bird or animal touches it. It is used a number of times in the New Testament for getting into trouble, but more especially spiritual trouble. The King James Version renders this "be offended," and other translations have "caused to stumble" or the like. However we render it, the verb draws attention to the ease with which Jesus' followers can take a course of action that will lead them into trouble. And the whole sentence speaks of Jesus' concern that this should not happen. "So that" indicates purpose: this is the aim of his discourse.

Jesus has just spoken of the Holy Spirit whom he would send from the Father to help them, and from that he turns to the kind of conduct his enemies would engage in as they sought to overthrow his followers. "They will put you out of synagogues," he says (v. 2), which would be a terrifying punishment for a Jew. As we have previously noticed, the synagogue was not only a place of worship, but a school and a center of social life for the Jewish community. To be expelled from it meant to be isolated from most of the activities that made up Jewish life. But the apostles must be clear that this was what they faced. If they thought that the Jews in general would give them a warm and sympathetic welcome, they were out of touch with reality.

Indeed, their enemies would go further. The word I have translated "indeed" is a strong adversative and often has meanings like "but, on the contrary." Here the force of it is, as a standard grammar puts it, "Not only this, but also," used to introduce a further point with some emphasis. Jesus is saying that, contrary to anything that might have been expected, there would be people who would think that killing his followers was a service to God. In due course this, of course, came to pass. It is one of the tragic ironies of history that from time to time the phenomenon recurs: people who are convinced that they are serving God oppose in the strongest way the real servants of God. The Spanish Inquisition is a striking illustration. The great tragedy of that inquisition was that it was run by sincere, godly men, men who thought they were doing God service as they tortured and killed people who professed the faith.

Why do people do things like this? "Because," Jesus says, "they have known neither the Father nor me" (v. 3). To say the right words about God and to know him are not the same thing. Jesus' words are a standing warning to his followers that they must give good heed to the things he said to them and to the things the Holy Spirit says to them as they go about their task of Christian service. There is no substitute for diligent study of Scripture and for taking with full seriousness what Jesus has said. It is very easy for us to be so sure that we know what the will of God is that we twist Scripture and make it say what we think it ought to have said.

The world does this sort of thing constantly. I am reminded of an incident related by the actress Helen Hayes. She says that she woke up one day to the fact that she had a reputation for being careless about her appearance, so decided to do something about it. She went to an exclusive dressmaker and had a special frock made, at a cost of $1,000. She wore it with a coral rose pin surrounded by diamonds and thought that for once she was doing things in style. But, after the press conference to which she wore it all, one of the reporters wrote: "There she sat, queen of the theatre, looking like a *hausfrau* in some costume jewelry and a little brown suit off the rack." That reporter was obviously interested not in what Helen Hayes was in fact wearing, but in what he thought she would be wearing.

And it is sometimes like that with the followers of Jesus. There are those in the world who are so sure of their own rightness and the error of true Christians that they are not going to give much attention to what they do and say. We do not like this, but we must reckon with it as one of the facts of life. The way of the true servant of God is never an easy way, and there will always be strong opposition from people who ought to know better but who are prejudiced.

Jesus has spoken in this way so that his followers will not be overtaken with surprise when they find this kind of opposition. It is not difficult to see why worldly people oppose the servants of God; that is only to be expected. But it is difficult to see why those who profess to be God's own children should oppose those who are faithful to the teachings of Jesus. In every generation that causes surprise. But Jesus says now, "I have spoken these things to you so that when the hour comes you may remember them" (v. 4). The end of the sentence is awkward but the words underline the point Jesus is making. His "I" is emphatic; no less than he is giving this solemn warning. Let them remember it in the day when they are in trouble. They will then know that what is happening is certainly not out of his control. He knew it would happen and he has provided for his own. They are facing a new situation, and this is why he gives this teaching. There was no need for it earlier "because I was with you." Jesus is now preparing his followers for a time when he would not be with them.

67

The Work of the Spirit

"But now I am going to him who sent me and none of you is asking me, 'Where are you going?' But because I have said these things to you sorrow has filled your heart. But I am telling you the truth, it is expedient for you that I go away. For, if I do not go away, the Paraclete will not come to you; but if I go away I will send him to you. And he, when he has come, will convict the world about sin and about righteousness and about judgment. About sin, because they do not believe in me; about righteousness, because I am going to the Father and no longer do you see me; and about judgment, because the ruler of this world has been judged.

"I still have many things to say to you, but you cannot bear them now. But when he, the Spirit of truth, comes he will lead you in all the truth. He will not speak from himself, but whatever he shall hear he will speak and he will declare to you the things that are to come. He will glorify me because he will take of mine and declare it to you. All things that the Father has are mine; for this reason I said that he takes of mine and will declare it to you" (John 16:5–15).

Jesus has spoken about the persecutions and other troubles his followers will have to face, and this note continues in chapter 16. In this chapter John uses the word *sorrow* four times, and he uses it nowhere else in his Gospel. But, as he speaks of the troubles the disciples will face, he speaks also of the resources they will have and particularly of the work of the Holy Spirit.

"But now" sets what follows in contrast to the preceding. Jesus is speaking of a whole new set of circumstances introduced by the fact that he is going off "to him who sent me" (v. 5). It is one thing for them to have Jesus visibly present among them and quite another for him to have removed to the other world. It is interesting that he does not say at this point, "I am going to my Father," but rather, "I am going to him who sent me." Right to the end he retains the language of mission. His time on earth had not been aimless, but he had been "sent" by the Father, sent for a purpose that was now about to reach its climax. We should also not miss the point that Jesus does not say, "I will be killed," or the like. He could have said something about the malice of those who were set on destroying him or about the sin of murder. Such things would indeed be important factors in the happenings that were about to unfold. It is true that what would happen would involve the murderous activities of his enemies, but that would not be the most important thing. What was significant was that he would be accomplishing the purpose of "him who sent me."

It seems a trifle curious that Jesus says that "none of you is asking me, 'Where are you going?'" for Peter had asked just that question (13:36; cf. also the remark of Thomas in 14:5). But Peter had been more interested in what it would mean for him to have Jesus go away than in where Jesus would be going (and Thomas also was more concerned with the fact that the disciples could not possibly know either where Jesus was going or the way to his destination than he was with what would befall Jesus). None of the little band had seriously asked what was about to happen to their Lord; their concerns had been for themselves, not for him. So in a very real sense they had not asked the question "Where are you going?" We should also notice that Jesus uses the present tense, "none of you is asking me. . . ." He is concerned with the present moment. And at that present moment the disciples were more concerned with the bleak future that lay ahead of them without Jesus than they were with what was going to happen to him.

Jesus turns, then, to the disciples' situation. They had understood enough of what Jesus said to know that they faced a decisive separation from him and a future that would be very different from those wonderful years in which they had been so constantly with him. So, Jesus says, "sorrow has filled your heart" (v. 6). John uses a somewhat unusual construction here. When something like sorrow is said to "fill" anyone it is usually put in the passive form—the person is filled with sorrow. This way of putting it almost personifies sorrow; it gives a picture of sorrow as invading the heart and taking possession of it. This signifies a deep and wholehearted grief.

An Expedient Departure

But, despite their grief, Jesus will go. Why? A number of reasons might well be suggested, but here Jesus says simply that it will be better *for them*. He precedes this with a solemn introduction: "But I am telling you the truth" (v. 7). There is more than one word for "but" in Greek, and the one we have here is a strong adversative, with a meaning like "contrary to what might have been expected." Jesus' departure from the disciples did not look at first sight as though it would be very helpful for them, no matter how necessary it might be. The construction John uses in conveying what Jesus said brings out the point that the Master is not speaking of a human assessment of the position. On purely human calculations it might have been thought that Jesus' continued presence would have been of incalculable value to the little group. The last thing they wanted was for him to leave them. They saw it as unmitigated disaster. So what he is telling them is far from what they would have expected or could have worked out for themselves.

Then we should notice that Jesus' "I" is emphatic. They should take notice of the words because they take notice of the speaker. They know enough about Jesus to know that his teaching on spiritual things is unmatched, and thus they must take good heed to what he is now telling them. In a way "I am telling you the truth" is unnecessary, for when did Jesus do anything other than tell the truth? But the expression adds a note of solemnity to what he is saying now; it makes it quite clear that he is adding to their knowledge, not simply saying something cheerful that would brace them when they faced hardships.

"It is expedient for you that I go away," Jesus says. "Expedient for you." That must have been very hard for them to realize. These people had left everything—homes, jobs, their whole way of life—in order that they might be with Jesus, and they had counted it all as very worthwhile. They had rejoiced to be so constantly with someone who taught them so much and drew them so close to God. This was the high point of all their lives. If he had to leave them, they would doubtless have said, that would be plain disaster. They would have to bear it as best they could, but it would be a catastrophe of unimaginable magnitude. But now Jesus is saying that it was expedient that he go away, and not that it was expedient for him or for some great cause, but for them! How could it possibly be expedient for them to lose their greatest source of support and hope?

That is the way we all argue, isn't it? We get so used to the sources of help that God supplies us with that we cannot bear to be parted from them. But sometimes it is in the sorrows and griefs and deprivations of life that we learn the most important lessons and make the most significant progress. Nobody likes suffering and loss, but Christians must realize that sometimes it is in such experiences that our best interests lie.

It is worth noticing that Caiaphas had used the same word about Jesus' death. "It is expedient for you that one man should die," the high priest had said (11:50) as he introduced the plot to bring about Jesus' death. That is the way the world reasons. The cynical politician was not thinking of profound spiritual truth, but of what would best serve his interests as a leading figure in the nation and one who wanted to preserve his place. For him it was "expedient" that Jesus should die. It did not matter to Caiaphas whether Jesus was guilty of some crime or innocent. He was concerned only with what was expedient, with what served his own interests.

The trouble was that he did not know what really served his best interests. For Caiaphas, what mattered was keeping his place as the most important political figure among the Jews. For Jesus, what mattered was the spiritual need of each individual. Thus both could refer to what was "expedient," but because they had such different ideas of what was desirable the meanings they attached to the word were so very different.

So, in a somewhat different way, was it with the disciples. For them, nothing could be better and nothing could be more in their own interests than that Jesus should remain with them physically. For him, it was important that he should die that death that would put away their sins and open up the way to the new life lived in the power of God's Holy Spirit. If he remained with them in the way they desired, they would have his physical presence from time to time (there would be the necessary breaks when for good reason they were apart). But if he went through with the program the Father had for him, then in due course the Spirit would be given, a divine presence that would be with them constantly with no intermission. The Spirit would lead them and empower them and be the mainspring of the life they would lead. On this side of Pentecost it is unthinkable that the church should be anything other than a Spirit-dominated church. But the disciples could not see that from the place where they stood.

Jesus brings this out with the double statement that if he does not go away the Paraclete will not come, but if he goes away he will send him. We do not know why it was necessary for Jesus to go away if the Spirit was to come. It is enough for us to know that this was so. And when the work of Jesus was consummated the Spirit, the Paraclete, would do his wonderful work in believers. As he does to this day.

Convicting About Sin

There are many things the Spirit does, and Jesus goes on to speak of some of them (v. 8). Generally speaking, in the New Testament the work of the Spirit is done in believers, but here we have an interesting glimpse of something he does in unbelievers. Jesus speaks of a threefold work of "convicting." The verb *convict* is not an easy one to translate. Phillips and Rieu each make use of four different translations for this verb in verses 8–11. Phillips has "convince," "expose," "reveal," and "show"; Rieu prefers "overthrow," "convict," "show," and "teach." In not one place do their translations agree! The same verb means "to cross-examine for the purpose of convincing or refuting an opponent (the word being specially used of legal proceedings)," as Bernard puts it. Jesus, then, is saying that the Spirit will accomplish a threefold work of convicting, and that the three aspects will refer to sin, to righteousness, and to judgment. The word is not invariably used in a legal sense, but it often is, and the context shows that it is so used here. Jesus goes on explicitly to refer to judgment (v. 11); thus we cannot exclude the legal force here. Christ's saving work can be viewed from other angles than the legal one, but the legal way of looking at it is important, and that is what is before us in this passage.

It needs a work of the Spirit to convict anyone of sin. We so readily hold to our own righteousness—it is other people who do wrong, we think. Someone has said that if you ask a sufferer, "How did you stub your toe?" a woman may well reply, "I walked into a chair," but a man will tend to say, "Some fool left a chair in the middle of the room and I walked right into it!" Whatever be the truth in the generalization, it cannot be disputed for a moment that we all tend to blame other people if we can. The natural person always tends to see others as sinners, and thus the natural person sees no reason for accepting Jesus as Savior. What has he to be saved from? It is only when the Holy Spirit has done a work of grace in a person's heart that this person sees his sins for the horrible reality they are.

Jesus adds to the words about convicting of sin "because they do not believe in me" (v. 9), an expression that can be taken in more ways than one:

1. It might mean that the essence of their sin consists in the fact that they do not believe in Jesus. It is failure to believe that is the basic sin.

2. It might mean that the Spirit will convict people of erroneous ideas about sin, as shown in the fact that they do not believe. They have got it all wrong, and it needs the Spirit to help them to see sin for what it is.
3. It might mean that sin reached its heinous depth in the failure to believe in Christ. The fact that they do not believe is the supreme illustration of what sin is.

All three interpretations are possible (and all three are true). It seems that we have here another example of John's habit of using expressions that can be taken in more ways than one and where he wants his readers to see more meanings than one.

Convicting of Righteousness

The Spirit's work of convicting has other aspects. He will convict the world "about righteousness" (v. 10). There is a somewhat different meaning in "about" here. To convict the world about sin means to show the world that it is sinful, but to convict it about righteousness does not mean to show it that it is righteous. That would be in contradiction of the work of showing that it is sinful. No, righteousness here must mean the righteousness that Christ brought about by his atoning death. Some scholars think it means that Christ is shown to be righteous, in contradiction to the world's verdict when it put him on the cross. It is, of course, true that Christ is righteous and that in later days even many in the world would come to recognize this. But it seems more likely that here Jesus means that one thing the Spirit would do would be to convict people of the fact that the only righteousness that avails in the end is the righteousness that believers have because of Christ's atoning death.

To outward appearance the death of Jesus was anything but a mighty divine act. To die on a cross was to come under a curse in the view of most Jews, in accordance with the words of Deuteronomy 21:23 (cf. Gal. 3:13). The very fact that Jesus died in this way showed that he was forsaken by God (as he himself said [Mark 15:34]), and to the Jews in general that proved that he could not possibly be the Messiah. Even apart from this Jewish view, Calvary does not look to worldly people like a mighty divine act. The world can see Jesus as a martyr, perhaps as a man who was misunderstood by his own people and was put to death on trumped-up charges. But his solitary death, with his followers forsaking him and running away (Mark 14:50), seems to show nothing but weakness and the inability to cope with the world. It needs the work of the Holy Spirit to teach us that this lonely death was the means of taking away sin and establishing the righteousness that sinners need and cannot achieve.

The cross is at the heart of the Christian faith. Millions of believers through the centuries and through all the world have been able to testify that it is through the death of Jesus that their sins have been put away and that they have been able to enter into righteousness. But it is believers who see this, people in whom there is a work of the Holy Spirit of God. Without that work of the Spirit, no one would understand what righteousness really is and no one would have righteousness credited to him in the sight of God.

Jesus links this convicting with his going to the Father and thus to their seeing him no more. This might be understood of the cross, for that was the event in which Jesus was taken away from the life he had lived with his followers. But it seems more likely that it should be understood as a short summary of the events that were about to be realized, which included the cross, the resurrection, and the ascension. This complex of happenings was one great work of God in which Jesus would accomplish salvation for sinners and would return to his Father in such a way that they would see him no more. And it is in this complex that the world's salvation would be wrought out.

Convicting About Judgment

The third work the Spirit will do in the world is to convict it about judgment (v. 11). The world, of course, stands under judgment because of the evil it does, and it needs the Holy Spirit to bring this home. But it seems that it is not this that is in mind here, for Jesus goes on to say that "the ruler of this world has been judged." "The ruler of this world" is, of course, Satan (as in 12:31). Once again Jesus is talking about the defeat of the evil one, and it is interesting that he speaks of it not in military terms but as an act of judgment. It is true that God is stronger than Satan and that Calvary can be viewed as a defeat of that fallen one. But here Jesus is saying that justice is done. We are saved in a way that is not only powerful but right. We should also notice that the verb "has been judged" is in the perfect tense, which points to something permanent. Jesus' victory is not in an unimportant skirmish that means little, but is a decisive triumph with continuing consequences.

And this salvation is something that has its effects on the saved. Jesus has overcome the evil one; as a result it can be said that his people have overcome him, too (1 John 2:13–14). The victory of Jesus spills over into victory for his church. The world is in the power of the evil one (1 John 5:19), but the evil one cannot touch the believer (1 John 5:18).

The Spirit, the Guide

The disciples should not think that they have learned all there is to know. Jesus goes on to tell them that he has many things yet to say to them (v. 12). Believers should be very careful here, for from time to time through the history of the Christian church, people have arisen who have said that they had new revelations and they have led people astray. It is important for us to keep a firm hold on the truth that the definitive revelation has been given in Scripture. Christian teaching is the teaching God gave through Christ and Christ's apostles. Nothing can claim to be authentic Christian teaching that does not agree with this.

But that does not mean that believers can adopt an attitude of "We know it all!" No generation of Christians can claim that it has exhausted all the possibilities in God's revelation. Sometimes a whole generation or more of Christians is blind to some aspects of Christian teaching, and it is a real awakening when a subsequent generation comes to see what has been lacking. Sometimes truths that have always been there, but whose significance has not been realized, come alive. It is accordingly important that we do not adopt a fossilized attitude to Christian teaching, but that we be ready to test anything that claims to be authentically Christian by the touchstone of God's Word. There must be an openness to the way the Spirit of God is leading as well as a firm grasp on the apostolic deposit of truth.

The Spirit, Jesus says, "will lead you in all the truth" (v. 13). There is a textual problem here, with some manuscripts reading "into all the truth," but we should probably not assume a great deal of difference between the two. The meaning is not that the Spirit will lead the church into new and different paths, for Jesus goes on to say that the Spirit will "not speak from himself." That is to say, the Spirit never leads people into paths different from those that Jesus advocated; the two are giving the same teaching and there is no conflict between them. But there is a greater depth and breadth in the truth than any of us realizes, and Jesus is saying that the Spirit will keep leading believers in this great and broad truth. The more we follow the leading of the Spirit, the more of the truth we come to know.

"He will declare to you the things that are to come" has been taken by some scholars to mean that the Spirit will enable Christians to forecast the future. But this does not seem to be what Jesus is saying, and in point of fact it is not the case that the more spiritually minded believers, those in whom the Spirit of God is powerfully at work, know more about the future than others. They are in much the same position as anyone else. God does not choose to make the future known in this way. This is not to deny that on occasion he has made such revelations to individual believers. That, of course, has happened. But it is not the way the Spirit normally works.

It is much more likely that Jesus is saying that the Spirit will lead the church in the whole Christian system. After the ascension of Jesus, there was a little band of believers but no ecclesiastical system of any sort. But in due course the Spirit of God led the apostles and their followers in the paths in which they should go. We cannot claim that every detail of the early church's practice was exactly in accordance with the mind of God. But we can say that, because the Spirit was leading and guiding, the Christian way that developed was essentially the right way. I say "essentially" because there is no reason for affirming that the early church never misinterpreted the Spirit's leading. But we can say that the Spirit so led the first followers of Jesus that the church that emerged was the people of his choice, doing the service he willed for them to do.

Glory

In this, Jesus says, "he will glorify me" (v. 14). The Spirit is in no sense in opposition to the Father or the Son. The three are united in this work of salvation; all three are involved in one way or another in the incarnation and in the saving death of Jesus. All three are concerned that believers have the right teaching and follow it in the right way. So the Spirit simply takes Jesus' teaching and "declares" it to the disciples. There is something final about that teaching, and the Spirit leads the disciples to see this.

Jesus goes on to remind his hearers that there is an essential community between himself and the Father. They are not at loggerheads in anything. Since all that the Father has belongs to Jesus, too, it is important that believers take notice of Jesus' teaching. And that is the reason why he says that the Spirit takes what is his and declares it (v. 15). Jesus is laying it down emphatically that all three persons are one in what they teach. Christian teaching comes to us with the fullest divine sanction. And we can never take as authentic teaching of the Spirit anything that is in contradition of what God has given us in his Word.

68

The Disciples' Joy

"A little while and you see me no longer, and again a little while and you will see me." Some of his disciples therefore said to one another, "What is this that he says to us, 'A little while and you do not see me, and again a little while and you will see me'? and 'Because I go to the Father'?" They said therefore, "What is this that he says, the 'little while'? We do not know what he is saying." Jesus knew that they wanted to ask him, and he said to them, "Are you inquiring with one another about this that I said, 'A little while and you do not see me, and again a little while and you will see me'? Truly, truly I tell you that you will wail and lament but the world will rejoice; you will be sorrowful but your sorrow will be turned into joy. When she gives birth, a woman has sorrow because her hour has come; but when the child is born she no longer remembers the anguish on account of her joy that a man has been born into the world. And you therefore now have sorrow. But I will see you again and your heart will rejoice and your joy no one takes away from you. And in that day you will ask me nothing. Truly, truly I tell you, if you ask the Father anything in my name he will give it to you. Until now you have asked nothing in my name; ask and you will receive so that your joy may be filled full" (John 16:16–24).

These last years of the twentieth century are marked by unparalleled advances in the technological sphere, yet coupled with human misery on an equally unparalleled scale. It is curious that with all the advances in science and technology we leave millions of our fellow humans to the slow death of malnutrition and disease. We make little effort to bring the benefits of medical knowledge and education to "backward" peoples. And, even in what we call the "advanced" countries, unhappiness and misery can be present on a large scale. This world with all its evil can be a sad and sorry place. Despite all its advances, our modern civilization has missed the truth that evil and misery tend to go hand in hand.

We are a curious race. We all like to be happy, and indeed many of us expend a lot of time and a lot of money in the pursuit of pleasure. Recreation has become a big industry in modern times, pointing to our deep-seated capacity to pursue what we see as the things that will make us happy. How tantalizing that it does not seem to work! The anticipation exceeds the attainment. Happiness proves to be something that we cannot secure by pursuing it. If we find something that gives us pleasure and keep pursuing it, we find that presently we become bored stiff. Even if we vary our goals a little, the same result is apt to follow. But if we forget out desire for happiness and find something that is worth doing, particularly some form of service of others, then happiness is apt to sneak in by the back door. But in its self-centeredness and its downright evil our generation seems not to notice this.

While it could not compete with our generation for the creation of human misery on a large scale, the first century was a time of sadness. Maurice Jones wrote of the ancient world: "It was a world where the burden of sin and of human misery was intensely realised." Stoicism was a grim creed, pessimistic at its heart. And Epicureanism, with its pursuit of pleasure, denied that the gods had any concern for mortals in their troubles—we are left to do the best we can for ourselves. Other philosophies and the religions of the day were little better. They brought no certainty of divine help, and people were conscious that their efforts did not measure up. There is evidence of widespread dissatisfaction with life but no solution to the quest for better things.

New Testament Christianity introduced something new into the world of religion—the note of real and deep joy. Few things are as important for an understanding of Christianity (and few things are as little noticed) as the recognition that the note of joy runs right through the New Testament. A. M. Hunter speaks of "that radiant optimism which began with the coming of Christ and which fills the pages of the New Testament from the four Gospels to the Revelation of St. John the Divine." William G. Morrice has a book entitled *Joy in the New Testament,* in which he examines twenty-four words the New Testament writers used to convey this sense of joy, words that occur a total of 326 times. Joy is not a minor part of New Testament Christianity but something that runs through and through the whole. It was not that the early Christians had it easy. Far from it, their lot was often a very hard one indeed. But they had learned that joy can be all-pervasive, so that it persists even in suffering (Rom. 5:3; Col. 1:24; etc.). It is this aspect of the Christian way that comes before us in the passage that forms our present study.

The "Little While"

It begins with Jesus saying to those with him in the Upper Room, "A little while and you see me no longer, and again a little while and you will see me" (v. 16). With the benefit of living on this side of the cross, we find little difficulty in seeing the meaning of these words. Jesus was referring to the fact that he would soon be on the cross. He would pass from this world in the way we call death, and the disciples would no longer see him. Never again would they know the experience of walking through Palestine with Jesus present in the body—going before them, eating and drinking with them, living among them as their leader. There is an important truth in "no longer": an era was coming to its close.

But that was far from being the whole story. If only "a little while" was to elapse before the apostles' whole world would collapse, it would be only a short period ("again a little while") before they would see their Lord again. After the resurrection he would come to them and they would see him and hear him. This would not be exactly the same as his presence with them throughout his earthly ministry, for he would come and go. He would appear mysteriously and just as mysteriously would disappear. But the point he is making here is that their loss of him would not be final. It would be real, but it would be for a limited time only.

Perhaps we should notice that some expositors have thought the reference to be not to the resurrection appearances, but to the coming of the Holy Spirit. Some have even thought that Jesus was talking about his ascension and his return at the end of the age. Now, it is true that he comes to all his people in the coming of the Spirit, and it is also true that we look to him to come again in glory at the end of this world. But neither of those comings fits the language used as well as Jesus' return to the disciples at the time of the resurrection. It was the well-known and well-loved Master that they would in due course recognize in his resurrection body.

But that was in the future. Not surprisingly, the disciples found it too hard to understand and said so to one another (vv. 17–18). On the other side of the cross it must have been impossible to get the meaning. When Jesus died it seemed to those who had been closest to him that all he had stood for had come to an end. He had not been able to defeat his enemies. They were too strong for him.

But the very reverse was the case. He defeated his foes and did so in the very thing that those foes saw as their victory. But until it had happened and God had set his seal on it all by raising his Son, the early followers of Jesus did not see that it was in the cross that God's mighty work of salvation and the defeat of evil was accomplished. So now the disciples fasten on the expression "a little while." Jesus had repeated it and clearly it was important. But what did it mean? With it they couple Jesus' words about going to the Father (v. 10), though Jesus himself had not linked them. They were on the right track in doing this, but even so it all remained mysterious. If Jesus really intended to bring in the kingdom of God of which he had spoken so often, why should he go away? If he intended no such thing, why should he come back? It must have seemed very puzzling.

Sorrow and Joy

Jesus took pity on them. They were puzzled and said so to one another, but they apparently did not think it right to ask Jesus for a solution. But he saw how it was with them. He asked, "Are you inquiring with one another . . . ?" (v. 19), which we should not understand as a quarrel. The word implies discussion but not dispute. Jesus recognized their genuine puzzlement and helped them a little.

He introduces his explanation with "Truly, truly" (v. 20), which we have seen used again and again in this Gospel when Jesus is beginning a statement his hearers are to recognize as both true and important. "You will wail and lament" signifies real anguish. The word *you* is the emphatic pronoun and is saved up until the last place in the clause, which increases the emphasis. It means *you—you* of all people. Jesus leaves no doubt that he is referring to something that they would experience—they in contrast to others, who are here described as "the world." Clearly in this passage "the world" means people outside the people of God, people who are opposed to God and to what God is doing among mankind. For such people the cross would mean rejoicing, for they would think that they had triumphed over Jesus and all that he was trying to do. The two verbs "wail and lament" point both to deep inner grief and to its outer expression in wailing. Jesus makes it clear that one result of what lay before him in the immediate future would be intense suffering for his followers.

This is an important lesson for them to learn, and Jesus repeats it in different words: ". . . you will be sorrowful but your sorrow will be turned into joy." The word for "but" is a strong word, one that points to an emphatic contrast. It was not something ordinary that their sorrow should become joy, but something totally unexpected.

We should notice further that Jesus does not say that their sorrow would be replaced by joy. That sometimes happens in this life, and we are always grateful when something that grieves us is taken away and replaced by something that refreshes us. But Jesus is not talking about this. He is saying that the same thing will mean for the disciples first sorrow, then joy. It will mean sorrow, but that sorrow will turn into joy.

Childbirth

We see this in the illustration that Jesus gives, that of childbirth (v. 21). The anguish of a woman in labor is very real. But when the child is born that is another matter. It is not that what caused the pain has been removed from the scene and replaced by something different that causes only joy. It is one and the same thing that caused first the pain, then the joy.

This is an unusual use of the illustration of childbirth. Elsewhere it is used to bring out something of the suddenness and the inevitability of the second coming (1 Thess. 5:3), or it may be used to emphasize the thought of pain (Isa. 13:6–8; Jer. 4:31). Sometimes the thought comes pretty close to that of resurrection after deep trouble (e.g., Isa. 26:17–19; Hos. 13:13–14), which may be held to be something of a foreshadowing of the deliverance that God would in due course accomplish in Jesus.

But nothing quite approaches the thought of the present passage. Here we have the thought that the very thing that is the cause of the pain is also in due course the source of the joy. Jesus emphasizes the thought of the joy by saying that when the childbirth is brought to its consummation the woman "no longer remembers the anguish." It is not that she forgets all that she has been through. Rather, it is that the present joy of the birth of a child is the thing that matters. The anguish is past, the joy endures. I have translated *anthropos* as "a man," but we should perhaps bear in mind that the term has no necessary emphasis on maleness. It would be pedantic to translate "a member of the human race" but it is something like this that the term denotes. It is not the thought that a son brings joy but rather that a child does this, whatever the sex.

Resurrection and Joy

"You therefore now have sorrow," says Jesus (v. 22). For the third time he has an emphatic "you" when he is speaking about sorrow (twice in v. 20). There is to be no doubt about the fact that it is the disciples—they and not some other people—who are about to undergo the uncomfortable experience of sorrow. This is the third consecutive verse with the word *sorrow;* Jesus leaves his hearers in no doubt as to its certainty or its seriousness. He is preparing his followers for some very difficult experiences. The point of "therefore" is not immediately obvious. Perhaps it arises from the illustration of the woman in labor. Because this is the way things are to be, *therefore* they must expect the sorrow of which Jesus speaks.

But though the sorrow is real and Jesus emphasizes it, the predominant note of this part of his discourse is joy. "I will see you again," he says. Previously he had said more than once, ". . . you will see me" (vv. 16, 17, 19). Probably the change draws attention to the new situation that Jesus himself will bring about by his resurrection. It is not that the disciples will find him by searching, but that he will find them by coming back from the dead.

The result of this will be that "your heart will rejoice." If anything, this is an understatement, for Good Friday would plunge the disciples into the depths of gloom. They had left everything for Jesus, and the cross would seem to them the denial of any possibility of their hopes being realized. "While there's life there's hope" runs our proverb, and though they did not have this wise saying, the truth that it expresses no doubt made its strong appeal to them. We must not minimize the sense of tragedy that must have taken firm hold of them in the face of Jesus' death.

That is why their joy was so extreme when they found that he had risen from the dead. Jesus is not speaking of some minor happiness but of a deep and exultant joy that the resurrection would in due course bring to them. That joy, he says, "no one takes away from you." The world had the capacity to plunge them into sorrow when it took their leader and put him on a cross. But the world could not keep them sorrowful once Jesus rose. The resurrection would bring them an imperishable joy, a joy that the world never gave and the world could never take away. It is this that makes the Christian experience so different from anything the world can provide. In the opening of this study I pointed out that the joy of first-century Christians stood in marked contrast to the gloom that was characteristic of so much of the best thought of the times. That was because there was the victory of the resurrection at the heart of the Christian faith, and there was no equivalent in the religions of the day.

It is still a source of joy that is open to Christians and to which the world has no access. It is one of the tragedies of the modern world that all too often Christians give no evidence of the joy that ought to be characteristic of them in all that they do. It is not easy to see why this should be the case. Christians today have just as open an access to the riches of grace as Christians in any other age. It is just as true for us as it was for the apostles that Christ died for us and rose again. It is just as true for us as it was for them that the Risen Christ comes to us and this ought to make us as joyful as it made the apostles. It would do a lot for us and for the world if we could recover that joy.

Prayer

More than once in this Upper Room discourse there are references to prayer, sometimes references that we would not have expected. So here. We could understand it if Jesus carried on with the message of joy, or if he went into a discussion of faith or peace. He does that in due course, but he follows his references to joy with this one to prayer. He first says "in that day you will ask me nothing" (v. 23). The meaning of these words is not beyond dispute for, while the verb *ask* can mean "ask a question," it can also mean "ask in prayer." In the next sentence Jesus refers to prayer, and some scholars think that he is doing that here and simply using two different words for prayer. But the strong expression "you will ask me nothing" is against this. In point of fact the disciples did pray to Jesus, so if this refers to prayer they did not fulfill it.

It seems more likely that we should take the verb in its more usual sense of asking a question. The disciples had been asking quite a lot of questions in the Upper Room, but the resurrection would answer so many of them that they would be in a completely new situation. The truth that Christ was stronger than death would come home to them as a flash of blinding inspiration, and in the light of the resurrection many questions that had loomed large for them would vanish into insignificance. The resurrection brought valuable new knowledge to the followers of Jesus as well as being the culmination of his saving work.

But Jesus does go on to prayer and introduces what he has to say with the strong beginning, "Truly, truly I tell you." This, of course, introduces something new and important. He goes on to say "if you ask the Father anything in my name he will give it to you." Prayer is to be in the name of Jesus. This does not mean that "the name" is a formula such that we should end each prayer with "through Jesus Christ our Lord" (though that is, of course, a very good way to end a prayer). It means that we should pray in all that the name means, the name of him who loved so much and did so much to be our Savior. Previously it had, of course, been possible to approach God in prayer and to know what answered prayer means. But in the light of the cross there would be something new. It would now be possible for believers to pray pleading "the name" of Christ, pleading all that is involved in the Son of God's coming to earth for sinners, in his living and dying and rising and ascending for them.

When Jesus says ". . . he will give it to you" this does not mean, of course, that every petition will be granted in the precise way the petitioner wants. Prayer "in the name" means prayer that agrees with everything that Jesus stands for. If, for example, we pray selfishly, then no matter how fervently we utter the name "Jesus" we are not praying "in his name"; such prayer does not harmonize with what Jesus is and came to do. We must also pray in faith and there are other things to be kept in mind.

But it still remains that this is a wonderful promise, and it opens up for believers some new vistas into what prayer is and can do. We should bear in mind that, with small variations, this promise is repeated six times in this discourse (14:13, 14; 15:16; 16:23, 24, 26; cf. also 15:7). Quite clearly Jesus means his followers to take prayer with much greater seriousness than we often do.

Jesus brings out the fact that this is something new by saying, "Until now you have asked nothing in my name" (v. 24). How could they? They had not known and still did not know what that name meant. The death and resurrection of Jesus would greatly enlarge their horizons. He is not asking them to carry on with their praying in the best way they had known up till this time. His dying for them would introduce a new and decisive factor into their prayer life and they should profit from that.

And then Jesus is back to the note of joy: "Ask and you will receive so that your joy may be filled full." Prayer does many things, but one of them is that it fills those who pray with joy. We noticed earlier that sometimes the note of joy is muted in modern Christianity. Could this be connected with the way we pray? Certainly Jesus looked for his followers to pray, to pray effectually, and to pray in such a way that they would not only be joyful, but that their joy might be filled as full as it could be. The deep joy of which Jesus speaks is connected with the love and the grace of God. It proceeds from what God has done in Christ, and this finds expression in fervent prayer, among other things. And when the redeemed pray effectually and see the answers to their prayers in Christ, then their joy is deepened, deepened so far that it cannot be deepened any more, deepened so that it can be said "your joy is filled full; it is as full as it can be."

69

The Disciples' Peace

"I have said these things to you figuratively; an hour is coming when I will no longer speak to you figuratively but I will tell you plainly about the Father. In that day you will ask in my name and I do not say that I will pray the Father for you, for the Father loves you himself because you have loved me and have believed that I came out from God. I came out from the Father and I have come into the world; again, I am leaving the world and am going to the Father." His disciples say, "Look, now you are speaking plainly, and you are using no figure of speech. Now we know that you know all things and you have no need that anyone question you; by this we believe that you came forth from God." Jesus answered them, "Do you now believe? Look, an hour is coming and it has come when you will be scattered each to his own home and you will leave me alone. And yet I am not alone, because the Father is with me. These things I have spoken to you so that in me you might have peace. In the world you have affliction, but be of good courage, I have overcome the world" (John 16:25–33).

In this section we come to the end of Jesus' discourse in the Upper Room. There remains only the great prayer recorded in chapter 17 before the Master goes forth to be arrested and crucified. The discourse ends with the majestic words "I have overcome the world," an extraordinary declaration to be made on the eve of his crucifixion. But the victory that Jesus would win is a victory of a sort very different from any that the world (or, for that matter, the disciples at that time) could ever have imagined. On the way to that great declaration we learn something about the disciples' faith and something, too, about the peace that Jesus would give them.

Our passage begins with an expression difficult to translate exactly. I have rendered it "I have said these things to you figuratively" (v. 25), but the problem is in the words translated "figuratively." More literally they mean "in dark sayings," which might be understood as "in parables" or "in metaphors" or "in figures of speech." The expression could be used for a parable (though it is not the normal word in the New Testament for this way of teaching), or it could be used for a proverb or for almost any kind of "wise saying." It has quite a range of meaning, but essentially it points to a way of speaking in which the meaning is not obvious. It requires some hard thinking to get through to the truths being expressed. Some parts of the discourse do not seem to be very difficult, but underlying the whole is the thought that Jesus would soon be dying for the sins of the world, a thought that the disciples could not understand at that time and that made some of what Jesus said quite incomprehensible to them. So Jesus used figures of speech.

But the time for such language would come to an end. "An hour is coming," Jesus says, when "I will tell you plainly about the Father." Evidently the disciples thought that this hour had come, for presently they say he is now speaking plainly and not figuratively (v. 29). They are probably mistaken. Indeed, they have been mistaken about a good deal in this discourse, as we see from their interjections from time to time. This was inevitable, for on the other side of the cross much was necessarily mysterious. The apostles cannot be blamed, but they seem to have been wrong at this point. Jesus is surely speaking of the time subsequent to the resurrection, when they would understand things much, much better than they could possibly do on the eve of the crucifixion.

The Father

We do not know much about the teaching Jesus gave after the resurrection, but we would expect it to concentrate on the meaning of the death and the resurrection and on the way these happenings were central to the good news they were to proclaim. Indeed, in view of the misunderstandings that are so plain in this narrative of what went on in the Upper Room (and in the accounts in the other Gospels), there must have been a good deal said about the cross and its significance. When we turn to the Acts of the Apostles we see that the early preachers were very sure of the message they proclaimed, as they made the crucifixion and resurrection central. Where could they have possibly obtained this teaching other than from Jesus during those forty exciting days?

But it is interesting that the Lord says now that he will tell them about the Father. The disciples professed to be worshipers of the one true God, but they knew all too little about him and needed further instruction about him. And we should also see that instruction about the cross and the resurrection must necessarily be instruction about the Father. We misunderstand the New Testament completely if we see the Son of God as accomplishing the world's salvation in isolation from the Father. That has been a temptation for some students of Christianity through the ages. The wonder of Christ's readiness to die and of his triumphant resurrection has been proclaimed as though it stood on its own as Christ's own solitary activity.

But it did not. Throughout this whole Gospel Jesus has made it clear that what he is doing the Father is doing. It is not that he does things like the things the Father does, but that the two are at work in the same things. The death on the cross would be an atoning act that involved the Father. It proceeded from and expressed the love of the Father (3:16). Paul speaks of the reconciliation Jesus wrought out as the action of God (2 Cor. 5:19). It is, of course, the case that it is the demand of the Father that we live uprightly that makes sinners of us all. And it is the wonder of New Testament teaching throughout that it is the love of the Father that brings us salvation despite the evil that we do. So, when Jesus spoke to the disciples after the resurrection, he would be speaking to them of the Father. His teaching would be teaching about the Father, and in the light of what he would say they would have a much better understanding of the kind of God the Father is.

Prayer

Several times in this discourse Jesus has emphasized the importance of prayer, and here he comes back to it again. He is not talking about the way they have prayed or the way they understood prayer at this point in time. He looks forward to the future with his "In that day . . ." (v. 26). He has already given teaching about prayer in his name (14:13f.; 15:16; 16:23f.), and his words now make it clear that it is this kind of prayer that is to continue. For Christians prayer must always be in the name of Jesus. It is because of who Jesus is and what Jesus has done that prayer is the mighty weapon it is for believers.

But we should be clear about what this means and what it does not mean. It certainly does not mean that the Father is reluctant to listen to the prayers of people like us and is grudgingly persuaded to do so because Jesus asks him. Prayer "in the name" does indeed bring to the fore all that Jesus is and does for sinners, but that being and that doing are fully in accordance with all that the Father is and does. Since God was in Christ in the work of reconciling the world to himself, to plead the name of Christ is to plead the work that God has done in Christ.

And, Jesus goes on, "the Father loves you himself" (v. 27). The Greek puts emphasis on "himself"; it is none less than the Father, it is the Father *himself* who loves you. It is not some angel who is near to God and can speak for you, not some great human dignitary whom you think is nearer to God than you and will have some influence on your behalf. No. It is God *himself* who loves you, and that is the great central truth that you must never forget. Ultimately everything depends on the fact that God is love (1 John 4:8, 16), and the whole of our salvation is the outworking of that love. So we may pray, knowing that we will be heard and answered as we pray in Christ's name, because the love of God undergirds it all. It is love that sent Jesus to this world for sinners. It is love that brought him in due course to the cross and all that this means. And it is love that means that the Father's ear is ever open to the prayer of the humblest of his children.

Love

Now the Father's love has its effects on those he loves. Disciples are people who respond to God's love with an answering love: "We love because he first loved us" (1 John 4:19). This means more than "we love him because he first loved us." It does mean that, but it also means that in the sense of *agapē,* the characteristic New Testament word for love, we love at all (God or our family or our friends or anyone) only because God first loved us. His love is creative; it makes of us something that we could never achieve by ourselves.

Love and faith go together, and faith has content. The disciples believed that Jesus came from God. To see him as nothing more than a great religious teacher is not to have faith in the sense that the New Testament writers understand it. For them faith is inextricably interwoven with a great divine act for our salvation, and we should see in it more than a general trust in divine providence. Faith and love belong together and faith is always "believing that. . . ."

When Jesus says the Father loves you "because you have loved me," we should not understand him to mean that the disciples' love for him is meritorious. He is not saying that the Father was disinclined to love them, but that he was persuaded to be different when he saw that they loved Jesus. Long ago Augustine wrote, "He would not have wrought in us something He could love, were it not that He loved ourselves before He wrought it." We must not lose sight of this truth. But it is also the case that the love we have for Christ matters in the sight of God. Jesus is saying that our love for him and God's love for us are inextricably intertwined. It is love that is the key to it all.

Faith

With this love there is linked the disciples' faith. Love is not, so to speak, a great, fuzzy benevolence, but a wonderful divine grace that finds its expression in the incarnation. The disciples, Jesus says, "have believed that I came out from God." Both verbs, "loved" and "believed," are in the perfect tense, which means permanence. Jesus is not speaking of passing attitudes but of that which lasts. It was the settled attitude of the disciples that they loved Jesus, their settled conviction that he had come from God.

Unless we see the incarnation as something that God has really done, unless we see that he sent his Son to be our Savior, we cannot put full meaning into the love of God. We know the meaning of love only in that it was none less than God that sent his Son to die for us (1 John 4:10). "I came out from the Father and I have come into the world," says Jesus (v. 28). Again the divine origin is brought out. Interestingly, the tense in the verb "I have come" is perfect: there is something permanent about Jesus' coming into the world (there are similar perfects about his coming in 12:46; 18:37). The incarnation did, of course, have an end, in that Jesus returned to that heaven from which he had come. He is not permanently limited to this world into which he came. But what he did here has undying consequences. This world is different because the Son of God lived here, and that Son of God is still here, as is evident in the changed lives of those who have received the salvation he wrought out.

But in addition to that permanent feature of the incarnation there is that which is temporary, and Jesus goes on to speak of it: ". . . again, I am leaving the world and am going to the Father." His tenses now are both present, pointing to what is imminent. He is on the point of leaving the world, and when he does he will return to the Father from whom he came out on his mission of salvation.

Trouble

For some reason the disciples say at this point that what Jesus is saying is quite plain (v. 29). From our standpoint it is plain, but we cannot see how they could possibly have understood it, and we feel that their subsequent conduct shows that they did not. But apparently they felt that they had made some progress in understanding, and they say accordingly that what Jesus says is plain to them.

But when they proceed with their statement they do not say that they now know all they should. They say that Jesus knows "all things" (v. 30). Their confidence is in his understanding, not theirs. Part of this at any rate comes from the fact that they recognized that he had read their thoughts (v. 19). He had known that they wanted to question him and answered the question even though they had not asked it. They make a general statement of this, reasoning that what he had done to them he could do to anyone. There is thus no need for anyone to question him.

This teaches them something about his heavenly origin. They had come to the conclusion that Jesus "came forth from God." Nobody could do the things that he did and think the things that he thought and teach the things that he taught simply on the basis of human achievement. There was much they did not know, but this they did know: that Jesus came from God. This conclusion was open to the Jews at large, but most of the Jews did not reach it. The disciples did, and this is evidence of their spiritual state. With all their faults in knowledge and conduct, at least they recognized that God was in Christ, that Christ had come to them from God, and that in him was the way of salvation—not only for them but for all people.

But their estimate of their faith was a little too confident, and Jesus raises a doubt about it. "Do you now believe?" he asks (v. 31), calling their faith in question. It was not that they had no faith at all; it was rather that they thought they were further along the way of faith than they really were. A time of trial lay ahead of them, and that trial would show up some of their deficiencies.

So Jesus goes on, "Look, an hour is coming and it has come when you will be scattered each to his own home" (v. 32). We are back at the thought that Jesus was about to be delivered into the hands of his enemies and that at that time the disciples would not stand loyally by him. They would all forsake him and flee (Mark 14:50). Jesus was not speaking of some distant trial for which they had plenty of time to prepare themselves. The "hour" was not only coming, but he could say that "it has come." Even as he spoke, Judas was doing his work of betrayal and the result would speedily become apparent. Each disciple would be concerned for his own skin when the time of trial came, and they would all run away and leave Jesus alone.

Alone? No, that is the wrong word. He would be in the hands of his enemies, who would take him before one authority and then another. He would be questioned by Annas and by Caiaphas among the Jews and by Herod and by Pilate among the rulers. He would not be short of enemies when the disciples ran away. The prisoner might well wish that he was alone when he found himself in such company.

But it was not these people Jesus had in mind when he said, "And yet I am not alone." They would be physically present, but no more. As far as what matters is concerned, he would be very much alone if simply in the presence of people like this. What Jesus meant when he said he would not be alone was "the Father is with me." He does not say "will be with me" but "is with me." He is talking about the most wonderful of realities, namely that no matter what evil people do, they can never cut God's Son off from communion with his Father. That spiritual presence would be with him throughout his ordeal and would sustain him.

Some find a problem in that while Jesus hung on the cross he said, "My God, my God, why have you forsaken me?" (Mark 15:34). But that passage refers to the way our salvation was accomplished. In some mysterious way the communion between the Son and the Father was broken as the Son bore the world's sins. The prophet Habakkuk could say to God, "Your eyes are too pure to look on evil" (Hab. 1:13), and the apostle Paul could write to the Corinthians, "God made him who had no sin to be sin for us" (2 Cor. 5:21). When Jesus was bearing the world's sin, part of what happened was this breaking of communion. There is mystery here, but there is also wonder. For us and for our salvation the Son of God underwent even the horrifying experience of separation from his Father.

But that was the divine way of dealing with sins. It did not arise because of what Jesus' human enemies did to him. Despite all that they could do to him, Jesus would never be alone. His communion with the Father would sustain him throughout the worst they could think up.

Peace

Jesus goes on to say that what he has spoken he has spoken to them "so that in me you might have peace" (v. 33). He has already spoken of the peace he leaves with them (14:27), and he comes back to the thought. "Peace," as the Hebrews understood it, is not the absence of war as it is with us (who have inherited much the Greek idea of peace). It is not negative but gloriously positive. It is not the absence of anything, but the presence of God's rich and full blessing. Jesus has spoken of the trouble that awaited his friends. That was real, but what was even more real and much more important was the peace he would give them.

There are three contrasts here. The first sets "in me" overagainst "in the world." This latter concept describes us all. The world is the place where God has set us to live out our lives, and the whole human race is "in the world." But overagainst that is "in me"; some of the human race are in Christ. They have put their trust in him and know this to be the significant thing. In him they have life (20:31). In him they bear much fruit (15:5). And now we find that in him they have peace.

The second contrast is between "you might have" and "you have." "You might have" does not throw any doubt on the reality of the peace that disciples have in Christ; it simply stresses that this peace is a peace for *disciples.* Those who are in deed and in truth in Christ have this among other possessions. Those who are outside Christ do not. There are many blessings that accrue to the believer, but no one gets them without becoming a believer. The contrast points to two different groups of people. We all belong to one; only believers belong to the other.

The third contrast is between "affliction" and "peace." "Affliction" is the lot of all who are in the world. The word points not to some minor irritation, but to very real hardship. It is used, for example, of the treading of grapes, of pressure to the breaking point. We all know what it is to experience something of this at some time in our lives. It is not that we are in fact broken, but that we are very conscious of the reality of the hardship we are undergoing. To be in the world is to be in trouble from time to time.

But the wonderful thing in this passage is the opposite member in the contrast: peace. We have already noticed that this is not the absence of strife and trouble. No believer goes through life without undergoing this part of being human. But peace means that there is a wonderful gift for the believer, such that trouble can be borne with equanimity.

I have read of an artist who wanted to paint a picture of peace. He chose, of all things, a storm beating against a rocky coast and depicted the waves, mountains high, crashing against the mighty rocks. He put a shipwreck in his picture, with a great ship driven up against the rocks and in the process of breaking up. In the water nearby there is the body of a drowned sailor. He has made it obvious that there is a wild storm beating against the coast and that this storm means danger and even death to people caught up in it. But in the foreground he has a mighty rock with a crack in it, and in the crack a dove has built her nest and is sitting on it, secure. Underneath the artist has written the one word: "Peace."

I do not know whether the picture is great art, but I do know that it expresses an important Christian truth. Believers are not immune to the storms of life. They must bear them, just as every member of the race must bear them. But they are secure. The Rock of Ages is their sure refuge and there they have peace.

Jesus' final word is one of encouragement and sheer audacity. About to face the cross that would look to everyone—his followers as well as his enemies—as total defeat, he gives a cry of victory. "I have overcome the world" does not express a wish or a hope but a fact—and a fact that is regarded as already complete (as the use of the perfect tense shows). As I have written elsewhere, "He goes to the cross not in fear or in gloom, but as a conqueror."

70

"Glorify Your Son"

Jesus said these things, and having lifted up his eyes to heaven he said, "Father, the hour has come. Glorify your Son so that the Son may glorify you, as you have given him authority over all flesh in order that he may give eternal life to all that you have given him. And this is the eternal life, that they may know you, the only true God and him whom you sent, Jesus Christ. I have glorified you upon the earth, having accomplished the work that you gave me to do. And now, glorify me, Father, with yourself with the glory that I had with you before the world was" (John 17:1–5).

The longest of Jesus' recorded prayers brings to a close his farewell discourse to his closest followers. It was not, of course, the longest of his prayers, for it is recorded that he prayed all night before choosing the Twelve (Luke 6:12), and doubtless there were many other occasions when he prayed at length. But of those prayers that have been written down this is the longest, and prayed as it was in the shadow of the cross it has always been vested with a peculiar solemnity for Christian people.

In the early fifth century, Clement of Alexandria said that in this prayer Jesus was a high priest acting on behalf of his people, and the prayer has often been called his high priestly prayer. Sometimes objection is made to this as, for example, when Barrett says that this does not do justice to the wide-ranging nature of the prayer. Perhaps there is more than one opinion on what we should look for in a high priestly prayer, and as there are no accepted rules to govern such a prayer the estimate is highly subjective. But the expression does draw attention to the fact that this is a very solemn and important prayer and one that is invested with deep interest for all Christian people, for it contains Jesus' final intercession for his people before the events of the passion.

I have spoken of the prayer as solemn, and so it is. But we should not overlook the fact that there is an air of triumph about it. Jesus knew that the cross loomed before him. In a very short time he would lay down his life. But he was not looking at his death as a tragedy. He was looking beyond it to the triumph that was sure. He has just told the disciples to cheer up; he had overcome the world (16:33). This prayer takes off from that starting point.

The prayer is a unity, but we may conveniently consider it as having three main sections. In the first (vv. 1–5) Jesus' prayer concerns himself and his relation to the Father. In the second (vv. 6–19) he prays for the disciples he is about to leave. Throughout the discourse in the Upper Room we have seen how his concern for them comes out again and again as he prepares them for the startling and unsettling events that were about to overtake them. Now at the close he prays for them. Despite everything he has said, they do not understand the terrifying nature of the events they face, and they will be badly shaken and extremely perplexed as those events unfold. So he commends them to the loving Father and prays that they may be kept. Then in the final section of the prayer (vv. 20–26) he looks beyond the immediate circle of his followers to the countless hosts of those who would in due course be brought within the household of faith. He prays that the great divine purpose be set forward in all of this.

Prayer to the Father

"Jesus said these things," John reports (v. 1), and clearly he is referring to the words of the preceding chapters, those final words in the Upper Room in which he gives the teaching that will prepare them for the trying days immediately ahead.

Then Jesus adopts the accepted posture for prayer. When they are praying, people tend to take up a posture that they do not use at other times. In Christian circles today if someone says, "Let us pray," people will probably bow their heads and close their eyes. In some places they will fall on their knees, in others they will stand, in others they will sit but bend forward, sometimes covering the eyes with the hand. There is no one proper posture for prayer, and any position that helps us in the activity of praying is acceptable. But among first-century Jews it was normal to raise the head, not bow it, and to open the eyes, not close them. In other words Jesus was simply taking the normal position for prayer among the people of his day. We see it, for example, in 11:41 and Mark 7:34 and in the ancient Scripture in Psalm 123:1. This was not invariable, and the sinner in one of Jesus' parables was so contrite that he did not dare to lift his eyes in this way (Luke 18:13). And, of course, there were occasions of special solemnity when the person praying would prostrate himself before God, as Jesus did in Gethsemane (Matt. 26:39).

He began his prayer with the simple address "Father." We have become used to this as a normal Christian way of beginning a prayer, but it was not usual in that day. The address was that used by a little child in speaking to his parent, but when God was addressed it was usual to add some qualifier; for example, a praying person might say, "Our Father in heaven." God was so great and so high that he must not be addressed in the language appropriate for familiar use within the family. But Jesus constantly used this way of speaking to his heavenly Father, and Christians picked up the habit from him. Notice the way it runs through this prayer (vv. 5, 11, 21, 24, 25). That God is Father was specially important at this point in Jesus' life.

The opening words of the prayer are "the hour has come." In earlier studies we have seen that the "hour" or the "time" of Jesus is referred to quite a number of times in this Gospel (2:4; 7:6, 8, 30; 12:23, 27; 13:1; 16:32). John never draws attention to it, but it is one of the ways he brings out the thought that from the beginning there was something that Jesus had set before him, something of great importance that he would do. It would happen in God's good time, and until that time arrived it could be said that his hour had not yet come. But in the shadow of the cross again and again it is said that the hour had come. We are to understand that this is the culmination of the purpose that has been before Jesus from the beginning. The death and resurrection were not surprising events sprung on Jesus so to speak, but were the climax toward which his whole life had moved. Jesus recognized that he was now coming to that climax, the consummation of God's purpose for him.

Glory

"Glorify your Son," Jesus prays. Glory is frequently before us in this Gospel from 1:14 on. John uses the noun *glory* eighteen times (which is more than in any other New Testament book except 2 Corinthians) and the verb *glorify* twenty-three times (no other New Testament book has it more than nine times). It is a very important concept for John. In chapter 3 of the first volume of these *Reflections* I have tried to draw out John's principal meaning when he used the terms for "glory" and I do not want to repeat here what I said then. But it cannot be said too often that John has a distinctive idea in mind when he uses the glory words. People commonly use them for majesty and splendor, for what is high and lifted up, for what is ornate and richly decorated. John does use the words for such things, and we may well discern that meaning in some of the ways they are used in this chapter. But John's great idea is that glory, real glory, is to be seen in lowly service. When someone who is high and powerful chooses to leave that secure and comfortable place in order to engage in a piece of humble service, that in John's eyes is real glory.

And the cross is the place where we see what real glory means. There the Son of God who is supreme in heaven accepted abuse and rejection and torture from evil earthlings. He could have destroyed them in a moment, but he accepted what they did to him, for this was the path by which forgiveness and salvation would become available to sinners. So it is not surprising that in this prayer the thought of glory is prominent. John is about to tell us of the cross, the lowliest of lowly service and therefore the most splendid revelation of glory.

It is possible that here Jesus is looking past the cross and all its shame and praying for the vindication that would be his when he returned to heaven. But it seems to me more likely that he is thinking primarily about the cross. That is where his glory would be consummated, for that is where he will render the supreme service to those he came to save. He is praying that there would be a real glorification of the Son in the events that lay immediately ahead.

He prays for his glorification "so that the Son may glorify you," for the glory of the Father and that of the Son are one. And specifically in this work of salvation it is important that we see that both are involved. It is quite wrong to picture the Father as a stern judge who lays it down that sinners are to be punished and who will not budge from that until the loving Son intervenes to deliver them. Salvation through the cross is salvation the Father as well as the Son brought about. In this very Gospel we have been told that "God so loved the world that he gave his only Son" (3:16), gave him so that whoever believes will not perish. Just as the Son is glorified in that act of lowly service we see on the cross, so is the Father glorified. The two are united in the great act of bringing salvation to people who otherwise would have perished, people who had no way of saving themselves.

The Gift of Life

Jesus goes on to refer to the "authority" that the Father has given him (v. 2), an authority "over all flesh," which means the entire human race. It is unexpected to have a reference to such a far-reaching authority when

Jesus was about to go to the cross; we find it easier to understand authority in the sense of the authority to execute judgment at the end of the world (5:27). But earlier John has spoken of the authority or the "right" of believers to become God's children (1:12), and it is something like this that is in mind here, though it is Jesus' authority and not that of the people he saves. The important thing is that it is authority that is concerned with the giving of eternal life. Though he is about to go to the cross, he is the one who will, with full authority, make the gift of eternal life.

In this chapter the verb *to give* is used with exceptional frequency; it occurs seventeen times in this prayer, thirteen times of the gifts the Father gives to the Son, and four of those the Son gives to his followers. John is fond of this verb and he uses it in his Gospel seventy-six times in all. It is noteworthy that he uses "grace" but little; he has it four times in his Prologue and not at all anywhere else in the Gospel. Someone has remarked that John uses "to give" in much the same way as Paul uses "grace." It certainly means a lot to John that God is a God who gives and gives and gives. But, while John emphasizes the truth that God gives habitually, here the aorist tense in the verb *have given* seems to point to the once-for-all gift that the Father gave the Son for his earthly mission.

The gift of authority is for a purpose, and that purpose is that the Son may make a further gift, the gift of "eternal life." As throughout this Gospel, life is God's good gift. It is not something that we achieve by our earnest endeavors, our good works, our devotional exercises, or the like. If we are to have eternal life, it will be because it has been given to us freely. As we have seen in the earlier volumes, eternal life is a most important topic in this Gospel. John sees Jesus as having come to bring people out of the darkness of their sinful and self-centered existence and to bring them into that life that is life indeed, the life that belongs to the age to come. For Christians the wonderful thing is that we do not have to wait until the afterlife before we experience that life. We have it now, for the Holy Spirit has brought about a new birth in God's people (see John 3) and thus given them life. It is a life that we begin here and now but that will go on through all the ages of eternity. But though it goes on and on, the time of its duration is not the important thing. What matters is rather the quality of the life in question.

Christ gives this life, he says in his prayer, "to all that you have given him." This points to the truth that it is the Father who takes the lead in this matter of conveying life, a truth we have seen expressed in other words elsewhere. For example, we find it in the discourse in the synagogue in Capernaum, when Jesus said, "All that my Father gives me will come to me" (6:37). There as here the neuter is used ("everything," not "everyone") a device that emphasizes the universality. There is no exception. Everyone who comes to Christ comes because God has first been at work in him.

There is an ambiguity in the Greek that is of interest. The word I have translated "in order that" may be taken with "Glorify your Son," which then would have two dependent statements: "Glorify your Son so that the Son may glorify you and also in order that he may give eternal life. . . ." That makes quite good sense and may be the meaning. Or we could take it with "given him authority"—"You have given him authority in order that he may give life. . . ." Either makes good sense, and competent scholars can be named behind each way of taking the words. But we have often noticed that John uses expressions that may be taken in more ways than one and that apparently he means us to take in both ways. Perhaps that is the truth of it here. It is important that the glorification of the Son was for the purpose of bringing life to believers, and it is also important that the authority God gave his Son has in mind the same purpose. We should accept both understandings of the word and rejoice in the emphasis the passage gives to the working out of the divine will. Our eternal life is no accident: the purpose of God was in it from the beginning.

Eternal Life

Now comes something of a definition of eternal life. Up till this point the prayer has moved smoothly, but now Jesus refers to himself, not as "the Son" nor as "I" but as "Jesus Christ" (v. 3), something he does nowhere else in the prayer. For that matter, the double name is found once in the Prologue (1:17) but nowhere in the body of the Gospel (though cf. 20:31). So it is unusual in this Gospel and many find it doubly unusual in a prayer. They bear in mind that in ancient documents there were no devices like our quotation marks, so that John would have no way of marking off words of his own from those of Jesus. They suggest that at this point the author has inserted a little explanation of his own, after which he resumes the prayer in the next verse.

But if it is difficult to see why Jesus should introduce a definition of eternal life and refer to himself in this way in a prayer, it is also difficult to see why John should wait until now to insert an explanation of eternal life in a Gospel that has used the concept on many occasions. It is also difficult to see why he should twice include "you" ("know you" and "whom you sent") in an explanation; this is the language of prayer, not explanation. It seems best to think that Jesus has used a somewhat unusual form in a prayer. Perhaps we should notice that there is an explanation in a somewhat similar passage, namely 1 John 5:20, although in that passage there is no "you"; the whole of the relevant section is in the third person.

Jesus then goes on to say that it is eternal life to know the Father and himself. He does not say that to know them *brings* life; he says that to know them *is* life. We can understand a little of this from some of our dealings with people. There are some people in whose company we would never do the worst things of which we are capable. Just the knowledge that we are with them lifts us a little. Again, there are people whose quality of life is such that when we know them we are lifted into an understanding of life we would not have reached if left to ourselves. In both cases it is the knowledge of other people that lifts us into a new dimension of living. The knowledge of God is, of course, on a much higher scale than this. But to know God, really to know God, is to enter a transforming experience. If we come to know God, we can never be the same sinful old people we were. To know God is life.

This is a Christian distinctive. In the Old Testament we read of people who ought to know God, but, while it is common for the prophets to complain that people do not know him (e.g., Jer. 9:3) and for them to call on people to know him, in fact it is not said that they do. We may get such a promise as that in the prediction of the new covenant: "'. . . They will all know me, from the least of them to the greatest,' declares the LORD" (Jer. 31:34). But the thought here is different. It means that people may know God here and now and, further, that to know him is to enter into eternal life.

The knowledge of God is linked with the knowledge of Jesus Christ, but that should not present the reader of this Gospel with too great a difficulty. Throughout, John has made it clear that we know God as he really is only through Jesus: there is no knowledge of God apart from Christ. There are two Greek verbs for "to know," and each of them occurs in John more often than in any other New Testament book. Knowledge matters for John, and it matters because Jesus has come to bring us knowledge and supremely, as we see here, because the knowledge of God and of Jesus is itself eternal life.

We should not overlook the reference to Jesus as "sent" by God. Mission ("being sent") is another of John's great thoughts and is a way of linking the Father and the Son very closely. It is because the Father sent the Son, sent him to be a Revealer and a Savior, that we know God for the God he is and that we know we cannot know God apart from Christ.

Glory Past and Future

"I have glorified you upon the earth," Jesus prays (v. 4). This is a backward look, and it points to something a little different from the glory of the cross that we thought of a little while back. Throughout his whole life Jesus glorified God, but he did it in lowliness and humility, not in splendid ecclesiastical pomp. In this we see a further illustration of the truth that "glory" in this Gospel usually points to lowly service. The life of Jesus was not "glorious" in the way the world understands glory. It was not lived in the corridors of power. At no time did vast crowds in the world's great cities acclaim him. He spent all his life in obscure Palestine and even there his visits to Jerusalem were few. Most of his life he was in rural parts or in country towns like Capernaum. There were some leading people among his converts, but not many. Most of his ministry was among humble folk, and most of his followers came from the lower strata of society. It is true that Jesus unflinchingly walked in the way of the Father. He had been sent by the Father and he did the will of the Father. But it was all in the path of humble service. It was as he understood glory that he could say "I have glorified you upon the earth," not in the way that worldly people understood glory.

"Having accomplished the work that you gave me to do" says much the same thing, though perhaps from a slightly different point of view. The expression certainly looks back over a life spent in patient service of God, but it also looks forward a few hours and includes the death Jesus would die on the cross. The word here translated "having accomplished" is related to the verb that Jesus used at the point of death on the cross, "It is finished" (19:30). Jesus came to bring people salvation and, now that the events had been set in train that would lead inevitably to the climax at the cross, it could all be seen as accomplished.

With all set in hand done, Jesus can look forward to restoration to the place that had been his with the Father "before the world was" (v. 5). He prays for the Father to glorify him and the cross is still in view. It was to Calvary that he would go, but the end would not be at Calvary. He will be restored to the glory he had before this whole creation made its appearance. Notice the plain assertion that Christ existed before his earthly life and indeed before anything was created (cf. 1:1; 8:58; 16:28). It is impossible to explain who he was in purely earthly terms. He existed before there was an earth.

His glory was the genuine article, not the tinsel affair that earthly glory so often is. We are so anxious to receive adulation that we may easily tarnish our genuine achievement. I like the little story of a certain outstanding fisherman who had caught a specially fine specimen. "Will you have it mounted as a trophy?" asked a friend. "Certainly not," was the reply, "I never have fish mounted. It stops them growing!" The sly dig at the way fishermen's tales tend to grow points us to a widespread tendency among us. Our "glory" all too often has spurious elements.

But it shines through this opening part of Jesus' prayer that his glory is the genuine article. He left his throne in glory, he served people in lowliness and humility, he died in pain and shame, and in all this what we see is not disgrace and humiliation. If we have eyes to see, it is real glory.

71

Prayer for the Disciples

"I have manifested your name to the men whom you have given me out of the world. Yours they were and to me you gave them, and they have kept your word. Now they know that all things whatever you have given me are from you, because I have given them the words which you gave me and they received them and know truly that I came out from you and they believed that you sent me. I pray for them. I do not pray for the world but for those whom you gave me because they are yours. And all mine are yours and yours are mine and I have been glorified in them. And no longer am I in the world, but they are in the world and I am coming to you. Holy Father, keep them in your name which you have given me so that they may be one as we are" (John 17:6–11).

Jesus has been speaking of the relationship between himself and his Father (which is so important for an understanding of the meaning of glory and of life). Now he turns his attention to the disciples. They do not know it, but they are standing on the threshold of a great crisis. In a matter of hours their Master will have been arrested, condemned in a travesty of a trial, and nailed to a cross. One of their number has already betrayed him, another will three times deny him, and they will all leave him and run away. It will be a testing time for them all, a time such as none of them has ever experienced. Jesus' prayer is to be understood as part of his tender concern for them, even in a time when he himself would be going through unimaginable horror. When he might well have been preoccupied with his own need and with the crisis for the salvation of the world, which was about to reach its climax, he yet thought of this little band and of its troubles.

"The Name"

"I have manifested your name to the disciples," he says (v. 6). There has been a good deal of discussion about the meaning of "your name," and some have thought that Jesus has disclosed to his followers a name for God that they had not known hitherto. The Jews treated the name of God with great reverence and, for example, they refused to pronounce the name that appears in the King James Version as "Jehovah," which these days is more commonly transliterated as "Yahweh." They felt that the name was so solemn and so holy that they must take no risk of misusing it ("taking it in vain"). If they never used it they would not misuse it, they thought. Some scholars think that it is this name that is in mind here. They hold that Jesus had explained to his followers something of what that name means. Akin to this is the idea that the name in question was "I AM" (cf. 8:58).

But this approach seems to be misguided. Had anything like this been in mind, there would surely be some place in this Gospel where the name and its meaning would have been made clear. How else could those that followed know the name? And if Jesus went to the trouble of disclosing it and its meaning to the intimate circle of his closest followers, it must certainly have significance for those who would in due course make up his church. It would surely have been recorded for them. It is further quite out of character with the Jesus who comes before us in this Gospel (and for that matter in the other Gospels) to be taken up with words and names and the meaning of a formula.

The explanation is surely to be sought along different lines. We have had occasion to notice a number of times that "the name" in antiquity had a richer and fuller meaning than it has with us. We use a name as little more than a distinguishing label and choose it because someone in the family has that name or because we like the sound of it or for some similar reason. But in biblical times it was widely held that "the name" in some way sums up the whole person. The giving of a name might indicate a position of superiority, as when Adam gave names to the animals (Gen. 2:19f.) or, in a different way, when a conqueror changed the name of a subject king. For example, when Nebuchadnezzar changed Mattaniah's name to Zedekiah (2 Kings 24:17) it meant that this king was now Nebuchadnezzar's man, and everybody who used the new name knew it. Or the name might point to some characteristic of the person. An interesting example is the occasion when Rachel, as she was dying, gave birth to a son and called him Ben-Oni, "son of my sorrow." The dying mother's anguish gives sense to this name, but the boy's father did not like it. He named him Benjamin, "son of my right hand" (Gen. 35:18).

Sometimes God changed people's names in a way that points to changes he has made in them and in the functions they would discharge in the working out of his purpose among mankind. Thus to Abram God said, ". . . your name will be Abraham, for I have made you a father of many nations" (Gen. 17:5). In similar fashion the name of Sarai, his wife, was changed to Sarah "princess" (Gen. 17:15), and later the name of Jacob was changed to Israel (Gen. 32:28; scholars dispute about the meaning of this name, but clearly it meant a lot to the man who bore it). When a certain Pashhur opposed the purpose of God by having Jeremiah beaten and put in the stocks, his name was changed: "The LORD's name for you is not Pashhur, but Magor-Missabib" (Jer. 20:3). The new name means "terror on every side" and points to the punishment that would come to Pashhur in due course.

There were other ways of using "the name" but we cannot survey them all. One that we should not pass by is the fact that the giving of a name may join the giver and the recipient in a close unity. This was the case when the husband gave his name to the wife (Isa. 4:1). Very importantly we see it when the Israelites became God's people: "The LORD will establish you as his holy people, as he promised you on oath, if you keep the commands of the LORD your God and walk in his ways. Then all the peoples on earth will see that you are called by the name of the LORD . . ." (Deut. 28:9f.). The prophet Jeremiah could appeal to God for help on the basis of the shared name: "You are among us, O LORD, and we bear your name; do not forsake us!" (Jer. 14:9b). This use of "the name" is important when we think of Christian baptism "into the name" (Matt. 28:19; Acts 8:16; etc.).

Sometimes "the name" is indistinguishable from the person. Thus the wiping out of the name means the total destruction of what the name signifies (Josh. 7:9). More interestingly, God's name may mean much the same as God: "See, the Name of the LORD comes from afar . . ." (Isa. 30:27); we would be more likely to say "the LORD comes. . . ." So with "your name is mighty in power" (Jer. 10:6), where we would say that God is mighty. The psalmist can link the name with love: ". . . deal well with me for your name's sake; out of the goodness of your love, deliver me" (Ps. 109:21).

Much more could be quoted, for "the name" is a rich and full concept in Scripture and is used in a variety of ways. But for our present purpose it is perhaps enough to say that Jesus has revealed to his followers what

God's "name" means in ways that they had never dreamed of before, and in doing this he has enlarged their understanding of the nature of God. To this day it is the case that people know what kind of God God is because of what Jesus has taught us about him in his formal teaching, in the way he lived out his life of communion with the Father and of service of the Father, and in the manner of his sacrificial death for sinners.

The Disciples

This revelation, Jesus says, he has made "to the men whom you have given me." These men are usually called his disciples and it is worth reflecting that the word means something like "learner," "student," though we should beware of transferring to the first-century "disciple" the associations we so firmly link with the twentieth-century "student." Perhaps the greatest difference was that of personal attachment, which was so much a part of being a disciple. It is, of course, the case that in modern times people will often want to study under a particular professor and will go to one university rather than another so that they may do this. But it is also the case that we are chary of being caught up in personal attachments and do not like to think that our studies are being affected by emotional bonds. We should also not forget that most of our learning comes from our study of books. We take it for granted that any serious student will spend a lot of time in libraries and that he will have a personal library of significant books. There are many things that cannot be taught by books, but there are also many things that can be so taught. One of the great advantages that students have in the more developed countries is just this, that they have access to so much more in the way of books and through their good libraries a vast literature is available to them.

But in antiquity every book had to be copied out laboriously by hand. That immediately limited the number of books and raised their price. And it put a lot more emphasis on the spoken word. A person who wanted to learn would carefully seek out a teacher and attach himself to that teacher. A good deal of what was learned was learned by heart, and it was common to have whole books committed to memory (a derogatory term was to call a man "a bag of books"—he had committed whole books to memory but had no wisdom in the way he used all this knowledge). The disciples would follow their teacher and live close to him. They would learn from what he did, from his whole manner of life, as well as from his words in class.

Jesus speaks of the disciples on this occasion as those "whom you have given me out of the world," and he puts some emphasis on this by repeating "Yours they were and to me you gave them." The fact that God works out his purpose is important. There is a mystery in the way the purpose of God combines with the freedom of our wills, and we will probably never work it out completely. But in this case what we are to see clearly is that the disciples did not attach themselves to Jesus purely because they thought it was a good thing to do so. While no doubt they felt quite free to join him and while they must have greatly enjoyed being his disciples, the prior and significant fact was that they were God's men. God had chosen them out for important service, and they followed Jesus because God gave them to him. When he says, "Yours they were," he has the word "Yours" first in its clause, which gives it emphasis, while the corresponding "to me" has a similar position. There is to be no doubt as to the priority of what the Father has done. This is brought out in a variety of ways in this Gospel. The Father "draws" people (6:44) and "gives" people the ability to come to Christ (6:65). Christ also "draws" them (12:32) and "chooses" them (6:70; 15:16). Whichever way it is put, there is an emphasis on the divine. We do not confer a favor on God when we decide to follow Christ. We are simply responding to what God has already done in us.

We should, of course, be mindful of this in our own lives. We are fond of speaking of a "call" to the Christian ministry and expect our clergy to be assured of a call when they accept a position. But we should be aware that God's purpose is much wider than that worked out in the official ministry of the churches. When he gives to any one of us abilities of one sort or another, we should reason that he expects us to use precisely those abilities. It makes a great deal of difference to our lives when we see our daily occupation, of whatever sort it is, as the occupation in which God has set us in order that we may serve him there. Any worthwhile occupation is one where we may render service, and if an occupation is not worthwhile a Christian ought not to be there.

Keeping the Word

Jesus goes on to say "they have kept your word." John has a good deal to say about keeping God's commandments and the like. He uses the verb *to keep* in this Gospel eighteen times, and it occurs also seven times in 1 John and eleven times in Revelation, whereas no other book in the New Testament has it more than eight times (Acts). A few of these passages say that God or Christ keeps believers, but most of them, as here, refer to the keeping of what God has said, his commandments or his teaching or the like. The "word" here stands for the teaching that God gives, teaching that leads to a whole way of life. The perfect tense of the verb points to something much more than a spasmodic act of obedience. This has been the settled attitude of the disciples, with whatever occasional lapses there may have been. Many people had heard Jesus casually with no heartfelt commitment. It was different with these men. Looking back over the whole period they had been together, Jesus can say that they have kept the word.

"Now" (v. 7) may be meant logically ("now this is what I mean") or it may be meant to indicate a point of time ("now, at this moment"). It seems probable that we should take it in the second way. Jesus is saying that the impact of the years they had spent together had had its effect and now, as his earthly ministry draws to a close, they have come into a state of knowledge, basically a state of knowledge about Jesus' mission. They have come to recognize that Jesus had come from the Father and further that it was the Father who had sent him (v. 8). "You" here is emphatic: "It was none other than you, none less than you that sent me."

God had given Christ many gifts so that he could accomplish that mission, and those gifts were unappreciated by most of the Jews and specifically by their leaders. But the disciples had come to recognize that these gifts were really gifts from God. This is a most important discovery and one that our generation for the most part has not made. We are all glad to recognize that Jesus was a great teacher; perhaps we say he ranks among the great religious teachers of all time, or we may even say that he was the greatest of them all. We see this as a truth that is widely appreciated; for example, we know that Gandhi esteemed very highly the teaching he found in the Sermon on the Mount. But all this is on the human level. It simply classes Jesus as one man among other men, and no matter how highly we place him in that class we are not being true to what he taught about his own person.

Jesus is saying here that the disciples have recognized the hand of God in what he said and did. Moreover he has passed teaching on to them, and this teaching is not of human origin. Jesus speaks of "the words which you gave me." His word for "words" is different from that in verse 6, but we should probably not put much emphasis on this fact. Both terms refer to what is spoken and in this passage both refer to a body of teaching. The plural here may put somewhat more emphasis on the different teachings Jesus gave, though we should notice that the singular occurs in a very similar context in verse 14. Rather than quibble about different terms and the difference between singular and plural, we should take in the truth that the disciples have wholeheartedly accepted Jesus' teaching and have come to recognize its heavenly origin.

"I Pray for Them"

Jesus goes on to say that he prays for them (v. 9). He adds, "I do not pray for the world," and this has presented a problem for many exegetes. It is not uncommon these days to have people say that the Johannine Jesus is different from the Synoptic Jesus. The Jesus of the earlier Gospels commanded his followers to love their enemies and to pray for their persecutors (Matt. 5:44), and he set the example by praying for those who crucified him (Luke 23:34). But, it is said, the Jesus of this Gospel is implacably opposed to those outside the number of his followers.

But this is to put a good deal of strain on the words actually used and it fails to take account of the fact that later in this prayer Jesus does pray for the world (vv. 21, 23). It would be better to think a little harder about what is actually meant. When we reflect on the meaning attached to "the world" in the Johannine writings we see immediately that it was impossible for Jesus to pray for the world as such. He could not ask that the world be encouraged in its worldliness, that it should experience God's blessing in its rejection of God, in its concentration on the here and now, in its self-centeredness, and in all the other things that go to make up worldliness. It was not possible for Jesus to pray that it would continue in its lightness and its refusal to give serious attention to ultimate realities. He could not ask God's blessing on its failure to repent and believe. The only prayer he could possibly pray for the world is that it should cease to be the world, and that is the prayer he does pray later. He asks that the disciples may be one so that the world may come to believe (v. 21) and that it may come to know that the Father had sent him (v. 23).

It is, of course, the case that what was true of the Son in this respect is true also of his people. We must live in the world but we cannot be of the world. And when we pray we must bear in mind the needs of the world in which we live, but we cannot pray for worldly people that they continue to be worldly. We can only pray for them to leave their worldliness and cleave to God in Christ.

Yours and Mine

The perfect unity between the Father and the Son comes out in the reason for Jesus' prayer; it is a prayer "for those whom you gave me because they are yours." There is a deep concern for the people who are the Father's. Jesus does not speak of them as in the first instance his followers and go on to see them as therefore the objects of the Father's love. The first thing about them is that they belong to the Father. They are Christ's because the Father gave them to him.

Jesus goes on to say "all mine are yours and yours are mine" (v. 10). There is a change in gender from the masculine to the neuter. Jesus is referring primarily to people, and the neuter can be understood to mean no more than the masculine earlier. But it is perhaps more likely that while people are included in the new expression, it extends beyond people. If it were confined to people it would be an extraordinary claim, but the wider extension makes it even more remarkable. There is nothing surprising about Jesus saying "all mine are yours," but it is a staggering assertion when he says "yours are mine." Since no creature can say this about God, the words point to Jesus' unique relationship to the Father.

With that Jesus links the idea of being "glorified," a concept that has meant much throughout this Gospel and has been a significant element in the earlier part of this prayer. We should probably see the element of humble glory here once more. The little band of disciples had not done anything remarkable, and Jesus was aware that the worst was yet to be. But, despite everything, they had entered to some extent into the mind of Christ and had learned the glory of lowly service. In this Jesus can say he has been glorified.

"Keep Them"

Again Jesus takes notice of the fact that his time in this world is nearly over (v. 11). Throughout this prayer he is conscious of the fact that his earthly course is run; he faces death in the very near future. But it is different for the little band. "They are in the world," Jesus says, "and I am coming to you." Up till now, ever since they had had the experience of being committed to the service of God in the way Jesus had shown them, they had had the visible presence of Jesus to inspire, encourage, and correct them. But now they are to face what it is to live in this world with Jesus back with his Father. This will be a more trying time than any they have previously faced, and it will also be a time when more depends on what they do and say. They do not know it yet, but they are to be the nucleus of the worldwide church that Christ would build. So Jesus prays for them in their new role in the world.

"Holy Father," he prays, a form of address found nowhere else in the New Testament. It is not without interest that holiness is not linked with God nearly as often in the New Testament as in the Old (except, of course, that there are constant references to the Holy Spirit). Perhaps this is because the men of the Old Testament had done their work so well. They had insisted on God's holiness and on the holiness of everything and everyone associated with him. The result was that Jews in general in Jesus' lifetime tended to think of God in terms of a remote holiness, an unapproachableness that cut off all thought of presumption, but which was in danger of leaving God's love without recognition. Be that as it may, holiness is not commonly ascribed to God in the New Testament, but that does not mean that it is not there. It is, and such an expression as this one reminds us of it.

So Jesus prays for the Father to "keep them." They will face all manner of trials and temptations and they will need divine aid. The "name" will have the same significance as earlier in the prayer. Since God is the kind of God he is, he may be looked to confidently for the answer to this prayer. And Jesus refers yet once more to the fact that the disciples have been given to him.

The end of this verse introduces a new thought, one that will be strongly emphasized as the prayer proceeds: ". . . that they may be one as we are." Unity among his followers matters immensely to Jesus, and he prays for a oneness that is like that between the Father and the Son. This is more than being fellow members of an ecclesiastical organization. It is not a shallow unity, with deep sub-surface tension and divisions. Jesus prays for his followers to have the same kind of unity as the unity he has with his Father. When we look at the state of the Christian church, this is a prayer that should make us think very hard about what we are doing to keep the unity that Christ gives us.

72

Disciples in the World

"While I was with them in the world I kept them in your name which you gave me, and I have guarded them and none of them was lost except the son of perdition, so that the Scripture might be fulfilled. And now I am coming to you and these things I speak in the world so that they may have my joy within them in all its fullness. I have given them your word and the world hated them because they are not of the world even as I am not of the world. I do not pray that you should take them out of the world, but that you should keep them from the evil one. They are not of the world even as I am not of the world.

"Sanctify them in the truth; your word is truth. Even as you sent me into the world I also have sent them into the world. And for them I sanctify myself in order that they also may be sanctified in truth" (John 17:12–19).

Jesus' prayer for the disciples continues. In this section he is concerned with the fact that they are to continue in the world, that world that throughout this Gospel we have seen is hostile to believers. The world has never understood those who commit themselves to the service of God and never will. Jesus' close followers have been sustained by their Master's presence, but they are about to enter a totally novel situation—they have committed themselves to be the servants of their Lord and will be without his visible presence. They do not yet know this and they cannot realize what a different situation they face. But Jesus knew what was before them and he knew their limitations (as he knows the situation and the limitations of all his servants). So he prays for them.

First Jesus looks back over the years of his earthly ministry. During that time he had been "with them" (v 12); there had doubtless been times when for one reason or another some or all of them were not in the same place as Jesus. But the characteristic of those years had been that the little band centered its whole life round the visible presence of their Lord. They had left their homes and their occupations to be with him in what they were sure was the most worthwhile thing they had done in their lives. He was teaching them important truths—truths about the God they professed to serve and about what their service implied. He also taught them something about himself. It would be important in the days that lay ahead of them that they should know that the Master to whom they had given their allegiance and for whose sake they would undoubtedly suffer persecution was no ordinary man. He was not even to be understood as a prophet. He was a prophet, but he was more. In him God had come to earth and it was important that they should know this.

Throughout those days, he now says, "I kept them in your name." His "I" is emphatic; none less than he had kept them. He does not elaborate on what "kept" means, but clearly the meaning is that he had kept them from going astray. They had made their mistakes and had had their misunderstandings, but through it all they had remained close to Jesus and faithful to God. This had not been due to their own tenacity, though doubtless that had been part of the story. Basically it was because Jesus had kept them in the Father's name. We saw in our last study that the "name" in some way stood for the whole person, and when Jesus says that the Father "gave" him this name, he means that God had revealed himself to him. It was because God is as he has been revealed that the disciples had been kept safe.

Jesus had "guarded" them from the assaults of the evil one. The result was that none of them had been "lost" but one. Of those before him at the moment of his prayer not one had been lost. They had persisted through all the assaults of Satan and were still loyal to God.

There was one exception, Judas. The past tense seems to show that the loss was irrevocable: Jesus does not see any possibility of his coming back again. There is a play on words in the original, meaning something like "none of them was lost except the son of lostness" (cf. NEB, "Not one of them is lost except the man who must be lost"). The exact expression is used of the man of sin in 2 Thessalonians 2:3. In both cases the thought is that the person's characteristic is "lostness"; neither of them belonged among the loyal and faithful. It is said in Acts 1:25 that Judas fell away "to go to his own place," and there is something of that thought here. His heart was not with Jesus; he really belonged elsewhere and would go where he belonged.

Jesus speaks of Scripture being "fulfilled." It is not certain which passage is specially in mind, but Psalm 41:9 and Psalm 109:4–13 have both been suggested. It does not matter which of them is to be preferred or even whether we can pin the prophecy down to any one passage. What Jesus is saying is that the purpose of God was fulfilled in the one as well as in the eleven. Judas might do an inherently evil act in handing over his Lord to the enemy, but that did not mean that the situation was out of God's control. His purpose was set forward as Jesus was brought into those events that would lead inevitably to the cross.

In thinking about this we should bear in mind the point made by Calvin: "It would be wrong for anyone to infer from this that Judas's fall should be imputed to God rather than to himself, in that necessity was laid on him by the prophecy." We must not think of Judas as caught up in some kind of blind fate, so that he was compelled to do something he did not want to do. Jesus is saying rather that Judas did exactly what he wanted to do. He was that kind of man. He was "the son of lostness."

But when he did exactly what he wanted he did not take God by surprise and upset what God had planned. Indeed, exactly the reverse is true. He set forward what God had planned, for God's plan took into account what a man like Judas would do. God foresaw what Judas's free choice would lead to and accomplished his purpose through Judas's act.

Separation and Joy

"And now I am coming to you," Jesus goes on (v. 13). The events that would bring him back to the Father had already been set in motion: he was in the process of return. He refers to the things he said, but it is not clear whether "these things" means the words of this prayer (a somewhat similar expression is used of another prayer, 11:42), the whole of the discourse in the upper room (cf. 15:11), or even the whole of the teaching he had given to the disciples. It is hard to see his entire teaching in the expression used, but either of the other two ways of taking the words is possible. Either way, Jesus is referring to the fact that he has been with the disciples and has spoken to them and in their hearing. But this state of affairs is about to pass away.

Partings among friends are not normally a source of happiness. We like to be together and see it as a source of pain when we are separated, especially if the separation is to be lasting. But Jesus is saying the things in question "so that they may have my joy within them in all its fullness." Jesus has said something very much like this earlier (15:11), and we should not miss the note of joy that runs through all he said in the Upper Room. He envisages a parting so complete that they would never again enjoy the kind of association they had had through the years of his public ministry. But he sees the separation as an occasion for joy, not sorrow. His departure and the world's hostility (to which he is about to refer) lead surprisingly not to sorrow but to joy.

They could not have known it at the time but subsequently were to find out that in the new situation they would have the presence of Jesus constantly. On earth, he was sometimes with them and sometimes not. After his return to heaven, he would be in their hearts always and that would be a source of unfailing joy. He calls it "my joy"; it was a joy closely linked to him and not obtainable apart from him. And this joy they would have in all its fullness. Jesus is not speaking of a minor moment of happiness. He is speaking of a never-failing joy, and that joy, no matter how difficult the outward circumstances may be, is the continuing possession of the servants of God.

Not "Of the World"

Jesus turns now to the problem posed by the facts that the eleven were his close associates and that they were to be living in a world that for the most part rejected him. He begins with "I have given them your word" (v. 14). The Greek term for "word" may be used to mean just one word as with us, or it may mean a saying as when Jesus said, "Remember the word that I said to you, 'A slave is not greater than his lord'" (15:20). Or it may stand for a whole subject such as the saying of Paul, "the word of the cross" (1 Cor. 1:18; this is often translated, "the preaching of the cross"; it means all the teaching given about the cross). Yet another use of the term is for a complete body of teaching, and we have seen that earlier in this prayer: "they have kept your word" (v. 6). We have the same usage here. Jesus is speaking of the whole body of teaching he has given the disciples, teaching that originates from God and may fitly be called his word. As he contemplates leaving them he looks to the Father's "word" that he has given them, for it is that body of teaching that will sustain them and be their guide in the very difficult days that lie ahead of them.

It might perhaps have been expected that the world would give a warm welcome to people who came with a body of teaching that originated with the Father, the Creator of all that is, the world included. But it turns out not to be so. The world, Jesus says, "hated" the disciples. It is not without its interest that John, who writes so often and so feelingly about love (is he not often called "the apostle of love"?), uses the verb *hate* more often than anyone else in the New Testament. He has it twelve times and nobody else has it more than seven times. The reason is that he uses it so often, as he does here, for the hatred the world has for God and the people of God. John likes to dwell on love, with all that love means. But he is clear-sighted. He does not shut his eyes to the fact that the world hates Christ's followers. In a way that is surprising, for the disciples are not hostile to the world. For them it is love that matters most of all. They have been loved by God and have come to see in Calvary what love costs. They have responded to God's love with an answering love, a love that overflows into a love for other people. Should not the world then welcome those who come to it in love and with a message of love?

But the world does nothing of the sort. It did not welcome Jesus and it fits that it does not welcome his followers. The world recognizes that "they are not of the world," just as Jesus was "not of the world." The love that Jesus brought and that his followers will in due course bring threatens the whole worldly way of life. The world has its moments of altruism, but the way of the world is at base a selfish way. The world is interested in those activities that set forward its pleasures, its prosperity, its aims for art and science and community ventures. Some of these activities are admirable and some of them lead to the squalidness that characterizes a good deal of modern society.

But whatever they are, they are the world's—and the world has no intention of giving up any of them, no matter how harmful they may be, in the interests of serving God and other people. The world may on occasion even admire the devotion of some outstanding servant of God, as it does, for example, Mother Teresa. But the world will not abandon its own self-seeking and follow such ways. It hates the way of life of believers and it hates believers, just as it hated the Son of God when he came among them.

We who serve God should be clear about this. The most we can expect from the world is that sometimes it will recognize that the servants of God are trying to do something worthwhile. But usually it will not even do this. The habitual attitude of the world to the people of God is a critical one. The world notices their faults and dwells on them: it is aware of the church's frequent preoccupation with its own life and worship, its lapses into conduct that befits the world and sometimes into conduct that does not reach the best the world can do. The world does such things because it has no intention of abandoning its chosen course and sees, however vaguely, that an acceptance of the Christian way means abandoning that chosen course.

The disciples, Jesus says, are not "of the world" and he goes on to say that he also is not "of the world." This expression refers to origin. He does not mean that believers ought not to be *in* the world. He will go on immediately to make it clear that he does not pray for their removal from it. This is their place of service and this accordingly is where they should be. But their essential being is not derived from anything worldly. It is derived from God.

The heart of the Christian message is that God in love sent his Son to live on earth among sinful people and finally to die on the cross to put away their sins. When sinners hear of this and repent and are converted, when they respond to the love of God with an answering love, they become different people. As Paul puts it, there is "a new creation" (2 Cor. 5:17). This does not mean that everything from the old life is done away with. Many things remain just as they were. Our bodies are the same, as are our family relationships, our friends, our jobs, and a whole host more.

But inwardly we are remade. The love of God changes those who respond to it into loving people. We begin in a measure to love as God loves. That means we not only love those people we find naturally attractive, but that we begin to see people as God does and love because of what we are, not because of what they are. And the more we respond to God's love, the more true this becomes of us.

It is all this that is in mind when Jesus says "they are not of the world." The outlook of believers, the fact that they are a new creation, that they have learned at least in some measure to love as God does—and the other fact that they have rejected the world's ambitions and hates and lusts and all the rest of it—all this means they do not belong to this world. Their essential being is something that derives from God in Christ, not from anything of the here and now.

But this does not mean that they are "other-worldly." Some believers are so taken up with what God has done for them and with their duty to God that they have forgotten that God has set them in a community. As members of that community they have a responsibility and a duty. They are to be the best that they can be as citizens, as family members, as friends, as members of this or that profession. It is no part of our Christian duty to try to contract out of the community as far as we can and to have the whole of our life lived within the circle of believers.

On the contrary. Jesus goes on to say, "I do not pray that you should take them out of the world" (v. 15). While it is true that believers are not "of the world" it is also true that their place is "in the world." It is there that they are to show what living in faith means. It is there that Christian love is shown for the robust and vigorous love that it is, and there that it may be contrasted with the sham loves and the lusts that so often pass for love in the world. It is there that they are to do their work of evangelism, a work that can scarcely be done if they do not identify with the community of which they are part. Jesus insists that his followers take their rightful place in the world. That is part of their Christian duty. We are to render to God what is God's, but we are also to render to Caesar what belongs to Caesar (Mark 12:17).

Life in this world can be hard for the servants of God, and many of them have asked to be taken from the world. This was the prayer of Moses (Num. 11:15), of Elijah (1 Kings 19:4), and of Jonah (Jonah 4:3, 8). In each case the request was refused, and we can see something of the reason why. In each case there was important work to be done here in the world, and it could not be done by the worldly.

If God's work is to be done, it will be done by God's people. When the going gets tough and we feel that everything is going against us and that it would be better if we were removed from the scene, it is well that we remember this. We may be impressed by the difficulties we face and our inability to do the things we would like to do, but we should bear in mind that God knows all about that and, knowing it, he has still set us where we are. Our task is not to complain, not to suggest that somebody else would do it so much better, but to get on with the business of living in the world as best we can. God asks us only for the best we can do. No more. But certainly also no less.

But if believers are not to be taken out of the world, Jesus prays that they may be kept from "the evil one" or perhaps "from evil." The Greek could mean either, and both give an excellent sense. I rather think that it is Satan that is in mind, but whether it is evil or the evil one, Christ looks for his followers to be kept away from wrong and to serve God and their fellows in the way that is right.

There is always the temptation for believers to live as the rest of the community does. That way often results in temporal success and, as we all want to get on, we are tempted to do as others do. And those others incline to do what will set forward their own interests. There is a story about a worker whose pay was a dollar short. He complained to the cashier, only to be met with the retort: "Last week we overpaid you a dollar. You did not complain then." "One mistake I can overlook," replied the worker, "but not two in a row!" We smile at this, but we can recognize the worldly habit of taking everything in the way that best suits the world's own advantage. There is, of course, a legitimate pursuit of things that will be to our advantage. To adopt a way of life that invariably brings us loss is not the Christian way. But to concentrate on worldly success is not the Christian way either, and resisting the temptation to do this is not easy. But it is that to which Christ calls all his people.

Jesus rounds off this part of his prayer with a repetition of the truth that "they are not of the world even as I am not of the world" (v. 16). Believers are to remember that they share this characteristic with Christ. Neither he nor they take their essential origin from this world.

We are to live here (as he lived here) doing the best we can, but remembering always that God has made us into people whose origin is not worldly. Therefore our horizon can never be bounded by this world.

Sanctification

Christ proceeds to pray, "Sanctify them in the truth" (v. 17). The essential idea in sanctification is that of being made holy, of being set apart to be God's. Holiness is not primarily connected with goodness, but depends on the deity. There are some "gods" who are cruel, and those who worship them tend to become cruel. But our God is a God of love, and those who worship him tend to become loving. Especially is this so with those who are genuinely sanctified, set apart to be his own. This is not something that we do or can do ourselves. Jesus prays that his followers may be sanctified, which means that he looks to God to bring about their sanctification. Those who are his do not simply exist in this world; they live in this world, but they also live on a higher plane. Their life is bound up with the things of God and lived out in the power of God.

This is emphasized with "in the truth." We have seen in our studies in the earlier parts of this Gospel that truth is an important concept for John. Truth is closely connected with the person of Jesus (14:6) and is a quality of action (3:21) as well as of speech. And when Jesus goes on to say "your word is truth," he ties truth closely with the revelation God has made, the revelation of old through the writers of the Old Testament books and the more recent revelation that he has now made through his Son. The word of God can, of course, be relied upon always and in whatever circumstances we find ourselves.

Those who are sanctified in the truth are set apart to serve, and this is characteristically explained in terms of mission. The Father sent the Son into the world on his mission of salvation, and now the Son says that he has sent the disciples into the world (v. 18). We are never to lose sight of the fact that those who are Christ's are saved not to satisfy their own desires but to serve. They are all on a mission.

Jesus ends this part of his prayer by saying that "for them" he sanctifies himself, so that they may be sanctified. The idea of sanctifying oneself is found only here in this Gospel and is rare elsewhere. It points to a solemn setting of oneself apart for the service of God. We should notice also that the verb is used in the Old Testament for the "sanctifying" of the firstborn of people and of animals. They were set apart for the Lord (Exod. 13:1), which meant, in the case of animals, that they were sacrificed (if not, they were killed in some other way); in the case of men, they had to be redeemed (Exod. 13:12–13). It was also used of animals for sacrifice (2 Chron. 29:33).

We should notice further Christ's "for them." This is the expression we meet elsewhere in this Gospel (and for that matter in other parts of the New Testament) in the sense of "on behalf of," "in the place of." Thus Jesus says he gives his flesh "for the life of the world" (6:51), where the sense is that he dies in place of the people he saves. Similarly the Good Shepherd gives his life "for the sheep" (10:11, 15), and there is no greater love than to give one's life "for" friends (15:13).

From all this there can be no doubt that here Jesus is saying that he is set apart to die "for" his people. It is unusual to refer to the cross in this way, but it is a very impressive way of bringing out the truth that this is the path of service of the Father to which the Son freely dedicates himself.

And there is a purpose behind it all, namely "that they also may be sanctified in truth." Again there is the thought that disciples are saved to serve. Christ's sanctification was to lead him to the cross, and in the light of that he asks that they may be sanctified, too. Clearly there is the thought of the wholehearted service that is to be the lot of every true servant of God. This is underlined by the addition "in truth." We have seen that truth is an important concept throughout this Gospel, and it is important that the service God's people render is no empty sham. Their sanctification is to be a sanctification in truth, wholehearted and setting forward the progress of God's truth.

73

Jesus' Prayer for All Believers

"Not for these only do I pray, but also for those who believe on me through their word, that they may all be one, even as you, Father, are in me and I am in you, that they also may be in us, in order that the world may believe that you sent me. And I have given them the glory that you have given me so that they may be one even as we are one. I in them and you in me, so that they may be perfected into one in order that the world may know that you sent me and loved them even as you loved me. Father, what you have given me, I will that where I am they also may be with me so that they may see my glory that you gave me, because you loved me before the foundation of the world. Righteous Father, both the world did not know you though I knew you, and these men knew that you sent me. And I have made your name known to them and I will make it known in order that the love with which you loved me may be in them and I in them" (John 17:20–26).

Jesus' prayer continues, but now he looks beyond the little group gathered with him in the Upper Room. His vision embraces those who will come to know him through the preaching in which the apostles will engage, and he prays further that this will have its effect on the world outside. Since our membership of the church arises only because of the outreach brought into being by the apostolic preaching, it is not fanciful to see in this part of the prayer a prayer of Jesus for all

Christians in their fellowship with all the other members of the church of God. He prayed for each one of us.

Jesus prayed for all believers (v. 20). We have had occasion to notice that throughout this Gospel there is continuing emphasis on believing. It is basic to the Christian understanding of things that nobody can be virtuous enough to gain a right standing before God; the fact is that we all come short of that which we ought to be. It is equally basic that it is only through what Jesus Christ has done for us that we can attain that right standing. And the saving action is the action of Christ in laying down his life for us on the cross and thus dealing with the situation our sins had posed. Sinners are not called upon to do some great and heroic deed to make up for the evil they have done, but simply to trust Jesus.

We see the Savior making that point here. He prays for those who believe. In the Greek "on me" is separated from "believe" and comes at the very end of the clause. As it immediately follows "their word," it is grammatically possible to understand it in the sense "who believe through their word about me." But few have been ready to take the words in this sense, and it seems that we should understand "on me" to go with "believe." The separation of the two expressions has the effect of giving a certain emphasis to "on me." It is Jesus and only Jesus who is the object of the Christian's faith, and it is Jesus and only Jesus who can deliver people from the results of their sin.

The importance of the church's evangelism is plain from the prayer. Jesus looks for people to become believers "through their word," an expression that reminds us of the recurring "your word" that refers to the divinely revealed message (vv. 6, 14, 17). The message of salvation comes from God, but it must be appropriated by the servants of God, and when they have made it their own it can be called "their word." It is now not something they have heard about, something they admire as divine, but something they have laid hold on. The whole Christian message is such that it is directed to bringing outsiders into faith and, having brought them, to build them up in Christian character.

Unity

Jesus prays for believers "that they may all be one" (v. 21). Seven times in this prayer Jesus prays "that they may be" (vv. 11, 19; twice in 21, 22, 23, 24), and four of the seven are prayers that his followers may be one. It is clear that Jesus was very concerned with what they would be in the days ahead and that he was particularly concerned that they should be united. It is clear throughout the New Testament that unity among the believers is thought of as extremely important (which is natural enough following the last prayer of Jesus for them), and it is also clear that the early Christians found it difficult to maintain unity.

Paul's letters make it very clear that there were those who attracted cliques and who sought to elevate themselves at the expense of the message. Indeed, through the centuries and right down to our own time, there have been and are self-willed people who call themselves Christians and who are accepted as church members in good standing, but who are more concerned with their own position than with doing the will of God.

The difficulty of maintaining unity is made manifest to all by the appearance of the various Christian denominations. There are hundreds of denominations and sects that call themselves Christian, which makes it very difficult to discern a unity. All the more is this the case in that quite a few of them maintain that they and they alone are the church of God, all others being outside the number of God's people. It is not surprising that in modern times there has arisen an ecumenical movement that tries to bring the sundered groups into one. Very often those in that movement have appealed to this prayer of Jesus. They say that in his last moments with the disciples Jesus prayed for unity and that accordingly—if we would do the will of Christ—it is important that we become one church with one organization and thus present to the world the unity for which the Savior prayed.

But it is far from certain that this is what Jesus had in mind. We may well be thankful for the extent to which the ecumenical movement has brought sundered Christians together. That they are even talking to one another and learning from one another is a gain. It is good for us all to learn that there are people outside our own immediate fellowship who are fine Christians with a deep insight into the ways of God, people who can teach us important spiritual lessons that we would not easily learn in our own group.

But we should be clear that Jesus was praying for something much more important than organizational unity. He was not praying for one big church with all believers outwardly united under one banner. He was praying for a deep spiritual unity, a unity like that between his Father and himself, for he says "that they may all be one, even as you, Father, are in me and I am in you. . . ." This kind of unity cannot be secured by an organization, no matter how large and powerful. Indeed the modern world shows that large and powerful organizations have a way of developing a life of their own and of forgetting the purposes for which they were originally established. A unity of heart and mind is much more difficult to establish. And much more important.

While the modern church has much to be repentant about in the way we have made or maintained divisions in the church of God, it is also true that sometimes there are striking manifestations of a unity of a profound and inspiring kind. I recall a service of worship in a remote village in Chile, where all the people obviously lived in poverty the like of which I have never known. They worshiped in a tiny church with crude benches for seats, a dirt floor, and very little in the way of comfort. I could not speak the language and preached through an interpreter. But I recall also the warmth of their welcome and the wonderful sense of unity in Christ that drew us all together.

I also remember a conference in Ecuador where I experienced warm fellowship with Quechua Indians and others and where we were all one in the faith. I have had a similar experience in large congregations in cities in the United States and Canada (where at least the language was no great barrier), in villages in Asian lands, in Africa, in sophisticated areas in Europe, in cultivated university circles as well as among the uneducated and the desperately poor.

While still being penitent for my part in maintaining divisions among the followers of Christ, I cannot but record my thankfulness for those many occasions when I have experienced a deep and satisfying unity with believers of many languages and nations, of differing degrees of affluence and education and outlook. And I cannot but record my deep thankfulness for the extent to which Jesus' prayer has already been answered. In a divided and apprehensive world it is good to see what that unity can do for believers, wherever they may be.

Jesus speaks of the unity between his Father and himself and prays "that they also may be in us." The unity he seeks comes about not by human effort and initiative, but by being "in" the Father and the Son. Paul speaks of our life as "hidden with Christ in God" (Col. 3:3), and it is this kind of life that brings unity. We will experience that unity for which Jesus prays when we live close to God, so close indeed that our real life is concealed from worldly people, hidden with our Savior in our heavenly Father. The closer we live to God, the closer we find ourselves to other Christians.

The World

It would be easy for the followers of Jesus to take up an other-worldly attitude in the face of this realization, and throughout history there have been all too many who have done just that. But as Jesus proceeds with his prayer it is clear that he does not look for his followers to cut themselves off from the communities in which they live. They are to be outward looking, interested in bringing people into a knowledge of God. Jesus prays that they may have their close unity "in order that the world may believe that you sent me." The unity is not an end in itself, but a means to evangelism.

Jesus prays that the world may come to believe that the Father sent him. This is in line with the emphasis on mission that runs right through this Gospel. That the Father sent the Son is the significant thing, sent him on a mission of salvation that would very soon cause his death on the cross. But there was no avoiding that, for it was in that way that salvation would be brought about. The world is to be brought into an understanding of the meaning of Christ's mission to the world. It is only in that way that the world may be induced to cease to be the world and become part of the people of God.

And in the process the people of God have an important part to play. In this life many situations arise in which we can help one another, often in ways that we do not anticipate. I like the story of a student who got married midway through his course. His friends were interested to notice that his grades improved markedly after the happy event, and one of them asked him why this was. "Well," said the new husband, "it's easier to explain poor grades to your mother than to your wife—especially if the wife is working to help you go through school!" It is perhaps not quite what we (and he) would have expected. But it is an interesting example of the way the young lady helped, even though she could not have anticipated it.

So with the church in the world. If church members really are living close to God, if their lives are hid with Christ in God (Col. 3:3), then the unity that results is impressive. It is all the more impressive in that it has to be done in a divided and strife-torn world. There is little that really binds people together in many a modern community. How can it be otherwise where people are concerned basically with their own prosperity? A united church, a church united in living close to Christ and in being concerned for one another and for the people outside, can stand out like a beacon in such a community.

And wherever the church manifests genuine unity in Christ it is attractive to some on the outside. The unity becomes a potent force for evangelism. We can put this in either of two ways. If believers are not living close to Christ, if the face they present to the world is that of a group of people bickering among themselves and criticizing others, then who in the world will want to join them? The world can be just as unhappy where it is and sees no need for change. Or we can say that if the world sees a church united in the bonds of Christian love, then it cannot but be impressed (the world cannot produce a unity like that). And some will gladly leave the world and link themselves with those who have come to understand the mission of the Redeemer.

Glory and Unity

Jesus moves on to the idea of glory. He says he has given them "the glory that you have given me" (v. 22). There is probably here the complex idea of glory that we have seen so often in this Gospel. John writes of a glory that centers on lowly service. When anyone is entitled to an exalted position in ease and comfort and leaves that position in order to render lowly service to someone in need, then we have real glory. That was what Jesus had done in living in the way he did and in facing up to the cross on which he would die, thus bringing about the supreme sacrifice and the supreme gift to sinners.

And that was the glory that he had given to his followers. The verb translated "given" is in the perfect tense, which points to a gift that remains; it is permanent. The world's glory comes and goes, but the glory of humble service that Jesus has given them will remain. As they had gone about Galilee with him they had not had an easy or comfortable or slothful existence. Those days had been hard and full of difficulty. They had known what it was to share with Jesus in the rejection he so often met, and they were about to go through the shattering experience of finding their Master arrested, tried, condemned, and crucified.

But that did not mean that they were called to a lot of misery and unhappiness. They were called to the path of glory. Jesus had brought them to see that their former way of life was incomparably impoverished in comparison to the path of service of God in the lowliness to which he had called them. Despised and rejected by many people they might be, but they had entered into something of the experience of glory. They had come to see that there was glory in the path of lowly service.

And that experience of glory was "so that they may be one." Again there is the stress on unity. We are not allowed to lose sight for one moment of the importance of the followers of Jesus being one. And again Jesus likens the unity he looks for in them to the unity between himself and the Father: they are to be one "as we are one." We should never forget the closeness Jesus looks for between us and our fellow Christians. He is not seeking some casual unity, easily accomplished and quickly lost. He is looking for something permanent and very close.

Jesus has earlier spoken of his being in the Father and the Father's being in him, and he has linked that with the disciples' being in the Father (v. 21). Now he speaks of himself as being in them and the Father as being in him so that they may be perfected into one (v. 23). It would seem that there are various ways of putting it; Jesus is not laying down an official formula. But however he puts it, he is emphasizing his own closeness to the Father; he may say that the Father is in him or that he is in the Father. It matters little which way it is put, for it is the closeness of the two that is important. And that is the model for believers. They are not to be content with some worldly model of what it is to be one. They are people who have been saved by Christ and must look at unity from the same standpoint as he does.

This time Jesus prays that his followers may be "perfected into one," where the verb for "perfected" is interesting. It derives from a root that conveys the idea of "end" or "aim"; to reach that aim is to be perfected. The point of this verb in this place is that it draws attention to the truth that unity is a necessary part of the perfection at which Christians aim. When we become followers of Jesus we are not embarking on a quest for individual blessing and happiness. These good gifts may well come to us, but our aim is to realize our salvation in the fellowship of Christ's people. We belong together in the church of God.

John Wesley reports that "a serious man" once said to him, "The Bible knows nothing of solitary religion. Therefore a man must find companions or make them." This is an important aspect of New Testament Christianity. It is not a faith that can be lived out in solitude. Someone has defined religion as what a person does with his solitariness. This may fit some religions, but not Christianity. We who follow Christ must bear in mind that Christ was one with the Father and in that spirit he expects his followers to be one with him and one with each other.

Once again Jesus ties this up with mission. His followers are to be perfected into one "in order that the world may know that you sent me." Here "you" is the emphatic pronoun: "It was none less than *you* that sent me" is the force of it. Jesus emphasizes his divine origin. The sense that he was accomplishing a divine mission runs through and through this Gospel, and Jesus brings it out again. It is important that his followers bring the world to see that it was none less than *God* who sent him. Jesus is not simply a very good religious teacher: he is the one sent by God to bring salvation. His followers can never escape the obligation to make that clear.

With this he links love: "you . . . loved them even as you loved me." Just as mission is one of the great concepts in this Gospel so is it with love. Indeed, the two belong together, for the mission is the outworking of the love of God. It is because God so loved the world that he sent his Son into it to be the Savior (3:16). God's love finds its expression in the mission of the Son, and it is important that our love find expression also.

On quite a different level there is the story of a newly married young man who came home from work at a time when his bride was immersed in some household chore that was occupying all her attention. That did not stop him from coming behind her, throwing his arms around her, and exclaiming, "Happiness is being married to you!" Her attention being firmly fixed elsewhere, she muttered "Okay, darling" and went on with what she was doing. Some time later a rather disappointed young man asked her if she remembered what he had said when he came in.

"No," she admitted. Then, feeling that she was getting to be on the losing end of the exchange and looking to get something back, she asked, "What is the nicest thing I ever said to you?" "I do" was the prompt and loving response from her husband.

There is no question here but that love was finding its expression, and that is an important part of being in love. And Jesus says that it is important for his people so to manifest the unity that results from the love of God for them that the world may come to recognize that love. They are to see the love of God in the people of God.

Seeing the Glory

The final petition in this prayer is that the followers of Jesus be with him and see his glory. He refers to them as "what you have given me" (v. 24), using the neuter, as in a number of other cases. As we have seen before, the effect is to make the expression somewhat more general. Whoever and wherever his followers may be, they are included. It is not without interest that, as he comes to the climax of the cross, when he is referring to himself Jesus says "not what I will, but what you will" (Mark 14:36); but now, when he is referring to his followers, he says "I will that . . . ." His concern for them is greater than his concern for himself. They will very soon be deprived of his presence and will feel themselves alone in the world. Jesus looks beyond that time of loneliness and deprivation and prays that they may be with him and see his glory.

We have seen that in this Gospel "glory" often refers to lowly service, but on this occasion it has the more usual meaning of splendor and majesty. Jesus has glory in heaven, and his prayer at this point is that his followers may see that glory. They had had a good deal to put up with in the opposition of the Jews. They had been well taught that real glory consists in gladly taking the lowly place. But Jesus wants them to see that that is not the whole story. The Father has given him the highest place of all, with all the glory that goes with the first place. We should not miss the point that it is only as they are with Jesus that they will see this glory. Nor should we overlook the fact that the glory is connected with the love the Father has for the Son. That is a love that antedates creation. The Father has always had a love for the Son, a love that existed before anything in all this universe had its being. It is an eternal love, with neither beginning nor end.

A Backward Look

The last two verses contain no petition, but in them Jesus looks back over the time the disciples have been with him. He addresses the Father as "Righteous Father" (v. 25), a form of address found here only in the New Testament. It reminds us of the fact that the Father is righteous in all his ways (Ps. 145:17). This may mean that he is righteous in eventually punishing those who consistently do evil (cf. 16:11). Or it may refer to his righteousness in acting in kindness toward his own (cf. 1 John 1:9: "He is faithful and righteous to forgive us our sins. . ."). In this context it is more likely to be the second meaning than the first. Jesus goes on to say two things: the first is that the world did not share Christ's knowledge of the Father, the second is that the disciples knew that the Father had sent the Son. Both are characteristic. Throughout this Gospel it has been made plain that the world did not know God. That was the trouble with the world. The world consistently misunderstood Jesus and set itself in opposition, and the basic reason for this was that the world had no knowledge of God.

Jesus does not say that the disciples had this knowledge. He says that they had knowledge of the divine mission of Jesus. It was not that they were people with a profound knowledge of sacred mysteries, people who had the spiritual perception to penetrate to a knowledge of God himself. But they had been with Jesus and had responded to what God had done through him. They had become aware of his mission and that was what mattered. With whatever spiritual fumbling and misunderstanding, they had come to know that it was God who was active in Christ. Jesus was not simply a pious man from Galilee with an unusual knowledge in things spiritual. He was a man who had been sent by God, and it was none less than God who was active in the things Jesus said and did. It was this response to Jesus of Nazareth that put his followers in the right when so many of their contemporaries were hopelessly in the wrong, including people like the Pharisees who were regarded as the religious experts.

"I have made your name known to them," Jesus goes on (v. 26). As we saw earlier, the "name" stands for the whole character; Jesus is saying that he has given them the authentic revelation of God. God is as Jesus has revealed him. Later Paul was to refer to God as "the God and Father of our Lord Jesus Christ" (Rom. 15:6), and that is still the way we know God. God is not some product of our fertile imaginations, but the God who has been revealed as Father by our Lord Jesus Christ. When Jesus goes on to say, "I will make it known," he draws attention to the fact that there is more to be known than had at that time been revealed. He would continue to make the name known among believers.

And it is significant that the prayer ends on the notes of love and unity. The Father had loved the Son and shown that love in many ways throughout his incarnate life. The object of the revelation of God that Jesus had made was not simply to increase the knowledge the disciples had of the deity. It was "in order that" (the construction expresses purpose) the love of God might be in them. We notice that Jesus speaks not simply of love but of "the love with which you loved me"; he is not expressing a hope that they would be the recipients of some different and inferior kind of affection. The love with which the disciples are loved is the same deep, unwavering love as that with which the Father loved the Son. God is love (1 John 4:8, 16), which means that it is his nature to love. He loves the disciples with the love that is the outshining of his essential being. There is no greater love than that.

Jesus adds, "and I in them." It is only as he abides in his people that they know the love of God. That love cannot be separated from the presence of Christ.

74

The Arrest of Jesus

When Jesus had said these things he went out with his disciples to the other side of the valley of the Kedron where there was a garden into which he and his disciples entered. Now Judas also who betrayed him knew the place, because Jesus often went there with his disciples. Judas therefore took the cohort and officials from the high priests and from the Pharisees and comes there with lanterns and torches and weapons. So Jesus, knowing all the things that were coming upon him, went out and says to them, "Who are you looking for?" They answered him, "Jesus of Nazareth." He says to them, "I am he." Now Judas also who betrayed him was standing with them. When therefore he said to them "I am he" they went away backwards and fell to the ground. So Jesus asked them again, "Who are you looking for?" and they said "Jesus of Nazareth." Jesus answered, "I told you that I am he; if therefore you are looking for me let these men go." [*He said this*] *so that the saying might be fulfilled that he had spoken, "Those whom you gave me, I lost not one of them." Therefore Simon Peter having a sword drew it and struck the high priest's slave and cut off his right ear; now the name of the slave was Malchus. Jesus therefore said to Peter, "Put the sword into the sheath; the cup that the Father has given me, shall I not drink it?"* (John 18:1–11).

At this point John's narrative takes up the same events as those recorded in the other three Gospels, but characteristically John does it in his own way. The point he makes emphatically throughout the whole passion narrative is that Jesus was supremely master of the situation. John will not let us miss the point that Jesus was not defeated by wicked people who were too strong for him; he acted in accordance with the will of his heavenly Father—and it was that will that was worked out in the events leading up to the crucifixion and the resurrection. The cry of the dying Savior "It is finished" or perhaps better "It has been accomplished" (19:30) points to the completion of a plan that had been worked out, not to a disaster that could not be averted. All four Gospels affirm this in one way or another, but John makes it plainer than do the others. For him it is supremely important that his readers do not miss the point.

The long period of instruction in the Upper Room has ended and Jesus' solemn prayer has concluded. Now Jesus is confronted with the events that would take him to the cross; it is only a matter of awaiting his enemies who would set the train of events in motion. So Jesus took his little band to a familiar spot to await the arresting posse. John says that they went "to the other side of the valley of the Kedron," where the word I have translated "valley" denotes something like "a winter torrent." It means a valley in which there was a stream that dried up in summer but where water flowed plentifully in winter. Some scholars remind us that "Kedron" can be understood in the sense "cedars" and translate "the brook of the cedars." But there were no cedars there, and it seems that this is the wrong way to take the words. In any case it is the location of the garden rather than the significance of the name of the valley to which John is drawing attention.

John is the only one of the Evangelists who tells us that they went to a garden. He does not tell us its name, but Matthew and Mark inform us that it was called "Gethsemane." Not only does John not tell us the name, but he says nothing of Jesus' agony as he prayed there. This has aroused a good deal of discussion, but we should probably take it as part of the way John worked out his purpose. He does not try to hide Jesus' agony. He specifically mentions the "cup" the Lord would drink (v. 11), and he has spoken of his troubled soul as he contemplated what would happen at the end (12:27). It is not that the agony is unimportant. Rather, we should remember that it was not possible for any of the Evangelists to tell the whole story. Each one makes his own selection from the large amount of material available about Jesus. Each one chooses the things that will bring out the significant points he wants to emphasize about the way the Savior went to the cross.

What John is saying is that in all the events accompanying the death of Jesus it was Jesus who was supremely in control. In the first century death on a cross was regarded as the most shameful (as well as the most painful) of deaths. It was something that would happen to a slave or a criminal. To most people it was unthinkable that anyone would voluntarily undergo such a death. If a man was crucified, that was evidence that he had been mastered, defeated, disgraced.

But John was not writing about a man who had been mastered or defeated or disgraced. He was writing about the strong Son of God who accomplished the world's salvation and did it by the way of the cross. His readers must not think that Jesus lost control, no, not for a moment. Resolutely he went forward on the path he had chosen, and all the actors in the great drama simply fulfilled their allotted tasks so that what God willed would be done.

J. O. F. Murray puts it this way: John "has no wish to conceal or deny the reality of the deep waters through which the soul of Jesus had to pass. He has already recorded (12:27) an agony in the Temple Courts. But he seems to have felt, as he looked back over the whole story, that there was another side even to the human experience than that which met the eye. We have already seen that to him the cross, so far from connoting humiliation and defeat, was the symbol of uplifting, of glory, and of victory. So here, he is content to recall the spiritual struggle by a single phrase (verse 11). He records exclusively words and deeds which shewed that Jesus remained throughout absolute master of the situation. He is so, of course, even in the Synoptic account: but there is so much else in the picture that the fact may easily be overlooked."

Judas

It is important for the narrative that Judas knew where to find Jesus, and John tells us specifically that he "knew the place" (v. 2). He also gives us the incidental information that the little band had often gone there. From the first three Gospels we would not gather that Jesus had been in Jerusalem often, let alone in a particular place in or near that city. While John does give more information about visits to the capital, he does not mention until now that this garden was a favorite spot. We are reminded that there is much about Jesus that we do not know.

John designates Judas as the one who betrayed Jesus. This tag is attached to Judas quite often: it was that by which he was remembered. It is not without its interest that none of the Evangelists goes out of his way to criticize Judas; none of them vilifies him. The worst any of them does is to say, as John does here, that Judas betrayed Jesus. They content themselves with recording the facts. Perhaps we might notice at the same time that the Gospels never praise Jesus. We never read of how wonderful Jesus was; none of the Gospel writers says that he was a great and good man. They simply recount the facts. The absence of praise or blame is remarkable and should be borne in mind. Those who wrote our

Gospels were interested simply in telling their readers what happened; those readers could work out for themselves how good or how bad were the people whose deeds were recorded.

The Arresting Party

Judas "comes" (the present tense makes it vivid), bringing a variety of people with him (v. 3). First John mentions "the cohort," a military term for the Roman soldiers. Strictly a cohort was the tenth part of a legion and comprised six-hundred men. Of course, a cohort was not always at full strength, and the number varied from time to time and from place to place. But the word clearly means a lot of soldiers, and some have drawn the conclusion that John was exaggerating wildly. It is impossible to think that six-hundred soldiers were sent to arrest one prisoner. To answer this some have pointed out that the word was sometimes used of a maniple, but as this meant a force of two-hundred legionaries it, too, seems too big. We must remember that the Romans were quite capable of using large numbers of soldiers for a comparatively small task. Were not "two hundred soldiers . . . seventy horsemen and two hundred spearmen" detailed to take the prisoner Paul on his way (Acts 23:23)? On this occasion they would not wish to skimp, for it was near a festival, there were many excitable pilgrims around, and there might be danger of a riot (cf. Mark 14:2).

But in any case John is probably using the term in a general sense, without any implication of the numbers involved. If we say, "The police came to arrest the man," we do not mean that the entire police force of a given city was mobilized for the event. John is using language of this sort. He is saying something like "Judas brought the soldiers," thus making it clear that the Romans were involved in the arrest as well as in subsequent proceedings. The Romans would have reasoned that it was important not to let any situation get out of hand; if the Jewish authorities were making an arrest, it was important it be accomplished with the minimum of fuss. So the Roman presence is quite natural.

There were also Jewish officials in the party. The linking of "the high priests" with "the Pharisees" probably means the Sanhedrin. This is the last mention of the Pharisees in this Gospel, which probably connects with the fact that they had little political power. They were a group of religious people, and it was people like the Sadducees and the high priestly families who were politically prominent and powerful. Throughout Jesus' ministry the Pharisees were his constant opponents, but at the end it was the high priests rather than the Pharisees who took the lead. The Sanhedrin was the highest assembly among the Jews and the "officials" they sent were probably the temple guard. Normally this guard was unarmed (weapons were neither needed nor appropriate in the temple), but on this occasion they had their weapons with them. They were obviously fearing trouble and were ready for it.

In addition to their weapons they carried "lanterns and torches." In earlier days these two terms seem to have been used interchangeably, but by New Testament times there was a difference. The "lantern" was apparently a cylindrical terracotta vessel with a handle on top for carrying purposes and with an opening at the side into which a lamp could be inserted. Now and then lanterns appear to have had built-in lamps. The "torch" consisted of strips of resinous wood fastened together and set alight. The combination indicates that the arresting posse had made sure of adequate lighting.

Which raises a little question: Why? The date of the Passover festival was fixed by the moon, and at full moon there would have been a good deal of light. It was probably clear rather than cloudy, for at a later time we read that the night was cold (v. 18). The probability is that the authorities thought that Jesus and his followers would flee and hide themselves when the posse drew near, so they were prepared.

"I Am He"

But in any event their detailed preparations were needless, for Jesus came out to meet them. John reminds his readers that Jesus knew "all the things that were coming upon him" (v. 4). This is another way of bringing out the truth that Jesus was in full control of the situation. He was not taken by surprise at the approach of the soldiers, for he knew what was going to happen to him. John does not tell us of Judas's kiss, by which the traitor identified his Lord, though this is found in all three of the other Gospels. Evidently it did not suit John's purpose to include it.

Strictly John does not speak of an arrest, but of Jesus' giving himself up. Jesus went out to the soldiers and asked them, "Who are you looking for?" We might say that this was obvious enough, but the question was important nevertheless. Jesus made them identify the object of their quest, and this made it clear that the disciples were not within the scope of the arresting officers. I have translated their reply "Jesus of Nazareth" (v. 5), for that is clearly the sense of it, but there is a curiosity in their wording. They use an expression meaning literally "Jesus the Nazoraios." In designating Jesus this last expression is found thirteen times, while "the Nazarene" occurs six times, so the former is the more usual. Linguists are puzzled as to how to get "from Nazareth" out of "Nazoraios," but clearly the ancients made the transition somehow. Fortunately, while there is a linguistic problem of some intricacy, there is no real doubt about the meaning. The soldiers are identifying the object of their search both by his name and his place of origin.

Jesus' reply is the solemn "I am," which we have seen used earlier in this Gospel (as in the seven "I am" sayings) and which we have noted is the language of deity. It is perhaps saying too much to say that Jesus is claiming to be divine by the use of the term in this place, but it is certainly striking. The soldiers had come out with their torches as well as their weapons to arrest a peasant who they were sure would be skulking away in some dark corner in the attempt to avoid certain arrest. Instead they are confronted by a commanding figure who boldly advances to meet them and who inquires what their business is.

John now adds the point that Judas was standing with the soldiers. We might say that it does not matter where Judas was standing; what mattered was what happened to Jesus. But John says again that Judas was the one who betrayed Jesus. The fact that he was standing with the soldiers was a physical demonstration of whose side he was on. The lines are drawn and Judas now belongs with the enemies of Jesus.

Awe

All this was too much for the soldiers. They were probably a mite superstitious and were certainly quite unprepared for the way things were going. The frightened peasant they thought they were pursuing turned out to be a strong and fearless figure who from the gloom of the garden strode out to meet them, asked them about their business, and addressed them in the language of deity. So it was not surprising that they were taken aback and "fell to the ground" (v. 6). The reference to their going away backwards may mean that the whole group paused and went backwards. Or it may signify that those in front stepped backwards at the sight of Jesus confronting them and collided with those behind, with the result that they tumbled to the ground. Some have thought that it was only Judas who fell, but this is not what the text says (those who hold this view have to amend the text to read "he fell," but there is no evidence for this).

John is telling us that even at the moment when he gave himself up to the soldiers Jesus was in complete control. So, far from overpowering him, at the sight of him they fell down. It is impossible to see them as in control. Jesus was carrying out the will of the Father and it was that will that was done.

A second time Jesus put the question "Who are you looking for?" (v. 7), and a second time the soldiers answered "Jesus of Nazareth." Both question and answer are identical with the previous inquiry and response. But Jesus now goes on "I told you that I am he" (v. 8). Again he has the solemn and emphatic "I am"; the reader is not to lose sight of the great claim he is making. And, having made it clear that the soldiers' business is with him alone, Jesus continues "if therefore you are looking for me let these men go." That was the point of his questions. Twice he had compelled the arresting party to say that they had come for him and twice they had mentioned no one else. "Therefore" (the word is important) he instructs them to let the disciples go; the soldiers have no business with them.

John simply adds "so that . . ." (v. 9); he leaves his reader to supply "This happened" or "He said this" or some other connective. This is a mark of John's style. He does this a number of times. There is no difficulty about the construction, for the connection is obvious enough: Jesus is referring to the words recorded in 17:12. There are minor variations, but they do not alter the sense. Those who commit themselves to the service of Jesus are not left to their own devices. Even at this moment, when he was delivered up to go to his death, Jesus made sure that his disciples would not be involved.

An objection is sometimes made that in his prayer in chapter 17 Jesus is referring to a spiritual happening: he kept them from falling away. Here, however, he is speaking about a physical peril, the danger of being arrested along with their Master. But perhaps the two are not as far apart as it might seem. Were they to have been taken off by the soldiers to appear before the high priest and eventually the Romans, it would have been a severe test of the disciples' faith and might well have done them irreparable harm. Jesus prevented any such thing from happening. At the end, as he went off to trial, condemnation, and death, he could say, "I lost not one of them."

Peter and Malchus

The disciples were not willing to give up their Master without a struggle, and Peter drew a sword in his defense (v. 10). The incident is related in all four Gospels, but John is the only one who tells us that the disciple was Peter. The word for "sword" may denote a long knife or a short sword (the word for a big sword is found in Luke 2:35 and several times in Revelation). It may at times be a little difficult to know whether an implement with this name is properly seen as a sword or a knife. Be that as it may, Peter was using it as a weapon of offense, and there is no reason for denying that a sword is meant.

It is sometimes said that the account cannot be accurate because Jewish regulations forbade the carrying of weapons at Passover. However, the German scholar J. Jeremias points to the dictum of a Rabbi recorded in the Mishnah that says that a man's weapons are his "adornments" and that therefore they are legal even at the feast. It has to be noticed, however, that the Rabbi in question was giving a dissenting opinion; most agree that weapons should not be carried at a feast. This does not mean that Peter did not have a sword. When people think there is danger they are apt to disregard regulations that would prevent them from doing what they think is necessary to safeguard their lives. There is no reason for doubting that Peter had a sword or that he was ready to use it.

But fortunately his zeal outran his skill. The light was probably bad, Peter was apparently not a skilled swordsman, and the man almost certainly presented a moving target. The result was that instead of inflicting a serious head wound Peter managed only to slice off the man's right ear. Some scholars with a knowledge of Jewish practices point out that the slitting of a man's ears was a means of disqualifying him from holding the office of a priest. They suggest that Peter was insulting the high priest in the person of his slave. This, however, is hard to see. The ear is a small target and it would be an expert swordsman who could inflict such a wound in such a light and at such a time. It is much more likely that Peter simply struck out at the man and managed only to clip his ear.

Anyway, at such a time why would anyone want to insult the high priest? Fighting off the arresting posse was much more important. Luke shares with John the information that it was the right ear and adds, as none of the other Evangelists does, that Jesus promptly cured the hurt (Luke 22:50–51). John alone tells us that the slave's name was Malchus. He speaks of him not as "a" slave of the high priest, but as "the" slave of that priest. Unfortunately there is no way of knowing just what that meant. The slave was being singled out in some way, but we can say no more than that.

Jesus immediately forbade further resistance, telling Peter to put his sword back into its sheath (v. 11). There can be little doubt that the "cup" that Jesus says he must drink is the cup of suffering. The other Gospels all speak of the cup that Jesus would drink, but they do so in their reports of the prayer in the garden, not in connection with the arrest (Matt. 26:39; Mark 14:36; Luke 22:42). The negative in Jesus' words "shall I not drink it?" is strongly emphatic. It leaves no doubt that Jesus was determined to go through whatever suffering lay ahead. He would suffer and he would die, but not because of the activities of the soldiers or those who sent them. He would do so because that was the cup the Father had given him. He would do it for the Father, not because evil men were too strong. They were not, and Matthew reminds us that Jesus could well have received an abundance of heavenly forces to deliver him had that been the way (Matt. 26:53). But it was not the way. He had come to save sinners and that meant drinking the cup that lay before him.

75

Peter's Denials

So the cohort and the commander and the officials of the Jews took Jesus and bound him, and they brought him to Annas first; for he was the father-in-law of Caiaphas who was high priest that year. Now it was Caiaphas who advised the Jews that it was expedient that one man should die for the people.

And Simon Peter and another disciple were following Jesus. Now that disciple was known to the high priest and he entered with Jesus into the high priest's courtyard. But Peter was standing by the door outside. Therefore the other disciple, who was known to the high priest, went out and spoke to the doorkeeper and brought Peter in. So the girl who kept the door says to Peter, "You aren't one of the disciples of this man, are you?" He says, "I am not." Now the slaves and the officials had made a charcoal fire, for it was cold and they were standing and warming themselves; and Peter was standing with them and warming himself.

The high priest therefore asked Jesus about his disciples and about his teaching. Jesus answered him, "I have spoken openly to the world; I always taught in synagogue and in the temple where all the Jews gather together, and in secret I have said nothing. Why do you ask me? Ask those who have heard what I said to them. Look, these people know what I said." When he had said these things one of the officials standing by gave Jesus a slap and said, "Do you answer the high priest like this?" Jesus answered him, "If I spoke wrongly bear witness of the wrong, but if well, why are you hitting me?" So Annas sent him bound to Caiaphas the high priest.

Now Simon Peter was standing and warming himself. They said to him therefore, "You aren't one of his disciples too, are you?" He denied it and said, "I am not." One of the slaves of the high priest, who was a relation of the man whose ear Peter had cut off, says, "Did I not see you with him in the garden?" Again, therefore, Peter denied. And immediately a rooster crowed (John 18:12–27).

The business in the garden being completed, John moves on. He tells us that the arresting party bound Jesus and led him away (v. 12). The word *cohort* seems to indicate that it was the Roman soldiers who were foremost in this, and this impression is reinforced by the use of the word I have translated "commander." Like that English word, it may be used quite generally of anyone who is in a position to give orders to others, or it may refer to the holder of a specific office, in this case that of the military tribune, the officer in charge of a cohort. While either "cohort" or "commander" may on occasion be used in a non-technical sense, the combination makes it tolerably certain that it was the Romans in the arresting party who were in charge, and it was they who saw to it that Jesus was delivered to Annas. This did not mean that they acted alone; John specifically tells us that the Jewish officials cooperated with them.

It is not clear why they bound Jesus. There is no indication that he intended to try to escape. Had he not come out to meet them and surrendered himself to them? It is possible that there was something of a reaction to the fear that they had experienced when they first saw Jesus. They were making sure that the situation was now completely under control. Or, of course, it may be that this was standard procedure when arresting people. We have little information about the details of what was done when prisoners were taken.

The Trial of Jesus

They took Jesus to Annas and thus began a rather lengthy period to which we may give the overall title of "The Trial of Jesus." None of the four Gospels gives us a complete account of what was done and in the end we are left with some uncertainties. What can be said, however, is that there were two main stages in the trial, a Jewish trial and a Roman trial. When the Romans conquered a country they did not proceed to set up a complex bureaucracy of their own to run it. In general they tended to say to the people in effect, "You may go ahead with your normal procedures, subject to our right to make changes where we think they are needed." In legal matters this meant that local courts went ahead in their normal manner, with the Romans reserving the right to take over a trial at any stage if they felt it expedient. One important feature was that they reserved the right to pass the death sentence (cf. v. 31). This was, of course, an elementary precaution from the Roman point of view, for without it a cunning local authority would be able to find in its own laws perfectly good reasons for executing those who supported the Romans. So the Romans kept the ultimate power in their own hands, while allowing conquered peoples to follow their own forms in matters that did not involve Rome's interests.

In the case of Jesus all this presented a problem. There seems little doubt that the Jewish leaders as a whole wanted him killed, but they wanted him killed for their own religious reasons. The Romans would not have regarded these religious reasons as sufficient justification for an execution. So they had to prepare two cases: one that would make it clear that Jesus was worthy of death according to their own Jewish laws, and a second that would convince the Romans that an execution was necessary according to the laws the Romans recognized. At this early stage they seem not to have given much attention to the Roman aspect. As we shall see later, Pilate's demand for a proper accusation according to Roman form seems to have taken them by surprise. But it must have been at the back of their minds.

Add to this the fact that they had to get it all done in a hurry. They had taken advantage of an opportunity for arresting Jesus that presented itself, and this happened to be at Passover time, one of the great occasions in the Jewish festal year. They had to be careful not to take the kind of action that would stir up a riot (Mark 14:1–2), and they had to keep themselves in a state of ceremonial cleanness so that they could take full part in the feast. Conforming to their established legal procedures in the time available to them presented them with a further problem. So we need not be surprised if we find the accounts a little difficult to follow at some points.

There are some uncertainties about the Jewish trial. There is not a great deal of information about the details of Jewish criminal procedure in the first century, but it is presumed that it did not alter greatly through the years and there is information from a later time. We can certainly follow the main stages of what went on, but we must bear in mind that there are uncertainties about some aspects of the trial that our best efforts cannot clear up.

The first in the chain of events is one such uncertainty. Why was Jesus brought before Annas? Caiaphas, not Annas, was the high priest, so it is not at all clear why Jesus was brought to Annas. The incident evidently did not greatly impress the Evangelists, for John is the only one of the four who tells us about it. Annas had been high priest but had been deposed by the Romans. It may be that some of the Jews regarded him as the real high priest, because they believed that the position of high priest was an office held for life. Patriots would hold that the pagan Romans had no right to depose God's high priest. Whatever the legalities of the situation, clearly Annas had a good deal of influence, for five of his sons were installed as high priest through the years, and at the time of which John is writing his son-in-law Caiaphas held the position. This meant that the wily old patriarch at the head of the family wielded a good deal of power, if only informally from the Roman point of view. For whatever reason, Jesus was brought to Annas first (v. 13).

John does not tell us much of what happened when Jesus was before Annas. As a matter of fact he tells us little about any stage of the Jewish trial; he prefers to concentrate on what went on when Jesus was brought before the Romans. But it is probable that the examination before Annas was an informal interrogation. It is likely that formal proceedings began only when Jesus stood before Caiaphas. Be that as it may, at this point John simply tells us of Annas's relationship to Caiaphas before going on to Peter's denials.

Some have seen a difficulty in John's statement that Caiaphas "was high priest that year," for high priests were not changed annually. But of course John does not say that they were. He is saying something like "In that fateful year, that year when the most important happening of all time took place, it was Caiaphas who was high priest."

John adds that it was Caiaphas who had said it was expedient that one man should die for the people (v. 14; see 11:49f.). In his mind it was this that marked Caiaphas out, this above all things. There is also probably a hint that a trial of Jesus before this man could not possibly be a fair trial. The judge had in effect sentenced the accused to death before he became a prisoner, before there was an arrest or a charge was brought. There could be no question of justice in a court presided over by such a judge.

Peter's First Denial

Now John returns to Peter. He gives him his full name, Simon Peter, and says he was following Jesus (v. 15). He gives no reason for Peter's action, but it may have been due to nothing more than a natural desire to see what the outcome of the arrest would be. John tells us also that "another disciple" was also following Jesus. He does not say who this man was, but many confidently identify him with the Beloved Disciple and see this as another example of John's unwillingness to speak openly about himself. Westcott says, "The reader cannot fail to identify the disciple with St. John." Calvin, however, calls the suggestion "a weak conjecture." In the end we must say that we do not know who this man was, though the Beloved Disciple is the most probable of the suggestions offered.

This other disciple had the advantage of being known to the high priest, and it seems agreed that the word *known* means more than casual acquaintance. It seems to indicate that the man belonged to the high priest's circle. At any rate he was able to get into the high priest's palace and bring in a companion when Peter could do no more than stand outside (v. 16). The way John puts it indicates that he was close by the door.

The other disciple (John repeats the information that he was known to the high priest) spoke to the doorkeeper. The word for "doorkeeper" is feminine; it was a female slave who supervised the entrance. The following expression is ambiguous. It may mean that the other disciple brought Peter in or it may mean that the doorkeeper admitted him. But the difference is not great; whichever way we take it, Peter got into the courtyard.

But clearly the lady had her doubts about this man and she proceeded to resolve them (v. 17). John slips into the present tense with greater vividness as he pictures her speaking to Peter. She asks whether Peter is a disciple, but her question is expressed in a way that shows that she expected a negative answer. She puts some emphasis on "you": "Surely *you* aren't among this man's disciples?" is the force of it.

When Peter followed Jesus, and more especially when he came into the courtyard, he must have reasoned that there would be some possibility of being challenged. But when the challenge came it was as gentle a challenge as can be imagined. It was not a man but a woman, not a free woman but a slave, not a mature matron but a girl. And she made no accusation; she did no more than ask a question. Her question, moreover, was phrased in such a way as to make it clear that a negative answer was expected. Clearly no one would expect a disciple of Jesus to be there in the courtyard, the lass who kept the door least of all. Peter was not being accused of anything great or small; he was being offered a way out of a difficulty. Nobody seriously thought he was a disciple is the suggestion, and unless he were to go out of his way to affirm that he was, he would be safe.

Peter promptly took the way out: "I am not." Clearly he did not have the time to think through the implications of his answer, but once he had spoken in this way he was committed. He would feel that he had to go through with it. A small step into evil not uncommonly leads to other steps. What happened to Peter is instructive for us all.

We would not have expected Peter to be the one who would deny his Lord. It seems quite out of character. But then people sometimes do act in quite unexpected ways. I was interested to read of the American Mathematical Society, which made an arrangement whereby its members got a discount of 25 percent on books it publishes. It began by simply sending a catalog with prices, leaving its members to calculate the amount of the discount. But the mathematicians made so many mistakes that the Society had to change its practice and send lists with a notice of "prices to members." Then all a member had to do was copy down the adjusted price. It can be a bit like that with all of us. We act out of character. And so did Peter.

John rounds off this part of his narrative by telling us that the slaves and others had made a charcoal fire (v. 18). It was a cold night and this was their way of keeping warm. John adds that Peter was with them, warming himself. It was perhaps dangerous to join the group round the fire, for he would be where he could be closely observed. But it would be equally dangerous not to join in. It was a cold night, and why would an unknown man be keeping to the shadows? Anyway Peter was cold. He joined the people in the only warm spot in the courtyard.

Questions for Jesus

"The high priest" here (v. 19) must be Annas, for Jesus had been brought before him (v. 13) and was not sent on to Caiaphas until after this examination had concluded (v. 24). Caiaphas was the functioning high priest, but no doubt Annas was still regarded by many as the real high priest, since the office was for life. An interrogation like that recorded here was certainly not legal in later times and was probably not legal at this time. Jewish law provided that an accused must not be invited to incriminate himself. His guilt had to be established by witnesses, and until witnesses had borne testimony there was no case to answer. Clearly Jesus' enemies were determined on a conviction right from the beginning and were not going to let themselves be hindered by the provisions of their law.

It is, of course, possible that Annas was treating this part of the proceedings as an informal inquiry, not a trial proper. If it was not part of a formal trial, he would see no reason why he should not interrogate the prisoner. The order Annas uses is of interest: he asks first about Jesus' disciples and then about his teaching. It seems that he was specially interested in the amount of success Jesus had had and the size of his following. The content and the rightness of his teaching were not so important for this cynical old politician.

But Annas was out of order in asking Jesus anything until he had produced witnesses, and Jesus' answer directs him to that truth. He points out that his teaching had been open; anyone could have heard him, so there should be no difficulty in producing witnesses. It is significant that Jesus ignores the question about his disciples and concentrates on the one that referred to teaching. Three times he uses the emphatic pronoun: "*I* have spoken openly . . . *I* always taught. . . . these people know what *I* said." Throughout this whole narrative Jesus takes care for his followers and will not let them be drawn into this discussion.

When Jesus says that he taught "openly" (v. 20), he uses a word that certainly has this meaning, but it is also used in the sense "boldly." He is making it clear that his teaching was no hole-in-the-corner affair. He had spoken where people could hear him and had spoken without fear or favor. There is no definite article with "synagogue"; the meaning of this is that he taught in synagogues generally, not in any one particular synagogue. But there was only one temple and when he moves to this he says "in the temple." All this means that his teaching was public and there was no difficulty in establishing what it was.

When he says "in secret I have said nothing," Jesus does not mean that he had never spoken in private. He is saying that the teaching he had given in the synagogues and in the temple was the only teaching he had given. In private he may have expounded this more fully and made its implications plainer for his closest followers, but it was the same teaching, not something different. He is making it clear that he did not have one kind of teaching, obviously harmless, for public consumption and another kind of teaching, of a revolutionary and inflammatory kind, for his intimate circle. His teaching was an open book, and if Annas really wanted to know what it was, he would have no difficulty in finding people who could tell him.

This was too much for one of the officials standing by (v. 22). This man struck Jesus and asked, "Do you answer the high priest like this?" The word *slap* originally meant a blow with something like a piece of wood, a rod. But in time it came to mean a blow with the hand and especially with the open hand, a slap. This seems to be the way it is used in the New Testament and therefore I have translated it "slap." But, no matter how we understand the term, it points to an illegality. A prisoner being examined should not be the subject of physical violence.

Once again Jesus calls for witness and the New English Bible brings out the legal flavor of the answer with "state it in evidence." The action of the man, like that of his master, was quite illegal, and Jesus simply invites them both to take notice of due process. If Jesus had said anything that was wrong, the man could point this out, but he had not done so. The other side of that coin is that if Jesus had spoken rightly, there was no reason for the physical violence.

There was nothing more, so Annas sent Jesus on to Caiaphas (v. 24). The King James Version has "had sent," which is the translators' way of getting round the difficulty of the reference to the high priest in verse 19. The King James men recognized that it was Caiaphas who was the functioning high priest at the time and apparently reasoned that it must be Caiaphas who was meant in verse 19. If that was so, then the verb in verse 24 must refer to an earlier action. But it is almost invariably accepted these days that the correct translation was "sent," not "had sent."

John tells us that Jesus was "bound," which may mean that the prisoner had been loosed from his bonds for the examination and was now bound again. Or John may be saying something like "bound as he was," which would mean that the bonds had remained throughout the questioning and were still in place when Jesus went on to Caiaphas.

Peter's Second Denial

John takes up the story of the denials once more. It is sometimes objected that John has placed one denial in the courtyard of Annas's house and then has moved the other two to that of Caiaphas. It is also pointed out that in the Synoptic Gospels the three denials follow on from one another, and it is suggested that John has dislocated the proper order. But on the first point it should be noted that John says nothing about the house of Annas. There is no reason for saying that Annas and Caiaphas were not in the same building. They were related by marriage and were both interested in the arrest of Jesus, so they may well have been in the one house. We should not be looking for a change of site: Peter was still in the same courtyard. And, as for the sequence of the denials, it is surely a mistake to think that they went off one after the other in immediate sequence. Nothing is more likely than that there were intervals (cf. Luke's reference to an interval of about an hour between the second and third denials, Luke 22:59). John's arrangement brings this out.

John resumes by reminding the reader that Peter was at the fire warming himself. "They" spoke to him, which presents a problem for some people as it is not what the other Gospels say. There are several differences in the personnel mentioned as questioning Peter. All four Gospels agree about the first inquiry: it came from a slave girl. But where John speaks of a number of people on this second occasion, Matthew and Mark have a slave girl (Mark seems to mean the same one as the first time; Matthew seems to mean a different one), while Luke speaks of a man. But we should not think of a deadly hush out of which emerges a lone questioner. We are talking about a group of servants gossiping around a fire while they await matters that will be decided by their lords and masters. Nothing is more likely than that when one of them raises the question of Peter's possible connection with Jesus, others round the fire would join in. This is clear in Matthew and Mark, where the slave girl does not question Peter but begins "This man was. . . ." She was addressing the others, and there is every reason for thinking that more than one of them would respond and throw an inquiry at the stranger in their midst. Different narrators of what happened would single out different speakers in the drama.

As John records the question there is still the presumption that Peter had nothing to do with Jesus. The question expects a negative answer. And gets one: "I am not."

Peter's Third Denial

There is more confidence in the challenger on the third occasion (v. 26). This is perhaps due to his closer involvement in what had gone on in the garden than were the earlier questioners. John tells us that this man was a slave of the high priest and a relation of that other slave whose ear Peter had cut off. He would have been more interested in who were and who were not Jesus' followers than the others round the fire. So he asks a question that expects the answer "Yes." He does not make an outright accusation and we may perhaps put this down to the circumstances. They were standing round a charcoal fire. Now a charcoal fire will glow red and give out a welcome heat, but it does not have flames. There would not have been much illumination. So the man was reasonably sure he had seen Peter before but could not be absolutely certain. Hence the form of his question. And for the third time Peter denied (v. 27). John records that straight away a rooster crowed. This fulfills Jesus' prophecy (13:38), though he does not specifically draw attention to this. He could trust those who had been following his narrative with close attention to work it out for themselves.

Interestingly, he says nothing at all about how Peter reacted. Elsewhere we learn that he wept bitterly (Luke 22:62), but John says nothing of this. In fact he says nothing about anyone's feelings in chapters 18 and 19, with the solitary exception of Pilate's being afraid (19:8). Throughout this section of his Gospel he concentrates on the facts. He is recording what happened; if people are interested in how any of the participants felt, he leaves them to work it out for themselves.

76

Jesus Before Pilate

So they bring Jesus from Caiaphas to the Praetorium; now it was early and they themselves did not enter the Praetorium so that they should not be defiled but might eat the Passover. Pilate therefore went outside to them and says, "What accusation do you bring against this man?" They answered him saying, "If this man were not an evil-doer we would not have handed him over to you." Pilate therefore said to them, "You take him and judge him according to your law." The Jews said to him, "It is not lawful for us to put anyone to death"; [this happened] so that the word of Jesus might be fulfilled which he spoke signifying by what death he would die (John 18:28–32).

John has told us very little about the Jewish stage of Jesus' trial. From the Synoptists we learn something of what happened when Jesus came before Caiaphas, but John says nothing about this. He has let us know that Annas sent him along to Caiaphas (v. 24), but he says nothing at all about what happened then. It was at that stage that the Jewish authorities went through the motions of condemning Jesus according to Jewish law. They established to their own satisfaction that Jesus was guilty of blasphemy and that accordingly he was (from their point of view) liable to the death penalty.

But they had a problem. They had no authority to carry out such a sentence. The only way of getting Pilate to agree to execute Jesus was to accuse him of an offense that the Romans thought serious. The Romans would certainly not have agreed that blasphemy of the God the Jews worshiped was serious. The authorities had to come up with something of quite a different character, though they did not forget their real accusation and on occasion this comes to the surface (e.g., 19:7). Though John moves quickly over what happened when Jesus stood before the Jewish authorities, he has quite a lot to tell us about the Roman stage of Jesus' trial. Indeed we owe to John most of our knowledge of what went on when Jesus stood before Pilate. This must have been very important for many of his readers, for they too were subject to the Romans and might at any time find themselves called on to give an account of themselves. It was good for them to know what Jesus had said and done when he was examined before Pilate.

One important aspect of John's account is the way he makes it so clear that Pilate found no crime in Jesus. Three times he tells us that Pilate declared that Jesus was innocent (v. 38; 19:4, 6). He makes it plain that it was no part of the intention of the Romans to move against the Lord; that took place because of the determined opposition of the Jewish authorities. And those authorities could not produce evidence of any wrongdoing. They were moved by the fact that Jesus had claimed to be God's Son, and for John's readers that was important.

How did John know what went on in the Roman trial? He does not tell us and, of course, may have had an informant somewhere within Pilate's circle. But Westcott long ago suggested that John himself may have gone into the Praetorium and thus have been an observer of proceedings there. It seems that the only reason the Jewish accusers did not go in was their fear of ceremonial defilement (v. 28), but ceremonial defilement would not have worried a close follower of Jesus. We must bear in mind that this is conjecture; we have no way of knowing whether or not it actually happened. But if it did, it would explain why this Gospel has so much more about what happened before Pilate than have the other Gospels.

At the Praetorium

John tells us then that "they," evidently the Jewish authorities, "bring Jesus from Caiaphas to the Praetorium" (v. 28). John has nothing to say about the Jewish trial but comes straight to the trial that mattered, the one that could sentence Jesus to death and whose sentence would be carried out. Notice that he uses the present tense, "bring," which makes it all so much more vivid. The Jews had done all that they could in their own jurisdiction and felt that they could now safely transfer proceedings to Pilate's court.

The Praetorium meant originally "the tent of the Praetor," i.e., the General's tent. "Praetor" denoted leadership of various kinds and in the army was the designation of the person we would call a general. The Praetorium was his headquarters. From that the term came to be used in a variety of ways for important places, much as we use "headquarters" in a variety of senses. With us "headquarters" may be a tent or may refer to a magnificent building or anything in between, but whichever way we use it, it denotes an important center. So with Praetorium. In a place like Palestine it meant the official residence of the governor. Pilate actually lived in Caesarea (cf. Acts 23:35), but when he came to Jerusalem the place where he stayed was for the time being called the Praetorium.

There is dispute about just which building this was. Traditionally it has been held that when he was in Jerusalem Pilate stayed in the Tower of Antonia. Herod the Great had rebuilt this tower at the northwest corner of the temple court and clearly it was a strong point guarded by a considerable contingent of troops. This was very important in a city where trouble could easily arise. The tower may well have been Pilate's Praetorium, as most scholars hold.

But it is also possible that he stayed in Herod's palace. The Jewish historian Josephus tells us that a later governor, Florus, stayed in this palace, and this may reflect a continuing practice. Another Jewish writer, Philo, says that Pilate once hung some shields in Herod's palace, which may possibly point to the same thing. It seems to mean that he had soldiers there, presumably his guard. Why else would he hang shields there? There is no indication given in this Gospel as to which was the correct place. Everyone knew where the Praetorium was in Jerusalem, so there was no need to point it out. In any case it would seem that the precise location was of little importance. What mattered was that Jesus was brought to the building that the governor had made his headquarters while he was in Jerusalem.

It was "early" when this happened, and the term may be understood in more ways than one. It could apparently denote the last of the four watches of the night (Mark 13:35), which would have ended at about 6:00 A.M. on our reckoning. But, though the ancients tended to start the day early, getting to the Praetorium before six in the morning seems a mite too early. Besides, there was a Jewish law that where a law case involved the possibility of a death sentence it could not take place at night, and the Jews may well have decided to have a daytime session after their nocturnal examination of Jesus in order to give at least the appearance of legality to what they were doing in the Jewish part of Jesus' trial. There was certainly a second stage to the Jewish trial (see Mark 15:1), and the Jews could not have gone to Pilate before this session. That legal matters could be dealt with quite early in the day is clear from Roman writers. For example, Seneca speaks of "thousands hurrying to the forum at break of day" and goes on to remark, "how base their cases, and how much baser are their advocates!"

Defilement at the Passover

But there was a problem for the Jewish leaders. It was Passover time and they very much wanted to keep the feast. But this stage of Jesus' trial was necessarily held in the Praetorium, a Gentile residence, and the Jewish rule was "The dwelling-places of Gentiles are unclean." To enter an unclean dwelling meant contracting ceremonial defilement; even to go into a tent where a dead man was lying meant defilement (Num. 19:14). A ceremonially unclean person must not eat of any sacrifice (cf. Lev. 7:20), and this effectively stopped him from keeping the Passover. Should anyone be unclean at Passover time, there was a special provision that enabled him to celebrate the feast a month later (Num. 9:6–13), but he could not observe it at the correct time with all the people. The rule about defilement from Gentile dwelling places applied only to the dwelling place itself; a courtyard or a colonnade did not matter. This meant that as long as they stayed in the courtyard the Jews were in the clear; but if they entered the Praetorium itself, they would become ceremonially unclean and would not be entitled to observe the Passover. As this was a very important feast they made sure that they were in the state of ceremonial cleanness that entitled them to take part in it.

This raises a big and difficult problem, which we may put this way. In Matthew, Mark, and Luke it seems that the Last Supper was a Passover meal, which meant that the Passover proper had been held before Jesus was arrested, whereas in John it seems that Jesus was crucified at the time the lambs and kids for the Passover observance were being sacrificed. This is part of the way that John brings out the truth that Jesus' death, viewed in one way, was a Passover sacrifice. Whole books have been written about how the problem should be resolved, and there is no space in a short study like this to go into it. It must suffice to state briefly my own opinion. (I have examined the problem more fully in my commentary, *The Gospel According to John,* Eerdmans, Grand Rapids: 1971, pp. 774–786.)

There is evidence that some groups in Israel used a different calendar from that observed by the temple authorities. For example, the community that produced the Dead Sea Scrolls used an ancient calendar and held that the priests in Jerusalem held all the festivals at the wrong times. The simplest solution to our problem, it seems to me, is that Jesus and his followers, following a different calendar, kept the Passover a day earlier than did the temple authorities. This would explain why the lamb or kid, the principal item in the Passover feast, is not mentioned in our accounts of the Last Supper. Since the animal had to be offered in sacrifice before being eaten, it could not be obtained without the approval of the temple authorities. The Synoptic Gospels refer to the Passover meal that Jesus and his apostles held together, John to the official celebration. And it was because the official Passover had not yet been held that the high priestly party would not enter Pilate's Praetorium.

We may profitably reflect on the fact that these people were very careful not to contract ceremonial defilement by entering a Gentile house, while at the same time not being in the slightest discomfited by the moral defilement of scheming to get an innocent man put to death. So can worldly self-interest blind people. One of the early church writers, Chrysostom, comments, "They who paid tithes of mint and anise, did not think they were polluted when bent on killing unjustly, but thought that they polluted themselves by even treading in a court of justice."

It is objected by some scholars that John cannot be right. They point out that when a person contracted ceremonial defilement he was required to bathe himself, but then he would be unclean only until the evening (Num. 19:22). So they hold that all that would be required of the high priestly party if they were defiled by going into the Praetorium would be a bath—and then at evening they would be clean and could go on to eat the feast.

But this overlooks the reason for the defilement. It was no minor defilement for a petty infringment of the laws of cleanliness that was involved, but, curiously as it seems to us, the defilement for the dead that was involved. It was held by the relevant Jewish authorities that the Gentiles were accustomed to cast aborted foetuses down their drains. Thus the defilement that would be contracted by going into a Gentile home would be the one arising from contact with the dead, and this lasted for seven days (Num. 19:14). Had the high priestly party contracted this defilement, they could not have eaten the Passover until the following month. Accordingly it was important for them that they stay out of Pilate's residence.

Pilate and the Jews

This is John's first mention of Pilate (v. 29), and he comes into the narrative without preamble or explanation. We might have expected that John would have informed his readers that this man was the governor or have qualified what he says in some other way, but he simply goes ahead and says that Pilate came outside. Clearly John expected that those who read his Gospel would have some knowledge of the basic facts and would not need to be told who Pilate was. It is perhaps surprising that Pilate came out; we might have thought that he would stand on his dignity and insist that if the priestly party wanted to conduct a case, they must observe the proper procedure and come into his judgment hall. But perhaps he was concerned to do all he could to avoid giving provocation to any section of Judaism at such a time. With the great festival so near there would be many excitable pilgrims in the city and it may have been diplomatic for Pilate to do what he could to preserve the peace. And, after all, what was required? Only that he come outside his own door and speak to the high priests there.

Pilate first asks, "What accusation do you bring against this man?" This does not necessarily mean that Pilate did not know what the Jews were doing; it is simply a request that they make a formal accusation in the proper form. A man would be on trial for his life and Pilate wants there to be no doubt that things were being done decently and in order.

But his question was something of an embarrassment for the Jewish leaders. They were quite sure in their own minds that Jesus must be put to death, and from the standpoint of Jewish law they were on familiar and safe grounds. As they saw it, Jesus had committed the terrible crime of blasphemy and therefore he must die. But they could not say this to Pilate, for they would be laughed out of court. The Romans did not regard blaspheming the God the Jews worshiped as a serious crime, certainly not one for which the death penalty was demanded. So they could not say what was really on their minds.

They must, of course, have known this before they approached the governor, and we wonder why they did not have a suitable charge ready, one drawn up in the accepted terms that the Romans would recognize. Perhaps they were taken by surprise. There had been Roman soldiers in Gethsemane when Jesus was arrested, so they had had Pilate's cooperation in making the arrest. We have no way of knowing exactly what had been arranged between the high priestly party and the occupying power, but it is not unlikely that the Jewish authorities thought that the arrest and the condemnation would go together. The Roman soldiers had helped in the arrest, the Sanhedrin had condemned Jesus. Surely the Romans would now carry out the death sentence?

But Pilate did not see things in this way. He was a Roman with a Roman love for justice. It was evidently important for him that the proper procedure be followed. The first stage in proceedings against any prisoner was a formal accusation. Only when this had been made could a trial go ahead. So Pilate made his request.

"Your Law"

But what could the Jews say? They had no accusation that would stand up in Roman law and they knew it. They had a good reason (as they saw it) for wanting Jesus executed, for he had blasphemed their God. But they could not make this a formal charge in a Roman court and expect the charge to stick. So they resorted to a generality: "If this man were not an evil-doer we would not have handed him over to you" (v. 30). The expression I have translated as "evil-doer" is more exactly "one doing evil," and the present tense in "doing" points to the habitual practice. If we thought of the modern expression "habitual criminal" we would get something of the force of it. Instead of making a specific accusation of some specific crime (which could be supported by evidence), they are saying in effect, "Trust us. We would not have brought him to you if he had not been a wicked person." Perhaps there is also the thought that the members of a conquered nation would not have handed over one of their own to the conqueror without a very good reason.

But this did not suit Pilate. If they had no accusation they wanted to bring in the proper Roman form, then let them look to it themselves after their own Jewish form. "You take him and judge him according to your law" (v. 31). The word *you* is emphatic here; Pilate is saying that if they have no formal accusation that a Roman can take note of, they should go away and look after the whole matter themselves. If *their* law has been broken, then that is no concern of the Romans.

To make sense of the trial narrative it is important for us to notice something of what the Romans did when they conquered a country. They did not bother to set up a cumbersome bureaucracy to administer the full body of Roman law. Instead, for the most part they allowed the conquered peoples to retain their own laws and customs and to administer them through their own legal systems. This would have made life a good deal more bearable all round. The conquered peoples would be able to carry on under their own familiar laws and with their own familiar officials, and the Romans would not be disturbed by petty matters that could so easily be handled by local officials. Crime was crime the world over and the conquered peoples could be trusted to deal with it.

But there was a danger in this of which the Romans were very conscious. If local officials were in complete charge of the legal system, they could systematically get rid of those who supported the Romans by bringing charges against them in the local jurisdiction and imposing heavy penalties. In extreme cases they would be tempted to impose the death sentence. The Romans would not know the details of local legal systems and might find their supporters fined heavily or put in jail or even executed.

To guard against any such thing the Romans insisted that at any stage of any case the Roman governor had the right to take it over and see it through in his own way. And, where the death sentence was in view, they allowed local officials no rights at all. The death penalty could be imposed only by the Roman governor. This system enabled the Romans to administer subject territories with a minimum of fuss and a maximum of security to themselves.

So what Pilate is doing at this point is saying to the Jews in effect: "If you have a charge that will stand up in a Roman court, then bring it. If you have not, then take him away and judge him in your own courts and inflict such lesser penalty as you see appropriate. If it is Roman law that is involved, we will follow Roman practices. If Roman practices are not to be followed, then by all means go ahead, but do so under Jewish law."

The Death Sentence

The Jews' response is "It is not lawful for us to put anyone to death," which makes it clear that they had made up their minds both that Jesus was guilty and that they would be satisfied with nothing less than the death penalty. They could have judged him according to their own law—in fact they had already done so—but they could not execute him. For that they needed Roman cooperation. What was galling to them was that they had thought they had it. Only now do they find that if they wanted a Roman execution, they had first to establish due cause by a Roman prosecution.

The situation is complicated a little by the fact that sometimes the Jews *did* put people to death. For example, a little later Stephen was stoned at the instigation of the Sanhedrin and without the permission of the Romans. This leads some to reason that the Jews did have the right to execute people, but only by stoning. They argue that the Jewish leaders wanted a death by crucifixion (which would mean that he died under the curse of God, Deut. 21:23), and if Jesus was to be crucified it had to be the Romans who did it. But no sufficient reason is given for the Jewish authorities to be so set on crucifixion. Granted that in their view a crucified man was under the curse of God, if they had stoned Jesus he would at least have been removed permanently from their sphere of operations and they would not have had all this pestilent business of trying to persuade the Romans to do things for them. They would surely have seen crucifixion as desirable but not necessary.

In any case Stephen's death appears to be a lynching. It is true that he appeared before the Sanhedrin and that when he was stoned the witnesses laid their clothes at the feet of Saul (Acts 7:58), which seems to give an appearance of legality. But at the critical moment we read "and they yelled with a loud voice and stopped their ears, and with one accord they made a rush at him, took him outside the city and stoned him" (Acts 7:57). This is not due process.

The Romans knew what they were about. The situation was clearly that they retained the right to inflict the death penalty. There were some occasions when the Jews could get away with a lynching. If the Romans were not interested in the person who was killed and if there was popular support for it, then they turned a blind eye. But that did not give the Jews license to carry out executions as and when they saw fit. And in the present case the Romans were not likely to let them get away with it. It was Passover time. The city was full of excitable pilgrims and an execution might well provoke a riot. If the Jewish authorities tried to take things into their own hands, they could expect Pilate to be very displeased. He would certainly take strong action against them. Somehow they had to get him to sentence Jesus to death.

The Death Jesus Would Die

To understand what was going on it has been necessary for us to see something of the legal and political situation. But John is interested in something far more important than that. He goes on to tell us that all this happened (as often, he omits these words, but leaves his readers to supply them for themselves) "so that the word of Jesus might be fulfilled which he spoke signifying by what death he would die" (v. 32). The Jewish leaders might scheme and plot, and the Roman governor might take up a righteous stance (and later be moved from it). But what happened most of all was that the plan of God was worked out.

More than once John has made it clear that Jesus came to die for his people. His death would put away their sins (cf. 1:29), and it would do so by his taking the curse that rightly should have fallen on them. John sees it as important that Jesus' death was by crucifixion (12:32–33), for in this way he would take the curse that otherwise would have rested on the sinners whose place he took. Annas and Caiaphas, the Sanhedrin, the Jewish mob, Pilate and his retinue, all these played their part, and no doubt each of them at one stage or another thought that he was doing the thing that mattered with Jesus. But John is telling us that in the end God carried out his purpose. Though there is a sense in which they all acted freely and did what they chose, there is a deeper sense in which they did nothing other than what God determined.

Nowhere is the will of God clearer than in the crucifixion of Jesus. There God's will was perfectly done.

77

Jesus' Kingdom

So Pilate went back into the Praetorium and summoned Jesus and said to him, "Are you the King of the Jews?" Jesus replied, "Do you say this of yourself or did others tell you about me?" Pilate responded, "I'm not a Jew, am I? Your own nation and the high priests handed you over to me. What did you do?" Jesus replied, "My kingdom is not of this world; if my kingdom were of this world my servants would be fighting in order that I be not delivered up to the Jews. But now, my kingdom is not from here." Pilate therefore said to him, "So you are a king?" Jesus replied, "You are saying that I am a king. For this reason I was begotten and for this reason I have come into the world, that I might bear witness to the truth. Everyone who is of the truth hears my voice." Pilate says to him, "What is truth?"

And when he had said this he went out again to the Jews and says to them, "I find no crime in him. Now you have a custom that I release someone to you at the Passover. Do you want me to release for you the King of the Jews?" They yelled again therefore saying, "Not this man but Barabbas." Now Barabbas was a brigand (John 18:33–40).

In this passage John paints a vivid picture of kingship—the kingship of this world as seen in the might of imperial Rome standing over against real kingship as seen in the lowly Son of God. That Jesus is King is a most important concept for John, and he brings it out again and again in the crucifixion narrative. But Jesus' kingship was exercised in a country where the Romans ruled, which points to a problem that is always before the people of God. In our day we face the fact that while we give our first loyalty to our God, we live out our lives in a situation where we must exercise other loyalties as well. We live as citizens, we pay our taxes and fulfill our civic duties. We live as members of a social order and must bear in mind our relationships to our fellow citizens. Then there are local community organizations to which we owe a greater or smaller loyalty. We have a certain obligation to be good neighbors and that gives rise to another loyalty. And this is different from our loyalty to our friends. We belong to families and this brings a host of other loyalties. And so we could go on. Life is a complex affair and our various loyalties do not always fit into a harmonious system. Sometimes they conflict, which inevitably makes for problems.

John is not trying to solve such problems, but in this narrative he is making it clear that the kingship of Jesus is very real and that it is very important. In the end it stands over against all the loyalties demanded by this world, and John brings this out by setting Pilate over against Jesus in solitary confrontation. At this critical moment all the other actors vanish from the scene: Annas, Caiaphas, the disciples, the Jewish mob. There are only Jesus and Pilate and the subject of their discussion is Jesus' kingship. In the last resort it is this that matters and it matters whether the Pilates of this world understand it or not.

Pilate, of course, does not understand Jesus' royalty. But John makes it clear that the governor recognizes Jesus' innocence. The story he is telling is that of the King who was wronged by a tyrant, even though he fully recognized that there was no fault in that King. It is a feature of John's account of the trial that quite early in the piece Pilate came to see that Jesus had committed no crime. From that point on it was never a question of guilt or innocence; it was a question of what Pilate would do when confronted with the King, and of the lengths to which evil men would go to bring about the condemnation of the King they rejected.

We who live in a world subject to the kingship of worldly authorities are to be clear that those authorities are not always swayed by considerations of justice and truth. We must clear-sightedly recognize that our world is one in which there can be evil and there can be weakness at the highest level. But as we live in our unjust world we are to remember that Jesus lived in this same world. And he suffered at the hands of evil people like the high priests who handed him over, and at the hands of a governor who saw what was right but nevertheless crucified him.

The King of the Jews

Pilate knew from the preceding conversation with the Jewish leaders that the case was a serious one. They would be satisfied with nothing less than the death penalty. So he left them standing outside and came back into the Praetorium (v. 33) to question the prisoner. Some translations have "went again into the Praetorium," but as there has been no previous mention of Pilate's being there, we should take the word in the sense "back." He had been standing outside in front of the Praetorium and now went into the room that had been behind him.

He called for the prisoner and began to question him. An interesting point arises from what John says. Did Pilate talk to Jesus directly and, if so, in what language? There is no mention of an interpreter so it seems that the two spoke to one another. The absence of any reference to an interpreter is, of course, not conclusive. John may have thought that this was so obvious that there was no need to mention it. But it is also possible that there was no interpreter. Pilate, as an educated Roman, would certainly have known Greek, for this language was spoken throughout the empire. But it is unlikely that a man like him would have taken the trouble to learn Aramaic, the language of a conquered and despised people. We do not, of course, know for certain that Jesus could speak Greek, but there is nothing improbable about it. The language was spoken all over the empire, and Jesus had been brought up in an area that could be called "Galilee of the Gentiles." So, while absolute certainty is impossible, there is at least a probability that John is relating this conversation in the language in which it was spoken.

Pilate's opening question shows that more had been said outside the Praetorium than John has narrated. He has not reported a specific accusation that Jesus was the King of the Jews, but that is the first thing that Pilate asks about. His question "Are you the King of the Jews?" is the first question he asks in all four Gospels (Matt. 27:11; Mark 15:2; Luke 23:3), in all four it is couched in exactly the same words, and in all four Pilate's "you" is emphatic: "Are *you* the King of the Jews?" Clearly, from what the Jews had said to him, he had been expecting a brigand or a revolutionary, a member of the resistance movement. One look at Jesus was enough to show him that all such ideas were wide of the mark and to wring from him this expression of incredulity. This lowly figure a king? That was quite impossible!

The expression "the King of the Jews" is applied to Jesus in Matthew 2:2, but apart from that only in the passion narratives. John uses it five times and clearly it was important for him that the crucified Jesus be seen to be King, though he meant, of course, a "king" in a very different sense from the sense in which Pilate understood the term. When Pilate spoke of a king he meant a political revolutionary; he was asking whether Jesus claimed to exercise secular sovereignty over the province in which he himself was the governor.

Jesus countered with a question of his own: "Do you say this of yourself or did others tell you about me?" (v. 34). This is not an attempt to avoid giving an answer, but a first step in clarifying what is at issue. If Pilate had asked the question of his own volition, the meaning would be "Are you a king like all the kings of the nations? Are you rebelling against Rome?" But if the question originated in what the Jews were saying about him, the meaning would rather be "Are you God's Messiah? Are you the King whom God will send?" The answer to the two questions would be quite different. Jesus would have to say "No" to the suggestion that he was a political ruler, but "Yes" to the question about Messiahship. So the point had to be cleared up before he could answer the question Pilate was asking.

Pilate's contempt for the Jews possibly comes out in his emphatic repudiation of being Jewish: "I'm not a Jew, am I?" (v. 35). His "I" is emphatic; whatever may be true of Jesus' accusers, this proud Roman must never be accused of Jewish citizenship! "Your own nation" has acted, Pilate says, and specifically "the high priests handed you over to me." The high priestly families were the most important politicians in the Jewish nation, and when they acted the nation could be said to be involved. Thus Pilate is saying that it was the Jews as a whole who accused Jesus of being a king.

But he is not really interested in the exact terms used; he wants to know what Jesus had done. Perhaps we should notice that a Roman governor in the provinces had considerable latitude about the way he treated a case. He was not obliged to follow any particular forms very closely, but simply to see that justice was done. A good deal was made of what was called his *cognitio,* which the Latin dictionary defines as "a becoming acquainted with" and in legal matters as "a judicial examination, inquiry." How he went about becoming acquainted with the facts was left for the most part to the initiative and the common sense of the governor. Clearly Pilate was not prepared to regard what the high priests had said as necessarily accurate; they may have had their own reasons for putting the accusation in the form they did. Anyway, Pilate was already doubtful whether Jesus was the kind of person to proclaim himself "King of the Jews." But the Jewish leaders had brought him to the Praetorium and made it clear that they wanted the death sentence. Obviously something lay behind it all. But what? What had Jesus done? It was that to which Pilate directed his attention. Was there or was there not some action that contravened Roman law?

A Kingdom "Not of This World"

Jesus does not respond to the suggestion that he has *done* something that offends the high priests, but gets back to the thought of kingship. He says "My kingdom is not of this world" (v. 36). The words are in effect an admission that he has a kingdom, though we should bear in mind that the Greek word for "kingdom" can have about it the thought of an activity, a reign rather than a realm. If it is this that is in mind, Jesus is saying that there is a sense in which he is sovereign over his followers, for he directs them as to how they should live. But he is not saying that there is any nation or area over which he claims to be the earthly and political ruler.

Pilate might well not have understood the distinction, but he could understand "not of this world." Jesus is definitely repudiating any idea that he was a political revolutionary. In common with most, I have translated "not *of* this world," but it is perhaps to be noted that the Greek has the preposition *ek,* which means "out of" or "from." It often points to origin and that seems to be the meaning here. Jesus' kingdom did not originate in this world; it is not the product of any of the forces that this world generates, nor does it conform to the ideas that this world produces. There is a sense in which it is in order to speak of his "kingdom," but if we do we should bear in mind that he is not referring to a kingdom anything like earthly kingdoms. This world did not originate it and this world cannot bring it in.

Jesus brings out the impossibility of seeing his kingdom as originating from this world by pointing to the fact that his followers were not engaging in the kind of military activity that characterizes this world's kingdoms. The form of the conditional sentence Jesus uses is one that indicates that the supposition is contrary to the facts. The force of it is: "If my kingdom were of this world (as it is not), then my servants would be fighting (as they are not)." The facts of the case show the absurdity of the charge. To establish a kingdom in the normal, worldly sense of the term military activity is essential. How can anyone establish a kingdom without overthrowing those who are currently ruling it? But no one has alleged that Jesus is leading soldiers. There has been no military activity. The thought is preposterous.

If Jesus had soldiers fighting for him, it would be "in order that I be not delivered up to the Jews." This is another way of bringing out the absurdity of the charge. The King of the Jews fighting in order not to be delivered up to the Jews? It would make no sense. Jesus dismisses out of hand the accusation his enemies are making before Pilate.

He goes on to say, "But now, my kingdom is not from here." He has just said that his kingdom does not take its origin from anything earthly, and this statement will repeat this in another form. "But now" introduces the real situation; it brings before us what is really the case, in contrast to the contrary-to-fact condition that we had in the previous expression. "Now, as things are" is the force of it. "From here" once again points to source; the kingdom of which Jesus is king does not take its origin in anything earthly. It is a kingdom, a rule, of a very different sort.

The King

Pilate seizes on the fact that Jesus has said "My kingdom," and he goes on to refer to Jesus in terms of kingship (v. 37). There is something of a problem with the Greek expression he uses. Pilate may mean "Since you speak of a kingdom, you are a king," or he may mean the words ironically, "So then, it is a king that *you* are!" But it seems better to take them as a question, still used with irony: "So you are a king?" But whichever way we take it, Pilate is clearly speaking of Jesus in terms of his being a king; whether the governor was ironical or not, John clearly means the words to be taken seriously. For him it is important that at this time, when Jesus is facing the cross, he is in reality supremely master of the situation and, for that matter, of every situation. He is King.

But, of course, there is a difference between the royalty that belongs to Jesus and the royalty that Pilate had in mind. To agree with what the governor has just said would be misleading, and Jesus replies that it is Pilate who is saying that he is a king. Jesus has spoken of his kingdom but has not said that he is a king. This is not simply a matter of words, for what he meant by his kingdom was his sovereignty over the lives of his followers, not a piece of territory over which someone might reign. But Pilate had in mind just that, a claim to a piece of territory, and that was not what Jesus was talking about. So Jesus reminds Pilate that it is he who has said that Jesus is a king. His "you" is emphatic. "It is *your* word, not mine" is the thrust of it.

Jesus goes on to contrast himself with Pilate. His "I" is emphatic, just as his "you" was when he referred to the governor. He sets the two in emphatic contrast. He goes on to give the reason that he was "begotten." The verb strictly means the action of the male parent, but in this place there is no reason for seeing a great difference from the usual translation "born." Jesus is here speaking of the process whereby he came into this world, and indeed he goes right on to say "and for this reason I have come into the world." This form of words tells us something about who Jesus was. We would not speak of ourselves as "coming into the world," but it comes natural for Jesus to say this. His essential being belongs to heaven and it was from there that he came into the world.

The Truth

The purpose of his coming, he says, was "that I might bear witness to the truth." This combines three expressions that occur with frequency in this Gospel: the conjunction "that" ("in order that") occurs one hundred and forty-seven times, "to bear witness" thirty-three times, and "truth" twenty-five times. In each case the word is found more frequently in John than in any other book of the New Testament. John is very interested in the working out of God's purpose, as he is also in the bearing of witness and in truth. So he now reports Jesus as saying that the purpose of his coming into this world was to bear witness to the truth. It is Old Testament teaching that God is "the God of truth" (Ps. 31:5; Isa. 65:16), while in the New we have expressions like "the truth of God" (Rom. 15:8) and Paul's teaching that idolaters exchange the truth of God for the lie (Rom. 1:25), teaching that seems to mean that truth is God's essential being. In this Gospel Jesus says, "I am the truth" (14:6), on which Bultmann comments, "So truth is not the teaching about God transmitted by Jesus but is God's very reality revealing itself—occurring!—in Jesus." We should not think of truth simply as the opposite of a lie. In this Gospel truth comes very close to the essential being of God, and it is this that Jesus reveals.

Jesus goes on to speak of "everyone who is of the truth." In this Gospel we read a number of times about people who are "of" something. Thus there are those who are "of the earth" (3:31), those who are "of the world" (15:19), those who are "of God" (8:47), those who are "of their father, the devil" (8:44). The expressions "from below" and "from above" in 8:23 have the same construction in the Greek: more literally they mean "of the below" (used of the merely earthly person) and "of the above" (which denotes Jesus' essential being). In all these cases to be "of" something points to origin or essential being or wholehearted commitment, so that when Jesus speaks of everyone who is "of the truth" he is referring to those who are wholeheartedly committed to the ultimate truth, to that truth that is associated with the Father's essential being and with which Jesus identifies himself. It is these people of goodwill who hear what Jesus is saying. People like the high priests do not hear it, despite their many temporal and religious advantages; but people like the disciples, with their limited opportunities, gladly hear him.

Pilate rounds off this part of the discussion with his question "What is truth?" (v. 38). One way of understanding his meaning is that which Francis Bacon made famous with his words: "What is truth? said jesting Pilate; and would not stay for an answer." It may be that Pilate was not interested in truth: he simply wanted to get this case over and out of the way. The sense of it would be "If it's only truth you're concerned about, then that is of small account over against something important like rebellion against Rome." Jesus had been accused of being "King of the Jews," but if he was doing no more than chasing truth, then for Pilate that was a small matter. As Lenski puts it, ". . . the tone is that of an indifferent worldling who by his question intends to say that anything in the nature of religious truth is a useless speculation." At least it was clear to Pilate that Jesus was no danger to the state. The state is not interested in the question of the reality of God.

But it is also possible that Pilate meant the question in a more significant sense. "What is truth? Where will we find it? How will we recognize it when we see it?" may have been the questions running through his head. He may have been saying that truth is a very difficult question; it is something that no one can ever find in its totality. And if Pilate asks the question in this sense, then again he is saying that Jesus is no danger to the state. However we understand his words, they mean that he has come to see that he ought to release Jesus.

John records no answer to Pilate's question, at least in words. But a number of commentators have pointed out that the whole sequence of events that followed is John's answer in action. Truth is seen in the quality of Jesus' action in going to the cross for the salvation of sinners. Truth is seen in the action of the loving Father in giving up his Son to effect this salvation. It is when we see the sinless Son of God hanging on Calvary that we come to understand what truth in action, real truth, means.

Barabbas

Pilate's reaction to his conversation with Jesus is to go out and tell the Jews, "I find no crime in him." John uses the present tense for his verb *says;* the scene is vividly present to his mind. Pilate's "no" is emphatic: "I find nothing at all in the way of crime in him" is the force of it. There is no justification for proceeding further with the trial, and Pilate ought therefore to have released Jesus without further ado.

But Pilate was inconsistent. This is a human failing that turns up from time to time. There was a small-town Chamber of Commerce that decided to encourage the manufacture and sale of locally produced goods. Among other things they ran an essay competition among the schoolchildren, who were asked to write an essay on the general subject. The kids joined in with some enthusiasm, and there were some good essays as the earnest students pointed out the virtues of encouraging local industry. The winner received a portable radio and was intrigued to find on it the words "Made in Hong Kong." It is one thing to know what should be done and quite another to do it, as that Chamber of Commerce found out.

So with Pilate. He knew that he ought to release Jesus, but he knew also that this would not please the Jews, so he tried a different course. He reminded them of a custom that a prisoner be released to them at

Passover time (v. 39). The custom is not attested anywhere but in the Gospels, but there is no reason for doubting its existence. Such a release of prisoners is known from other parts of the ancient world and would be a way of pacifying conquered peoples. It seems that Pilate, having come to the conclusion that there was no reason for Jesus to be condemned, chose this way of attempting to secure his release. If he could get the people to accept Jesus' release, then at one and the same time he would be treating him as a condemned criminal (which he doubtless hoped would satisfy the Jewish leaders) and letting him go (which would satisfy his sense of what was right). But it was the people who would choose which prisoner would be released, not the governor (Mark 15:6), so it was necessary to persuade them to accept Jesus. Pilate accordingly took the initiative and suggested that he release "the King of the Jews." Doubtless he chose the title to make the release of this prisoner more attractive.

But this did not suit the mob. Since few, if any, can have thought that Jesus was really a criminal, the thought of wasting their opportunity by getting an innocent man released (instead of one of their own who had been sentenced for activities against the Romans) cannot have been attractive. So they asked for Barabbas (v. 40). They did not make their request halfheartedly but "yelled" for the man of their choice. John tells us that this man was "a brigand," which probably means a member of the resistance movement. Luke tells us that there had been a rebellion and that Barabbas had killed someone in that rebellion (Luke 23:18–19). Clearly he was the kind of fighter that the mob would love to get released.

His name is interesting. Barabbas is not really a name at all. "Bar" is an Aramaic expression meaning "son of"; thus "Simon Bar-Jona" (Matt. 16:17) means "Simon, son of John." Again, "abba" is the Aramaic for "father." "Barabbas" is thus the transliteration into Greek of an expression that means "son of father." It is not unlikely that John intends his readers to see that the people's choice meant that one who was a very earthly "son of father" was released, while one who in the most meaningful sense was "the Son of the Father" was killed instead.

Another possibility arises from the fact that several manuscripts of Matthew give the name as "Jesus Barabbas" (Matt. 27:16–17). That the name is not used elsewhere is natural enough; Christians would not want to call this criminal by the name of their Savior and Lord, and "Barabbas" was sufficient to indicate who they had in mind.

But it is a significant thought that the sinless Jesus, the Son of the heavenly Father, went to the cross instead of the sinful Jesus, the son of an earthly father.

78

Power—And Sin

So then Pilate took Jesus and scourged him. And the soldiers plaited a crown of thorns and put it on his head and they clothed him with a purple robe. They kept coming to him and saying "Hail, King of the Jews" and slapping him. And Pilate went outside again and says to them, "Look, I am bringing him outside again so that you may know that I find no crime in him." Jesus came out, therefore, wearing the crown of thorns and the purple robe. And he said to them, "Look, [here is] the man." When the high priests and the officials saw him therefore they yelled saying, "Crucify! Crucify!" Pilate says to them, "You take him and crucify him, for I find no crime in him." The Jews answered him, "We have a law, and according to our law he ought to die, because he made himself the Son of God."

When Pilate heard this saying he was more afraid and went into the Praetorium again and says to Jesus, "Where are you from?" But Jesus gave him no answer. Therefore Pilate says to him, "You don't speak to me? Don't you know that I have power to release you and I have power to crucify you?" Jesus answered him, "You would have no power against me unless it were given you from above; for this reason he who handed me over to you has a greater sin." Upon this Pilate tried to release him, but the Jews yelled saying, "If you release this man you are not Caesar's friend. Everyone who makes himself a king speaks against Caesar" (John 19:1–12).

Pilate had tried to get Jesus released by making him the subject of the normal release of a criminal at Passover time. But that had failed because the mob refused and made it clear that they wanted Barabbas. But Pilate was still convinced that there was nothing criminal about Jesus, and he still wanted to release him. So he tried another tack. He had Jesus scourged and either induced or allowed the soldiers to engage in some crude horseplay, mocking Jesus as a "king."

It is possible that in all this the governor was making an appeal to the pity of the people. When they saw one of their own suffering a scourging and being mocked by the crude soldiery, perhaps they would change their minds? If this was what Pilate intended, it was a complete failure, for there was no change in anyone's mind. It is perhaps more likely that he was making it quite clear that there was no possibility of seeing Jesus as a rebel leader. When he was ill-treated and mocked in this way it would be plain to all that he could not be seen as a leader of a guerilla band. But the mob would not go along with this either. They were not concerned with Pilate's scruples. They wanted a crucifixion and would not be content until they had it.

John's "So then . . ." (v. 1) seems to mean that the scourging took place at this point. There is a little problem in that in our first two Gospels it seems to take place after Jesus had been sentenced to be crucified (Matt. 27:26; Mark 15:15). Scourging was a normal preliminary to crucifixion, and a casual reading of Matthew and Mark would lead us to believe that Jesus was sentenced to crucifixion and that the execution proceeded in the normal way, with the usual preliminary scourging. However, if we look more carefully we will see that neither of those two writers actually mentions a formal sentence. They knew that Jesus was scourged, as was the normal procedure at a crucifixion, and they say so. But they do not locate it precisely in the sequence of events. Luke does not specifically mention the scourging but says that Pilate spoke of "chastising" Jesus (Luke 23:16, 22) and evidently this took place at more or less the same point in the proceedings as in John's record of the crucifixion events. We should probably understand Matthew and Mark to mean that Jesus was in fact scourged before he was crucified, but that they are not telling us at what point this took place. John lets us see that Pilate had Jesus scourged, not as the preliminary to crucifixion, but as a possible way of avoiding crucifixion.

Scourging was a terrible punishment, carried out with a whip made of several thongs. Each thong had pieces of metal or bone bound into it, so that a whipping could do a great deal of damage. The historian Eusebius tells us that in the time of Polycarp (early in the second century) some people "were torn by scourges down to deep-seated veins and arteries, so that the hidden contents of the recesses of their bodies, their entrails and organs, were exposed to sight." The Roman writer Cicero speaks of people being "scourged to death." We do not know how many strokes Jesus received, but if his scourging was severe it would explain why he needed help to carry the cross to the place of execution and why he died so soon. We should not miss the point that none of the Gospels dwells on the agonies Jesus must have suffered; they all say simply that Jesus was scourged. There is no attempt to stir up the readers' emotions. There is only a straightforward account of what was done.

The Mockery

The soldiers now proceed to indulge their sense of humor. It is not every day that a "king" is brought to execution, and they let themselves go in what doubtless seemed to them a very funny charade. The prisoner was a "king"? Very well, they would crown him, and they did so with a very unpleasant crown, one made of some thorny material (v. 2). None of the Gospels enables us to identify with certainty the material out of which the crown was made. Traditionally it has been thought to have been made from some thorny plant whose sharp thorns would add to Jesus' suffering, and in the end that seems the most probable understanding. But some scholars think that the "thorns" were "spikes," which would stick up and out (not into the wearer) in the form of a "radiate" crown, a crown that meant the wearer was the divine ruler (and this was part of the mockery). Evidently the point was not important for the Gospel writers, and they simply tell us that the crown was "of thorns."

They also put a "purple robe" on Jesus. Purple was a very expensive dye, made from a shellfish (called *murex*) that was not easy to obtain. Thus purple was costly and came to be associated with royalty. Matthew speaks of a scarlet cloak (Matt. 27:28) and, while scarlet dye was not as expensive as purple, it was far from cheap. It was made from the dried bodies of a little insect that lived on the oak tree. Thus scarlet clothing was associated with the wealthy. Scarlet cloaks were used by military officers, and the probability is that the soldiers came up with an old cloak from one of their officers. It was not exactly what kings wore, but it was close enough to give the general idea and was certainly a long way from anything that Galilean peasants ever wore!

Matthew seems to have the mockery later (probably Mark also), after Jesus' condemnation. Westcott thought that there were two stages in the mockery. This one he holds was due to Pilate, who was still trying to bring about Jesus' release. If Jesus could be shown to be insignificant, there might be no barrier to letting him go, and mockery was part of the process. Later, when he was handed over to the soldiers for crucifixion, they apparently took up the idea on their own initiative. They may have been happy at the idea of mocking a "king" and in doing so to show that they were contemptuous of the nation of which they declared him to be sovereign.

So they "kept coming to him" (v. 3; the tense of the verb points to continuous action), evidently in some formal manner as people approach royalty at an official function. This is the case also with the greeting, "Hail, King of the Jews." A greeting beginning "Hail" could be used in ordinary society. It was used, for example, by Judas when greeting Jesus in the garden (Matt. 26:49), and it is the way Gabriel began his conversation with Mary (Luke 1:28). But it was also used of royalty, as in the expression "Hail, Caesar." So it suited the soldiers well enough. Their form of words conveys a meaning something like "Hail, you 'King'!" They use the language of royalty, but clearly in mockery. Their slapping was evidently meant as a caricature of some way of expressing homage.

Clearly the soldiers relished their role as humorists and saw themselves as making the most of a highly ironical situation. Here was a peasant, they were apparently reasoning, accused of being a king. Well, then, they would take that peasant and treat him as a king, everything being done obviously as a joke. But John sees a deeper irony in that situation. The one whom the soldiers were treating so cavalierly was indeed a king, not a petty ruler like even the great Caesar, but King of kings and Lord of lords. John's readers are to see the real kingship shining through, even though none of those taking part in the events at that time realized quite what they were doing.

"Look, the Man"

Pilate went outside again (as in 18:38). John does not tell us when he went inside, but clearly he did. Now he came out and told the people what he planned to do (v. 4). He would bring Jesus out to the courtyard, he says (notice John's use of the present tense for greater vividness), in order that those there may know that he has found no crime in him. He does not explain how he thought they would come to this knowledge. Perhaps his meaning is that, with Jesus having been scourged and with the tokens of the soldiers' mockery upon him, it would be obvious to all that there was no truth in the suggestion that he was leading a rebellion. As "King of the Jews" Jesus, in Pilate's view, amounted to no more than a figure of fun.

So Jesus came out (v. 5) just as he was when the soldiers were through. John specifically says that he was wearing the crown of thorns and the purple robe. "Look," says Pilate, "look and you will see for yourselves, just as I have seen for myself, that this man is no revolutionary. He has committed no crime. He is no more than a poor creature from Galilee." The expression "Look, the man" is sometimes used in the classics with a meaning like "the poor man," "the poor creature." It will express Pilate's contempt and his complete dismissal of the charges as lacking all substance.

But John may be at work with his irony again. Contempt was what Pilate was trying to express when he used the words, but John may well have seen a meaning like "Look, *the* man." Others are but pale shadows of what being "man" means, but here we see one in whom there is perfect manhood. There may conceivably be more. The Hebrew word *Adam* means "man," and Adam was created to be sovereign over creation (Gen. 1:28). But the first Adam failed miserably to fulfill his destiny and instead brought a curse to creation (Gen. 3:17). But whereas the first Adam brought disaster, the last Adam brought life (1 Cor. 15:22, 45). It may be that John, in recording the expression, is looking away from Pilate's meaning to a much deeper significance than the governor ever dreamed of.

"Crucify! Crucify!"

But both Pilate's and John's meaning are lost on the Jews. The high priests and their associates had come there for one purpose only, to secure the crucifixion of Jesus. They were not greatly interested in Pilate's little plan for releasing Jesus. They were concerned with securing a crucifixion. This is the first time the word *crucify* has appeared in the narrative (v. 6), and it is interesting to notice that it comes not from the mob, but from the high priestly group. That was their aim and they make it clear.

This leads Pilate to say, "You take him and crucify him," which is rather puzzling. We saw in an earlier study that the Jews had no authority to execute people, and in any case if they did put anyone to death it would be by stoning (as they did with Stephen). We should notice that Pilate uses emphatic pronouns: "*You* take him and crucify him, for *I* find no crime in him." He sets himself in emphatic opposition to the Jews: *they* may want a crucifixion, but *he* is aware of no offense in Jesus. That is clear enough, but why Pilate should talk of the Jews' crucifying Jesus is not. They could not do it. It may be that this is just a wild statement coming from a man who was exasperated beyond measure. "You are not listening," Pilate may be meaning. "I find no crime in the man. He does not deserve crucifixion. I want none of it. If you are not going to take notice of me and of my processes of law, go and crucify him yourselves—if you can!"

The Jews make no direct answer to what Pilate has just said but speak of their own legal system. This does not carry on the conversation along the lines on which it has been going, but it gives the real reason for their hostility to Jesus. "We have a law," they say, "and according to our law he ought to die, because he made himself the Son of God" (v. 7). Their "we" is emphatic, "*we,* as opposed to the Romans and, for that matter, anyone else." The word *law* is characteristically used to mean the first five books of the Old Testament (e.g., Matt. 7:12) and sometimes even for the whole of it (e.g. John 15:25). But it may also be used for just one of the regulations in the Law, and that is the point of it here. The Jewish leaders are referring to the words "anyone who blasphemes the name of the LORD must be put to death . . ." (Lev. 24:16). From their point of view, what Jesus said and did constituted blasphemy—and for that crime the only penalty was death.

The way they put the offense is "he made himself the Son of God." They put "Son of God" in an emphatic position: "it was nothing less than the Son of God that he made himself!" From the standpoint of Roman law Pilate had been able to discern no crime in Jesus, no offense that merited the punishment of death. Now the Jews invite him to look at Jesus from *their* point of view. They had correctly discerned what Jesus' teaching meant for his position over against the Father. They did not stop to ask whether what he said was true. It was enough for them that it contradicted all that they thought was possible. For them it was quite impossible for any man to be the Son of God, so for Jesus to make the claim was to commit a horrible blasphemy. And to blaspheme the one God was to commit the worst crime they could envisage. The penalty had to be execution.

This made Pilate "more afraid" (v. 8), but as he has not been described as afraid previously, this raises a question or two. We are probably right in seeing fear behind his hesitancy in dealing with Jesus. We would have expected that a Roman governor would normally have gone right ahead with the case, acting decisively either to condemn or acquit the prisoner. But Pilate has dithered up till now, and this is evidence of some deep-seated conviction that there was something here that he did not understand and of which he was to some extent afraid.

Now John says he was *more* afraid and does not give the reason for this. It may be that it was the expression "Son of God" that troubled him. Pilate would not have accepted this in the sense that either Jesus or the Jewish leaders used it. But people in the Greco-Roman world had a rich mythology that told of demigods and heroes, and there was a good deal of speculation about "divine men," beings who evidently shared in the nature both of the gods and of people. There were many stories of gods and goddesses appearing in human form, and superstitious people would put no limit to what might happen when divinity appeared among humankind. It is possible that Pilate shared in a superstitious fear of what could follow a manifestation of divinity in human form, and the words of the Jewish leaders may have led him to fear the worst. This would have been reinforced by his wife's dream, of which Matthew tells us (Matt. 27:19).

Another suggestion is that Pilate was concerned about his own future. The Romans were generally very respectful of local religious practices, for obvious reasons. It made for good government to have Roman administrators who took care not to stir up opposition by heavy-handed practice towards religious observances that meant nothing to them but very much to the local people. Pilate may have feared that what he was doing would appear to the powers in Rome to be paying insufficient attention to local religious ideas. Yet another interpretation is that this statement alerted him to the possibility that he would not be able to carry through his idea of releasing Jesus.

Thus there are quite a few possibilities. We cannot be sure that it was any one of these to the exclusion of the others that swayed the governor, and it must remain possible that more than one of them stirred up his fears. What is clear is that it was the statement that Jesus claimed to be God's Son that scared Pilate.

Power on Earth

So Pilate went back into the Praetorium to interrogate Jesus again (v. 9). Jesus had been brought out of the Praetorium (v. 5), and John does not say when he was brought back in. But it must have happened, for Pilate now went back in to talk to him. This time he is interested in origins. "Where are you from?" he asks. This is perhaps not the question we would have expected, but evidently Pilate thought that this was the significant thing. If Jesus was from Nazareth, that was one thing. If he was from heaven, that was quite another.

But Jesus said nothing. Jesus is said to have been silent at one point or other of his trial in each of our Gospels (Matt. 26:63; 27:14; Mark 14:60f.; Luke 23:9). In this, some of the commentators of the early church saw a fulfillment of the prophecy of Isaiah 53:7. It is not clear why he remained silent at this point, for earlier he had spoken quite freely to Pilate. It may be that Jesus felt that the governor would not have understood if he told him the real facts; it was not a simple question he had asked. It is also possible that the answer was already before Pilate, for Jesus had told him of his being born and having come into the world to bear witness to the truth (18:37). Or Jesus may have felt the question was not relevant. In the earlier part of the narrative Pilate had been doing his duty and trying to find the facts in the case so that he would know whether Jesus was innocent or guilty. He had discovered that there was no crime in Jesus, and that was all that concerned him. Jesus' origin was not relevant to the case. Whatever the reason, Jesus kept silent.

This outraged Pilate, and in his further question he puts the word *me* in an emphatic position: "*To me* you don't speak?" (v. 10). Jesus might keep silence before anyone else in the trial, but Pilate was convinced that he was the one who mattered. It was incredible that the prisoner should refuse to answer any question that he might put to him. Was he unaware of the realities of the position? There was no restriction on the power of the governor in such a case as this.

Pilate brings out what he saw as the essentials of the situation with a further question: "Don't you know that I have power to release you and I have power to crucify you?" In both places he puts emphasis on "power" by putting it first: "*power* I have to release you and *power* I have to crucify you." Pilate is in no doubt that he is completely master of the situation. In the end it is *his* word that will determine whether Jesus lives or dies. His word for "power," incidentally, is one that means "authority"; Pilate is not talking about physical power, but the power that comes from occupying the supreme position.

Power from Above

But the highest authority in the land had made a mistake, and Jesus proceeds to point this out. These are the last words Jesus says to Pilate in this Gospel and indeed his only recorded words to anyone after the scourging. He points out that all earthly power is held only by divine permission and says to the governor, "You would have no power against me unless it were given you from above" (v. 11). "From above," of course, means "from God in heaven," not "delegated from Rome." That God rules in the affairs of men is clear throughout the Bible and mattered a great deal to the early Christian church. For the most part believers were the world's "little people," and it was important to them that in the last resort what mattered was what God decreed, not what earth's tyrants said. Paul develops the idea that the earth's ruler is "God's deacon [or servant]" (Rom. 13:4). This is not the way it appears to those who wield power, but Jesus makes it clear that this is the truth. Power does not rest with Pilate but with God.

Jesus goes on to say, "he who handed me over to you has a greater sin." This does not mean that Pilate is guiltless: "greater sin" implies that there is a "lesser sin," and even though we must look elsewhere for the great sinner, Pilate is to be blamed for the way he exercised the power that God had given him. But the real offender, of course, was Caiaphas. Some have instead suggested Judas, for there was an important sense in which he "handed Jesus over" to the arresting authorities. Indeed the verb used here is often used of Judas in the words usually translated "who betrayed him" and similar expressions (e.g., 6:64; 12:4). Actually it can be used of others also and even of Pilate himself (v. 16), but in a slightly different sense. But Judas was only a tool of whom Caiaphas availed himself, and Pilate was one whom Caiaphas saw could be persuaded to do what the high priest thought was expedient. He was the power behind it all, and to him attaches the "greater sin."

Caesar's Friend

Something about Jesus' words greatly affected Pilate, for he now tried to release Jesus (v. 12). There is a difficulty in the words I have translated "upon this"; more literally they mean "out of this" and may mean "for this reason" or "from this time" (the same expression and the same ambiguity are found in 6:66); perhaps in the Johannine manner both are meant. John does not say what it was that Pilate actually did, but he goes on to speak of what the Jews yelled, so that Pilate must have gone out of the Praetorium to the courtyard where the Jews were. Evidently he did something in the way of trying to bring the Jewish leaders to a better frame of mind.

But Pilate's trouble was that he wanted things both ways. I am reminded of a story about Sir Thomas Beecham, who conducted in operas where mostly the sopranos were ladies of considerable stature. On one occasion a friend asked him why he did not choose ladies who ate less. "Well," Sir Thomas said, "I would like to. But unfortunately those who sing like birds eat like horses. And vice versa." Sir Thomas could not have it both ways and was forced to make his choice. And that was also the way it was with Pilate. He wanted to stand in well with his Jewish subjects and his Roman superiors on the one hand, and he wanted to release Jesus on the other.

But the Jews immediately showed him that it was not going to be possible for him to have it both ways. "If you release this man," they said, "you are not Caesar's friend." It is not certain whether they are using the term "Caesar's friend" in a general sense, of one who acted in Caesar's best interests, or whether they are referring to a select group of people who were admitted into the category of "Friends," people honored by the ruler, perhaps for rendering special service. A. N. Sherwin-White says that the expression "becomes markedly official in imperial documents, with the suggestion that so and so is the official representative of the Princeps." Many hold it unlikely that a man like Pilate would have been admitted to such a select company. Our answer must be that we do not know. He certainly was the emperor's representative in Palestine, and he may have had the official title "Friend."

Whether or not it was used as an official title, there is no doubt about the general sense. The Jews are issuing a veiled threat that if Pilate lets Jesus go, this will become known in Rome and the consequences for the governor may well be very serious. Of course, Pilate could contend that he had done nothing other than release an innocent man, but it was not as simple as that. If the Jews were to report him to Rome, his whole record would come out, and there was much that Pilate would want to keep hidden. The Jewish writer Philo speaks of another occasion when the possibility arose that the Jews would send an embassy to the Emperor, and Pilate feared that if they did so they would tell the emperor of "the briberies, the insults, the outrages and wanton injuries, the executions without trial constantly repeated, the ceaseless and supremely grievous cruelty." We need not doubt that Philo is overplaying his hand a little, but it is obvious that Pilate could not afford to have his record scrutinized closely in Rome.

"Everyone who makes himself a king speaks against Caesar," said the Jews, and Pilate recognized what they meant. He recognized also that this gave him a valid excuse for putting Jesus to death. From that moment there was no doubt that a crucifixion would take place.

79

No King But Caesar

So Pilate, when he had heard these words, brought Jesus outside and sat on the judgment seat in a place called Stone Pavement, but in Hebrew Gabbatha. Now it was the Preparation of the Passover; it was about the sixth hour. And he says to the Jews, "Behold, your King!" They yelled therefore, "Away with him! Away with him! Crucify him!" Pilate says to them, "Shall I crucify your King?" The high priests replied, "We have no king but Caesar" (John 19:13–15).

The story moves remorselessly to its climax. "So" (v. 13; the word might be translated "therefore") points to the necessary sequence. It was because the Jews said, "Everyone who makes himself a king speaks against Caesar" (v. 12), that Pilate proceeded to act as he did. John makes it clear that it was the enmity of the Jews that was the decisive thing. Pilate had no wish to take action against Jesus, but he was not ready to face an accusation that he had failed in his duty as "Caesar's friend." It was hearing the words about Caesar that decided him.

There is a small point about the Greek that we should notice. There are two constructions that may be used after the verb *to hear.* If it refers to hearing a person, the verb is followed in Greek with the genitive case; but if it is a matter of hearing a sound or a voice or a word or the like, it is followed by the accusative. But when John is saying that a voice or a word is heard with appreciation and understanding, he follows the verb with the construction usually reserved for persons, the genitive. That is what he does here. It was not only that the words the Jews said fell on Pilate's ears. He understood what they meant and what they implied. We would say today, "He got the message!" He knew that he would be in trouble with Rome if he released Jesus. And that meant that the execution would certainly go ahead.

The Judgment Seat

Pilate prepared for the official sentencing and brought Jesus outside. I have translated the name of the place as "Stone Pavement," and this is certainly one of the meanings of the word. But it can also mean "Mosaic Pavement," and a few scholars have thought that this is the meaning we should give it here. This, however, seems improbable. It is likely that this was an area where there was a good deal of traffic, and a mosaic would be unlikely in such a place. It is uncertain whether Pilate had made his Praetorium in Herod's palace or in the Tower of Antonia, but the case for the latter is supported by the fact that excavation has revealed a court paved with large stones, which might well be the pavement of which John writes. It covers an area of about 2,300 square yards, so it was quite a considerable court and might well have a name of its own. Raymond E. Brown says that the stones are more than a yard square and a foot thick. Incidentally, scratched in the stones in more than one place are the patterns of what was evidently a game (a gambling game?) played by the soldiers during the times they were waiting there.

The identification cannot be regarded as certain, for some archaeologists think that Herod's palace is much the most likely place for the events of which we are thinking. But at least the courtyard of Antonia shows us the kind of place that was in mind and may well be the very spot on which these events took place.

John gives a second name for the place, the Hebrew, or (as we would say) Aramaic, name. Gabbatha is not the Aramaic equivalent of "Stone Pavement" but a quite independent name for the same place. The word is found here only and is of uncertain meaning. Some think it means "the hill of the House," which would mean the hill on which *the* House (i.e., the temple) was built, but it is not easy to see the appropriateness of this. Others think the meaning has to do with height, "elevated place, ridge," and this would fit either Antonia or Herod's palace. But however the word be understood, it is clear that John had exact knowledge of the place and of the various names it was called.

There Pilate had set up his "judgment seat." The word means "step" (it is used in much this way in Acts 7:5). It came to be used of a seat with steps leading up to it and thus of an important seat. The seat that a judge would use when delivering his judgments was such a seat, and the term is regularly used in the sense "judgment seat." This is the one place in the New Testament where it is used without the definite article. That is to say, John is speaking of "a" judgment seat, rather than "the" judgment seat. This seems to mean that it was not "the" judgment seat, the judgment seat normally employed. That judgment seat would, of course, have been inside the Praetorium, where cases were habitually tried. But on this occasion there was a difficulty because the Jews would not enter the building. It looks as though Pilate set up a portable judgment seat outside in order to accommodate their scruples.

We should notice a little peculiarity in the way John expresses what happened there. In English the verb to sit may be either transitive or intransitive; we may say, "the hostess sat him at the head of the table" or we may say "he sat at the head of the table." There is a similar ambiguity about the Greek word John uses. If we take the verb as intransitive, we will understand it as I have translated: Pilate "sat on the judgment seat." But it would be quite possible to understand it as transitive; in Greek the object "him" could be understood, and some scholars have translated it ". . . brought Jesus outside and sat him on the judgment seat" (Moffatt, for example, understands the Greek in this way). I do not think we should translate it like this, as it would lead to an understanding of the text that seems quite impossible. Would Pilate really have sat his prisoner on the judgment seat? Surely not.

But it seems that John has quite intentionally used a piece of Greek that could be understood in this way. John is interested not only in the way the events unfolded but in what they meant. Who really was being judged that day? To outward appearance it was Pilate who was in charge of things and who gave sentence, and it was Jesus who was the subject of Pilate's activity. But in a much more meaningful way Jesus was and is supreme. It is before his judgment seat that we will all stand one day (2 Cor. 5:10), Pilate as well as everyone else. And Pilate will be judged for what he did that day in Jerusalem. He thought he was giving judgment, when in fact he was doing something for which he would one day come into judgment himself. Who was really on trial that day? John will not want his readers to overlook the irony of the situation.

The Preparation of the Passover

John puts in a little time note that must have been clear to his readers but unfortunately presents problems for us. He says it was "the Preparation of the Passover" (v. 14), which is a difficult expression. The Jews regularly used the word *Preparation* to designate Friday, for they used that day to prepare for the Sabbath. Indeed a standard dictionary of terms in the principal Indo-European languages says, "The day before the Sabbath was called 'Preparation.'" There is no question about this widespread use; if we take the word in this way here, it will mean "Friday in Passover week."

However, there are some scholars who point out that just as the Jews prepared on Friday for the coming of the Sabbath, so on the eve of any great festival they prepared for that festival. These scholars point out that the Passover was approaching and think it would be natural for the Jews to use "Preparation" for the day before the Passover, whether it was Friday or not. But a difficulty in the way of this view is that no evidence has been brought forward to show that the Jews used "Preparation" for the eve of any holy day other than the Sabbath. The Jews would certainly have prepared for the coming of a festival like Passover, but we have no evidence that when they said "the Preparation" they meant the day on which they made ready for that feast (or for that matter any other feast). It was the day they got ready for the Sabbath.

It is better to stick with what we know. I like the story of the mother who discovered her bright son had a habit of leaving money in the pockets of his jeans, and she had laundered dollar notes on more than one occasion before she found out. It made no sense to her, so she asked him, "Why don't you keep your money in your wallet?" "Well, Mom," came the reply, "I may not remember where I left my wallet, but I always know where my pants are." He stuck to what he knew.

We know that "Preparation" was a way of referring to Friday. In view of the preparations for the great festivals it seems logical to us that they would use the same word in that context. But the point is that we have no knowledge of any such usage. If the term was in fact used for the Preparation on the eve of Passover (or any other festival), no evidence of this survives. It is much better to stick with the evidence and to see John as saying that it was the Friday in the week that the Passover took place. This is supported by the fact that Mark, writing about the same day, says that it was "the Preparation, which is the day before the Sabbath" (Mark 15:42).

John proceeds to give the time of day as "about the sixth hour," which puzzles us as Mark says that Jesus was crucified at "the third hour" (Mark 15:25). One way of reconciling the two statements is to change the sentence division in Mark. There was very little punctuation in ancient manuscripts, and it is modern editors who put in full stops, commas, and all the rest of our apparatus for understanding the text. There is usually no great trouble in doing this, but just occasionally there is more than one possibility. One scholar has suggested that in Mark 15:25 we should put our full stop after "third hour," in which case the time refers to the soldiers' casting of lots. For most of us this does not help for we see this as taking place at the time of the crucifixion, but this scholar thinks it took place at the time of the scourging. If we could accept this there would be no problem: Mark would be referring to the time of the scourging and John to that of the crucifixion. But that seems a very unlikely understanding of what Mark has written. It does seem as though he is referring to the time of the crucifixion.

Another way of looking at the problem was put forward by B. F. Westcott, a great scholar of an earlier day. He thought that throughout his Gospel John was using Roman time, when the day went from midnight to midnight, and the other Gospels were using Jewish time, when the day began at sunset and the hours were reckoned first as the hour of the night and then as the hour of the day. On this way of looking at it, John is referring to a time about six in the morning (as on our time scale), whereas Mark, with the day beginning at around 6:00 A.M., is speaking of somewhere around 9:00 A.M. As John refers to the trial as coming to its climax and Mark to the actual crucifixion, this would fit in nicely.

Unfortunately, however, the so-called Roman time does not seem ever to have been used in telling the time. The Romans did count from midnight when they were dealing with legal matters like leases. If a lease ran out on a given day, at precisely what time of the day did it terminate? They solved the problem by picking on the middle of the night, when most people were in their beds asleep, as the beginning or end of the official day. But when it came to telling the time they seem always to have meant the hours since sunrise or since sunset, just as everyone else did. The Roman writer Pliny points out that people in different places use different ways of reckoning time: "The actual period of a day has been differently kept by different people: the Babylonians count the period between two sunrises, the Athenians that between two sunsets . . . the common people everywhere from dawn to dark, the Roman priests and the authorities who fixed the official day, and also the Egyptians and Hipparchus, the period from midnight to midnight." But we have no record of anyone in antiquity beginning at midnight when he counted the hours of the day. Sundials, for example, had VI at the middle of the day, not XII.

Other suggestions have been made. Thus the Greek form of the sign for three was very similar to that for six, and some have thought that an early scribe mistook what Mark had written. Another possibility is that by "hour" Mark meant "watch," and as the third watch would begin at noon Mark meant essentially what John meant. Such suggestions, while interesting, lack probability.

It seems that the best way of solving the problem is to remember that for the ancients time was always approximate. People did not have watches or clocks; they looked at the sun and guessed what the time was. Mark's "third hour" will mean nothing more precise than some time about the middle of the morning, and John's "about the sixth hour" a time getting on towards noon. Unless we have some reason for thinking that one (or both) was striving for absolute accuracy, a time in late morning would suit either reference. No such reason has ever been put forward.

"Behold, Your King!"

John goes on to tell his readers that Pilate, having had Jesus brought out, says (he uses the present tense for greater vividness) to the Jews, "Behold, your King!" We should probably think of Jesus as still wearing the crown of thorns and the purple cloak (v. 5). We might have expected that Pilate, sitting on the judgment seat as he was, would simply pass the official sentence. Instead he points the Jews to their King. From Pilate's point of view this is possibly one last attempt to get the representatives of the conquered nation to see the impossibility of taking seriously the accusation that Jesus claimed to be a king in the political sense. Was this bedraggled figure clad in the robes of mockery "King of the Jews"? For Pilate it was impossible.

But from John's point of view the words are a formal statement from the governor sitting on his official judgment seat of the reality of Jesus' dignity. He was indeed the King of the Jews. Indeed he was much more than that. He was the King who fulfilled all that to which Old Testament prophecy pointed, the Lord's Messiah. Long ago Gideon had refused to be a king over Israel, saying, "The Lord will rule over you" (Judg. 8:23), and when the people wanted a king "such as all the other nations have," God said to Samuel, ". . . it is not you they have rejected as their king, but me" (1 Sam. 8:5, 7). The people of the Old Testament looked forward to that day of which the Lord had said, "You are my Son; today I have become your Father. Ask of me, and I will make the nations your inheritance, the ends of the earth your possession. You will rule them with an iron scepter . . ." (Ps. 2:7b–9a). Now God had raised up that Son of whom he had spoken, that Son who would be King forever, and there was a profound truth in Pilate's invitation, "Behold, your King!" It was indeed their King, the King promised through the ages, who stood before them.

Caesar

And in the face of their King these representatives of Judaism yelled their renunciation (v. 15). Pilate's well-meant attempt to stir up feelings of compassion and the like failed, as it was bound to fail. The people "yelled," the word pointing to a great shout. Probably there had been something close to silence as Pilate from the judgment seat spoke about Jesus, but the reference to him as "King" brought a spontaneous shout of repudiation.

Far from recognizing Jesus for what he was, the mob called for him to be removed and crucified. It is difficult to give the exact force of their cry in English. They use the imperative of the verb "to take up, take away" and it stands by itself. Their one-word imperative is repeated and we have something like "Take away, take away!" In English we must insert the object and in doing this we lose something of the force of the sharp imperative. The mob is calling for Jesus to be removed in no uncertain terms. They want none of this King of whom Pilate speaks.

There may be another typical piece of Johannine irony here. In earlier studies we saw that John uses the language of exaltation to refer to crucifixion, as when Jesus speaks of being "lifted up" and in this way drawing all people to him (12:32). The verb here is a different one, but the idea of lifting up might conceivably be in mind. Jesus would indeed be taken up (and from the Jewish point of view, out of the way). But his being taken up would fulfill the divine plan whereby the sin of the world is taken away (cf. 1:29, where the verb used here is used of the Lamb of God taking away the sin of the world).

The mob calls for Pilate to have Jesus crucified, which elicits from the governor the question "Shall I crucify your King?" Literally he puts "King" first for emphasis: "Your King shall I crucify?" He still insists on using the word for royalty, but the mob is in no mood for reasoning. They want blood, and nothing less will satisfy them. But we should not miss John's emphasis on Jesus' royalty. Throughout this narrative John keeps recording the use of terms that bring out his deep conviction that Jesus is King in the fullest sense. Even those who call for his death cannot alter the fact that he is King. And Pilate, with his feeble attempts to set Jesus free, keeps bringing out the fact of his royalty.

John rounds off this part of his story with another of those sayings that are meant by those who use them in one way and yet convey a profound truth in another. "We have no king but Caesar," they say, meaning that they are loyal subjects of the emperor. It is of no use for Pilate to keep drawing attention to a person who claims to be a king, for they themselves recognize no such claims. They look to Caesar as their sovereign and Pilate as the lawful representative of that sovereign. They want nothing to do with a king from Nazareth.

This is a phony explanation. I am reminded of a rather nervous old lady on her first flight in an airplane. When darkness fell she called to a steward and asked, "How does the pilot know where he is going when he is away up in the air like this and he cannot see the way?" The steward pointed to a place outside the window where a green light was flickering on the wing. "Do you see that green light?" he asked. "Yes," she replied. "Now look through the window on the opposite side. Do you see that red light?" "Yes, I do," said the lady. "Well, as long as he keeps between those two lights he is okay," said the steward and put her mind completely at rest, even though there was not a shred of truth in what he said.

The Jewish leaders here are talking as cynically as the steward. They have their Scriptures, which make it clear (as we have just noticed) that God is their King and, despite what they say to Pilate, they do not want to repudiate their Scriptures. Their words to the governor are no more than a strong way of distancing themselves from Jesus. But in uttering them they are in fact stating the truth. Whatever they might say in their religious moments, they have no king but Caesar. In the last resort they give their loyalty to those who walk the corridors of human power. They live like shrewd and cynical politicians, people who know how to manipulate others in order to get the result at which they aim. They are not concerned in the slightest to set forward the purposes of God if those purposes do not fall in with what they see as politically expedient. They really have no king, at least in the fullest and most meaningful sense of that term, other than Caesar.

80

The Crucifixion

Therefore he delivered him to them then to be crucified. So they took Jesus. And carrying his cross he went out to a place called "The place of a skull," which is called in Hebrew "Golgotha," where they crucified him and with him two others, one on each side and Jesus in the middle. And Pilate wrote also a title and put it on the cross: and it was written "Jesus of Nazareth, the King of the Jews." This title many of the Jews read, because the place where Jesus was crucified was near the city, and it was written in Hebrew, Latin, and Greek. Therefore the high priests of the Jews said to Pilate, "Don't write 'The King of the Jews,' but that he said 'I am King of the Jews.'" Pilate replied, "What I have written, I have written" (John 19:16–22).

Pilate's conversation with the chief priests has shown him that they were bent on having Jesus crucified. He had tried a number of different approaches with a view to delivering the man from Nazareth, and they had all failed. The issue boiled down to this: if he set this penniless Galilean free, he would probably find himself defending his far-from-perfect record as a governor before a tribunal in Rome. Pilate was not prepared to face such a trial. So he gave Jesus over to crucifixion and thus got himself off the hook. John's "therefore" at the beginning of verse 16 looks back to the words of the chief priests: "We have no king but Caesar" (v. 15). It is because of the line the chief priests took that Pilate acted as he did. They are saying in effect that whatever happens to poor men from Galilee, our place before Caesar must be safeguarded. "We are serving Caesar faithfully by putting down a revolutionary," they are reasoning. "But you, Pilate? Are you putting down this rebel? Or are you countenancing revolt?"

Pilate gave in: ". . . he delivered him to them then to be crucified." These apparently simple words form another of John's enigmatic statements. What actually happened must have been that Pilate called for some soldiers and handed Jesus over to those who would take him out and crucify him. How else would matters be handled?

But in strict grammar the words refer to the chief priests. John says, ". . . the high priests replied, '. . . .' Therefore he delivered him to them. . . ." John is surely reminding his readers that, although it was Pilate who gave the sentence and Roman soldiers who performed the actual work of crucifixion, it was the chief priests who were responsible. Neither Pilate nor the soldiers would have acted if the matter had been left to them. But the chief priests were implacable. It was due to them that the crucifixion took place, so that in a very meaningful sense it was really to them that Jesus was handed over.

Crucifixion

Putting people to death by fastening them to crosses was widely practised in antiquity, both in the Roman Empire and outside it. Not as much is known about it as we would have anticipated from its widespread use, and it has been pointed out that the accounts in our four Gospels are the most detailed that have come down to us. Crucifixion was regarded as a very shameful thing, and the writers of antiquity apparently did not care to dwell on it; they certainly shrank from recording details. The words of Cicero are often quoted, when he spoke of crucifixion as "that most cruel and disgusting penalty." We should perhaps notice also the words of the Jewish writer Josephus who spoke of it as "the most wretched of deaths."

And it was painful. The Roman philosopher Seneca speaks of the very slow and painful way the crucified died and asks whether anyone would willingly die in this way: "Can anyone be found who would prefer wasting away in pain dying limb by limb, or letting out his life drop by drop, rather than expiring once for all? Can any man be found willing to be fastened to the accursed tree, long sickly, already deformed, swelling with ugly weals on shoulders and chest, and drawing the breath of life amid long-drawn-out agony? He would have many excuses for dying even before mounting the cross" (cited from Martin Hengel, *Crucifixion* [London, 1977], pp. 30–31).

Crucifixion was a torment largely restricted to the lower classes. It was frequently inflicted on slaves and on criminals, but rarely on those in the upper social classes. It was a matter for very serious concern when a Roman citizen was crucified. This did happen on very rare occasions, but it was widely felt that it should never occur. But where the lower classes were concerned it was judged a proper form of execution. It was thought to be specially valuable where slaves were involved, for there was a large population of slaves and the upper classes seem to have been perpetually nervous about the possibility of a successful slaves' revolt. The judicious use of crucifixion was seen as a way of keeping the slaves in their place.

We are familiar with the traditional shape of the cross on which Jesus was crucified, but this was not the only shape. It seems that originally a single stake was used, but in time other forms were used as well. The shape might be that of a T, with the crosspiece at the top, or a Y or an X. A cross was simply a device for killing a person, and its shape was unimportant as long as it served the purpose. The victim was fastened to the cross either by nails or by cords. There was usually a projection like a horn, which the victim straddled and which enabled him to take some of the weight from his arms.

There appears to have been considerable variety in the way people were crucified, for this form of execution allowed wide scope for the sadistic to devise ways of torturing their victims. Sometimes people were crucified upside down. The remains of a man have been discovered in Judea in which the legs were twisted so that one large nail could be driven through both heels. Flogging was the regular precursor to the actual nailing to the cross, so that the victim was invariably in great agony.

It is not known what actually brought about death (and fortunately our scientists cannot watch a crucifixion to find out). The circulation and the respiration would certainly have been affected, and long exposure would not have helped. One possibility is that the combination of all the various phases of ill treatment, together with the prolonged strain of being held in an unnatural position, brought about heart failure. Another suggestion is that the constriction of the lungs over a prolonged period of time had a fatal effect. A further possibility is that the supply of blood reaching the brain was greatly reduced and terminal brain damage resulted. Whatever the ultimate cause, it is certain that death did result.

Golgotha

It was to this frightful method of execution that Jesus was led out. John tells us that he carried his cross (v. 17). It was normal practice for the victim to carry all or part of his cross (why waste the energy of someone else on this task?). The other Gospels tell us that somewhere along the way a man called Simon, who came from Cyrene, was made to carry Jesus' cross (Matt. 27:32; Mark 15:21; Luke 23:26). None of them says that Jesus carried it at first (that is something we owe to John), but Mark and Luke tell us that Simon was coming "from the country." This plainly means that he was not there at the beginning but encountered the procession somewhere along the way. Putting all this together, it seems that Jesus carried the cross at first, but that he was in a weakened state (his scourging may well have been a very heavy one). When it became obvious that he was having difficulty in reaching the place of execution, the soldiers pressed this passer-by into service. They would not carry the cross and Jesus could not, so someone else had to be found; a man coming in from the country would serve very well.

They took Jesus to a place called "the place of a skull," which cannot now be identified with certainty. It is not known why it was given this name. One suggestion is that the skulls of people who had been crucified lay around, but it is highly unlikely that Jews with their strict ideas of ceremonial purity would allow such a defiling practice. Nor would Joseph have had a tomb carved out for himself in such a place. Further we are told that there was a garden "in" the place where Jesus was crucified (v. 41), which makes it practically certain that no parts of bodies would be lying round. Origen, an early Christian scholar, mentions a pious tradition that Adam was buried there. It is, of course, impossible to know where Adam was buried, but even if this was the place, that scarcely forms a reason for giving it the name "skull."

The usual explanation these days is that the place of Jesus' crucifixion was on a hill shaped something like a skull. Our hymns and sermons are full of references to "the green hill far away," and it is almost a dogma among Christian people. There is nothing unreasonable about this, and it is supported by the fact that a crucifixion was public. The authorities wanted people to see criminals on their crosses so that they would be warned not to break the law. A crucifixion on a low hill would serve this purpose very well. But there is no ancient tradition to that effect, and we must bear in mind that there is nothing in any of the four Gospels that says explicitly that Jesus was crucified on a hill.

John proceeds to give us the Hebrew (or rather, Aramaic) name for the place as "Golgotha." This word also means "skull" as incidentally also does the Latin *calvaria*, from which we get "Calvary." Clearly "skull" is closely bound up with the place of Jesus' crucifixion even if we do not know the precise reason.

The Crucifixion of Jesus

John says simply "they crucified him" (v. 18). Like the other Evangelists, he dismisses the frightful horror that was crucifixion in one word.

It is interesting that not one of the four writers of Gospels tries to arouse our pity or play on our emotions. They all content themselves with the facts. They tell us what happened and that is all. It is important that we get it clear that Jesus died for us. It is not important that we harrow our feelings by reflecting piously on the details of what he endured for us.

It is perhaps worth reflecting that Christians have usually not sustained this attitude. A little reflection on the hymns about the passion that Christians of all denominations find attractive will remind us that we do tend to dwell on the sufferings of Jesus. I do not want to say that it is morbid or unhealthy to call to mind that Jesus suffered greatly for us or even to remind ourselves of what those sufferings were. But it is important that we go along with the Gospel writers in seeing that it was the theological significance of Jesus' death that is of primary importance, not the harrowing of our feelings.

All four tell us that there were two others crucified with Jesus and that he was in the middle. His enemies may well have meant this as a final insult. They knew that he had lived a godly life, but they were seeing to it that he died the death of a criminal and brought it about that he was right in the middle of a pair of criminals when he died. From their point of view there was no mistaking the fact that he was one with evil people.

And the Evangelists all record the fact because from their point of view, too, it was important that when he died Jesus was one with evil people. He did not come to earth to live solely among the pious. He came to call sinners to repentance, and one gibe that was hurled at him was that he was the "friend of sinners." For the writers of the Gospels this was not an insult but the expression of an important truth. Jesus came to save sinners. He died to save them, and the fact that on the cross he hung between people who were obviously grievous sinners graphically illustrated that truth. His death was a death on behalf of sinners, and his position when he died brought that out for those who had eyes to see.

Pilate's Title

Pilate proceeded to write "a title" (v. 19). John's "also" probably means that this was an addition to all the other things the governor had done to show his contempt for the Jews. He had been compelled to crucify Jesus when he did not want to do it, but he had also said and done things that he knew would irritate the Jewish leaders, and this is another example. As he died Jesus would be proclaimed as "the King of the Jews."

It is not easy to see how the Greek word *titlos* should be translated here, and I have kept close to the original with "title." Others render it "notice" or "inscription" and there are other translations as well. What the word denoted was a kind of placard, which was often used in antiquity to bring out the crime for which a person was being punished. The Roman Suetonius, for example, tells of an occasion when the emperor Caligula ordered that a slave's hands be cut off and that he be led among the emperor's guests with a placard hung from his neck that gave the reason for his punishment.

Pilate, then, decided on a *titlos* for Jesus. It gave his name, place of origin, and his crime. There are slight differences in the other Gospels, but this is not surprising, as John tells us that it was written in three languages and we do not know which form each of the Evangelists has in mind. What is important is that the writing said plainly that Jesus was "the King of the Jews." As we have seen in our earlier studies, John emphasizes the kingship of Jesus throughout his passion narrative and here we see him bringing it out right to the last. It is important for him and he wants his readers to be in no doubt about it. The Jews might reject Jesus, and the Roman authorities might be too spineless to resist the Jewish leaders' attack on him, but for John the really significant thing in all that was happening was that Jesus was (and is) King.

John goes on to the point that "many of the Jews" read this title. There would probably not have been a great number who had seen and heard what went on previously. The number of people who could crowd into the courtyard of Pilate's Praetorium would have been limited, and even among them there would not have been many who had actually heard what had been said. But a crucifixion was a public occasion and many would go to see it. As the crucified were normally left on their crosses for a long time, there was plenty of scope for people to come and gape. So Pilate's title would become widely known. John's readers will see that the kingship of Jesus was noised around Jerusalem.

This was helped by the fact that the inscription was in three languages, "Hebrew, Latin, and Greek." "Hebrew" in the New Testament usually means Aramaic: it stood for the language of the local people over against that of those from outside. And, of course, since Hebrew and Aramaic are related languages, there is reason for the usage. It is generally accepted that Aramaic was the language of the Jews of Palestine of that day, so that it was a natural language for Pilate's title. Latin was the official language, the language of the governing authorities. And Greek was the language used throughout the Roman world, the *lingua franca* of the day. The result of using all three languages was that almost anyone who could read would be able to understand what was written in one of the languages at any rate.

Only John has the information about the three languages; the fact that he mentions it shows his interest in Jesus' universal kingship. Jesus, it is true, is here called "the King of the Jews," but this notice of his royalty is given in three significant languages. John is interested in the fact that Jesus is King of the Jews, but he is also interested in the fact that his kingship does not stop at that nation. So he brings out the universality with which it was made known.

But the enemies of Jesus did not care for the words Pilate used. They knew that Jesus did not claim to be a king in the sense in which Pilate used the word. He had told Pilate that his kingdom was not of this world (18:36), and, while they were not there when Jesus spoke these words, they well knew from his whole ministry that this was indeed the case. Their accusation that he was a political revolutionary was completely false. But since it was that accusation and not anything else that had been the basis for bringing about the crucifixion, Pilate would see his "title" as completely justified. But while the chief priests were ready to make their accusation before Pilate more or less privately, they did not like a public proclamation that Jesus was what they had claimed he was in order to bring about his execution.

So they now come to Pilate saying, "Don't write 'The King of the Jews,' but that he said 'I am King of the Jews'" (v. 21). It is one thing to use a convenient accusation, another thing to have what you say blazoned abroad. Incidentally they are here called "the high priests of the Jews," an expression that is found only here in the New Testament (though Acts 25:15 comes pretty close). It is not necessary to add "of the Jews," because there is no question about which high priests are in mind. But John may be intending to draw some kind of parallel with "the King of the Jews." These high priests were denying the kingship of him who in fact was supreme over the nation of which they were the high priests, and this fact pointed to the truth that they ought to have given him full loyalty. There is irony in that it was "the high priests of the Jews" who objected to his rightful title being given to "the King of the Jews."

Of course, it was a little late to say "Don't write"; Pilate had already written the words that offended them. While they say "Don't write," they seem clearly to mean, "Alter what you have written." C. F. D. Moule, however, is not convinced and includes this passage in a list of those where "the reason for the use of the tense is difficult to detect." This is certainly so, but we cannot get round the facts that the words were already written and the priests wanted something different. Whatever the grammatical problems in the expression, they want this notice taken down and another substituted that would make it clear that Jesus had been no more than a false claimant to royalty. The notice as written sounded to them too much like the truth.

But Pilate would not budge. Clearly he had had enough of the high priestly group. They had forced him into a condemnation of a man he recognized to be innocent, but they could not force him into writing a notice of their choosing. So he says firmly, "What I have written, I have written" (v. 22). "Could any playwright have given Pilate a more effective or impressive final line?" (Raymond E. Brown).

I am reminded of a coach driver who, when he stopped at a certain town, said to his passengers, "This is a half-hour meal stop. I am not allowed to recommend to you any restaurant as superior to any other. But if any of you should want me during the next half-hour, I simply let you know that I will be at the Elite Cafe, four doors down the street on the right." Strictly speaking, he did not break the letter of the regulations. But he did get his point over very plainly.

So with Pilate. The priests were a long way from being satisfied, but Pilate was within the regulations. What he wrote may not have been tactful, but the priests had chosen to make their case against Jesus that he was a rebel and that they were loyal—they had "no king but Caesar." From the position they had taken up there was surely no real ground for complaint. So Pilate would not budge, and the result is that the last word from the governor expressed the kingship that the priests were so anxious to deny. And that John is so firm in affirming!

81

The Death of Jesus

So the soldiers, when they had crucified Jesus, took his clothes and made four parts, a part for each soldier, and the tunic. Now the tunic was seamless, woven from the top right through. They said therefore to one another, "Let us not tear it, but cast lots for it, to decide whose it will be"; in order that the Scripture might be fulfilled which says, "They divided my garments among themselves and they cast lots over my clothing." The soldiers therefore did these things.

Now there stood by the cross of Jesus his mother and his mother's sister, Mary the wife of Klopas, and Mary Magdalene. When Jesus therefore saw his mother and the disciple whom he loved standing by, he says to his mother, "Woman, look, your son." Then he says to the disciple, "Look, your mother." And from that hour the disciple took her into his own home.

After this Jesus, knowing that all things had now been finished in order that the Scripture might be fulfilled says, "I am thirsty." There was a jar full of cheap wine set there; so they put a sponge full of the wine on hyssop and brought it to his mouth. When therefore he had received the wine Jesus said, "It is finished!" and he bowed his head and delivered up his spirit (John 19:23–30).

John turns his attention to some of the things that happened while Jesus hung on the cross and includes some information that is found nowhere else. He begins with the soldiers who had been charged with the duty of crucifying Jesus.

People were usually crucified naked, and it was the custom that the soldiers who performed the duty took the clothes of their victims as one of the perks of their office. John tells us that these soldiers did their duty first: they crucified their prisoner (v. 23). Having done that they turned their attention to his clothing. Strictly speaking, the word John uses means the outer garment, the robe (it is used in this way of the scarlet cloak the soldiers used in their mockery, v. 2). But it can also be used quite generally of any garment; here the plural is used for all of Jesus' clothing.

The usual clothing of a first-century Palestinian man was a loincloth, an undergarment (a tunic), an outer garment (a cloak), a belt, a covering for the head, and a pair of sandals. John tells us that Jesus' clothes were divided into four parts, providing a part for each soldier (which is what tells us that there were four soldiers in the crucifixion party; we are left to guess whether the same four crucified the thieves or whether there were four soldiers for each cross). It is not easy to see how this pile of clothing could be divided into four more or less equal shares. It may be that the cloak was divided at the seams and distributed among the parts, or perhaps there were unequal shares. If the latter, this may point to different parts in the work of crucifixion; or, as they did later over the tunic, they may have done a little gambling to see who got the biggest share. This seems to be the meaning of Mark's account that "they divide his clothes, casting lots over them, what each should take" (Mark 15:24). The point is unimportant. What matters is that the soldiers proceeded to divide the clothing.

The Seamless Robe

But when they came to the tunic they found that it was not made in the usual fashion, with a number of sections of cloth sewn together, but was seamless, woven in one piece. This does not mean that it was a luxury item, but it does point to some special care. We are left wondering who thought so much of Jesus that this special tunic was provided, but there is no way of deciding the point. The soldiers clearly thought that such a tunic demanded special attention and thus decided not to tear it but to cast lots for it (v. 24).

The Jewish historian Josephus tells us that the high priest's robe was seamless: ". . . this tunic is not composed of two pieces, to be stitched at the shoulders and at the sides: it is one long woven cloth, with a slit for the neck, parted not crosswise but lengthwise from the breast to a point in the middle of the back" (it was this slit that the high priest prolonged when he tore his robes, as in Mark 14:63). It is possible that John is hinting at Jesus' priestly activity when he mentions this seamless robe at the time of his death, but the point cannot be insisted upon. In any case we do not know how many people other than priests wore seamless tunics.

Christians have often seen symbolical significance in this seamless robe. Many think of a reference to the unity of all Christ's people, gathered together into one through his death, though it is hard to think that this is John's meaning. M. F. Wiles has an interesting comment on the way the seamlessness was viewed by a number of the early church writers: "Christ's seamless robe woven from the top, which suggested to Origen the wholeness of Christ's teaching, to Cyprian the unity of the church, and to Cyril the virgin birth of Christ, receives from Theodore [i.e., Theodore of Mopsuestia] no other comment than that such methods of weaving were common in the time of Christ, although in his day they had died out except for soldiers' uniforms." We may take the item as an interesting piece of information that may well point to someone as having bestowed special care on Jesus, but we have no real reason for going beyond that.

John sees a fulfillment of Scripture in this gambling, and he quotes Psalm 22:18. He introduces his quotation by using the conjunction that means "in order that"; it expresses purpose and thus brings out John's point that God's will was done throughout these sad events. Strictly speaking, it should be preceded by "they did this" or some similar expression, but John frequently omits words like these, which the reader could be expected to supply. He concentrates on a word that conveys the idea of purpose. The death of Jesus on the cross did not mean an overthrow or defeat of the divine purpose; it was that in which the divine purpose was supremely worked out. John sees this not only in the great central fact, but also in the details, and it is this to which he directs attention at this point. He adds that the soldiers "therefore" did these things. They saw themselves as doing no more than engaging in some gambling that enabled them to make a satisfying division of the spoils. John saw them as doing what God had determined to be done and had prophesied through the sacred writer centuries before.

The Mother of Jesus

Crucifixions were public affairs. The authorities liked to have people see them, for this would warn them to be careful and keep the laws. So there was no problem in people gathering round the cross. On this occasion the followers of Jesus may well have thought that there would be danger in coming too close, which may explain Mark's recording that there were some women standing at a distance (Mark 15:40). It may be that they were standing close to the cross at first, but that later they felt it more prudent to be at a distance. Or the authorities may have required them to move away as Jesus' death drew near. However we understand the situation, they were there—and John proceeds to relate an important happening.

First he tells us what women were there (v. 25), but unfortunately in such a way that we cannot be sure whether there were three or four of them. The problem centers round "his mother's sister." Three ladies are clearly distinguished (all of whom were called "Mary," though, as always in this Gospel, the name of Jesus' mother is not given). But it is uncertain whether ". . . his mother's sister, Mary the wife of Klopas . . ." means that his mother's sister was Mary, the wife of Klopas, or whether, after mentioning "his mother's sister" (without giving her name) John moves on to list "Mary the wife of Klopas." If the former, there would have been three ladies; if the latter, there were four. It is unlikely that two sisters would bear the same name, so it is probable that we should see this Mary as from a different family. Further, it is not unlikely that John has listed four believing women to stand over against the four unbelieving soldiers who gambled over Jesus' clothing.

I have translated "Mary the wife of Klopas" but in fact John says no more than "Mary the of Klopas," which might be understood as "the daughter of Klopas" (or even "the sister of Klopas," but there seems no reason for this view). This Mary appears to be the one Mark mentions as the mother of James the less, and Joses (Mark 15:40), which convinces most people that she should be understood as Klopas's wife. It is most improbable that a woman with children of her own would still be characterized as someone's daughter; in conformity with the usage of the time she would be linked with her husband.

But the importance of the incident depends on the presence of Mary the mother of Jesus and of the Beloved Disciple. The other women were there and John mentions them, but he tells us nothing of what they said or did or what was said to them. But as he hung on the cross Jesus took thought for his mother. As William Barclay says, "There is something infinitely moving in the fact that Jesus in the agony of the Cross, in the moment when the salvation of the world hung in the balance, thought of the loneliness of His mother in the days when He was taken away. Jesus never forgot the duties that lay to His hand." Earlier in this Gospel we are told that Jesus' brothers did not believe in him (7:5), and we may fairly infer that they were out of sympathy with Mary. So it was important that there should be somebody who would look after her when Jesus was no longer there.

Jesus said to Mary, "Woman, look, your son" (v. 26). Clearly Mary was to take the words to mean that from then on the Beloved Disciple would be in the position of son to her and that he would take responsibility for her. These words are balanced by equivalent words to the Beloved Disciple, "Look, your mother" (v. 27). As elsewhere, in this Gospel, this disciple is not named, but as we have seen in earlier studies, we should probably understand him to be John, the son of Zebedee, a man who clearly stood very close to Jesus and was the object of his special regard.

"From that hour," John tells us, "the disciple took her into his own home." Actually this last expression means more literally "into his own things" (as in 1:11; 16:32), but it is commonly used with reference to one's own home and that is surely the meaning here. John is telling us that in obedience to Jesus' words he took Mary into his home. The implication is that he took responsibility for her from that time on. "From that hour" has been understood by some to mean that Mary and John left the crucifixion at that point. They point out that Mary is not mentioned in the list of women who were there when Jesus died (Matt. 27:56; Mark 15:40) and suggest that the reason is that John had already taken her home.

But the reference to "that hour" need not necessarily mean the time of day and indicate that John and Mary took immediate action. We have seen that throughout this Gospel there are references to "the hour" (or "the time") of Jesus, which mean the significant hour, the hour of his death. This may well be the meaning here. This is supported by the fact that the Beloved Disciple writes as an eyewitness of the events of verses 31–37 and it is not easy to see how he could have gone home with Mary and returned in time to see the death of Jesus. The meaning is surely that when Jesus died John took responsibility for Mary.

The Death of Jesus

"After this" (v. 28) in Johannine usage probably means a short time later. It is possible to take the words to mean that the next happening followed immediately, but we should probably not press the words to mean this. But clearly John is not writing about a lengthy interval.

It is not completely certain whether the words "in order that the Scripture might be fulfilled" should be taken with what precedes (in which case Jesus knew that the events that had taken place had fulfilled Scripture) or with what follows (in which case it is his thirst to which the Scripture points). Probably this is another example of John's using an expression with two meanings and expecting his readers to see both. This is the only place in the New Testament where this particular verb is used of the fulfillment of Scripture. It may be no more than a stylistic variant of the verb more commonly used. But this verb has the meaning of bringing something to its appointed end or aim, and John may be using it of set purpose. What was being done meant not simply the fulfillment of what one particular passage of Scripture foretold, but the fulfillment of the great purpose of God prophesied in so many places. Indeed, it might be said that Scripture as a whole was being brought to its intended aim in the death of Jesus as the outworking of the purpose of God for the salvation of sinners.

Jesus says (again John uses the present tense for greater vividness), "I am thirsty," which leads us back to Psalm 69:21. Thirst was a natural accompaniment of crucifixion, of course, but it is not without interest that this, too, can be found in the Old Testament. John is the only one of the Evangelists to mention Jesus' thirst while on the cross.

He proceeds to tell us of a jar of wine set there (v. 29). The word for "jar" is quite a general one and can be used for almost any object. A standard lectionary notes a place where it is used with the meaning "table," while in Luke 17:31 it stands for any possessions that a person might own. It is the context that tells us the meaning, and here an object that holds wine is clearly a jar. The word for "cheap wine" is often translated "vinegar." It means a sour wine that was in common use. The lectionary suggests as translation "sour wine, wine vinegar" and explains this: "it relieved thirst more effectively than water and, because it was cheaper than regular wine, it was a favorite beverage of the lower ranks of society and of those in moderate circumstances . . . esp. of soldiers." Obviously it was there primarily to relieve the thirst of the soldiers, but someone took advantage of its presence to help Jesus when he was thirsty.

There was obviously a difficulty in offering a drink to a crucified person. A cup of any sort would be difficult to get to his lips and in any case might not be easy to manage. So the method used was to fill a sponge with the wine and put it on a stick long enough to reach the mouth of the person on the cross.

Hyssop

John says that they put it on "hyssop" and so brought it to Jesus' mouth. But this has aroused a good deal of discussion, the objection being raised that hyssop is a small bushy plant that would not produce a long enough stem to reach the mouth of anyone hanging on a cross. It is pointed out that hyssop was a good plant to use in such ceremonies as sprinkling and that it was in fact prescribed to be so used in some Old Testament ceremonies (e.g., Lev. 14:4–7; Num. 19:18). From this it is reasoned that John is not really telling us what happened but saying symbolically that some form of purification was being effected. This interpretation is very unsatisfactory, however. Cheap wine was not used in purification, nor is it easy to see why Jesus should need such a purifying ceremony. If indeed a sprinkling of some sort was being effected, it is more likely that John is making a reference to the Passover (cf. Exod. 12:22), for he sees Jesus as the perfect Passover sacrifice.

But it is so difficult to see hyssop functioning in any such way that some scholars have abandoned the attempt. They draw attention to the fact that the Greek word for "hyssop" is very like a word for a "javelin," and that this word is indeed found in one late manuscript at this point. The idea is that the soldiers would certainly have a javelin with them and that it would be an ideal means of raising the sponge to Jesus' lips.

Against it is the fact that it is not easy to see how almost the whole manuscript tradition should have been corrupted to read "hyssop" while only one eleventh-century copy has the right word. There is a further difficulty in that it is not certain that the soldiers in Palestine would have had this particular kind of javelin. G. D. Kilpatrick points out that it was used by legionary soldiers, but not by the auxiliaries who were found in Palestine. There seems no convincing reason for accepting the conjecture, though the New English Bible translates "javelin" with a marginal reading: "*So one witness; the others read* on marjoram." It is not easy to see why they do not mention the lateness of their one witness, nor why they have picked on marjoram as the alternative. "Hyssop" seems clearly to be what John wrote.

But what he meant by it is another matter. It is curious that some writers are so sure they know what "hyssop" was. Thus a standard lexicon says it means "a small bush w. blue flowers and highly aromatic leaves," and such certainty is far from unusual. But W. E. Sherwell-Cooper, who has written a book entitled *Plants and Fruits of the Bible,* notes a number of possibilities but says, "I find it difficult to discover what hyssop really is." Similarly Raymond E. Brown says that eighteen different plants have been suggested. It seems that the word was used of a number of different plants (why we do not know) and that more than one of them would have a stem long enough and firm enough to convey a sponge full of liquid to the mouth of a man on a cross.

We should also keep in mind that a very long stick was probably not required. Our artists often paint pictures of the crucifixion with three very high crosses, such that perhaps the feet of the crucified were on a level with the heads of the spectators. But we should bear in mind that a cross was no more than a means of killing a man. As long as it was high enough to keep the sufferer's feet off the ground, it served its purpose. It is true that sometimes a high cross was used, but this seems to have been the case only when there were special circumstances, for example when the powers-that-be were contemptuous of the person being executed. It is unlikely that Pilate would have ordered anything other than the usual form of crucifixion in the case of Jesus. Accordingly it would not require a very long cane to bring the sponge to his lips.

Matthew and Mark tell us that Jesus refused a drink, but this was *before* the crucifixion (Matt. 27:34; Mark 15:23), and it is not the wine for normal drinking that we find here, but drugged wine to dull the senses of the crucified to some extent. In the Talmud we read: "When one is led out to execution, he is given a goblet of wine containing a grain of frankincense, in order to benumb his senses, for it is written, *Give strong drink unto him that is ready to perish, and wine unto the bitter in soul.* And it has also been taught: The noble women in Jerusalem used to donate and bring it." It is heartwarming to read of this humane custom in a rather callous age. But Jesus refused the kindly act. It would seem that he was intent on keeping his mind clear while he went through that suffering that was to mean so much. Now, however, as he was approaching the climax of it all, he needed to be able to speak so that people could hear and he accepted the drink that would serve his purpose.

"It Is Finished!"

Jesus' expiring cry (v. 30) is one word in the Greek. John says nothing about the manner of the utterance, but the other three Gospels all say that Jesus cried in a loud voice just before he died (Matt. 27:50; Mark 15:37; Luke 23:46); the first two say that Jesus was given a drink just before he spoke. There seems little doubt that John has given us the word Jesus used and that the others let us know that it was a loud shout. The word he used means "It is finished," a word that has already been employed in verse 28. As so often in this Gospel, the term could be understood in more ways than one. It could mean that Jesus' earthly life was over: he was about to die. But, while that was true, the more important truth is that the death of Jesus meant the completion of that work of salvation for which he had come to earth.

John goes on to say that Jesus "bowed his head," a detail found only in this Gospel. Interestingly this same verb is used when Jesus said that the foxes had their holes and the birds their roosting places, ". . . but the Son of man has not where he may lay his head" (Luke 9:58). That place that the Son of man did not have during his earthly life he found when he gave up his life. The early Christian scholar Origen comments that Jesus "bent the head and took His departure in the act of resting it, as it were, on the lap of the Father, who could cherish it and strengthen it in His bosom."

John describes Jesus' death by the words "he . . . delivered up his spirit," which is not the usual way of referring to death. Actually none of the four Gospels says simply that Jesus died or uses any of the customary ways of indicating the end of this mortal life. John's verb is used in the Greek translation of Isaiah 53:12 of the death of the Suffering Servant, but there it is said that he delivered up "his soul," whereas John has "his spirit." It is possible that this way of putting it indicates a certain element of voluntariness. Jesus did not stand in the same relation to death as do the rest of us. Some have taken "spirit" here to refer to the Holy Spirit and think that Jesus either gave the Spirit back to God or that he gave the Spirit to his followers. But the language does not require this, and we have no reason for thinking that John would have included a reference to such a far-reaching activity without making it much more clear.

John, then, is describing a death that differed from other deaths. This death was the means of bringing about the salvation of sinners throughout the world and throughout the ages. John tells the story in such a way as to bring out the accomplishment of the divine purpose. In the end it was this that mattered, not the treachery of Judas, nor the scheming of the high priests, nor the weakness of Pilate. In and through them all God worked out his purpose, a loving purpose, a purpose that issues in salvation for all believers.

82

Jesus' Pierced Side

The Jews therefore, since it was the Preparation, in order that the bodies might not remain on the cross on the Sabbath, for that Sabbath was a great day, asked Pilate that they might have their legs broken and that they be taken away. So the soldiers came and broke the legs of the first man and of the other who was crucified with him. But when they came to Jesus, as they saw that he was already dead, they did not break his legs, but one of the soldiers pierced his side with a spear and straightaway blood and water came out. And he who saw it bore testimony and his testimony is true and that one knows that he says true things in order that you too may believe. For these things happened so that the Scripture might be fulfilled, "A bone of him will not be broken." And again another Scripture says, "They will look on him whom they pierced" (John 19:31–37).

Our information about this part of the crucifixion story we owe to John alone: the other Evangelists do not mention the breaking of the legs nor the spear thrust that pierced Jesus' side. But clearly this immediate sequel to the death of Jesus greatly impressed someone who was there. It was apparently a most unusual series of happenings. It would have been expected that Jesus' legs would have been broken like those of the men on the other crosses, but they were not. Moreover, soldiers did not usually thrust spears into people on crosses as they did to him, and the issue of water and blood from the dead body was unparalleled. That all this brought about the fulfillment of two passages from the Old Testament was impressive.

The incident begins with a reference to "the Jews" (v. 31). This is the way John often refers to those of his own nation, particularly the leaders, who were hostile to Jesus. A little earlier he has spoken of "the high priests of the Jews" as having come to Pilate with the request that the wording of the placard he had had set on Jesus' cross be altered (v. 21), and we need not doubt that the same people are in mind here. It was the high priests who would be particularly concerned that the Sabbath be properly observed.

The Great Sabbath

As we saw when we were looking at verse 14, "the Preparation" was a name given to Friday, the day before the Sabbath. The Jews were very strict about the way the Sabbath was kept and on the preceding day did everything they could to get ready. They took with great seriousness the requirement that no work be done on the Sabbath. For example, they used to prepare on Friday the meals they would eat on the Sabbath, which meant that they did no cooking on the Sabbath itself. With this kind of activity going on, the day of Preparation became a very significant day.

On this occasion there was a problem about the bodies. The Jews did not want dead bodies to be left hanging on crosses. It was explicitly laid down in their Law: "If a man guilty of a capital offense is put to death and his body is hung on a tree, you must not leave his body on the tree overnight. Be sure to bury him that same day, because anyone who is hung on a tree is under God's curse. You must not desecrate the land the LORD your God is giving you as an inheritance" (Deut. 21:22–23). It would not worry the Romans, and indeed they might be very happy to have this happen, for they saw crucifixions as so many opportunities of showing people the penalty for wrongdoing. The more who saw the crosses the better. But they responded to Jewish scruples in the matter, and it was the custom in Judea for the crucified to be taken from their crosses and not left there overnight. Josephus, the Jewish historian, says that "the Jews are so careful about funeral rites that even malefactors who have been sentenced to crucifixion are taken down and buried before sunset."

This would be the case on any day and especially so when the Sabbath was approaching, but John points out that there was a particular reason for action to be taken on this occasion: "for that Sabbath was a great day"; more literally John says, "great was the day of that Sabbath." The reference to the day of the Sabbath does not appear to be specially significant (it is found in other places, such as Luke 13:14; 14:5), but "great" singles out *that* Sabbath as specially noteworthy. John appears to mean that, while all Sabbaths were important, that Sabbath was even more important than others, for—whereas they were simply the ordinary weekly observances—this one coincided with a solemn feast day, the day of the Passover. There does not appear to be any example of the use of "great" to qualify a Sabbath before this time, though it is found among the Jews at later periods. One Jewish scholar even thinks that, as this is the first example of the use, the Jews copied the term from the Christians! But this is most unlikely, for the Jews were too hostile to the new faith to take over terminology for their holy days from people they saw as heretics.

We are somewhat in the position of a certain teacher of some children with hearing difficulties. The children were helped with every aid that modern technology made possible, including electronic hearing devices. One day a mysterious hissing noise made its appearance and the class was somewhat disrupted. Every switch and setting was adjusted, but the noise did not go away; if anything, the students complained that it got louder. The frustrated teacher said, "I can't hear any unusual noises," which caused one of the children to mutter, "How can he hear it? He isn't deaf!"

Like this teacher of the deaf we are on the outside; we do not share the position of those involved. And, as we do not share the attitude to life of first-century Jews, we find it difficult to be sure that we completely understand when a holy day of theirs was called "great" and precisely which days merited this description. But we can see that a day that was both a Sabbath and the Passover could surely be called "great" if any day could. It should be observed with proper solemnity and, among other things, dead bodies should be put out of sight and buried.

Broken Legs and Pierced Side

Evidently two of those crucified were still well and truly alive, and it looked as though they would not die before the Sabbath came. They would thus not be eligible to be taken down and buried before sunset (when the Sabbath, of course, began). So the Jewish leaders asked Pilate to have the process hastened by breaking the legs of those on the crosses. This of necessity would not be done gently (it was done by striking the legs with a heavy mallet), and there would be the shock attendant on the brutal blows as well as the damage done by having broken legs added to all the other traumas the men on the crosses had experienced. It was also the case that those on crosses could gain minor relief by taking some of their weight on their feet, but if their legs were broken, this would be impossible. Their whole weight was then suspended from their nailed hands, with the consequential constriction of the lungs. It added to their misery, but at least it cut it short to some extent, for it hastened their death. Sometimes the mallet was used to break other bones, but in this case only the legs. Incidentally, the remains of a crucified man recently discovered in Palestine show that his legs had been broken in this way.

John uses an unusual construction, which (in the endeavor to keep as close to the Greek as possible) I have translated "that they might have their legs broken," but which is often understood as "that their legs might be broken" (RSV). But there is not a great deal of difference in meaning and, whichever way we translate, it is clear that the Jews were looking for a brutal act that would enable them to preserve their ceremonial purity. They wanted three dead bodies taken away and out of sight before the Sabbath began.

John does not say explicitly that Pilate gave permission, but clearly he did. John moves immediately to the action and tells us that the soldiers got to work and broke the legs of the two criminals who had been crucified with Jesus (v. 32). It is not clear why he speaks of the first and the third. Did the soldiers see that Jesus was already dead and pass him by? Or did John get the less important ones out of the way before turning his attention to the person of central importance?

Whichever the correct solution, in due time they came to Jesus and found that he was already dead. No reason is given for his dying before the others. Perhaps he had had a heavier scourging than they, or they may have been stronger physically. We do not know. We can say no more than that Jesus' death took place before that of the others and earlier than was expected.

But one of the soldiers wanted to be sure that there was no mistake, so he thrust his spear into Jesus' side (v. 34), a thrust that would kill him if he was not already dead. The word for "spear" is *longchē* (in Latin *lancea*), which means a long slender spear. This word may be the reason the early church said the soldier's name was Longinus (cf. our "Lance"). There was a belief in the early church that Longinus was converted and in due course became a Christian martyr, but we have no way of knowing whether or not this was the case. John records that immediately there came out "blood and water."

Blood and Water

There has been a good deal of Christian speculation on this. John does not tell us what significance he saw in it, but it is clear that it struck him as important; otherwise he would not have included it in his narrative. He may well have seen some spiritual meaning as well, but he records it in the first instance because it happened.

Some with a medical interest suggest that this points us to the manner of Jesus' death. William Stroud argued that it means a physically ruptured heart, with the result that the blood "separates into its constituent parts, so as to present the appearance commonly termed blood and water." R. V. G. Tasker quotes the opinion of John Lyle Cameron that the passage means that there was a flow of blood from the heart and great blood vessels and of water from the distended stomach (cf. the thirst of v. 28), both of which would be pierced by an upward blow from a spear.

According to the ideas of antiquity this may be a way of bringing out the actuality of Jesus' death. It was held among the Jews that the body is half water and half blood. Thus a Jewish writing says: "Man is evenly balanced, half of him is water, and the other half is blood." The passage goes on to draw an edifying moral: "When he is deserving the water does not exceed the blood, nor does the blood exceed the water; but when he sins, it sometimes happens that the water gains over the blood and he then becomes a sufferer from dropsy; at other times the blood gains over the water and he then becomes leprous." We may pass by this interesting medical theory of the way sin and certain diseases are connected; the significant point for our present purpose is that the human body is understood in terms of blood and water, so that when both are shed there can be no doubt about the factuality of the death. There were some early heretics who held that Jesus did not really die, that he only seemed to die. If John was confronted by people who thought like that, he may have included the reference to the blood and the water as a way of showing that Jesus really died; there was no "seeming" about it.

Others discern spiritual significance. Some see a reference to the sacraments, blood pointing to the Holy Communion and water to baptism. It should certainly be accepted that both get their meaning from the death of Jesus. The Holy Communion is a proclamation of Christ's death (1 Cor. 11:26), and baptism is a being baptized into Christ's death (Rom. 6:3). But whether they are in mind in this passage is quite another thing. As far as I know, there is no evidence that the early church used the term "blood" to refer to Holy Communion or "water" when it meant baptism. We have no reason for thinking that these two sacraments were in mind when the terms "blood" and "water" were used without qualification or explanation. A minor objection is the order in which the two are mentioned. Surely it is more natural to put first the reference to baptism, the service of initiation into the Christian church, and follow it with one to Holy Communion, which is open only to those who have already been baptized.

If we look at the way John uses the terms elsewhere in his Gospel we find that he uses "blood" in the statement that those who respond to Christ are not born "of bloods" (1:13; the word is plural), and again four times in the passage about eating Christ's flesh and drinking his blood (6:53–56). Life comes from the blood of Christ. As for water, there are several passages, but we should notice particularly the reference to being born of water and the Spirit (3:5), which again links life with Christ. This is the case also with the "living water" that Christ will give (4:10–11), which will be a fountain "leaping up into life eternal" (4:14). Nor should we overlook the fact that "living water" will flow from the believer, an interesting happening linked with the Spirit's activity (7:38f.). John thus links both terms with the life Christ gives, and there seems no reason to doubt that he is saying here that real spiritual life is available only through Christ's death.

The Witness

It is plain that the point means a great deal to John and he insists that there is good testimony to it, although the precise meaning of the words in which he expresses the thought is not clear. Somebody saw what happened, and John uses the perfect tense in both "he who saw it" and in "bore testimony" (v. 35). The force of this is to stress the continuing efficacy of a past action. That this person had seen what occurred is a fact that continues to be important and so is the testimony that the witness bore. Both are permanently on the record, so to speak. John is sure that there is solid evidence continuing into the day of the writing of his Gospel. He goes on to say that "his testimony is true" and further that someone knows this. Our problems are that it is not clear who the witness is who bore his testimony, nor who it is who knows that he speaks the truth.

The most obvious way of understanding the witness is to see him as the author of the Gospel, the Beloved Disciple. An objection sometimes urged is that this writer has twice recorded sayings that a man's witness to himself is not acceptable (5:31; 8:13). But this is seen to lack force when we reflect that here the witness is not bearing witness to himself. He is bearing witness to an observed fact, and there is no reason why he should not say, "I saw it. I know it is true for I was there and my own eyes witnessed what happened." We should also bear in mind the similar language in 21:24, where there is no doubt that it is the Beloved Disciple who is in mind. It would be quite in character for him to refer to himself in just this way here.

The alternative is to see the witness as some unnamed person who is not the author but to whom the Beloved Disciple gives his approval. The difficulty with such a view is that there is no clear indication that a person other than the author is intended or who this other person might be. This may be a somewhat curious way for the writer to refer to himself, but it is an even more curious way for him to refer to someone else.

It is more difficult to identify "that one." It may, of course, refer to the witness himself. Then he is saying that he has borne witness and that he himself is convinced of the truth of what he has said. If we see the witness as the Beloved Disciple, then this is a statement giving solemn emphasis to his deep conviction of the truth of what he has just written. This is the way *The Living Bible* sees it, with its paraphrase: "I saw all this myself and have given an accurate report so that you also can believe." This must surely be the best way of understanding the sense of the Greek, however free the translation may be.

Another way of taking the words is given in Rieu's translation: "This is vouched for by the man who saw it, and his evidence may be relied on. Also, to assure you, the writer knows that he is telling the truth." This may be supported by the fact that "that one" might very naturally be taken of the author of the whole and be understood in distinction from the person bearing the witness. C. C. Torrey maintains that the expression may well reflect an Aramaic expression that is "a common Jewish substitute for the pronoun of the first person singular." That is to say, the Aramaic equivalent of "that one" may mean "I." Further, it would be very natural to see the witness and the person who vouches for the witness as two different people. In my opinion this is not as likely as the earlier view, but it is not impossible.

A third way of viewing it is to see "that one" as a reverent way of referring to God or to Christ (reverent, because it avoids using the divine name). This is the way Moffatt takes the passage: "He who saw it has borne witness (his witness is true; God knows he is telling the truth), that you may believe." Hoskyns and Davey point out that "that one" is used in this Gospel and in 1 John a number of times to refer to Christ and that similar expressions in 21:24 and 3 John 12 "introduce an additional witness." From all this they deduce that "it seems almost necessary to regard this phrase as the attestation of the witness of the Beloved Disciple by the Lord Himself." But this is a little too confident. While "that one" does sometimes refer to the Lord, it quite often refers to someone else; it all depends on the context. And while similar expressions may introduce an additional witness, the words here are not such as to require such a conclusion. The reasons for accepting Moffatt's view that we should understand God as the one who confirms the witness are much the same as those for Christ, and they are subject to much the same objections.

The expression is thus far from obvious, but the simplest and most likely way of understanding the words is to see them as the Beloved Disciple's way of saying emphatically that he saw what happened and that he is certain of what he saw.

Faith

What John has recorded he has not written aimlessly but "in order that you too may believe." There are a couple of ambiguities here. The one arises from the fact that "in order that" may be taken in more ways than one. It may refer to the immediately preceding verb, which will give the meaning "He says true things in order that you may believe." Or it may refer to the whole of the preceding part of the sentence, in which case John is saying that the person who saw what happened has borne his witness in order that readers may believe. It seems probable that we should take it in this second way. It is the purpose of the witness that people may be brought to believe, a purpose that we later find lies behind the whole Gospel (20:31). In the words of C. K. Barrett, "It indicates the general aim of the veracious testimony of the witness. 'You' (the readers of the gospel) 'are not merely to believe that blood and water did in fact issue from the side of the Crucified, but to believe in the full Christian sense.'"

The other ambiguity arises from a variation in the manuscripts. Some of them read the present tense in the verb *believe,* which, if used strictly, would give the meaning "that you may keep on believing," while others have the aorist, which would mean "that you may come to believe." In the first case it means that the words are addressed to believers: they are to be strengthened in their faith. In the second it means that the words are addressed to unbelievers: they are to be brought to see what God has done for them in Christ and because of this to put their trust in him. There seems no way of resolving this problem. Both are true and both are important, and the manuscripts do not give decisive support to either. Perhaps we are given an indication that the first way of looking at it is to be preferred by the inclusion of the word *too:* the readers as well as the witness are to do the believing in question. There is no doubt that the witness is already a believer, so perhaps the inference is that the readers are expected to be believers also.

Fulfillment of Scripture

John rounds off this section of his narrative by drawing attention to the fact that two passages in the ancient Scripture were fulfilled in these happenings. These things, he says, happened "so that. . . ." There was a divine purpose in them. Certain things were foretold in Scripture; therefore corresponding things happened. God is working out his great purpose, a purpose that had been foretold in many parts of the Bible. Now that the consummation of it all was occurring, there was the fulfillment of those foretellings. Neither of the things to which John draws attention would have been expected; they were unusual, given the circumstances of crucifixion, and that makes them very significant.

There is some doubt about which is the first passage John has in mind, for the words "A bone of him [or, it] will not be broken" occur more than once. They are found twice in connection with the Passover, namely in Exodus 12:46 and Numbers 9:12 (there is a third such reference in Exod. 12:10 in the Greek translation of the Old Testament, but this one does not occur in the Hebrew). The words occur also in Psalm 34:20, which refers to the Lord's protection of the righteous man. It is true that in both John and the Psalm the words are a prediction, whereas in the other passages they are a command. But this seems to be outweighed by the fact that the Psalm is concerned with saving the righteous man from death, whereas both John and the Pentateuch are concerned with the way a dead body is treated. The wording in Exodus and Numbers is closer to John, too, and it seems best to see a reference to the Passover.

John is surely saying through his first quotation that the deep spiritual truth that the Passover foreshadowed finds its full expression in Jesus' crucifixion. The Passover in Old Testament times pointed to the deliverance of Israel from slavery, to the emergence of the people of God. In a fuller and more meaningful sense this is what happened at Calvary. Sinners were delivered from their slavery to sin and there followed the emergence of the people of God in more than a merely national sense. The fellowship of the redeemed in the Christian church was made possible by Christ's death.

The other passage is Zechariah 12:10 (cf. Rev. 1:7). Some scholars think that "they" here means the soldiers who performed the crucifixion and, of course, the words would refer to them. But it is likely that John is thinking of "the inhabitants of Jerusalem," who are explicitly mentioned in the Zechariah passage and who were responsible for bringing the crucifixion about (cf. v. 16). In the days of the prophet the Jerusalemites had rejected their God, and John is seeing the same words to apply to what happened at the cross.

We should not miss the point noticed at the beginning of this chapter that both facts were unusual. It was common for the legs of the crucified to be broken, and in this case both of those who died with Jesus were mistreated in this way. But he was not. His bones remained whole. But soldiers did not usually thrust spears into people on crosses. The piercing of Jesus' side was a most unexpected happening. John cannot be accused of manufacturing fulfillments of prophecy to cover what always happened at crucifixions. These passages from the Old Testament point to two highly unusual aspects of Jesus' death. They bring out the truth that the plan of God was fulfilled thereby.

83

Jesus' Burial

After this Joseph from Arimathea, being a secret disciple of Jesus for fear of the Jews, asked Pilate that he might take Jesus' body and Pilate gave permission. He came therefore and took his body. Nicodemus, who first came to him by night, came too, bringing a mixture of myrrh and aloes, about a hundred pounds. So they took the body of Jesus and bound it with linen cloths with the spices as the custom of the Jews is for burial. Now there was a garden in the place where he was crucified and in the garden a new tomb in which no one had ever been placed. There therefore they laid Jesus on account of the Preparation of the Jews, because the tomb was close (John 19:38–42).

"After this" (v. 38; more literally "after these things") is an expression John uses a number of times, apparently with a meaning like "some time later." It does not mean "immediately after," so John is not saying that Joseph went to Pilate straight after the incident with the spear. He is not following a strict chronological timetable, but saying that at some unspecified time later Joseph made his approach to Pilate.

A Man Called Joseph

Joseph of Arimathea appears in all four Gospels at this point in the story of Jesus and at this point only. Evidently the early church remembered that he had taken the initiative in securing Jesus' burial, but did not remember other things about him. It is not known where Arimathea was situated. Luke tells us that it was "a city of the Jews" (Luke 23:51), but this does not locate it with any precision. One suggestion is that Arimathea is another name for Ramathaim-Zophim (1 Sam. 1:1), but as the location of this place is also unknown that is not particularly enlightening. Other suggestions have been made, but none is completely convincing. All the credible suggestions, however, make it clear that the location was in Judea, so Joseph was not a Galilean; he was one of those in the territory of Jesus' bitterest enemies who had come to believe in Jesus. As Joseph had had a tomb hewn out for himself near Jerusalem it is clear that he had now moved from Arimathea and was living in Jerusalem or nearby.

John tells us that Joseph was "a disciple," as does Matthew, though that Evangelist expresses it slightly differently: he says that Joseph "had been discipled" (Matt. 27:57). Neither Mark nor Luke speaks of him as a disciple, but both say that he was looking for the kingdom of God (Mark 15:43; Luke 23:51), which amounts to much the same thing. The Synoptists add other information. Joseph was wealthy (Matt. 27:57), and a member of the Sanhedrin (Mark 15:43; Luke 23:50). Luke tells us both that he was a "good and righteous man" and that he had not given his consent to the action of the Sanhedrin when Jesus was condemned (Luke 23:50–51). John has none of this information. He concentrates on the facts that Joseph was a secret disciple and that he was active in securing the burial of Jesus. Secret disciples are not described in glowing terms in 12:42–43, but clearly Joseph had now come out of hiding and by going to Pilate had in some sense allied himself to the group of Jesus' followers. It is, of course, possible that he would be seen not so much as a disciple as a Jew who was anxious to see that Jewish burial customs be followed, for the Jews took very seriously the obligation to see that burials were carried out properly. But under the circumstances Joseph could scarcely have done what he did without its being known that he was a disciple of the crucified Jesus.

To go to Pilate and ask for the body took courage, as Mark makes clear (Mark 15:43; he went in to Pilate "boldly"). And it probably explains Jesus' honorable burial. Criminals were not normally given the burial accorded to upright citizens; they were buried without ceremony in a common grave. But Joseph was clearly an important citizen, and when he made the request for the body Pilate was quite ready to let him have it. A minor point is that none of the other Evangelists uses John's words for "came" and "took." Matthew has a different verb for "take," while Mark and Luke use a compound meaning "take down." But all four make it clear that Joseph took charge of the body to make sure it was given proper burial.

Nicodemus

John links Nicodemus with Joseph (v. 39). This is another piece of information we owe to John; none of the other Evangelists mentions his part in the burial. In fact none of them mentions Nicodemus anywhere; it is only John who tells us anything about him. Early in his Gospel he says that Nicodemus first came to Jesus by night (3:2), a fact that he recalls here. Evidently it had made a deep impression on John. He also tells of an ineffectual defense of Jesus that Nicodemus made before the Sanhedrin (7:50ff.). Evidently, like Joseph, he had not made a public profession of his faith in Jesus. It is not without its interest that at a time when all the apostles forsook Jesus and fled, at a time when all hope for the movement associated with Jesus' name seemed gone, it was these two secret disciples who boldly came out into the open and saw to it that Jesus was given a proper burial. Perhaps they felt that this was their last opportunity to do anything for him and they were not going to waste it.

People sometimes surprise us. You never know how they will turn out. There was a mother who happened to meet the teacher of her young son. "I'm Johnny's mother," she said, and then, "Is that bragging or apologizing?" The mother evidently was not too sure about her boy but was prepared for the worst. People, including small boys, sometimes develop in ways other than we would anticipate.

Nicodemus was perhaps like that. He did not turn out as we might have expected from the earlier references to him. Not only did he associate himself with Joseph, but he came "bringing a mixture of myrrh and aloes." These were evidently to be used in the burial. The Jews did not embalm bodies in the Egyptian manner, which involved mutilation by the removal of the viscera. Instead they washed the body, anointed it, and wrapped it. It was the Jewish custom to put such spices as Nicodemus brought in the folds of the linen about the body. The combination of myrrh and aloes is not found in any New Testament passage other than this, though it does occur in Psalm 45:8 and in Song of Songs 4:14. Myrrh was one of the gifts the Wise Men brought to the infant Jesus (Matt. 2:11; the only other New Testament use of the word), while aloes is mentioned in the New Testament only here (it seems not to have been common in burials). The other Gospels do not mention the spices that were put with Jesus' body on the Friday, though they refer to the women as preparing spices for use on the Sunday morning (Luke 23:56; 24:1; cf. Mark 16:1). They could not have been unaware of what Nicodemus had brought (Mark 15:47), but evidently they wanted to add their own personal tribute to their dead Messiah.

A Royal Burial

John explains that what Joseph and Nicodemus were doing was according to "the custom of the Jews for burial" (v. 40). Actually the expression John uses means more literally "to prepare for burial" (it is used, for example, of the woman who anointed Jesus, Matt. 26:12), but obviously here the preparation and the burial are closely connected. Some suggest that we should take the expression literally; they understand John to be saying that Joseph and Nicodemus did not really carry out the burial. They recognized that they would not be able to do all they wanted before the Sabbath began at sunset, so they simply prepared for the burial that would take place three days later. This, however, seems to be reading something into the use of the unusual verb. There is nothing in any of the four Gospels that leads us to think that the men were not really burying Jesus, but doing no more than get the body ready for burial. The time would run out before they could do all they wanted, and this left scope for the women to come back to complete the process after the Sabbath. But Joseph and Nicodemus were clearly engaged in a real burial according to the customs of the day.

There is a suggestion that John and the Synoptists are in contradiction here, with the burial taking place on Friday in this Gospel and the women doing what was necessary on Sunday in the others. It is argued that in view of the large amount of spices that Nicodemus provided, there was no necessity for the women to do anything more. Each account, it is said, tells of a complete burial. But a little reflection shows that this explanation is not adequate. If we may refer to our own practice, no matter how many floral tributes are found at a funeral, close friends would never overlook the importance of adding their own. So with the women. It may well be that Nicodemus had done all that was necessary. But they still wanted to add their own personal tribute, and that was what they tried to do on the Sunday morning.

The men then took the body and got it ready to put in the tomb. They wrapped it in linen, where there is some uncertainty about the meaning of the word I have translated as "linen cloths." There is evidence that in Egypt at any rate it meant not any ordinary material but fine linen, and we need not doubt that it has such a meaning here. Joseph was wealthy and would scarcely stint in a burial that was accompanied by such a generous quantity of spices.

But does it mean strips of linen that were wound round and round? It is often held that it does and that this marks a contrast with what we read in the Synoptists about the "shroud" in which Jesus was buried (Matt. 27:59; Mark 15:46; Luke 23:53). There is no doubt that the word used by the three Synoptists means a large sheet, for the same word is used of the linen sheet a young man wrapped around his body (Mark 14:51–52). Nor is there any doubt that strips like bandages were sometimes used in burials, for that is what happened at the burial of Lazarus (11:44), though with the use of a different word from that used here.

John's word occurs again in Luke 24:12, but otherwise in the New Testament only in this Gospel (here and in 20:5–7). It is a diminutive and may possibly refer to narrow strips, in which case we should think that Joseph and Nicodemus used strips to bandage the body, then wrapped the whole in a linen shroud. But possibly we should not understand the language quite so strictly: it may mean nothing more precise than "linen cloths."

All this was in accordance with the normal Jewish customs of burying. What was not in accordance with custom was the amount of the spices. John tells us that there were about "a hundred pounds" in weight, which was far in excess of what was normal. The *litra* was a weight equal to 327.45 grams, so that a hundred of them came to a significant weight, much more than would normally be used at a funeral.

We should probably find the reason for the large amount in expressions that refer to royal burials. At the burial of Asa we are told that a very large though unspecified amount of spices was used (2 Chron. 16:14). The Jewish historian Josephus tells us that at the burial of Herod the Great there were five hundred servants carrying spices; so this funeral was celebrated in royal fashion. In the Talmud there is the story of an incident in which a proselyte named Onkelos burned more than eighty minas of spices at the funeral of that great teacher, Rabbi Gamaliel the elder. When asked why he did it he drew attention to the words about King Zedekiah: "As people made a funeral fire in honor of your fathers, the former kings who preceded you, so they will make a fire in your honor . . ." (Jer. 34:5). He went on to ask, "Is not Rabbi Gamaliel better than a hundred kings?" Clearly it was expected that in a royal funeral large quantities of spices would be used.

We have seen how throughout the narrative that tells of Jesus' arrest and trial and execution John has stressed the kingship motif. It seems that he is keeping it up right to the end and bringing out the thought in the burial arrangements. Jesus may have been crucified in the manner of a criminal, but he was buried in the manner of a king. Despite what the chief priests and the Romans might think, in his death Jesus was sovereign. John does not let the reader forget this.

The Garden Tomb

Another piece of information that we owe to John is that there was a garden there (v. 41). It would seem that the garden was quite extensive, for the crucifixion took place there and this would require a good deal of room. There had to be space for three crosses and the spectators that were inevitable at such a public function, and there was also room for the tomb. It is interesting that John tells us both that the tomb was new and that no one had ever been placed in it, whereas Matthew confines himself to saying that it was new (Matt. 27:60). Mark says nothing about its condition, and Luke says no one had ever been put in it (Luke 23:53). A tomb hewn out of rock was, of course, quite expensive, so it was not uncommon to have more than one person buried in such a tomb. Sometimes there was a series of chambers with room for several bodies in each. But this tomb was new. No one had ever been buried there before. John emphasizes the point by using an emphatic double negative; evidently he saw it as important. That the tomb was new makes it seem that Joseph had had the tomb prepared for his own burial in due course (Matthew tells us that it was Joseph's tomb, Matt. 27:60).

The newness of the tomb will have its importance when we come to consider the empty tomb on Easter morning. There can scarcely be any question of the women making a mistake in being unable to find Jesus in a tomb that contained several bodies. This tomb was new and no other body than that of Jesus had ever been placed in it. It would not be easy for a mistake to be made when the women came looking for Jesus' body.

John goes on to say that it was "the Preparation," and therefore they buried Jesus in this tomb that was so close (v. 42). As we have seen, the Preparation was the name for Friday, the day before the Sabbath, but in this place there will be some emphasis on the fact that there was only a limited time for getting ready for the Sabbath. Had the burial been arranged for some place at a distance, time would have been lost in making the journey. As it was, they were practically at the tomb and were able accordingly to get the burial completed before the Sabbath began. We should not understand this to mean that the burial was accomplished so hastily that anything of significance was omitted. The Mishnah says that a body should not be left overnight without burial, but if burial was delayed "by reason of the honor due to it" (that is, to perform some necessary duty such as securing a coffin or proper burial clothes), then there has been no sin in the delay (*Sanhedrin* 6:5). We may be sure that all that was proper was done, even though Jesus' body was buried before sunset.

John then conveys to his readers some interesting information about Jesus' burial, including quite a few things of which we do not read elsewhere. But in the end the outstanding impression with which he leaves us is not so much that he has useful information to which no one else has access, but that he is writing about the burial of a King. The greatness of Jesus that shines through this whole Gospel is not lacking when we come to the funeral arrangements.

84

The Empty Tomb

Now on the first day of the week Mary Magdalene comes to the tomb early while it was still dark, and sees the stone taken up from the tomb. She runs therefore and comes to Simon Peter and to the other disciple, whom Jesus loved, and says to them, "They have taken the Lord out of the tomb and we do not know where they have put him!" So Peter and the other disciple went off and they were going to the tomb. Now they were both running together and the other disciple ran in advance, faster than Peter, and came to the tomb first. And having stooped and peeped in he sees the linen cloths lying; however he did not go in. So Simon Peter comes too, following him, and he entered the tomb; and he sees the linen cloths lying and the small cloth that had been on his head not lying with the other cloths but wrapped together apart in one place. So then the other disciple, the one who came to the tomb first, entered, and he saw and he believed. For they did not yet know the Scripture that he must rise from the dead. So the disciples went away again to their homes (John 20:1–10).

There is impressive agreement in all four Gospels on the main fact—that Jesus rose from the dead. There is also a great deal of difference in detail; each writer has his own approach to the subject and his own stories of things that happened on that memorable morning. None of the stories that John records is found in the other Gospels. But then he does not have Luke's story of the walk to Emmaus or Matthew's account of Jesus meeting the women as they went away from the tomb or Mark's mention of the young man in white who told the women that they would see Jesus in Galilee. Plainly each of the Evangelists had his own understanding of what the really important things were that happened on that great morning, and each tells the story in his own way.

John begins with the time note that what he is about to relate took place "on the first day of the week" (v. 1). It is not without interest that in their resurrection accounts none of the Gospels uses the expression "on the third day" or the like to draw attention to the prophecies Jesus had made that he would rise on the third day after evil people had put him to death. They all content themselves with the fact that it was the first day of the week, the Sunday after the crucifixion. Actually the word for "week" is simply "sabbaths"; the Jews used this expression to denote the time between two Sabbaths and in doing so brought out the truth that the Sabbath, the day set apart for God as holy, was the important day. Of course, for Christians the day when Jesus rose from the dead became the important day; every Sunday is for them a reminder of resurrection.

John begins with a reference to Mary Magdalene. All our Gospels tell us that this lady was early at the tomb, but there is variety in the way we read of her companions. John, of course, mentions none of them; he concentrates on Mary. But Matthew says that she was accompanied by "the other Mary" (Matt. 28:1); Mark mentions these two and adds Salome (Mark 16:1); while Luke speaks of the two Marys and of Joanna (Luke 24:10). Evidently there was quite a group who came, but it was Mary Magdalene who first saw the risen Jesus, and John concentrates attention on her. That Mary was the first to see Jesus is explicitly said in Mark 16:9. This is not in the oldest manuscripts, and scholars are agreed that it formed no part of the original Gospel of Mark. It may even have been a deduction from what John says, but it is certainly an early and explicit witness to Mary's place in the resurrection appearances.

Mary is given the name "Magdalene" (as in 19:25). This is the feminine form of a place name, Magdala, and the expression means "Mary of Magdala." The Talmud tells us that there was a town called Magdala about twenty minutes' walk from Tiberias (on the western side of the Sea of Galilee). The word means "tower," and evidently there was a tower of some sort that gave the place its name; perhaps it was a guard tower or fort. The town seems to have been the center of a thriving fishing industry.

Mary came to the tomb "early." In the translation I have tried to bring out the fact that John uses several present tenses: the scene is evidently vivid to him and he sees it as he describes it. Mary then comes to the tomb quite early. The word for "early" was used in 18:28 of the time when they took Jesus from Caiaphas to the Praetorium. The trial that would lead to Jesus' death began early in the day, and those events that were to bring his followers the certainty that he had risen also began early in the day. John says "it was still dark," which sets us a little problem, for Mark says that the sun had risen (Mark 16:2). There are two ways of dealing with this. Some suggest, quite reasonably, that the ladies did not all set out at the same time: the earlier ones came while it was still dark, the others a little later when the sun had risen. It is also possible that when they set out it was still dark, but that by the time they reached the tomb the sun had risen. What is clear from all the accounts is that they were on the move quite early in the day.

John does not say why Mary was there, but from the other Gospels it is clear that the women were bringing spices to place with the body. The burial on Good Friday must have been rather hurried, and they wanted to make sure that the burial was completed with all due reverence. So they brought their spices, their own tribute to Jesus, to add to what Nicodemus had provided on the Friday. It is even possible that Nicodemus had not had time to use all the spices he had brought (he had provided a large quantity) and the women may have wanted to finish what he had started. None of the Evangelists clears up this point for us.

The Empty Tomb

Mary saw that the stone that had been rolled across the entrance to the tomb (Mark 15:46) was no longer there. The verb John uses is not the one we would expect for rolling a stone (though curiously *The Living Bible* translates "the stone was rolled aside"); it means rather something like "lift up." It seems as though John means us to understand that the stone was lifted out of its groove. What had taken place was no ordinary phenomenon, but the result of an exercise of divine power (cf. the earthquake of which Matthew tells us, Matt. 28:2). The stone had been moved in an extraordinary fashion. John uses the perfect tense of the verb, which may be meant to indicate permanence. A closed tomb has no more relevance to Jesus.

Matthew tells us that an angel spoke to the women (Matt. 28:5), while Mark says that they went into the tomb and that a young man in a white robe spoke to them (Mark 16:5ff.). Luke also says that the women entered the tomb and adds that they were confronted by two men in shining clothes (Luke 24:3–4). John says nothing of all this. It is possible that Mary was not in fact with the other women (who on this view came a little later) and that she simply reacted to the sight of the stone that had been moved. Against this she says a little later "*we* do not know . . ." so that she had obviously been with other people at some stage. Probably she came to the tomb with other women and simply left them. It is clear that her immediate thought was that the men must be told, so she took off and ran to them (v. 2). She had seen enough to know that the tomb was empty, and it was important to her that Peter and others be informed. It was urgent that they be told without delay, so she ran. It is interesting that she ran to Peter (here given his full name, "Simon Peter"). He had three times denied his Lord, but clearly the followers of Jesus still regarded him as the leader of the little band.

John adds "and to the other disciple, whom Jesus loved." In the Greek there is the repetition of the preposition *to,* which is unexpected if the two were together. It is possible that John means that Mary ran to Peter first and then ran to another place where the Beloved Disciple was and told him the same thing. But this scarcely seems likely and we should not read too much into the repetition of a preposition. More likely Peter and the other disciple were together and Mary ran straight to them.

Why does John speak of "the other disciple"? Were there not many other disciples? Perhaps because he was earlier associated with Peter (13:23–24), perhaps because he had been spoken of in the account of the crucifixion (19:26; cf. 19:35), and John is referring back to that. This disciple is further described as the one "whom Jesus loved." When John refers to Jesus as loving this disciple he normally uses another Greek word for "to love," and curious conclusions are sometimes drawn from the verb he uses here. But we should probably see the difference as no more than a stylistic variation. This verb makes it just as clear as the other that the man was the object of Jesus' affection.

Mary conveyed her startling news in one brisk sentence: "They have taken the Lord out of the tomb and we do not know where they have put him!" Her "they" may be no more than the equivalent of the passive: "The Lord has been taken out. . . ." Or Mary may have in mind people like the chief priests and their allies. Who else would do such a dastardly thing? Mary apparently does not give a thought to the possibility of a resurrection. The empty tomb means only one thing to her—a grave robbery.

It is easy, of course, to jump to a wrong conclusion. There is a story of certain medical personnel who were giving some high school children a tour over a large hospital, pointing out important features that had been installed to safeguard their health. In an operating theatre the visitors were told that during an operation the surgeon and his attendants all wore masks. "Why do they do that, do you think?" they were asked. It puzzled them for a moment, but then one young man explained it: "So that if they make a mess of it, no one will know who did it."

This sounded reasonable to the boy, and a grave robbery sounded reasonable to Mary. What other explanation could there possibly be? So she produced her explanation with confidence. Apparently in her mind there was no doubt at all. She goes on to say "we do not know . . ."

indicating that other women had been associated with her, even though John does not say who they were. He is apparently well aware that a number of women had come to the tomb, but he does not speak of them, for his concern is to tell what happened to Mary. The others come in only incidentally, because Mary happens to use the plural and thus draws attention to her companions.

They did not know "where they have put him." It was perhaps a little early for such a conclusion; Mary might conceivably have allowed a little time for a search to be made and inquiries to be begun. But we misunderstand what happened if we apply rational considerations like that. Mary loved her Lord and it was a bitter tragedy for her that he had been nailed to a cross and killed. The bottom had dropped out of her world. She had probably gained a little solace by engaging in the only thing left to her—seeing that Jesus was given a reverent and decent burial. And now even that was rudely taken away from her! Evil people had violated the tomb and Mary had no idea what they had done to the body. So she tells Peter and John.

John at the Tomb

The startling news triggered off a hasty trip to the tomb so that they could see for themselves what had happened. "Went off" (v. 3) is more literally "went out" and some have drawn the conclusion that Peter was in hiding. It is probably not necessary to suppose this (though after the crucifixion it is likely that Jesus' followers were keeping a low profile). John pictures the journey as in process with his use of the continuous tense "they were going." When he says that they were running "together" (v. 4) he means "at the same time"; his subsequent narrative makes it quite clear that John does not mean in physical proximity to one another. One ran faster than the other (or knew a better way), but they ran at the same time.

The other disciple got to the tomb first. Some decide that he was the younger man and thus could run faster. This may well have been the case, but the narrative does not prove it. The youngest does not always run fastest, and in any case we have no way of disproving the suggestion that the other disciple knew the locality better, so could take another (and quicker) route. But John does say that he ran faster. In fact he makes quite a point of it. Most translations say simply that the other disciple "outran" Peter or that he "ran faster" than that disciple. But John has two words, a verb that means "run ahead," "run in advance," and an adverb signifying "faster." He leaves us in no doubt that in this race "the other disciple" was well ahead of Peter and that he got to the tomb first.

We would have expected him to go right into the tomb to check immediately on what was there, but he did not. He stayed outside, which is somewhat surprising after he had been so eager to get to the tomb that he ran all the way there. Perhaps he saw this as one of the situations in life in which it is well to be careful.

Such situations arise from time to time. I was reading of an insurer who approached Lloyds of London with an inquiry about a difficulty or two. "Would you insure a show cat for a plane trip?" was the request. "And also would you insure a special parrot against physical harm?" There was a pause while the requests were considered. Then the answer came: "Yes, we would be prepared to insure them, but not both together!" We can understand Lloyds' hesitation and appreciate that sometimes great caution is needed.

It may be that the disciple at the tomb was a trifle hesitant in the face of something highly unusual. Even from outside the tomb it was plain that something very unusual had taken place, and perhaps he hesitated to thrust himself forward into the midst of action so to speak. Another suggestion is that he waited out of respect for Peter. After all, Peter was the leader of the little band, and the other disciple may have felt it would be presumptuous to go in before him. For whatever reason, he stayed outside.

But that did not stop him from looking in (v. 5). John makes use of a verb that a standard lexicon defines as "stoop sideways," which it says is used of "a bad harp-player"! The verb also signifies "stoop for the purpose of looking" and is sometimes used of peeping out of a door or window. In this place the lexicon says that the meaning is "of persons outside a place, *peep in, look in.*" So the other disciple peeped into the tomb.

John tells us that he saw the linen cloths lying there. At this point he says nothing about their arrangement (cf. v. 7); he just says that they were there. The body would normally have been placed on a shelf, and John seems to be saying that there is where the cloths were.

Peter at the Tomb

No indication is given as to how long afterwards Peter arrived at the tomb, but in due course he came there, "following" the first disciple (v. 6). Peter apparently did not hesitate but went straight into the tomb. There he saw the linen cloths as the other disciple had done, but he also saw the cloth that had been around Jesus' head (v. 7), which the other disciple evidently had not been able to see from his position outside the tomb. John calls this the *soudarion,* which is a word taken over from the Latin *sudarium,* a cloth used for wiping off sweat *(sudor).* John has already used the word in connection with a burial, for he speaks of a *soudarion* as round the head of Lazarus (11:44). The same word is used of the small towel in which the lazy servant hid the money his master had given him to trade with (Luke 19:20) and of the small cloths ("handkerchiefs"?) taken from the body of Paul and placed on sick people (Acts 19:12). It clearly denotes any small towel, though the word does not indicate the precise size. It has been suggested that in a burial it would have been passed under the chin and then tied on top of the head as a way of ensuring that the dead person's mouth did not fall open. Whether this was the way of it or not, it was used in Jesus' burial, and John specifically mentions that Peter saw it.

He says that the small towel was not with the other burial cloths "but wrapped together apart in one place." The expression "in one place" is unusual, but it seems to be used in opposition to another place: the cloths that had been around the body were not in the same place as the one that had been around the head. This has sometimes been understood to mean that all the grave cloths were left in the position they had been in when Jesus rose. The idea is that the body of Jesus had simply been raised (through the cloths?), leaving the cloths as they were. This may or may not have been the case, but it is not easy to understand the Greek as saying it. John simply seems to mean that the cloths were not all together and that the small cloth was rolled up or folded up. If the meaning was that all the cloths were in the position they had occupied when round the body, the small towel would have been right alongside the other cloths. The use of the same word in connection with the raising of Lazarus perhaps justifies us in noticing that when that man was restored to this mortal life, he had to have someone help him remove the grave cloths. But when Jesus rose, he needed no help. He simply left the cloths behind as he rose into his resurrection life.

It is important that John is describing a tidy and orderly scene, not the mess that would have been the result of grave robbers or the like defiling the tomb. Chrysostom, an early commentator on the passage, remarks: "For neither, if any persons had removed the body, would they before doing so have stripped it; nor if any had stolen it, would they have taken the trouble to remove the napkin, and roll it up, and lay it in a place by itself; but how? they would have taken the body as it was. On this account John tells us by anticipation that it was buried with much myrrh, which glues linen to the body not less firmly than lead." Schnackenburg quotes another early church father, Ammonius of Alexandria: "If he had been abducted by enemies, then, on account of the gain, they would not have left the clothes behind. If it was friends, then they would not have permitted the corpse to be dishonoured in its nakedness. . . . That shows rather that the body which passes over into immortality has no need of clothing in the future." The orderliness in the tomb shows that the absence of the body is not to be explained by the actions of grave robbers.

Seeing and Believing

After Peter had gone into the tomb, the other disciple followed his example (v. 8). Probably both "so" and "then" are important. "So" translates a conjunction that we could render "therefore"; it gives a reason for what follows. It was because Peter entered that the other disciple followed suit. "Then" puts his entrance in the correct temporal sequence: it was after Peter's entrance. This is the third different verb for "see" in this chapter, and the fact that there are differences has led some students to try to find significant differences in meaning. This is probably wasted ingenuity. It is a mark of John's style that he uses words of similar meaning without making any precise difference between them, and this is true of his verbs for "seeing" as well as other words.

John does not say what he saw, but presumably he means that he saw the same things as Peter had seen: the grave cloths and the way they were arranged. J. B. Phillips translates "saw what had happened," but this is reading something into the passage. It is not what John says and is a highly improbable interpretation. He saw the grave cloths and the place where Jesus had lain.

He not only saw but "believed." Unfortunately John does not say what it was that he believed. One way of taking the expression, which is as old as Augustine, is to understand John to mean that he believed what Mary had said. When they first heard it, it sounded incredible, but he now saw that it was true. Some scholars hold that this way of taking the words is the most straightforward way and point out that it relieves us of the difficulties attendant on taking "believed" in a deeper sense. But most find this view unsatisfying.

With our knowledge of the wonderful thing that God had done that morning, it is easy to guess that he believed Jesus had risen. This may possibly be true, but it goes beyond what John has said. And if that is what he meant, why does he go on immediately to say, "For they did not yet know the Scripture that he must rise from the dead" (v. 9)? That would be a very curious comment on a statement that a man believed that Jesus had risen. Because they hold that the whole story brings out the pre-eminent faith of the Beloved Disciple, some commentators are very sure of this. Schnackenburg, for example, holds that the passage "undoubtedly" refers "to the full faith in the resurrection of Jesus. . . . The point of the story lies in the clear and strong faith of the beloved disciple." But this is surely not so. The point of the story lies in the bodily resurrection of Jesus. That the Beloved Disciple came to some kind of faith is important, but it is not "the point of the story." To move to any sort of human achievement or excellence is to miss the wonderful thing that John is saying about what God has done.

We should also bear in mind that a little later John records words of Jesus to Thomas: "Do you believe because you have seen me? Blessed are those who have not seen and yet have believed" (v. 29). It is difficult to escape the impression that the thought of verse 29 is not out of mind when John writes "he saw and he believed." Whereas Schnackenburg and others see a glorification of the Beloved Disciple, it is surely the case rather that this disciple is humble. He does not see himself as an outstanding example of faith, as one who early penetrated into an understanding of the resurrection. He sees himself as one who had to see before he believed.

It is probable accordingly that we should understand "believed" to mean that what he saw in the tomb convinced him that something wonderful had happened. And whatever the wonderful thing was, it was a means of strengthening his faith. He did not attain to the blessing attendant on believing without seeing, but he did attain to the blessing of believing.

The Scripture

John adds that "they did not yet know the Scripture that he must rise from the dead" (v. 9). "Not yet" surely means that in due time they did come to this knowledge. Luke tells us that in due course the risen Jesus would instruct the two on the way to Emmaus in the things about himself "in all the Scriptures" (Luke 24:27), and he records Jesus' words, "So it stands written that the Christ should suffer and rise from the dead on the third day" (Luke 24:46). John seems to be saying much the same. At this point, early on the resurrection morning, they did not know the teaching of Scripture on the point (and thus were not looking for a resurrection). But in due course they would come to know what the relevant Scripture meant. The plural "they," where the preceding words lead us to expect "he," is curious. But John seems to be moving on to the point that this understanding of Scripture would come not only to him but to Peter and to others also.

He completes this part of his story by saying that the two went off home. The expression for "to their homes" (v. 10) is not the usual one, but there seems no doubt as to the meaning. John is saying that after they had seen the empty tomb they went home. Why should they stay there? Quite plainly the body of their Lord was gone and they could do no good by staying where it had been buried.

Let us end this study by reflecting that John does not say that the Scripture teaches that Jesus *would* rise from the dead but that he *must* rise. There is a compelling divine necessity about the resurrection. It is not that, as things turned out, this is what happened. The resurrection was in the plan of God and therefore it *must* take place.

85

Mary Sees Her Lord

But Mary was standing by the tomb, outside it, weeping. As then she was weeping she stooped and peeped into the tomb and she sees two angels in white sitting, one at the head and one at the feet where the body of Jesus had lain. And they say to her, "Woman, why are you weeping?" She says to them, "They took my Lord away, and I do not know where they put him." Having said these things she turned round and she sees Jesus standing and did not know that it was Jesus. Jesus says to her, "Woman, why are you weeping? Who are you looking for?" She, thinking that he was the gardener, says to him, "Sir, if you have carried him off tell me where you put him and I will take him away." Jesus says to her, "Mary." She turned and says to him in Hebrew "Rabbouni" (which means "Teacher"). Jesus says to her, "Stop clinging to me, for I have not yet ascended to the Father. But go to my brothers and say to them, 'I am going up to my Father and your Father, and my God and your God.'" Mary Magdalene comes telling the disciples, "I have seen the Lord," and that he had said these things to her (John 20:11–18).

Each of the Gospels deals with the resurrection appearances in its own way. It is possible that Mark had none at all, for the oldest manuscripts finish at 16:8, which may have been the original end of that Gospel. It is also possible that Mark did go on to speak of appearances of the risen Jesus and that this part of his Gospel has been lost. If so, we do not know what was in it. But the other three recount a number of appearances, and none of them simply agrees with the others: they all have their own stories. This gives us a variety of accounts and enlarges our knowledge. It also presents us with problems, and it is not unusual for scholars to say that the accounts of the appearances cannot be harmonized. This, however, is not so. Long ago B. F. Westcott gave the following "provisional arrangement of the facts connected with the first Easter-Day."

1. Just before 6:00 P.M. on Saturday Mary Magdalene and Mary the mother of James go to see the tomb (Matt. 28:1).

2. Later Mary Magdalene and Mary the mother of James and Salome buy spices (Mark 16:1).

3. Early on Sunday, the resurrection, then the earthquake, the coming of the angel, and the opening of the tomb (Matt. 28:2–4).

4. Mary Magdalene, Mary the mother of James and Salome, probably with others, set out for the tomb in the twilight. Mary Magdalene goes ahead and returns at once to Peter and John (John 20:1ff.).

5. The other women reach the tomb when the sun had risen (Mark 16:2), see an angel, and receive a message for the disciples (Matt. 28:5ff.; Mark 16:5ff.).

6. Other women, among whom is Joanna, come later, but still in the early morning (Luke 24:1ff.); there is a vision of "two young men" (Luke 24:4ff.).

7. Peter and John come to the tomb (John 20:3–10). Mary Magdalene sees two angels (John 20:11–13). Other women take news to the apostles (Luke 24:10f.).

8. The Lord appears to Mary Magdalene (John 20:14–18; Mark 16:9).

9. The Lord appears to other women who are returning to the tomb (Matt. 28:9f.).

10. The Lord appears to the two disciples on the way to Emmaus (Luke 24:13ff.).

11. In the late afternoon the Lord appears to Peter (Luke 24:34; cf. 1 Cor. 15:5).

12. The Lord appears to the eleven and some others (Luke 24:36ff.; John 20:19ff.).

This may or may not be the correct sequence of the events. But it shows that the accounts in the various Gospels are not as difficult to reconcile as is sometimes alleged. Other commentators have made a slightly different arrangement. I am not concerned to advocate any particular position. I simply point out that, while it is not easy to work out exactly the order in which the various events took place, competent scholars have been assured that our accounts do fit in with one another.

But our primary concern in this study is not with how we should relate the various events on that wonderful morning, but with what happened to Mary Magdalene. We return to her experiences.

Mary and the Angels

Peter and John had clearly left Mary Magdalene far behind when they ran to the tomb. But she was headed in the same direction as they and in due course arrived. She may have reached the tomb before the apostles left; if so, she did not go away when they did (Augustine made the comment, "A stronger affection riveted to the spot one of a weaker nature"). Or she may have taken so much longer to make the journey that they had gone before she arrived. John does not tell us. He contents himself with saying that after the disciples had gone home she was standing by the tomb (v. 11).

John's "but" contrasts Mary with Peter and John: they went off *but* she stayed on. His expression means that Mary was close to the tomb, not simply in the general vicinity. He says that she was outside and that she was weeping. He leaves us in no doubt about the depths of her grief. It was bad enough that Jesus had been killed by his enemies. It was even worse when they would not leave him alone in death, for the Jews attached great importance to proper burial. The empty tomb could mean for Mary only that Jesus' enemies had stolen the body. Why would they do that? It must have seemed to her that they were going to heap indignities on the body of Jesus and thus insult his memory as well as kill him. So Mary wept.

Still weeping, she stooped and looked into the tomb. John uses again the picturesque word he had used of the Beloved Disciple in verse 5. Mary stooped and peeped in to get a better view of what was inside. John's narrative becomes vivid with the use of the present tense as he writes "she sees two angels in white" (v. 12). The Gospels have an interesting variety of references to those in the tomb. Matthew speaks of "an angel" (Matt. 28:2), Mark of "a young man" (Mark 16:5), and Luke of "two men in dazzling clothes" (Luke 24:4), though these are apparently also called "angels" (Luke 24:23). It would seem that the heavenly visitants could be spoken of either as "men" or as "angels." Either way of putting it, they were heavenly beings sent by God to bring his message (the word we normally translate "angel" means a "messenger" and is used in this way of John the Baptist in Matt. 11:10 and of the messengers Rahab received in James 2:25).

But should we speak of one of them or two? On this point Temple comments, "It is not to be presumed that angels are physical objects reflecting rays of light upon the retina of the eye. When men 'see' or 'hear' angels, it is rather to be supposed that an intense interior awareness of a divine message leads to the projection of an image which is then experienced as an occasion of something seen and heard. That divine messengers were sent and divine messages received we need not doubt; that they took physical form so that all who 'saw' anything must 'see' the same thing we need not suppose." It is possible that Temple's explanation is the right one. Some people have more spiritual perception than others. What is quite clear is that in the different Gospel accounts different people are reported as having seen different things. Some saw one and some two of the angelic beings. It is, of course, also possible that all saw two, but as one of them was more prominent and was the speaker, he alone is mentioned in some accounts.

John tells us that the angels were robed in white (the normal color for angels in the visions of which we have a record). They were sitting, and their places were determined by the position of Jesus' body in its burial, one being at the place of the head, the other where the feet had been. Matthew is the only one of the Evangelists who speaks of an angel as outside the tomb; he tells us that an angel rolled the stone away and sat on it (Matt. 28:2). In Mark the young man in the white robe was "sitting on the right side" (Mark 16:5). Luke speaks of the two in dazzling robes as standing by the women (Luke 24:4). We should not put too much emphasis on the position of the angels; there is no reason for thinking that they did not move. The Evangelists are simply telling the story as they knew it, and such things as changes of posture do not come into their accounts.

In the other Gospels the angels reassure the women by telling them that Jesus had risen. In the story of the appearance to Mary Magdalene this feature is absent, though the question put to Mary (v. 13) might conceivably be understood as having much the same effect, for the angels are possibly implying that there was no need for tears. At any rate they ask her why she is weeping, and Lenski points out that it is a good question: "Indeed, why does she weep?—when we should all have had cause to weep to all eternity if what she wept for had been given her, the dead body of her Lord!"

They address her with the term *Woman,* a form of address that sounds harsh in English, but which did not have this effect in Greek. John tells us that Jesus used this form of address when speaking to his mother at the time of the turning of the water into wine and again when he spoke to her from the cross. In the other Gospels he uses it in speaking to women for whom he was about to do miracles (Matt. 15:28; Luke 13:12). So we should not see this salutation as formal or distant.

Mary's reply essentially repeats her words of verse 2, though with two alterations. Instead of "the Lord" she refers to "my Lord," and in place of "we do not know" there is "I do not know." Both alterations make the statement more personal. Mary's strong attachment to Jesus, and the depth of her feeling at what she could see only as a disaster, come out in her words. She is quite definite: "They took my Lord away." This, of course, goes beyond her knowledge, but to Mary there was no other possibility. She knew that the body had been placed in that tomb on Friday. Now on Sunday it was not there. What else could possibly have happened? Grave robbers must have been at work.

Mary and "the Gardener"

Mary abandoned a conversation that promised so little. Perhaps, as Chrysostom suggested long ago, the angels made some movement when they saw Jesus standing behind Mary. Perhaps she herself heard footsteps of someone approaching. For whatever reason, she turned round (more literally "to the things behind") and saw Jesus standing there (v. 14). She did not recognize him, though John does not tell us how this came about. That she was not expecting to see Jesus will be part of the answer. She was preoccupied with her own ideas (someone had stolen the body) and was not ready to recognize what did not fit in with those ideas. It is well worth reflecting that this is a mistake we repeat all too often. We expect our Lord to act in ways that accord with our own thoughts, and when he does not we do not recognize him. There is a bit of Mary in all of us at times.

Her eyes were full of tears, and this may have impaired her vision at that moment (though we should add that tears do not usually prevent us from recognizing someone we know well). But we should bear in mind that a number of times the risen Jesus was not recognized by his followers. Notably was this the case with the two who walked with him to Emmaus without recognizing him (Luke 24:13–31), but Matthew records the doubts of some who saw him (Matt. 28:17), and Luke speaks of some disciples, startled when Jesus appeared among them, who thought that they were seeing "a spirit" (Luke 24:37). A little later in this Gospel there is a story of fishermen who did not recognize Jesus when he stood on the shore of the Lake of Galilee (21:4). Evidently there was something different about the risen Jesus such that even his close followers did not always recognize him. Resurrection means transformation (cf. Paul's "we will all be changed," 1 Cor. 15:51).

Jesus puts to Mary exactly the same question as the angels had done: "Woman, why are you weeping?" (v. 15), but he adds "Who are you looking for?" The form of the second question may be significant: Mary was looking for a thing, a body, whereas she should have been looking for a person, Jesus. But Mary apparently was still too much taken up with her grief to take in the significance of what was said to her. She wanted a body and would settle for nothing else.

John tells us that she supposed that Jesus was "the gardener." She apparently simply jumped to this conclusion, and jumping to a conclusion can lead us wildly astray. There was a householder with a pleasant home in a seaside resort, about half a mile from the sea. It was his practice to use seaweed as a fertilizer and it apparently worked, for he had a very attractive garden. The time came when he had to move and the house was put up for sale. To his surprise there were no bids for it at all. He discovered why when one of the people who had attended the auction pointed to the seaweed on the garden and asked, "How often does the tide come up as far as here?" Jumping to this conclusion on the evidence of the seaweed was preventing potential buyers from acquiring a very pleasant house.

And Mary's assumption held her back from the wonderful blessing that was before her. John does not tell us why she thought she was talking to the gardener, but he has already told us that the tomb was in a garden (19:41)—and who would appear early in the morning in a garden but the man charged with the responsibility of taking care of it? Intent on finding the body of Jesus, it occurs to Mary that the gardener may well know where it is. He may have decided he did not want a body in his beautiful garden and have put it somewhere else. Incidentally Tertullian, a Christian writer of the second century, tells us that some of the Jews said the gardener removed the body of Jesus so that "his lettuces might come to no harm from the crowds of visitants"!

So Mary says to him, "Sir [she is respectful even to one she thinks is no more than a gardener], if you have carried him off tell me where you put him and I will take him away." If enemies have stolen the body, there would be little chance of an answer to such a request. But a gardener may mean no disrespect to the deceased and—if he has removed the body for his own reasons—may well be prepared to disclose its whereabouts. At any rate Mary is not going to overlook this possibility. It is somewhat curious that she does not say whose body she is looking for or even that she is looking for a body; she says no more than "him," a pronoun she uses three times. It was the Lord who was preoccupying her thoughts at this time, and she was probably so overwhelmed with grief that she did not think how she could express her thoughts in carefully chosen words.

It accords with this that she says she will take him away. It is unlikely that Mary unaided would have been able to carry a man's body, and she would have no tomb ready into which she could place it if she did. But a person as overcome with grief as Mary was does not work out exactly how much she can lift and how she will overcome problems like this. The one thing that mattered to her was that the body was gone and she wanted it back.

Mary and Her Lord

Jesus speaks only one word, "Mary" (v. 16). This immediately dispels any thought of a gardener, for it shows that he knew who she was. The name is given in the form "Mariam," which appears to be Aramaic (John has used the form "Maria" in 19:25; 20:1, 11). Jesus is speaking in the language of ordinary people in Palestine in that day.

Mary turned, which puzzles us a little. Earlier she had turned to see the "gardener" (v. 14), and she should have been facing him now. But perhaps once she had glanced at him without recognizing him, she had turned back to the tomb, where her deep interest clearly lay. Or John may mean that she now turned her full attention on the man to whom she was talking. Whatever the explanation, it was in the pronouncing of her name and her immediate response to it that she came to realize that it was Jesus to whom she was speaking.

She responded with one word, "Rabbouni," which, like "Mariam," is Aramaic (Aramaic and Hebrew are closely related and when the New Testament writers use the term "Hebrew" they usually have in mind what we call "Aramaic"; perhaps we could say that Aramaic was the form of Hebrew used in first-century Palestine). John explains that "Rabbouni" means "Teacher," but it is an unusual form of address. W. F. Albright thought that there was a note of affection about the word and that we should see the meaning as "My dear Master." Understood in this way, it expresses some of Mary's affection for Jesus. This seems more likely than the opinion of some that it means much the same as "Rabbi." If Mary wanted to say no more than "Rabbi," there seems no reason why she should not have used that word. An interesting feature of its use is that it is often employed when people spoke of God, the heavenly Master. It may be used to refer to people, but when this is done the word seems always to be used in talking about them, never as a way of addressing them. We should probably say then that Mary's use of the term as a form of address indicates something of her love and respect for her Lord.

Touching and Clinging

There is a little problem about Jesus' next words to Mary (v. 17). They have been understood in the sense "Touch me not" (KJV), but there seems no reason why Mary should not have touched him. Indeed, in Matthew's account of the resurrection we find that the women held Jesus' feet as they worshiped him, and there is no record of any objection (Matt. 28:9).

We should probably understand John's report in terms of the way Greek verbs are used. Here we have the present imperative with a negative and this normally has the meaning "Don't keep on [doing whatever the verb means]," rather than "Don't start [whatever the verb denotes]." The implication here is that Mary was already touching Jesus and he is telling her to stop. And, while the verb John uses may be used of touching, a standard lexicon says of it, "prop., *to fasten to*" and goes on to give as some of its meanings, *"to fasten oneself to, cling to, lay hold of."* More than a casual touch is meant. There is little doubt that in her joy at the sudden discovery that Jesus was alive Mary was clinging to him. Jesus tells her to stop doing it.

He goes on to say "for I have not yet ascended to the Father." It is not easy to see the reason for this. We can say that after Jesus had ascended to the Father there was going to be no possibility of touching him or clinging to him physically. Moreover, as we know from Luke that the ascension did not take place until forty days after the resurrection (Acts 1:3), Jesus may be saying in effect: "There is plenty of time. I will not ascend to my Father for some weeks!"

There are some scholars who hold that John has a different idea and that he thought of the ascension as taking place on Easter Day. They often suggest that we should take no notice of what Luke says about the ascension's being weeks later, for John is not necessarily viewing the ascension in the same way as Luke sees it. But this overlooks the fact that John does not picture Jesus as ascending that day. In this very chapter he speaks of Jesus as appearing to the disciples a week later (vv. 26ff.). There is no indication that John thought of Jesus as ascending on Easter Day and subsequently coming back to earth again. We should also bear in mind that the tense of the verb here is perfect—it points to an ascending that is complete and final. That, Jesus says, had not taken place.

It may well be that Jesus is correcting a misapprehension. Mary's reaction to seeing Jesus seems to show that she thought he had come back to resume the old life so that things would now be as they had been before the crucifixion. It may be that she was envisaging a situation not unlike that when Lazarus was raised. That friend of Jesus died, indeed, but he was raised to resume the life he had left. She had not yet realized that Jesus' resurrection was different. He was risen into a new life, nothing like the old one he had left, and Mary should not misunderstand.

Jesus' going to be with the Father was still future. Mary was holding on as though if she let him go she might never see him again! But this was wrong. The ascension that would signal the end of Jesus' earthly mission was still some time away. There would be other opportunities for seeing him.

Mary's Message

Jesus proceeds to give Mary a message she is to take to people he calls "my brothers" (in Matthew's account also the risen Lord gave the women a message for "my brothers," Matt. 28:10). Does this mean brothers in our sense of the term, male members of the same human family? Or is it a way of referring to disciples? We would have expected that Jesus would want Mary to take his message to his disciples, and in fact she does go off to them and tell them what had happened to her and what Jesus had said (v. 18). But Jesus does not usually call his disciples his "brothers." We could infer that he thought of them in this way from some words that Matthew reports: "Whoever does the will of my Father who is in heaven, he is my brother and sister and mother" (Matt. 12:50). And we should bear in mind that a little later in this Gospel John speaks of the disciples as "brothers" (21:23). It is, of course, possible that Jesus has in mind the brothers in his earthly family, and in favor of this is the fact that as early as Acts 1:14 we find them with the disciples. He must have seen them at some time after he rose, for during the time of his ministry they "did not believe in him" (cf. 7:5). The possibility that he had them in mind in his words to Mary must be allowed, but on the whole it seems more likely that he was thinking of the disciples. We must presume that Mary knew whom he meant, and she went to the disciples.

The message referred to Jesus' going up to "my Father and your Father, and my God and your God." This way of putting it unites Jesus with his followers because it is the same Father and the same God that they revere. But it also makes a difference, for Jesus does not say "our Father and our God." He seems deliberately to be making a difference between his relationship to the Father and theirs. Augustine, the early church commentator, said: "He saith not, Our Father: in one sense, therefore, is He mine, in another sense, yours; by nature mine, by grace yours . . . my God, under whom I also am as man; your God, between whom and you I am mediator."

Mary did as she was told (v. 18). She went to the disciples and gave the message. John retains her exact words as she utters the amazing and significant truth: "I have seen the Lord," but then he turns to indirect speech with "he had said these things to her." Mary's experience as she saw the risen Lord receives the emphasis.

86

Jesus' Appearance to the Disciples

So then, when it was evening on that day, the first day of the week, and the doors where the disciples were having been shut for fear of the Jews, Jesus came and stood in the middle and says to them, "Peace be to you." And when he had said this he showed them his hands and his side. Therefore the disciples rejoiced when they saw the Lord. So Jesus said to them again, "Peace be to you; even as the Father has sent me, I also am sending you." And when he had said this he breathed on them and says to them, "Receive Holy Spirit; if you forgive the sins of any, they have been forgiven to them, if you hold those of any, they have been held" (John 20:19–23).

There can surely be no doubt at all that this is John's account of the same appearance as that which Luke tells us took place on the evening of that first Easter Day (Luke 24:36–49). Two of Jesus' followers had walked with him as far as Emmaus without recognizing him, but as they began a meal together they recognized him. Then they hastened back to Jerusalem to let the disciples there know what had happened. And when they had brought this exciting news something even more exciting happened—Jesus appeared in the middle of the little group.

There are, of course, important differences. Luke says nothing about Jesus' breathing on the disciples, nothing about the Holy Spirit, nothing about the forgiveness of sins. John does not tell his readers about the disciples' terror at the sight of Jesus or that the little group thought they were seeing a ghost or that Jesus calmed them by eating a piece of fish.

But both locate the incident in Jerusalem in the evening of Easter Day and say that it happened in a gathering of Jesus' followers in that city. Both say that Jesus gave the greeting of peace. Both tell us that Jesus showed his followers the wounds he had received: John speaks of his hands and his side, while Luke refers to his hands and his feet. It seems plain enough that it is the same incident, but that the two tell about it from different points of view. Some things mattered to Luke, while other things seemed important to John. We may just feel thankful that we have both accounts and thus are in a better position than if we had but one.

The Locked Doors

John begins this section of his story with a time note (as he often does throughout his Gospel; it is perhaps a little mark of an eyewitness who remembered when things happened). It was evening on "that day," further explained as "the first day of the week" (v. 19). In this way John ties in what he is about to say with the preceding story of the appearance of the risen Jesus. Indeed, the tie may be a little closer, for the word I have translated "so then" is one that mostly means "therefore," and if we were to take it in that way here John would be saying that what he is about to narrate took place because of the preceding: Jesus rose and appeared to Mary and *therefore* soon after appeared also to the disciples. We cannot insist on such a strong link, but we can say that John is telling us a continuous story, not embarking on something quite unrelated to the preceding.

He goes on to say that "the doors where the disciples were" were shut. Christians usually speak of this as the "Upper Room" (I have also done this in earlier chapters.), and it may well have been. But none of the Gospels says this, and the idea is apparently derived from the room in which they were met in Acts 1:13. This is not at all improbable. I am simply drawing attention to the fact that John does not say anything about this one way or the other. He contents himself with referring to the doors.

He uses the plural "doors," not "the door," and we should take notice of this because the plural of this word is found in John only here and in verse 26. It is possible that the room was entered through double doors, but more likely that he is thinking of the door into the house and then the door into the room where the group was assembled and saying that both were firmly closed. When he says they were "shut" he uses the perfect tense of the verb, which we should take in this context to denote that they were locked, all the more so in that John adds that this was done "for fear of the Jews."

All the Gospels speak of someone or other experiencing fear at the time of the resurrection (see Matt. 28:4, 5, 8; Mark 16:8; Luke 24:5). There is a difference, however, between John and the others. The first three seem to link fear with the experience of the supernatural. It was the fact that a dead body had been brought to life that caused the fear. Clearly some mighty and unusual force was at work and those near to it were afraid. But in John it is the Jews who are the cause of the fear.

There is no evidence of which we are aware that would indicate that the disciples were in real danger. We know that the Jewish leaders were hostile to Jesus and that because of this they took the action that brought about his death, but there is no indication that they carried this over into persecution of Jesus' followers. When the disciples a few weeks later began to preach about Jesus and to lay the responsibility for his death on the Jewish authorities, they did begin to persecute them. But that was in the future. At this point in time, the evening of the first day of the week, that day on which Jesus rose, the Jewish authorities seem to have been content to let the followers of Jesus alone. They may well have felt that without Jesus the movement was of no importance.

Or the disciples may have had another possibility in mind. It must have occurred to them that the authorities might well think that they had stolen the body of Jesus. In this case they would probably accuse some of them of grave robbing. Whichever way it was, it is understandable that the disciples were nervous. They had been closely associated with Jesus, and the Jewish authorities had brought about the crucifixion of their Master. Who could tell when they might turn their hands against his followers? While they did not think the danger so great that they fled from Jerusalem, they did take their precautions. And on this evening they met behind locked doors.

John speaks of those present as "the disciples," a general term covering people who had attached themselves to Jesus and were taught by him. It does not, of course, mean all to whom this description applied, but some of them. There seems no reason, however, for confining the term to the apostles, as some suggest. A little later John speaks of "the twelve" (v. 24) and if that was what he had in mind here, there seems no reason why he should not have said so. In any case Luke makes this clear. He says that when the two to whom Jesus appeared on the road to Emmaus returned to Jerusalem they found assembled "the eleven and those with them" (Luke 24:33). In addition to the apostles there were thus the two who went to Emmaus and other followers of Jesus, who were simply said to be "with" the apostles.

Now there came an unexpected joy to the little group. This sometimes happens in life. I like the story of the somewhat harassed housewife who went to a travel agent and made a series of arrangements for her children to go to a variety of holiday camps and for her husband to go off on a lengthy business trip. When it had all been arranged to her satisfaction the travel agent asked, "Now when can I arrange a holiday for you?" She thought for a moment, then produced a dazzling smile as she said, "You just did!" It was not the object nor the expected outcome of her visit to the travel man. But it happened. And at this point in the Gospel the disciples did not come together explicitly to get a great blessing. But they did. Something they had not planned came to pass and in doing so brought them great joy.

Jesus Came

John says that Jesus came and stood "into" the middle, which is not quite the way we would have expected him to have put it. The preposition has about it the idea of motion towards something or someone—Jesus moved towards them. This is not expressed so strongly that we need to bring it out in our translation, but it is an interesting way of putting it. They were assembled together, talking about the facts that Jesus had appeared to Simon Peter and to the two on the way to Emmaus (Luke 24:34–35), and suddenly—Jesus had come to them. He was there. He was standing in the middle of them.

John has made it clear that the doors were closed when Jesus came. This means that the Lord came to be with them without first opening the doors and thus that his resurrection body was not bound by the limitations that attend us all in this earthly life. Paul tells us that those who are still alive when Jesus comes back at the end of the age will "be changed" (1 Cor. 15:51–53), and perhaps we are seeing here something of what that means. At any rate John makes it clear that the risen Jesus did things that the incarnate Jesus did not do.

Jesus gave them the greeting of peace: "Peace be to you" (characteristically John uses the present tense "says" for greater vividness; it was a dramatic moment). It is not completely certain that this was the standard greeting at that time, but it was certainly used and had been for centuries (e.g., 1 Sam. 25:6). But it was used on occasion as a way of giving assurance, as it was when the Lord said to Gideon, "Peace! Do not be afraid. You are not going to die" (Judg. 6:23; for some reason NIV omits "to you" after "Peace," but this is found in the Hebrew). Whether or not this was the standard greeting between Jesus and his followers, on this occasion there will certainly be the note of reassurance. The disciples were afraid. They did not understand how their Master could really be there among them when he had been killed a day or two before. Jesus speaks to reassure them.

Not only did he give assurance by his words, but he proceeded to show them marks made on his body by the wounds when he was crucified (v. 20). His hands bore the marks where the nails had been driven in, and his side the wound where the spear had been thrust (John is the only one to tell us that Jesus showed them his side). This would show them, despite the fact that there were significant differences (locked doors did not keep him out), that it was the same Jesus who had been crucified who now stood before them. The sight of the wounds convinced them. "Therefore" indicates that it was on account of what Jesus had done that they rejoiced. Their fear gave way to joy as they were struck by the realization that it was no ghost that was standing there, but that very same Jesus who had suffered on the cross so recently. There was no longer any doubting that Jesus was alive. Nor was it possible to doubt that it was the very same person who had suffered on the cross. The wounds proved this. There was joy in that room.

Mission

Now comes a very solemn moment. Jesus proceeded to commission and empower his followers for service. First let us notice John's "so" (v. 21), which is the same Greek word as that rendered "therefore" (v. 20). What followed arose out of the assurance the disciples had received that it was Jesus, the same Jesus who had been crucified, who was alive and standing with them. It is still the fact that effective Christian service arises from the conviction that Jesus died for us and that this same Jesus who died rose again from the dead. Throughout the New Testament the death and resurrection of Jesus are at the heart of the Christian message, and it is on the basis of a deep conviction that God has acted in these striking happenings that believers are sent into the world to do service for God.

Jesus repeated the greeting of peace and the repetition gives it emphasis. That it now follows the disciples' realization that the Jesus who died has really risen perhaps means that peace in a fuller sense comes to those who have appreciated what God has done in Christ's atoning death and resurrection. God can be called "the God of peace" (Rom. 16:20), and the peace he brought about for sinners he brought about through the cross (Col. 1:20; cf. Eph. 2:14–18). On the basis of Jesus' death and resurrection peace in the fullest sense comes to those who trust him.

Jesus went on, "even as the Father has sent me, I also am sending you." That the Father "sent" Jesus is one of the great thoughts that runs through this Gospel, and it is appropriate that Jesus now reminds his followers of that great truth. His life here on earth was no aimless idyll, but a serious doing of the Father's will. He had been sent to accomplish a work of salvation and had now brought that to its triumphant conclusion in the cross and the resurrection. Throughout the New Testament it is clear that this remains the basis of the Christian movement. Without this great act of God there is no basis for its existence.

Now comes the staggering consequence: "I also am sending you." There is emphasis on the "I"—"no less than *I* am sending you." It is the crucified and risen Lord, the one who has done so much for their salvation, who sends them forth. And that, of course, remains the justification for the church's mission. The church is not a group of religiously minded busybodies, anxious to interfere in other people's lives and turn them into replicas of themselves. It is a group of people who have been saved by Christ's saving death and resurrection and who, on the basis of that death and resurrection, have been commissioned to bring the message of salvation to sinners everywhere. The powerful act of God that lies behind salvation and brought it about demands that believers should be active everywhere in spreading the gospel.

Perhaps we should notice that John uses two different Greek words for "send," for sometimes people put emphasis on this and draw such conclusions as that the mission of the church is not the same as the mission of the Christ. This is, of course, true, but we cannot prove it by the use of the two verbs. As previously mentioned, John has a habit of using words like these without putting any real difference of meaning; it is a stylistic feature. Sometimes he repeats a word, and indeed in 17:18 he tells us that Jesus prayed "even as you sent me into the world I also have sent them into the world," where exactly the same word is used of both Jesus and the disciples. But more commonly John varies his words without any significant difference of meaning. That is surely what he is doing here.

The Gift of the Spirit

Now comes something of which we read only in John. Jesus "breathed on" the disciples (v. 22). It is not easy to get an English form of words that will translate this exactly. In common with almost all translators I have inserted a "them," which is not in the Greek; in English we cannot say simply "he breathed on and says" so we insert "them" (Schonfield makes a valiant attempt with "he expelled a deep breath," but this misses the "on"). The point of this is that John is not saying that Jesus went round the little group breathing on each one of them individually. He breathed on the group as a whole. The gift of which he is about to speak is a gift made to the church rather than to individual members. It will, of course, be exercised through individual members, and there is an aspect of it in which what happens in and through individuals is important. But first we should notice that it is given to the church as a whole.

Then Jesus said, "Receive Holy Spirit." There is no definite article here, and a few translators suggest "Receive a holy spirit," but it is hard to fit this into either the teaching of Jesus or the theology of John. There is no warrant for thinking that Jesus was thinking of a good spirit (like an angel?) and giving that spirit as a gift to the believers. It is surely the Holy Spirit of whom he is speaking. But as he makes the gift he is putting his emphasis on the character of the gift (as Holy Spirit) rather than on the person of the Holy Spirit (as a personality distinct from others). The church is indwelt by someone who is nothing less and nothing other than Holy Spirit. And it is that Holy Spirit who leads the church through all the ages.

We should perhaps bear in mind that in Greek the word we translate "Spirit" also means "breath" or "wind." It was thus very appropriate that Jesus should use breath as an outward sign of the gift of the Spirit that he was giving the disciples. Sometimes Christians have taken this kind of thing very literally. R. E. Brown tells of a time when the Coptic Patriarch in Alexandria used to breathe into a skin bag, which was then firmly tied and taken up river to Ethiopia. There it was released on the man chosen to be head of the Ethiopian church! We cannot think that Jesus meant anything like this to happen, but the custom shows how suitable it was in the ancient world to use breath to convey teaching about the Spirit.

It is not obvious how we are to relate the gift Jesus made that evening to what happened on the Day of Pentecost as narrated in Acts 2. Some have held that this is John's version of the way the Spirit was given to the church and that we should choose between Luke's account and that given here. This seems quite unwarranted. Luke is telling us of something that, even though it was not a happening in the public domain, was immediately followed by preaching before a large number of people from a large number of places and of whom a large number were converted. John is describing something that happened to a little group of Jesus' close followers who met in a private room. The two accounts are quite different and clearly refer to different happenings.

We should bear in mind that "there are diversities of spiritual gifts, but the same Spirit" (1 Cor. 12:4). The New Testament makes it plain that there are many gifts of the Spirit, and Christian experience through the centuries confirms this. We are to think accordingly of two distinct workings of the Spirit, one on the day of the resurrection and another, made for a different purpose, several weeks later.

Forgiving and Retaining

Jesus went on to utter a difficult saying, one that has been understood in a variety of ways in the history of the Christian church (v. 23). First there is an ambiguity about whether we should translate "If you forgive . . ." with the meaning I have given in my translation, or whether we should render it "Whose soever sins . . ." (KJV). But this is a small problem and it does not matter which way we solve it. In the end the meaning is much the same.

The verb I have rendered "hold" should be taken to mean "refuse to forgive," in opposition to "forgive" earlier in the sentence. We should perhaps notice that there are some who think we have a reference to rabbinic practice, in which some things were "loosed" in the sense that they were declared permitted and others were "held" in the sense that they were forbidden. In that case Jesus is saying that the Holy Spirit will guide the church to declare authoritatively what things are acceptable for the Christian and what things are forbidden. But forgiveness is the more probable meaning.

The passage has been made the justification for the practice of some groups of Christians whereby an ordained clergyman "forgives" or "retains" sins. The right to do this is restricted to the ecclesiastical figure because, it is said, those present on this occasion were the apostles through whom the ministry was transmitted to the church. But we have already seen that there were others than the apostles present on this occasion. There are no grounds in the text of John for restricting the gift (whatever it was) to clergy or ecclesiastical officials of any kind. R. H. Strachan emphasizes this and holds that "any disciple of Christ" may make the declaration of which this verse speaks. This may be true, but I doubt that it is what Jesus is saying. The gift was made to the church as a whole. It is true that gifts made to the church must in the end be exercised through individuals, but there is nothing in the passage that says who these people are or even hints that they must be clergy. The Spirit-filled church is not to be limited by the actions of an ecclesiastical hierarchy.

One feature of the discussion is that most of those who take part in it concentrate on the power of forgiving; they spend their time talking about the way in which God's forgiveness is to be mediated. But we should not overlook the fact that in the context this is linked with the power of retention, and it is impossible to think that God places this power in the hands of any individuals, however godly.

Let me put it this way. People make mistakes. Through the centuries it is certain that individuals, be they clergy or authorized officials or Strachan's "any disciple of Christ," have made mistakes and that they still do make mistakes. When the mistake is made of declaring forgiven someone who ought not to be forgiven, I can imagine (I do not say I think it would happen, but I can imagine) that God might go along with the mistake. God might conceivably endorse what his representative said and let someone into heaven who ought not to have been there.

But I cannot imagine God's endorsing a mistake made in the opposite direction. If the person in question declined to declare forgiveness when he should have done so, I am sure that God would never endorse that mistake, no matter how highly the ecclesiastical person was regarded or how supreme his place in the church. It is unthinkable that God would allow someone to be in hell who ought not to be there, simply because some fallible human said so. But the power to retain sin is on all fours with that to forgive. We do not have the one without the other.

Another point may be significant. The verbs "forgive" and "hold" are in the perfect tense, and this points to an already existing fact. God does not forgive or withhold forgiveness because his representative on earth utters these or those words. Jesus is saying that when the Spirit-filled church makes its statement that such-and-such sins are forgiven they have in fact already been forgiven, and when it says that other sins are retained they are in fact not forgiven.

And there is yet another feature of the passage to which we should give attention, namely that the word I have translated "any" is in the plural both times, not the singular. Jesus is not saying "if you loose the sins of any man" but "if you loose the sins of any men." It is classes of people, not individuals, of whom he is speaking. Of course, what is laid down with respect to groups has its application to individuals. But we must not interpret the passage as though Jesus were speaking of the individual sinner in the confessional. Basically he is referring to sinners in the plural. He is saying that the Spirit-filled church has the right (and the duty) to say that such-and-such sins are forgiven and such-and-such sins are not.

We should not overlook the fact that the words are spoken in the context of the mission of the church. Believers are sent by Christ into the world, just as Christ was sent by the Father into the world. And when they go they go to proclaim the salvation Christ has won for them and in the proclamation let their hearers know what sins are forgiven and what sins are not. W. Milligan and W. F. Moulton long ago wrote a commentary in which they say on this passage, "It is not a direct address by one person to another that is thought of,—'I declare that *thy* sins are thus authoritatively remitted or retained.' It is a proclamation from one collective body to another,—from the Church to the world." The church is still required to convey this authoritative message to a world of sinners.

87

Thomas the Doubter

But Thomas, one of the twelve, who is called Didymus, was not with them when Jesus came. So the other disciples said to him, "We have seen the Lord." But he said to them, "Unless I see in his hands the mark of the nails and thrust my finger into the mark of the nails and thrust my hand into his side, I will certainly not believe."

And after eight days his disciples were again indoors and Thomas was with them. Jesus comes, the doors being shut, and stood in the middle and said, "Peace be to you." Then he says to Thomas, "Bring your finger here and see my hands, and bring your hand and thrust it into my side and be not unbelieving but believing." Thomas answered him saying, "My Lord and my God." Jesus says to him, "Because you have seen me you have believed? Blessed are those who have not seen and yet have believed."

Therefore Jesus did many other signs before his disciples which have not been written in this book; but these have been written in order that you may believe that Jesus is the Christ, the Son of God, and that believing you may have life in his name (John 20:24–31).

In modern times there are some people who have thought that at first the disciples did not believe that Jesus had risen from the dead. They were stunned by what happened on Calvary. Surely the Jesus they knew so well could not have been defeated by his enemies and killed! Bit by bit they convinced themselves that he could not have been overcome by death, and then stories began to appear. He was alive and people had seen him! In the opinion of some of our contemporaries, this kind of self-hypnotism is the way we should account for the resurrection appearances.

But this was not the way of it, according to Scripture. Certainly the followers of Jesus at first had no thought of a resurrection, but there was no gradual accustoming of themselves to the thought until eventually they accepted it. The New Testament writers tell us that on the first Easter Day there were five appearances of Jesus: he appeared to Mary Magdalene, then to the other women, later to the two who were walking to Emmaus, then to Peter, and in the evening to the ten apostles and those gathered with them in Jerusalem. Over the next forty days there were five more appearances at irregular intervals, and then they finished (except for the appearance to Saul of Tarsus on the Damascus Road). This is not the gradual building up of a story. There is a sudden, shattering happening that burst on an astonished group. And quite soon the appearances cease.

The story of Thomas is very important. Thomas was a robust doubter. He would not be persuaded by the combined testimony of all the rest of the apostolic band. He had lived with them for years and knew them to be trustworthy people, but he still did not believe. Evidently he wondered what had got into them. For Thomas the idea that a dead man was alive again was crazy nonsense. He was not going to fall for such a silly story. He could not understand why all the apostles, sensible men whom he knew well, had accepted it. And no matter how stupid they had been, he was not going to follow their example. Later in the New Testament we read of Paul's account of some people who said, "Dead men don't rise!" Thomas would have fitted in well with them.

The Twin

John is the only one of the Evangelists who tells us anything about Thomas other than that he was one of the Twelve. Outside this Gospel he appears only in lists of the names of the apostles. So John has put us in his debt by the things he tells us about this interesting man.

He starts his account of this incident by introducing us to Thomas. He has mentioned him before in his story of the raising of Lazarus. On that occasion, when Jesus announced his intention of going up to Jerusalem, Thomas rather gloomily said to the rest of the Twelve, "Let us go, too, so that we may die with him" (11:16). It was not a cheerful utterance but it shows us something of the devotion this man had for his Master. We meet him again in the Upper Room. Jesus said to the group, "I go to prepare a place for you. . . . And you know the way where I am going" (14:2–4). But Thomas did not know the way and would not pretend that he did. So he said to Jesus, "Lord, we don't know where you are going; how can we know the way?" (14:5). Thomas appears in this Gospel as a hardheaded man, a practical man, an honest man, one who did not pretend. So his reaction to the resurrection story is of great interest and importance.

John tells us now that Thomas was "one of the twelve" (v. 24). Without Judas, of course, there were only eleven, but "the twelve" was clearly a name for the group and it was retained even though the group now lacked one member. Matthew, Mark, and Luke all use the expression "the twelve" quite often; it was clearly a recognized way of referring to the group of close followers of Jesus. (They were also called "apostles," for they were the people Jesus "sent" as his representatives in a special way, but this term is not frequent in the Gospels.) While John, of course, knows that they were called "the twelve" he does not often use the expression. In fact we find it only in the story of the feeding of the five thousand and its sequel (6:13, 67–71), and here. It was quite unexpected that one of the Twelve was at first so slow to accept belief in the resurrection. So John makes Thomas's standing clear before he goes on to the story.

He tells us again that Thomas was called Didymus. As we saw in an earlier study the word is a Greek word meaning "twin," and this is the meaning of the Hebrew word we transliterate as "Thomas." It seems that in the first century when twins were born the parents sometimes had a name for one of the children but called the other one simply "Twin." That was evidently the way of it with this apostle. There have been speculations as to the identity of the other twin, but we have no way of knowing and it does not matter. Our business is with this one of the two.

A Refusal to Believe

Thomas was not with the others when Jesus came to them on that first Easter Day. John does not tell us why. It has been conjectured that it was because Thomas was a pessimist: he saw the death of Jesus as the end of everything that the little band had stood for and therefore there was no point in continuing to meet. But this goes beyond anything the Bible says. John gives no reason for Thomas's not being with the others on that occasion, and he does not criticize or blame him for it. He simply records it as a fact.

The others, of course, told Thomas what had happened. "We have seen the Lord," they said (v. 25). It was the most wonderful thing and they must have been full of it. The tense of the verb John uses for "said" is imperfect and we should understand it in the sense "they kept telling him."

But, despite their confident repetition of the story, Thomas was not convinced. He had to see for himself. And not only see, he had to feel. "Unless I see in his hands the mark of the nails," he said, "and thrust my finger into the mark of the nails and thrust my hand into his side, I will certainly not believe." There is a small uncertainty about the wording here, arising from the fact that in Greek the word for "mark" (*tupos*) is very much like the word for "place" (*topos*). Most manuscripts have "mark" here, but some have "place." The New English Bible has one example of each: "Unless I see the mark of the nails on his hands, unless I put my finger into the place. . . ." These translators evidently thought that John used both words. The point is a small one and does not greatly affect the sense. What matters is that Thomas demanded both visual and tactile evidence: he had both to see and to feel—and only then would he believe.

Thomas, of course, was mistaken in this. In the end the presence of Jesus was enough of itself to sweep away his doubts. But we often make a mistake about what will enable us to recognize what we are looking for. There is a story about a little old lady who parked her car in a fairground and when it was time for her to go home could not remember where she had put it. She looked without success in all the places she thought likely. Some kindly people noticed her distress and asked whether they could help. She told them of her problem and when they asked what sort of car she described it as a blue Chevrolet with a dent in the door on the driver's side. She remembered the registration number, too, and the helpful strangers began a search. After a short interval a young man came back and said, "I've found a car that looks like it, but it has a five-meter canoe on the roof rack." "Oh, dear," said the old lady, "I forgot to mention that!" The old lady thought that the dent in the driver's door was the thing that would enable recognition and did not even remember what was far more distinctive.

So with Thomas. He laid down with some emphasis what he thought were the necessary prerequisites of belief. He was, of course, quite wrong. All his doubts were in due course going to be swept away simply by his finding himself in the presence of the risen Lord. But that does not alter the fact that he had a load of doubt to remove, nor that he had very firm ideas about what it would take to remove it. And the fact that in due course it *was* removed has been a source of inspiration and help to believers ever since.

Thomas ends his little speech with a very emphatic statement, which I have translated "I will certainly not believe." For him belief in a resurrection was a sheer impossibility. It could not happen. He refused to allow the possibility for a moment. Earlier in this Gospel, in the story of the healing of the nobleman's son, we have some words of Jesus: "Unless you people see signs and wonders you will not believe" (4:48). Thomas is here coming perilously close to that position of unbelief.

Some have felt that Thomas was not so much of a doubting disposition as deeply shocked by what had happened at the crucifixion. They suggest that a profound shock may have unsettled him and made it impossible for him to think that the cause of it all could be taken away, as the other disciples were saying. This is supported by pointing to Thomas's emphasis on the wounds, which is felt to be somewhat morbid. All this is, of course, speculation; we have no way of knowing whether or not there is substance in it. What we do know is that whether it was due to Thomas's innate hardheadedness or whether it was due to shock, this disciple was quite unable to go along with what the others were telling him. For Thomas at this time talk of a resurrection was sheer nonsense.

Faith Replaces Doubt

In first-century Palestine people used an inclusive method of counting, which meant that in defining the limits in a period of time they included the first day as well as the last. When they said "after eight days" (v. 26) they meant what we would say as "seven days later" or "a week later." John does not say what it was "after," but we should probably understand him to mean a week after "Jesus came" (v. 24). He is unlikely to mean that it was a week after the ten had a conversation with Thomas. The whole thrust of what he has just said implies that they had had repeated conversations with him as they tried to get him to see reason. Their first discussion of what had happened would probably have been on the Monday after the resurrection, but it is improbable that John here means the next Monday. It is much more likely that he means a week after the resurrection. In the earlier part of the chapter he has been concerned with what happened on the Sunday Jesus rose. Now he moves on to the next Sunday.

Again the disciples were met together, again they were indoors, and again the doors were shut (with the perfect tense carrying the implication that they were firmly closed, i.e., locked). A teasing question is "Where did this happen?" John does not mention any change of scene, and it is natural to take what he says as meaning that the disciples were still in Jerusalem. But Jesus' message to the disciples through the women was that they were to go into Galilee (Matt. 28:10; cf. Mark 16:7), and that is where John has them in chapter 21. He does not say when they made the trip, and it is quite possible to hold that they moved north during the week and that this appearance was in Galilee. But we have no information to decide the point and can only conclude that both possibilities must be left open.

This time Thomas was in the group. And, as on that earlier Sunday, suddenly Jesus "stood in the middle and said 'Peace be to you.'" The words are the same as those used of the appearance on the previous Sunday except that John here uses the past tense "said," rather than the present tense "says" that he employed on the previous occasion. But when he moves to the words that Jesus spoke to Thomas he uses the vivid present (v. 27).

These words include some unusual ways of putting things. We would not usually say "bring your finger" nor, when we are speaking of a finger, would we say "see. . . ." But in both cases the meaning is plain and we can only guess at the reason for the unusual expressions. Jesus' body still bore the marks of his crucifixion and he invited Thomas to see them for himself.

"Be not unbelieving" translates a construction that implies that Thomas has been unbelieving and that Jesus now tells him to desist. There is no verb in the final expression, but the clear implication is that Thomas is to move out of a state of continuing unbelief into one of continuing belief. A profound change of attitude is looked for, a change that would begin with a recognition of the resurrection but would continue through the whole of life.

Lord and God

But Thomas was not as great a sceptic as he thought he was. When Jesus stood before him, he did not need to feel the wounds of his Savior. Jesus called on Thomas to make the very tests that disciple had said were needed when he rejected what his fellow disciples were saying. This shows that Jesus knew exactly what his unbelieving disciple had demanded. Was it this that brought conviction to Thomas? Or was it simply the sight of the risen Lord? John does not say and we do not know. But we do know that Thomas did not now want to make the tests he had previously thought necessary.

It is true that some students of this Gospel think that Thomas did do this. They reason that when Jesus told him to do so he must have obeyed. But surely if he did John would have said so. In any case the whole supposition is highly unlikely. John is surely telling us that Jesus' appearance and his words to Thomas were all that was necessary. He goes on to speak of Thomas as a believer (v. 29) and there says that it was because of his seeing Jesus that Thomas believed, not because of his touching the wounds. It is also legitimate to hold that Thomas would not have been a believer in the sense in which John uses the term if he had in fact had to feel the wound prints before accepting the truth about Jesus' resurrection.

No, it was not because he had physically handled the body that Thomas believed. It was because in one dazzling moment he had come to realize that he was standing before a Jesus whom he must now call "My Lord and my God" (v. 28). This is an address to Jesus in almost the same terms as the psalmist of old addressed his God (Ps. 35:23).

We have had occasion to notice that "Lord" may be used in ordinary polite address, very much like "Sir" in our society, and that it may also be used of the deity one worships. Throughout this Gospel it has been used occasionally by the disciples when referring to Jesus, but after the resurrection it is more frequent and charged with fuller meaning. It has been suggested that here we should understand it in an earthly sense, as though Thomas were saying something like "It is our Master, and he is divine!" But it is much more likely that Thomas is using the term with the full implication of deity. He is using the word with its fullest meaning to bring out his new conviction that Jesus was divine in the fullest sense of that term.

When he goes on to add "my God" there can be no doubts. This is the first time that anyone in this Gospel has greeted Jesus in this way. In the opening verse John has said that "the Word was God" (1:1), but this is his way of bringing out the greatness of the Word before he got down to his story of the Word incarnate. Jesus had come to earth as a man and had moved among people as a man. They had always recognized him as such, sometimes thinking of him as a very great and good man (and sometimes not). But in this moment, when he made a gigantic leap of faith, Thomas recognized that Jesus could not be understood in purely human terms. With all the difficulties that this recognition involved, he must be seen as God.

Seeing and Believing

Jesus gives his approval to the words of his servant (v. 29). It is not certain whether the Master's words should be taken as a question or as a statement. The Greek could mean either, but in this case there is not really a great difference of meaning. If we take the words as a question, it is not the kind of question that people ask in order to elicit some information that was not known to them previously. Jesus knew quite well that Thomas believed and what had brought about that belief. He is directing his servant's attention to the process and reminding him that he had lacked faith until he saw his Lord. He believed on the basis of what he had seen.

This should not be taken as an indication that there was something inferior about Thomas or that his faith was of a poorer quality than that of other people. It is easy to see him as a disciple, class 2. I am reminded of Lester Pearson, the great Canadian, whose mother had always hoped he would be ordained and made a minister of the church. Instead he went into politics and found his sphere of service there. The day he was admitted to the Cabinet he telephoned his mother and said to her, "Mother, I'm a Minister now!" "Delighted," she replied, "even if it is the second-class kind." There may perhaps be a difference of opinion about the extent to which this woman's opinion is to be accepted, but there is no doubting that she saw clearly that in the service of God some do better than others. So with the way people look at Thomas. There are those who put him firmly in a lower class.

But this is unwarranted. After all, all those who have so far said to have believed after the resurrection did so *after* they saw. This was true of the Beloved Disciple, as he says expressly (v. 8; we are not in a position to say precisely what it was that he saw that caused his faith, but we should notice his explicit statement that for him sight preceded faith). This was the case also with Mary when she saw Jesus standing outside the tomb and with the ten when Jesus met them in their closed and locked room. While Thomas had been more forthright than any of the others in expressing his refusal to believe until he saw Jesus, his faith must not be downgraded. At the very least we must admire his straightforwardness in expressing his doubts and his immediate change of opinion when he stood before Jesus. Faith arising because we have seen Jesus in some way is not a bad thing.

Jesus went on to say, "Blessed are those who have not seen and yet have believed." He does not say "more blessed," as though to indicate that he is moving from a less worthy faith to a better one. Both groups of believers are "blessed." At the time the words were spoken there cannot have been many who were in the position of believing without seeing: all those of whom we have knowledge had seen and then believed. But, of course, there were others who had trusted Jesus in his lifetime and no doubt some of them believed on the basis of what the apostles told them. Jesus pronounces a blessing on them.

After Jesus ascended the possibility of seeing him here on this earth was taken away. There might be occasional exceptions, like the appearance to Saul of Tarsus as he journeyed to Damascus. But for most Christians this was not the way. They believed without seeing, and this is characteristic of discipleship to this very day. We who have not had the privilege of being with the Lord as he moved about Palestine in ancient times or of seeing him when he rose from the dead may yet rejoice that this benediction has been pronounced on us. It is a very blessed thing indeed to believe when we have nothing visible to point to. We have our Lord's own word for this.

The Purpose of This Gospel

John adds a few words to convey the reason for writing his book. He begins by making it clear that he has not given an exhaustive account. There were many things he knew but did not include (v. 30). And in saying this he does not even refer to incidents in which Jesus took a part or to teaching he imparted to his followers. He speaks only of "signs." As we have seen in earlier studies, this is one of the ways in which John characterizes the miracles of Jesus. It is not the only way. He sometimes speaks of them as "works," the kind of thing he does just as naturally as we do our "work" of whatever kind it is.

But when he speaks of them as "signs" he is referring to them as "significant." They are deeds of power and they are marvels that people are quite unable to explain. But more important than that is the fact that they are meaningful. Those who have eyes to see look beyond the miracle and see the hand of God. Rightly understood, Jesus' "signs" bring a powerful message to those who are open to receive it. John says now that he has done no more in this Gospel than make a selection from the host of signs that Jesus did. There were many more, as we can see for ourselves if we read what is written in the other Gospels. John does not give us the same selection of miracles as do the others, but even when we have added what they say to what John says we have no reason for thinking that we have a full account of all Jesus' wonderful deeds. We do, however, have enough to see that God acted in a special way through Jesus.

John says that Jesus did the signs, written or not, "before his disciples." This does not mean that he did no signs without an audience, as though he were a public performer. He may have done other signs in private; there is nothing we know about his methods that rules out the possibility. But throughout this Gospel John has drawn attention to the importance of bearing witness and is here speaking of those things Jesus did to which his disciples can bear this witness. These things are well attested. The reader is assured that there is ample testimony to justify believing.

Karl Heim, a great German scholar, finds it important that John says nothing about a great number of signs. He points out that disciples collect everything they can about a dead prophet: that is all they have of him. But with a living person it is different. Then disciples say only what is necessary to introduce him to other people. John's Lord was (and is) living, and John says only what is necessary to introduce him to his readers.

Now he moves from what is not written to what is. "These," John says, "have been written in order that you may believe. . ." (v. 31). The verb translated "written" is in the perfect tense, like Pilate's "What I have written, I have written" (19:22). There is something permanent about it. John's account is on record and stays there. And his purpose is evangelistic: ". . . that you may believe."

There is a textual problem of some importance here. The manuscripts are divided, with some reading the aorist tense of the verb and some the present. The difference between the two is slight (only one letter), and whichever is original it would be very easy for a scribe to write the other by mistake. If the letter is included, we have the aorist, which strictly means "that you may come to believe"; in that case the Gospel has a straight evangelistic purpose. If it is omitted, we have the present with the meaning "that you may keep on believing"; in that case the Gospel is meant to help believers go on in the faith. But perhaps we can make too much of the difference. Whichever tense we read, we should discern an evangelistic thrust but also the demand for a continuing attitude: John wants people to make an initial commitment to Christ, but also to go on in the faith. He looks for them to believe and to keep on believing.

John proceeds to put some content into Christian faith. It is not enough simply to believe: it matters *what* we believe. So John says he wants his readers to believe "that Jesus is the Christ, the Son of God." As we look back over his Gospel we can see that this aim is abundantly clear. He has written in such a way that the attentive reader may indeed come to believe that Jesus is the Christ, the very Son of God. In what he said and what he did and what he was Jesus made that abundantly plain. In modern times there have been people who have thought that Jesus was nothing more than a good man, a humble teacher who taught important truths. This is true as far as it goes, but it does not go far enough for John. For him it is important to see that Jesus is the Christ, God's Son, and from the beginning he has had before him the aim of making that clear to all his readers.

Faith in Jesus as the Christ, the Son of God, does not leave people where they were. It leads to eternal life, life which John here says is "life in his name." The "name," as we have seen, means all that the person is. John is saying that life, real life—life that lasts through eternity—is life that comes from Christ in all his being. When we put our trust in him, we have life and we have it through eternity.

88

A Wonderful Catch of Fish

After these things Jesus manifested himself again to the disciples by the Sea of Tiberias; and he manifested himself like this. There were together Simon Peter and Thomas who is called "Twin," and Nathanael from Cana of Galilee and the sons of Zebedee and two others of his disciples. Simon Peter says to them, "I'm going fishing." They say to him, "We're coming with you." They went out and embarked in the boat and that night they caught nothing. When it was already becoming early in the morning Jesus stood on the beach; the disciples, however, did not know that it was Jesus. So Jesus says to them, "Lads, you haven't caught anything, have you?" They answered him, "No." He said to them, "Cast the net on the right side of the boat and you will find something." Therefore they cast it, and they were no longer able to haul it in for the number of the fish. Therefore that disciple whom Jesus loved says to Peter, "It is the Lord." So Simon Peter, when he had heard that it was the Lord, girded on his tunic, for he was stripped, and threw himself into the sea. But the other disciples came with the little boat, for they were not far from the land, but about two hundred cubits off, dragging the net of the fishes. When therefore they had disembarked on to the land they see a charcoal fire set and a fish set on it and bread. Jesus says to them, "Bring of the fish which you have now caught." Simon Peter therefore went up and dragged the net to the land, full of large fish, a hundred and fifty-three of them; and although there were so many of them the net was not torn. Jesus says to them, "Come and have breakfast." Now none of the disciples dared to ask him, "Who are you?" knowing that it was the Lord. Jesus comes and takes the bread and gives it to them and the fish likewise. This is now the third time that Jesus was manifested to the disciples after he had risen from the dead (John 21:1–14).

Many scholars think that this Gospel originally ended at what we now call the close of chapter 20. They think that either the original author or someone else later added chapter 21. The most important reason for holding this view is that 20:30–31 looks so very much like the end of a book and this is supported by the fact that to some people chapter 21 looks something like a postscript rather than something that was intended from the first.

There is no way of proving either that this chapter was or was not part of the original Gospel. We can say that we know of no manuscript that lacks it, so that if it was an addition, that addition was made very early. We can say also that the style is much the same as that of the first twenty chapters, so that the probability is that it was written by the same author, whether at the time he wrote the bulk of the Gospel or some time later. The point is not important; as there is no real evidence to decide it we simply notice the difference of opinion and pass on. What is certain is that it forms part of John's Gospel as that Gospel has always been known in the church.

John links what follows with the preceding with the words "After these things" (v. 1). This, of course, refers not to 20:30–31, but to the preceding accounts of the appearances of Jesus. What John is about to relate did not take place on the first Easter Day or in the days that followed immediately; it was later. How much later he does not say, and as the other Gospels do not mention this appearance we have no way of knowing. This is the longest account we have of a post-resurrection appearance in Galilee; most of the accounts concern appearances in and around Jerusalem. John says that Jesus "manifested" himself, where the verb has a meaning like "revealed himself," "showed himself." It is not often used of the post-resurrection appearances (again only in Mark 16:12, 14). The word implies that Jesus certainly existed, even if he was not seen or heard by his followers. His existence was in another world, but he could, as on this occasion, "show himself" to people here and now.

A Fishing Trip

This showing of himself took place, John says, "by the Sea of Tiberias." We usually refer to this sheet of water as the Sea of Galilee, and it seems likely that our way was the way it was named in the time of

Jesus (in the Old Testament it was also called the Sea of Chinnereth, and in Luke 5:1 it is the Lake of Gennesaret). But about A.D. 20 a town was founded on its shores and called "Tiberias" after the emperor. The sea adjoining the town eventually came to be called by the same name, but it took quite a few years for this to happen. John is apparently here using the name by which it was known at the time he was writing his Gospel.

It seems that the apostolic band no longer remained together, and John proceeds to list those who were concerned in the incident he is about to narrate (v. 2). As is his custom he gives us the full name, "Simon Peter" (which he does seventeen times, a strong contrast with the Synoptists, who have it no more than six times between the three of them). He goes on to list Thomas (and explain that he was called "Twin") and Nathanael (whom we have not met since he was brought to Jesus by Philip in chapter 1). The next expression must be translated "the sons of Zebedee," but the word "sons" is missing. There is no doubt about John's meaning, for he has the masculine form of "the" so that the expression means "Zebedee's men," and in this context these men must be his sons. John does not use the expression elsewhere; indeed he does not name Zebedee elsewhere. And, of course, he never names either of the sons. It is all in keeping with the fact that he does not name the members of his family. But he is letting us know that he and his brother James were members of the fishing party. There were also two others, but apart from the fact that they were disciples of Jesus he says nothing about them. Evidently in this context it did not matter who they were.

It was Peter who started things moving. "I'm going fishing," he says (v. 3). It has sometimes been thought that this means "I'm going back to the old life. I'm going to resume living as a fisherman." In support of this it is urged that Peter uses the present tense and that this naturally refers to a continuing activity. So it does, but it is reading a lot into it to see it without any supporting evidence as referring to a change of lifestyle. We should rather understand Peter to refer to one occasion. Quite clearly the band of apostles was in a rather uncertain mood during the time between the resurrection and the ascension. The appearances that took place from time to time were wonderful, but the apostles could not predict them, and with only five recorded over a period of six weeks they were not the kind of thing that set the pattern of one's whole life. At the time of the ascension they were commissioned to take the gospel to the whole world, and not many days later, on the day of Pentecost, they were given the help of the Holy Spirit to fulfill their commission. From then they were men with a mission, men who knew what they stood for and what they were going to do.

But in this intermediate period they must have been very uncertain. The gloom of Good Friday had been replaced by the joy of Easter Day.

Life would never be the same for them. But what were they to do? Did Jesus plan to resume the old life and lead them as they moved through Palestine? Did he have something else for them to do? They did not know, and until they did know their position was a difficult one.

So on this day Peter announced a fishing trip. At least it was something to do, it meant engaging in a craft where they were very much at home, and it was a useful thing to increase the supply of food. So Peter's announcement rang a bell. They all immediately agreed to join him and the band of seven set out. P. Loyd commends them for this and draws a useful lesson. "When the pause comes and the vision begins to be less vivid," he writes,"we are not to be idle or despondent. We are to go on with the obvious tasks of every day." He goes on to exclaim, "How wise were these disciples who calmly went back to their fishing." Whether this is a complete explanation of the disciples' position or not, at least it is useful for us to reflect that our moments of vision and exaltation are high points. They are not the staple of everyday life. And in everyday life there are humdrum tasks that we do well not to neglect.

John tells us that the little party "went out" but does not say from where. It may be that they were in a house together, but the verb is a very general one and we do not know. He goes on to say that they "embarked in the boat" but does not explain this either. "The" boat seems to indicate a definite boat, perhaps the boat they had in the past habitually used for fishing, but again the expression does not tell us.

But John does tell us that the expedition was a failure. Nighttime was held to be the best time for fishing, and not only in Palestine. Aristotle, the great Greek philosopher, says "Fishermen, especially, do their fishing before sunrise and after sunset." And, of course, fish caught during the night could be sold bright and early in the market. It was clearly the best time. So this party had the favored time for fishing but to no avail. "They caught nothing." Fish can be exasperating!

A Great Catch

As the day was breaking Jesus stood on the beach (v. 4). The word for "early" is connected with "first" and points to "first light," "dawn." "Becoming early in the morning" is a very awkward piece of English, but I have put it that way to bring out the force of the Greek as I see it. Some manuscripts have "it had become," but the best reading appears to be the present "it was becoming." John is not saying that day had already begun, but rather that it was already coming into existence, beginning to dawn.

John has another unusual piece of Greek when he says that Jesus "stood on to the beach." We expect him to say that Jesus stood "on" the beach (as in my translation), but he uses a preposition that conveys the thought of motion toward. He has done the same thing twice with his statements that the risen Jesus "stood in the middle" in his appearances to the disciples in Jerusalem (20:19, 26). Perhaps on all three occasions John is hinting at the mysterious nature of Jesus' appearances. At one moment he was not there and the next he had come "into" the middle of them, here "on to" the beach.

But, from the boat away out on the sea and in the half light of early dawn, it would not have been easy for them to recognize him. We must also bear in mind that on a number of occasions the risen Jesus was not immediately recognized, even by disciples who had been very close to him. We saw that in the story of Mary Magdalene in the previous chapter (cf. 20:14), and, of course, the classic illustration is the walk to Emmaus, when for a lengthy period two people who knew Jesus well walked and talked with him without knowing who he was. Whether it was the dimness of the morning light or the unusualness of the appearance of the risen Jesus, John does not say. But the important thing was simply that they did not know who it was who was there on the beach.

Jesus called out to them (characteristically John makes it vivid with the use of the present tense, "says"): "Lads, you haven't caught anything, have you?" (v. 5). The word for "lads" more literally means "little children," and John uses it for the nobleman's little boy in 4:49 and even for a newborn baby in 16:21. But it can be used to address adults, as for example in 1 John 2:18. For that matter, in many languages we have a similar usage. In French *garçon* may mean "boy," but it is also used of men of any age in certain contexts. Moulton and Milligan cite a use of the term for soldiers, and in another place for "slaves." John's word does not appear to have been used often as a form of address to men, but it is not unexampled, and "lads" brings out the force of it.

Jesus' question looks for a negative answer. He knew that they had had no success. In passing we may notice that John often uses the Greek construction that looks for a negative answer, but in the words of Jesus he does this twice only (in 6:67 and here). His verb more literally means "you don't have," but there is evidence that this is the way a person speaking Greek in antiquity would put to a hunter or a fisherman the question about whether he had been successful. I have used the word "anything" because the term John employs does not strictly mean "fish." In those days bread was the staple food and made up the most part of the meal, especially for the poor. But something would be eaten in addition to bread, and it is this addition that John's word strictly means. But in many places what was eaten in addition to bread was fish, and thus it was a natural term to be used in a question directed to fishermen who had obviously been engaged in their craft over a long period.

They responded with a monosyllabic "No." It had been a disappointing night and they clearly did not want to talk about it. Human activity can be fruitless. I am reminded that Igor Stravinsky when he was eighty-eight years old pointed out that there is "a very lively business being done with one's demise." Obviously at that age Stravinsky had no long life expectancy, and he went on to say, "I have been consulted about memorial concerts, record albums, posthumous TV programs—and offered good fees too. But I would like to know how I am supposed to collect them!" We can understand that all sorts of people would want to cash in on the good man's death, but as far as he was concerned it was a fruitless pursuit and he wanted none of it.

The disciples were just as disinclined to talk about their fruitless pursuit. But a surprise was in store for them. The man who stood on the shore did not want to talk about their failure. He simply gave them a command for success: "Cast the net on the right side of the boat and you will find something" (v. 6). The Greek here is very unusual, but fortunately the meaning is fairly clear.

But why should the disciples cast the net on the right side? That is not so clear. Some have suggested that at that time people normally cast the net on the left side, and they hold that Jesus was telling the fishermen to do something different from their normal custom (as he did in Luke 5:4, when he told them to let their nets down in daytime and was met by Peter's reply that they had already fished all night without success, v. 5). But I have not been able to find any reference in ancient writings that tells us which was the favored side or even whether there was a favored side.

Another suggestion is that the right side was the lucky side. This may well have been the case in pagan circles, but John does not speak of luck and it is impossible to think of the risen Jesus telling the fishermen to trust in luck. Yet another idea is that from the shore Jesus could see a school of fish appearing on the right side of the boat and was accordingly directing the fishermen to cast their net there. But there is no hint of this in the narrative, and it seems highly unlikely.

Rather, John is telling us that the risen Jesus was able to bring about something that the fishermen could not bring about. They, with all their knowledge and skill, caught nothing. He, with a word, brought about a catch the like of which they had not seen before (except possibly the one in Luke 5). They did as Jesus suggested and found so many fish in their net that they were no longer able to haul in their catch. It was a spectacular change in the state of affairs. All night—nothing. Now one cast—and the net was full.

"It Is the Lord"

That was enough to enable one of the fishermen to know who the stranger on the shore was. We have not been told hitherto that the Beloved Disciple was among the fishermen. He must have been one of the two "sons of Zebedee" or one of the two unnamed disciples (v. 2). From other considerations it seems that we should understand that he was John the son of Zebedee. When he saw the catch he said to Peter, "It is the Lord" (v. 7). As we saw earlier, this is the way the followers of Jesus tended to refer to him after the resurrection. It is certainly very suitable at this point when such a stupendous miracle has been wrought.

Peter immediately took action. We read that he did this "when he had heard that it was the Lord"; evidently he could not see this for himself. This may be because of the distance from the shore and the uncertain light. Even when he was told who it was he may have been unable to discern Jesus' features in those conditions. But there may be the thought that he did not have the spiritual perception to work it out for himself. After all, the light and the distance were the same for the Beloved Disciple, and in any case we read that it was because that disciple saw the miraculous catch—not because it was now light enough for him to recognize who was standing on the shore calling out to them—that he said, "It is the Lord." It still takes spiritual perception to see the Lord in what happens to us in everyday life.

There is a bit of a problem in what followed. Some translations tell us that Peter was "naked" (e.g., KJV), but this is probably incorrect. Complete nudity would offend Jewish ideas of what was right, and in any case it is unlikely that a man would work through the cool hours of the night with nothing on at all. I have translated it "stripped," which means "stripped for work," "stripped of his outer garments." The "tunic" that he now girded on is not the name of a specific garment; it means an outer garment, whatever it was. "Tunic" seems a reasonable word, for that is probably what a fisherman would have as his outer clothing.

A further difficulty is why Peter "girded on" some clothing prior to jumping into the sea to swim ashore. We would have expected the reverse procedure. A man commonly removes what will impede him in swimming; he does not add to his clothing before getting into the water. There are two real possibilities to consider. One is that among the Jews a greeting was a religious act and for them a religious act could not be performed naked. We see this in the fact that Jews did not greet one another in the baths. There all were naked and therefore a religious greeting was impossible. Peter may have had it in mind that he would need to be properly clothed when he met the Lord, so he girded on his tunic.

The other possibility lies in the meaning of the word I have translated as "girded on." It is not a common word; in the New Testament it is used only of Jesus girding himself preparatory to washing the disciples' feet in the Upper Room (18:4, 5) and here of Peter. There is no other example. So Peter now, so to speak, "tied his tunic round himself." The tunic may have been what Brown calls a fisherman's smock; if this was all Peter was wearing, he was naked underneath it and therefore could not take it off. The alternative was to tuck it into his girdle, and that was what he did. In this case there is no addition of clothing before swimming; there is simply a sensible rearrangement of the very simple garment Peter was wearing.

Whichever be the true explanation of Peter's clothing, that apostle "threw himself into the sea," which presumably means that he swam ashore. But John does not say this. In fact he says nothing more about Peter until he drew the net ashore (v. 11). Did any of the others follow Peter's example? John does not say. He does not even tell us how and when Peter got ashore, so it remains uncertain whether his impulsive leap into the sea gained him anything (Hoskyns, for example, thinks that the people in the ship got to shore before Peter did! It all depends on how fast a swimmer Peter was and how fast the ship was). For John these things were not important. What was important was that the Beloved Disciple was the first to recognize Jesus and that Peter was the first to act.

Breakfast on the Shore

The rest of the crew came ashore with the boat (v. 8). This time John uses a diminutive, "little boat," but this is probably no more than a stylistic variant. The diminutive termination was often used in the first century with no real difference from the general form (for that matter, in common speech these days we often refer to "the little old—" without meaning either that the object in question is ancient in years or diminutive in size). The disciples in the boat did not have far to come, and John gives the distance as "about two hundred cubits" (a cubit was the distance from the elbow to the tip of the middle finger, about eighteen inches). Evidently they still found the net full of fish to be too heavy to haul on board, so they simply dragged it along.

When the party landed they found a charcoal fire (v. 9; John had earlier spoken of a charcoal fire in the high priest's courtyard, 18:18; he is the only New Testament writer to refer to charcoal). "A fish" was evidently cooking on the fire, but we need not think that the bread was being cooked as well; it was simply there.

Jesus called on the mariners to bring some of the fish they had caught (v. 10). This time the word for "fish" is in the plural, which contrasts with the singular in the previous verse. Some scholars think that Jesus' call for the disciples to bring some of the fish is merely in order that they may exhibit it; they think that Jesus was going to supply the meal for them all in something like the way he fed the five thousand with a few loaves and fishes. But there is nothing in the narrative to indicate this. It seems rather that John is saying that Jesus invited them to bring what they had caught in order to make their contribution to breakfast.

This brought Peter into the action once more. We do not know exactly when he reached the shore or what he did when he got there, but he was certainly there and available when Jesus asked for the fish. Clearly the fishermen had still not brought the fish to land, for Peter went up and dragged the net to the shore (v. 11). We have already discovered that the net full of fish was too heavy to be hauled into the boat (v. 6), so this probably means that Peter organized the bringing of the net to land rather than that he engaged in a virtuoso performance on his own.

At this point John tells us that there were "a hundred and fifty-three" fish. There has been endless speculation as to why John records this number and the meaning he found in it. Probably the simplest explanation is the best: he records it because that was the number actually caught. The fishermen would have to count them, for the catch would be divided among them all and a count was a necessary preliminary. Quite apart from that, fishermen have always delighted to remember the details of unusual catches. All this is true, but there was no imperative reason to record the number in the gospel account, and we may well recall that there is no number in the marvelous catch narrated for us in Luke 5. It is possible that John saw some significance in the number, and perhaps we should look at some of the suggestions that have been put forward.

It is often said that a hundred and fifty-three is the total number of kinds of fish in existence according to the ancients and that John records it as a way of saying that the gospel gathers in people of every kind. This is attractive, but unfortunately it does not seem to be well based. That there were held to be a hundred and fifty-three kinds of fish rests on a statement found in Jerome to the effect that a writer called Oppianus Cilix, "a very learned poet," says this. But unfortunately no one else has been able to find this statement, and the suspicion arises that Jerome is simply giving a plausible reason for an edifying interpretation. Pliny, who is much nearer the date of the New Testament, wrote a book entitled *Natural History* in which he says that there were seventy-four kinds of fish. It seems clear that this interpretation, while popular in some circles, is not soundly based.

Others point out that a hundred and fifty-three is the sum of all the numbers from one to seventeen. That means it is the sum of ten, the number of the Law, and seven, the number of the sevenfold gifts of the Spirit. Others point to seventy-six, the sum of the numbers symbolized by the letters of Simon's name, which, if added to seventy-seven, the sum of those in the word for "fish," gives us the total of the fish here. They suggest that John's use of the number is in order to tell us that Simon is the divinely commissioned fisher of men. Others see a reference to the Trinity, for the number is three times fifty plus three. There seems no point in going further with this sort of interpretation. The possibilities are limited only by the imaginations of ingenious thinkers. But there is no real reason for thinking that John meant any of them. He is surely doing no more than recording a fact noted at the time.

John adds the point that despite the great number the net was not torn (as it was in Luke 5:6). This could possibly be meant to draw attention to the power of the risen Lord; believers with him at their head are never in danger of being overpowered. But again it may be no more than a detail that John has recorded.

Jesus called the little group to breakfast (v. 12) and indeed personally distributed the bread and the fish to them (v. 13). John tells us that none of the men dared to ask Jesus "Who are you?" since they knew who he was. This is all rather curious. Why should they ask such a question? We should probably understand that they were nervous because of the very unusual circumstances in which they found themselves. They had gone out for a normal fishing trip and had caught nothing though they fished all night. Then, in response to a command from on shore, they had let down their net and caught an extraordinary number of fish. The Beloved Disciple had told Peter that it was the Lord, so they knew it was he. But everything was so strange. They were probably somewhat nervous and strained and did not know what to say.

John rounds off the story by telling his readers that this was "the third time that Jesus was manifested to the disciples after he had risen from the dead" (v. 14). It was not his third appearance; he had appeared to Mary Magdalene and to others. But this was the third time that the members of the apostolic band had experienced such an appearance (the previous two being the appearances narrated in the previous chapter to the disciples without Thomas and then a week later with him).

89

Peter Restored

When therefore they had breakfasted Jesus says to Simon Peter, "Simon, son of John, do you love me more than these?" He says to him, "Yes, Lord, you know that I love you." He says to him, "Feed my lambs." He says to him again, a second time, "Simon, son of John, do you love me?" He says to him, "Yes, Lord, you know that I love you." He says to him, "Tend my sheep." He says to him the third time, "Simon, son of John, do you love me?" Peter was grieved because he said to him the third time, "Do you love me?" and he says to him, "Lord, you know all things, you know that I love you." Jesus says to him, "Feed my sheep. Truly, truly I tell you, when you were younger you used to gird yourself and walk where you willed; but when you are old you will stretch out your hands and another will gird you and lead you where you do not will (to go)." This he said signifying by what death he would glorify God. And when he had said this he says to him, "Follow me" (John 21:15–19).

Throughout Jesus' public ministry the Gospels make it clear that Peter was the leader of the apostolic band. But then, at the time of the crucifixion, three times he had denied to Jesus' enemies that he was a follower of Jesus, denied that he even knew him. Probably in the general gloom that overwhelmed the little group when Jesus was crucified not much notice was taken of this. After all, at the critical moment they had all forsaken Jesus and fled away. After he died there was not much room for distinguishing one lack of heroism from another and not much point in it either.

But then Jesus rose.

Now the gloom had gone and the disciples could face life again. From time to time, as we have seen in the last few studies, Jesus appeared to his followers, sometimes to one or two individuals, sometimes to groups. It was clear that he had not been defeated by death but had conquered it. During those weeks it could not have been clear to them where their path of duty lay, but it was quite plain that there was a future for those who had followed Jesus. No longer were they a dispirited little band with no purpose and with no hope. They did not know what Jesus would want them to do or where he would want them to go. But he was alive and would certainly want them to do something. Doubtless he would make it all clear in due course.

Where did Peter stand in all this? They had always looked to him and he had not failed them. But in the crisis he had failed Jesus. Would Jesus replace him with someone else? Would Jesus remind them sometime of those terrible denials when Peter had hobnobbed with the enemy at the very time that the Master was going through the legal processes that in due course would lead to his crucifixion? It must have been an unsettling time for them all, as well as a time when they rejoiced in the great truth that Jesus was alive.

All this is the background to the story to which we now come. The general thrust of it is quite clear—Jesus was restoring Peter to his place as leader and spokesman for the little group. Publicly before a few of his followers he was charging Peter to follow him and to be a shepherd to others who likewise followed him. But, while the general thrust is so plain that it cannot be mistaken, there are several problems about details. We shall note them as we go along.

Love More Than These

The incident now to be narrated followed the breakfast Jesus had with the little group of disciples on the shore of the sea of Tiberias. Jesus addressed a question to Simon Peter, and John makes it clear that this was a solemn and important occasion, first by using the full name "Simon Peter" as he introduces this disciple and then with the formula "Simon, son of John" in the opening of Jesus' question (v. 15). It is an interesting minor point that although Jesus gave to Simon the name Peter (1:42; Mark 3:16), there is only one occasion on which he is reported to have addressed him by this name (Luke 22:34; cf. Matt. 16:18). Usually he calls him simply "Simon." The other disciples often call him "Peter" and, as we have noted, John mostly has the full name "Simon

Peter." On this occasion Jesus includes the fact that he was the son of John, which makes the address somewhat more formal and solemn than would otherwise be the case.

The question put to him is this, "Do you love me more than these?" where the comparison raises a problem: to what does "these" refer? The word might be masculine, with the meaning "Do you love me more than these men?" Or it might be neuter: "Do you love me more than these things?" And if it is masculine, it might be understood as "Do you love me more than you love these men?" or "Do you love me more than these men love me?" There is something to be said for each of these ways of taking it.

Did Peter love Jesus more than he loved the disciples with whom he had gone fishing? He had three times denied that he even knew Jesus, but his loyalty to his fellow disciples was unquestioned as far as we know. Right there and then he had just completed a fishing expedition in which he was their partner. Clearly he was prepared to associate with them and work with them. So it is possible that Jesus was forcing Peter to look at the question "To whom is your love really directed?" Whatever fine words he might say, did Peter's deep affection rest on his comrades, men with whom he was working in the old familiar way, or on Jesus, the Lord whom he had denied?

We might think it unlikely that Jesus would ask Peter to compare his love for Jesus with the love others had for the Master. But it is not an impossible meaning of the words, and Peter had given reason for such a comparison. In the Upper Room Peter had said to Jesus, "Even if all should take offense [RSV, "fall away"] because of you, I will never take offense" (Matt. 26:33; Mark 14:29). He used the emphatic pronoun for "I," and this sets him in sharp contrast with the others. He had certainly claimed a higher loyalty if not a warmer love. And in this Gospel it has been reported that Peter said he was ready to lay down his life for Jesus (13:37), which we should possibly take in conjunction with Jesus' later words that "no one has greater love than this, that one lays down his life for his friends" (15:13). Peter had claimed a readiness to give the supreme proof of love for Jesus, and he is certainly implying that his love was greater than that of others, even if he does not say this in set terms. So it is far from impossible that Jesus is now asking him whether he still stands by his claim.

Or Jesus may be referring to the boat and the nets and the fish and the comradeship of people who had worked together all through the night, even against the discouragement of catching nothing. This stood for a whole way of life. Peter had been a fisherman before he came to Jesus and right at that moment was a fisherman again. What was at the center of his love? Peter had been through some difficult times with the arrest and the crucifixion of the Master for whose sake he had left "home and toil and kindred." That period must have been a harrowing one for all those who had cast in their lot with Jesus of Nazareth. Then came the wonder of the resurrection and of the intermittent appearances of Jesus to some of his followers. It must have been a wonderful time but must also have caused its strains; it certainly was not a tranquil time. After all this, was Peter ready to say, "Enough is enough. I'm going back to the old, familiar life. It may not have many mountaintop experiences, but it is without the deep valleys through which I have had to go!"?

All three ways of understanding the question are possible, even though legitimate objections may be raised against each. Perhaps in the end we should conclude that there is most to be said for the second view, the view that Jesus is asking Peter whether, in view of all that has happened, he still stands by his boast that he would stand by Jesus when everybody else failed. Had his loyalty been shaken by all that he had gone through since that night in the Upper Room? Or did he still adhere to Jesus with a deep and lasting love?

Peter's reply is that he does love Jesus. He uses the address "Lord," which shows that he still claims to be a follower, a servant of his risen Master. He is not claiming a high place, but a low one, and in doing so is maintaining the link with Jesus. And he goes on to appeal to Jesus' knowledge of the facts. He does not say, "I certainly do love you" or "Of course I love you" or anything like that. He says, "*You* know that I love you" and he employs the emphatic pronoun *you.* The force of it is "Whatever be the case with other people, surely *you* know my love for you."

Words for Love

But in Peter's reply we have a different word for "love" from that used by Jesus, and the question arises as to whether this change of vocabulary signifies a change of meaning or whether it is no more than a matter of style. Jesus uses the verb *agapao,* but Peter replies with *phileo.* The same is true in the second question, but in the third Jesus changes and uses Peter's word *phileo.* When we meet either of these verbs alone we have no hesitation in translating it as "love," but when the two occur in the one context it seems reasonable to many people to look for a difference in meaning.

Here it is possible to take the passage in the sense given in *The Living Bible,* where Jesus' question is "Do you love me?" and Peter's reply is "You know I am your friend" (the same distinction is found in the margin of NEB). This understands the verb *agapao* to denote a higher kind of love than *phileo,* and this is often the way the distinction is understood.

Indeed, at the present time I think it is the distinction most often accepted.

William Hendriksen sets out this distinction in these terms: "we believe that *agapao in this story* (and generally throughout the Gospels, though *with varying degree of distinctness in meaning*) indicates love, deep-seated, thorough-going, intelligent and purposeful, a love in which the entire personality (not only the emotions, but also the mind and the will) plays a prominent part, which is based on esteem for the object loved or else on reasons which lie wholly outside of this object; while *phileo* indicates (or at least tends in the direction of) spontaneous natural affection, in which the emotions play a more prominent role than either the intellect or the will." This way of understanding the two words takes the passage to mean that Jesus is asking Peter whether he has the higher and richer kind of love for him, and Peter is replying that he does not claim so much, but that he does have a real, if lesser, kind of love. When they come to the third question Jesus comes down to Peter's level.

Such a way of understanding the variation makes a good deal of sense and it is not surprising that many people take it this way. But we should perhaps notice that in an earlier day exactly the same verbs were understood in practically the opposite way. Thus R. C. Trench wrote an important book on synonyms in the New Testament. It was published in 1854, went through several editions, and is still used as a standard work. In the edition I have Trench notes that Jesus' question uses the verb *agapao* and proceeds: "At this moment, when all the pulses in the heart of the now penitent Apostle are beating with a passionate affection toward his Lord, this word on that Lord's lips sounds far too cold; to very imperfectly express the warmth of his affection toward Him. The question in any form would have been grievous enough (ver. 17); the language in which it is clothed makes it more grievous still. He therefore in his answer substitutes for the *agapas* of Christ the word of a more personal love, *philo se* (ver. 15). And this he does not on the first occasion only, but again upon a second. And now at length he has triumphed; for when his Lord puts the question to him a third time, it is not *agapas* any more, but *phileis*."

This second way is understood by a number of scholars. Thus C. B. Williams holds that *agapao* means "to love intelligently, with devotion" and *phileo* "to love tenderly, with personal affection." He translates Jesus' question with "Are you really devoted to me?" and Peter's reply as "I tenderly love you." G. H. C. MacGregor sees the distinction most likely to be made as that the first verb denotes "the esteem existing between benefactor and recipient" and the second "the personal affection existing between members of the same family."

It would be possible to go on for a long time citing opinions, for many have committed themselves to a difference in meaning between the verbs and come down heavily on the side of their favored view. But unfortunately others come down just as heavily on the other side. We find an interesting illustration in the translations of E. J. Goodspeed and H. J. Schonfield. Goodspeed translated Jesus' question as "Are you devoted to me?" and Peter's reply as "I love you," while Schonfield exactly reversed the translations.

The fact that those who find a difference in meaning are not able to agree as to which is the higher and which the lower form of love arouses the suspicion that they are reading something into the text and that the difference is not something John intended when he recorded the dialogue. And to see a difference is to ignore the fact that John habitually uses words that are near synonyms but without putting a difference in meaning between them. For example, Greek has two words for "to send," and John uses both with considerable frequency but in much the same sense. He has five words for "seeing," and it is impossible to say that they consistently denote different kinds of sight. So is it with two verbs for "to know"; there may be significant differences in the way they are used by some authors, but it is impossible to find a difference in meaning in John. There are other such words but there is no point in making a lengthy list.

It seems clear that he does this with the two words for "love." Thus he speaks of "the disciple whom Jesus loved" with the use of the verb *agapao* in 13:23, 25 and other places, but with *phileo* in 20:2. Are we to think of two "beloved disciples," one of whom Jesus loved rather more than the other? It seems clear that this is no more than John's liking for variation. The fact is that he habitually varies his use of words with no appreciable difference in meaning, and it is best to understand him as doing this in the present passage. Jesus asks Peter whether he loves him, and Peter replies that he does.

This is strengthened by the fact that it is not easy to see a consistent difference between the two verbs in the way John uses them. He has a marked preference for *agapao,* which he uses thirty-seven times, whereas he employs *phileo* only thirteen times. We must expect accordingly that there will be some ways of using *agapao* for which there is no parallel with *phileo.* But for almost every use of *phileo* in this Gospel there is a parallel with *agapao.* Thus John uses the former verb for the Father's love for the Son in 5:20 and the latter in 3:35. The two verbs are used for the Father's love for the disciples (16:27 and 14:21), for Jesus' love for his followers (11:3, 36 and 13:1), and for Jesus' love for the Beloved Disciple (20:2 and 13:23). When we turn to the love that people exercise *phileo* is used of loving one's life and *agapao* of loving glory

(12:25 and 12:43); both are used of the disciples' loving Jesus (16:27 and 14:15). In the passage we are presently discussing the former verb is used several times for Peter's love for Jesus, while the latter is often used elsewhere of the disciples' love for him (8:42; 14:15, 21; etc.). The only use of *phileo* that seems to lack a parallel to *agapao* seems to be that for the love of the world for its own (15:19), and even here we may perhaps say that the love of believers for one another (love within a given group) forms an analogy (13:34; 15:12, 17).

This is reinforced by the fact that the conversation between Jesus and Peter would have taken place in Aramaic, and John is reporting it in Greek. The choice of the verbs would thus be John's and should be understood in terms of John's literary habits. We should also not miss the significance of Peter's reply. He begins with "Yes, Lord"; he is not correcting what Jesus said, but accepting it. Bernard asks, "Why should he say 'Yes,' if he means 'No'?" Our best understanding of the passage is that Peter is grieved that Jesus is raising a doubt about the reality of his love, not as to the exact quality of that love. (Perhaps I should make it clear that I am denying a difference in the meanings of the verbs *in John*. I am not saying that other writers do not make a difference in the ways they use the words. I have elsewhere put a good deal of emphasis on the difference between the nouns *agape* and *philia*, but that is another thing. Those differences are real, but they do not affect the fact that John appears to use the two verbs in much the same way.)

Tend the Flock

Jesus replies with a commission to Peter that it seems we should understand as "Feed my lambs." There are problems in the threefold charge that Jesus gives to Peter (vv. 15, 16, 17). Some of these concern the manuscripts, which vary as to whether we should read "lambs" or "sheep" or "small sheep." I do not think these variations are very important, and in this study in each case I plan simply to take the reading that seems generally accepted. It is not unlikely that John varied his terminology, so that he sometimes spoke of sheep and sometimes of lambs, but this is probably not important.

Another problem is whether we should take the different words to mean different people. Thus some think that when we read of lambs the reference is to children in the church, and when we read of sheep it is to adult members. There is no reason why Peter should not be given instruction about a variety of members, but it does not seem probable that in a passage like this it is different members that are in mind. Rather it would seem that we have another example of John's love for variation. Throughout the section Jesus is commissioning Peter to fulfill the role of shepherd to Christ's flock. Whatever the word, Peter is being charged to look after the whole flock.

Yet another problem concerns the verb used to instruct Peter in his duties about the flock. Here in verse 15 it is a verb with the meaning of feeding the flock, grazing them, and this verb is repeated in verse 17. But in verse 16 it is a more general term, with a meaning like "act as a shepherd to the flock," so that Peter is being instructed to do all that a shepherd should do. It is, however, unlikely that when Peter is told to feed the lambs or the sheep the meaning is that he should do no more than provide them with fodder. Once again we seem to be confronted with the Johannine habit of varying the language. Whatever the verb and whatever the precise meaning of that verb in isolation, in all three passages Peter is being instructed to be all that a shepherd ought to be to the sheep in his care.

Repetition of the Charge

Jesus thus put a question to Peter about his love and, having received the answer, went on to charge Peter to look after the feeding of the flock. Then the Lord repeated the process (v. 16). Again he asked Peter, "Simon, son of John, do you love me?" but this time he does not add "more than these." Whatever the precise meaning of this expression, it had served its purpose and does not figure in the subsequent dialogue. Peter's reply is exactly the same as the first time. He appeals to Jesus' knowledge of his servant as he affirms his love.

A third time the question and the answer come (v. 17), but this time Jesus' verb is the one Peter has been using throughout the exchange. As we saw earlier, this probably does not mean a significant difference in meaning and is underlined by the fact that Peter was grieved "because he said to him the third time. . . ." If there was a significant difference, this was not the third time Jesus had asked the question, but the first. What caused the apostle's grief was apparently not that Jesus was asking a new question, but that he had now asked the same question (with a different verb) three times. It was bad enough being compelled to face up to it once, worse to do it twice, and a cause for grief that the question came a third time.

This time Peter's answer is a little fuller. Previously he has said that Jesus knows his love; now he says, "Lord, you know all things"; as he omits the "Yes, Lord" of the two previous answers, he is apparently relying entirely on Jesus' knowledge. When he moves on to "you know that I love you" his verb for "know" is different from the one he has used in the two previous answers, but there seems no difference in meaning. In this exchange John has given us several examples of change of word without significant change of meaning, so this one should not surprise us. What is important is that Peter is aware of Jesus' knowledge of what goes on in the hearts of people (and in this third answer his knowledge of "all things"). And because of that knowledge Jesus must know of the love his unworthy servant bore him.

There can be not the slightest doubt that this incident means the restoration of Peter to his position of leadership. When he denied his Lord three times in the face of his enemies he acted in a way unworthy of a follower of Jesus. But now three times he has been given the opportunity of acknowledging his love for his Lord, and three times he has been commissioned to act as a pastor to the flock. It was a clear declaration before the other disciples that Peter was restored to his place.

We should not overlook the fact that in this expression of confidence in Peter the one thing Jesus asks concerns his love. He does not ask about his leadership abilities or his capacity to preach or his understanding of the gospel or anything except just this—does he love? In God's church today we are apt to pay attention to a great number of qualities before we think of love. It is salutary to reflect on the place of love in the New Testament understanding of Christianity. "The greatest of these is love" (1 Cor. 13:13). We should reflect on this more often than we do.

A Prophecy of Peter

Now Jesus looks to the future and utters a prophecy about what would happen to this apostle. He introduces it with the solemn "Truly, truly" (v. 18): what follows is significant and is to be noted carefully. Then Jesus reminds Peter of his experience during youth. He used then to gird himself, where the verb points to tying a belt or girdle of some sort to keep one's loose robes from hindering freedom of movement. With that is coupled "walk where you willed"; in those days Peter had complete freedom of movement.

But it will not always be thus. In Peter's old age he will stretch out his hands. It is not quite clear why this should be included, for there is nothing corresponding to it in the previous words, as there is for each of the other items. Thus young and old are contrasted, as are girding yourself and being girded, and walking where you willed and being led where you do not will to go. Perhaps it is a general expression to bring out the helplessness of the aged, who depend on other people for everything.

These words may be a prophecy of the preparations for crucifixion. At least that is the way the words were understood by many in antiquity. A standard lexicon points to a use of the word in this sense in Epictetus, and the Jewish historian Josephus speaks of people who were "stretched out" in a context in which he also says they were crucified. We cannot be sure that the word would of itself in this context carry the notion of crucifixion, but it certainly points to a situation in which Peter would be unable to determine his movements, and this leads naturally enough to the thought of his death as a martyr.

John explains that in this saying Jesus was speaking about the death that Peter would in due course die (v. 19). The explanation was needed, for the words of verse 18 do not point unambiguously to death. Evidently they were clear enough to Peter, but John adds a little explanation for the reader who might not see the point. Jesus was not speaking simply about Peter's being bound and detained, but about his death. And in his death he would glorify God. This is another example of the "humble glory" we see so often in this Gospel. The death Peter would die would not obviously be glory from the point of view of the heathen who saw it. But it would be a deliberate taking of a lowly place, and for John that is really glorious. He is saying that Peter would in due course die in lowly fashion and in that there is real glory.

And John rounds off this section of his narrative with Jesus' command to Peter, "Follow me." The present tense is used and that normally has a continuous sense; in this place it would mean "Keep on following me." That would have real point because in the past Peter's following of Jesus had been somewhat erratic. Sometimes he had been very, very right, but sometimes also he had been very, very wrong. Jesus is commanding him to keep on following him. Constancy is an important part of discipleship.

90

The Beloved Disciple

Peter turned and sees the disciple whom Jesus loved following, who also reclined on his breast at the supper and said, "Lord, who is it who is betraying you?" Peter then saw this man and says to Jesus, "Lord, what of this man?" Jesus says to him, "If I will that he remains until I come, what is that to you? You follow me." Therefore this saying went out among the brothers that that disciple would not die. But Jesus did not say to him that he would not die, but "If I will that he remains until I come, what is that to you?"

This is the disciple who testifies about these things and who wrote these things, and we know that his testimony is true.

Now there are many other things that Jesus did which if they were written every one, I suppose the world itself would not contain the books that would be written (John 21:20–25).

Peter must have been very greatly encouraged by the little session of question-and-answer that Jesus has just conducted with him. While clearly he did not like the repetition of the question about his love, it was undeniable that Jesus had now restored him to his position of leadership in the little group of apostles and thus in the little church as a whole. After the shame of Good Friday and the uncertainties in the weeks following the resurrection, it must have meant a great deal both to Peter and to the others to have his position clarified and his place of leadership endorsed by none less than the risen Lord himself.

Now Peter turned and saw his friend the Beloved Disciple following (v. 20). The verb "to follow" is sometimes used in the sense "follow as a supporter, an adherent" (in some such sense as that in mind when we say that some leader or would-be leader has secured a "following"), and this has led some scholars to hold that this is very much in mind at this point. Some suggest that whereas Peter had had to be told to follow Jesus (v. 19), the Beloved Disciple was doing this quite spontaneously: he did not need to be told. Others think that the Beloved Disciple was following Jesus to death (and they sometimes make this part of an argument that this disciple had died before these words were written). That there is included the thought that the Beloved Disciple was following in the way a disciple should may well be included, but more than that is probably not implied. We should beware of fanciful interpretations. As they walked the Beloved Disciple was behind Peter, so that when Peter turned round there he was.

John proceeds to make quite clear who was in mind by referring to the incident at the Last Supper when at Peter's suggestion this man, reclining as he was on Jesus' breast, had leaned back and asked the question, "Lord, who is it who is betraying you?" (13:23–25). Actually the question John had asked had been "Lord, who is it?" In the context of Jesus' prediction this had been all that it was necessary to say. But in recalling the question it is necessary to expand it a little to bring out the meaning of what was said then. The betrayal had obviously made a deep impression on the disciples and they remembered everything that was connected with it. We might have expected this identification of the Beloved Disciple to have been made when he was first introduced in this chapter (in v. 7). But John writes in his own way and does not necessarily do things as we would.

What of the Beloved Disciple?

Peter, now restored to leadership, saw his friend and took action. It is not clear why he did so; John's place would certainly be assigned him when and as his Lord determined, and that was really nothing to do with Peter. But perhaps, being the leader in the band, he wanted to know what was expected of those he would lead—and there was no one better to start with than the man behind him at that moment. So he asked, "Lord, what of this man?" (v. 21). His question is very terse: in the Greek it is literally "Lord, but this man, what?" This leaves it open to interpretation in more ways than one. Peter may be asking what work John will do, or where he will stand in the hierarchy now that the place of leadership has been made clear, or what will happen to him. It is not a precise question.

We might have been able to work out precisely what Peter wanted to know if Jesus had answered precisely as Peter expected. But he did not. He made it clear that what would happen to John was no concern of Peter's. "If I will that he remains until I come," Jesus said, "what is that to you?" (v. 22). The "if" construction implies nothing as to the fulfillment or otherwise of the condition. Jesus is not saying that he *does* will that John will remain, but simply suggesting the possibility. The thrust in his answer is that John's sphere of service and such matters as the length of his life have nothing to do with Peter. Whatever was involved in his tending Christ's flock, it did not include access to information about the service the Beloved Disciple would render.

"Remains" means "remains alive" (as, for example, in 1 Cor. 15:6), though perhaps we should remember that this same verb is the one used in the memorable passage in which Jesus speaks of the disciple as remaining in him and of himself as remaining in the disciple (15:4). There may be a hint at the mutual indwelling that would take place throughout the Beloved Disciple's life, but the main thrust of Jesus' words refers to remaining alive until the second coming. He says "until I come," but it is the second coming that is in mind ("second coming" is, of course, our convenient way of referring to the decisive event at the end of this age; the New Testament never speaks of the "second" coming; it is always simply the coming, as here). Jesus' final question is as terse as that of Peter, "What to you?" In English we put in "is that" to bring out the meaning. This is not necessary in the Greek, and the short question is impressive.

Jesus ends with "*You* follow me," and his "*you*" is emphatic. There was a similar command back in verse 19, but on that occasion there was no emphatic pronoun. Its use now is probably to contrast Peter with the Beloved Disciple. Peter is to keep following Jesus right up to death. The Beloved Disciple may or may not follow in that way, but either way it does not alter the fact that Peter's task is clear. Peter has enough on his plate with concentrating on following Jesus. He need not concern himself with questions that do not concern that following. This is something that all Christians do well to take to heart. We all find it so very easy to comment on the service other Christians are rendering or, in our opinion, are not rendering. Criticism comes easy, but it is not part of being a disciple. Our job (as was Peter's) is to follow Christ. Working out in what way others should serve him is no part of discipleship.

We should not miss the force of the present tense in the verb *follow*. In Greek the present tense has continuous force, so that the thrust of this command is "keep following me." Discipleship is a business that can never be done and got out of the way. It is something that concerns all of life, whether life be long or short. We would all be ready to be disciples in short bursts, but the test of discipleship is seen in the long haul. Being a disciple day after day through year after year is demanding. But it is to nothing less than this that Peter was called. And it is to nothing less than this that we are called in our very different place.

John Will Not Die?

John turns now to a misunderstanding of Jesus' words that arose among some of the early disciples. People are sometimes apt to draw wrong conclusions and to misinterpret the evidence that is before them. I like the little story of the man who had lived all his life in the country and who came to the big city for the first time. His friends there did their best to make his stay memorable and showed him all the sights. One night they took him up on a nearby hill from which there was a magnificent view of the city lights. The countryman gazed at it all in wonder. Then he gave his verdict: "Looks like everyone is home tonight!" Clearly he had a lot to learn about city-dwellers.

Some of the disciples now drew just as wrong a conclusion from the words Jesus spoke to Peter; they held that Jesus' meaning was that the Beloved Disciple would not die (v. 23). Jesus had, of course, not said that. He had been concerned with what Peter should do, not with what would happen to John. Jesus' question was a way of helping Peter see that John's sphere of service was no concern of his, but some of the brothers understood it to mean that they had learned something about that sphere of service. They thought that at least they had learned that it was a sphere in which John would be active right up till the time the Lord comes back again.

We should perhaps notice the use of the term "brothers" as a means of referring to the Christian group. This has passed into general Christian use and spread to other organizations, but we should not take it too lightly. In the New Testament it refers to the truth that those who follow Christ are members of one heavenly family. We have one heavenly Father, and that makes us all brothers and sisters in the family that matters. So here John refers quite naturally to Christians generally as "the brothers." John makes it clear now that Jesus did not make a prophecy about the Beloved Disciple's longevity. Jesus was telling Peter that what happened to John was none of his business. He was not saying anything about the length of John's life at all.

He repeats the words used in verse 22 exactly, which is a rare phenomenon in this Gospel. John usually makes some small variation when words are repeated, even when he is quoting. As the words would have been spoken in the Aramaic language and the exact form in Greek was due to John, we should take this as significant; this is the way John writes. The precise form of the words is important and John cites them exactly. We should perhaps notice also that his word for "but" is a strong adversative: it marks a definite contrast. Jesus did not say that he would not die. "But, on the contrary," he said no more than "If I will that he remains until I come. . . ." Some scholars hold that this shows us that this Gospel was written after John's death, but this seems an erroneous deduction. After that disciple died people would not keep repeating "He will not die." We should rather draw the opposite conclusion. The Beloved Disciple must have been alive and, with people repeating this erroneous understanding of what Jesus had said, John saw it as important that the point be cleared up. If people really thought that John would live until the second coming, then when he died they would be disillusioned. It was necessary to make it clear that there was no prophecy that he would live right through the age.

The Author of This Book

The last two verses appear to have been written by someone other than the author of the Gospel up to this point, for his "we know" (v. 24) shows that at any rate he joins others with him in this statement. In verse 25 there is a reversion to the singular, but there is no indication of a change of author. Our best understanding of all this is that some people banded together to commend this book, and they united to say that the Beloved Disciple was the author. The one who actually wrote down this attestation then added a few words on his own initiative.

Throughout this Gospel there has been a good deal of emphasis on witness or testimony, and now we are told that it is the man who was referred to in the previous verse, the Beloved Disciple, who bears witness to what has been written in the book. That is to say, there is good authority for what has been written. The verb is in the present tense, which is most naturally understood to mean that the Beloved Disciple was still living at the time the attestation was added to the book. It does not prove it, for even of a dead person it would be possible to say: "He is the witness behind this book." But that is not the most natural way of taking the words.

In this connection the word *testimony* is important, for testimony is borne by a witness who tells what he knows. It is not a matter of opinion to which the word refers, but a matter of knowledge. There is a difference. It is important to tell what is known.

There is a story of a junior lieutenant who was posted to field headquarters. There he found that one of his tasks was to rouse the regimental commander each morning. On the first morning he approached the great man's tent with some trepidation and made his announcement: "It's six A.M., sir, and time to get up."

Nothing happened, other than the sound of gentle snoring. He repeated his announcement a little louder. When nothing happened once more he spoke much more loudly. This third time he got a response. A rather sleepy voice emanated from the tent with the words, "Lieutenant, you announce the time. I'll make the decision!"

So in this matter it was the function of the Beloved Disciple to say what he knew. It was not his task to write a theological treatise or even a manual for evangelists who went forth to preach the gospel. His job was to tell his readers what he knew of his own knowledge, that is to say, what he had seen and heard, what Jesus had said and done. This Gospel is a monument to the way he carried out the task.

The writer goes on, "and who wrote these things." Some have held that this means no more than that the Beloved Disciple bore his witness and that someone else wrote down in his own way what he recollected of the testimony. But the most natural way of understanding the words is that it was the Beloved Disciple who wrote the book. This would be a very curious way indeed of expressing the idea that there was one person who bore testimony and another who wrote the book. The words surely assign both tasks to the same person.

A more difficult problem is the exact meaning that is put into "wrote." This may mean that the disciple penned the actual words of the book: he wrote it all out in his own handwriting. But it might also mean that he dictated a book to someone else who did the actual writing. This, of course, is commonplace to this day. I suppose most modern books are typed by a secretary, but we do not say that the secretary wrote the book. The author wrote the book, even though he or she did so through the hands of a secretary. A third way of taking the words finds favor in some circles, namely that the Beloved Disciple "caused to be written" what he had said as he bore his testimony. Depending on the meaning put into "caused" this might leave room for a considerable contribution from someone who did the actual writing. It has been pointed out that nobody thinks that Pilate did the actual writing of the words on the cross, though it is said that he "wrote" them (19:19). But surely this means much the same as the secretary hypothesis: nobody thinks that the words were anything other than those chosen by Pilate himself. Yet another view is that the Beloved Disciple bore his witness and that someone who heard him wrote a book of his own based more or less on his recollections of what the Beloved Disciple said. On this view the general ideas would be those of that disciple, but the exact form of expression would be due to some unknown author.

Such views must be mentioned because they have been sincerely held. But if we are going to stick to what is actually said, our choice must be limited to the first and second views. The words mean that the

Beloved Disciple wrote the book himself, either with his own hands or with the help of a scribe.

It is possible to take "these things" to mean the words describing the last incident or incidents, but this seems highly improbable. The words surely mean the book as a whole. Why would anyone want to append a solemn attestation to one or two incidents and neglect the rest of the book? What was there about such incidents that would cause a group of people to attest them so solemnly if they cared little about the greater events narrated earlier? We must take the words as a brief description of the whole book.

"We know that his testimony is true" the attestation goes on, but unfortunately we do not know who is meant by "we." We can say that it must refer to some very early Christians, for there is no manuscript of this Gospel that lacks the words. We cannot say that they were added after a century or two to help the book along. The evidence indicates that they were there from the time the book was written. Evidently when this book was started on the circulation that was to take it right round the world and right through the centuries there was a little group of people who knew who it was who vouched for it. As the group did not need to be identified for those first readers, they effaced themselves and let all the emphasis rest on the book. All that we can now say is that at the time this Gospel was published there were people who solemnly asserted that the author was the Beloved Disciple and that to their knowledge what he said was true. There is thus more than one witness. There is the Beloved Disciple who wrote the book and there is the group of people who testify both to his authorship and to the truth of what he has written.

Many Other Things

With the use of the first person singular ("I suppose," v. 25) we are apparently back with the author of the book. He has before told us that he has made a selection from what was known about Jesus and has written simply that people may know that Jesus is the Christ, God's Son, and that in this faith they may have life eternal (20:30–31). Now he comes back to the thought that there is much more that could have been written. When he talks about the impossibility of the world's containing all the books that would have to be written for a complete account, he fits into a pattern we find in antiquity.

Thus a saying of Rabbi Jochanan b. Zakkai (who died somewhere around A.D. 80) survives: "If all the sky were parchment, and all the trees were writing pens, and all the seas were ink there would not be enough to write down my wisdom which I have learned from my teachers; and yet I have had the pleasure of only as much of the wisdom of the wise as a fly, who plunges into the ocean, takes away." Or we might notice some words of Philo, the great Jewish scholar: "Were [God] to choose to display His own riches, even the entire earth with the sea turned into dry land would not contain them."

We should not try to interpret this final statement of the Gospel by working out precisely how many books could be fitted into the world. John is not giving an exact number of books, but is speaking of the vast amount that would have to be put down if all that Jesus said and did and the meaning of his life and death and resurrection were to be recorded.

And perhaps those of my readers who have continued with me through four volumes as we have studied the twenty-one chapters of the Fourth Gospel will not be disposed to quibble about what John has written. We have by no means exhausted the meaning of this Gospel, and the more we have thought about it the more we have realized the smallness of our perception. But also the more we have realized the greatness of the treasure God has given us in this part of Scripture.

To God Be the Glory.